Teacher Preparation Classroom

TEACHER PREP
MERRILL
PRENTICE HALL

See a demo at
www.prenhall.com/teacherprep/demo

Your Class. Their Careers. Our Future. Will your students be prepared?

We invite you to explore our new, innovative, and engaging website and all that it has to offer you, your course, and tomorrow's educators! Preview this site today at www.prenhall.com/teacherprep/demo. Just click on "go" on the login page to begin your exploration.

Organized around the major courses pre-service teachers take, the Teacher Preparation site provides media, student/teacher artifacts, strategies, research articles, and other resources to equip your students with the quality tools needed to excel in their courses and prepare them for their first classroom.

This ultimate online education resource will provide you and your students access to:

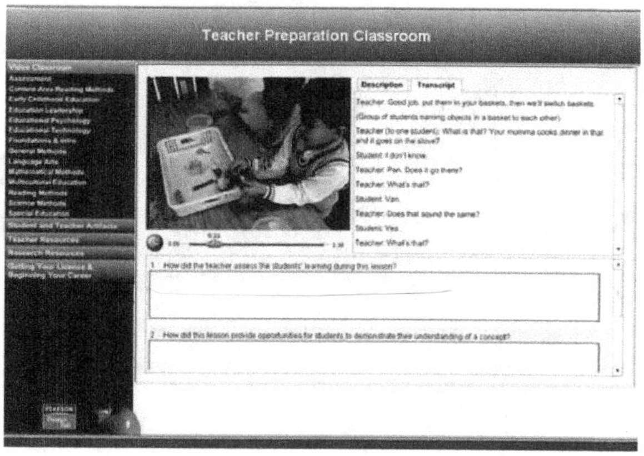

Online Video Library More than 250 video clips—each tied to a course topic and framed by learning goals and Praxis-type questions—capture real teachers and students working in real classrooms.

Student and Teacher Artifacts More than 200 student and teacher classroom artifacts—each tied to a course topic and framed by learning goals and application questions—provide a wealth of materials and experiences to help your students observe children's developmental learning.

Lesson Plan Builder Step-by-step guidelines and lesson plan examples support students as they learn to build high-quality lesson plans.

Articles and Readings Over 500 articles from ASCD's renowned journal *Educational Leadership* are available. The site also includes Research Navigator, a searchable database of additional educational journals.

Strategies and Lessons Over 500 research-supported instructional strategies appropriate for a wide range of grade levels and content areas.

Licensure and Career Tools Resources devoted to helping your students pass their licensure exam; learn standards, law, and public policies; plan a teaching portfolio; and succeed in their first year of teaching.

How to ORDER *Teacher Prep* for you and your students:

For students to receive a Teacher Prep Access Code with this text, instructors **must** provide a special value pack ISBN number on their textbook order form. To receive this special ISBN, please email **Merrill.marketing@pearsoned.com** and provide the following information:

- Name and Affiliation
- Author/Title/Edition of Merrill text

Upon ordering *Teacher Prep* for their students, instructors will be given a lifetime *Teacher Prep* Access Code.

FIFTH EDITION

Teaching Children and Adolescents with Special Needs

Judy L. Olson

Jennifer C. Platt
University of Central Florida

Lisa A. Dieker
University of Central Florida

PEARSON
Merrill
Prentice Hall

Upper Saddle River, New Jersey
Columbus, Ohio

Library of Congress Cataloging in Publication Data
Olson, Judy L.
Teaching children and adolescents with special needs/Judy L. Olson, Jennifer C. Platt, Lisa Dieker. —5th ed.
p. cm.
Includes bibliographical references and index.
ISBN-10: 0-13-240285-8
ISBN-13: 978-0-13-240285-9
1. Special education. 2. Teaching. 3. Classroom management. I. Platt, Jennifer M. II. Dieker, Lisa.
III. Title.

LC3969.047 2008
371.9—dc22

2007022181

Vice President and Executive Publisher: Jeffery W. Johnston
Executive Editor: Ann Castel Davis
Development Editor: Heather Doyle Fraser
Editorial Assistant: Penny Burleson
Production Editor: Sheryl Glicker Langner
Production Coordination: Ann Imhof, GGS Book Services
Design Coordinator: Diane C. Lorenzo
Photo Coordinator: Maria B. Vonada
Cover Designer: Jason Moore
Cover Image: Super Stock
Production Manager: Laura Messerly
Director of Marketing: Davis Gesell
Marketing Manager: Autumn Purdy
Marketing Coordinator: Brian Mounts

This book was set in Galliard by GGS Book Services. It was printed and bound by Edwards Brothers Malloy. The cover was printed by Phoenix Color Corp.

Photo Credits: p. 2, 260 by Anne Vega/Merrill; pp. 20, 56, 94 by Anthony Magnacca/Merrill; pp. 132, 292 by Tom Watson/Merrill; pp. 166, 234 by Scott Cunningham/Merrill; p. 194 by Lynn Saville/Prentice Hall School Division; p. 332 by Liz Moore/Merrill; p. 366 by Patrick White/Merrill.

Pearson Education Ltd.
Pearson Education Singapore Pte. Ltd.
Pearson Education Canada, Ltd.
Pearson Education—Japan
Pearson Education Australia Pty. Limited
Pearson Education North Asia Ltd.
Pearson Educación de Mexico, S.A. de C. V.
Pearson Education Malaysia Pte. Ltd.

PEARSON
Merrill
Prentice Hall

5 6 7 V069 17 16 15
ISBN-13: 978-0-13-240285-9
ISBN-10: 0-13-240285-8

To Larry R. Olson,

To Chris Platt and the memory of Virginia F. Cox,

To Rich and Joshua Dieker,

and

To our students, who inspired the writing of this text: those we have worked with in the past, those we are currently teaching, and those still to come.

PREFACE

This fifth edition is based on a personal philosophy that has evolved from the literature in special and general education and from our professional experiences. Research on teacher effectiveness in both special and general education provides many exemplary teaching practices that we include in this text. Our professional experiences include teaching both elementary and secondary students in general and special education settings, supervising interns, teaching and mentoring pre-service and in-service teachers, and participating as learners in our own professional development activities involving effective teaching practices.

The basic philosophy that keeps us actively involved in the profession after more than 30 years is that, as teachers, we can "make a difference" in the lives of our students. When the pre-service and in-service teachers we work with express concern about not affecting the lives of each of their students to the degree they wish, we remind them of the following story of a young boy walking along the beach. To paraphrase:

> That morning the tide had brought in thousands of starfish and scattered them on the hot, dry, sandy beach. A young boy was walking along the beach, tossing starfish back into the cool, blue water. As he was doing this, a man approached him. The man looked at what the young boy was doing and said, "Why are you doing that? Don't you see it's impossible? Look at the thousands of starfish. You can't possibly make a difference." The young boy slowly looked up at the man, picked up another starfish, and threw it back into the water, saying, "It makes a difference to this one."

We hope you continue to find ideas and suggestions in this fifth edition to make a difference in your students' lives. You have the power to make a difference, for you have chosen to teach.

FEATURES OF THE TEXT

We continue to use an informal, personal tone of writing. Additionally, we structure and organize the text around evidence-based practices, including the following:

- **Advance Organizers and Post Organizers.** We begin each chapter with an advance organizer by providing an outline that highlights the key topics within the chapter along with an opening chapter scenario. We close each chapter with a section called "Putting It All Together," along with discussion questions that challenge you to reflect on your professional practice and to think critically about the chapter content.
- **Reviewing/Checking for Understanding/Monitoring Progress.** Throughout the chapters, we include several checkpoints so you can monitor your progress as you read. These checkpoints take the form of "Important Points" found in each section of the chapter.
- **Active Involvement.** We provide opportunities for you to become actively involved by providing engaging activities in each of the chapters. They are interspersed

throughout the chapter to give you opportunities for application and practice. Remember the Chinese proverb: "I hear and I forget, I see and I remember, I do and I understand."

- **Visual Aids.** We include tables, figures, diagrams, photographs, and illustrations throughout the text. We hope you use them to clarify concepts and to increase your interest.
- **Reflections on Practice.** Throughout each chapter, we have included sections called "Reflections on Practice". These sections provide supplementary, extension, and enhancement opportunities for the reader to connect research to practice.

NOTEWORTHY CHANGES

As a result of feedback from reviewers, colleagues, and our students, along with input from users of the fourth edition and changes in our field, we have made important additions and revisions to this edition. As our field is constantly evolving, we have updated information in all of the chapters, described new legislation and national education policies, and reorganized the chapters in the text to provide additional clarity. We have included much new information such as examples that apply to inclusive settings; new ideas for communication and collaboration among general and special education professionals, paraprofessionals, and families; ways to actively involve and include students in content areas; more examples of how students construct their own knowledge by interacting with others; suggestions for transition from teacher-directed to student-directed classroom activities; and website information.

We believe that special educators must be adept at teaching content, setting up for the school year, communicating with general educators in inclusive classes, using assessments, and planning and teaching lessons for all learners. Therefore, we have expanded the information in Chapter 8, *Content Instruction*, and enhanced Chapters 2–5 (*Beginning-of-the-Year Planning and Organization, Communication and Collaborative Consultation, Informal Assessment*, and *The Instructional Cycle*) to reflect changes in our field. Throughout all chapters we have added the new features of opening chapter scenarios, Putting It All Together sections and Reflections on Practice. In addition, we have included websites at the end of the textbook to help you and your students access even more information about each chapter topic.

Based on a literature review of effective practices for teaching students with mild disabilities, we have included information on universal design for learning, response to intervention, best practices in content instruction, functional behavior assessment, scaffolding instruction, and adapting lesson plans. We believe that the fifth edition is a text that contains practical, evidence-based teaching strategies; relates to everyday occurrences in the schools; and describes motivating, experience-based activities. We hope that, like the boy and the starfish, our ideas and suggestions make a difference to you and your students.

ACKNOWLEDGMENTS

We wish to acknowledge the contributions of everyone who assisted us in the completion of this text. Our thanks to Colleen Klein-Ezell and Dan Ezell, who wrote Chapter 11, *Technology for Teaching and Learning.* We also wish to thank Beth Christner for her extraordinary contributions. Beth, a general and special education teacher, wrote the opening chapter scenarios, prepared many of the reflections on practice sections, and assisted with literature reviews and editing. She also prepared the Instructor's Manual and PowerPoint Slides. Thanks goes to Shelby Robertson for her help in completing literature reviews, editing, and handling permissions and Kara Rosenblatt and Evadne Ngazimbi for their literature searches and editing. To Ann Davis, Heather Fraser, Penny Burleson, and Sheryl Langner, and all the Merrill/Prentice Hall staff, we express our gratitude for making our dream a reality.

Thanks to our reviewers for their critical analysis, valuable input, and suggestions: Kathryn A. Lund, Arizona State University; Alma K. Miller-Sennett, Kutztown University; and Craig Rice, Providence College. Without the input of our students at the University of Central Florida and the support and encouragement of our families, colleagues, and friends, we would not have had an opportunity to make a difference in the lives of students with special needs. We are deeply grateful for these many contributions.

Discover the Merrill Resources for Special Education Website

Technology is a constantly growing and changing aspect of our field that is creating a need for new content and resources. To address this emerging need, Merrill Education has developed an online learning environment for students, teachers, and professors alike to complement our products—the *Merrill Resources for Special Education* Website. This content-rich website provides additional resources specific to this book's topic and will help you—professors, classroom teachers, and students—augment your teaching, learning, and professional development.

Our goal is to build on and enhance what our products already offer. For this reason, the content for our user-friendly website is organized by topic and provides teachers, professors, and students with a variety of meaningful resources all in one location. With this website, we bring together the best of what Merrill has to offer: text resources, video clips, web links, tutorials, and a wide variety of information on topics of interest to general and special educators alike. Rich content, applications, and competencies further enhance the learning process.

The Merrill Resources for Special Education Website includes:

- Video clips specific to each topic, with questions to help you evaluate the content and make crucial theory-to-practice connections.
- Thought-provoking critical analysis questions that students can answer and turn in for evaluation or that can serve as basis for class discussions and lectures.
- Access to a wide variety of resources related to classroom strategies and methods, including lesson planning and classroom management.
- Information on all the most current relevant topics related to special and general education, including CEC and Praxis™ standards, IEPs, portfolios, and professional development.
- Extensive web resources and overviews on each topic addressed on the website.
- A search feature to help access specific information quickly.

To take advantage of these and other resources, please visit the *Merrill Resources for Special Education* Website at

http://www.prenhall.com/olson

BRIEF CONTENTS

CONTENTS

PART 1

Foundations for Instruction

CHAPTER

1

Students with Special Needs

KEY TOPICS

- Student Characteristics
- Cultural Diversity
- English Language Learners
- Effective Teaching Strategies
  - Reductionist Paradigm
  - Constructivist Paradigm
  - Sample Lessons Based on Paradigms
  - Combining Paradigms for Effective Instructional Practice
- Inclusion
- National Education and Standards-Based Reform
- Professional Commitment
- What We Believe
- Putting It All Together

"Hey Todd! How's it going?" asked Liz O'Malley as she stepped into the cafeteria line behind Todd Davis. Todd is in his first year of teaching Intensive Reading to ninth- and tenth-grade students at Lincoln High. Liz however is in her 21st year as an ESE teacher at this rural location, and has served as Todd's mentor since his arrival earlier this year.

"Whew! I am really looking forward to our break next week," said Todd as he juggled his cafeteria tray while trying to count out the correct change. "I'm hoping to find some time to relax, but I'm also thinking it will be great to have some time to regroup and make a few changes in my classroom."

"I know exactly what you mean," Liz replied as both took a seat in the teachers' lounge. "I'm traveling to the city to spend time with my grandkids, but before I come home, I'm attending a conference that will review the latest IDEA regulations. I should have a lot to report when I get back."

Todd shook his head as he replied, "I don't know how you do it. I am so busy with lesson plans, behavior plans, IEPs to write, and a million other things! I'm worried I'll miss out on policy changes and legal regulations that I should know about."

"Don't worry Todd. Most first-year teachers feel like that. Until you get your first few years behind you, it is best to rely on the county updates we receive by e-mail and the professional development programs like the online module we completed together last month. I know you are a member of several professional organizations. Make sure you are on their e-mail list and they will send you electronic updates. And of course as your mentor, I'm not going to let you miss anything!"

"Thanks Liz. I'll look forward to hearing about that conference."

It can be challenging to keep up with the latest information in the field of special education. Look back for a moment at the advice that Liz gave to Todd. Can you think of any other suggestions she could have given him? What actions do you currently take as an educator or a future educator to stay abreast of the latest federal, state, or local school district changes?

INTRODUCTION

The field of special education will continue to grow and change in the 21st century, supported by federal legislation, such as the Individuals with Disabilities Education Act (IDEA) reauthorized in 2004. Current legislation has impacted students with disabilities and reframed the roles of general and special education teachers, administrators, other professionals, and families. Furthermore, as schools are restructured to meet the mandate of the No Child Left Behind Act (2001), designed to reform federal education policy, special educators are studying the impact of this legislation on students with disabilities.

In this chapter, we begin by focusing on the diverse needs and characteristics of children and adolescents with learning and behavior problems. Being knowledgeable about student characteristics means that you know your students' academic levels, can identify the skills they bring with them to the learning situation, and understand their cultural backgrounds. Children and adolescents with special needs often exhibit problems with academic and social skills that make it difficult for them to meet the demands of school, home, and/or community.

For optimum learning to occur, you must use effective teaching strategies based on sound research. Therefore, we provide an instructional framework based on proven educational practice, which you can use in planning, implementing, and evaluating instruction. You must also be aware of the issues related to the standards-based movement, the legislation that regulates what is considered a highly qualified special education teacher, the focus on creating Universally Designed Instruction (UDI) for all learners, the increased availability of technology to assist students with disabilities and the emphasis on inclusion of students with disabilities in general education settings. More information on these important topics will be provided throughout the various chapters. We conclude this chapter with the Council for Exceptional Children Standards for Professional Practice and ask you to make a commitment to students with exceptionalities, their families, and the teaching profession.

STUDENT CHARACTERISTICS

Students with special needs often have problems in academic areas, social interactions, motivation, and transition to adult roles. In many school districts, these students are referred to as having learning disabilities (specific learning disabilities), mental disabilities (mental handicaps, mental retardation, educable mental handicaps), emotional disabilities (emotional disturbance, behavior disorders), or high incidence disabilities. Often, placed into the group of students with mild disabilities or varying exceptionalities, these students have many similarities and often spend much of their school day in inclusive settings. The U.S. Department of Education Programs (2002) reported that close to half of the students with disabilities in regular school buildings were educated for most of their day in regular classrooms.

Some of the characteristics that students with special needs or mild disabilities may display include:

Inadequate academic achievement. Often, students are two or more years behind their grade-level peers in reading, mathematics, spelling, written expression, and/or oral language skills.

Inappropriate school behaviors. Students may be physically or verbally aggressive. They may be easily frustrated or unable to cope with the demands of the school environment. Other signs of inappropriate school behavior include noncompliance with teacher directions and instructions and lack of teacher-pleasing behaviors, such as being prepared for class, maintaining eye contact, and raising hands.

Poor attending behaviors. Students with special needs may have trouble following teacher directions and instructions. They seem to have difficulty attending to the relevant information in a message and are frequently unable to concentrate on an assignment or task.

Poor memory. Being unable to remember information from one week to the next or from one day to the next is another characteristic common to many students with special needs. These students frequently have problems remembering spelling words, basic math facts, and two or more directions.

Poor metacognitive skills. Often, students do not have the necessary organizational and learning strategies to become self-regulated learners. They do not monitor their understanding of new information or develop effective strategies to complete a task.

Poor self-concept. For many students with special needs, school is not a comfortable, rewarding place. Instead, it is a place where they often fail to meet the standards for success.

Inadequate social skills. Students with disabilities often cannot maintain satisfactory interpersonal relationships, are less socially accepted by peers, and demonstrate impaired communication (pragmatic language) skills. The lack of social skills precludes adequate adjustment not only to the demands of the school environment, but also to the postschool environment. Students with special needs are frequently less accepted and less successful in the world of work due to lack of social skills.

These areas are what you are expected as the special educator to remediate in your work with students with disabilities and their families. Your job is to get to know the strengths of all the students you meet and to use their assets to assist them in overcoming areas of deficit. Throughout this textbook we focus on students with special needs being served to the maximum extent appropriate in the general education setting.

CULTURAL DIVERSITY

Within the population of students with special needs are students who are not members of the Anglo-American culture. These students are from Native American, Asian, Hispanic (Latino), African American, and other cultures.

The school culture frequently reflects Anglo-American values and because of this many children are being left behind (Hodgkinson, 2002) As indicated by Nieto (2000), most prospective educators are female, white, and English speaking. Nieto (2004) challenges educators to see their role as interrupting the cycle of inequality and oppression based on one dominant culture. This need for support is especially critical for students who are culturally and linguistically diverse students with disabilities. This particular population experiences some of the greatest language difficulties in the general education setting (Rodriquez, Parmar, & Signer, 2001).

As a teacher you see that our world is changing (Friedman, 2005), especially in our classrooms, and your role is to advocate and provide appropriate evidence-based education to all students. Remember some of your students may find that their culture is at odds with the school culture. Yet too often students whose cultures do not match a traditional definition of "appropriate school behavior" are viewed from a deficit model (Allen & Hermann-Wilmarth, 2004; Delpit, 2002). As a special education teacher, your job is to view students from a strength-based model. Children and adolescents from different cultural backgrounds have already demonstrated incredible skills by being able to acclimate to a new culture (Darling-Hammond, Chung, & Frelow, 2002). We urge you to use these strengths to help students be successful learners in your classroom.

Some strategies to use in your classroom that embrace different cultural values include:

1. Allowing students to help and assist each other at times, instead of requiring students to complete work independently all the time, and giving some assignments that require collaboration (e.g., group projects).
2. Using cooperative learning groups and peer tutoring.
3. Giving students alternatives for the completion of assignments (e.g., a hands-on exhibition; a demonstration using technology).
4. Encouraging students to meet important deadlines by reminders of due dates.
5. Remembering to include both affective and academic objectives on the Individualized Education Program (IEP).
6. Teaching students to reach daily goals before asking them to monitor monthly goals.

We encourage you to become familiar with the cultural values of the community and invite community members to share their expertise and cultural knowledge. You should always be respectful of all cultures and try to bring in materials and perspectives from various cultures. For example, when coteaching a unit on Western expansion in the United States, Ms. Wright brought in materials that considered the Native Americans' viewpoint in addition to that of the white settlers' viewpoint.

ENGLISH LANGUAGE LEARNERS

In addition to the cultural differences in your classroom, you may have students who are not native English speakers. The term *English language learners* (ELLs) refers both to students who are not proficient in English and to students who use adequate conversational English but struggle with the language of the academic curriculum (Gersten & Baker, 2000). Schools attempt to meet the needs of these students by offering immersion programs, English as a second language (ESL) programs, or bilingual programs (Gollnick & Chinn, 2002). In the structured immersion model, the teacher teaches content information through adaptations in the English language with the goal that students acquire proficiency in English while at the same time achieve in content areas. An ESL program is based on a special curriculum that typically focuses on learning the English language as opposed to content and is usually taught during specific times. Every bilingual education program has an ESL component (National Clearinghouse for English Language Acquisition). Bilingual programs use two languages (the native language and English) for teaching and learning. Usually, the native language is used to teach concepts and knowledge, and English is used to reinforce the information (Baca & Cervantes, 1998).

To meet the needs of students identified as ELLs, Gersten and Baker (2000), along with other researchers, recommend a shift of focus from arguing over which programs (i.e., immersion, ESL, or bilingual) should be selected to identifying the best methods for teaching these students. In a review of 24 intervention studies (research-based and descriptive) and interviews with professional educators and researchers, they identified the following "critical components" for instruction:

1. Reinforce auditory information with visual aids, such as graphic organizers and word banks.

2. Build the background knowledge of students. Going over the new vocabulary in a reading assignment and discussing what the class knows about a topic before it is presented are ways to build group knowledge.
3. Implement peer tutoring and cooperative learning.

Throughout the rest of this textbook, we describe additional effective strategies for teaching students from a variety of cultures and English language learners with disabilities.

IMPORTANT POINTS

1. Students with special needs may display one or more of the following characteristics: inadequate academic achievement, inappropriate school behaviors, poor attendance behaviors, poor memory, poor metacognitive skills, poor self-concept, and inadequate social skills.
2. Anglo-American values may be at odds with those of the many other cultures of the students in your classroom.
3. The term *English-language learners* (ELLs) refers both to students who are not proficient in English and to students who use adequate conversational English but struggle with the language of the academic curriculum (Gersten & Baker, 2000).

Activity 1.1

Find someone who has a different cultural background than your own and then compare the values of your cultures to those of the school culture. Discuss how well the school culture meets the needs of your different cultures.

(Answers for this and other activities are found in the Instructor's Manual.)

EFFECTIVE TEACHING STRATEGIES

In a meta-analysis of over 1,000 research studies, Forness, Kavale, Blum, and Lloyd (1997) identified effective, possibly effective, and ineffective special education interventions. The ineffective strategies included special class placement, perceptual training, the Feingold diet, modality-based instruction, and social skills training. They identified psycholinguistic training, peer tutoring, computer-assisted instruction, stimulant drugs, reduced class size, and psychotropic drugs as possibly effective. Effective strategies included early intervention, formative evaluation, cognitive behavior modification, direct instruction, behavior modification, reading comprehension instruction, and mnemonic training. Effective teaching strategies in special education are currently based on two paradigms of the learning process. One view is the ***reductionist paradigm*** (also referred to as scientific, modern empiricism, or Newtonian mechanistic), and the other is the ***constructivist paradigm*** (also referred to as holistic or social constructivism). In the reductionist paradigm, learning tends to be teacher-focused, skill-based, product-oriented, and highly prescribed (Johnson, 2004). In the constructivist paradigm, learning tends to be student-focused, meaning-based, process-oriented, and loosely structured (Johnson, 2004).

Both paradigms influence instructional interactions and generate heated debate in the special education field. For our discussion, we concentrate on a comparison of the two paradigms in regard to their views of the role of the teacher, the role of the student, and their influence on instructional and assessment practices.

REDUCTIONIST PARADIGM

The reductionist paradigm views the teacher's role as one of providing direct instruction through detailed lesson plans, systematic instruction, and feedback. Teachers structure the school day by providing ample instructional time and high task management. They introduce and orient, model and demonstrate, check for understanding, maintain a brisk pace and a high success rate, and monitor seatwork and progress (Englert, Tarrant, & Mariage, 1992). The teacher is in charge of instruction, and knowledge is transmitted from teacher to student. The students frequently are not involved in decision making and often engage in rote learning. Through the use of task analysis, the curriculum is separated into components with scope and sequence checklists. Reductionism emphasizes lecturing, telling, showing, and explaining (Johnson, 2004), and direct, explicit teaching (Schug, Tarver, & Western, 2001).

CONSTRUCTIVIST PARADIGM

In the constructivist paradigm, the teacher's role is more like that of a facilitator as students assume responsibility for their own learning. The teacher embeds implicit instruction in meaningful contexts, promotes classroom dialogues, demonstrates responsive instruction, links students' prior knowledge with new knowledge, and establishes classroom learning communities (Englert, Tarrant, & Mariage, 1992). Students often lead discussions, select their own objectives, and learn from other students. They construct their own knowledge through active involvement and integration into their schema. Assessment includes authentic, real-life processes, and errors provide insights not into students' weaknesses but into how students think. Subject areas are taught in authentic contexts (Englert, Tarrant, & Mariage, 1992).

SAMPLE LESSONS BASED ON PARADIGMS

An examination of sample lessons may assist in understanding the effects of the two paradigms on instruction. We begin with a sample lesson from a reductionist viewpoint. Then we present the same lesson based on the constructivist principles, adapted from a lesson presented by Englert, Tarrant, and Mariage (1992). Both lessons are centered around opening morning activities, a beginning routine in many primary inclusive classrooms.

Reductionist-Based Lesson

TEACHER: It's time for our morning message. Today is Tuesday. What is today, everyone (hand signal to cue unison response)?

STUDENTS: Tuesday.

TEACHER: Correct. Today is Tuesday. (Teacher writes the sentence on the board.) Let's read our first sentence together. Everyone (signal).

STUDENTS: Today is Tuesday.

TEACHER: Good reading, everyone. Jim, what is happening today?

JIM: We are going on a field trip.

TEACHER: Yes, we are. Where are we going?

SAMANTHA: To the fire station.

TEACHER: Let's say that in a complete sentence, Samantha.

SAMANTHA: We are going to the fire station.

TEACHER: Now that's a complete sentence. (Teacher writes: We are going on a field trip to the fire station.) Everyone, let's read that sentence together (hand signal).

STUDENTS: We are going on a field trip to the fire station.

TEACHER: Good reading, everyone. So where are we going, Sherry?

SHERRY: We are going to the fire station.

TEACHER: Correct. When are we going to the fire station, Kenisha?

Constructivist-Based Lesson

TEACHER: Anything special to write about today in our morning message?

JOSH: We are going to the fire station today.

MEGAN: A field trip.

TEACHER: Let's see. (Teacher writes: We are going to the fire station today, a field trip.) Oh! That doesn't sound right. What do you think?

KENISHA: Something's wrong with field trip.

SEBBIE: Maybe it needs a period.

TEACHER: Let's see. (Teacher adds a period before field trip and a capital A.) I added a period so now I need a capital. Let me read it, A field trip. What do you think?

STUDENTS: No.

TEACHER: Maybe, I can say for. (Teacher writes: We are going to the fire station today for a field trip. Teacher reads sentence.) What do you think?

STUDENTS: Yes.

TEACHER: What do you want to say about the field trip?

MEGAN: We leave at 11:00.

ROY: I want to say 11:00 o'clock.

STUDENTS: (Some say Yes, and some say No.)

TEACHER: Let's vote on adding o'clock. Thumbs up for Yes. Thumbs down for No.

Activity 1.2

Work with a partner to compare and contrast the two lesson samples based on the reductionist and constructivist paradigms. Before reading the next section of the chapter, predict when you might use each of the paradigms in your instructional practice. Now read the next section.

COMBINING PARADIGMS FOR EFFECTIVE INSTRUCTIONAL PRACTICE

Many experts feel that the selection of an effective instructional practice in special education depends on the task and the individual. Research indicates explicit instruction grounded in the reductionist paradigm is more effective in teaching basic decoding skills, and implicit instruction grounded in the constructivist paradigm is effective when the focus is on comprehension process or higher-level skills (Stanovich, 1994). Howell, Fox, and Morehead (1993) suggest that students who have poor prior knowledge and encounter initial failure on the task may need explicit instruction, whereas students who have good prior knowledge and early success may need implicit instruction.

Harris and Graham (1994), proponents of the constructivist paradigm, argue that extensive, structured, and explicit instruction does not need to "equate with decontextualized learning of meaningless skills, passive learning, or the teaching of gradually accruing basic skills as a prerequisite to higher-order thinking and learning" (p. 238). Instead, they urge teachers to be responsive to individual needs, styles, and differences. We agree with Harris and Graham; therefore, in this text, we incorporate practices based on both paradigms. For example, we discuss assessments such as precision teaching (reductionist-based), the use of portfolios (constructivist-based), strategies such as direct instruction (reductionist-based), and reciprocal teaching (constructivist-based).

Planning lessons that address the needs of all learners should take both paradigms into consideration. The concept of Universal Design for Instruction (UDI) focuses on instruction that does not have to be retrofitted to meet the needs of various learners (Hitchcock, Meyer, Rose, & Jackson, 2002) but is created with the needs of all learners in mind during the initial planning phase and through all phases of instruction. Therefore, we have framed this textbook in the concept of UDI wrapping around the instructional framework. However, it is important to note that our instructional framework embraces both reductionist-based and constructivist-based paradigms as we talk about planning, presentation, independent practice, and evaluation (see Figure 1.1). In this instructional framework, the teacher, the students, or the combined efforts of the teacher and

Figure 1.1 INSTRUCTIONAL FRAMEWORK

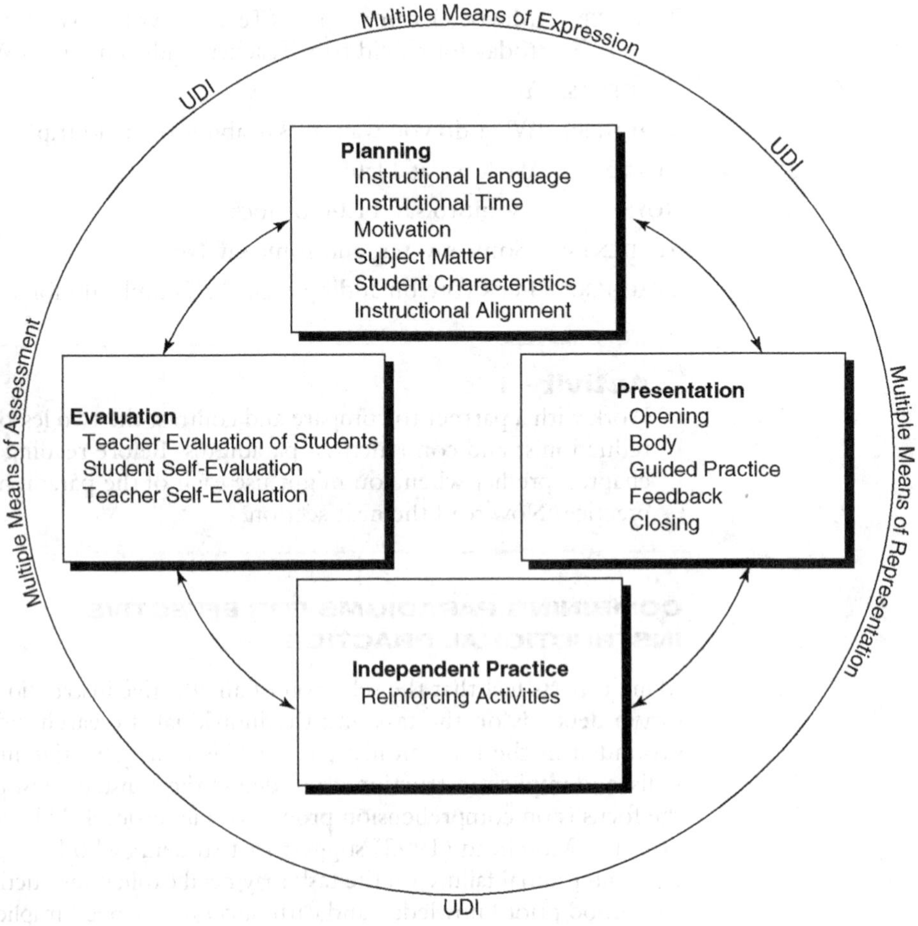

students may lead to the planning of a lesson that is created for a range of learners with various disabilities in the general education setting.

During the planning of a unit or a lesson, the various types of disabilities are used to frame a lesson that teaches to students' various strengths and provides tools (e.g., metacognitive strategies or assistive technology) to navigate areas of weakness. Using a dialogue, the teacher may at first present the lesson and then turn over the lesson presentation to the students; or in classroom communities, the students may learn from one another. In the feedback and evaluation process, the involvement of both the teacher and students is essential. Students may self-evaluate or self-monitor and/or teachers may evaluate and monitor. We discuss the instructional framework in detail in Chapter 5.

IMPORTANT POINTS

1. In a meta-analysis of over 1,000 research studies, Forness, Kavale, Blum, and Lloyd (1997) identified early intervention, formative evaluation, cognitive-behavior modification, direct instruction, behavior modification, reading comprehension instruction, and mnemonic training as effective strategies.
2. Effective teaching strategies in special education currently are based on either the reductionist or the constructivist paradigms of the learning process.
3. The reductionist paradigm views the teacher as the primary transmitter of information and decision maker; students as active participants in rote learning with little input; assessment as leading to sequential and hierarchical instructional objectives; and instruction as fast paced and teacher directed.
4. The constructivist paradigm views the teacher as a facilitator and one of the decision makers; the students as major decision makers as they learn from each other; assessment as occurring in authentic, real-life procedures; and instruction as purposeful and matched to students' interests and experiences.
5. Many special educators feel that both paradigms include practices that are effective for students with special needs, depending on content and student characteristics.
6. Understanding the principles of Universal Design for Instruction, teachers can use the instructional framework of planning, presentation, independent practice, and evaluation to create lessons for all learners that incorporate practices based on both paradigms.

Activity 1.3

Now that you have read this section, reflect on the different practices suggested by the two paradigms. Discuss with a partner when you feel the different practices may be effective.

INCLUSION

The inclusion of students with disabilities into the general education setting is an increasing trend due to numerous changes in laws that require students to meet the same state standards as their nondisabled peers. The push for more inclusive placements is also supported by parents and educators who believe that students with disabilities have the right to be in the same classes as their nondisabled peers (Hitchcock et al., 2002). As a special educator you should assume that all or at least part of your day will be spent in the general education setting either coteaching or providing support to students who are expected to not only be provided the general education curriculum but to pass rigorous standardized tests. Therefore, your understanding of effective research-based strategies as well as a strong grounding in how to help students included in content areas across grade levels is critical.

Although some people see the inclusion of students with disabilities as a recent trend, throughout history society has become more inclusive. Students who used to be institutionalized are today allowed into schools and this trend continues with a greater acceptance of the wide range of differences found in the general education setting. For example, Kavale and Forness (2000) share that just 50 years ago students with learning and behavioral challenges were not even allowed to attend public school. Today, however, denying a child access to the general education curriculum is the exception, whereas it was formerly the norm (Weiner, 2003; Bloomfield & Cooper, 2003).

The term or concept of inclusion actually took flight in American schools in 1986 when Madeline Will, Assistant Secretary of Education, proposed that we educate more students with disabilities in general education settings. She advocated a shared responsibility and commitment between general and special education and the use of effective special education techniques beyond the special class setting, called the Regular Education Initiative (REI). This initiative led to one of the major reform issues currently facing the field of education, that of inclusion.

According to the *Twenty-Fourth Annual Report to Congress* the inclusion of students with disabilities in general education classrooms has continued to gain momentum over the last several years (U.S. Department of Education, 2002). The Individuals with Disabilities Education Act (IDEA) throughout all revisions and reforms continues to support the use of a continuum of services, which emphasizes that the first placement to consider is the general education setting to serve students with disabilities. Yet what often occurs is that students with certain labels (e.g., behavior disordered) may be denied progression through this continuum because in some schools a label determines placement. In strong inclusive schools teachers believe that all students are capable of being successful in the general education setting. Despite this belief and the continuum of services that includes the general education setting as the first option to consider, the topic of inclusion remains a controversial one and at times ill-defined. As you work as a special education teacher, make certain you listen as well as look carefully within your teaching, team, school, or district to determine if the actions match the definition of inclusion (Salend, 2005). Some professionals support full inclusion (placing all students with disabilities in general education classrooms), whereas others favor inclusive schools that welcome students with disabilities, but at the same time, realize that the general education placement may not be the best educational option. Still others describe "responsible" inclusion, a school-based education model that is student centered and bases educational placement and service provisions on the needs of each student (Dieker, 2007). Most models advocating full inclusion include the following:

1. All students attend their home or neighborhood school—where they would attend if they did not have a disability.
2. A natural proportion (i.e., representative of the school district at large) of students with disabilities can be found at any school site and within each classroom.

3. A zero-rejection policy exists, so that no student is excluded on the basis of type or extent of disability.
4. Placements are age and grade appropriate, without any or limited self-contained special education classes operating at the school site.
5. Cooperative learning and peer instruction methods receive significant use in general instruction at the school site to provide natural peer supports.
6. Special education supports (e.g., coteaching) are provided within the general education setting.
7. A climate is created that embraces celebrating student differences and acknowledging a need for change from the traditional models of instruction, collaboration, and assessment.

Originally adopted at the annual conference of the Council for Exceptional Children (CEC) in 1993, the CEC Policy on Inclusive Schools and Community Settings calls for a continuum of services but supports inclusion as a meaningful goal (see Figure 1.2). Leadership organizations in the United States such as the American Federation of Teachers as well as many organizations in other countries also have created policies or statements similar to the one in Figure 1.2 related to inclusion. As a teacher you should be prepared to support a diverse student population in inclusive settings and facilitate collaboration among families, educators, businesses, and agencies to prepare students for membership in inclusive communities (Platt & Olson, 1997).

Figure 1.2 CEC POLICY ON INCLUSIVE SCHOOLS AND COMMUNITY SETTINGS

The Council for Exceptional Children (CEC) believes all children, youth, and young adults with disabilities are entitled to a free and appropriate education and/or services that lead to an adult life characterized by satisfying relations with others, independent living, productive engagement in the community, and participation in society at large.

To achieve such outcomes, there must exist for all children, youth, and young adults a rich variety of early intervention, educational, and vocational program options and experiences.

Access to these programs and experiences should be based on individual educational need and desired outcomes.

Furthermore, students and their families or guardians, as members of the planning team, may recommend the placement, curriculum option, and the exit document to be pursued.

CEC believes that a continuum of services must be available for all children, youth, and young adults.

CEC also believes that the concept of inclusion is a meaningful goal to be pursued in our schools and communities.

In addition, CEC believes children, youth, and young adults with disabilities should be served whenever possible in general education classrooms in inclusive neighborhood schools and community settings.

Such settings should be strengthened and supported by an infusion of specially trained personnel and other appropriate supportive practices according to the individual needs of the child.

Source: From *CEC Policy Manual,* 1997, Chapter 3, "Special Education in the Schools," Section Three, Professional Policies, Part 1, p. 4. Reston, VA: The Council for Exceptional Children. Reprinted by permission.

BOX 1.1

Reflections on Practice

As a special education teacher, you may be hired to serve children with disabilities in an inclusive setting in your school (which is a belief framing our work in this textbook). One part of your job responsibilities is helping shape people's beliefs about the education of students with disabilities, a role you may not have anticipated. Remember, many of our students' parents and grandparents did not go to school with students with disabilities included in the general education setting. As a result, they may have questions or concerns about how inclusive education works. As a special educator you should anticipate what these questions may be and prepare yourself to educate others about accepting differences within a classroom. This education may need to include students without disabilities, their parents, other faculty members, administrators, community members, and/or school board members. A proactive approach to explaining inclusive education will help everyone understand why students with disabilities have the right to be in the general education setting.

You may want to look at www.inclusiveschools.org and learn about inclusive schools week. This site provides interesting ideas to use in your classroom as well as week-long activities to raise awareness of administrators, teachers, students, and your community about inclusive education. In addition to this, we invite you to visit the informational websites in Table 1.1 that focus on inclusive practices.

A new emerging dimension of inclusion in our field has been students with disabilities being included in local and state assessments. With the legislation of No Child Left Behind and IDEA (2004) being passed, more and more students are being included in local and state standardized assessments. For example, the U.S. Department of Education National Assessment of Education Progress (NAEP) now defines criteria for students with disabilities to be included in assessments.

According to the current criteria, a student with a disability is to be included in the NAEP assessment except in the following cases:

1. The student's IEP team determines that the student cannot participate; *or*,
2. The student's cognitive functioning is so severely impaired that she or he cannot participate; *or*,
3. The student's IEP requires that the student has to be tested with an accommodation or adaptation that NAEP does not allow.

The Working Forum on Inclusive Schools (1994), a consortium of 10 national education associations, identified 12 characteristics of inclusive schools:

1. A sense of community (e.g., all students belong and can learn in the mainstream of the school and community).
2. Leadership (e.g., principals should involve faculty in planning and decision making).
3. High standards (e.g., all students are given the opportunity to achieve high educational standards and outcomes).
4. Collaboration and cooperation (e.g., there is an emphasis on collaborative arrangements and support networks among students and staff).
5. Changing roles and responsibilities (e.g., roles of school professionals change, and everyone becomes an active participant in the learning process).
6. An array of services (e.g., varied school/community services are available, all coordinated with the educational staff).

7. Partnerships with parents (e.g., parents are full partners in the education of their children).
8. Flexible learning environments (e.g., flexible groupings and developmentally appropriate experiences are provided to meet students' needs).
9. Strategies based on research (e.g., practices include cooperative learning, curriculum adaptation, peer tutoring, direct instruction, reciprocal teaching, social skills instruction, computer-assisted instruction, study skills training, and mastery learning).
10. New forms of accountability (e.g., there is less emphasis on standardized tests and more on assessment to monitor progress toward goals).
11. Access (e.g., adaptations, modifications, and assistive technology ensure access).
12. Continuing professional development (e.g., staff members continue to improve their knowledge and skills).

Many professionals agree on the value of integrating students with disabilities into general education classroom settings. There is disagreement, however, as to how inclusion is implemented. Collaborative models that ignore the individual learning needs of students can be problematic (Zigmond & Magiera, 2001). Many educators believe that inclusion is most effective when the integration of students with disabilities is combined with a broader restructuring that includes multiage classrooms (Irmsher, 1996). Others recommend guidelines for "responsible" inclusion: "(1) the student and family are considered first; (2) teachers choose to participate in inclusion classrooms; (3) adequate resources are provided; (4) models are developed and implemented at the school-based level; (5) a continuum of services is maintained; (6) the service delivery model is continuously evaluated; and (7) ongoing professional development is provided" (Vaughn & Schumm, 1995, p. 264).

Emerging from our field is a number of instructional practices that are essential for successful inclusion of students with disabilities. These practices include coteaching, cooperative learning, peer support strategies, positive behavioral support, embedded learning strategies, and content-enhancements (Ehren, Lenz, & Deshler, 2005; King-Sears, 1997). As the debate over how best to meet the needs of students with disabilities continues, we urge you to evaluate the effects of separate programming and integrated settings on student achievement. Table 1.1 provides informational websites that we

Table 1.1 Informational Websites

The United Nations Educational, Scientific and Cultural Organization (UNESCO)—www.unesco.org
Inclusion.com provides materials and resources on inclusion—www.inclusion.com
ERIC Clearinghouse on Disabilities and Gifted Children—www.ericec.org
National Association of State Directors of Special Education—www.nasdse.org
National Center on Educational Outcomes—http://education.umn.edu/nceo
National Center to Improve Practice in Special Education (NCIP)—www2.edc.org/NCIP
National Information Center for Children and Youth with Disabilities (NICHCY)—www.nichcy.org
National Center for Education Statistics—nces.ed.gov
Special Education Resource Center (SERC)—www.ctserc.org
U.S. Department of Education Office of Special Education and Rehabilitative Services (OSERS)—www.ed.gov/offices/OSERS
Federation for Children with Special Needs—www.fcsn.org
Parent Advocacy Coalition for Educational Rights (PACER)—www.pacer.org
Family Village: A global Community of Disability-Related Resources—www.familyvillage.wisc.edu
Parent Education and Assistance for Kids (PEAK) Parent Center, Inc.—www.peakparent.org

believe are helpful to teachers and may also help you shape your thinking about inclusive practices.

Activity 1.4

Part 1: Visit a school and talk to as many people as possible about their thoughts on inclusion. After you have interviewed people, re-read this chapter and write a summary of your thoughts on inclusion.

Part 2: Arrange your class to sit in two circles (one on the outside and one on the inside). The inner circle discusses what they learned about inclusion and their own thoughts on the topic while the outer circle listens. Next, students in the outer circle talk while the inner circle listens. Then each group writes a summary of what they heard as they listened to their peers.

IMPORTANT POINTS

1. Inclusive education is still somewhat controversial but is an emerging trend for many students with disabilities.
2. The inclusion of students in the general education setting is often argued as a human rights issue and that a student's label should not determine placement.
3. The premise for inclusion is that students with special needs benefit academically and socially by being served alongside normally achieving students as opposed to being separated from them.
4. Many organizations around the globe have created statements related to inclusive practices.

NATIONAL EDUCATION AND STANDARDS-BASED REFORM

"The participation of students with disabilities in standards-based reform was mandated with the 1997 amendments to the Individuals with Disabilities Act (IDEA). IDEA (1997) requires states to include all students with disabilities in their accountability programs and to provide students with disabilities the accommodations they need to be so included" (Fuchs & Fuchs, 2001, p. 174). The Individuals with Disabilities Education Act (1997):

> assures that all children with disabilities have available to them . . . a free appropriate public education which emphasizes special education and related services designed to meet their unique needs, to assure that the rights of children with disabilities and their parents or guardians are protected, to assist states and localities to provide for the education of all children with disabilities, and to assess and assure the effectiveness of efforts to educate children with disabilities. (IDEA, 20 U.S.C.: 1400[c])

The recent reauthorization of IDEA affirmed the 1997 legislations and paralleled the statements in the No Child Left Behind Act (NCLB) representing a national initiative for education reform to improve our systems, policies, standards, and most importantly, outcomes for all students. The four basic components of this new act from the Fact Sheet (2002) were:

a. ***Accountability for Results:*** Creates strong standards in each state for what every child should know and learn in reading and mathematics in grades 3–8. Student progress and achievement will be measured for every child, every year.

b. ***Unprecedented State & Local Flexibility & Reduced Red Tape:*** Provides new flexibility for all 50 states and every local school district in America in the use of federal education funds.

c. ***Focusing Resources on Proven Educational Methods:*** Focuses educational dollars on proven, research-based approaches that will most help children to learn.

d. ***Expanded Choices for Parents:*** Enhances options for parents with children in chronically failing schools—and makes these options available immediately in the 2002–03 school year for students in thousands of schools already identified as failing under current law. (http://www.whitehouse.gov/news/releases/2002/01/20020108.html)

This law, NCLB, set high expectations for public education on the national level. We recommend that you check with your state department of education and examine the education reform initiatives that your state has established and are being implemented in your area, and monitor the impact these initiatives are having on students with disabilities and on teacher preparation. We hope you will make staying current with legislative policies and advocating for the needs of the students you serve as one of many of the goals you commit to as a life-long learner and educator.

PROFESSIONAL COMMITMENT

This level of strong commitment to the field of special education by parents, educators, and leaders is the reason our field continues to evolve and move forward towards parity between general education and special education. The primary international organization that represents the special education field is the Council for Exceptional Children (CEC). The mission of CEC is to improve educational outcomes for individuals with exceptionalities:

> The Mission of the Council for Exceptional Children (CEC) is to promote professional excellence to meet the educational needs of individuals with exceptionalities worldwide. CEC supports professionals, families, and all others working on behalf of individuals with exceptionalities; advocates for the needs of culturally and linguistically diverse individuals; advances research and evidence-based practice; advocates for appropriate governmental policies; sets professional standards; provides continuing professional development; and helps professionals achieve conditions and access resources necessary for effective special education professional practice.

Members of the special education profession are responsible for upholding and advancing certain standards for professional practice (CEC, 2003). These standards include:

1. Identify and use instructional methods and curricula that are appropriate to their area of professional practice and effective in meeting the individual needs of persons with exceptionalities.
2. Participate in the selection and use of appropriate instructional materials, equipment, supplies, and other resources needed in the effective practice of their profession.

3. Create safe and effective learning environments that contribute to fulfillment of needs, stimulation of learning, and self-concept.
4. Maintain class size and case loads that are conducive to meeting the individual instructional needs of individuals with exceptionalities.
5. Use assessment instruments and procedures that do not discriminate against persons with exceptionalities on the basis of race, color, creed, sex, national origin, age, political practices, family or social background, sexual orientation, or exceptionality.
6. Base grading, promotion, graduation, and/or movement out of the program on the individual goals and objectives for individuals with exceptionalities.
7. Provide accurate program data to administrators, colleagues, and parents, based on efficient and objective record-keeping practices, for the purpose of decision making.
8. Maintain confidentiality of information except when information is released under specific conditions of written consent and statutory confidentiality requirements (p. 2).

With your acceptance of these responsibilities, you make a commitment to students with exceptionalities, their families, and the teaching profession. We hope you will give careful thought to these responsibilities.

WHAT WE BELIEVE

Our text is centered around five beliefs:

1. There are generic research-based instructional techniques that all teachers of students with special needs should know how to apply and assess.
2. These research-based techniques may be used in teaching various content areas/ subject matter and for various ages and levels of students with mild disabilities in a variety of settings.
3. In the 21st century, special educators must modify curriculum and adapt instruction as they work in collaborative partnerships with general educators, administrators, families, and other school professionals to meet the needs of students in increasingly diverse and inclusive classes.
4. As external partnerships become more critical to the success of students prior to entering school, during school, and in postschool situations, special educators will need a varied repertoire of collaborative skills to initiate and maintain these relationships.
5. All instruction should be student-centered, family-centered, and embrace the cultural and diverse backgrounds of today's learners.

Currently, many texts focus on mathematics, reading, and other content areas. Instead, we thoroughly discuss research-based instructional techniques and apply them, with examples, to various content areas, levels, and settings. We feel that in most inclusive settings, special educators will be responsible for modifying curriculum and adapting instruction, while relying on general educators for their expertise in curriculum areas. We believe our text fulfills the need for pre-service and in-service teachers to have a solid foundation in effective research-based methodologies built around reflective practice. From this solid foundation, teachers, through practice and successes, will add their own adaptations to best meet the needs of individual learners, as no one method works for all students.

PUTTING IT ALL TOGETHER

As you think about your role as a special educator, remember that at the core of our profession is protecting and ensuring the rights of students with disabilities and their families. Students with disabilities can come from all walks of lives and all cultures from around the globe. As a special educator you are expected to use teaching techniques that embrace the wide range of learners that you serve while ensuring these students are successful not only in school but also in life. Students with disabilities have the right to be an equal member in all aspects of society including being part of the general education setting. As a professional you can be guided by national organizations but the bottom-line is your dedication and commitment to ensuring the best possible outcome and future for the students you will be privileged to serve in your career as a special education teacher.

IMPORTANT POINTS

1. Participation of students with disabilities in standards-based reform was mandated with the 1997 amendments to the Individuals with Disabilities Act (IDEA), reauthorized in 2004.
2. The reauthorization of the Elementary and Secondary Education Act (ESEA), also known as the No Child Left Behind Act, was signed into law in 2002 with an emphasis on accountability, local control, expanded parent options, and doing what works.
3. A career in special education carries with it many professional responsibilities that are stated in the CEC Standards for Professional Practice.
4. In this text, we focus on research-based instructional techniques that may be used for teaching in various content areas for various levels of students. These techniques can be used by special educators to modify curriculum and adapt instruction as they work in partnership with general educators to meet students' needs.

DISCUSSION QUESTIONS

1. Discuss with a partner the implications of national education and standards-based reform on children and adolescents with disabilities.
2. Examine the CEC Standards for Professional Practice. Reflect on what the standards mean to you as a member of the special education teaching profession.
3. Discuss some of the common characteristics of students with special needs. Relate the characteristics to students with disabilities whom you have taught or worked with previously.

Websites: Useful websites related to chapter content can be found in Appendix A.

CHAPTER

2

Beginning-of-the-Year Planning and Organization

KEY TOPICS

It was the first day of pre-planning with one week to go before the start of school. Ivey Leonard was standing in the middle of her classroom surveying the blank slate before her. The boxes around her feet contained the materials she had accumulated throughout her years in college and now she was finally ready to create the classroom community she had dreamed was possible. In her first assignment as a special education teacher at an urban elementary school she knew she would face many challenges in the days to come, but for now the biggest challenge was where to begin.

She remembered from her internship experience that the daily schedule seemed to be somewhat difficult to establish so she decided to start there. She pulled out the folder she had received at the faculty meeting that morning with all the tools she would need for planning. In the folder there were grade-level lists of students sorted by their classroom teacher's name, planning period schedules, and lunch schedules for the entire school. For the next few hours she sat at her computer and checked her students' IEPs for the services they would need to receive. Eventually she pulled it all together into a schedule that appeared to meet everyone's needs and allowed for time spent in planning with other teachers. Her biggest block of time would be spent with Cheryl Gleason, the third-grade teacher with whom she was assigned to coteach for language arts and mathematics. Ivey would also need to work with fourth and fifth graders in her pull-out classroom. After e-mailing the schedule to all the teachers who would be impacted, she went to see Cheryl Gleason in her third-grade classroom.

Ivey was a little nervous about the coteaching portion of her teaching assignment. What if Cheryl didn't like her or didn't want to coteach? What if Cheryl had a totally different philosophy of teaching than she did? Ivey had heard stories about coteaching assignments where the special educator was little more than a glorified teaching assistant. However, Ivey had strong feelings about the power of teacher collaboration for meeting the needs of students, and she kept this in mind as she entered the third-grade classroom.

She needn't have worried. Cheryl Gleason was very pleased to see her, and for the rest of the afternoon, they put their heads together and worked out a plan that would involve sharing responsibilities for both whole-group and small-group instruction. They reviewed IEP goals and objectives for the third graders with learning disabilities, discussed grading, record keeping, classroom rules, and plans for guiding and managing behavior. Since Cheryl had been a part of a coteaching team before, she was able to share some of her perspectives on what had worked best to meet the needs of all the students in the classroom. In fact, by the time Ivey had left, Cheryl had encouraged her to think of it not as "Cheryl's third-grade class" but as "their third-grade class," their community of learners.

At the end of the day Ivey returned to her pull-out classroom and again surveyed the boxes she had left unpacked. She smiled to herself as she mentally reviewed all she had accomplished on that first day. "I wonder what I should do first tomorrow?" she thought to herself.

Beginning-of-the-year planning and organization is really all about prioritizing. Do you think Ivey Leonard made wise choices in how to spend her time on her first day? After a good night's sleep, what do you think Ivey should do tomorrow?

Responses to these questions are found in the Instructor's Manual.

INTRODUCTION

The Council for Exceptional Children (2003) has identified the knowledge and skill base for all entry-level special education teachers of students with exceptionalities, and among the essential knowledge and skills are an emphasis on planning and managing the learning environment. The planning, management, and organization decisions you make prior to and during the first week of school can establish the climate and set the tone for the rest of the school year (Ammer, Platt, & Cornett, 2004). The beginning of the school year is the ideal time to establish a safe, risk-free classroom learning community where all students are welcomed, valued, respected, and supported; where they are given opportunities to be active participants in the learning process; where they know and understand the rules and expectations; and where they will experience success. Taking a proactive approach at the start of the school year, quickly establishing systems and routines, and clearly communicating expectations to students will minimize the likelihood of problems later in the year. Therefore, in this chapter we present information to guide you in your efforts to plan and manage your teaching and learning environments particularly at the beginning of the year. We focus on what you should do prior to and during the first week of school as you review individualized education programs (IEPs), develop goals and objectives for students, prepare for a variety of instructional grouping arrangements to promote student participation, establish and communicate grading practices, record-keeping procedures, and classroom rules, and develop schedules.

DESIGNING INDIVIDUALIZED EDUCATION PROGRAMS AND PLANS

With the passage of PL 94–142 in 1975, the development of an Individualized Education Program (IEP) for students with disabilities became a requirement. The 1990 amendments renamed the law the Individuals with Disabilities Education Act (IDEA) and added the requirement that plans for transition services be made part of the IEP no later than age 16.

The IDEA Amendments of 1997, PL 105–17, amended and reauthorized the Individuals with Disabilities Education Act. The 1997 IDEA amendments placed a greater emphasis on providing access for students with disabilities to participate and progress in the general education curriculum including provision of the supports needed to enhance that participation and progress (Katsiyannis, Ellenburg, & Acton, 2000; Pugach & Warger, 2001). The 1997 reauthorization of IDEA called for substantive participation by general education teachers as active members of IEP teams who are essential to the development and implementation of instructional strategies, interventions, accommodations, and services. The emphasis on providing access for students with disabilities to the general education curriculum has increased the attention given to the selection of appropriate accommodations that can be used in general education settings (Etscheidt & Bartlett, 1999). Furthermore, "The 1997 IDEA amendments specifically addressed the need for students with disabilities to be included in state and district-wide assessment practices (with or without accommodations or through alternate assessments)" (Katsiyannis, Ellenburg, & Acton, 2000, p. 119). In addition, the 1997 amendments changed the age from 16 to 14 for developing a statement of transition service needs. This change emphasized the importance of early planning and preparation by students, parents/families, and teachers. Students' IEPs should reflect the courses that relate to their desired postschool outcomes, such as business and technology courses for a student interested in computer-related employment, and should contain content that addresses postschool desires and needs.

The reauthorization of IDEA in 2004 changed the name to the Individuals with Disabilities Education Improvement Act, but it is still referred to as IDEA (Smith, 2005). The changes that affected IEPs included adding flexibility to attendance requirements at IEP meetings; establishing a pilot project for multiyear IEPs in effect in some states; allowing modifications to IEPs during the year without the presence of the entire team; deleting the requirement of writing short-term objectives unless students are assessed with alternate assessments; and requiring a statement of transition goals beginning with the first IEP to be in place when the student reaches 16 years of age (Smith, 2005). Notice the 2004 IDEA amendments changed the age for the development of transition services back to age 16. Along with these revisions to the IEP are other procedural safeguards that were amended regarding procedures when students move to a different school or state in terms of who can call for assessment of a potential disability. These new provisions of IDEA regarding IEPs took effect on July 1, 2005.

COMPONENTS OF THE INDIVIDUALIZED EDUCATION PROGRAM

"The IEP is the cornerstone of IDEA-2004 and outlines the accommodations, goals and services a child needs to receive an appropriate education" (Burns, 2006, p. 3). It is like a road map for special education instruction, because it tells where students are going and how they are going to get there. It describes what the student needs and what will be done to address those needs. One of your essential tasks at the beginning of the year is to become thoroughly familiar with each student's Individualized Education Program. IEP forms vary by state, school district, and sometimes by category within the same district. Although some states are beginning to adopt statewide IEPs, these documents across all states must contain the following components:

1. The student's present levels of academic achievement and functional performance, including a statement of how the disability affects the student's involvement and progress in the general education curriculum.
2. A statement of the annual goals (academic and functional) that the student is expected to attain and how and when the goals will be measured.
3. For students with disabilities who take alternate assessments, a statement of benchmarks or short-term objectives.

4. A statement of the special education and related services, supplementary aids, program modifications, or supports that will be provided
5. The extent, if any, to which the student will not participate with nondisabled students in a general education classroom
6. Projected dates for initiation and duration of special services
7. Modifications needed for participation in statewide or districtwide assessments or if it is determined the student cannot participate, why the assessment is inappropriate and how the student will be assessed
8. Needed transition services (from school to work or postsecondary education) beginning with the first IEP to be in place when the student reaches 16 years of age
9. Rights that transfer at age of majority and focus on students who are in their last year of receiving services, informing them of any services that will transfer upon reaching the age of maturity
10. Signatures of participants at IEP meeting.

We encourage you to visit the U.S. Department of Education Website, http://www.ed.gov/policy/speced/guid/idea/idea2004.html, and go to the page for IDEA 2004 resources. Under technical assistance tools you will see information on model forms including guidance on required content and information on procedural safeguards.

Present Levels of Academic Achievement and Functional Performance

The student's present levels of performance are usually based on results from both formal and informal measures. Formal assessment measures contain specific rules for administration, scoring, and interpretation. They are typically based on a comparison with the performance of students of the same age and grade level (that is, they are norm referenced). Informal measures do not contain rigid rules for administration, scoring, and interpretation. They may consist of inventories, observations, criterion-referenced tests, or probes. Chapter 4 presents a detailed description of informal assessment.

In examining the sample IEP in Figure 2.1, notice that both formal tests, such as the Florida Comprehensive Assessment Test (FCAT), and informal measures, such as a Directed Reading Activity (DRA), were administered to determine the current levels of educational performance.

Annual Academic and Functional Goals

A student's annual goals are developed by IEP team members after they examine the student's present levels of performance. Examples of annual goals appropriate for students with special needs are:

1. Master basic computation facts at the first-grade level.
2. Read the 220 Dolch words.
3. Apply note-taking techniques in content area classrooms.
4. Comply with teacher's requests.

Progress toward goals may be assessed by using the IEP as a tool to monitor students' progress. In Figure 2.1 three annual goals are written for Jimmy. Two of them are academic and one is functional. Notice that the statewide assessment test and teacher observation are among the evaluation methods that will be used.

Individualized Education Program

Student Information

Name: Jimmy Smith Date: 12/8/06

Student ID: ______ Date of Birth: 10/5/91

Address: 654 Sunset Avenue, Smalltown USA

Phone: (407) 543-1234

School: Enterprise Elem Grade Level: 5

Parent Notification Box
(If not attending meeting)

Date	Type of Attempt	By Whom	Results

Present Level of Academic Achievement and Functional Performance

Jimmy is a 5th grade student who is currently reading at a 3rd grade level, as indicated by a score of 38 on a DRA (administered 10/21/06). He demonstrates adequate phonemic awareness but he struggles with phonics, fluency, vocabulary, and comprehension.
His current oral fluency rate is 93 words correct per minute which places him in the second quartile for 5th grade. Jimmy has not yet mastered basic addition facts (10 correct/5 wrong in 1 minute probe on 11/4/06) or subtraction facts (8 correct/5 wrong in 1 minute probe on 11/5/06). Jimmy's scores for the 2005 FCAT were as follows: Reading 262 (level 1) Math 281 (level 2), Science 260 (level 2).

IEP date: 12/8/06

IEP review date: 12/8/07

In Attendance at IEP Meeting

Parent/Guardian Lorna Smith Student Jimmy Smith

ESE teacher Ivey Leonard Regular Education Teacher Eve Peabody

School Psychologist Maria Hayes LEA representative Steve Palladino

Other ______ Other ______

Annual Academic and Functional Goals

Indicate short term objectives for those students who participate in alternate assessments

		Evaluation Method	Date Initiated	Date Completed
Goal 1	Jimmy will improve grade level reading and language arts skills.	CBM	12/11/06	
Goal 2	Jimmy will improve grade level math skills.	CBM	12/11/06	
Goal 3	Jimmy will improve homework completion skills.	Checklist	12/11/06	

Jimmy's progress towards meeting annual goals will be reported through progress reports (3 times yearly) report cards (3 times yearly), and periodic parent/teacher conferences.

Special Education and Related Services

Program or Service	Amount of Time per Week	Projected Initiation Date	Anticipated Duration	Person Responsible	Supplemental Aids and Services	Accommodations
SLD	5 hours/ week	12/11/06	12 months	Classroom Teacher		AlphaSmart

Figure 2.1 SAMPLE IEP

A Statement of Benchmarks or Short-Term Objectives

As a means of reducing paperwork, IDEA 2004 requires IEPs to include short-term objectives *only if* a student is being assessed with alternate assessments (Smith, 2005). Please keep this in mind when you are trying to decide whether you need to write short-term objectives as part of a student's IEP. We include this section because you may have students who are assessed with alternate assessments. In addition, your state or school district may still require short-term objectives as part of the IEP. Be sure to determine what your state and school district require.

Informal measures, such as curriculum-based measures or Directed Reading Activities, may be used to identify and evaluate the attainment of short-term objectives. Short-term objectives should be stated in instructional or behavioral terms. For example, "Lucy is hyperactive" is not written in behavioral terms, whereas "Lucy got out of her seat 32 times during her 25-minute music class" is written in behavioral terms. A behavioral objective includes four components: the learner, the target behavior, the condition, and the criterion.

The target behavior identifies what the learner is asked to do. It should be observable and specific so it can be measured. Following are some sample target behaviors frequently found in the IEPs of students with special needs. Notice that the target behaviors are observable and measurable.

1. Write the answers to subtraction facts.
2. Rephrase the main idea of a paragraph.
3. State verbally two expectations of an employer.
4. Follow teacher's requests.

The condition of a behavioral objective usually relates the circumstances under which the behavior will occur. It frequently tells when or how. Following are examples of conditions:

1. Given a worksheet . . .
2. Without use of a dictionary . . .
3. Using a calculator . . .

The criterion of a behavioral objective describes the minimum level of performance for mastery of the target behavior. The criterion may be expressed in terms of the following:

1. Accuracy—90%, or 15 correct.
2. Rate—15 correct in 1 minute.
3. Time—10 minutes.

Academic behaviors are usually measured in terms of accuracy or rate. To ensure mastery of an objective, an overlearning measure is frequently suggested (Alberto & Troutman, 2006). The overlearning measure requires that the student perform this behavior more than one time. Examples of overlearning include the following:

1. three days
2. four sessions
3. five attempts

Now, putting all four components of a behavioral objective together along with the overlearning measure, the following examples represent behavioral objectives appropriate for students with special needs:

1. Upon request, Jerome will apply the steps of a test-taking strategy to a practice test within 40 minutes for three sessions.
2. When asked, Penny will read aloud a passage at 150 correct words per minute with two or fewer errors for three days.
3. When asked to begin, Zita will say the names of 20 targeted states and their capitals within 3 minutes for three trials.
4. Without prompting, Joe will begin the teacher's assignment within 2 minutes for three sessions.

A Statement of Special Education and Related Services, Supplementary Aids, Program Modifications, or Supports

Special education and related services appropriate for each student must be included in the IEP. Special education services include direct and indirect services. Direct services are those provided by a special education teacher to the student, whereas indirect services are those provided by a special education teacher to the general education teacher. Special education teachers may provide these indirect services by helping classroom teachers identify effective instructional techniques and adapt materials. Related services, provided by specialists, include counseling, social work, adapted physical education, psychological testing, and transportation. The roles, responsibilities, and amount of time allocated for special education and related services must be clearly stated in the IEP. Figure 2.1 shows that Jimmy receives specific learning disabilities (SLD) services for 5 hours a week and participates in regular/general education for 25 hours a week. It also shows that the supplementary aids, accommodations, or supports include assistive technology in the form of an AlphaSmart.

Participation with Nondisabled Students in General Education

The amount of time a student will participate with nondisabled peers, must be noted on the IEP (see Figure 2.1).

Projected Dates for Initiation and Duration of Services

The projected dates for the initiation and duration of services must be indicated on the IEP. For example, Figure 2.1 shows that Jimmy will spend one hour a day receiving special education services beginning 12/10/06 (initiation of services), for 12 months (duration of services).

Accommodations in Statewide and Districtwide Assessments

One section on the IEP describes participation in statewide and districtwide assessments. In some cases, the student will participate in these assessments, but will need an accommodation in the administration of the tests (e.g. use of AlphaSmart). A space is provided on the IEP to describe the accommodations. In cases in which the student will not participate in state and district assessments, the IEP team needs to state a reason along with a description of an alternate assessment. Figure 2.1 shows that Jimmy did participate in statewide assessment and needed an accommodation.

Transition Services

The transition planning section of the IEP includes a place for the IEP team to include transition goals, academic/instructional activities, related services, community experiences, employment and adult living objectives, and functional evaluation information. Because Jimmy is only 12, no mention of transition services appears on the IEP. Chapter 12 provides a detailed description of transition IEPs.

Rights at Age of Majority

The purpose of this section of the IEP as provided by the U.S. Department of Education is, "Beginning not later than one year before the child reaches the age of majority under State law, the IEP must include a statement that the child has been informed of the child's rights under Part B of the IDEA, if any, that will, consistent with 34 CFR 300.520, transfer to the child on reaching the age of majority," Basically, this statement is included to help students understand their rights for services once they are of legal age to make their own educational decisions. Notifying parents and students of this transfer of rights one year in advance allows the parents and students to discuss how they will make this transfer or seek legal documentation necessary if students need continued support to create their educational plans once they reach the age of majority.

Signatures of Participants at IEP Meeting

Appearing on the IEP is a section that includes the names of those who attended, their roles (e.g., parents, special education teacher, student), and the date of the meeting. Visit the U.S. Department of Education Website (http://www.ed.gov/policy/speced/guid/idea/idea2004.html) and go to the page for IDEA 2004 resources. On this page under the Technical Assistance Tools you will find the information on Model Forms, including guidance on the required content, as well as information on the Procedural Safeguards.

WEEKLY AND DAILY PLANS

"Effective teachers are expert at planning and preparation for instruction" (Nougaret, Scruggs, & Mastropieri, 2005, p. 219). Planning guides teachers for a year, a 9-week term, a day, or a lesson. It requires identification of learner needs, goals and objectives, materials, instructional strategies, and evaluation procedures. In addition to the IEP, which is mandated by law, weekly planning is required by many school principals. Often, teachers turn in plan books on Friday for the principal's approval of the next week's lessons. When teachers write their plans for the week in a plan book, they typically include times, names of texts or materials, and page numbers. Sometimes, special and general education teachers record information such as the levels of the students in each of the curriculum materials used in the class, the groups to which they are assigned, and the names of students receiving related services. In pull-out programs, teachers list the names of students and the subjects they are assigned to in general classroom settings.

Weekly plan books do not provide teachers with specifics about presenting lessons or adequate space to add much detail, which may be a problem if there are 10 students working on different objectives. Therefore, in addition to using a weekly plan book, resource teachers and teachers who coteach with classroom teachers in general education classrooms need to use an additional planning format to enable them to be aware of their objectives, procedures, materials, and evaluation methods for each lesson. Figure 2.2, which contains an example of a lesson from a science unit on the rainforest, includes the essential parts of a lesson. Please see Chapter 5 for a detailed discussion of lesson planning and presentation.

Activity 2.1

Contact your local school district for a copy of the IEP that is used in that district. Look for the IEP sections that were described in this chapter. They may be found in different locations on the form you have because IEP forms vary from district to district.

1. Write two annual goals for Carl (description follows).
2. For each annual goal, write two short-term objectives. Remember to include the learner (i.e., Carl), the target behavior, the condition, and the criterion.

Carl is in seventh grade and attends Sprague Middle School. In mathematics, he is functioning on a fifth-grade level. However, his reading difficulties make it hard for him to solve word problems unless someone reads the problems to him. He can add and subtract well, but has difficulty with multiplication, division, and all operations involving fractions.

Carl has difficulty decoding words and therefore does not comprehend what he reads if the level of the material is higher than fifth grade. His teacher has discovered that he enjoys reading materials that involve science topics. With these materials, he has better success with decoding, fluency, and comprehension.

(Answers for this and other activities are found in the Instructor's Manual.)

IMPORTANT POINTS

1. The planning and organization decisions you make prior to and during the first week of school can establish the climate and set the tone for the rest of the school year.
2. An Individualized Education Program (IEP), mandated by law, includes the accommodations, goals, and services a student with disabilities needs in order to receive an appropriate education.
3. The components of an IEP describe (a) the student's present levels of academic achievement and functional performance; (b) annual academic and functional goals; (c) a statement of benchmarks or short-term objectives only if a student is being assessed with alternate assessments; (d) a statement of special education and related services, supplementary aids, program modifications, or supports; (e) participation with nondisabled peers in general education; (f) projected dates for initiation and duration of services; (g) modifications in statewide and districtwide assessments; (h) transition services; and (i) signatures of participants at the IEP meeting.
4. In addition to the IEP, planning includes using a weekly plan book and designing specific lesson plans that include objectives, procedures, materials, and evaluation procedures.

BOX 2.1

Reflections on Practice

Individualized Education Programs (IEPs) are one of the special education teacher's responsibilities. However, there is increasing interest in engaging students in IEP development and in student-led IEP meetings particularly at the secondary level. After all, when students take ownership for what they are going to learn, there is a greater chance they will learn it. Therefore, increasing a student's responsibility for IEPs can positively impact student buy-in and participation in the IEP process (Mason, McGahee-Kovac, & Johnson, 2004). Students can and have been assisted to lead their own IEP meetings (Eisenman, Chamberlin, & McGahee-Kovac, 2005). Mason, McGahee-Kovac, Johnson, and Stillerman (2002) found that when students took responsibility for leading their IEP conferences, they tended to know more about their disabilities, legal rights, and needed accommodations than other students. By law, students of any age must be invited to be part of their IEP meeting if the purpose is to plan transition services, and transition planning must begin at age 16 (Kupper & McGahee-Kovac, 2002).

Preparing students to lead their IEP meetings requires preparation and training. Mason et al. (2004) identified three general levels of student participation ranging from presenting limited information to assuming responsibility for all aspects of the IEP meeting:

Level 1: Student presents information about or reads from his or her transition plan for the future.

Level 2: Student explains his or her disability, shares information on individual strengths and weaknesses (present levels of performance), and explains the accommodations needed. Students present Level 1 information and may suggest new IEP goals.

Level 3: Student leads the IEP conference, including Level 1 and Level 2 responsibilities, introductions, and closing. (p. 19)

If students are to become advocates for their in-school and postschool activities and outcomes, they will benefit from participating in the IEP process. By participating they will learn to speak for themselves, explain their disability to others, contribute to the decision making, and become more involved in their own education (Kupper & McGahee-Kovac, 2002). For more information about the student-led IEP process, consult:

Eisenman, L., Chamberlin, M., & McGahee-Kovac, M. (2005). A teacher inquiry group on student-led IEPs: Starting small to make a difference. *Teacher Education and Special Education, 28*(3–4), 195–206.

Kupper, L., & McGahee-Kovac, M. (2002). *Helping students develop their IEPs. Technical assistance guide* (2nd ed.) (and) *A student's guide to the IEP* (2nd ed.). Washington, DC: NICHCY.

Mason, C. Y., McGahee-Kovac, M., & Johnson, L. (2004). How to help students lead their IEP meetings. *TEACHING Exceptional Children, 36*(3), 18–25.

McGahee, M., Mason, C., Wallace, T., & Jones, B. (2001). *Student-led IEPs: A guide for student involvement.* Arlington, VA: Council for Exceptional Children.

Figure 2.2 A LESSON FROM A SCIENCE UNIT

Subject:
Science (1:45–2:30)—"The Rainforest"

Objective:
After instruction, the students will write in their journals three facts about the rainforest, with 95% accuracy, for 2 days.

Procedures:

1. Introduce the lesson by asking students if they can describe a rainforest.
2. Read *A Day in the Rainforest.*
3. Discuss the story with the students.
4. Have the students generate words from the story that describe how it feels to be in the rainforest.
5. Write their suggestions on an overhead transparency.
6. Give a 10-minute presentation on life in the rainforest.
7. Have students name things that live in the rainforest.
8. Write these on an overhead transparency.
9. Have students write in their rainforest journals three facts about the rainforest that they learned in the lesson.
10. To close the lesson, have the students share one fact that they have written about the rainforest.

Materials:

1. The book, *A Day in the Rainforest*
2. Overhead projector, transparencies, and pen
3. Journals

Evaluation:
Students will be evaluated by checking their journals to be sure they wrote three accurate facts about rainforests.

CREATING INSTRUCTIONAL, ASSESSMENT, AND MANAGEMENT DECISIONS

Due to the varied and complex demands placed on special education teachers (e.g., implementing the goals and objectives of IEPs, planning appropriate learning activities, adapting instruction, and modifying materials), many tasks must be accomplished before the start of the academic year. Careful attention to these tasks eases the transitions students experience as they return to school. Part of beginning-year planning and organization involves making decisions about how to coordinate instruction, assessment, and management. This planning includes attention to instructional grouping arrangements, student variables, grading and record-keeping procedures, setting up the learning environment for technology and establishing management procedures such as classroom rules.

INSTRUCTIONAL GROUPING ARRANGEMENTS

One of the challenges teachers face as they begin the year is organizing and managing the classroom environment for instruction. Polloway, Patton, and Serna (2005) underscore the critical importance of classroom organization, which has taken on even more significance with the inclusive education movement. Teachers must consider instructional arrangements that are conducive to learning and yet minimize distractions, and that promote student engagement and academic achievement.

Instruction may be provided in a variety of ways: large groups, small groups, one-to-one, with peers, or independently. Individualization of instruction may be achieved by using any of these instructional arrangements. As Christenson, Thurlow, and Ysseldyke (1987) point out, individualization does not limit the grouping arrangement to situations in which a student works alone or in a one-to-one arrangement with a teacher. Individualization refers to "helping students succeed, to achieve a high percentage of correct responses and to become confident in his/her competence" (p. 6).

Factors influencing decisions about how to provide instruction include (a) the characteristics and needs of the students, (b) the type of learning planned—whether the teacher is teaching a skill for the first time (i.e., acquisition learning) or students are practicing and maintaining a skill that has already been taught (i.e., fluency and maintenance learning), (c) the task or activity (e.g., engaging in a dialogue about a literature selection, discussing job interviewing, building a model of the digestive system, or writing and reflecting in journals), and (d) the types of instructional methodology that are available. Callahan, Clark, and Kellough (1998) recommend that you consider the types of instructional methodology that are available, including:

- Cooperative learning
- Debates
- Games
- Laboratory experiments
- Multimedia and other types of technology
- Problem solving
- Peer tutoring
- Simulations
- Textbooks
- Learning centers
- Computer-assisted instruction
- Demonstrations
- Guest speakers
- Lecture/presentations
- Panel discussions
- Questioning
- Role-playing
- Think-pair-share
- Coteaching.

Teachers should choose instructional arrangements that meet students' needs as documented in their IEPs and that address cultural and linguistic diversity. In addition, as they plan these arrangements, they should consider how to set up the learning environment for technology for both students and teachers. A method to incorporate technology is to check students' IEPs for any mention of technology. For example, Jimmy's IEP calls for him to use the AlphaSmart. Special education teachers in pull-out programs need to set up their classrooms with appropriate technology, and those working in inclusive settings need to plan with coteachers for the use of technology in general education settings (e.g., computer work stations off to the side; large-group seating to view a DVD; availability of assistive technology tools to enable students with special needs to access the general education curriculum). As you read the next section, think about how you would use technology within each of the instructional arrangements. Please see Chapter 11 for a complete description of technology for teaching and learning.

Large-Group Instruction

There are many opportunities for using large-group instruction. For example, you could use large-group instruction to introduce a strategy for taking notes. Lewis and Doorlag (2006) suggest providing guided practice for the whole class at once. Have the students practice taking notes by watching a videotape of a content lesson (e.g., global warming), while you circulate around the room to monitor use of the note-taking strategy. Other appropriate uses of whole-class instruction include the viewing of multimedia presentations, large-group discussions of content area subjects, and demonstrations. Fister and Kemp (1995) recommend the use of the Ask, Pause, Call technique during presentations to large groups. The teacher asks a question, pauses to allow students to process the question and formulate a response, and then calls on someone.

Large-group instruction is used extensively in general education classroom settings. Now that greater emphasis is being placed on coteaching of classes by general and special educators (Dettmer, Thurston, & Dyck, 2005), special education teachers who coteach in inclusive classrooms can share with general education teachers the responsibility for providing instruction to the whole class. Be aware that when using large-group instruction, not all of the students will learn all of the content you present. You still need to think about individual student needs. Dyck, Sundbye, and Pemberton (1997) use an Interactive Lesson Planning Model to determine the topic of a lesson, the content of the lesson, and what parts of the content can be learned by all, most, or some of the students given their varied levels and skills. This planning model, particularly useful for coteachers, serves as a basis for differentiating activities, objectives, and assessments for students.

When providing instruction to the entire group, many teachers arrange the desks in rows. This structure may be appropriate when you are lecturing and making presentations through directive teaching or giving a PowerPoint presentation. When utilizing this type of arrangement, move around the room, and direct comments and questions to students seated in various parts of the classroom to keep all students engaged. Cegelka (1995) emphasizes the importance of arranging the desks so that all students can see the whole-group instructional area and yet not face areas that could distract them, such as learning center activity areas, windows, or doors.

Small-Group Instruction

Small-group instruction is appropriate when teachers present different material to different students (Lewis & Doorlag, 2006). Small groups are frequently used in acquisition learning to teach a specific skill (Polloway, Patton, & Serna, 2005). Groups should be flexible: Sondra, Tim, Rahji, and Bertha may be grouped together for instruction in mathematics but be members of other groups for spelling. If Bertha progresses more rapidly than the others, she is moved to another, more appropriate group.

Small-group instruction usually consists of groups of two to five students. It is used when teachers want to work closely with students, give them the opportunity to express what they know, provide them with frequent feedback, and allow them to receive feedback from other students (Vaughn, Hughes, & Moody, 2001). Small groups may also be used in cooperative teaching situations to divide the class into different skill groups. Small groups are frequently used in general education classes because of the heterogeneity of the population and thus they would work well in inclusive settings.

Small-group arrangements are particularly effective for teaching academic skills. Reading is frequently taught in small groups. Small-group arrangements also are useful for cooperative learning activities (activities in which students work together and teach each other), role-playing activities, and review sessions. A detailed description of cooperative learning is provided in Chapter 9. When working with a group, some teachers prefer to seat students in a semicircle facing them in order to provide optimum feedback and attention; there is support for this grouping arrangement for low-achieving students in the areas of mathematics (Carnine, Silbert, & Kame'enui, 1997) and reading (Carnine, Silbert, Kame'enui, & Tarver, 2004). Small-group instruction may be appealing to students who have language differences because they may feel more comfortable asking for clarification in a small group and because they may have more opportunity to participate.

Small groups are not always used for purposes of direct instruction. Frequently, small groups are led by students who take turns assuming the role of the leader and guiding instruction through question asking and dialogue (Vaughn, Hughes, & Moody, 2001). In Chapter 7, we present a description of reciprocal teaching in which students assume responsibility for their own learning as they link their prior knowledge with new knowledge through questioning, summarizing, clarifying, and predicting text information. Reciprocal teaching is often used with small groups of four to seven students.

One-to-One Instruction

Working on a one-to-one basis with the teacher allows students to ask questions, receive corrective feedback, and interact directly with the teacher, which is highly advantageous for students. Individual instruction is appropriate for students who are working on acquisition learning, having difficulty learning in a small-group setting, or needing assistance with specific aspects of assignments (Polloway, Patton, & Serna, 2005). The disadvantage of one-to-one instruction is that the special education teacher's time and attention can be focused on only one student at a time.

Teachers using one-to-one instruction must plan for the rest of the class, perhaps by including cooperative learning activities and peer tutoring. Some teachers utilize the skills of paraprofessionals or volunteers to provide one-to-one instruction to students. Other teachers ask paraprofessionals or volunteers to monitor the rest of the class while they work with individual students. Some coteaching arrangements are conducive to one-to-one instruction. While one teacher works with most of the class, the coteacher assists other students on a one-to-one basis (see Chapter 3 for other suggestions). In arranging the classroom, teachers can set up tables or desks away from the rest of the class for one-to-one instruction.

Peer Tutoring

Vaughn, Schumm, Klingner, and Saumell (1995) found that students with learning disabilities prefer to work with a peer than alone or in a large group. In peer tutoring, one student receives instruction from another under supervision of the teacher. Peer tutoring is effective for fluency and maintenance learning, such as practicing mathematics facts and spelling words. Tutors may also check answers to end-of-chapter questions, provide positive reinforcement and corrective feedback, and teach or reteach specific skills to other students who need extra help. When instruction is provided through tutorial arrangements, you may want to arrange areas in the classroom for peer tutors by putting two desks together or by providing small tables set aside from the rest of the class. Peer tutoring is often combined with other instructional options, such as large- and small-group arrangements. A detailed description of peer tutoring is provided in Chapter 9.

Independent Learning

Independent learning may include a student's independent practice of something that has already been taught (e.g., completion of a learning center activity on addition of like fractions; preparation of a first draft of an essay). For example, when students have acquired a skill and need additional practice, you should provide practice opportunities for them. It is helpful to include a self-correcting component in this type of independent practice work (e.g., provide an answer key in the learning center on fractions).

Independent learning may also include the student's completion of an independent project (e.g., preparing entries for a portfolio; conducting research in the library/media center for a science project). While those students who are capable of independent learning with little or no assistance are engaged in independent work (e.g., adding work to a portfolio), you can assist other students individually or in small groups.

Classrooms may be set up to contain individual work areas where students can work quietly and independently. Students may also work independently at a table, desk, or computer workstation. The challenge for teachers is to place the individual work areas away from the more active areas of the classroom.

In summary, there are a variety of ways to arrange the classroom for instruction including whole class, teacher- and student-led small-group instruction, peer tutoring, one-to-one instruction, and independent learning. You can use any of the previously described arrangements or a combination of one or more of them, depending on your instructional purpose(s) and the needs and characteristics of your students. Flexible grouping arrangements allow you to individualize instruction in a variety of ways. Figure 2.3 contains examples of possible arrangements for large- and small-group instruction. Notice how these groupings may be used effectively in both pull-out and inclusive classrooms, and how they allow the teacher to move around the room to provide instruction and monitor progress while keeping students interested and engaged.

Activity 2.2

Think of examples of lessons you could teach using large-group, small-group, and peer-tutoring instructional arrangements. Choose the grade level and subject area. Now sketch the classroom arrangement for each of the lessons.

Figure 2.3 LARGE- AND SMALL-GROUP INSTRUCTIONAL ARRANGEMENTS

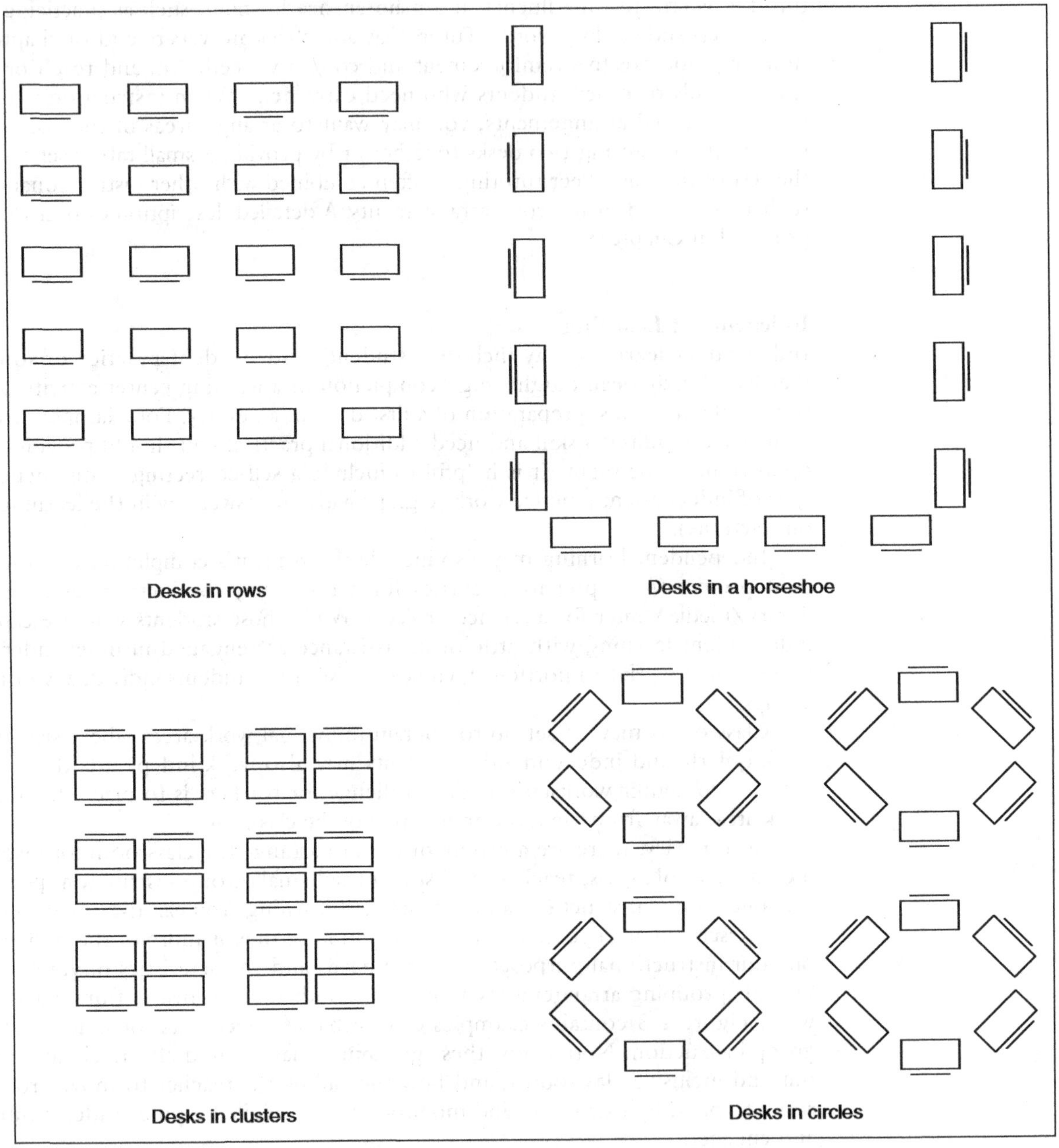

STUDENT VARIABLES

Student variables that affect instructional decisions and classroom organization include the number of students in the class, their age and grade levels, their skill levels, cultural and language differences, and related challenges students have (mobility, language, behavior, etc.). You may, therefore, arrange the room to accommodate students who are working at various levels and who are focusing on different content and skills by including learning centers, computers, a variety of instructional grouping arrangements, and modified curriculum materials written for several different grade levels. Heron and Harris (1987) suggest that verbal communication moves across, not around, tables. Therefore, they recommend that a student with low verbal skills be seated across from a student with high verbal skills to maximize the reception of verbal messages and nonverbal cues (that is, facial expressions and gestures). Student placement is something to keep in mind as you work with coteachers in inclusive settings.

Consider cultural differences in setting up the classroom. In some cultures students participate freely in group discussions while in other cultures they do not. This fact is important to remember as you plan your instructional activities so you do not mistake limited participation due to cultural differences as lack of ability. Students from cultures that are people oriented or that endorse working together for the good of the group may benefit from cooperative learning activities, group projects, and other collaborative activities. Teachers may want to consider using physical arrangements and activities to complement various cultural preferences by including tables, peer-tutoring areas, activity areas, and independent work areas.

GRADING AND RECORD-KEEPING PROCEDURES

As part of the assessment decisions you make at the beginning of the school year, decide how you are going to grade student work, monitor progress, and keep records of student performance, and how you will communicate these procedures to your students. We suggest that you do this verbally, in writing, as part of the classroom rules, or in all three ways.

Grading

Grading is an essential part of educational practice, providing feedback to students, their families, and others (Miller, 2002). More and more students with disabilities are receiving instruction in general education classrooms and, therefore, are being graded there. Grading students with disabilities is particularly perplexing in inclusive settings. In a grading survey, 368 general education teachers rated pass-fail grades and checklists as appropriate for students with disabilities (Bursuck, Polloway, Plante, Epstein, Jayanthi, & McConeghy, 1996). Both general educators (Bursuck et al., 1996) and secondary students (Munk & Bursuck, 1997) felt that grade adaptations only for students with disabilities were unfair. As a special education teacher, you may be responsible for assigning grades, you may not assign grades at all, or you may assign grades in collaboration with a general education teacher. Bursuck et al. (1996) found that 50% of the general educators in their survey assumed complete responsibility for grading, whereas 40% shared grading responsibilities with special educators. Remember that in true coteaching the special educator and the general educator should co-plan, co-instruct, and co-assess, so grading should be part of your role in an inclusive classroom.

General techniques such as assigning multiple grades, basing grades on a variety of assignments, factoring in growth rate (Guskey & Bailey, 2001; Munk, 2003), contracting for grades, and establishing criteria for grades have been found to be effective in grading students with special needs (Bursuck & Munk, 1997). Written narratives may also be used to supplement the use of letter grades (Munk & Bursuck, 2004). A modified grading system can be used for students with disabilities, but it must be available to all students unless the student with disabilities is taking the general education class for no credit or is not required to master the course content (Salend & Duhaney, 2002). Check with your school district to see what the grading guidelines are and whether you have the flexibility of utilizing alternative grading systems with your students. Also make sure to consult the student's IEP as grading modifications listed in the IEP are binding (Friend & Bursuck, 2006).

Assigning Multiple Grades Assignments may be evaluated with multiple grades. For example, you may assign two grades for a report—one for content and one for mechanics. Giving two grades takes into consideration the ideas (content) as separate from the mechanical aspects (punctuation, spelling, grammar), which present stumbling blocks for many students with special needs. Munk (2003) and Guskey and Bailey (2001) suggest the use of multiple or balanced grades as a way to assign students grades on their report cards. Munk and Bursuck (1997) found that general education teachers and secondary students believed assigning separate grades for effort and product to be a helpful adaptation for students with special needs. For example, Ms. Barbour assigned a grade of C for the quality of the writing of one of her student's essays and a grade of A for effort for the time and effort the student devoted and the research the student completed on the topic.

Basing Grades on a Variety of Assignments Miller (2002) recommends basing grades on multiple dimensions such as tests, homework assignments, projects, and extra credit work. Additionally, you have the option of determining the final grade by giving more weight to reports and homework scores than exam scores.

Factoring in Growth Rate Grading based on improvement is another adaptation that is effective for students with disabilities (Munk, 2003). One of the authors based students' spelling grades, in part, on the increase in the number of words spelled correctly from the Monday pretest to the final spelling test on Friday. For example, both Marcus and Bridget earned an A grade. Marcus improved by 10 words from the spelling pretest to the posttest, which boosted his grade to an A. Bridget improved by only one word, yet earned an A grade as she scored 100% on the posttest.

Contracting for Grades Contracting with students for grades based on a certain level of proficiency on IEP objectives is another suggestion (Polloway, Epstein, Bursuck, Roderique, McConeghy, & Jayanthi, 1994). In this grading procedure, you discuss short-term objectives with the students and agree on the level of proficiency to be reached by the end of each grading period. Reaching the predetermined level of proficiency results in a higher grade than not reaching it.

Establishing Criteria for Grades In addition to percentages, make sure that you provide your students with grading criteria. For example, is it possible for a paper with a grade of A to have spelling errors? Discuss with the students the characteristics of outstanding work, average work, and poor work, and show them examples. Mr. Lucas teaches students how to take notes so that they can improve their performance in history class. As part of his teaching procedure, he shows them examples of good and poor notes. He specifies his criteria for grading students' notes for the content (e.g., key points of the lecture) and the technique (e.g., accurate use of a note-taking sstrategy).

Using Written Narratives In addition to assigning letter and number grades you can also add written narratives about student performance (Munk & Bursuck, 2004). Frequently, these written descriptions of student performance provide more meaningful and specific information to students and their families than a letter grade does. These narratives can also be used to set or adjust the student's goals (Miller, 2002) and/or identify what students must do to improve (Friend & Bursuck, 2006).

Some effective instructional practices that support grading procedures for students with disabilities in inclusive settings are (Salend & Duhaney, 2002):

1. Communicate expectations and clear guidelines to students and families. Sharing information may be accomplished during an open house or on the Internet by posting your grading criteria and guidelines.
2. Show models of exemplary work before assigning projects.
3. Provide nongraded assignments to students first with feedback and additional instruction if necessary before grading the final product.
4. Give extra credit.
5. Calculate grades based on median, not mean, scores.
6. Involve students in the design of grading rubrics.

One of the most troublesome questions for you as a teacher is whether students with special needs should fail in classes for which you have the responsibility of assigning grades. Special education teachers are supposed to provide students with an appropriate education plan. If a student is failing, the teacher should ask such questions as, Did I design an appropriate education plan? Did I implement it correctly? Is there something else I might do? Should I add other incentives? We feel that students should not fail in a special education setting if they truly have been provided with an individualized education program. Whatever grading system you use, be sure you explain it thoroughly to your students and their parents and implement it in a consistent manner, giving each student what he or she needs for success.

Record Keeping

"Record keeping consists of collecting, maintaining, and utilizing student information and data for instructional and/or administrative purposes" (Polloway, Patton, & Serna, 2005). Teachers should keep careful, written records on a daily basis regarding student performance. "The most important factors are that data are collected regularly, recorded in a systematic fashion, and then utilized to determine whether instructional modifications should be made" (Lewis & Doorlag, 2006, p. 170). Record-keeping systems may be designed prior to the start of the school year. Charts, graphs, checklists, and other forms may be developed to accompany the activities and materials that students will use in the classroom. In some classes, the record-keeping system is visible to everyone, as in Mrs. Murphy's fourth grade, where the names of the books each student has read are posted. In other cases, the record-keeping system is kept in a digital format, as in Mr. Russo's high school class, where mathematics students are studying probability. In addition, Mr. Russo's school uses a tool that allows parents to review their child's progress via the web. A checklist containing mathematics vocabulary and rules is available on the computer and in a format that Mr. Russo and each student can access and update on a daily basis.

Teachers may develop other record-keeping systems by recording the date and score for computer and learning center activities; progress toward mastering specific skills; attendance records; precision teaching; scores on tests, homework, and other assignments; and progress in portfolios, journals, and group projects. Having these records available in digital format may be particularly helpful for teachers. For example, using grading software allows teachers to manipulate the data, a significant advantage over looking at information on paper (e.g., sorting students to see if they are experiencing difficulty in multiple subjects; looking for a correlation between poor academic performance and absences or tardiness)(Cohen & Spenciner, 2005).

Students may be responsible for some of their own record keeping. Lewis and Doorlag (2006) recommend involving students in checking their answers with an answer key and

BOX 2.2

Reflections on Practice

Rubrics can be a valuable tool for grading and record keeping. Teachers who use rubrics have found them helpful in monitoring student progress in academic and social skill areas, and parents gain a better understanding of which skills their children have mastered and which ones they need to work on. When a rubric system is used, the ratings can be used to create IEP goals, determine class rank, and monitor student learning gains. The rubric shown illustrates how students are performing in relation to skills needed for success in school and is being used to generate IEP goals.

IEP Data Collection Tool

	Tom	Jim	Bill	Sue	Matt	Quincy	Deon	Tyler
Respects others and property	•					•		
Shows positive attitude/behavior	•	•				•		
Completes tasks	•					•	•	
Stays on task	•		•	•	•	•		
Completes homework	•		•	•			•	•
Uses assignment book	•		•	•				
Initiates tasks	•		•					
Breaks down and completes tasks on time					•		•	
Seeks support when needed – academic – medical					•			
Organizes materials								•
Checks work								•
Follows directions								•

Just imagine the different ways the information from this rubric could be used for one or all of the students listed. The squares that are marked could represent a pretest, posttest, or progress monitoring of specific skills in a cotaught environment. In this case, the squares that are marked are going to become goals for the students' IEPs. When using rubrics, remember to clearly define each of the terms so that your students know exactly what is expected. For example, "uses assignment book" means that students write down each day's homework assignment in an assignment book, which is checked by the teacher at the end of school/class each day. We encourage you to use a rubric system with your students as part of your grading and record-keeping systems.

then recording or graphing the results. For example, Ms. Broxton has her students practice their multiplication facts with flash cards and then graph their own performance. Figure 2.4 contains a graph of Shamika's performance for one week (see Figure 2.4). This record keeping on the part of students provides them with immediate awareness of their performance and may lead to application of strategies to improve that performance.

Whatever record-keeping procedures you develop, be sure they reflect the instructional objectives and levels of performance designated for each student in each area of the academic and social skills curriculum. Records of student performance in pull-out and inclusive settings may be used to plan, modify, and evaluate instruction and to motivate students to greater achievement.

Figure 2.4 SHAMIKA'S MATHEMATICS RECORD

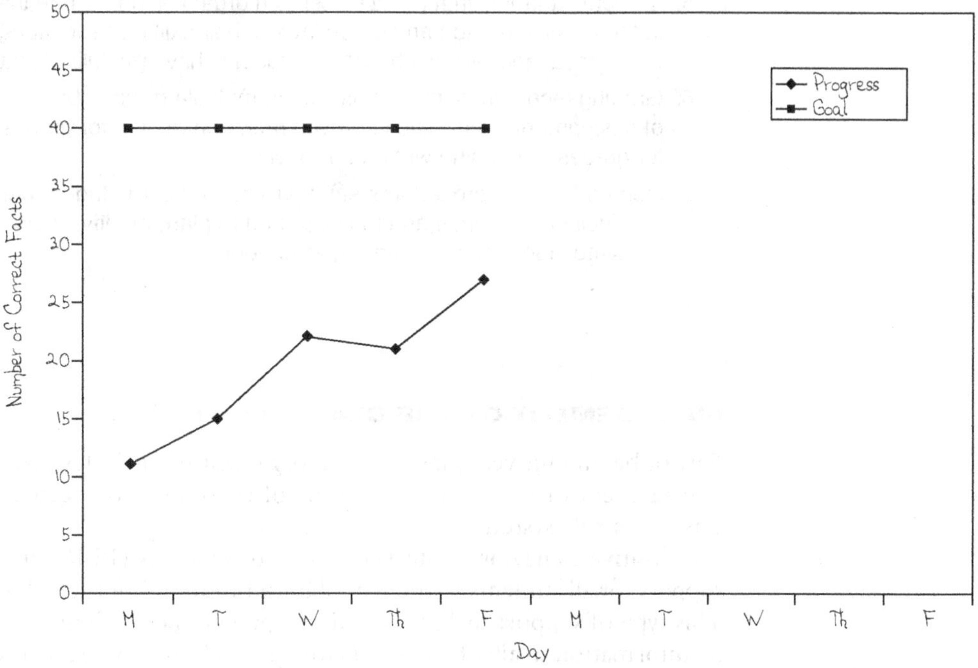

Activity 2.3

Part 1: Work with a partner for this activity. You are coteachers in a sixth-grade classroom. Design a record-keeping system to keep track of your students' daily performance in mathematics (you choose the particular mathematics skill).

Part 2: Work with your partner again. Design a self-assessment record-keeping system for a high school class (you choose the grade, subject, and skill).

IMPORTANT POINTS

1. Large-group instruction is appropriate for guided practice activities, the viewing of multimedia presentations or videotapes, large-group discussion of content area subjects, and demonstrations and is frequently used in general education classrooms.
2. Small-group instruction is used to present different material to students and is effective for acquisition learning, teaching of academic skills, and student-led activities in which students take turns assuming the role of the leader as in reciprocal teaching, cooperative learning activities, and role-playing.
3. Peer tutoring is effective for fluency and maintenance learning, monitoring progress, providing feedback, and teaching and reteaching specific skills to students who need extra help.
4. Independent learning may include a student's independent practice of something that has already been taught or a student's completion of an independent project with little or no assistance needed from the teacher.

5. Student variables that affect classroom organization include the number of students in the class, their age and grade levels, their skill levels, cultural and language differences, and related challenges students have (mobility, language, behavior, etc.).
6. Grading techniques include assigning multiple grades, basing grades on a variety of assignments, factoring in growth rate, contracting for grades, establishing criteria for grades, and using written narratives.
7. Record-keeping procedures can be used to record student performance in pull-out and inclusive settings and may be used to plan, modify, evaluate instruction, and motivate students to greater achievement.

MANAGEMENT OF THE CLASSROOM

Part of beginning-year planning and organization includes making decisions about the management of the classroom. Some of these decisions center around establishing a classroom rule system.

Positive Behavioral Interventions and Supports (PBIS) are ***school-wide*** systems of support for all students in the school both inside and outside classrooms (e.g., hallways). This type of support includes the development and implementation of rules. According to information available at the National Technical Assistance Center's PBIS website (www.pbis.org):

> Emphasis is on school-wide systems of support that include proactive strategies for defining, teaching, and supporting appropriate student behaviors to create positive school environments. Positive Behavioral Interventions and Supports (PBIS) represent an application of a behaviorally-based systems approach to enhance the capacity of schools, families, and communities to design effective environments that improve the link between research-validated practices and the environments in which teaching and learning occurs.

Rules are consistent from class to class throughout the school; students know the expectations; positive behaviors are rewarded instead of negative behaviors punished; and a continuum of support is used to address students' behavioral needs (particularly useful for students with behavioral disabilities) instead of using a one size fits all approach. In a PBIS school, more attention is given to a student's positive behavior (i.e., getting to school on time) than a negative behavior (i.e. being tardy for school). In a middle or high school where students change classes all day, the PBIS model may be particularly helpful for students with social or behavioral problems because the rules are consistent throughout the school and students do not have to figure out the expectations for each class. Also helpful in inclusive schools, the PBIS model can assist co-teachers to work together more consistently and effectively. However, since it is likely you will find yourself in a school in which faculty members are responsible for setting expectations and establishing rules in their individual settings, we present ideas for establishing a classroom rule system as part of your beginning-year planning and organization. For a thorough description of how to use the PBIS model to teach students positive social behaviors, please see Chapter 9.

You will notice as you are reading this section that many of the suggestions are very teacher directed, even though we strongly encourage the use of student input in formulating the rules and selecting choice strategies. Eventually, we feel that self-management should replace teacher direction, but this is a gradual process. Self-management strategies are discussed in Chapters 4 and 7.

Establishing Rules

Rules let students know what you expect. Students react differently during the completion of independent assignments when the teacher expects talking in a low voice and when the teacher expects total silence. One effective way to identify class rules is to make a list of your behavioral expectations ahead of time (Sprick, 2006). Another is to ask if there are any schoolwide rules (Sprick, 1985). An examination of the list of schoolwide rules will let you know what behaviors administrators and teachers feel are necessary for maintaining order.

Once you define your expectations, you should establish rules. Following are some guidelines:

1. ***Provide opportunities for students to give input concerning the rules.*** Involving students in the development of rules gives them a sense of being part of the decision-making process and a sense of ownership, but leaves the teacher without rules for the first day of school (Sprick, 2006). Sprick (1981) suggests that if you want students to design their own rules, you should post temporary rules for the first three or four days, until students become familiar with the routines. Emmer, Evertson, and Worsham (2006) report that students in secondary settings do not typically share in the development of rules because of the nature of the secondary school with teachers teaching multiple sections and the use of schoolwide rules are not up to compromise. In this setting specifically a PBIS model can be very effective especially to help students with the transition from middle school to high school.
2. ***Base rules on acceptable behaviors.*** In deciding on the rules, keep in mind the behaviors that are expected in the general classroom setting. It may be acceptable for a student to complete work standing at a table in a pull-out setting, but this behavior may be totally unacceptable in an inclusive setting. In many school districts, there are certain rules that all students are expected to follow. If this is the case, incorporate these rules into your system. Other considerations for deciding which behaviors to include in rules are to select those that promote the ease of functioning as a classroom community.
3. ***State rules positively.*** Positive rules lead to a positive atmosphere in the classroom and clue the students into appropriate behavior. "Speak politely to others by saying thank you and please" is a much better rule than, "Don't shout at others." The first rule suggests an appropriate behavior, whereas the latter just warns the students not to shout.
4. ***Select only about three to six rules.*** A rule cannot be invented for every slight infraction that may happen in class. Sprick (2006) suggests three to six rules, and no more than six. Some schools use three simple rules all focused on respect. The rules are respect yourself, respect others, and respect property. Almost any issue that arises can fall under these three rules.
5. ***Select rules for both academic and social behaviors.*** Rules usually deal with academic behaviors, such as "Complete all assignments," or social behaviors, such as "Keep hands and feet to yourself." Often academic rules will prevent inappropriate social and affective behaviors.
6. ***Relate rules to specific behaviors, but be general enough to cover many classes of that behavior.*** A rule such as "Be kind to others" is general; it can cover many classes of behaviors, including "Say nice things to other students" and "Keep your hands to yourself." Thus, the use of a general rule reduces the number of rules needed. However, students may not understand what is meant by the rule if no specific behavior is identified. This problem may be solved by listing examples of specific behaviors next to the rule or by discussing and role-playing specific behaviors.

7. ***Change rules when necessary.*** If being unprepared for class is a problem for your third-period class, this behavior should become the focus of a new rule. If students are completing all work, it may be time to remove the rule that deals with completing all assignments. This change does not mean that students no longer have to complete the work; rather, since everyone is remembering it, a written rule is no longer necessary.
8. ***Relate rules to IEP objectives.*** For many students with special needs, functional goals as well as academic goals are written in the IEP. These goals may be added to the rules for each individual student as individual goals or, if many students have similar objectives, may become part of the group list of rules (e.g., completion of homework).
9. ***Consider cultural differences.*** In some cultures, student involvement in class is often vocal, exuberant, and physical, so students may be on task even though they are not sitting quietly in their seats. You may want to incorporate such factors into rule selection. For example, "Finish all assignments" may be a better rule than "Work quietly at your seat."

Activity 2.4

As a special education teacher, you may be working in both pull-out and general education classrooms. It is important to establish rules in both of these settings in order to let students know what you expect.

Part 1: Make a list of five or six rules you might use in an elementary level pull-out classroom. Describe how you could involve students in developing the rules.

Part 2: Make a list of five or six rules you might use in a middle or high school inclusive classroom. Be sure to describe how you would work with the general education teacher to establish these rules.

Teaching Rules

Once rules are selected, the next step is to teach and discuss them frequently. Particularly at the beginning of the school year, the class rules should be discussed, demonstrated, and for younger children, practiced. Good and Brophy (2003) recommend that you state rules clearly and include a rationale.

The following techniques, adapted from Direct Instruction procedures (Engelmann & Carnine, 1991), are suggested for teaching rules. They include defining or describing the relevant attributes of the behavior, modeling examples and nonexamples, and asking students to discriminate between them (Morgan & Jenson, 1988). For example, with the stay-on-task rule, define for the students what "stay on task" means (e.g., "Stay on task means you write or listen or read when you work"). Next, give positive examples (e.g., "When you are doing a mathematics paper, you are on task if you are writing down the problems, figuring out the answers, or thinking about how to solve the problem") and negative or nonexamples (e.g., "You are not on task if you are looking out the window, thinking about lunch, or talking to a friend"). Then model examples and nonexamples of on-task behaviors and ask the students to identify and explain why the behavior is an example or a nonexample of on-task behavior. In response to this question, a student may say, "You are on task because you are looking at the mathematics book," or "You are not on task because you are looking around the room." Next, have students model the appropriate or inappropriate behavior and have others identify whether the students are displaying on-task behaviors. During this role-play activity, the students are not only practicing the rule, but also learning to evaluate behaviors.

Post the rules in the room or in individual notebooks to help students remember them. Many adolescents write the rules on a sheet of paper to keep in their notebooks. One creative student teacher incorporated the rules into a class constitution to parody the United States Constitution.

Prompting the Use of Rules

Having rules does not mean students will automatically follow them immediately. Students often need prompts to internalize or perform behaviors independently (Rosenshine, 1990). Prompts are ways to remind students to follow the rules. For example, verbal prompts such as "Remember, raise your hand," or visual prompts, such as a finger over the lips, may prevent talk-outs. The visual prompt of standing near the whispering students often stops off-task behavior. Other prompts include sharing expectations, peer modeling, positive repetition, and issuing either warning or choice statements. Sometimes students can remind their peers to follow classroom rules.

Sharing Expectations Sharing expectations is a way to explain to students what rules are in effect or what behaviors you expect for that particular activity (Sprick, 2006). Rules often vary, depending on whether the activity is to be completed by individuals or by small groups. Stating behavior rules at the beginning of a lesson is especially effective for students with problem behaviors (Emmer, Evertson, & Worsham, 2006).

An example of sharing expectations about behaviors appears in these sample instructions given to secondary students: "Today, we begin our study of the Roman Empire. As we discuss the beginning of Roman civilization, please remember to listen to others' ideas without interruptions, to copy the notes from the board, and to participate in the discussion." With many elementary students, you must share your expectations before academic and nonacademic activities. For example, "Rashida, remember, when we stand in line for lunch, we keep our hands to ourselves and face the door."

Peer Modeling Peer modeling may also serve as a prompt for following rules (Alberto & Troutman, 2006). To use peer modeling, praise students who are following the rule by identifying specific behaviors (e.g., "Good, Jason, you are standing quietly in line") and ignore the student who is not (e.g., ignore Trae). Then, when the student displays the appropriate behavior, praise him or her (e.g., "Good, Trae, that's the way to stand quietly in line").

Positive Repetition Positive repetition is similar to peer modeling in that you first tune in to positive behaviors of the students who are following the rules. Then you repeat the directions or instructions you gave. For example, if Jane, a middle school student, is refusing to follow your directions to take out her science book and turn to page 45, ignore Jane and say to Ramone, "Thank you, Ramone. I can see you have your science book out. I appreciate your turning to page 45, Vayola. This side of the room is ready to begin."

Praising other students instead of tuning in to the inappropriate behavior of a student is difficult even for seasoned teachers. The natural reaction to this type of situation is to focus on the deviant or noncompliant behavior immediately, instead of praising the students who are following the rules. Deviant or noncompliant behaviors can make teachers fearful that their authority is being questioned and that they are losing control. Yet being positive as a first step is frequently sufficient to stop inappropriate behavior. In addition, praising teaches students that teacher attention, often a powerful motivator (Alberto & Troutman, 2006), may be secured through appropriate behaviors instead of inappropriate behaviors.

Issuing Warning Statements and Choice Statements We recommend the use of warning statements and choice statements only after you have tried to change the behavior by positively attending to the appropriate behaviors of other students. If, after praising others, you find that a student is still not following the rule, you may want to use a warning or a choice statement. A warning statement alerts the student to the rule infraction. For example, "You are forgetting our rule to listen to others, Sam. This is a warning," lets Sam know that he needs to display appropriate behavior immediately. Warning statements are often used with younger children.

With a choice statement, you present the appropriate behavior that relates to the rule and some sort of unpleasant option to the student, for example, "Sally, you are breaking Rule 4. Either remember to raise your hand (rule) or leave the group (option). It is your choice."

Once you issue a choice statement, give the student an opportunity to think about the choice. Move out of the student's vicinity to avoid a direct confrontation and continue with other activities. That way, a student can save face and even mumble nasty things out of your hearing range (or, at least, you can pretend not to hear them). Be certain always to acknowledge an appropriate choice in some way, such as "I see you've made a good choice, Sally. Thank you."

In issuing choice or warning statements, you should remain calm and speak in a quiet, firm voice. Lower your voice at the end of a warning statement. Be aware of nonverbal behaviors, such as eye contact. When issuing a warning statement, avoid pointing a finger at the student, which is a clue to the student that he or she is upsetting you. Instead, if your hands are resting at your sides, you convey an air of confidence.

Emmer, Evertson, and Worsham (2006) suggest that teachers give students a list of options when they break a rule. With this strategy, teachers focus students' attention on ways to solve the problem, instead of focusing on noncompliance. For example, options for Sally, who is not raising her hand, may include: "Sally, talking out is not appropriate. You may raise your hand when you need help, go on to the next problem until I can help you, or reread the directions."

The type of prompt given depends on the type of behavior and the time of the year. You would not administer a choice statement for behaviors that are physically detrimental to a particular student, other students, the teacher, or school property. Samantha cannot be given a choice if she is hitting Jim. You must stop her immediately. Typically, more prompts are given at the beginning of the year until students become familiar with the rules.

Activity 2.5

Work with a partner for this activity. Share with your partner an example of how you would teach and prompt rules in an elementary and a secondary setting. Now ask your partner to give you an example of a warning statement and a choice statement at both elementary and secondary levels. Make sure all of the examples are age and grade appropriate.

Enforcing Rules

The next step is to decide what you are going to do when students follow rules and when they do not. You may want to use specific praise or positive attention intermittently to call attention to students who are following the rules, and then award certificates or free time at the end of the week based on particular criteria.

Specific praise statements identify the praiseworthy aspects of students' behaviors. When using a specific praise statement, include a description of the specific behavior the student is demonstrating and the student's name, for example, "I like the way you are working quietly, Terri" for the young student and "That was a good decision when you ignored Hugo's remark, Josh." For many adolescents, positive public praise from a teacher is unpleasant or embarrassing, as they don't want to be singled out from their peers (Sprick, 2006). Thus, you may want to praise adolescents in private or praise the group effort instead of individuals. This is also true for various cultural groups who prefer quiet, private, specific praise.

Specific praise and positive attention may be interwoven into your daily routine; neither is time consuming. Attending to the student with a raised hand and ignoring the one shouting out requires no extra time. Stopping at secondary students' desks to compliment them for staying on task during independent practice activities is appropriate for students who enjoy being praised or singled out for teacher attention in private (Sprick, 2006).

What are your options when, even after prompting, a student continues to break the rules? Usually, the options are (a) withholding something the student likes, or (b) presenting the student with something he or she doesn't like. Many teachers withhold points, privileges, or free time from students who do not follow the rules; others write referrals or require students to eat lunch alone. In a PBIS school, the options should be articulated in advance and consistent across all classrooms.

Whatever consequence you use, remember to remain calm and follow through. Some students try to talk teachers out of the consequence, such as "Oh, Mr. Jones, please don't send me to the principal's office. I'll do my work now." A teacher who does not follow through at this time is teaching students that they can wait to do their work until the teacher threatens to take them to the office, and then they can talk the

IMPORTANT POINTS

1. Positive Behavioral and Intervention Supports (PBIS) are ***school-wide*** systems of support for all students in which rules are consistent from class to class throughout the school; students know the expectations; positive behaviors are rewarded instead of negative behaviors punished; and a continuum of support is used to address students' behavioral needs (particularly useful for students with behavioral disabilities) instead of using a one size fits all approach.
2. In a middle or high school where students change classes all day, the PBIS model may be particularly helpful for students with social or behavioral problems because the rules are consistent throughout the school and students do not have to figure out the expectations for each class.
3. Guidelines for establishing rules are to incorporate student input, base rules on acceptable behaviors, state rules positively, select only about five or six rules, select rules for both academic and social behaviors, make rules specific, change rules when necessary, relate rules to IEP objectives, and consider cultural differences.
4. Teaching rules requires defining or describing the important attributes of the behavior, modeling examples and nonexamples, and asking students to discriminate between them.
5. Prompting the use of rules includes the sharing of expectations, peer modeling, positive repetition, and the issuing of warning or choice statements.
6. Teachers must be consistent in enforcing rules and following through when students do not follow rules.

teacher out of taking them there. You need to follow through with the consequence, or your effort becomes just an empty threat.

In addition to following through with consequences, consistency is a prime consideration in enforcing rules. If "Raise your hand to speak" is a rule, then all students should have to follow it or in a PBIS school these rules are consistent as are consequences. Be careful not to fall into the trap of giving attention to a student who is shouting out because that student happens to be blurting out the correct answer. Consistency allows students to learn that there are expectations in your class accompanied by rewards for following them and consequences for not complying.

Finally, remember to provide appropriate feedback. For example, Mr. Anderson gave his secondary students the following feedback at the end of fifth period: "Most of today's class went well. All of you followed directions, copying the notes from the board, but I had to prompt you not to interrupt when someone was talking. Let's work on this during tomorrow's class. Tomorrow I will write the goal on the board, Try not to interrupt when others are speaking."

SCHEDULING FOR INSTRUCTION

In the chapter opening scenario Ivey Leonard chose to make the scheduling of her students in her own pull-out class and in general education classes her highest priority. We agree with Ivey that scheduling is an essential part of effective teaching and should be given priority at the beginning of the school year. Schedules provide structure and organization and allow teachers to accomplish the goals and objectives that they have planned for their students. Students with learning problems can benefit from the routine that systematic scheduling provides (Mercer & Mercer, 2005). Teachers should let students know what activities they are to accomplish and when they should complete them. Thus, the use of systematic scheduling may increase self-directedness and independence among students by eliminating the need to check with the teacher about each assignment.

Polloway, Patton, and Serna (2005) underscore the importance of a carefully planned schedule: Students are intrinsically motivated, the use of schedules maximizes the appropriate use of time, and teachers can provide an educationally relevant program with appropriate transitions between instructional activities. It is important to provide students with a schedule that will maximize learning opportunities and address the goals and objectives of students' IEPs.

SCHEDULING IN ELEMENTARY SCHOOLS

As teachers develop schedules in elementary schools, they should use the following information in making instructional decisions: (a) each student's needs, which can be prioritized and taken from the IEP; (b) the amount of time the student is supposed to work in the special education setting; (c) the amount of time the student is scheduled in other settings; and (d) the schedules of general classroom teachers.

Consultative Services and Cooperative Teaching

Many students who have special needs are capable of functioning in inclusive settings with modifications and adjustments made by their teachers. These modifications and adjustments are accomplished through collaborative consultation between special and general educators. Special education teachers provide indirect services by participating on school-based assistance teams and by helping general education teachers modify the curriculum, develop and adapt materials, and assess students' academic and social behavior. Chapter 3 provides a detailed description of collaborative consultation.

At other times, special education teachers are called on to provide direct services in the general education classroom. These services may involve coteaching, that is, working with classroom teachers to coteach students in inclusive classrooms. When both special and general education teachers share the responsibility for providing instruction, they should plan schedules together.

Pull-Out Programs

Scheduling in the elementary pull-out program can be time consuming and challenging because students usually participate in multiple settings with several different teachers. Scheduling is typically accomplished in cooperation with general education teachers and others (such as speech/language pathologist, counselor, etc.). Students attend the pull-out program for part of the day to work on specific academic and social behaviors identified in their IEPs and spend the rest of the time receiving instruction in the general education classroom and/or in various related services. Because students attend pull-out programs for varying amounts of time, teachers are faced with many challenges in scheduling students for instruction. For example:

1. Students may range in age from 6 to 14.
2. Students may have varied and specific needs.
3. Students may be functioning on many different levels.
4. General education teachers may have preferred times for sending students to the pull-out program.
5. Communication with many general education teachers may be difficult and time consuming.
6. Locating materials appropriate for many levels, ages, and interests may be challenging, but should be tied to the general education curriculum.

Despite the difficulties in scheduling students in a pull-out program, special education teachers may develop effective schedules by following a few guidelines:

1. Collect the schedules of all teachers who have students with mild disabilities assigned to their classrooms.
2. List the academic and social skill areas with which students need help.
3. Group students by area of need, making an effort to keep primary and intermediate students separated.
4. Plan individual and group times to keep class size reasonable and instruction workable.
5. Revise the original schedule until it works.

In addition to providing direct services to students in a pull-out program, you will also need to consult with general education teachers. This collaboration is important because of the responsibility for students that is shared by special and general education teachers and because you will want to reintegrate your students into the general education classroom to the extent that is appropriate. Reintegration requires close communication and collaboration. Table 2.1 provides an example of an elementary pull-out program schedule.

SCHEDULING IN SECONDARY SCHOOLS

At the secondary level (middle school and high school), special education teachers may serve as consulting teachers and coteachers in general education classrooms or they may provide instruction in a pull-out program.

Table 2.1 Elementary Pull-Out Program Schedule (One Week)

	Monday	Tuesday	Wednesday	Thursday	Friday
8:00–8:30	Problem-solving committee meeting	Consult with classroom teachers	Consult with classroom teachers	Consult with classroom teachers	Consult with classroom teachers
8:30–9:30	Work with 1st-, 2nd-, and 3rd-grade students (Teacher-directed instruction in reading)	→ (Learning Centers)	→ (Teacher-directed instruction in comprehension)	→ (Process writing)	→ (Teacher-directed instruction in comprehension)
9:30–10:30	Work with 4th- and 5th-grade students (Listening)	(Comprehension monitoring)	(Summarization)	(Comprehension monitoring)	(Paraphrasing)
10:30–11:15	Coteach in 3rd grade	Coteach in 4th grade	Coteach in 5th grade	Coteach in 1st grade	Coteach in 2nd grade
11:15–12:00	Assessment	Adapt materials	Assessment	Adapt materials	Assessment
12:00–12:30	Lunch	Lunch	Lunch	Lunch	Lunch
12:30–1:00	Work with 4th- and 5th-grade students in mathematics (Small group)	→ (Small group)	→ (Computer)	→ (Learning center)	→ (Small group)
1:00–1:30	Work with 2nd- and 3rd-grade students in language arts (Small group)	→ Games	→ (Small group and self-correcting materials)	→ (Computers)	→ (Small group)
1:30–2:30	Assist in general classrooms on "as needed" basis in content area subjects (science, social studies, health)				
2:30–3:00	Planning/ Consulting	→	→	→	→
3:00	Dismissal	Dismissal	Dismissal	Dismissal	Dismissal

Consultative Services and Cooperative Teaching

Special education teachers at the secondary level fulfill the roles of consulting teachers the same way that special education teachers at the elementary level do. Services to students with special needs may be both direct and indirect. However, secondary schools are typically larger, which means there are more teachers to work with, more schedules to work around, and more subject area classes. Special education teachers may coteach with classroom teachers in general education classrooms. For example, Mr. Jessup teaches an outlining strategy to a science class to help the students organize the content Mrs. Lange presents in science. He also works with her in adapting some of the material in the textbook. Table 2.2 provides an example of a middle school teacher's block schedule. In the first period language arts program, Mr. Fletcher uses the first 10 minutes of class for attendance, general directions, orientation to the day's activities, and a brief review. He spends the next 30 minutes of class providing direct instruction and guided practice to students.

Table 2.2 Middle School Teacher's Block Schedule—Consultative Services in General Education Classrooms

	Monday	Tuesday	Wednesday	Thursday	Friday
First Period 9:00–10:32	Language Arts (7th Grade)	Language Arts (7th Grade)	Language Arts (7th Grade)	Language Arts (7th Grade)	Language Arts (7th Grade)
Second Period 10:36–11:46	Coteach Social Studies (8th Grade)	Coteach Social Studies (8th Grade)	Coteach Social Studies (8th Grade)	Coteach Social Studies (8th Grade)	Coteach Social Studies (8th Grade)
Second Period (Continued) 11:46–12:23	Lunch	Lunch	Lunch	Lunch	Lunch
Third Period 12:27–1:55	Adapt Materials for Content Teachers	Adapt Materials for Content Teachers	Adapt Materials for Content Teachers	Adapt Materials for Content Teachers	Evaluate and Select Software Programs
Fourth Period 1:59–3:20	Learning Strategies (7th Grade)	Learning Strategies (7th Grade)	Learning Strategies (7th Grade)	Learning Strategies (7th Grade)	Learning Strategies (7th Grade)
3:20	Dismissal	Dismissal	Dismissal	Dismissal	Dismissal

The next 30 minutes are devoted to small groups, where students work cooperatively to complete assignments. The final 15 minutes of class are used for whole-class discussion, in which students report the results of their group work. The final 5 minutes is used for wrap-up activities. In addition to teaching language arts, Mr. Fletcher coteaches and consults with classroom teachers and adapts materials.

Pull-Out Programs

Students at the secondary level may attend pull-out programs for assistance in academic skills, social skills, job-seeking skills, learning strategies, and leisure skills (Deshler & Schumaker, 2006). Teachers in pull-out programs at the secondary level are responsible for providing direct services to students and may also be responsible for assessment of students. In addition, they may have consulting responsibilities, such as working with teachers to adapt materials and instruction. They often work with guidance counselors to schedule students into their classes and into select general education classes. Secondary schools operate with fixed class periods that are approximately 50 minutes long. Good and Brophy (2003) suggest that the first 8 minutes of class be used for review, the next 20 minutes for teacher presentation and guided practice, and the next 15 minutes for independent practice.

Mrs. Hefter uses the first 5 minutes of class for attendance, general directions, orientation to the day's activities, and a brief review. She spends the next 20 minutes teaching her students how to monitor errors in their written work and providing guided practice. Then the students spend 15 minutes in independent practice with feedback. The next 10 minutes are allocated to addressing pressing individual student needs, such as clarification of an assignment from a general education class, organization of notes and materials from a content area classroom, or a quick review for a test or report from a general education classroom. These final few minutes of class are also spent giving a post organizer, such as previewing the next day's class schedule, reinforcing work completed, reporting progress toward class or individual student goals,

Table 2.3 Secondary Schedule—Learning Strategies Class (One Class Period)

8:00–8:05	• Take attendance. • Announce next week's exam schedule. • Explain activities for class period.
8:05–8:25	• Review previous lesson in error monitoring. • Teach students how to detect and correct punctuation errors in paragraphs. • Use overhead projector and handouts (cue cards). • Have students take turns practicing on overhead projector and orally as a group.
8:25–8:40	• Hand out paragraph worksheets. • Have students work independently to detect and correct punctuation errors. • Circulate to monitor and check work.
8:40–8:50	• Check with students on regular class assignments, homework, etc. • Recap day's activities and preview tomorrow's lesson on detecting and correcting spelling errors.
8:50	• Dismissal

and announcing schedule changes. By scheduling this way, Mrs. Hefter has effectively used all of the class time and met her objectives and curricular responsibilities while providing time for individual student needs (see Table 2.3).

Some special education teachers at the secondary level use a folder system. Students come into their classrooms, get their folders, and examine the schedule in the folder. This system gives them a preview of the activities for the class period. While some students are receiving teacher-directed instruction, others complete work in their folders or work with a partner or a small group. Some teachers rotate students in and out of learning centers or cooperative learning activities. When not involved with other instruction, the teacher circulates around the room, providing instruction to individuals and groups, monitoring progress, and giving feedback and reinforcement.

Like pull-out program teachers at the elementary level, these teachers at the secondary level wear many hats. They must fulfill consulting responsibilities with general education teachers, be curriculum and materials specialists, have knowledge of secondary diploma options and the classes students must have to graduate, possess good public relations skills, and be prepared to help students make the transition from school to work and adult living.

Students with special needs may receive instruction in mathematics, English, science, and other subjects from a special education teacher in a pull-out setting. Materials are available to present the same subject matter that is covered in a general education class, but with less emphasis on reading. For example, students with special needs may take a class called Oceanography, which parallels the class that other students take, but they complete it using modified texts and adapted curriculum materials.

STUDENTS WHO NEED MORE TIME

Despite all your efforts at scheduling, you will find that it is next to impossible to plan one schedule and expect it to work for all students. Some students need more time than others to complete assignments. Scheduling becomes especially problematic in inclusive classrooms, as the same students always seem to be the last to finish if they finish at all. For students who show a willingness to work hard but who need more time because of a learning problem, limited English proficiency, or other factors, we recommend the

BOX 2.3

Reflections on Practice

There are a variety of ways to get to know your students at the beginning of the school year in order to create a classroom community, build rapport, and establish effective classroom management. Following are several ideas that may help teachers of students with special needs at the elementary and secondary levels. The activities are appropriate for both special and general education settings.

Interviews. Secondary students, in particular, enjoy interviewing another student in the class to collect biographical information. Give the students 10 to 15 minutes to talk with a partner. Have the students develop two headlines that can be put up on a bulletin board. One headline should be a school-related achievement and the other a personal accomplishment. Then, have the students present their information. For example, Manny Owens introduced another senior, Jerard Collins, with the school-related headline, "Collins Makes Honor Roll at End of Junior Year" and the personal headline, "High School Senior Lands Summer Job at the Wilmington *Sentinel*."

Life Lines. Many students enjoy constructing a life line (i.e., time line) of their personal and school-related activities. Have the students draw a horizontal line and write in major events along the line. (This is also an excellent sequencing activity.) Have the students begin with the time of their birth and continue to the present. Let the students present their life lines orally in class or transfer them to a bulletin board.

Games. After students introduce themselves to the rest of the class, collect cards on which the students have written introductions. As you read what it says on each card, such as hobbies and favorite food, let the rest of the class guess which student is being described. You may also include a card for yourself.

Vanity Plates (Graves & Bradley, 1997). Give students a sheet of oak tag the size of a license plate and ask them to create a vanity plate that gives important information about themselves using letters, numbers, pictures, and other symbols. After creating their vanity plates, have the students share them with the class.

Whatever you choose to use, make sure you spend time getting to know your students at the beginning of the year. The time spent in building a classroom community through getting-to-know-you activities is well worth it.

following strategies adapted from Kellough and Carjuzaa (2006) in combination with our own ideas.

1. Learn as much about the student as you can.
2. Adjust your instruction to the student's preferred learning style.
3. Use all modalities when you teach.
4. Help the student learn content in small, sequential steps with frequent checks for understanding.
5. Use frequent positive reinforcement (verbal and written).
6. Check readability level of materials.
7. Adapt instruction and modify materials if needed.

8. Maximize the use of cooperative learning, peer tutoring, role-play, student-led group activities, and hands-on activities.
9. Be less concerned about the quantity of content coverage and more concerned with the student's understanding of the content that is covered.
10. Teach study skills, strategies, and survival skills (such as listening strategies, test-taking strategies, teacher-pleasing and class participation skills, and time-management skills).
11. Use peer pairing for support and to enhance learning.

EFFICIENT USE OF TIME

In observation of 230 elementary students with mild disabilities, Rich and Ross (1989) found that noninstructional time such as transitions, wait time, free time, snacks, and housekeeping accounted for almost 3 hours of the school day. An examination of 52 high school programs for students with learning or mental disabilities indicated that the students spent an average of 24% of their time in nonacademic activities (Rieth, Polsgrove, Okolo, Bahr, & Eckert, 1987). Since research shows that time spent on academic learning tasks increases achievement, you should schedule the day to maximize student involvement in direct learning activities. As a teacher, you can control the time dimensions of housekeeping and transition times by the way you schedule.

Housekeeping Time

Housekeeping time is the time spent in performing such routine chores as taking attendance, collecting homework assignments, and writing on the board. If they are well organized, these activities make a class run smoothly. If they are not managed correctly, these activities can cause behavior problems and loss of valuable teaching time. Housekeeping questions that need to be resolved include how to sharpen pencils, ask for assistance, and get permission to leave the classroom. If you spend time planning routines, you will spend less time on housekeeping activities during class, thus maximizing instructional time.

Transition Time

Transition time involves changing from one activity to another or from one setting to another. Again, valuable teaching time may be lost without smooth transitions. For young students, role-playing transition times, such as moving from the desk to the reading group, is helpful. Posted schedules make both secondary and elementary students aware of subject changes. Teachers who circulate throughout the room to answer questions and monitor students' behavior promote more on-task behavior during transition times (Englert & Thomas, 1982). Frequently, much time is lost in transition from pull-out programs to the general education classroom. Incentives are often necessary to motivate students to arrive on time. Extra points, public posting of the names of on-time students, and on-time clubs with special privileges are effective solutions for late arrivals.

Activity 2.6

Work with a partner to develop a list of ideas for creating a community of learners and getting to know your students at the beginning of the school year. Do this for elementary, middle, and high school levels.

IMPORTANT POINTS

1. Tips for scheduling in the elementary school include (a) identifying student needs, (b) attending to the amount of time that students should spend in general and special education, and (c) examining the schedules of classroom teachers.
2. Pull-out program scheduling at the elementary level requires attention to general education classroom schedules, the needs of students, grouping arrangements, and flexibility.
3. Secondary schools operate with fixed class periods that include review, teacher presentation, controlled practice, and independent practice.
4. For students who need more time to complete assignments, teach using all modalities; check frequently for understanding; use positive reinforcement; adapt instruction and modify materials; use cooperative learning, peer tutoring, role-playing, student-led group activities, and hands-on activities; focus on understanding of content; teach study skills, strategies, and survival skills; and use peer pairing.

PUTTING IT ALL TOGETHER

The decisions you make and the plans you put in place at the beginning of the year will set the tone for the rest of the school year. In this chapter we discussed how the IEP serves as a map to guide each student, and how daily and weekly plans are the vehicles through which student needs are addressed. We presented ideas for organizing and managing the learning environment including creating appropriate instructional arrangements for the delivery of instruction, establishing grading and record-keeping procedures, and setting up classroom rules to communicate expectations and guide behavior. We shared strategies for scheduling in elementary, middle, and high school settings. Finally, we gave you some ideas for getting to know your students during the first days of school. We hope that the ideas presented in this chapter will help you build a classroom community that will be welcoming and supportive of all learners.

DISCUSSION QUESTIONS

1. A parent of a student in a general education class questions how a student with disabilities who is included in that class can receive a grade of A. How would you explain your grading rationale to the parent?
2. Discuss when you would use the following instructional arrangements in your classroom: large group, small group, one-to-one, peer tutoring, and independent learning. Draw a sketch of your classroom to reflect the instructional groupings you would use.
3. Defend the statement, "Thoughtful and thorough planning is essential for effective teaching and learning to occur."

Websites: Useful websites related to chapter content can be found in Appendix A.

CHAPTER

3

Communication and Collaborative Consultation

KEY TOPICS

It was only the second week of the school year, but already Mr. Washington, Jamaal's fifth-grade teacher, had contacted Jamaal's mother, Ms. Johnson, to come in for a conference. He and Mrs. Shoemaker, the special education teacher, were sitting in Mr. Washington's classroom when Ms. Johnson came to the door.

"We have noticed some issues that need to be addressed concerning Jamaal's social skills," began Mr. Washington.

"I'm not surprised," said Ms. Johnson. "Every year it takes Jamaal the first few weeks to adjust to being back in school. Since we moved this summer, I even sent him to summer camp just so he could have some time to spend around kids his own age. You see, I am a single mom and Jamaal is my only child."

Mrs. Shoemaker, special education teacher who coteaches with Mr. Washington, looked up from her paperwork and replied, "Well, we have some great ideas for how to channel his energy and improve his relationships with his peers. Now, how about if we start by having you tell us what strategies have worked well for Jamaal in the past."

"To be honest, one of the reasons I moved here was because nothing seemed to be working well for Jamaal in his last school. He just gets messier and messier and he can't seem to make and keep any friends. I am hoping that a fresh start will help him break his bad habits."

Mrs. Shoemaker smiled, "Disorganization and difficulty with peers are very common characteristics of children with learning disabilities. There are many strategies we can use both as teachers in the classroom and that you can use at home. In fact, we wanted to talk to you today about those strategies so that you can practice them with Jamaal. Also, what about friends? You mentioned that he has a hard time making and keeping friends. Why do you think that is true?"

"Jamaal comes on a little strong with most kids his own age. In our family we often hug each other, but then he gets in trouble for that same thing at school. I suppose he is a little immature for his age, but he just wants so much for the other kids to like him. Do you really think these strategies can help?"

"Yes, we do," replied Mrs. Shoemaker. "You can see on this list that we have begun by identifying twelve specific social skills and replacement behaviors we want to target for Jamaal. For example, to help him learn about respecting the personal space of others, we want him to replace his urge to hug with a smile and direct eye contact instead. Over the next few days we will model this skill and openly discuss it within our classroom setting. Mr. Washington and I like to have our students role-play situations so that all students can practice the skill. Then the next step is to practice the skill outside of the classroom. In order to do that, we have arranged for our class to be reading buddies with a first-grade class. Jamaal will be assigned a buddy that he can read with three times a week, and once each month they can even eat lunch together in the cafeteria. In this way Jamaal will have opportunities to practice his social skills with someone who looks up to him in different settings."

"OK," said Ms. Johnson, "How can I help at home?"

"We're glad you asked," replied Mr. Washington. "Let's start by discussing how we can best communicate with you at home. . . ."

Often after meetings with parents we think back and realize we could have said or done things differently or offered additional suggestions. Look back over the above scenario. Find three things that were handled well by the faculty in this situation and three things that could have been improved. After you have read the first half of the chapter, look at your response to see if you want to add or change anything.

Responses to these questions are found in the Instructor's Manual.

INTRODUCTION

The field of special education is undergoing many changes. Major reform efforts and legislation have focused on redefining and restructuring the relationship between general and special education. Among the recommendations for this restructuring and redefining of relationships are that general and special educators increase their collaborative efforts in planning and providing instruction to students with disabilities in inclusive settings (Deshler & Schumaker, 2006). Because the number of students with special needs who receive services in general education classrooms has significantly increased, the question is no longer *what* to teach, but *where* to teach. Voltz, Brazil, and Ford (2001) recommend that general and special education practitioners focus on including students with disabilities in general education classrooms in active, meaningful ways; that all students share a sense of belonging, and there is a shared ownership among faculty. To provide successful experiences for students with special needs, teachers need to become more involved in collaborative planning and problem solving (Voltz, Brazil, & Ford, 2001). Collaborative interactions are occurring in inclusionary schools, where students who were previously excluded are now included in general education classrooms (Friend & Bursuck, 2006). It has become more the norm than the exception that teachers of children and adolescents with special needs are working less in isolation and more as members of an educational team. Thus, the ability to communicate and collaborate with other members of a team (general classroom teachers, administrators, paraprofessionals, other direct- and related-service providers, and families) may have a significant impact on the quality of services that special educators provide for their students.

"Good communication skills are a prerequisite for collaboration" (Pugach & Johnson, 1995, p. 62). "Working with colleagues in a collaborative manner is hard work that requires a special set of skills to facilitate communication" (Johnson, Pugach, & Hawkins, 2004, p. 9). Therefore, in this chapter, we begin with the topics of communication, strategies for effective communication, and specific techniques to use with parents/families. We also provide the rationale for collaborative consultation, describe the options for implementing collaborative consultation, and share with you some of the barriers to collaborative consultative interactions along with suggestions for prevention and success. Finally, we provide recommendations for planning and implementing paraprofessional programs, and leave you with some final thoughts about collaborating with other partners in the school and community.

COMMUNICATION

The importance of communication skills has been well documented in the literature (Bos & Vaughn, 2006). We believe that communication is the key to effective working relationships with teachers and other members of the school team and is essential for successful interactions with parents/families. Dettmer, Thurston, and Dyck (2005) report that people spend approximately 70% of their day communicating in one form or another (i.e., listening, speaking, and writing), and therefore, good communication among special educators, general educators, and parents is essential to the success of students with special needs in the general education classroom.

FACTORS TO CONSIDER IN COMMUNICATION

Because communication is vital to your success as a professional, we hope that you will consider skills in communication to be as important as skills in subject-area content; strategies for planning, teaching, and assessment; classroom management; and adapting materials and instruction. Attention to the following attributes will assist you in building rapport, respecting and accepting differences, and building and sustaining productive partnerships with others.

Nonverbal Skills

Nonverbal communication is essentially all communication other than the spoken or written word. It includes facial expressions, gestures, nods, open and closed body positioning, eye contact, and posture, and is a powerful component of overall communication (Lincoln, 2002). Often a discrepancy exists between what the speaker is feeling and actually saying (Scott, 1990). For example, if a teacher greets a parent by saying how great it is to see her so they can discuss her child's progress, but the teacher is dreading the meeting and has a negative expression on her face and a closed body stance, this nonverbal communication will overshadow the verbal statement and may create a negative, distrustful atmosphere. Therefore, nonverbal communication is as important as verbal communication in interactions with others. Nonverbal communication consists of proxemics, kinesics, and paraverbal components.

Proxemics. Proxemics refers to personal space, or the amount of distance you need to feel comfortable in your interactions with others; an imaginary circle that surrounds your body and is your comfort zone. When others cross into your space, you become uncomfortable. Problems may occur for students who are unaware of this unwritten rule and stand too close or do not respect the personal space of others.

Culture influences a person's comfort zone. Many Asian Americans require more personal space and are uncomfortable with the physical closeness of a teacher, whereas people from the Hispanic culture frequently need less personal space (Briganti, 1989). In the Middle East, people tend to stand close to each other when speaking; in Latin America, two people of the same gender tend to stand closer than do those in North America; and Africans tend to stand much closer than Anglo Americans (Bulusu, 1998). The personal space you are comfortable with is often influenced by the gender, age, culture, and size of the other person. Anxiety also plays a part in personal space. A person who is anxious usually requires more personal space. When communicating with parents during a conference, you may want to place the chairs so that there is room for the parents to move and adjust their comfort zone.

Kinesics. Body language, such as posture and gestures, also conveys a message. There is great diversity among the codes of nonverbal behavior such as body movements, posture, and gestures (Chesebro & McCroskey, 2002). Again, cultural effects are evident in this nonverbal communication. For some cultures, looking down and not at the teacher is a sign of respect, while in other cultures, children are taught to make and maintain eye contact to show interest and respect. Keep this in mind as you interact with parents and professionals.

In regard to posture, it is important when communicating with other professionals and parents and families to maintain a supportive stance. A supportive stance requires physical positioning so you are not sitting or standing directly in front of a person since this may be perceived as authoritarian. Instead, try sitting or standing to the side or at an angle.

Activity 3.1

Part 1: With about 7 feet between you, stand directly across from another member of your class. Looking at this individual, have him or her walk toward you. Hold your hand out and say stop when you begin to feel uncomfortable. Now reverse roles. Were your comfort zones similar or different?

Part 2: Discuss the implications of proxemics and kinesics for the seating of students in cooperative learning groups. Consider age, culture, and gender.

(Answers to this and other activities are found in the Instructor's Manual.)

Paraverbal Communication. The tone, volume, pitch, and cadence of your voice along with the use and timing of silence are involved in paraverbal communication or paralanguage (Friend & Cook, 2003). Lincoln (2002) reports that about 38% of received information comes from paraverbal communication. Therefore, it is important to use a relaxed, pleasant tone of voice with the appropriate inflection and pauses in your interactions with others (e.g., parent-teacher conference) and in your presentations (e.g., a speech to the Parent Teacher Association) in your school.

Being a good, responsive listener is essential for effective communication. Dettmer, Thurston, and Dyck (2002) offer two comments by humorists in regard to listening:

> It takes six letters of the alphabet to spell the word *listen.* Rearrange the letters to spell another word that is a necessary part of responsive listening (Did you get *silent*?).
> In the middle of listen, the *t* doesn't make a sound. (p. 134)

Other suggestions for desirable nonverbal communication skills are found in Table 3.1.

Verbal Skills

The verbal skills of active listening, rephrasing, open-ended questioning, and summarizing can be effective during communication (Turnbull & Turnbull, 2005). Coupled with nonverbal skills and the avoidance of educational jargon, they can lead to productive communication sessions.

Active Listening Many teachers use active listening. In active listening, you communicate to others that you are interested in what they have to say, will work to understand what they mean, and are comfortable with the feelings underlying their message. You echo what others say, including their emotions, and they can either confirm or correct the accuracy of your understanding. For example, if a parent or professional says, "I just can't understand why Janae is the way she is!" an active listening response is, "You

Table 3.1 Nonverbal Communication Skills

Desirable	Undesirable
Facial Expressions	
• Direct eye contact (except when culturally proscribed) • Warmth and concern reflected in facial expression • Eyes at same level as client's • Appropriately varied and animated facial expressions • Mouth relaxed; occasional smiles	• Avoidance of eye contact • Eye level higher or lower than client's • Staring or fixating on person or object • Lifting eyebrow critically • Nodding head excessively • Yawning • Frozen or rigid facial expressions • Inappropriate slight smile • Pursing or biting lips
Posture	
• Arms and hands moderately expressive; appropriate gestures • Body leaning slightly forward; attentive but relaxed	• Rigid body position; arms tightly folded • Body turned at an angle to client • Fidgeting with hands • Squirming or rocking in chair • Slouching or placing feet on desk • Hand or fingers over mouth • Pointing finger for emphasis
Voice	
• Clearly audible but not loud • Warmth in tone of voice • Voice modulated to reflect nuances of feeling and emotional tone of client messages • Moderate speech tempo	• Mumbling or speaking inaudibly • Monotonic voice • Halting speech • Frequent grammatical errors • Prolonged silences • Excessively animated speech • Slow, rapid, or staccato speech • Nervous laughter • Consistent clearing of throat • Speaking loudly
Physical Proximity	
• Three to five feet between chairs	• Excessive closeness or distance • Talking across desk or other barrier

Source: From *Direct Social Work Practice: Theory and Skills,* Sixth Edition, by Dean H. Hepworth, Ronald H. Rooney, and Jo Ann Larsen. ©2002 by Brooks/Cole. Reprinted by permission.

sound very concerned about Janae." Active listening provides parents and professionals the freedom to express and acknowledge what they think and feel. Coupled with nonverbal communication (e.g., head nods, smiles, and open body positioning), active listening plays a critical role in interactions between parents and professionals.

Rephrasing. When you rephrase or reframe what parents and professionals say, you use your own words to restate what the individual said. Unlike active listening, in which you concentrate on both the affective and cognitive parts of the message, in rephrasing you concentrate on the meaning or cognitive part. For example, look again at the speaker's message, "I just can't understand why Janae is the way she is!" A possible rephrasing response is, "You are having difficulty understanding Janae's problems." With this response, you are not attempting to describe the feeling (e.g., concern), but the cognitive part of the message. Rephrasing changes the words to help parents and professionals hear what they are saying and perhaps approach their problems from a different perspective.

Open-Ended Questioning Open-ended questions encourage parents and professionals to share information and to actively participate. They typically begin with *how, what,* and *tell me about* (Bos & Vaughn, 2002, 2006). The questions may be unstructured (e.g., "What do you think about Hector's program?") or structured, which limits the responses (e.g., "What have you found that works with Sarah when she begins to cry?") (Turnbull & Turnbull, 2005). According to Hepworth, Rooney, and Larsen (2002), open-ended questions are used to elicit information and elaboration (e.g., "Tell me how the notes are working with Juan." or "I'd like to know how the notes are working with Juan."). Focusing on open-ended questions does not mean that you should never ask a closed-ended question, such as "Do you feel Lashonda is making progress?" or "Does Lashonda frequently appear tired?" Such closed-ended questions are useful for finding factual information, but a preponderance of these questions limits discussion.

Summarizing To summarize, simply restate what the parents or professionals said, highlighting the major points. Summarization helps to acknowledge that a topic has been exhausted and the major points are understood.

Activity 3.2

Work with a partner to complete this activity:

Part 1: A general classroom teacher tells you that Miranda is taking up too much of his time in his math class. Write down two active listening statements and an open-ended question in response to the teacher's comment.

Part 2: Horace's parents complain to you that you are giving him too much homework to do. Write down two active listening statements and an open-ended question in response to this comment.

IMPORTANT POINTS

1. Communication is the key to effective working relationships with teachers and other members of the school team, and is essential for successful interactions with parents and families.
2. Nonverbal communication is essentially all communication other than the spoken or written word and includes proxemics (personal space), kinesics (posture and gestures), and paraverbal communication (tone, volume, pitch, and cadence of your voice along with the use and timing of silence).
3. Effective verbal communication skills include active listening, rephrasing, open-ended questioning, and summarizing.

COMMUNICATION AND COLLABORATION WITH PARENTS AND FAMILIES

"Parents are an integral part of efforts to improve student performance, their insights critical to educational change" (Hernandez, 2001, p. 82). Interactions among parents and families and school professionals result in benefits to both students and family members (Hoover-Dempsey, et al., 2005). Parents are able to assist their children at home, and children and adolescents benefit from increased opportunities to learn. Teachers and school systems also benefit from increased family involvement because teachers learn more about their students through the wealth of information that families can contribute, and attitudes toward schools are enhanced through home–school collaboration (Dettmer, Thurston, & Dyck, 2002, 2005).

Involving family members in the education of students with disabilities is not only educationally sound, but also mandated by law (Salend, 2001, 2005). The Individuals with Disabilities Education Act (IDEA) Reauthorized 2004 strengthened parent participation in decision making and in resolving home–school disputes, by including family members in the educational process.

Families of students with special needs face the typical challenges of child rearing and, in addition, must cope with the issues involved with a child with a disability (Blalock, 2001). Additional characteristics of families, such as the increasing number of women in the workforce, a reliance on day-care centers and extended family members (Platt & Olson, 1997), the number of single-parent families (Ascher, 1987), ethnic-cultural identities (Friend & Bursuck, 2006), and employment patterns (Wehmeyer, Morningstar, & Husted, 1999) make it imperative for teachers to be sensitive and responsive to family issues. Encouraging parents to visit school; increasing the frequency of communication by making phone calls, sending home positive notes, e-mails, or newsletters; and using telephone answering machines for recorded messages are just a few techniques that encourage a collaborative relationship between the school and family members (Blalock, 2001).

The foundation for any collaborative effort between families and school personnel is based on clear, open communication. Sometimes what seems like a lack of home cooperation turns out to be a problem in communication (Johnson, Pugach, & Hawkins, 2004). We hope you will incorporate the verbal and nonverbal communication skills mentioned earlier in the chapter in your interactions with family members. Throughout this chapter, and the entire text, the terms *families* and *parents* are used interchangeably, and may refer to mothers, fathers, stepparents, foster parents, aunts, uncles, grandparents, guardians, older siblings, and others.

BARRIERS TO COMMUNICATION

Unfortunately, not all communication with family members has been positive. To encourage school–home collaboration, you must be aware of some of the barriers to communication as well as ways to manage conflict. Johnson, Pugach, and Hawkins (2004) identified attitudes of professionals that interfere with communication with parents and families. These attitudes include the beliefs that parents are helpless, that parents are responsible for the child's conditions, that parents' opinions are not worthwhile, that parents are pushy or adversarial, and that parents and professionals should not become overly friendly. A belief particularly attributed to family members from minority cultures is that they lack interest in their child's development (Rounds, Weil, & Bishop, 1994). As Harry (1992) explains, this belief is exacerbated by the fact that some cultures stress respect for and deference to authority, which interferes with active participation at IEP and other meetings. The National Parent Teacher Association (PTA) conducted a survey of PTA presidents to determine why more families are not getting involved in their children's education and found the following reasons: lack of time, difficulty understanding the system, language and cultural differences, transportation difficulties, problems arranging child care, and feelings of intimidation and not being welcome (Kroth & Edge, 1997).

A first step in communicating with parents is viewing parents as partners, showing trust and respect, and having empathy for their problems. An attitude of respect and trust is particularly important when working with parents from various cultural groups (Olion, 1989). Several factors contribute to a feeling of mistrust of the school including parents who are overwhelmed with daily life issues, those for whom English is not the predominant language used at home and those who are intimidated by school personnel (Wood, 2006). Teachers need to be aware of the feelings parents have (e.g., mistrust) and the challenges they face (e.g., working several jobs or lack of transportation) and consider the perspectives and experiences that parents bring to the communication process (e.g., information about the child's prior educational experiences). Remember, the parent is the child's first teacher and typically the one constant variable over the child's entire life.

CRISIS CONFRONTATION

You should always assume that interactions with parents will be positive, but when you do communicate with parents who are upset, it is never easy, even for veteran teachers. Conflict can be particularly daunting for new teachers. The use of effective communication techniques can reduce the competitive nature involved in conflict and assist in resolving situations between parents and educators (Melamed & Reiman, 2000). But how do you handle communication when you are surprised by an irate parent? There are steps you can take to diffuse the situation:

1. ***Remain calm, confident and listen to what the parent is saying.*** If possible, move the parent to an office or classroom where you can speak privately. Use appropriate verbal (i.e., active listening) and nonverbal (i.e., a calm voice and supportive stance) communication skills to keep the situation under control.
2. ***Avoid arguing and becoming defensive*** (Johnson, Pugach, & Hawkins, 2004). Instead, use some of the nonverbal communication skills in Table 3.1 as the parent speaks.
3. ***As you listen to the parent, write down key information and restate it*** (Johnson, Pugach, & Hawkins, 2004). Writing down the concerns may have a calming effect on the parent, gives you a record of what has been said, and presents an opportunity for follow-up (e.g., scheduling a future meeting with all interested and involved parties).
4. ***Conclude the meeting in an assertive, yet understanding manner with an action plan.*** Ensure that the parent knows that you are serious about resolving the problem, but that you cannot solve it at that time. An unexpected confrontation may occur when students are present and school is in session. Although you cannot take time away from your teaching responsibilities to continue the conversation, you can agree to work with the parent on the problem at a future date.

Crisis confrontations with parents are not typical. In fact, most interactions with parents are positive and productive. You can increase the number of positive interactions with parents by maintaining ongoing communication with them and practicing effective verbal and nonverbal communication techniques with parents when you meet. We suggest you always start the year with positive phone calls home to set the tone for a productive collaborative relationship.

PARENT/FAMILY-TEACHER CONFERENCES

"The very nature of the educational process makes the relationship between home and school an important one" (Hernandez, 2001, p. 82). Communication with parents and family members can be strengthened by improving parent and family-teacher conferences (Salend, 2001, 2005). Effective communication skills should be used during conferences with family members. In a longitudinal survey conducted by Harry, Allen, and McLaughlin (1995), parents of preschool students in special education from the African American culture identified four deterrents to participation: inflexible scheduling, limited conference time, emphasis on documentation rather than parent participation, and role structure of professionals as authoritarians. Hopefully, you can avoid these deterrents with the following suggestions for successful parent/family-teacher conferences. These conferences generally include three steps: (a) planning the conference, (b) conducting the conference, and (c) following through after the conference. We present a checklist identifying procedures for these three steps in Figure 3.1. The procedures were adapted from the University of New Mexico/Albuquerque Public Schools Center for Parent Involvement.

Planning the Conference

If parents feel threatened when asked to attend a conference, they may try to make excuses for not attending (Johnson, Pugach, & Hawkins, 2004). Therefore, be specific about the purpose of the conference and work with parents to find a time when family members can attend. You may notify parents of the parent-teacher conference by a note or by phone. A phone call provides an opportunity for the parents to ask questions and for you to check their understanding of the purpose of the meeting. Some parents, such as single parents, may feel more comfortable if they invite someone to attend the conference with them. If parents do not speak English well or at all, it is important to consider using interpreters and to have materials translated into the native language of the family (see Box 3.1).

Before the conference, review the student's cumulative folder, gather examples of work, and prepare materials, including a skeleton script of what you are planning to say. Scripting the content allows you to check your communication to determine whether it is free of educational jargon, to organize your thoughts, and in many cases, to listen carefully to the parents (because you have planned the important points you want to mention). A script also allows you to check with other teachers to obtain their input. In a coteaching situation, it is essential that you meet with the general education teacher ahead of time for his or her input. In fact, you may want to sit down together and complete the script or have the general education teacher join you for the conference.

Educational jargon often interferes with communication. If you must use educational jargon, define or give examples of the terms. For instance, if you use the term

Figure 3.1 CONFERENCE CHECKLIST

Planning the Conference

_____ 1. Notify
- Purpose, place, time, length of time allotted

_____ 2. Prepare
- Review student's folder
- Gather examples of work
- Prepare materials

_____ 3. Secure co-teacher's input, if appropriate

_____ 4. Script important points you wish to make

_____ 5. Arrange environment
- Select site
- Choose comfortable seating
- Eliminate distractions

Conducting the Conference

_____ 1. Build rapport
- Welcome
- Introduce yourself and others
- Describe roles of all individuals at conference

_____ 2. Preview meeting
- Purpose
- Time limitations
- Note taking
- Emphasize importance of parents' input

_____ 3. Share information
- Use open-ended questions
- Use active listening/rephrasing
- Discuss strengths, concerns, and solutions
- Pause once in a while
- Look for nonverbal cues

_____ 4. Complete parent-conference form

_____ 5. Summarize information
- Review high points
- Schedule other meetings or follow-ups
- Thank them for taking the time to come and for their contributions

Following Up on the Conference

_____ 1. Review conference with student, if appropriate

_____ 2. Share information with other school personnel, if needed

_____ 3. Mark calendar for planned follow-up

_____ 4. File parent-teacher form

short-term objective, add a definition, "the small steps students must master to reach a goal," or an example, "Josiah must master the short-term objective of changing percentages, such as 70%, to decimal numbers, such as 0.70, before he can figure out sales tax."

When scripting the content, include student strengths, your concerns, and possible solutions. Remember to be aware of cultural implications. For example, in many cultures, such as Asian American (Chinn & Plata, 1987), Latino (Briganti, 1989), and Native American (Walker, 1988), child rearing is shared by grandparents or others who live in the home. Therefore, consistency in helping children and adolescents with disabilities can be achieved only if whole families agree to participate in the intervention.

BOX 3.1

Reflections on Practice

The number of parents, families, guardians, and others who interact with school professionals come from a variety of cultural groups and speak a number of languages other than English as their primary or only language. Therefore, we share with you the recommended practices of Ohtake, Fowler, and Santos (2001) for working with language interpreters. We recommend including interpreters in conferences and IEP meetings with families whose first or only language is not English, and suggest the following when interacting with interpreters as part of conferences with parents of English language learners.

Before the Meeting:

- Have a list of interpreters.
- Encourage the family to choose an interpreter who is the most satisfactory to the family.
- Discuss the importance of neutrality.
- Encourage the interpreter to be self-reflective.
- Discuss how clear communication could be prompted with interpreters. Do not discuss attitudes of families toward the plan proposed by the team.
- Provide the interpreter with written documents as advance organizers. Discuss the agenda of the meeting on the basis of the documents.
- Provide the interpreter a glossary that plainly explains terms used in special education.
- Encourage the interpreter to take an introductory course in special education at the college level.
- Discuss the duties and vital roles of interpreters and other team members.
- Encourage the interpreter to be a cultural broker.

During the Meeting:

- Create an informal atmosphere.
- Avoid using professional jargon.
- Use visual aids and concrete examples.
- Avoid idiomatic words, slang, and metaphors that are difficult to translate.
- Be aware of long words.
- Use simple sentences.
- Speak slowly and clearly.
- Use consecutive interpretations.
- Encourage the interpreter to take notes and ask questions whenever he or she needs.
- Be sensitive to reactions shown by the interpreter to identify if the interpretation process is going well. However, your eye contact should be with the family.

After the Meeting:

- Evaluate the meeting with the interpreter using the guidelines described in "Before the Meeting" and "During the Meeting."
- Encourage the interpreter to ask questions and clarify issues about the meeting.

BOX 3.1

(continued)

- Identify problems that the interpreter may have encountered during the meeting.
- Encourage the interpreter to advise you if you communicate with the family in a culturally inappropriate manner.
- Brainstorm ways to address those problems for future meetings.

Taken from Ohtake, Y., Fowler, S. A., & Santos, R. M. (2001). (p. 9). ***Working with interpreters to plan early childhood services with limited-English-proficient families*** (Technical Report #12) [electronic version]. Champaign-Urbana, IL: Culturally and Linguistically Appropriate Services for Early Childhood Research (CLAS) Institute.

Another consideration in offering solutions is to recognize that some resources may not be available to the parents. For example, you would not want to suggest that Mario complete his homework on a computer if the family does not have a computer or the transportation to take him to the public library where they do have computers. For these reasons, it is important to secure parent input concerning solutions; the ones you write during the planning should never be etched in stone. A sample script appears in Figure 3.2.

A final part of planning is selection of the environment for the conference. Try to use the classroom. There, you have immediate access to the files, plus the parents can see the setting that serves as their child's or adolescent's learning environment (Turnbull & Turnbull, 2005). Be certain to provide all participants with adult-sized

Figure 3.2 SAMPLE SCRIPT

Student's Name _Bill_

Grade _Ninth_

1. *Strengths* (Check vocabulary.)
   - Participates in discussions.
   - Makes insightful comments that often describe the point the author is trying to make.
   - Is a leader during cooperative learning groups. (Cooperative learning groups involve students of different ability working together on a project.) For example, Bill helps organize the other students by suggesting how they might all work together, asking such questions as, Who wants to draw the graph? and Who wants to look up the information in the encyclopedia?

2. *Concerns* (Check jargon and specific examples.)
   - Bill is constantly late for his first-period history class, which is resulting in a failing grade.
   - His ninth-grade class teacher and I kept a record of the number of times late the past 3 weeks—late 11 of 15 days an average of 20 minutes each day. On time about 1 day a week.
   - Bill says he oversleeps or he rides with a friend who oversleeps. (Ask parents for thoughts about why he is late.)

3. *Possible Solutions* (Initiate by asking parents if they have any solutions. If none, ask them about each of the following and see if they think any one would work.)
   - Bill rides the bus instead of riding with a friend.
   - Set up a home reinforcer system. At the end of the week the teacher will call the parent. If Bill is on time 3 out of 5 days, he can go to the football game or dance or out on Friday night. If not, he stays home.
   - Bill and both teachers write out a contract. If Bill is on time 3 out of 5 days, he earns the negotiated reinforcer at school, such as leading a small-group discussion with materials provided by the teacher.

Figure 3.3 CONFERENCE FORM

Parent-Teacher Conference Form

Student's Name: Bill Jacobs Grade: 9th

Date: 10/12

Place: Milton High School

Purpose: To discuss Bill's lateness to his first-period history class, which is resulting in a failing grade. Tardy 11 out of 15 days the past 3 weeks. On time 4 out of 15 days, about once a week.

Possible Solutions:

Solutions	Evaluation
1. Parents will talk with Bill.	Determine effectiveness.
2. If late for more than two days during the week, he must ride the bus the entire week.	Negative, too long of a punishment.
3. If on time for three days during the week, Bill's father will take him out to drive the car on Saturday.	Positive, must do every week.
4. If on time for three days a week for five or six weeks, Bill's father will take him to a professional football game.	Positive, six weeks' time.

Solution Selected: #4

Bill's parents feel he will work for football and they want him to take driving lessons at school. His teachers will make up a chart for Bill, so he can see his progress.

Follow-Up Procedures:

Ms. Gonzalez will call Bill's parents on Tuesday and Thursday to report Bill's progress.

Signatures: Diane Jacobs (parent/s)

Linda Gonzalez (teacher)

chairs and make sure that the room is comfortable. It is always advisable to have tissues available for parents who may become upset or emotional.

Conducting the Conference

Establishing rapport, previewing the conference, sharing information, and summarizing the information are ingredients for successful completion of a conference. We also recommend the completion of a conference form during the conference to serve as a written verification of the content. A completed form dealing with the problem of Bill's being late for class is found in Figure 3.3. Beginning with possible solutions, the information was completed with the input of family members.

Establishing Rapport Greeting parents at the door is a way to add to the comfort of parents from diverse cultures (Kuykendall, 1992). Begin the conference by introducing yourself and any other individuals, indicating their responsibilities. Be certain to address the parents respectfully. Dettmer, Thurston, and Dyck (2005) suggest using greeting words in the family's language. If you are part of a coteaching situation and the general education teacher and you are both present, the person who contacted the parents should take charge. If you are in charge, remember to ask opinions of your coteacher as well as the parents as you conduct the conference. Arrange adult seating for the parents and place your chair next to the parents and not directly across from them.

Previewing the Conference At this time, state the purpose of the meeting, identify time limitations, and emphasize to the parents their importance in providing input and solutions. If you plan to take notes, inform the parents and ask them if they would like a copy. Take notes openly, so they can see what you are writing (Johnson, Pugach, & Hawkins, 2004). If you are going to complete a conference form similar to that in Figure 3.3, show and explain the form.

Sharing Information In sharing information, remember to use open-ended questions, active listening, and rephrasing. Make every attempt to involve the parents actively. In many cultures, parents are passive receivers of information in school matters. For example, in some cultures, schooling is viewed as the responsibility of the school and parental involvement in school matters is not expected or encouraged. It is important to know this so you do not misinterpret a lack of participation as a lack of interest.

Always start on a positive note, mentioning the strengths of the student. Next, move to the concerns, using specific examples of student work. You may want to ask parents if they see similar behavior at home. Once your concerns are thoroughly discussed, move to possible solutions, asking for parent input. Throughout the conference, remember to listen to the parents, refrain from interruptions, and give the parents many opportunities for input. Wait for the parents to respond before adding another point: In some cultures, it is impolite to interrupt others.

Summarizing the Information Before concluding the conference, review the major points, including the concerns and the solution agreed upon. Schedule any future meetings, phone calls, or follow-through plans. Be certain to thank the parents for their ideas and contributions, and offer to send them a copy of your notes or the conference form.

Following Through After the Conference

If you are planning to review the conference with the student, you should mention this at the end of the parent conference and ask the parents for their permission, or summarize what you plan to say. If you need to share the information with other professionals, remember that any written information that is shared with other school personnel must be revealed to parents upon request (Morgan & Jensen, 1988). As a follow-up after the conference, send a note to the parents thanking them for attending and include a copy of the conference form or something in writing that restates actions to be taken and persons responsible. Finally, be certain to file the conference form and follow up on any of your responsibilities. For example, the solution agreed upon for Bill's tardiness requires the teacher to contact the parents twice a week.

Activity 3.3

Examine the description below and script the information using the script in Figure 3.2 as an example. Be sure to include strengths, concerns, and possible solutions.

Frequently, Marie does not turn in her homework. She tells the fifth-grade teacher that she did it, but forgot to bring it to school. At this time, her grade is a D due to her incomplete homework assignments. She is able to score Bs and Cs on the weekly quizzes.

IMPORTANT POINTS

1. Interactions among families and school professionals result in benefits for students, family members, teachers, and school systems.
2. The Individuals with Disabilities Education Act (IDEA) Reauthorized 2004 strengthened parent participation in the educational process.
3. During a crisis confrontation, teachers should stay calm, isolate, listen, restate, question, keep the communication simple, view it as not personal, and be assertive.
4. Parent-teacher conferences involve (a) planning the conference, (b) conducting the conference, and (c) following through after the conference.

COLLABORATIVE CONSULTATION

Collaboration is thought by professionals in inclusive schools to be the key to their success (Friend & Cook, 2003). According to Idol, Nevin, and Paolucci-Whitcomb (2000):

> Collaborative consultation is an interactive process that enables people with diverse expertise to generate creative solutions to mutually defined problems. The outcome is enhanced, altered, and produces solutions that are different from those that the individual team members would produce independently. The major outcome of collaborative consultation is to provide comprehensive and effective programs for students with special needs within the most appropriate context, thereby enabling them to achieve maximum constructive interaction with their nonhandicapped peers (p. 13).

In collaborative consultation, participants such as general and special education teachers, families, students, administrators, paraprofessionals, school counselors, employers, and speech pathologists serve as consultants in their respective areas of expertise, so that all participants have the opportunity to share their knowledge and skills (Blalock, 2001). Through this collaborative effort, it is possible to exchange information about a student's strengths and weaknesses and to identify potential teaching strategies and curricular adaptations that could prove beneficial (Knackendoffel, 1996). Successful resolution of problems is dependent on the skills of the collaborators. Because most educators may not possess a strong background in collaborative strategies, it is recommended that they receive training in order to serve in collaborative roles (Idol, Nevin, & Paolucci-Whitcomb, 2000; Roache, Shore, Gouleta, & Butkevich, 2003).

RATIONALE AND NEED FOR COLLABORATIVE CONSULTATION

Collaboration between special and general educators is viewed as an essential component in the success of students with disabilities who are being served in general education classes (Dettmer, Thurston, & Dyck, 2002; Voltz, 2003). Today, special educators must operate as part of a team in many aspects of their roles, such as planning, placement, assessment, instruction, and monitoring progress, necessitating greater collaboration among school professionals and others (Blalock, 2001). "Effective collaborative consultation relies on the parity and equity of contributions from all collaborators" (Idol, Nevin, & Paolucci-Whitcomb, 2000, p. 13). Friend and Cook (2006) have identified several characteristics of collaboration, including the following: Collaboration is voluntary, requires parity among participants, is based on mutual goals, depends on shared responsibility for participation and decision making, requires the sharing of resources, includes shared accountability for outcomes, involves trust, and builds a sense of community.

Studies have revealed that the use of collaborative consultation has resulted in (1) improved student outcomes, (2) effective instruction of students with special needs in general education classrooms, (3) a reduction in the number of students referred for special education, (4) support for the implementation of the collaborative consultation model, and (5) improved mutual problem solving, sharing of knowledge, and communication among general and special educators (Saver & Downes, 1991). Support for consultation among general educators was shown in a survey by Myles and Kasselman (1990) in which half of the teachers surveyed reported using collaborative consultation, even though a formal consultation program was not available in their schools. Kamens (1997) found that collaborative activity increases job satisfaction and self-esteem, promotes better working relationships, and contributes to professional development. When teachers collaborate, they tend to become more knowledgeable about their fields, become more involved in school decision making (Sindelar, Griffin, Smith, & Watanabe, 1992), and improve their skills and those of their students (Elliott & Sheridan, 1992). According to Dynak, Whitten, and Dynak (1997), teaching should not be an isolated act; elementary education, special education, and content area teachers should collaborate as part of their regular school day. You have probably noticed that schools today are focused on building collaborative learning

Activity 3.4

"Coming together is a beginning; keeping together is progress; working together is success" (Henry Ford).

Imagine yourself as a special education teacher who is working as part of a team with general education teachers, families, students, administrators, paraprofessionals, school counselors, psychologists, speech pathologists, and other school personnel. As a member of this team, what kinds of things would you be able to accomplish for students with special needs that you could not do as well on your own? Give examples at the elementary and secondary levels.

IMPORTANT POINTS

1. The ability to communicate and collaborate with members of a team (general classroom teachers, administrators, paraprofessionals, other direct- and related-service providers, and families) may have a significant impact on the quality of services that special educators provide for their students.
2. Collaborative consultation is an interactive process that enables people with diverse expertise to generate creative solutions to mutually defined problems (Idol, Nevin, & Paolucci-Whitcomb, 2000).
3. Studies have revealed that the use of collaborative consultation has resulted in (a) improved student outcomes, (b) effective instruction of students with special needs in general education classrooms, (c) a reduction in the number of students referred for special education, (d) support for the implementation of the collaborative consultation model, and (e) improved mutual problem solving, sharing of knowledge, and communication among general and special educators.

communities to meet the increased accountability for student learning (Marchant, 2002), and educators are making use of each other's knowledge and expertise (Lieberman, 1995).

OPTIONS FOR IMPLEMENTING COLLABORATIVE CONSULTATION

Several options or models have been found to be effective in the implementation of collaborative interactions (i.e., mutual problem solving and shared decision making) among professionals. They include teacher assistance teams (Chalfant & Pysh, 1989), prereferral intervention (Friend & Cook, 2006; Winzer & Mazurek, 1998), response to intervention (Vaughn & Fuchs, 2003), consulting teacher (Idol, 1988), and cooperative teaching (Friend & Cook, 2006).

Teacher assistance teams and prereferral interventions are examples of a team approach to problem solving. Members of these teams range from general education teachers to special education teachers, administrators, English language learning personnel, counselors, social workers, and other members of the school community. In these two approaches, the intent is to work collaboratively through formal, structured stages to solve problems and make decisions about students. These approaches tend to reduce the number of inappropriate or unsuitable referrals for special education placement (Blalock, 1997), provide support to students (Bos & Vaughn, 2006), and expand the instructional alternatives that teachers have at their disposal (Olson & Platt, 2004). Many of the students who are referred to these teams may be experiencing difficulty in the classroom because of cultural and linguistic differences (Craig, Hull, Haggart, & Peréz-Selles, 2000), which should be taken into consideration as part of prereferral interventions. Teacher assistance teams and prereferral interventions can assist teachers to make changes in their instructional practices and respond to the increased diversity of student needs in their classrooms (Craig, et al., 2000).

Response to Intervention (RTI) is part of a multitiered service delivery system for students with academic difficulties as a means of providing them with quality instruction and remedial assistance within the general education setting: Special education is provided for students with disabilities who need more specialized services than can be provided in the general education environment (NJCLD, 2005). Response to Intervention is described as a way to provide help more efficiently to struggling students. This intensive instruction separates students with disabilities from students who are struggling for other reasons. The RTI process is expected to reduce enrollment in special education since the provision of services does not depend on an intelligence test score (Fuchs, Mock, Morgan, & Young, 2003). Like teacher assistance teams and prereferral interventions, RTI may reduce the number of inappropriate referrals to special education and the overidentification of minority students (NJCLD, 2005; New Report, 2005).

The consulting teaching and cooperative teaching options both involve close collaboration between general and special education teachers in actual classroom settings. These teaching options should reflect a culturally responsive approach to the ever-increasing diversity in schools. Where teacher assistance teams, prereferral interventions, and RTI involve more of a problem-solving approach, consulting teaching and cooperative teaching focus more on collaborative consultation and interactions among participants in the general education classroom.

Teacher Assistance Teams

Teacher assistance teams (TATs) are school-based teams that serve as support systems for classroom teachers (Bos & Vaughn, 2006). Such teams provide opportunities to brainstorm solutions to problems and exchange ideas, methods, and techniques for developing instructional alternatives to help students referred to the team (Hayek, 1987). The philosophy behind TATS is that classroom teachers have the skills to teach students with learning and behavior problems by working together in a problem-solving, collaborative manner. Teacher assistance teams have been utilized in schools for years (Westling, Herzog, Cooper-Duffy, Prohn, & Ray, 2006) and are typically composed of general education teachers, administrators, and support personnel. These teams function to help the referring teachers resolve classroom-based problems. The use of TATS has resulted in benefits to students, their families, and professionals (Chalfant & Pysh, 1989). Pysh and Chalfant (1997) emphasize the importance of providing time for teams to meet and ensuring that teams receive external reinforcers when they meet outside of their daily activities.

Teacher Referrals A teacher who is having difficulty with a student submits a referral to the team. The referring teacher describes the student's performance, strengths, and weaknesses; the interventions already attempted; and other pertinent information, such as health history or assessment results.

Reviews of Referrals The team coordinator reviews the referral and asks the team members to read it prior to a team meeting so that the team members may devote the meeting time to actual problem solving (Chalfant & Pysh, 1981).

Requests for Specific Information The team coordinator responsible for the case may contact the referring teacher for clarification of information submitted or for additional information, may observe in the classroom if necessary, and develops a problem-interaction diagram that summarizes the concerns (Chalfant & Pysh, 1989).

Classroom Visits It may be helpful if one of the team members observes the student in the classroom. This team member may collect additional pertinent information through observation of the student and the environment.

Problem-Solving Meetings The TAT meeting lasts for 30 minutes and includes the following steps recommended by Chalfant and Pysh (1981):

1. Reach a consensus about the nature of the problem.
2. Negotiate one or two objectives with the referring teacher. Be sure that the objectives specifically state the behaviors the student should achieve.
3. Brainstorm alternatives.
4. Select the methods the referring teacher would like to try and define the methods.
5. Assign responsibility for carrying out the recommendations (who, what, when, where, how).
6. Establish a follow-up plan for continued support and evaluation.

Recommendations The meeting should result in recommendations for the referring teacher to implement, recommendations for informal assessment for the teacher or a team member to complete, or a referral for special help.

Prereferral Intervention

Prereferral intervention refers to "a systematic set of activities in which students believed to be at risk for school failure are evaluated with regard to their learning and educational needs as well as their abilities" (Blackhurst & Berdine, 1993, p. 51). Prereferral intervention is designed to prevent inappropriate placements in special education and to help general classroom teachers interact effectively with students who have special needs. Implemented in a highly collaborative manner (Welch, et al., 1990), prereferral intervention focuses on instructional and behavioral interventions as opposed to testing and placement. In other words, it involves the use of interventions with students who have diverse needs outside of special education (Baca & Almanza, 1991). Some professionals dislike the use of the term *prereferral*, as it implies that referral to special education is imminent (Graden, 1989). The term *intervention assistance teams* is used by some to describe a team approach to assisting teachers with students, prior to considering referral for special education (Friend & Cook, 2006).

Through prereferral interventions, teachers gather data on a student's learning and behavior, design a support system to assist the student in general classrooms, and adapt curriculum and modify the classroom environment (Winzer & Mazurek, 1998). Thus, prereferral intervention has two areas of emphasis: problem solving and adaptations, and modifications. Problem solving involves collaborative consultation among members of a school-based problem-solving team to which referrals are sent and whose members suggest instructional interventions. Adaptations and modifications are recommended when students' needs are not being met in the existing classroom setting. Studies conducted on prereferral interventions demonstrated that schools could reduce referrals and testing for special education, and increase the use of consultation (Safran & Safran, 1996). Table 3.2 contains examples of modifications for prereferral recommended by Winzer and Mazurek (1998).

Stage 1: Referral for Consultation The classroom teacher requests assistance from a consultant (such as a school psychologist, a social worker, a special education teacher, or a counselor) or seeks assistance from a school-based problem-solving and screening team (school psychologist, other classroom teachers, special education teacher, principal, social worker, or a counselor).

Stage 2: Consultation The consultant or team collaborates with the classroom teacher to define the problem, explore intervention strategies, try them, and evaluate the outcomes. If the intervention attempts are successful, the process ends. If they are not, the process moves to a third stage.

Stage 3: Observation During the observation stage, additional information is collected through observation of the student and the environment. Then alternate intervention plans are implemented and evaluated. At Stages 2 and 3, the participants must specify the roles and responsibilities of those implementing the plan. For example, the school psychologist may be responsible for observing the student, the classroom teacher may be responsible for collecting work samples and performing an error analysis, and the special education teacher may be responsible for adapting instructional materials.

Stage 4: Conference At this stage, a conference is held with a child review team to communicate the results of interventions and make decisions. This team comprises some of the school resource people mentioned in Stage 1 (school psychologist, general classroom teachers, special education teachers, etc.). All information is reviewed and the team makes recommendations to continue the interventions, try alternative interventions, or refer the student for consideration for special education placement.

Stage 5: Formal Referral At this stage, the student may be referred for an educational assessment. Information previously gathered and interventions tried during the previous

Table 3.2 Modifications for Prereferral

Materials modifications	Make materials self-correcting. Highlight critical features. Block out extraneous elements.
Instructional modifications	Use mnemonic devices. Shorten directions. Provide mediators. Use advance organizers. Preface all remarks with a title or the main idea of the lesson. Use cognitive learning strategies.
Cues, feedback	Provide more prompts. Use corrective feedback. Provide visual cues.
Management	Use contingency contracts. Change seating. Use cooperative strategies. Use peer tutoring.
Content	Slow pace; use wait time.
Grouping	Use learning centers.
Test taking	Teach test-taking skills.
Study	Teach study skills. Note all assignments on a special bulletin board.
Psychosocial	Use the following: Counseling Support groups Social services Cross-cultural counseling

Source: From Winzer, M. A., & Mazurek, K. M. (1998). *Special Education in Multicultural Contexts.* Upper Saddle River, NJ: Merrill/Prentice Hall. Reprinted by permission.

stages can be vitally important. The team members may want to ask themselves what additional data are necessary to make a decision. They may want to reexamine student work samples, records of assignment completion, observations of classroom behavior and participation, screenings of academic skills, and modifications made in the classroom. Further assessment could include curriculum-based assessment, criterion-referenced testing, and additional observation measures.

Stage 6: Formal Program Meeting A formal meeting of the child study team is held to review information from the first five stages. The team discusses alternative placements and services and writes IEP goals, if appropriate.

Response to Intervention (RTI)

Response to Intervention is an objective examination of the relationship between an academic or behavioral intervention and the student's response to the intervention (Brown-Chidsey & Steege, 2005). RTI is based on three core concepts: (1) application of scientific, research-based interventions in general education; (2) measurement of a student's response to these interventions; and (3) use of the RTI data to inform instruction. The consensus of fourteen organizations forming the 2004 Learning Disabilities Roundtable (2005) was that data from an RTI process should include the following:

1. High-quality, research-based instruction and behavioral supports in general education.
2. Scientific, research-based interventions focused specifically on individual student difficulties and delivered with appropriate intensity.
3. Use of a collaborative approach by school staff for development, implementation, and monitoring of the intervention process.
4. Data-based documentation reflecting continual monitoring of student performance and progress during interventions.
5. Documentation of parent involvement throughout the process.
6. Documentation that the timeliness described in the federal regulations are adhered to unless extended by mutual written agreement of the child's parents and a team of qualified professionals.
7. Systematic assessment and documentation that the interventions were implemented with fidelity.

Although there is no universal model of RTI, it is generally thought of as a multitiered model or service delivery system that provides quality instruction, differentiated instruction, and remedial opportunities (NJCLD, 2005). A three-tiered model would include:

Tier 1: High-quality instructional and behavioral supports are provided for all students in general education.

Tier 2: Students whose performance and rate of progress lag behind those of peers in their classrooms, school, or district receive more specialized prevention or remediation within general education.

Tier 3: Comprehensive evaluation is conducted by a multidisciplinary team to determine eligibility for special education and related services.

Like TATs and prereferral interventions, the RTI approach involves professionals from general and special education, administrators, parents, and others as appropriate. The process may be initiated by a parent or teacher and as with other interventions, proceeds through steps. The National Joint Committee on Learning Disabilities (2005) suggests five steps.

Step 1: Identifying and analyzing the problem, including collection of baseline data

Members of the collaborative team meet to define the problem and collect data to document it using multiple assessments (e.g., curriculum-based measures).

Step 2: Generating possible strategies or interventions

Based upon assessment data, team members generate a list of possible interventions and evaluate each one for its potential.

Step 3: Implementing an intervention plan

Team members implement the intervention plan and assign roles to those who will be involved.

Step 4: Monitoring student progress to determine success

Team members collect data and continuously monitor student progress.

Step 5: Reviewing and revising plans as needed

Team members regularly review the implementation plan using progress monitoring data, and revise or adjust as needed.

RTI, as a collaborative problem-solving approach, appears to be a refinement of TATs and prereferral approaches. Potential benefits include (1) earlier identification of students with learning disabilities using this problem-solving approach instead of an ability-achievement discrepancy formula, (2) reduction in inappropriate referrals to special education and the overidentification of minority students, (3) data that relate to instruction, (4) a focus on student outcomes, and (5) an emphasis on collaboration and shared responsibility (NJCLD, 2005). However, many questions remain to be answered such as whether the RTI process can identify a learning disability, how students will move through the process, what happens if a student is unresponsive to intervention, how parents will be involved with the process, and what additional human resources will be needed to implement RTI. We encourage you to study the research that is being conducted nationally on response to intervention as you try different instructional approaches and make decisions about your students.

Consulting Teacher

Consulting teaching is "a process for providing special education services to students with special needs in which special education teachers, general education teachers, other school professionals, or parents collaborate to plan, implement, and evaluate instruction conducted in general classrooms for the purpose of preventing or ameliorating students' academic or social behavior problems" (Idol, 1986, p. 2). As a problem-solving process, it is meant to be highly collaborative, with general and special education teachers working as partners in planning instruction. Idol (1988) feels that consultation should *support, not supplant*, general education programs. We suggest that consulting teachers should possess excellent listening, interpersonal, communication (verbal and nonverbal), problem-solving, and teaming skills, as well as effective technical skills (e.g., task analysis, questioning).

The role of the consulting teacher requires knowledge of large- and small-group instruction, familiarity with the general education curriculum, ability to adapt and modify materials and instruction, flexibility, and expertise in working with others. For example, a high school teacher was concerned that the readability level of her history textbook was too high for many of her students, that the text failed to represent the contributions of different cultural groups to the development of the United States, and that it did not present a balanced perspective. She worked with the consulting teacher in the development of materials to supplement the text. They used DVDs, books that represented different ethnic groups, and reference materials from the media center and websites. Consulting teachers may also design curriculum units, participate in prereferral systems, and coteach with general classroom teachers.

Figure 3.4 contains an example of a cooperative planning guide, which employs four steps in consultation (i.e., define the problem, analyze the problem, implement a plan, and evaluate the plan). Notice that the form was completed cooperatively by the special education teacher, Ms. Hernandez, and the classroom teacher, Mr. Whitley. They began by defining the problem. Through an exchange of information including listening, questioning, and clarifying, they were able to target Marcus's problem—he does not pay attention in science class and this affects his performance on tests and projects. Second, they analyzed the problem. They did this by listing (a) the factors in the classroom that might be contributing (e.g., the class is primarily lecture), (b) the behaviors of the student that might be contributing (e.g., he doesn't write anything

Figure 3.4 AN EXAMPLE OF A COOPERATIVE PLANNING GUIDE

Cooperative Planning Guide

Student's Name: Marcus Wyler
Date: 11/10

1. Define the problem:	Marcus doesn't pay attention in science class and this affects his performance on tests and projects.
2. Analyze the problem: a. List the factors in the environment that may be contributing to the problem	• The pace is fast. • The class is large. • The class is primarily lecture.
b. List the behaviors of the student that may be contributing to the problem	• He doesn't come to class prepared with pencil and paper. • Ho doesn't watch when information is put on the board. • He doesn't write anything down, so he probably doesn't study.
c. Discuss the student's strengths	• He likes working with peers. • He has excellent attendance. • He learns well from visuals.
3. Implement a plan: a. List and prioritize five recommendations b. Go back and write the initials of the person responsible for implementing each recommendation next to that recommendation	• Award points for coming prepared. (1) D.W. • Present material on transparencies when possible. (4) D.W. • Cue him when to write something down.(3) D.W. & J.H. • Teach him to take notes. (2) J.H. • At the end of class, review the key points of the presentation and let him compare his notes to a peer's. (5) D.W.
4. Evaluate the plan: For each recommendation listed in 3(a), specify how it will be monitored and evaluated	• Science teacher will keep a record of points earned. • Special education teacher will check notes for technique and science teacher for content. • Science teacher will keep track of the effectiveness of cueing. • Science teacher and special education teacher will check notes for evidence of material presented on transparencies. • Science teacher and special education teacher will check notes for key points.

Special education teacher: Judy Hernandez
Science teacher: Don Whitley
Comments: Let's meet next Thursday after school to review Marcus's progress.

down), and (c) the strengths of the student (e.g., he learns well from visuals). As you can see by examining Figure 3.4, they learned a great deal about Marcus by using environmental variables and student strengths and weaknesses to analyze his problem.

Third, they implemented a plan. They did this by first generating and then prioritizing several recommendations. They also decided who would be responsible for carrying out each recommendation. For example, their first priority was to award points to Marcus for coming to class prepared, with the science teacher assuming the responsibility for implementation. The next priority was to teach Marcus to take notes. The special education teacher assumed responsibility for this priority.

Finally, the teachers determined how they would evaluate the plan. They did this by deciding how they would fulfill their roles and responsibilities. For example, the science teacher kept a daily record of the points Marcus earned by coming to class prepared. The special education teacher agreed to evaluate Marcus's notes for technique, and the science teacher assumed responsibility for checking the notes for content.

The consulting teacher may use any of the previously mentioned methods for collaborative problem solving. The key is to use teamwork and shared decision making to create, implement, and evaluate realistic alternatives for students.

Cooperative or Coteaching

Given the increased diversity in today's public school classrooms, it is essential to develop alternative forms of service delivery within the general education setting (Weiss & Lloyd, 2002). According to Hourcade and Bauwens (2001), educators can no longer segregate students by ability levels or cultural and/or linguistic diversity. Cooperative or coteaching has emerged as an effective way to facilitate the inclusion of students with diverse needs and occurs when two or more educators (general educator and special educator or other specialist) share the instruction for students in a classroom (Friend & Cook, 2003). In coteaching, cooperative planning, instructing and evaluating are emphasized. Both the general and special education teachers are present in the classroom and assume responsibility for instruction. Roles and responsibilities are determined on the basis of the strengths and skills of the teachers.

By combining the planning and teaching skills of general and special education professionals in a cooperative arrangement, it may be possible to achieve successful reintegration of students with special needs into general education classrooms. Most general education teachers are skilled in content and curriculum and in providing instruction to large groups, whereas most special education teachers are adept at analyzing and adapting materials and are knowledgeable in special teaching methodologies. In planning instruction, general educators typically identify a theme or topic related to district or state competencies and then develop activities, whereas special education teachers, who are accountable for student mastery of IEP objectives, focus on student learning first and then generate activities to help students meet the objectives (Dyck, Sundbye, & Pemberton, 1997). Figure 3.5 illustrates the interaction of curriculum content (the specialty of general education) and specialized methodology (the specialty of special education) to produce a more effective instructional situation through cooperative teaching (White & White, 1992). To be successful, coteaching

Figure 3.5 INTERACTION CURRICULUM CONTENT

Regular Education	Collaborative Teaching	Special Education
Content knowledge Curriculum objectives Curriculum materials Content resources support Content development Curriculum sequence Learning environment	Shared teaching Evaluation Classroom management Student supervision Team problem solving Communication skills Response to change Professional growth Social and emotional needs addressed	Knowledge of each disability Individual learning styles Adaptation of curriculum Learning strategies Modifications to learning environment Legal issues Motivational techniques

Source: From "A Collaborative Model for Students with Mild Disabilities in Middle Schools" by A. E. White & L. L. White, 1992. *Focus on Exceptional Children, 24*(9), 7. Copyright 1992 by PRO-ED. Reprinted by permission.

requires administrative support, professional development and training, adequate planning time, a willingness and comfort level to work with a colleague in the classroom, ongoing communication, parity among partners, trust, and flexibility.

Friend and Cook (2006) recommend the following six approaches to coteaching all of which include the collaboration of a general education and special education teacher. Both teachers are part of the planning, teaching, and evaluation process. The roles of the teachers should be reversed regularly and selection of each approach should be made with the goal of successfully integrating students with disabilities with their peers without disabilities.

One Teach, One Observe One teacher leads the lesson, while the other observes students and collects data. In this way, the teachers gain valuable information about students' abilities to listen, pay attention, and follow directions. They may also identify which teaching techniques and instructional strategies will be most effective.

One Teach, One Assist In this approach one teacher leads the lesson and the other circulates around the classroom to monitor progress, answer questions, clarify aspects of the lesson or assignment, assist students to stay on task, and check student work.

Station Teaching The students are divided into heterogeneous groups and work at stations around the classroom. Some students may be working with the general education teacher, others with the special education teacher, and others with volunteers or peers.

Parallel Teaching This approach consists of dividing students into two heterogeneous groups to receive similar instruction, but in smaller groups. Each teacher instructs half the class, which ensures students a better pupil-teacher ratio and thus more opportunities to ask questions and respond.

Alternative Teaching In this approach, one teacher works with most of the class, while the other works with a small group. Teachers use the small group to preteach, reteach, review, and/or enhance and enrich learning.

Teaming In the teaming approach, general and special educators share the responsibilities for planning and presenting content to students. At times, one teacher may take the lead for some aspect of instruction, such as teaching the steps for a bill to become a law. At other times, the other teacher takes the responsibility for part of a lesson, such as instructing students in how to interpret the graphics in their social studies texts. The two teachers may role-play or model an activity. The decision of who teaches what depends on the preferences, training, and strengths of the teachers (Snell & Janney, 2000).

Activity 3.5

Work with a partner for this activity. One of you will be the general education teacher and the other the special education teacher. Choose one of the six approaches to coteaching, other than teaming, and develop a lesson planning guide (see Box 3.2). Choose the level (elementary, middle, or high school) and the content area and decide what each will do before, during, and after the lesson.

BOX 3.2

Reflections on Practice

Throughout this chapter we have talked about the importance of collaboration, and believe it is absolutely essential when participating in coteaching. Therefore, we have developed a *lesson planning guide* for coteachers and others to use before, during, and after a cotaught lesson based upon some of the ideas of Villa, Thousand, and Nevin (2004).

Who: General educators, special educators, paraprofessionals

What: Example of a Lesson Planning Guide

When: 2:00–2:50 Monday

Where: Mr. Webster's eighth-grade social studies classroom

How: Teaming approach to coteaching

	Mr. Milaki, Special education Teacher	Mr. Webster, General education Teacher	Ms. Parrish, Paraprofessional
Before the lesson	• Meet to jointly plan and prepare the lessons for the week with Mr. Webster and Ms. Parrish.	• Meet to jointly plan and prepare the lessons for the week with Mr. Milaki and Ms. Parrish.	• Meet with Mr. Milaki and Mr. Webster for clarification of roles and responsibilities. • Prepare vocabulary lists and distribute in class.
During the lesson	• Use KWL approach with entire class. • Introduce new vocabulary. • Circulate and monitor cooperative learning group activity on "how this class would be run under a democracy, dictatorship, and parliamentary government."	• Present a lesson on the different forms of government with frequent pauses to check for understanding. • Circulate and monitor cooperative learning group activity on "How this class would be run under a democracy, dictatorship, and parliamentary government."	• Listen to lesson presentation. • Distribute vocabulary lists. • Assist in monitoring group work.
After the lesson	• Speak briefly after class with Mr. Webster and Ms. Parrish to adjust the next day's lesson and determine how you will assess student learning.	• Speak briefly after class with Mr. Milaki and Ms. Parrish to adjust the next day's lesson. • Ask Ms. Parrish to provide students' comments resulting from group activity to both teachers by the next morning to assist with assessment.	• Put together students' comments from groups and e-mail them to Mr. Milaki and Mr. Webster by the next morning.

BARRIERS TO AND INGREDIENTS OF EFFECTIVE COLLABORATIVE CONSULTATION

Although collaboration has many benefits as a service option, a number of barriers may interfere with its effectiveness (Bondy & Brownell, 1997; Mitchell, 1997). In this section, we discuss some of the barriers to collaboration and provide suggestions for overcoming them.

1. **PROBLEM:** ***Insufficient time and overwhelming caseloads***

   Lack of time is frequently cited as a barrier to developing interactive relationships (Pugach & Johnson, 2002). Because of the demands of multiple roles and responsibilities, some teachers state that consultation is just one more thing to do (Nowacek, 1992).

   SOLUTIONS: In situations in which cooperative teaching has been implemented, time has not been found to be a problem, perhaps because with more efficient communication, duplication of instruction to students with mild disabilities is minimized (Bauwens, Hourcade, & Friend, 1989). Furthermore, as teachers gain more experience with the roles of consulting teacher and coteacher, responsibilities may become more evenly distributed. Teachers who participate as members of collaborative consultation teams, as they do in prereferral intervention, teacher assistance teams, and response to intervention, may initially find the procedures time consuming; however, with increased use, these structured procedures may expedite decisions about students. Finally, school administrators can play an important part in easing the time and scheduling problems of teachers. Administrators may help alleviate the time problem by providing adequate planning and scheduling time for teachers and by assigning concurrent preparation periods to those who need them. West and Idol (1990) report several strategies for increasing consulting time that have been successfully used in elementary and secondary settings. We present an adapted version of their work in Table 3.3.

2. **PROBLEM:** ***Lack of administrative support***

   Lack of administrative support can be a barrier to productive collaborative consultation efforts between general and special education teachers.

   SOLUTIONS: School administrators can create a climate in which collaborative consultation is valued. Their involvement in promoting consultation, controlling caseloads, providing adequate time for consultation, financing programs, facilitating

Table 3.3 Strategies for Increasing Consulting Time

1. Have the principal or other support staff member teach a period each day on a regular basis.
2. Cluster students for independent assignments and study activities in large rooms with fewer staff supervising.
3. Ask a business or community organization that has adopted your school to supply a permanent floating (no cost) substitute.
4. Use teaching assistants or volunteers to supervise at lunch and as classes change.
5. Ask the principal to assign a specific time each week for professionals to collaborate.
6. Use part of regularly scheduled in-service days for collaborative teams to meet, or designate a half day each month without students (third Monday afternoon of each month) to use for collaboration.

Source: West, J. F. & Idol, L. (1990). Collaborative consultation in the education of mildly handicapped and at-risk students. *Remedial and Special Education, 11*(1), 30. Copyright 1990 by PRO-ED, Inc. Reprinted by permission.

teachers' efforts, breaking down barriers, and addressing implementation issues is crucial to the success of consultation-based programming. Teachers should share their ideas and suggestions for how to schedule cooperative planning time with their principals, provide incentives and support for teachers engaged in consultation, and solve implementation issues. When administrators include teachers from the initial planning stage through implementation and evaluation, they significantly increase support for new programs. Platt and Olson (1997) provide the following suggestions for school administrators:

- Promote a climate that is conducive to collaboration.
- Take a leadership role in promoting collaborative consultation and model collaboration for faculty and staff.
- Have a clear understanding of the basic principles of collaborative consultation and facilitate similar understanding by others (by providing speakers, written information, visits to other sites, and ample opportunities for dialogue).
- Develop an awareness of probable roadblocks to consultative efforts and effective solutions for managing them.
- From the beginning, include faculty and staff in participatory planning and decision making and secure their ownership.
- Provide necessary professional development for all participants.
- Know how to plan, finance, implement, and evaluate collaborative consultation.
- Provide incentives and support for professionals engaging in collaborative consultation. (p. 174)

3. **PROBLEM:** ***Differences in background and areas of expertise***

Historically, the roles and responsibilities of special and general educators have been different. According to Glatthorn (1990), "the special education teacher is more often concerned with one student and how learning might be individualized; the classroom teacher worries about the entire class and how overall achievement might be advanced. The special education teacher tends to be concerned with developing a wide range of learning and coping skills; the classroom teacher focuses on academic skills and content" (p. 307). The beliefs general and special educators have about each other may pose barriers to collaboration (Bondy, Ross, Sindelar, & Griffin, 1995) and may cause each to question the credibility of the other.

SOLUTIONS: The options for implementing collaborative consultation, such as consulting teacher or coteacher, may reverse negative attitudes, misunderstandings, and resistance. Combining a professional who possesses knowledge in curriculum, content, and large-group instruction with a professional who is skilled in adapting instructional materials and implementing effective teaching strategies may enhance the progress of all students and assist with the integration of students with special needs into the general education classroom. Once teachers experience the power of collaboration, they will not view their differences as weaknesses, but as strengths. The competencies presented in Table 3.4 are derived from the work of Friend and Cook (1992); Idol, Paolucci-Whitcomb, and Nevin (1994); and Platt and Olson (1997). They represent the types of technical skills and personal qualities that are likely to facilitate effective collaboration for all professionals regardless of field, background, and training.

Table 3.4 The Top Ten Technical Skills and Personal Qualities of Effective Collaborators

Technical Skills	Personal Qualities
Effective collaborators typically know how to	*Effective collaborators typically are*
1. Manage resistance	1. Respected by others
2. Facilitate change	2. Socially competent
3. Resolve conflict	3. Warm, sensitive, understanding
4. Adapt curriculum and instruction	4. Flexible
5. Use principles of effective instruction	5. Risk-takers
6. Manage the learning environment	6. Knowledgeable and experienced
7. Use effective communication skills	7. Good listeners
8. Monitor student progress	8. Confident
9. Work as a member of a team	9. Able to think on their feet
10. Engage in problem solving	10. Energetic

Source: From Platt, J., & Olson, J. (1997). *Teaching Adolescents with Mild Disabilities.* Pacific Grove, CA: Brooks/Cole Publishing Company. Reprinted by permission of Wadsworth Publishing Company.

4. **PROBLEM:** ***Differences and difficulties in communication***

Special education teachers use a communication code that may not be easily understood by general education teachers. Teachers of students with special needs may use abbreviations such as LRE, IEP, FAPE, ITP, CRT, RTI, and CBM, unaware that classroom teachers may not understand these terms.

SOLUTIONS: Use a shared language to communicate about students and school-related activities. This may help strengthen the bond that should exist among professionals who share responsibility for the same students. Suggestions for enhancing communication include:

- Using a common language that is easily understood by all participants (avoiding jargon, abbreviations, and vocabulary specific to one person's experiential background, but not to others) (Platt & Olson, 1997).
- Using effective communication techniques, which we described earlier in the chapter, such as active listening, reflective statements, nonverbal techniques, questions, and adequate verbal space.
- Showing respect for others' knowledge, valuing their expertise, and pooling the talents of all team members (Platt & Olson, 1997).
- Developing an attitude of shared ownership for ideas and activities, and assuming joint responsibility, accountability, and recognition for problem resolution (Phillips & McCullough, 1990).

Activity 3.6

Assume the role of a special education teacher in a high school. Convince a general education colleague that collaborative consultation is a worthwhile activity in which to participate. Be sure to address issues such as planning time, paperwork, and communication. How will the two of you convince your principal that you need common planning time?

IMPORTANT POINTS

1. Options for implementing collaborative consultation include teacher assistance teams, prereferral intervention, response to intervention, consulting teacher, and cooperative teaching.
2. Barriers to effective collaborative consultation include insufficient time and overwhelming caseloads, lack of administrative support, differences in background and areas of expertise, and differences and difficulties in communication.
3. Ingredients of effective collaborative consultation include adequate time, administrative support, combining the strengths of professionals, and use of a shared language.

COLLABORATION WITH PARAPROFESSIONALS

The efforts in special education to expand services to students with disabilities by including them in general education classrooms along with changes in the Individuals with Disabilities Act (IDEA) Reauthorized 2004 have prompted increased participation of paraprofessionals as facilitators of instructional and behavioral support and members of the educational team (Beale, 2001; Wallace, Shin, Bartholomay, & Stahl, 2001). It is currently estimated that from 250,000 to 280,000 paraprofessionals are employed in special education nationally (Drecktrah, 2000). "According to the Individuals with Disabilities Education Act (IDEA) Reauthorized 2004, paraeducators are defined as persons who work directly under the supervision of licensed professionals and who often deliver instructional and direct services to students and their parents" (Werts, Harris, Tillery, & Roark, 2004, p. 232). Throughout this text, we use the terms *paraprofessional, paraeducator*, and *teaching assistant* interchangeably.

GROWTH OF PARAPROFESSIONALS

The Individuals with Disabilities Act (IDEA) of 1997 placed emphasis on the training and supervision of paraprofessionals to provide special education services (Wallace, et al., 2001). IDEA of 1997 specified, "Paraprofessionals who are adequately trained and supervised may assist in the delivery of special education and related services" (Part b, Sec. 612 (a)(15). IDEA Reauthorized 2004 strengthened that emphasis by requiring paraprofessionals to have a two-year degree or equivalent. Over the last several years, the substantial growth in the use of paraprofessionals in special education has had a positive impact on the delivery of services to students with disabilities (Tillery, Werts, Roark, & Harris, 2003). A typical urban district is likely to employ 80% of its paraprofessionals in special education and related services with the remaining hired in bilingual, remedial, and general education (Blalock, 1991). Pickett (1996) indicates that, among the many reasons for employing paraprofessionals, the main reason is to improve the quality of education and other services to students and their parents and families.

The phenomenal growth rate of paraprofessionals has been attributed to (a) the high marks that paraprofessionals have received in serving exceptional students (Killoran, Templeman, Peters, & Udell, 2001); (b) the ability of paraprofessionals to work with a wide range of exceptionalities in a variety of settings (Stanovich, 1996; Wadsworth & Knight, 1996); (c) the improvement of teacher–pupil ratios (Skelton, 1997), thus providing a cost-effective manner to extend the impact of professionals

(Blalock, 1991); (d) the expanding roles of paraprofessionals from performing routine clerical and housekeeping tasks to providing instructional support, assessment activities, and observing and documenting student performance (Beale, 2001; Blalock, 1991); and (e) the introduction of various reform initiatives and/or legislation such as the Individuals with Disabilities Education Act (IDEA), Reauthorized 2004.

Teachers have reported the many advantages of having paraprofessionals in their classrooms such as assistance supervising and monitoring students, clerical support, assistance with small groups, and having another individual with whom to share ideas (Tillery, et al., 2003). Unfortunately, although paraprofessionals have a great deal to offer, they are frequently assigned responsibilities and assignments for which they have not been trained (Beale, 2001). Training and supervision have been informal, haphazard, or nonexistent (French, 2001; Hilton & Gerlach, 1997), and placement decisions have not always been made systematically. According to Blalock (1991), many schools are not providing training at all for paraprofessionals, which is contrary to what is recommended in the literature (United States Office of Special Education Programs, 2001). Furthermore, pre-service and in-service programs rarely prepare teachers to work with paraprofessionals in a manner that will result in improved student performance (Wallace, et al., 2001), nor do they provide instruction in supervision (NJCLD, 1999). Therefore, it is necessary to examine ways to improve current practices and maximize the positive effects that these important members of the educational team can have on students.

PLANNING PARAPROFESSIONAL PROGRAMS

To best utilize the skills and talents of paraprofessionals to meet the needs of teachers and students, certain aspects merit consideration. Skills needed include matching paraprofessional's skills with students' needs, utilizing paraprofessionals with culturally and linguistically diverse populations, and defining roles and responsibilities.

Matching Skills with Needs

The activities assigned to a paraprofessional should be determined by a teacher or service provider based on the education, skills, and interests of the paraprofessional and the needs of the students (NJCLD, 1999). In this way, a paraprofessional who is skilled at the modification of materials and the adaptation of lessons is assigned to help a teacher make these kinds of adjustments, whereas someone with effective instructional skills and good rapport with students is assigned to a teacher who needs someone to go over vocabulary with the students, monitor progress during practice activities in an inclusive setting, or help students review for tests. Those with skills in monitoring, collecting data, and providing feedback could assist with the reintegration of students into general education classrooms or help students make the transition to work settings.

Utilizing Paraprofessionals with Culturally and Linguistically Diverse Populations

Teachers are expected to possess the knowledge, skills, and experience to be effective with students from increasingly diverse cultural, linguistic, and socioeconomic backgrounds (Ortiz & Garcia, 1989; Stanovich, 1996). Therefore, it is helpful to have a paraprofessional who can work effectively with culturally and linguistically diverse groups and can speak multiple languages. Miramontes (1990) recommends the selection and training of paraprofessionals who can provide links between the students' home and school languages and cultures, make home visits, act as translators at staffings, and serve as tutors to help with special education interventions.

Paraprofessionals can and have assisted non-English-speaking students and students from culturally diverse backgrounds (Miramontes, 1990). One of the authors of this textbook set up a program that utilized volunteers to work individually and in small groups with students to teach them to speak English. Through the volunteers, the students were able to share some of their culture, language, and customs with their peers. An assistant who can explain in two languages and who can create learning activities compatible with student characteristics and interests is a tremendous asset.

Another way to involve assistants in ensuring that students from culturally and linguistically diverse backgrounds succeed is to have them develop games, computer activities, and multimedia in which material can be learned in a variety of ways. Assistants may also help monitor diversified grouping patterns, such as cooperative learning and peer tutoring, and participate in coteaching activities. These instructional arrangements allow more students to participate, regardless of their cultural and linguistic backgrounds.

Defining Roles and Responsibilities

The lack of a clear job description appears to be one of the problems most commonly experienced by paraprofessionals. In fact, the greatest frustration between professionals and paraprofessionals is the lack of specificity regarding roles and responsibilities (Blalock, 1993). According to Frith and Mims (1985), "Paraprofessionals who possess

Figure 3.6 EXAMPLE OF A PARAPROFESSIONAL'S SCHEDULE

	Monday	Tuesday	Wednesday	Thursday	Friday
8:00–8:30	Plan with special education teacher.	→	→	→	→
8:30–10:30	Assist with small-group instruction in reading in pull-out program and monitor independent work.	→	→	→	→
10:30–11:30	Monitor student progress in 4th-grade language arts class.	Monitor student progress in 5th-grade math class.	Monitor student progress in 3rd-grade reading class.	Monitor student progress in 2nd grade in process writing.	Monitor student progress in 1st-grade reading class.
11:30–12:30	Make study guides for 5th-grade social studies class.	Make reading games for 3rd-grade class.	Adapt materials in science for 4th-grade class.	Adapt materials in social studies text for 5th-grade class.	Make chapter outlines for 6th-grade math class.
12:30–1:00	Lunch	→	→	→	→
1:00–2:00	Assist teacher in monitoring cooperative learning groups in math in pull-out program.	Assist in whole language in pull-out program.	Assist in math in pull-out program.	Assist in whole language in pull-out program.	Assist in math in pull-out program.
2:00–2:45	Work one-to-one with specific students in pull-out program.	→	→	→	→
2:45–3:15	Assist in supervising peer-tutoring arrangements in 6th grade.	Check student folders in pull-out program.	Assist in supervising peer-tutoring arrangements in 6th grade.	Check and update files in pull-out program.	Assist in supervising peer-tutoring arrangements in 6th grade.
3:15–3:30	Meet with special education teacher to review and plan.	→	→	→	→

a realistic perception of what is expected of them are more likely to perform admirably and to be more satisfied with their work" (p. 226). Teachers should clearly specify what the teaching assistant is expected to do within the areas of instruction, behavior management, assessment, classroom organization, and clerical support. As you can see from Figure 3.6, a paraprofessional can accomplish many tasks in the special education setting and in the general education classroom. The key is careful communication of tasks, roles, expectations, and responsibilities.

BOX 3.3

Reflections on Practice

French (2002) has devised a set of suggestions to help you make the most of your work with paraprofessionals and, in turn, with your students. We provide an adaptation of her suggestions with our own examples.

- ***Provide an orientation.***

  Just as teachers need to know the expectations of their positions, so do paraprofessionals. Provide a description of roles, responsibilities, policies, and procedures.

- ***Analyze your work style and preferences and those of the paraprofessional.***

  Take stock of your own work style first (e.g., organized, well planned, or more casual and spontaneous), then talk to the paraprofessional to see if you have similar or different work styles. This will help you make decisions about how you will work together.

- ***Identify your program and student needs.***

  Figure out what your program will include (e.g., cooperative learning groups) and what your students need (e.g., cues and encouragement from the paraprofessional for those students who are reluctant to participate).

- ***Identify the needs of classroom teachers.***

  Find out what the classroom teacher needs and how the paraprofessional can meet those needs (e.g., distributing corrected homework papers or supporting students as they complete activities at a learning center or station).

- ***Determine the skills of the paraprofessional.***

  Paraprofessionals have different strengths, which can be matched with the needs of teachers and ultimately benefit students (e.g., listening to students read, conducting a review after the teacher has taught students how to check their own work for errors).

- ***Determine and provide the training that the paraprofessional needs.***

  Once you have determined the ways you want the paraprofessional to assist you, make sure you have prepared the paraprofessional in those areas (e.g., teaching a test-taking strategy, assisting students as they write their own stories).

- ***Teach, coach, and provide feedback on the performance of new skills.***

  Everyone benefits from coaching as they learn something new and from feedback regarding their performance of a skill. It is important to be positive and constructive in your comments.

(continued)

BOX 3.3

(continued)

- ***Develop an assignment and schedule for the teaching assistant.***

  Leave nothing up to the imagination. Provide an assignment in writing and establish the routine of giving the paraprofessional a schedule so he or she will know where to be and what to do throughout the day. At some point, you and the paraprofessional will be able to develop the schedule together.

- ***Delegate judiciously and skillfully.***

  Carefully choose what the paraprofessional will do (e.g., monitoring progress during independent practice activities) and what will remain your responsibilities (e.g., communicating with parents). Clarify the specifics of an assignment (e.g., how to complete it, when it is due, and how it will be evaluated).

- ***Monitor and document performance.***

  Remember to monitor the performance of the paraprofessional by providing feedback, correction, and positive reinforcement.

- ***Hold regular meetings.***

  Having regularly scheduled meetings with the paraprofessional will prevent problems and misunderstandings from occurring.

- ***Manage conflicts.***

  Even under the best circumstances, there may be conflicts. Use a problem solving approach to work these out. Remember to keep the welfare of the students as your primary goal. You may discover that when you focus on the students, you take the pressure off yourselves and can more easily identify solutions.

To access French's article, see French, N. (2002). 20 ways to maximize paraprofessional services for students with learning disabilities. *Intervention in School and Clinic, 38*(1), 50–55.

IMPLEMENTING PARAPROFESSIONAL PROGRAMS

There are several things to consider when organizing a paraprofessional program. To implement the program effectively, you should include orientation and training; clarification of expectations, planning, and scheduling; communication; feedback; and evaluation.

Orientation and Training

Prior to employment, Blalock (1991) recommends that paraprofessionals attend an orientation to learn about the types of programs, individuals who will be served, roles and responsibilities, and physical sites. Paraprofessionals who receive professional development feel more skillful (United States Office of Special Education Programs, 2001). Riggs (2001) reports that some school districts begin with a district-wide orientation that starts with policies and procedures and eventually addresses training in specifics (e.g., instructional strategies, computer technology, and special education law). Lindsey (1983) suggests that paraprofessionals attend an initial meeting with other members of their school faculty and staff. Such a meeting should include the following activities: (a) introductions, (b) definition of the paraprofessional's role, (c) information about assessment and instructional techniques, (d) presentations, (e) simulations, and (f) a question-and-answer session. An initial building level session may include discussions about confidentiality, rules, and school procedures including safety and security considerations. Then a general orientation from a building-level administrator may occur, followed by specific training by a teacher or other service provider.

Training is necessary at the outset and on an ongoing basis (Demchak & Morgan, 1998; Hilton & Gerlach, 1997; Wadsworth & Knight, 1996). Training may be provided in the classroom by the teacher and in separate training workshops as needed. Separate training sessions may focus on topics such as how to work with culturally diverse populations, implement coteaching, supervise cooperative learning activities, use effective questioning, and work effectively in inclusive settings. After initial training, professional development activities should be provided throughout the school year to provide ongoing instruction and support.

Clarification of Expectations

Paraprofessionals report that they feel successful in their roles when they clearly understand what is expected of them (Bos & Vaughn, 2006) and clarifying roles decreases the likelihood of misunderstandings (Cohen & Spenciner, 2005). Therefore, teachers should communicate to paraprofessionals what they expect them to do. When a teacher and paraprofessional clarify expectations, they decide on (a) the specific tasks the paraprofessional will complete and where they will complete them, (b) the skills necessary to accomplish the tasks, and (c) any training or modeling of strategies that would help the paraprofessional complete the tasks. For example, if a paraprofessional is being asked to help a teacher implement literature circles in the classroom, he or she will need specific instruction in the use of literature circles and perhaps the opportunity to observe the teacher using literature circles with students. The teacher should work with the paraprofessional to decide how the paraprofessional will acquire the skills, such as through observation and on-the-job training or by attending in-service workshops, or by viewing a presentation on the topic.

Planning and Scheduling

It is important for special education teachers to meet with paraprofessionals to plan and schedule activities. Often paraprofessionals are assigned to several different classrooms and may be under the supervision of more than one teacher. In the case of coteaching situations, it is essential that you work out the roles and responsibilities in advance. For example, in the station teaching approach to coteaching, the general and special education teacher may teach the same content to two groups of students, while the paraprofessional may work with a third smaller group in a review session.

Once identified, the tasks or job descriptions should be written on a schedule (see Figure 3.6). Daily and weekly schedules are helpful in clarifying assignments and structuring the activities of an assistant. In the course of a school day, teachers and paraprofessionals will probably spend time in a variety of classrooms due to the focus on reintegrating students with special needs into the general education classroom. Therefore, the use of a schedule becomes critical. The responsibilities of a paraprofessional may change as the needs of the students change. Teachers should use IEPs to guide their planning for students and work with paraprofessionals to implement changes.

Communication and Feedback

"On-going communication between professionals and paraprofessionals is vital to their collaborative relationship and to positive educational outcomes for students" (Demchak & Morgan, 1998, p. 13). Cohen and Spenciner (2005) suggest that teachers and paraprofessionals schedule regular meetings. The meetings can be used to plan, schedule, discuss student progress, make modifications and adjustments in instructional and behavior management programs, or revise the paraprofessional's job responsibilities.

Activity 3.7
Assume the role of a special education teacher in an elementary school. Look back in the chapter at the section on coteaching. How would you utilize the skills of a paraprofessional in parallel teaching, alternative teaching, and teaming?

Evaluation

Effective programs for paraprofessionals include an evaluation component. Paraprofessional competence is often documented through performance evaluations, direct observation, work samples, and videotapes (Killoran, et al., 2001). The greater the specificity of the assistant's duties and the greater the structure in identifying the tasks in writing, the easier it is to evaluate performance. If paraprofessionals are to provide services to students with special needs, then teachers must provide them with adequate training and supervision, clarify their roles, schedule their time effectively, and give them ample feedback and recognition.

COLLABORATION WITH OTHER PARTNERS

Throughout this chapter, we have focused on collaboration with parents and families, general educators, and paraprofessionals. However, a variety of other partners are critical for the success of school and community programs (Blalock, 1997). These partners include administrators (e.g., principals, assistant principals), other teachers or specialists (e.g., bilingual, transition specialists), related-service providers (e.g., speech-language pathologists, counselors, school psychologists, social workers, occupational and physical therapists, and assistive technology specialists), community and state agency personnel, and job coaches. The key to success in working effectively with these and other partners is through communication and collaboration. Many of the techniques and procedures we have suggested that you use with teachers, paraprofessionals, and parents and families will work effectively with these partners as well. In particular, see our suggestions for administrators in the section of this chapter on barriers to and ingredients of effective collaboration. In addition, we have included an example of the desired qualities of an exemplary collaboration inspired by the work of Hunt (1995). We believe that these seven suggestions (Table 3.5) can be used in collaborative interactions with all partners.

Table 3.5 Desired Qualities of an Exemplary Collaboration

1. Unconditional support based on shared goals, mutual decision making with the agreement to disagree.
2. Positive attitudes and interactions combined with mutual respect among partners and collaborators.
3. Shared responsibility and no-fault teaming.
4. A total commitment by the partners to resolve problems and conflict.
5. Team spirit that is enhanced by building on existing strengths and skills of partners.
6. Professional development and support of partners to learn and grow.
7. Ongoing, positive interactions with the community.

PUTTING IT ALL TOGETHER

In this chapter, we have focused on communication and collaboration—two essential ingredients for success with parents and other members of the school team. We have addressed parent-teacher conferences, options for collaborative consultation, and the contributions of paraprofessionals in facilitating instruction for students with special needs. The work is not easy. It requires cooperation and compromise, but the benefits are great: access to the general education curriculum for students with special needs and improved student learning. Armed with strategies to enhance communication and collaboration with all stakeholders, we are confident that you will be prepared to interact positively and productively with families and members of the school community.

IMPORTANT POINTS

1. The use of paraprofessionals in special education has grown substantially, and this growth has positively affected the delivery of services to students with special needs.
2. A paraprofessional, sometimes called a teaching/educational assistant or paraeducator, is a person who either instructs or delivers direct services to students and/or their parents, and who serves in a position for which a teacher or other professional has ultimate responsibility for the design and implementation of IEPs and other services.
3. In planning paraprofessional programs, it is important to (a) match the skills of the paraprofessional with the needs of the teacher, (b) examine ways to utilize the skills of paraprofessionals in working with culturally and linguistically diverse populations, and (c) clearly define role expectations and responsibilities.
4. Implementation of paraprofessional programs should include (a) orientation and training, (b) clarification of expectations, (c) scheduling, (d) communication and feedback, and (e) evaluation.
5. A variety of other partners are critical for the success of school and community programs, including administrators, other teachers or specialists, related-service providers, community and state agency personnel, or job coaches.

DISCUSSION QUESTIONS

1. Give examples of the verbal and nonverbal communication skills that you, as a teacher, feel would be most effective in the following situations:
   a. A planning meeting with a general education colleague in which the two of you are collaboratively completing a cooperative planning guide for a student (see Figure 3.4).
   b. A feedback session with a paraprofessional.
   c. A meeting with parents who are concerned about their child's progress. Think back to the chapter opening scenario with Mr. Washington (fifth-grade teacher), Mrs. Shoemaker (learning disabilities teacher), and Ms. Johnson (Jamaal's mother).
2. Discuss the potential impact of response to intervention on student learning.

Websites: Useful websites related to chapter content can be found in Appendix A.

CHAPTER

4

Informal Assessment

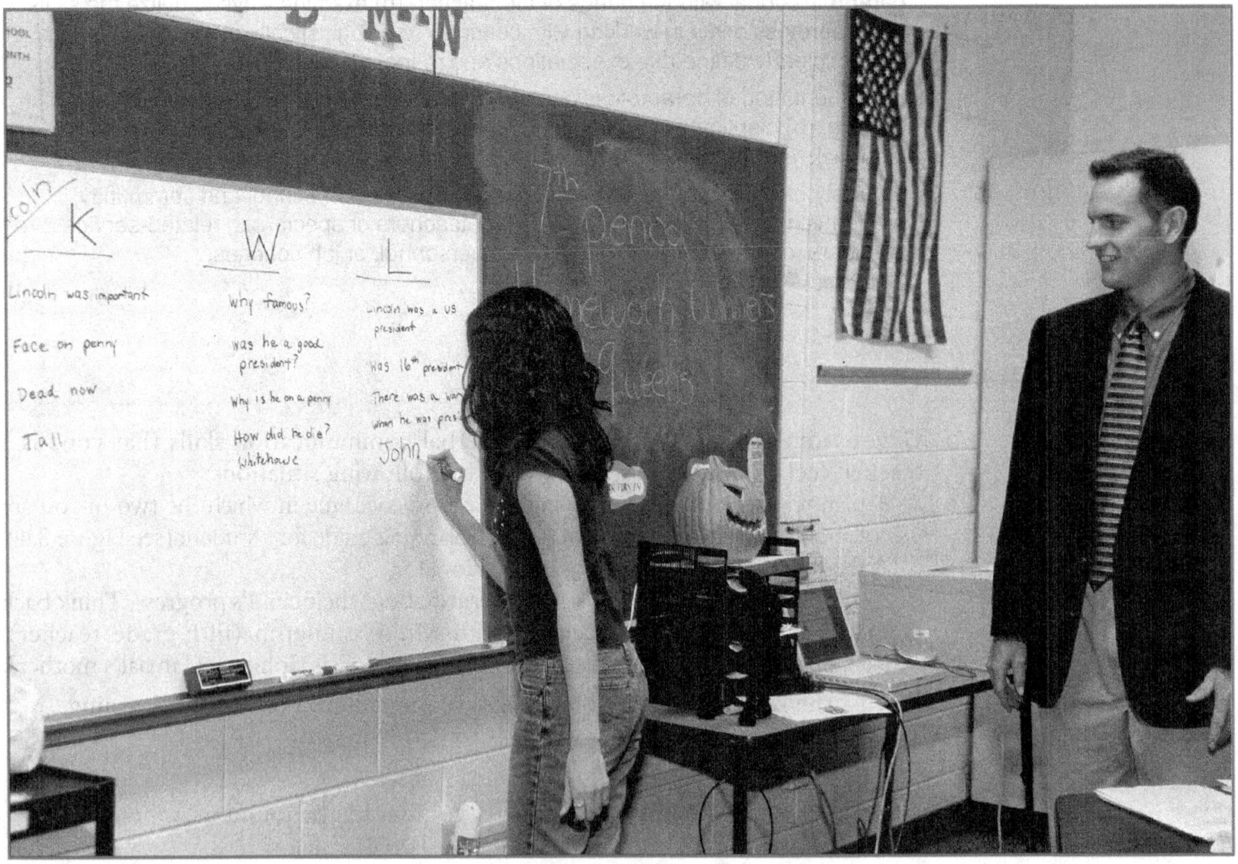

KEY TOPICS

"Welcome back to school!" began Mrs. Consuelas, one of the ESE teachers at Mountaintop Middle School, "I am excited to be leading our professional development today focused on assessing students with disabilities in your classroom."

"As most of you know, our school has been increasing the number of students with special needs that we serve inclusively in general education classrooms every year. This coteaching model benefits all our students in many ways, and the purpose of today's presentation is to eliminate any confusion you might have about how teaching teams should informally assess students with special needs."

"Let's start by taking a look at the charts you created on your way in today. On the first chart I asked you to write down one thing you already know about assessing your student with special needs, and on the second chart you wrote questions you have that you would like to learn more about today. When I look at the first chart, I see that there seems to be some confusion about preparing students with special needs for our yearly state-mandated standardized tests. And on the second chart I see that many of your concerns center around who is responsible for informal assessment documentation in coteaching situations, the general education teacher or the special education teacher."

"First of all, let's talk about standardized tests and clear up one very important detail: The law now states that all students, including those with disabilities, must participate in both district and statewide assessments. A wonderful tool that you all have at your disposal is the Individual Education Program, or IEP. Every child who has been identified with a disability has an IEP, and every IEP has a section that details what types of accommodations a child with special needs will have when they take district and statewide standardized tests. Therefore, a good place to start when planning informal assessments is to create a rubric that shows each student on an IEP and what accommodations they are allowed. This step will make it easier for both general education and special education teachers to ensure they are practicing the accommodations during informal assessments throughout the year."

"I am glad to see the number of questions regarding the responsibility for assessment in coteaching situations. These questions indicate to me that our teams need to do a better job of communicating with each other, and that is partly what today is all about. During the remainder of our morning I intend to cover topics such as different types of informal assessments, record-keeping tips, and how to use these assessments to guide your instruction of students. We will give general and special education teachers plenty of time to share ideas and communicate with each other in small groups. If you think of additional questions as we go, don't worry, we'll have plenty of opportunities to add to our charts, and before we break for lunch we will wrap up with a quick list of what we learned today."

Pretend for a moment that you are a faculty member participating in this professional development program. Mrs. Consuelas was obviously modeling the ***K-W-L*** *(****K****now,* ***W****ant-to-Know, and* ***L****earned) approach to learning. Name one thing you would have written on the chart that asked what you already* ***K****now. Then think of at least one question you* ***W****ant to know more about and write that down as well. We hope that by the time you reach the end of this chapter, your question will have been answered.*

Responses to these questions are found in the Instructor's Manual.

INTRODUCTION

We begin the chapter by discussing some of the changes in assessment brought on by No Child Left Behind (NCLB) and the reauthorization of the Individuals with Disabilities Act Amendments (IDEA) 2004. Assessment is a critical component of both NCLB and IDEA 2004 in the ruling that students with disabilities will be included in district and state assessments. Children who are not meeting state standards will be monitored through annual yearly progress evaluation and functional behavior assessment will be used as a means to address problem behaviors of students with disabilities.

We provide information in this chapter related to different types of informal assessments teachers can use that tie closely to local and state assessment tools. These tools may be used in a range of learning environments. Criterion-referenced tests, precision teaching, probes, curriculum-based measurement, and error analysis all suggest systematic data collection procedures that have a history of use in special education. The informal assessments of exhibitions, portfolios, probes, self-monitoring, interviews, and checklists have less systematic data collection procedures. Portfolios are often identified as authentic assessments. Authentic assessments are based on the constructivist paradigm with its emphasis on "assessing real-life processes and accomplishments" (Heshusius, 1989, p. 412). The authentic assessment approach is fairly new to the special education field, and the effectiveness is still uncertain, even though it is being implemented in a growing number of large-scale assessment programs at district and state levels.

Teachers may use these data collection procedures to plan programs for students and to monitor their effectiveness. The relevancy of these procedures has become even more important in this time of Response to Intervention (RTI). Most states are focusing on a three-tired system that uses informal assessment data to determine if students are in need of more intensive special education services. The focus of RTI is to provide adequate support and effective interventions to learners at the elementary levels to remediate as many issues as possible. The intended outcome is that less support will be needed when a student is at the secondary level because the issues will be remediated.

The interventions used both in RTI and the field of special education related to informal measures must be linked to state standards and used in both pull-out and inclusive settings. These assessments may be used alone or in combination with other assessments but for students with mild to moderate disabilities must be focused on the general education curriculum. Tools available include interviews, checklists, and error analysis, which may be used with other informal measures discussed in the chapter. We conclude the chapter with ways to involve students in data collection procedures.

ASSESSMENT COMPONENTS OF IDEA AMENDMENTS OF 1997 AND 2004

The reauthorizations of IDEA in 1997 and again in 2004 provided clarity to the field that students with disabilities are to learn the same curriculum and meet the same state standards as their nondisabled peers. Students with more significant disabilities can be exempt from meeting grade-level state standards but still must be assessed using an alternative form of assessment. The reauthorization allows a maximum of 3% of students in a state or district to be considered for alternative types of assessment.

Therefore, the majority of students with disabilities are expected to be included in state- and district-wide assessment programs. The core academic subject areas of math, science, social studies, and language arts are typically assessed in state-wide programs and many districts link the standards to graduation, funding, and pass-fail rates (Goldberg, 2005; Thurlow, Lazarus, & Thompson, 2005). Changes from NCLB and IDEA have held districts accountable and many districts are failing to meet Annual Yearly Progress due to students with disabilities not meeting state standards. The test scores of students with disabilities are being used in district and state measures of accountability (Kleinert, Haig, Kerns, & Kennedy, 2000), and the results must be made available to the public with the same frequency and detail as those of students without disabilities (OSEP, 2002). No longer do states have the option of whether to include or exclude students with disabilities in state testing, which makes ongoing progress monitoring and informal assessment even more critical in today's classrooms.

Most of the students we discuss in this text will be involved in state assessments with accommodations. All students on 504 plans or IEPs are eligible for accommodations on state assessments as determined by the IEP team. These accommodations may include extending the time, allowing frequent breaks during testing, using assistive technology (e.g., alphasmarts, using a scribe for written responses, or administering the test in small groups or in separate settings) (Thurlow, et al., 2005). However, according to Wood (2002), accommodation strategies are typically decided by states and not teachers, so you must be aware of the accommodations allowed in your district and state.

We recommend that classroom teachers become familiar with all accommodations available and that those listed on students' IEPs be used throughout the year not just on state tests. Too many times students are provided with accommodations on state testing but fail to use these supports adequately because they may not have learned the skill needed to use these tools (e.g., how to use a scribe).

BOX 4.1

Reflections on Practice

Go to your local state department's website and see if you can find the accommodations that are allowed for students with disabilities at the state level. Remember that students can have a variety of supports ranging from a scribe, to extended time on a test, to having test items read aloud. The accommodations or modifications allowed on testing must be used daily in practice by students if they are to be successful when it comes time for state-wide assessments.

Most state departments provide guidelines for how to provide extended time. Other examples often found for each state include:

- The number of times questions can be repeated
- How to read aloud numbers in math questions
- When calculators may be used
- How written responses are to be recorded if a scribe is used
- If spell checkers or dictionaries are allowed

Note, as you review the list of accommodations and modifications allowed in your state, whether they are consistent across various types of disabilities or if some types of disabilities (e.g., reading disabilities) are not allowed the same level of support as other types of disabilities.

Another emphasis in the reauthorizations of IDEA 1997 that affects assessment is the mandate that the "IEP Team shall in the case of a child whose behavior impedes his or her learning or that of others, consider, when appropriate, strategies, including positive behavioral interventions, strategies, and supports to address that behavior" [IDEA, 20 U.S.C. (section) 1414 (d)(3) (B) (i)]. The ruling allows IEP teams to decide the behaviors that constitute the need for interventions and if the behaviors are impeding a student's learning (Drasgow & Yell, 2001). These problem behaviors may include verbal and physical abuse, noncompliance, disruptive behaviors, property destruction, and aggression (Van Acker, Boreson, Gable, & Potterton, 2005). To arrive at the appropriate interventions, a functional behavior assessment (FBA) is conducted.

Additionally, a behavior intervention plan (BIP) must be created by the IEP team for students who have been referred to alternative placements, suspended from school for more than 10 school days in a school year, and placed in an alternative setting for a weapon or drug offense (Gartin & Murdick, 2001). Because teachers will not be conducting FBAs or making decisions about interventions for problem behaviors alone, we include a basic description of FBAs and their use with students with mild disabilities.

FBAs require the following:

- Identification of problem behavior (e.g., Jim runs out of class).
- Analysis of the frequency, duration, and intensity of the target behavior (e.g., event recording for five days finds that the behavior occurs on the average of three times from 9 A.M. to 12 P.M. each day).
- Description and analysis of the antecedents and consequences of the behavior (e.g., when teacher introduces centers, student runs, and teacher chases after student).
- Hypothesis of the purpose the behavior is serving (e.g., to get teacher attention).

- Selection of positive supports or BIPs for the appropriate behavior that achieves the same function as the inappropriate one (e.g., before introducing centers, the teacher has Jim come to the front and model how to go to centers quietly; she then praises Jim for appropriate modeling).
- Collection of data on the effectiveness of the intervention in changing behavior (e.g., event recording for 30 days and then intermittent event recording for 6 months). (Drasgow & Yell, 2001).

Reid and Nelson (2002) reviewed 14 studies of FBA procedures used with students with learning disabilities and emotional and behavioral disorders in school settings. They report promising results of the FBAs to decrease inappropriate behaviors, but that more research needs to address the maintenance of appropriate behaviors over time. Some other findings include:

1. Problem behaviors were related to escape (e.g., task too difficult) or attention (e.g., peer or teacher) in a majority of the children.
2. Insufficient data exists to assess the practicality of FBA in school settings because direct-service providers such as teachers and other IEP members were not instrumental in conducting the FBAs in any of the studies.
3. Simple curriculum modifications such as student selection of academic activity, moderation of task difficulty, student participation in preferred activity or task, and the addition of prompts resulted in improvements of behavior.

Activity 4.1

With a colleague discuss the steps of creating an FBA given the following information.

A student taps someone in class once every 10 minutes. This behavior has lasted for more than a month and data have been collected over the last 2 weeks. A specific peer seems to be the trigger for the behavior.

Using the steps provided, discuss each step as outlined for creating a functional behavioral analysis including an intervention you might try and how you would measure effectiveness.

(Answers for this and other activities are found in the Instructor's Manual.)

PORTFOLIO ASSESSMENT

Portfolios are "purposeful, collaborative, and self-reflective collections of student work" generated during the instructional process (McRobbie, 1992, p.2). All states have in place some type of alternative assessment for students with more severe disabilities and often portfolios are the chosen tool. For students with mild disabilities portfolios are often used as a way to document academic progress. Moreover, many software programs exist to help teachers and students organize and monitor portfolios.

Portfolios have both advantages and disadvantages (Johnson & Arnold, 2004). Advantages include (a) a variety of ways to measure progress and to demonstrate what learners can or cannot do, (b) the incorporation of student ownership and self-reflection, (c) the measurement of both process and product, (d) the linkage to real-life situations, and (e) the emphasis on students' strengths. Disadvantages include (a) the amount of time required, (b) the lack of reliable scoring procedures, (c) the lack of empirical evidence of effectiveness, (d) cost efficacy, and (e) subjective assessment. In a recent newsletter from the Association of Supervision and Curriculum Development (2006), they discuss the incompatibility of using portfolio assessment and then assessing students on state standards using more traditional assessment tools. This issue is one that requires additional research to determine the compatibility of these two types of activities.

Most states now have specific guidelines for using portfolio assessments for students with more moderate to severe disabilities who will be exempted from taking traditional state tests (Johnson & Arnold, 2004). However, Salend (2000) recommends the use of portfolios in inclusive classrooms for all students as portfolios may easily be tied to the annual goals and standards of the general education curriculum. Although there are no typical portfolios, common characteristics include (a) teacher-assigned work (teachers often determine the number and types of pieces), (b) rationale (purpose for forming it), (c) student intent and goals for the material they are including (showing beginning, middle, and end of the year growth), (d) table of contents as well as written summary to introduce each section, (e) relation of each section to state standards, and (f) a summary of the content.

We recommend the following steps in creating a student portfolio: (a) plan the focus, (b) select the content, (c) select the times for adding materials, (d) design scoring procedures, (e) teach students to self-assess and reflect, and (f) arrange periodic conferences that include conferences where students present their work to their parents.

PLAN THE FOCUS

To prevent the portfolio from becoming a hodgepodge of papers, focus on the key goals of instruction (Valencia, 1990). Cohen and Spenciner (1998) recommend a focus on academic progress and students' self-understanding for middle school students and a focus on career planning and graduation requirements for secondary students. Wesson and King (1996) suggest that affective behaviors are also appropriate for the portfolio focus. We recommend the selection of goals and short-term objectives based on students' IEPs.

SELECT THE CONTENT

Portfolios may contain, among other items, samples of students' work in all content areas, samples of projects, periodic self-evaluations, progress reports, pictures or videotapes of a student's project (Wesson & King, 1996), a student-generated list of books and genres read each month (Flood & Lapp, 1989), and community service projects (Cohen & Spencimer, 1998). Wesson and King (1996) report that videotapes, instructor observations, self-observations, and home progress reports serve as content for a behavior portfolio. You may wish to include originals, copies, or summaries of the materials. McRobbie (1992) also suggests that students organize the portfolio with a table of contents, a letter of introduction that explains its organization, dates on all examples, a short explanation of the selection of each piece of work, and references.

SELECT TIMES FOR ADDING MATERIALS

Wolf (1989) schedules monthly student checks for his eighth-grade students. At this time, the students remove some papers and keep those that best exemplify their progress.

Table 4.1 English Rubric

English Paper		
Parts	**Attributes**	**Points Possible**
1. Title	Engaging, concise, legible	5 points
2. Introduction	Depicts a position or point of view, gives a clear rationale, presents a framework for related issues	5 points
3. Body	Articulates and defends the author's position, examines sources of information, considers various positions	5 points
4. Summary/conclusion	Restates major premise and supportive data	5 points
5. References	Accurate, adequate to support the author's position, presented according to style manual	5 points
6. Mechanics	Proper grammar usage, legible, correct punctuation, correct spelling, appropriate use of syntax	5 points
Strengths		
Weaknesses		

DESIGN SCORING PROCEDURES

Rubrics are scoring guides that are frequently used in portfolio and other authentic assessments. Numerous websites provide examples of rubrics. Table 4.1 shows an example of a rubric that could be used to score a student's portfolio in a secondary English class.

Levels identify the degree to which the performance meets the criteria, for example, Highly Acceptable, Acceptable, or Not Acceptable. The numbers in the rubric system identify the specific requirements for each level and criteria. For example, an indicator for the criteria of mechanics and the level of Highly Acceptable may be that the student has written a paper with no spelling errors, total subject and verb agreement, no grammar errors, and complex sentence structures.

Analytic and holistic scoring strategies are another feature of a rubric. An analytic scoring rubric is often used for diagnostic purposes, is specific, is frequently in matrix form, and designates a score for each criterion (Marzano, Pickering, & McTighe, 1993). A holistic rubric promotes an overall impression of a student's performance, is broad and general, is frequently in hierarchical form, and designates one score for the product. You may use either or both scoring strategies.

Rubrics make teacher expectations clear, show students how to reach the expectations, and assist students to evaluate quality (Goodrich, 1996–1997). Table 4.2 presents a partial scoring rubric with the various features identified. Using the sample holistic math rubric, Jimmy may score a 4 or Competent on his entire math portfolio.

Table 4.2 Partially Completed Sample Rubric for Math Portfolio

SAMPLE ANALYTIC MATH RUBRIC

	Highly Acceptable (3)	Acceptable (2)	Not Acceptable (1)
Problem Solving	Superior reasoning in problem solving; Answers justified; Valid conclusions drawn; Reasonable predictions made	Satisfactory reasoning in problem solving; Most answers justified; Conclusions usually valid; Usually reasonable predictions	Very limited reasoning in problem solving; Answers often not justified; Many conclusions invalid; Predictions generally unreasonable
Communication	Clear and consistent language, including terminology and symbolism to communicate the problem-solving approach	Generally appropriate language, including terminology to communicate the problem-solving approach in a satisfactory way	Limited language, including terminology to communicate the problem-solving approach in a marginal way

underline = levels
bold = criteria
regular print = sample indicators
Adapted from http://www.ebe.on.ca?DEPART/RESEAR/RUBRIC.HTM, January 1998.

Using the sample analytic math rubric, Jimmy may score a 3 or Highly Acceptable in problem solving and a 2 or Acceptable in communication. Check the website www.teach-nology.com for rubrics designed for reading skills, paragraph writing, behaviors, and oral expression.

TEACH STUDENTS TO SELF-ASSESS, SELF-REFLECT, AND SELF-ADVOCATE

Often, students are directed to self-assess and self-reflect in portfolios. Some students with disabilities have problems with this type of metacognitive task (see Chapter 7). To assist a student in self-reflection, you may either use the rubric or you may identify questions for the students to answer and then model your answer to these questions. For example, Mr. Jordan identifies three questions: (1) What is characteristic about this new piece of work I am including in my portfolio? (2) What has changed between my old work and my new work? (3) What remains to be done? He then presents two pieces of his own work and models out loud his answer to the questions before he asks the students to do the same with their works. The concept of self-advocacy in Chapter 12 focuses on transition from school-to-work, yet students at all levels can be taught to use their portfolios to reflect on their strengths and to learn how to advocate for themselves. This skill can be taught as early as first grade by simply telling a student that it is his or her job to remember that they only do 10 of the 15 spelling words each week. These simple tasks empower students and can be shown in their portfolios.

ARRANGE PERIODIC CONFERENCES

Regular sessions for portfolio discussions between teachers and students should be scheduled throughout the year (Valencia, 1990) and should include components that teach students how to advocate for their needs as appropriate. Wesson and King (1996) suggest monthly reviews and a check of one portfolio a week. During a conference, you should discuss a student's progress (Valencia, 1990), plans for inclusion of other pieces for the portfolio (Valencia, 1990), and the student's thoughts about the portfolio. Ask such questions as, "What is your favorite thing?" "Why did you organize the portfolio the way you did?" (Farr, 1989). Asking these types of questions assists students in self-reflection.

INTERVIEWS

Another type of informal assessment includes interviews in which students are asked to share their thought processes. It is important to establish rapport and provide a safe, secure environment in which students can risk being wrong without penalty. An interview may proceed in the following manner. First, you instruct the student, "Kari, please complete these problems (e.g., 85 + 19, 67 + 18, 34 + 17) out loud so I can hear how you figure them out." As Kari is calculating the problems, she replies, "Well, 85 plus 19 means to add. Five plus 9 is 14, and 8 plus 1 is 9. So the answer is 9-1-4 [nine, one, four]." She proceeds with similar explanations and mistakes in the other two problems.

In analyzing Kari's thought processes and her answers, you find that she knows that *plus* means to add and she knows the addition facts. She also knows to begin in the ones column, but she does not know place value and the regrouping process, nor does she monitor her computation by checking to see whether the answer of 914 makes sense.

Sometimes, interviews are accompanied by recommended questions for the teacher to ask the student, as in the following spelling interview (Baskwill & Whitman, 1988). To measure spelling using this procedure, select a list of 20 words from either the spelling or reading text that the student is using in the inclusive setting. To introduce the task in a nonthreatening manner, tell the student that you are really looking for a better way to teach spelling and that it doesn't matter how many mistakes the student makes. Next, give the words in isolation. Then give the same words in context. Add definitions if the student requests them.

Sit down with the student and go over the list together, asking such questions of the student as, "Which words do you think you spelled correctly?" "Which ones aren't you sure about?" "Why did you decide on this particular spelling?" "How else could you have tried to spell this word?" "If this word is incorrect, how could you find the correct spelling?" (Baskwill & Whitman, 1988). Remember, when using the interviewing technique, assess both error patterns and strategies.

EXHIBITIONS

Exhibitions provide students with ways to demonstrate their knowledge through areas of strength instead of weakness. This tool can be used at key points to support transition across skills and to celebrate student-learning outcomes (Pearlman, 2002). Just because schools have always used letter grades or just because schools send home report cards and have conferences twice a year does not mean this is the best way to support the learning of all students. The Coalition for Essential Schools (2006) suggests that exhibitions be used as a tool to promote authentic learning in classrooms. On their website they define exhibitions as "presentations in which students demonstrate what they know and what they have learned in face-to-face meetings with teachers, parents, and other community members. Exhibitions are a way in which schools and their communities can assess students' mastery of both a body of knowledge and the thinking skills that are required in the real world." Exhibitions

BOX 4.2

Reflections on Practice

Self-advocacy and self-determination skills for students with disabilities are critical to their success in life beyond school. Providing students with options to demonstrate their knowledge supports the development of the skill of making choices. Just as we like to choose the activities we complete or the courses we take, students with disabilities are no different. Remember, students with disabilities like to not only be provided with assistance as they demonstrate their learning, but they also like to help others. Make certain your assessments embrace students' strengths by allowing them the chance to shine in front of their peers.

assist students in doing self-assessments so they are better prepared to advocate for their needs. This type of assessment is typically paired with a rubric to assist in evaluating the learning.

PROBES

These types of assessments are usually short in length and are typically used to reinforce a critical skill such as math computation or remembering factual information. Keeley, Eberlee, and Farrin (2005) used formative *assessment probes* in their work with students in science to address difficulties identified in the research on student learning. Their work focused on science teachers using the information gathered from the probes to quickly analyze and design instruction explicitly targeted to students' faulty ideas in science and to guide the students through a conceptual change. Teachers can make weekly or monthly informal assessment probes to summarize the critical skills and then start each class daily with various 1–3 minute probes.

CHECKLISTS

The use of checklists can provide insight into the ways in which students approach tasks and the types of errors they make. You may also use checklists to gain information concerning any subject area, to find out about interests, to monitor a student's

Figure 4.1 A STUDENT'S WORK SAMPLE

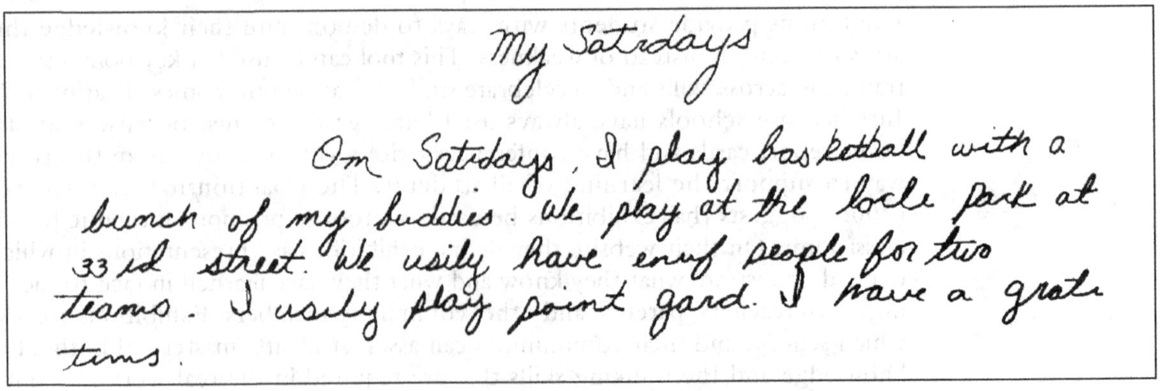
My Satrdays

Om Satrdays, I play baskatball with a bunch of my buddies. We play at the locle park at 33 id street. We usily have enuf people for two teams. I usily play point gard. I have a grate tims.

Figure 4.2 SCORING OF THE STUDENT'S WORK SAMPLE IN FIGURE 4.1

1. **Is the student able to write a topic sentence?**
   Yes.
2. **Is the student able to write supporting sentences?**
   Yes, rest of sentences relate to topic.
3. **Does the student use descriptive words?**
   No, limited adjectives—"point, great."
4. **Is the student able to use a variety of sentences (simple, compound, complex)?** No, all simple.
5. **Does the student use dialogue?** None used.
6. **Are there many mistakes in grammar?** None.
7. **Is the story organized?**
   Yes, it begins with a topic sentence and has details and a closing.
8. **Are there many spelling errors?**
   Yes, 10 out of 40 words.

progress in an inclusive setting, or to use for creating alternative grading structures (see Chapter 2). Checklist items are frequently phrased positively to assess what a student can do instead of emphasizing the problems. You may complete checklists using work samples (see Figure 4.1) or during observations. You may use the checklist found in Figure 4.2 to evaluate written expression as this teacher did in evaluating the work sample in Figure 4.1.

Students may also use self-assessment checklists to monitor their work. For example, you may have students answer whether they identified the relevant information, selected the correct steps, calculated the problems correctly, and verified their results as they solved word problems.

A way to use checklists as communication devices for inclusive settings is to ask the general education teacher to monitor specific behaviors during the class and to have the students return the checklist to you. Behavior and academic achievement items are often included on checklists. Some checklists even have a place for the students or teachers to write in homework assignments (see Figure 4.3). Many special education

Figure 4.3 TEACHER MONITORING CHECKLIST

	Periods											
	First		Second		Third		Fourth		Fifth		Sixth	
	Y	N	Y	N	Y	N	Y	N	Y	N	Y	N
Came on time	✓			✓	✓		✓					
Brought supplies	✓			✓	✓		✓					
Followed directions	✓		✓		✓		✓					
Completed work	✓		✓		✓		✓					
Grade on assignment	B		C (late work)		C		B					
Teacher initials	GEO		JMP		RC		BOT					
Homework assigned	None		Page 91, 1–22		Page 102, 12–45		None					

teachers include the return of checklists among their classroom rules and provide consequences for return and nonreturn of checklists.

IMPORTANT POINTS

1. With the reauthorization of IDEA, students with disabilities must be included in state assessments.
2. Functional behavioral assessments require (a) identification of problem behavior; (b) analysis of the frequency, duration, and intensity of the target behavior; (c) description and analysis of the antecedents and consequences of the behavior; (d) hypothesis as to the purpose the behavior is serving; (e) selection of positive supports or behavior intervention plans for the appropriate behavior that achieves the same function as the inappropriate one; and (f) collection of data on the effectiveness of the intervention in changing behavior.
3. Portfolio assessment is the collection of samples of the physical ongoing evidence of a student's progress.
4. Rubrics are scoring guides that include the three features of criteria (e.g., mechanics), levels (e.g., highly acceptable), and indicators (e.g., no spelling errors).
5. Teachers may use checklists to gain information concerning subject areas, to identify students' strengths and interests, and to monitor behaviors in inclusive settings.

ERROR ANALYSIS

The analysis of students' errors helps you to focus instruction. For example, if you find that Paul correctly calculates all facts except those involving the basic addition facts of 9 (i.e., 9 + 1 through 9 + 9), you know you must teach just these addition facts. Errors also provide insights into how students think and reason (Heshusius, 1989). Error analysis may be combined with all informal assessments.

Before using error analysis, you should consider language differences. Many experts argue that language differences, especially those dealing with phonemes, or sounds, should be of concern only if they impair meaning (Ortiz & Polyzoi, 1989). For example, if a Hispanic student reads *easy* as "iysi" or an African American student reads *they* as "dey," but each understands the content of the message, you should note these substitutions as language differences and not reading errors. Remember, varieties of English are equally effective and valid forms of communication (Grossman, 1994). Some common language differences found in black English include omission of the *s* suffix (e.g., "The girl play" or "I have two penny"), the use of *be* as a main verb (e.g., "He be busy"), and the deletion of contracted forms of *is* and *are* (e.g., "He here" or "They here") (Gollnick & Chinn, 2002). Spanish speakers often omit the *s* suffix, (e.g., "four bell" for "four bells"), trill the *r* when two *r*'s are together (e.g., "sorrrrel for sorrel"), and pronounce the following sounds the same: *sh* and *ch*, *s* and *z*, *n* and *ng*, *b* and *v*, *d* and *th*, *y* and *j*, *t* and unvoiced *th*, unvoiced *th* and *s*. Native Americans rarely use final consonants; omit articles *a*, *an*, and *the*; and have difficulty with prepositions (e.g., "get on car" for "get in the car") (Gollnick & Chinn, 2002). Many Asian Americans have difficulty pronouncing *sh*, *ch*, *r*, *x*, *l*, and *j* (Chan, 1987).

READING

In the *Qualitative Reading Inventory,* Leslie and Caldwell (2006) discuss the following decoding errors: (a) omissions (the student omits words when reading), (b) substitutions (the student substitutes a similar word that often makes sense in the sentence), (c) insertions (the student adds words), and (d) reversals (the student reverses letters or phrases). Leslie and Caldwell do not count repetitions (repeating a word or phrase when reading), hesitations (pausing longer at some words when reading), or omissions of punctuation (e.g., not pausing at the end of a sentence) as errors because scoring is unreliable for such factors, and repetitions and hesitations do not alter the text's meaning. In another common error, called an aided word, the teacher supplies the word for the students (Mercer & Mercer, 2001).

Reading comprehension errors frequently include mistakes in text-explicit, text-implicit, and script-implicit comprehension (Pearson & Johnson, 1978). Table 4.3 contains examples that measure each of these areas of comprehension. Text-explicit comprehension, also termed *literal comprehension,* requires the reader to recall information specifically found in a selection. When you ask students to identify the main characters, or actions of the main characters, or to sequence events, or recall significant details, you are checking text-explicit comprehension. Question 1 in Table 4.3 is an example, because students should find the answer directly in the first sentence of the paragraph.

Text-implicit comprehension, also referred to as *inferential comprehension* (Tindal & Marston, 1990), requires the reader to interact with information that is implied and not found directly from any one source in the passage. Forming opinions, predicting the next event in a story, and identifying the influence of the setting on the actions of the main character in a story are examples of text-implicit comprehension. Question 2 in Table 4.3 checks this type of comprehension, because the reader must assimilate the information from more than one sentence.

In script-implicit comprehension questions, the reader must use the information from the text and provide additional personal information (Tindal & Marston, 1990). Undoubtedly, a person who is not familiar with the sport of basketball will not answer Question 3 correctly. This type of comprehension question is generally difficult for students who lack the necessary background experiences.

SPELLING

Common spelling errors include omission of silent letters (e.g., clim for climb) and sounded letters (e.g., cimb for climb), phonetic substitutions (e.g., clime for climb), letter reversals (e.g., cilmb for climb), addition of letters (e.g., climbe for climb),

Table 4.3 Sample Comprehension Errors

A student reads the following paragraph:

> There were 25 seconds left in the championship basketball game. The winner of the game would be high school state champion. The score was tied 98 to 98, but no one could believe that the Tigers were in contention. After all, the tallest player of the team was only 6′5″, the height of the shortest player of the opposition team, the Braves. But the Tigers had been deadly on the 3-point plays and had not missed a free throw.

After reading the paragraph, the student responded to the following sample questions:

1. How much time was left in the game? *Answer:* Twenty-five minutes. (text-explicit error)
2. What was the main idea of the paragraph? *Answer:* There was only a little time left in the game. (text-implicit error)
3. Why is height such an advantage when playing basketball? *Answer:* I don't know. (script-implicit error)

words with apostrophes (e.g., possessives and contractions), and rule overgeneralizations (e.g., add an *s* for plurals such as deers for deer) (Evans, Evans, & Mercer, 1986; Salvia & Hughes, 1990). Spelling is often a problem area for many students with disabilities.

MATHEMATICS

Roberts (1968) identified the following mathematics error categories: (a) wrong operation (the student selects one operation, such as subtraction, when another operation, such as addition, should have been selected), (b) obvious computational error (the student incorrectly recalls a basic number fact 7 + 8 = 16, instead of 15), (c) defective algorithm (the student employs the correct operation and knows the basic number facts but does not use the correct process or procedure, such as 112 − 46 = 76, in which the student forgot to regroup in the tens place), and (d) random response (the student answers incorrectly without any apparent relationship between problem solving and the problem). Cohen and Spenciner (1998) summarized the following word problem errors: difficulty in reading and understanding language and vocabulary, identifying relevant and irrelevant information, using all the steps for solving a problem, and performing the correct mathematical operations.

BOX 4.3

Reflections on Practice

Have you ever wondered how you can turn research-based practices into strategies you can actually use in your classroom? The research team of Zrebiec Uberti, Mastropieri, and Scruggs (2004) asked a third-grade special education teacher to target a skill deficit in her inclusive classroom, design an intervention plan, and put it into practice while documenting the outcome. The resulting study demonstrated that teachers and researchers can team up to effectively make use of research-based practices in an inclusive classroom.

The teacher in this study noticed that her students with learning disabilities and the students for whom English was a second language struggled with the skill of addition with regrouping. She used error analysis to create individualized self-monitoring checklists, two research-based strategies combined, and the results were very positive.

This study demonstrated once again that error analysis can be part of an effective technique to use when teaching mathematics. For some students with processing issues it is critical that error analysis is used to determine how they learned a process incorrectly. If this correction does not take place, particularly with basic computations, it is quite possible that a student will continue the same error pattern for years to come.

Whenever possible, try to involve students in the analysis of their errors. In the Zrebiec Uberti, Mastropieri, and Scruggs study, the teacher used error analysis to create individual self-monitoring checklists that guided the students through a correct learning pattern. You could also choose to ask students to provide either a verbal or written description of the errors in their thinking on one or two problems. Combining an error analysis approach with individual student checklists, think-alouds, or written responses can be a very effective use of research-based practices.

PROCEDURES

We recommend the following steps for analyzing errors:

1. After scoring the items, list the student errors (e.g., on the addition fact worksheet, Jan is missing 9 + 8, 7 + 8, 6 + 8).
2. Make a hypothesis about the error pattern (e.g., computational error, basic addition facts, especially the 8 facts).
3. Test the hypothesis by examining the correct problems to see if any have the same pattern (e.g., Jan calculated 6 + 4, 5 + 6, and 9 + 2 correctly, so none of the correct ones involved the basic addition facts of 8).
4. If not correct, redo the hypothesis (e.g., steps 1–3 again).
5. Teach correction of the error (e.g., Jan needs to be retaught the basic addition facts of 8).

Sometimes, asking the student to think out loud helps in error analysis.

Activity 4.2

Identify the following error patterns.

C = correct; X = incorrect (The student's incorrect responses are in parentheses.)

Reading Words

1. That X (thit)	3. of X (off)	5. for C
2. was X (wiz)	4. man X (min)	6. top C

Math Problems

1. 36 +19 (55) C	3. 47 +16 (63) C	5. 26 +87 (13) X	7. 26 +13 (39) C
2. 29 +68 (97) C	4. 55 +79 (34) X	6. 45 +65 (20) X	

Spelling Words

1. mat X (mit)	3. ran X (rin)	5. man X (min)
2. run C	4. flop C	6. sky X (ski)

CRITERION-REFERENCED TESTS

Criterion-referenced tests (CRTs) measure the extent to which a student has mastered a skill or task based on an established criterion (Mercer, 1992). Unlike formal tests, which compare a student's performance to that of other students, a criterion-referenced test compares the student's performance to some expected mastery level. A commonly used CRT measure in special education is the *Brigance* diagnostic inventories (Brigance, 1999). The *Brigance* diagnostic inventories are multiskill batteries that contain subtests measuring skills in areas such as reading, mathematics, employability, life skills, and spelling.

Commercial CRTs focus on hierarchies of skills found in the general education curriculum and are not specific to a school district's curriculum. For example, the scope of the mathematics curriculum for kindergarten through eighth grade, no matter the particular mathematics series, usually includes mathematics readiness (e.g., recognizing numerals), number facts (e.g., reciting basic facts, such as 4×6), whole numbers (e.g., adding two-digit numbers with regrouping), fractions and mixed numbers (e.g., adding fractions), decimals (e.g., reading decimals), percents (e.g., converting percents to decimals), measurement (e.g., telling time to the hour, recognizing different coins), metrics (e.g., reading Celsius temperature), and geometry (e.g., recognizing squares) (Brigance, 1999). In the sequence, mathematics readiness skills such as rote counting are taught before basic facts, which are taught before fractions.

STEPS

We recommend the following steps: (1) select the test, (2) administer the test, (3) select the expected level of mastery, (4) identify objectives, and (5) monitor progress in CRT assessment. We discuss these steps as related to commercially produced CRTs. (For discussion of the creation of CRTs by teachers, see Jones, 2001a, 2001b.)

Select the Test

A basic knowledge of the curriculum scope and sequence for various grade levels can help you in test selection. For example, if you are selecting reading tests to assess a first grader's reading performance, you are not likely to select a reading test that measures comprehension of colloquial and figurative expressions, because this skill is usually introduced much later. Instead, tests that measure basic sight vocabulary, initial consonant sounds, and short vowels are more appropriate because these skills are introduced in the primary-grade reading curriculum. Most series have a scope and sequence that you can check for the various grade levels. Additionally, many states and districts identify standards that students are expected to achieve at various grade levels.

Discussing a student's problem with the general education teacher is also helpful. For example, if Mr. Gonzalez, Jim's second-grade teacher, tells you that Jim has problems telling time, you should, as a first step, select a criterion-referenced test that measures math skills, especially one that contains items dealing with measurement of time.

Administer the Test

Many of the commercially prepared instruments provide guidelines for where to start and stop testing and general directions and procedures for easy and quick administration. Additionally, you may make adaptations during the testing process. For example, if you wish to hear Latasha's thoughts as she solves the math problems, you may ask her to think aloud as she writes the answers.

Select the Expected Level of Mastery

There are no absolutes for selection of a mastery criterion. For profitable academic learning, students should maintain an accuracy level of 80% during lesson presentation and between 90% and 100% during independent practice (Christenson, Thurlow, & Ysseldyke, 1987). Some CRTs suggest mastery levels.

Identify the Objectives

Mastery levels assist in the identification of objectives. For example, if you expected Sharon to score 80% on a reading comprehension test but she scored only 60%, you should target reading comprehension for remediation. Furthermore, you should examine the specific questions that Sharon missed. Did she miss questions that required her to order and sequence events, or did she miss questions that required her to remember significant details?

Monitor Progress

Usually, teachers monitor mastery of the objectives at the end of the year using the same CRT. The results of this posttest are often recorded on the IEP.

Sample Plan

We have presented the steps for using a CRT, but to help you better understand the process, we relate Consuela's experience to each of the steps.

1. ***Discuss the student's problem with the general education teacher.*** In a conference, Consuela's fifth-grade teacher indicates that Consuela has problems reading words with silent letters and two or more syllables.
2. ***Check the curriculum scope and sequence of the subject area and grade level.*** A check of the reading scope and sequence from Consuela's classroom text shows that silent letters, prefixes, suffixes, and syllabication are word analysis skills that students should master by fifth grade. Additionally, the school district identifies these skills in the performance standards for the state assessment exam.
3. ***Select a CRT.*** Consuela's teacher selected the *BRIGANCE Comprehensive Inventory of Basic Skills—Revised* (CIBS-R) (Brigance, 1999) because it measures all of the skills found in the classroom text.
4. ***Administer the CRT.*** The teacher administered the following tests from the *Brigance:* (a) phonetic irregularities to check silent letters, (b) suffixes, (c) prefixes, and (d) division of words into syllables.
5. ***Decide on a criterion of mastery.*** The teacher selected 95%.
6. ***Compare the student's performance to the mastery level.*** Consuela reached the established criterion on phonetic irregularities (silent vowels) only. She did not reach mastery on the tests dealing with reading suffixes and prefixes, nor was she able to apply the rules for syllabication.
7. ***Identify short-term objectives for initial instruction.*** (a) Presented with a list of 50 words, Consuela will read words containing the suffixes *-ous*, *-ment*, *-ation*, *-ward*, and *-ist* and the prefixes *de-*, *mis-*, and *fore-* with 90% accuracy and (b) presented with a list of two-syllable words, Consuela will apply the syllabication rules dealing with like consonants between two vowels (*bot\tom*) and unlike consonants between two vowels (*con\form*) to divide the words with 90% accuracy.
8. ***Monitor progress.*** The teacher plans to test Consuela at the end of the year, unless the teacher feels that Consuela has reached the short-term objective before then.

Activity 4.3

Write a short-term objective in mathematics based on the following performance on a test of two-digit addition. The criterion for acceptable performance is 90%. Correct = +. Error = −.

1. 24 + 42 = 66 +	5. 18 + 31 = 49 +	9. 42 + 19 = 51 −
2. 35 + 29 = 54 −	6. 27 + 14 = 31 −	10. 29 + 32 = 51−
3. 62 + 21 = 83 +	7. 17 + 52 = 69 +	
4. 59 + 35 = 84 −	8. 82 + 11 = 93 +	

IMPORTANT POINTS

1. Language differences should be considered as errors only if they impair meaning.
2. In reading, decoding errors include omissions, substitutions, insertions, reversals, and nonresponses, whereas comprehension errors include problems with text-explicit, text-implicit, and script-implicit comprehension.
3. Common spelling errors include omission of silent letters and sounded letters, phonetic substitutions, letter reversals, addition of letters, words with apostrophes, and rule overgeneralizations.
4. Mathematics errors include wrong operation, obvious computational error, defective algorithm, random response, and word problems.
5. The following steps are recommended for analyzing errors: (a) list the student errors; (b) make a hypothesis about the error pattern; (c) test the hypothesis by examining the incorrect problems to see if any of these have the same pattern; (d) if not correct, redo the hypothesis; and (e) teach correction of the error.

PRECISION TEACHING

Precision teaching is a precise and systematic way to measure student performance in academic skills at both the elementary and secondary levels. Although precision teaching is not a specific teaching strategy, it helps you decide on and evaluate the effectiveness of instructional strategies. Precision teaching has demonstrated effectiveness in both inclusive and resource room settings (Stump, et al., 1992). Keel, Dangel, and Owens (1999) recommend it as one of the effective strategies to use for students with mild disabilities in inclusive classrooms.

Using rate of response, precision teaching emphasizes direct and continuous measurement of behavior (West, Young, & Spooner, 1990). Rate is the number of behavior movements divided by the number of minutes observed. In precision teaching, the average number of correct and incorrect responses per minute is calculated. The underlying principle is that a skill is mastered only if it can be performed both accurately and quickly. A student who is able to take notes at 30 words a minute will be more successful in an inclusive setting than one who is just as accurate in writing words but can transcribe only 10 words a minute.

A time limit of 1 minute is specified for measuring most academic skills, although the time limit may vary according to the amount of curriculum measured and student characteristics. For example, 3 minutes may be used when addition, subtraction, multiplication, and division facts are measured at once, compared with 1 minute when measuring addition facts alone. Fifteen seconds may be used for students who are highly distractible and cannot focus on a task for 1 minute (Binder, Haughton, & Eyk, 1990).

Activity 4.4

Using the opposite hand you would typically write with give yourself 15 seconds to write the A, B, Cs. How did you do? Can the letters be read? How many times did you have to repeat the A,B,C's aloud as you wrote. You probably found this task to impact both accuracy and fluency. Now, reverse hands and do the same task for 15 seconds. How are your letters this time? They can probably be read, but how many letters did you write in the 15 seconds? Unless you are ambidextrous, you probably wrote more letters the second time. If a professor told you that you could take notes with your nonwriting hand only, your accuracy would be somewhat affected, but your fluency would be more affected, and you would miss many notes. This activity helps you understand how many students with disabilities feel.

STEPS

The steps to precision teaching lead to planning and monitoring decisions and include: (a) pinpoint the behavior to be taught, (b) design or select a probe, (c) take a baseline, (d) select an aim, (e) decide whether the skill is appropriate, (f) write an objective, (g) decide on an intervention, (h) teach and test, (i) graph scores, and (j) monitor progress. A discussion of each step follows.

Pinpoint the Behavior

Pinpointing is choosing a behavior to change. In precision teaching, each behavior is counted, so the behavior must be repeatable and observable, and it must have a beginning and end (White & Haring, 1980). The skill of reading initial consonant clusters is appropriate to pinpoint. This skill is repeatable, as words requiring initial consonant clusters may be read again and again. It is observable, as you may listen while the student reads. Finally, each initial consonant cluster has a beginning and an end. Other appropriate pinpointed behaviors are spelling words, writing letters, and saying letter sounds.

Design a Probe

Once the skill is pinpointed, you can either design an informal test, called a probe, or use commercial probes. If you plan to design your own probe, you should first allow a standardized count in order to assess the skill accurately. To ensure a standardized count, the student must have freedom and opportunity to move (White & Haring, 1980). To allow the student freedom to move, design the probe so that you do not place physical constraints on the student. For example, if you use flash cards to test basic sight words, you are probably interfering with how fast the student can read the

Table 4.4 Sight Word Probe

about	after	be	five	its	must	seven	there	well	sleep	(10)
call	from	him	let	old	upon	ask	Cold	why	around	(20)
after	five	must	there	sleep	from	let	around	upon	cold	(30)
about	be	its	seven	well	call	him	Old	ask	why	(40)
around	why	cold	ask	upon	old	let	Him	from	call	(50)
sleep	well	there	seven	must	its	five	Be	after	about	(60)
about	call	after	from	be	him	old	Its	let	five	(70)
upon	must	ask	there	cold	well	why	around	sleep	must	(80)

words, because the student's performance depends, in part, on how quickly you manipulate the cards. Thus, changes in performance during assessment may be due to your dexterity in presenting the flash cards. You are less likely to interfere with a student's freedom to move if you use a typed list instead of flash cards.

Opportunity to move requires that students never run out of problems to complete. (Remember, a 1-minute time limit is usually imposed.) White and Haring (1980) argue that an overabundance of items allows for a more accurate picture of the student's performance, because it avoids ceiling effects. Having more items on a probe than students can possibly finish does not mean including 140 different words or math facts. Ten words or 10 facts may be repeated 14 times to reach 140, or 2 words or facts may be repeated 70 times. See Table 4.4 for an example of a sight word probe. Notice that even though there are 80 total words on the sample probe, there are only 20 different words, repeated 4 times. Thus, a student is actually being assessed on 20 words, not 80.

Once you have decided the content of the probe, you should identify the input and output channels for measurement (Hefferan & Diviaio, 1989). Input channels are the ways in which a student receives the information. In a school setting, input channels are usually visual or auditory. The student either sees the information when reading a text or hears the information when listening to the teacher read the text. Output channels are the ways in which a student expresses information. In a school setting, this is often done with an oral or a written response; for example, the student either says the answer to a math question or writes the answer.

The input and output measures may vary for any task; for example, you may test a student's addition skills by presenting a worksheet of addition problems. This is a visual (*see*) input as the student looks at the problems on the worksheet. However, you can change this input to an auditory (*hear*) input simply by reading the problems from the worksheet instead of giving the paper to the student. In the same way, the output measure can be either a *say* response, if the student responds by orally telling you the answer, or a *write* response, if the student responds by writing the answer.

The identification of the input and output channels leads to decisions concerning how to teach. For example, if Juan performs better on a hear-say spelling probe than on a hear-write one, you may suggest to Ms. Mueller, his second-grade teacher, that she allow Juan to spell the words orally to a volunteer in the back of the class during the traditional Friday spelling test. The last information to record on the probe is the cumulative score for each row of problems (see Table 4.4).

Take a Baseline

To take a baseline, you administer the same probe at least three times without teaching. For most academic skills, this administration takes a minute. It is a good idea to tell the student that it is impossible to finish all of the problems but to do them as quickly as possible. If the student hesitates for more than 2 seconds on any item, tell the student to proceed to the next item. It is also important to stress to the student to be as accurate as possible.

Select an Aim

Just as in criterion-referenced assessment, you select a mastery level, which shows that the student has learned the skill for automatic application to different situations and is ready to proceed to a different skill. In precision teaching, the mastery level is expressed in terms of an aim, which consists of correct responses (count correct or cc) and error responses (count error or ce) per minute (a rate measure), with an overlearning component (more than one session). A sample precision teaching aim is 80 correct responses and 2 error responses (80 cc/2 ce) per minute for three sessions.

Before discussing the different techniques for calculating an aim, we need to describe the scoring procedures. You score items differently following precision teaching procedures than you do normally. For example, to score reading you frequently count sounds, letters, or words, and to score spelling, you count letters. To score math problems, you count each digit so 25 + 42 = 67 is scored as two correct answers. Conversely, the problem 25 + 42 = 87 results in one correct answer (the 7) and one wrong (the 8). Items on a probe are scored only as far as the student progresses. Thus, a student who finishes only 10 of 50 problems on a probe is not penalized for failing to complete all 50 problems as only the 10 completed problems are scored. Skipped problems are usually counted as errors only to where the student finished.

You may calculate a precision teaching aim by using performance standards, peer assessment, student baseline, or the adult-child proportional formula (Eaton, 1978; Haring & Gentry, 1976; Koorland, Keel, & Ueberhorst, 1990). Remember, the idea of an aim is to set a mastery criterion so that the student generalizes the skill at various times and in various settings. You are hoping that when the student reaches the aim of 80 correct and 2 incorrect digits a minute on an addition probe, he or she will be able to add at home or during the math class on Friday. If you find that a student meets the aim but then forgets the skill 2 days later, you probably did not set an appropriate mastery level.

Determine the Appropriateness of the Skill

As a general rule, a student must have at least five correct responses (cc) and not reach the aim for two of the three sessions of baseline (White & Haring, 1976) for a skill to be considered appropriate for teaching. If the student makes fewer than five correct responses, the skill is probably too difficult. If the student reaches the aim, the skill is too easy.

When the student makes fewer than five correct responses, you may either slice back or step down on the curriculum scope and sequence (White & Haring, 1980). To slice back, simply cut the curriculum into smaller pieces; for example, use a probe of 0 through 4 multiplication facts to replace the probe of 0 through 9 multiplication facts. To step down, select an easier skill in the curriculum scope and sequence. For example, the student still does poorly on 0 through 4 multiplication facts, so the teacher decides to assess the student's knowledge of addition facts, an easier skill. You should take another baseline if you change the amount of curriculum or the skill. The rule of five correct responses for selection of an appropriate skill is not absolute but a beginning guideline.

Identify the Objective

The objective consists of the input and output channels, the pinpointed behavior, and the aim. For example, Consuela will see/say (input/output channels) initial consonant clusters in words (pinpointed behavior) at 70 cc and 2 ce per minute for 3 consecutive sessions (aim).

Decide on an Intervention

Although precision teaching may be used with any intervention, guidelines for the selection of a strategy are linked to the learning stages of acquisition, fluency, and maintenance or proficiency. Usually, anyone who learns a new skill, whether driving a car or recalling multiplication facts, proceeds through these three stages. In the first stage, acquisition, the driver attempts to keep the car in the correct lane between the middle line and the shoulder, while the mathematics student tries to answer problems such as 4 + 5 accurately. Modeling, immediate feedback, questioning, and direct instruction are effective strategies for the acquisition stage.

In the next stage, fluency, the student is making few errors and is concentrating on pace or speed. At this stage, the driver is no longer worried about keeping the car on the road in the proper lane (accuracy) but is attempting to drive more than 10 miles an hour (fluency) while remaining in the proper lane. The mathematics student is trying to answer 4 + 5 before a second passes. Flash cards, drill activities, and reinforcements are frequently recommended for this stage (Haring & Eaton, 1978).

The final stage, maintenance or proficiency, is reached when the aim (both cc and ce) has been obtained. The teaching strategy is to move to another skill because the student has mastered the content. Now, the driver drives on the freeway at the speed limit and the mathematics student adds accurately and quickly. Table 4.5 presents a summary of the decision-making procedures involved in determining the appropriateness of the skill, identifying the learning stage, and deciding on the intervention.

Teach and Test

Each day, after instruction is completed, you administer the same probe to monitor the effectiveness of the intervention. Remember, if you are worried that the student will memorize the answers, you may require the student to start at different items each day as long as the student started at different items during the baseline sessions.

Graph the Scores

Once you record a raw score, you must convert it into a count per minute (rate) for display on a semilogarithmic chart or graph. In a semilogarithmic graph, the distances between the lines are adjusted proportionally. Proponents of this type of graph argue that a change from 10 to 20 is the same proportionally as a change from 20 to 40; both are a doubling.

Many teachers graph data on a standard celeration chart (SCC) (Lindsley, 1990). Other teachers use adaptations of the SCC, such as the ABC–5 graph (Figure 4.4). We explain how to chart data using the ABC–5 graph. The vertical lines on the ABC–5 graph are called day lines (Hefferan & Diviaio, 1989). You can chart behaviors from Sunday through Saturday for 11 weeks, or 77 days. The short, dark marks at the top of the chart are Sunday lines, an easy way to locate the beginning of the week. The horizontal lines are often referred to as number lines (Hefferan & Diviaio, 1989).

On the ABC–5 graph, we are able to count from 0.1 to 500 counts per minute. The graph is rarely marked above 300, because few behaviors may be accomplished at more than 300 counts a minute. Notice that there is a one-to-one correspondence between the numbers 0.1 through 10. However, from 10 to 100, the numbers proceed 10, 15, 20, and then skip in increments of 10 until 100. The count continues 100, 150, 200, 300, 400, and 500. Therefore, to chart counts between 10 and 500, you must estimate.

Table 4.5 Calculation of Aims for the Pinpoint of See-Say Words in Fifth-Grade Reader

PERFORMANCE STANDARD	
Procedures	**Examples**
1. Find the skill in the performance standards most like the one on the probe. Look under the *Pinpoint* heading.	The pinpoint of See-Say words in fifth-grade reader is most like the See-Say words in context (oral reading).
2. Select the suggested standard under the *Standard* heading.	It is 200+ words/min. So student's aim is 200 cc/2 ce per minute.
PEER ASSESSMENT	
Procedures	**Examples**
1. Administer the probe for 1 minute to three students who perform the skill appropriately.	Peter: 100 words correct in 1 minute. Rosa: 150 words correct in 1 minute.
2. Find the average of the peers' scores.	Amy: 134 words correct in 1 minute. 100 + 150 + 134 = 384 384 ÷ 3 = 128 cc So student's aim is 128 cc/2 ce per minute.
STUDENT BASELINE	
Procedures	**Examples**
1. Administer the probe for 1 minute to student for 3 days.	Student scored the following words correct on the three days of baseline: Monday: 50 cc Tuesday: 60 cc Wednesday: 40 cc
2. Find the average of the three baseline assessments.	50 + 60 + 40 = 150 ÷ 3 = 50
3. Take the average score times 2.	50 (average score) × 2 = 100 So student's aim is 100 cc/2 ce per minute.

Students can be taught even at a young age to chart their own progress simply using an Excel spreadsheet. They then can print out graphs of their progress. Steps for charting include (1) complete the student information, (2) mark the record floor, (3) mark the aim, (4) record the raw data, (5) convert the raw data to counts per minute, (6) chart correct and incorrect responses per minute, (7) identify ignored and no-chance days, and (8) connect data points.

1. ***Complete the student information.*** Identify the name and age of the student, the pinpointed behavior, and the aims at the bottom of the graph.
2. ***Mark the record floor.*** The record floor identifies the amount of time that you administer a probe. Record floor figures are found on the right side of the graph.
3. ***Mark the aim.*** Mark the aim on the graph by finding the acceptable performance criteria of correct and error responses per minute on the count lines.
4. ***Record the raw data.*** Enter the raw scores in the data boxes at the right of the graph. Enter the correct raw data at the top and the error raw data at the bottom for each day that assessment occurred.

5. ***Convert the raw data to counts per minute.*** Data you record on the graph must be converted to a count per minute. In most spreadsheet programs you can simply create a formula dividing the score by the number of minutes. Thus, to record a student's score of 3 incorrect responses in 5 minutes, you would first divide 3 by 5, then locate 0.6 on the chart. To show a 0 count, mark the data point just below the record floor. A count of 1 always falls on the record floor line.
6. ***Chart correct and incorrect responses per minute.*** Enter the data on the date that the student performed the task and put a FINISH HERE *x* to mark the incorrect responses per minute. To mark the correct responses on the chart, locate the first day you administered the probe on the day lines. Then locate the count on the number lines. Follow the lines until they intersect and place a dot at the intersection. Follow the same procedures to chart incorrect responses, only place an *x* at the intersection.
7. ***Identify ignored and no-chance days.*** Before you connect any of the data points, consider no-chance days and ignored days. No-chance days are days when you do not have an opportunity to assess the student, such as over the weekend or during an absence. Ignored days are days when you have an opportunity to assess the student but decide not to. Code IG for ignored and NC for no-chance in the raw data boxes.
8. ***Connect data points.*** Connect the correct data points and then connect the error data points. Do not connect data points across no-chance days or phase change lines. Phase change lines (vertical lines) denote whenever something is changed, for example, a change in intervention, pinpointed behavior, or mastery aim. Always draw a phase change line between the last session of baseline and the first day of intervention to note that teaching has started. Once you have connected all the data points, you will have a learning picture. Figure 4.4 presents a pictorial summary of all the charting procedures.

Activity 4.5

Using a computer program, such as Excel, chart the following data from a precision teaching assessment on a semilogarithmic graph.

Behavior: See/write addition facts with sums 0–18.

Aim: 80 cc, 2 ce.

Observation time: 1 minute.

Baseline:

Monday—10 cc, 10 ce.

Tuesday—15 cc, 10 ce.

Wednesday—5 cc, 15 ce.

Intervention:

Thursday—20 cc, 10 ce.

Friday—20 cc, 8 ce.

Monday—24 cc, 8 ce.

Tuesday—Ignored.

Wednesday—30 cc, 0 ce.

Figure 4.4 SUMMARY OF STEPS FOR CHARTING

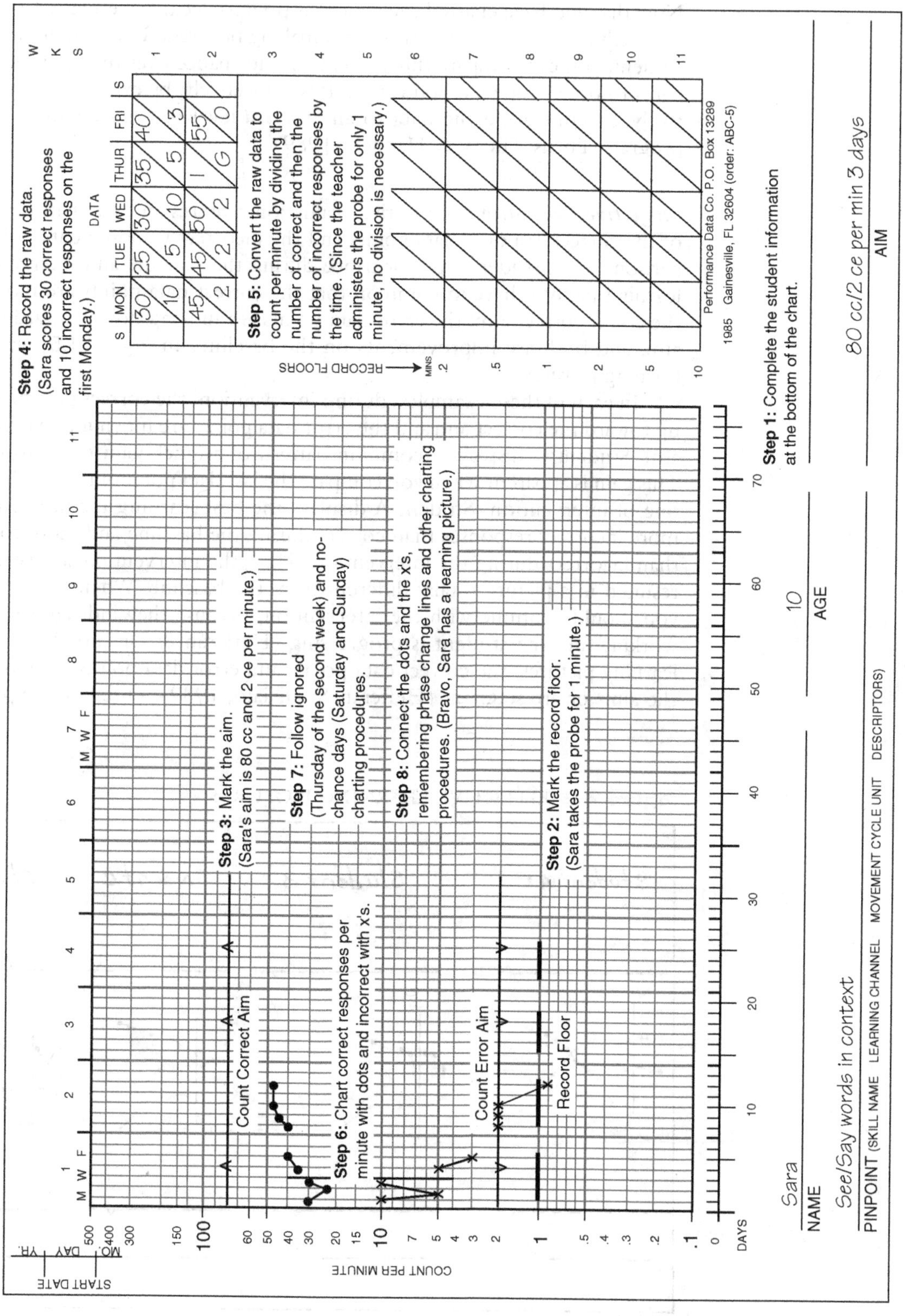

Monitor Progress

Now that you have charted the data, it is time to decide whether the intervention plan is effective and whether the student is making progress. Using multiple sheets for each student, you can compare this student's performance over time as well as how it compares to other students. You can do this subjectively, by eyeballing the data, or objectively, by comparing the data to an *expected* level of progress or an *actual* level of progress (Fuchs, Fuchs, & Hamlett, 1989).

Subjective Evaluation Subjective evaluation requires an examination of the direction of the correct response data points and the incorrect response data points and a comparison of the student's performance during the baseline and intervention. Effective learning pictures have in common that the correct data points are moving up toward the count correct aim, the error data points are moving down toward the count error aim, and both are improvements on the baseline. In Figure 4.5, we show effective learning pictures.

In each of these examples, during intervention, the correct data points are moving up toward the correct aim and the error data points are moving down toward the error aim. Student C displays a common pattern of a quick gain once instruction begins. This gain is apparent when you compare the last data point of the baseline with the first one of intervention. Student A displays the best learning picture. This student had more incorrect responses than correct during the baseline and more correct responses than incorrect during the intervention. Thus, the intervention was very effective, as it resulted in a picture totally different from the baseline. When you see such pictures, you should continue with the intervention, because they indicate the intervention is working and the student is progressing (Hefferan & Diviaio, 1989). In ineffective learning pictures, the correct data points and error data points are moving away from the aims or are stagnant (Hefferan & Diviaio, 1989). Often, a comparison with the

Figure 4.5 EFFECTIVE LEARNING PICTURES

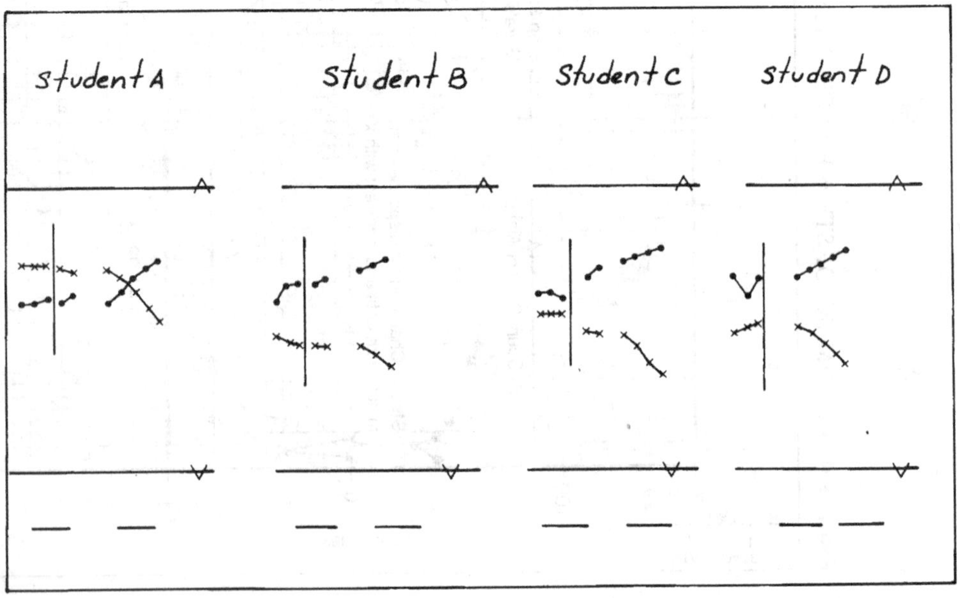

Figure 4.6 STUDENT MONITORING

Key
| = one assignment

		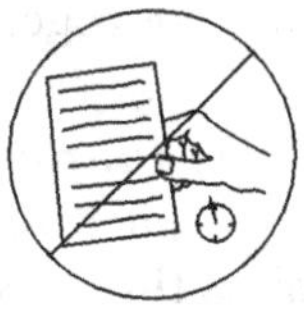	Total # of history assignments due
Week of April 3–7	| | 50%	| | 50%	4
Week of April 10–14	| | | 75%	| 25%	4

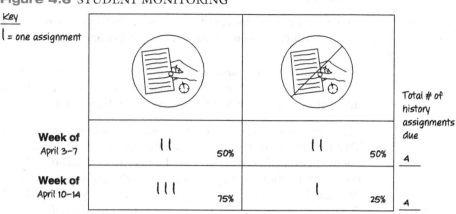

baseline shows that there is not much difference in progress. Figure 4.6 displays some ineffective learning pictures.

Student A is not progressing, because the correct data points have flattened out. When you see three consecutive sessions of flat data, it is an ineffective picture. Student B is not progressing either, because correct responses are decreasing and incorrect responses are increasing. Note, too, that for Student B, incorrect responses remain higher than correct responses during the intervention. If you consider the intervention data only, you may think that Student C's picture is effective, because the correct data points are ascending and the error data points are descending; however, when you look closer, you see the correct data points are lower and the error data points are higher than they were at baseline. In Student D's picture, the error data points are decreasing, but so are the count correct data points. When you see pictures like these, you should change your intervention or make other program changes (e.g., take multiple timings and average the score or change the goal) because the student is not making adequate progress.

Sometimes, the data do not present a clear picture of progress, especially when there is much fluctuation. In these cases, an objective evaluation is much more effective.

Objective Evaluation In objective evaluation of a student's progress, you analyze data trends and make changes following certain decision rules. Data trends use either *expected* or *actual* rate of student progress. When you measure *expected* rate of student progress, you have a preconceived date and aim in mind that a student must meet to show progress. When you measure *actual* rate of student progress, you do not have a preconceived date or aim in mind; instead, you rely on student behavior (the number of correct responses per minute during intervention) to evaluate performance.

Fuchs, Fuchs, and Hamlett (1989) found that teachers who evaluated progress using *actual* student performance produced more achievement gains than did a control group of teachers who monitored progress with end-of-unit math tests, unsystematic observations, and workbook and worksheet performances. However, teachers who evaluated progress using *expected* student performance did not produce more achievement gains than did the control group.

SAMPLE PLAN

Now that we have discussed all of the steps to precision teaching separately, we bring the steps together to write an instructional program for Rosa, a ninth grader.

1. ***Pinpoint a behavior.*** After a discussion with the general classroom teacher or based on Rosa's IEP or an examination of the district standards, Ms. Kornig determines that Rosa was having problems simplifying fractions to lowest terms.

2. ***Select a probe, input and output channels, a time, and scoring procedures.*** The teacher-designed probe contains 40 different problems, like 4/12 and 8/20. Each of the problems is repeated once, for a total of 80 problems. Rosa takes the probe for 1 minute using the see/write channels, because she is expected to perform the skill in an inclusive setting as a paper-and-pencil task. Ms. Kornig counts each digit of the answer (e.g., 1/4 counts as two digits) only to where Rosa stops.

3. ***Take a baseline.*** Rosa scores 10 cc (count correct) and 5 ce (count error) responses on Day 1, 10 cc and 10 ce on Day 2, and 15 cc and 9 ce on Day 3.

4. ***Select a mastery aim.*** Ms. Kornig selects an aim of 70–90 correct digits and 2 incorrect digits per minute for three sessions based on the performance standard chart skill of "See-Write Math Facts" (Table 4.6).

5. ***Determine the appropriateness of the pinpoint.*** Examining the baseline scores, the skill is appropriate for Rosa, because she has at least five correct responses and has not reached her aim.

6. ***Write a short-term objective.*** The objective is "Presented with an 80-item probe, Rosa will see/write fractions to lowest terms at 80 cc and 2 ce per minute for 3 consecutive days."

7. ***Select the intervention.*** Because Rosa is in the acquisition stage (she scored 5–19 correct responses), Ms. Kornig plans to use modeling of the simplification procedures as a teaching intervention.

8. ***Begin teaching and testing.*** Every day, after a 10-minute teaching session, Ms. Kornig administers the same probe that was administered in baseline.

Table 4.6 Decision Making with Precision Teaching

Is the skill appropriate?	Why?	What is the learning stage?	Why?	What is the teaching intervention?
Yes	5 or more are correct. Aim not met.	Acquisition	5 to 19 correct in a minute.	Direct teaching. Give immediate feedback.
Yes	5 or more are correct. Aim not met.	Fluency	20 or more correct and 10 or fewer wrong in a minute.	Drill and practice. Use reinforcers.
No (too easy)	Aim reached.	Maintenance	Reached mastery level.	Go on. Take baseline on the new skill in the scope and sequence.
No (too hard)	Less than 5 correct.	Preacquisition	Scored less than 5	Slice back or step down.

9. ***Graph scores.*** Rosa graphs her scores to create a learning picture.

10. ***Monitor progress.*** Ms. Kornig decides to measure progress using the *actual rate* of progress, drawing a celeration line after 7 days of data collection. She plans to change the intervention if Rosa is not making progress.

IMPORTANT POINTS

1. In precision teaching, behaviors that are repeatable and observable and that have a beginning and end are pinpointed.
2. Probes should not interfere with a student's opportunity or freedom to respond and are administered for 3 days without any intervention to collect baseline data.
3. In subjective evaluation, a learning picture is effective when the correct data points are moving up to the count correct aim, the error data points are moving down to the count error aim, and both are improvements over the baseline.
4. Objective evaluation requires the drawing of celeration lines based on either the *expected* rate of student change or the *actual* rate of student change.
5. Teachers may change the intervention, take multiple timings, or select a different goal when a student is not progressing.

CURRICULUM-BASED MEASUREMENT

Curriculum-based measurement (CBM) is a measurement and evaluation system developed at the University of Minnesota Institute for Research on Learning Disabilities by Deno, Fuchs, Mirkin, and their colleagues (Deno, 1985). Curriculum-based measurement is a type of curriculum-based assessment (Fuchs, Fuchs, & Hamlett, 1989) that considers accuracy and time. CBM employs brief, frequent assessment based on the student's classroom curriculum and provides teachers with a technique for monitoring progress (Frisby, 1987). Thus, if the school district has adopted a specific reading series, material for assessment is selected from the series texts. This procedure ensures that students are assessed on skills that have been or will be taught. The matching of assessment and instructional materials is also recommended for students with cultural and linguistic differences. Such students often perform better when they are tested on material that is presented in the classroom (Sugai, Maheady, & Skouge, 1989).

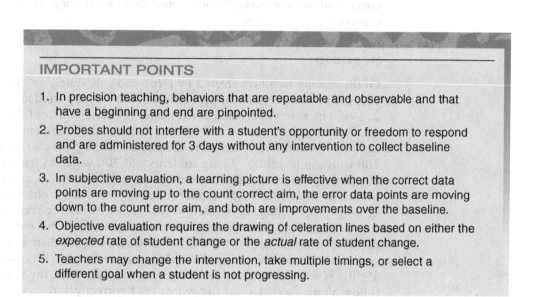

The systematic procedures of CBM demonstrate technical adequacy and validity, are well-supported in the special education literature (Elliott, 1998), and have been effectively used in inclusive settings (Salend, 2000). Like precision teaching, CBM uses frequent, direct measurement of academic performance in reading, math, spelling, and the writing curriculum. However, CBM focuses on general outcomes measured over time, whereas precision teaching involves mastery measurement of subskills of the curriculum (Fuchs & Deno, 1991). For example, in spelling, a precision teaching probe may contain only silent *e* spelling words and once students meet mastery on that skill, another probe is created with a different spelling skill. Instead, with CBM procedures, alternate probes of 20 words randomly selected from the 400 words in the second-grade curriculum are created; some of these words contain silent *e* spelling words. Thus, CBM is measuring student performance across the entire yearlong curriculum. Fuchs and Deno (1991) note that this general outcome approach to assessment is more attuned to holistic and integrated learning outcomes. We first discuss the administration and scoring procedures for reading, spelling, math, and written expression.

READING

Of the reading measures created by Deno and colleagues, we discuss oral reading fluency per minute and the maze procedure. Both are supported in the research as reliable and valid measures of reading performance (Fewster & MacMillan, 2002).

To measure a student's oral reading fluency, ask the student to read three passages, each for 1 minute, from various reading texts. These passages should be approximately 100 words in length for young students and 300 words in length for older students. Select one passage from the beginning, one from the middle, and one from the end of various grade-level texts. Be careful to select prose paragraphs without much dialogue or many proper nouns or unusual words (Deno, Mirkin, & Wesson, 1984).

To begin the assessment process, instruct the student to read the passage as quickly as possible. If the student hesitates on a word for more than 2 seconds, say the word and tell the student to go on. Time the selection for only 1 minute (Salvia & Hughes, 1990). While the student is reading each passage, mark the student responses on a follow-along sheet. Count the words read correctly and incorrectly by the student through the last word read for each passage, and rank the number to find the median scores. Words misread (e.g., *house* for *horse*), words omitted (e.g., leaving out *horse*), words reversed (e.g., *was* for *saw*), and phrases reversed (e.g., *the beautiful, wild horse* for *the wild, beautiful horse*) are counted as errors. Misread proper nouns, self-corrections, and insertions (e.g., adding the word *the* to the phrase *the wild "the" dark horse* instead of *the wild, dark horse*) are not counted as errors (Tindal & Marston, 1990).

Another reading task frequently used in CBM procedures is the maze or closure task, which permits testing of students in group settings (Shin, Denon, & Espin, 2000). The maze probe presents a reading selection with every seventh word deleted after the first sentence. The deleted word is replaced with three multiple-choice alternatives, one correct word and two clearly incorrect words. During the 3-minute reading session, students select one of the three alternatives to fill in the blank correctly.

Activity 4.6

Select a 100-word passage from a fifth-grade social studies text. With a partner, create a closure or maze task by deleting every seventh word after the first sentence.

SPELLING

Spelling measures typically include 20 words. Lists are randomly selected from either the spelling series used in the district or basal readers (Deno, et al., 1984; Marston & Magnusson, 1985). Begin by dictating words for 2 minutes, directing the student to write as many letters of each word as he or she can. Give about 10 seconds to spell each word and do not present any new words in the last 3 seconds of the test (Deno & Fuchs, 1987).

BOX 4.4

Reflections on Practice

In a study conducted by the Center for Applied Linguistics (Howard, Arteagoitia, Louguit, Malabonga, & Kenyon, 2006), researchers developed an English spelling assessment tool that was designed to assess the spelling progress of Spanish-English bilingual children from second through fifth grade. They determined that in order to reduce the cognitive load when assessing students who have language needs, offering a partial spelling of a multi-syllabic word enables students to better demonstrate their true attainment of the desired skill. For example, if the target skill is to assess various vowel patterns, a potential dictation format that could be used for the word *complained* is *compl*_____ _____.

Building on the research of Howard et al. (2006), consider what you might do in your classroom. Instead of giving a standard spelling test consider making a list of three words and ask students to identify the correct word. This type of spelling test reflects what students are asked to do when they use a word processing program. Using this procedure also eliminates some level of cognitive load by asking students to identify correct spelling instead of writing complete words. Furthermore, this type of activity can be especially useful for students with writing processing or physical disabilities. An example of an item from this type of spelling test is:

☐ complein ☐ complained ☐ compleined

Score the test by counting the number of correct letter sequences within the 2-minute sample. Counting correctly spelled words by letter sequences usually results in one more count than the number of letters; for example, the word *agent* consists of six possible correct letter sequences: one before *a*, because the student knew where to start (beginning to *a* = +1); one from *a* to *g* (+2); one from *g* to *e* (+3); one from *e* to *n* (+4); one from *n* to *t* (+5); and one after *t*, because the student knew where to end (*t* to end +6) (White & Haring, 1976). Thus, *agent* is marked in the following manner: $^{+1}a\ ^{+2}g\ ^{+3}e\ ^{+4}n\ ^{+5}t\ ^{+6}$.

MATHEMATICS

Curriculum-based measurement for math consists of multiple tests of the types of problems found in the year's curriculum (Fuchs, Fuchs, Hamlett, & Stecker, 1991). Thus, you are measuring a student's performance on the entire math curriculum over time.

You administer the various 25-item tests, directing the students to proceed as quickly as possible. As in precision teaching, score the sample by counting each correct digit. Fuchs, Fuchs, Hamlett, and Whinnery (1991) recommend a test time of 1 minute for Grade 1, 1.5 minutes for Grades 2 and 3, 3 minutes for Grade 4, 4 minutes for Grade 5, and 5 minutes for Grade 6. Others recommend a 2-minute time limit (Shinn, 1989).

WRITTEN EXPRESSION

CBM measures for written expression consist of three story starters or topic sentences (Deno, Marston, & Mirkin, 1982). An example of a story starter is, "The score was tied. As the soccer ball rolled in front of my feet, I. . . ." An example of a topic sentence is, "He went shopping at Wal-Mart."

You may either read or write the story starter or topic sentence for the student. Administer the three story starters or topic sentences at one sitting or at three sittings. Give the student a minute to think about the stories, 3 minutes to complete the stories, then count the number of words in each story. Do not count numbers (Deno & Fuchs, 1987).

Determining what constitutes a word is the teacher's decision. Salvia and Hughes (1990) suggest considering grade level and linguistic backgrounds in scoring words. They recommend counting misspelled words as words for older students (e.g., *summer* spelled *sumar*) and counting any letter sequence that can be identified as a word for younger students (e.g., *summer* spelled as *sum*). For children whose first language is not English, they suggest counting word sequences that are acceptable translations of the native language.

STEPS

Now that we have discussed the assessment procedures, we identify the steps you may follow to use CBM for planning and monitoring student progress. We provide examples from the area of reading.

Table 4.7 Suggested Instructional and Mastery Standards

	Instructional Standards	Mastery Standards
Reading (1-minute sampling)*		
1st & 2nd grade	11 to 20 wpm 10 to 30 wpm, <7 errors	50 to 70 wpm
3rd–6th grade	41 to 50 wpm 30 to 60 wpm, <7 errors	70 to 100 wpm
Spelling (2-minute sampling)		
1st & 2nd grade	20 to 30 correct letter sequences (cls)	60 to 80 cls
3rd–6th grade	40 to 59 correct letter sequences	80 to 140 cls
Math (time varies based on grade level)		
1st grade	11 or fewer correct digits	Weekly increase of one digit
2nd grade	12–22	
3rd grade	23–30	
4th grade	31–46	
5th grade	47–60	
6th grade	>60	
Written Expression (3-minute sampling)		
1st grade	Student's median	14.7 words
2nd grade	score of 3 samples	27.8 words
3rd grade		36.6 words
4th grade		40.9 words
5th grade		49.1 words
6th grade		53.3 words

*Deno, Fuchs, and Marston (2001) identify mastery standards of an increase of 2 wpm per week for beginning readers and an increase of 1 wpm per week for Grades 2–6.

Source: From the works of Deno, Mirkin, & Wesson, 1984; Fuchs, Hamlett, & Fuchs, 1990; Fuchs & Shinn, 1989; Hasbrouck & Tindal, 1992; Marston, Dement, Allen, & Allen, 1992; Marston & Magnusson, 1985

Administer and Score the Probe and Select Instructional and Mastery Standards

We have already discussed the administration and scoring procedures, so we concentrate on discussion of the instructional and mastery standards. Instructional standards often determine the grade level of the materials appropriate for instruction. Mastery standards identify the goals students must reach to show that they have learned the information. Fuchs and Shinn (1989) caution that further research is needed as to the technical adequacy of the determination of instructional and mastery standards. Therefore, this information serves as a guideline. Many school districts are establishing their own instructional and mastery standards for CBM measures. See Table 4.7 for suggestions from the literature concerning instructional and mastery standards.

EXAMPLE 1:

Mr. Smith administered probes from the first-, second-, and third-grade curriculum to Manu, who was in third grade. Based on the suggested instructional standards for third grade (see Table 4.7), Mr. Smith selected an instructional standard of 30 wpm with less than 7 errors. He then instructed Manu to read the three third-grade passages as quickly as possible for a minute each and ranked his median reading score, which was 10 correct words and 17 errors. This score was below the instructional standard, so Mr. Smith then administered selections from the second-grade reader. Manu read 25 wpm correctly with only 2 errors on the first passage of the second-grade text, 35 wpm correctly with only 3 errors on the second passage, and 30 wpm correctly with 2 errors on the third passage. A ranking of the number of words per minute correct (25, 30, 31) resulted in a median score of 30 wpm correct. Thus, Mr. Smith began instructing Manu in the second-grade text.

Write an Annual Goal and Short-Term Objectives

Deno, Mirkin, and Wesson (1984) recommend that teachers compare the instructional and mastery standards along with the IEP review date to write an annual goal and short-term objectives. Fuchs, Fuchs, and Hamlett (1989) recommend that teachers or students select ambitious mastery goals for the best results.

EXAMPLE 2:

Mr. Smith, with Manu's input, selected the mastery standard of 50 words per minute with less than 7 errors (see Table 4.7 for second-grade level). Based on this information, Mr. Smith wrote the following annual goal: "When placed in Reader 2 of the Houghton-Mifflin series, Manu will increase his reading from an instructional standard of 30 wpm correct to a mastery standard of 50 wpm correct, with less than 7 errors before the next IEP review." Next, Mr. Smith subtracted the instruction standard from the mastery with the result that Manu would have to read 20 more words by the end of 12 weeks, the date of the IEP review. Because Mr. Smith was measuring Manu's reading progress weekly, he arrived at the following short-term objective: "Every week, when presented with a random selection from the Houghton-Mifflin second-grade reader, Manu will read aloud with an average increase of about 2 wpm correct (20 divided by 12)."

Teach and Test

During teaching and testing, parallel assessment forms are given to the student at least once a week. Do not allow the student to practice the material before assessment. Wesson (1987) suggests that teachers select 10 pages from the beginning, middle, and end of each assigned text for measuring reading progress. The text and 30 slips of paper with page numbers written on each slip are then placed in a container. A student randomly selects a slip of paper, turns to the page number in the assigned text, reads the passage, and initials the back. Once a student has read and initialed the slip three times, he or she can no longer use that page as a measure of reading progress.

EXAMPLE 3:

Mr. Smith instructed Manu from the second-grade text and selected parallel passages for monitoring Manu's progress. He assessed Manu once a week with 1-minute samples.

Graph the Scores

Data is charted on an equal interval graph. An equal interval graph is a linear graph in which the distance between lines occupies equal space; that is, the distance between 5 and 10 is the same as the distance between 10 and 15 and between 15 and 20. It is probably the graph you used in school. Fuchs, Hamlett, and Fuchs (1990) have designed a software program, *MBSP: Monitoring Basic Skills Progress*, which contains graded reading passages, spelling lists, and arithmetic probes. Students enter responses on the computer, and the computer graphs the data.

EXAMPLE 4:

Mr. Smith helps Manu chart his scores on an equal interval chart. They chart the results after the scoring of each probe.

Evaluate Progress

Fuchs, Fuchs, and Hamlett (1989) recommend that teachers consider both the *expected* and *actual* rate of student change to evaluate intervention effectiveness. Their software program, *Monitoring Basic Skills Progress* (Fuchs, Hamlett, & Fuchs, 1990), displays aimlines and regression lines. The program also communicates the appropriate intervention decision. Additionally, the software conducts a skills analysis of students' responses to the test items (Fuchs, Fuchs, Hamlett, & Whinnery, 1991). Allinder (1996) found that special educators who knew the measurement systems and the software, scheduled frequent assessments, examined students' graphs, implemented decision rules, and had adequate planning time produced more significant math gains. See Figure 4.5 for a sample of the decision rules used to evaluate progress.

EXAMPLE 5:

Based on the decision rules, Mr. Smith finds that Manu is making good progress.

As we discussed the various informal assessments, we attempted to point out some of the similarities and differences. Table 4.8 shows a comparison of the various informal assessments.

INVOLVING STUDENTS IN DATA COLLECTION

Student involvement in data collection increases motivation and makes them feel more responsible for their own learning, plus it often saves teacher time. If you decide to incorporate precision teaching or CBM procedures, teaching students to grade their own probes and to chart the results promotes active student participation in the learning process. Research shows that self-graphing maintains students' performance at high levels (McDougal & Brady, 1998; Trammel, Schloss, & Alper, 1994).

Table 4.8 Comparison of Various Informal Assessment Measures

	Criterion-Referenced Tests	Precision Teaching	Curriculum-Based Measurement	Portfolio
Administration	Individual/Group	Individual/Group	Individual/Group	Individual (work selected by student)
Content	Curriculum scope and sequence	Curriculum scope and sequence	Classroom texts	Work samples
Mastery measure	Percent	Rate Reading—words per minute Math—digits per minute Spelling—letters per minute	Fluency Reading—words per minute Math—digits at varied times Spelling—letters in 2 minutes Written expression—words in 3 minutes	Varies
Uses	Identify goals, objectives	Identify goals, objectives, learning stages, teaching strategies	Identify goals, objectives, materials	Identify objectives
	Measure progress with pre- and posttests	Measure progress with repeated measurement	Measure progress with repeated measurement	Measure progress with rubrics
Assesses	General outcomes, Skills	Skills	General outcomes, Skills	Skills, Strategies, Interests
Setting	Pull-out, inclusive classes	Pull-out, inclusive classes	Pull-out, inclusive classes	Pull-out, inclusive classes

Wesson (1987) suggests setting up a measurement station in the class to involve the students. Place all materials, such as pencils or pens, a stopwatch with an audible beep, a tape recorder, assessment materials (probes or texts), direction sheets, answer sheets, and graphs, at the center. It is best to file the answer sheets, graphs, probes, and texts in a box for easy access. The direction sheet should contain step-by-step directions, explaining how to use any equipment. For example, Bott (1990), in giving directions for collecting oral reading samples, tells the students to "find the cassette tape labeled with your name, rewind it to the beginning, and press the record and play buttons down at the same time" (p. 287) to assist students in using a tape recorder. You may arrange the probes and texts according to subject areas. Schedule the students at the measurement station and assign them to the assessment materials based on their IEP objectives. Have the students proceed to the center, select the required assessment materials identified on their schedules, follow the assessment procedures, chart the information, and return all materials to their proper places.

Goodrich (1996–1997) suggests that students help create scoring rubrics. She recommends that teachers show and discuss examples of good and poor work. From these examples, students list criteria, levels, and indicators. She then suggests they use the rubrics for peer and self-assessment. For example, eighth-grade students in cooperative groups identified the following criteria for their language arts portfolios: neatness, range of characteristics, effectiveness of story, use of unusual vocabulary, and sharpness of ideas and arguments. They then added the levels of "Yes; Yes, but; and Not Quite." They next defined indicators of a "Yes" level for neatness to include minimal erasures on the paper, straight margins, page numbers, proper heading, and legible handwriting. Lastly, they defined the other indicators.

Learning logs represent another way for students to participate in their evaluation (Baskwill & Whitman, 1988). In learning logs, students enter what they have learned in any subject area. The students date and compile the logs in a notebook. Logs indicate whether students can describe what they have learned, relate isolated ideas, and recognize relevant information (Baskwill & Whitman, 1988). For example, at the end of each day, Ms. Anderson has her students write one thing they learned and how they felt about the day in their logs.

Self-monitoring of academic and social behaviors is another way to involve students in data collection. McDougal and Brady (1998) found that self-monitoring along with other self-management strategies increased math performance and engaged time of students with disabilities in inclusive settings. To teach students with special needs to monitor their own progress in an inclusive setting, use the following steps compiled from practitioners (Hughes, Ruhl, & Peterson, 1988).

1. ***Define the behavior for monitoring.*** Behaviors selected for self-monitoring should be easily identified as having occurred or not occurred. Behaviors such as turning in homework assignments, raising hand to speak, writing headings on papers, and bringing paper and pencil to class are appropriate for self-monitoring.

2. ***Teach students to discriminate the behavior.*** Model examples and nonexamples of the behaviors and then ask students to discriminate between them.

3. ***Design the form for data collection.*** On the form, be sure to include the behaviors, dates, and key for coding. See Figure 4.6 for an example of a form. This form was used with secondary students to count how often history homework was turned in on time.

4. ***Demonstrate how to record using the form.*** Model how to record on the form and explain the scoring code.

5. ***Use a time routine.*** Scheduling a specific time for students to complete the forms increases the chances that students will remember to monitor the behaviors when you are not around. Schedule the time for monitoring as close to the completion of the task as possible.

6. ***Use teacher reliability checks.*** A reliability check is easier if the student is monitoring a paper-and-pencil type of task, which leaves a permanent record. For example, a quick check of the general education teacher's grade book will let you know whether the student is correctly monitoring the turning in of history homework on time. Many times, teachers reward students when their counts match. Actually, checking the use of the form is more important than checking accuracy. After all, the objective is for students to monitor their own progress.

7. ***Introduce self-monitoring in one inclusive class setting first, and then generalize to others.*** Anderson-Inman (1986) reports that allowing students to decide when and where to use the self-monitoring form makes them feel more committed to using it. Perhaps next a secondary student may want to monitor the turning in of math homework on time.

PUTTING IT ALL TOGETHER

In this time of high-stakes testing comes high-stakes accountability for teachers and students to demonstrate mastery of state standards. In this chapter we have provided you with a range of assessment ideas to help monitor ongoing student progress and growth. Remember as a special educator you may need to use a range of tools to ensure that students master the content on an ongoing basis and to be prepared to remediate areas in which gaps exist. In early elementary years closing these gaps is critical to student success in the future. Overall, we suggest that as a special educator

Activity 4.7

Assume you have three students in your class with the following characteristics. How would you involve each in data collection and advocating for their needs at the elementary or secondary level?

Student A: Has a learning disability in reading comprehension and spelling, loves to please the teacher but reads a year below grade level and spells two years below grade level.

Student B: Is strong academically but her behavior often gets in the way of her learning. She has poor peer relationships and often has difficulty working in groups. She is not motivated by pleasing the teacher but does like to get good grades.

Student C: Overall this student is at a lower level in all academic areas but constantly seeks peer and teacher attention.

IMPORTANT POINTS

1. Curriculum-based measurement uses classroom materials for assessment, measures performance using fluency, and compares a student's score with suggested instructional and mastery standards or criteria.
2. The oral reading fluency measure requires a student to read passages for 1 minute from various reading texts to determine the instructional reading level (the grade level for instruction), and the maze or cloze procedure requires students to select the appropriate word from a choice of three words to fill in the blank correctly.
3. The spelling measure requires students to write as many spelling words as they can in 2 minutes and is scored by counting letter sequences.
4. In mathematics assessment, sample problems from the whole-year's math curriculum are selected and scored by counting the number of digits correct.
5. In written expression assessment, students are given three story starters or three topic sentences and instructed to write a story for each within 3 minutes.
6. Student involvement in data collection increases motivation and makes them feel more responsible for their own learning, plus it often saves teacher time.

your assessment of students must be planned, methodical, and ongoing to ensure their success across grade levels and content areas.

DISCUSSION QUESTIONS

1. Discuss some of the difficulties encountered in establishing and maintaining a monitoring system such as Precision Teaching and Curriculum-Based Measurement. Brainstorm some solutions.
2. Discuss ways to involve students with special needs at both elementary and secondary levels in data collection procedures.
3. Present the pros and cons of using CBM compared to portfolio assessment.

Websites: Useful websites related to chapter content can be found in Appendix A.

CHAPTER

5

The Instructional Cycle

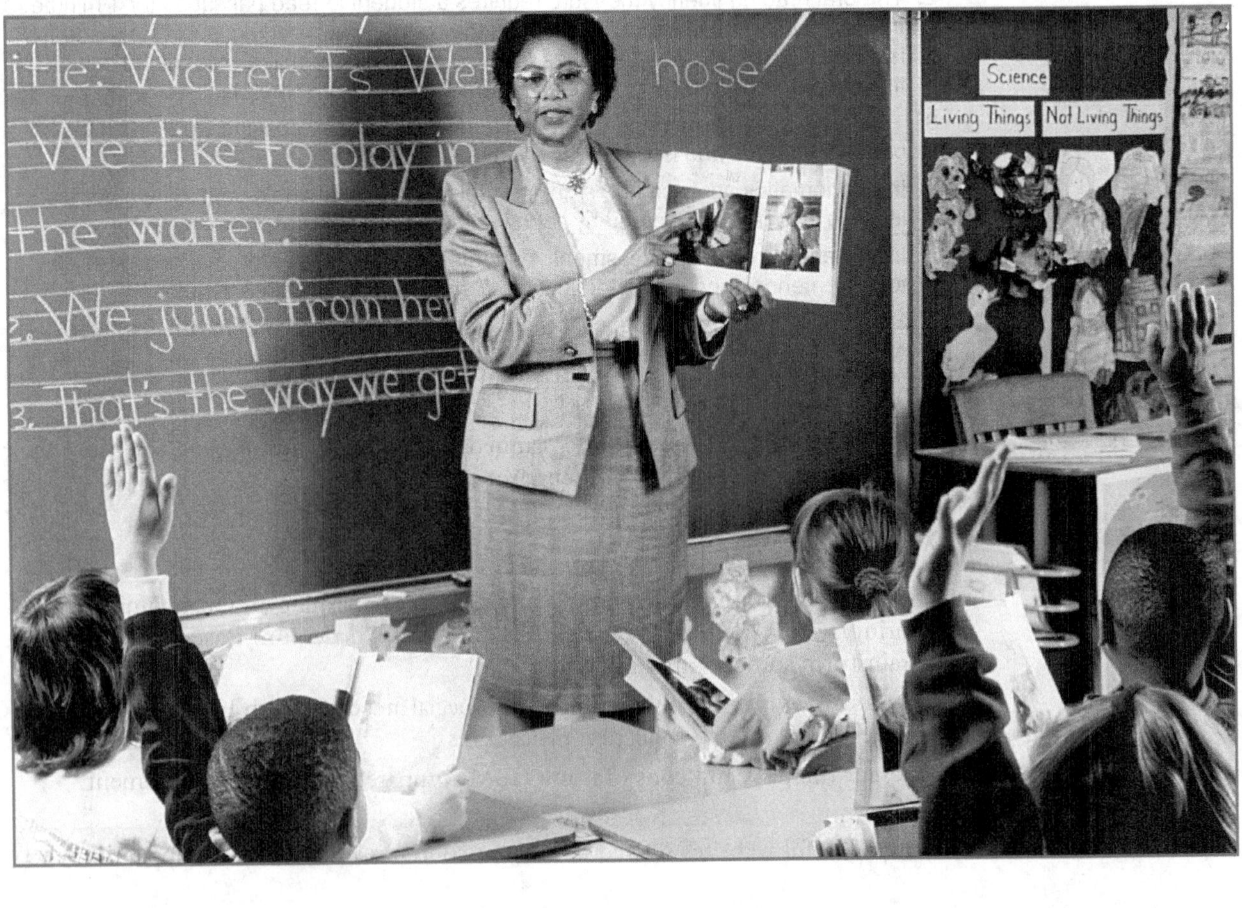

KEY TOPICS

Universal Design for Learning

Planning
- Instructional Time
- Motivation
- Academic Content

Presentation
- Opening
- Body
- Guided Practice
- Closing
- Feedback

Independent Practice
- Monitoring Student Practice

Evaluation
- Specify the Criteria
- Vary Ways to Evaluate
- Teach Students to Self-Evaluate
- Complete a Self-Evaluation

Lesson Plan
- Putting It All Together

"Mrs. Chen, welcome to Southwest High. I'm Eric Roland, and I'm one of the Intensive Reading teachers here at Southwest. How are things going so far?"

"Okay, I think!" Mrs. Chen replied. "The summer flew by, and now here I am, ready or not, starting to teach biology."

"I wanted to stop by and touch base with you about some students we'll be sharing this year. Do you have a few minutes to chat?"

"Sure! I noticed on my class roster for second period that I have two students on IEPs and I was told you could tell me about their needs."

"Right. You will have Jocelyn Herro and Tiffany Romano. Here are copies of their IEPs for your planning purposes.

"Jocelyn and Tiffany both have specific learning disabilities, but that is where any similarity between them ends. Tiffany also has behavior problems and can be quite a challenge to control. She needs to be on a positive behavior plan that focuses on target behaviors at all times. Jocelyn, however, has an attention deficit disorder so you need to monitor her closely for staying on task. She is very quiet and tends to drift off."

"I remember in my interview, the principal mentioned that all of you at Southwest High use Universal Design for Learning as an instructional planning tool. I have a lot of questions about how to put that into everyday practice."

"Well, this is our third year of using Universal Design principles school-wide, and our faculty members are excited about the impact that it has had on driving instruction of all our students, not just those with special needs."

"Basically," continued Mr. Roland, "Universal Design simply means that when you are conceptualizing your lessons you will want to plan for diversity of needs right from the start, rather than trying to change lessons to fit needs later. I know that may sound tough at first, but we will work together to make sure Jocelyn and Tiffany, as well as the rest of your students, are learning."

"Sounds good," said Mrs. Chen, "but you will be working with them in a pull-out program during first period and I will be on my own in this classroom of twenty-five students during second period. I understand how the instructional cycle works but how do we coordinate our daily plans?"

"Good question. I will be planning my lessons around the concepts you teach each week. In my classroom I'll provide both guided reading, and independent practice in a small-group setting to support what I know you are working on in the larger classroom setting. You will also need to present information in a variety of ways and allow your students to express what they have learned in multiple formats, and I can help you with planning for that."

"Let's work together," he continued, "to draft a plan for your first few weeks. In the meantime be thinking about a good 'hook' to get their attention on your first day."

"Terrific!" said Mrs. Chen. "I can hardly wait to get started!"

What kind of "hook" could Mrs. Chen use to engage her students on the first day? How can you ensure that your planning addresses a variety of learners in your classroom?

Responses to these questions are found in the Instructor's Manual.

INTRODUCTION

In Chapter 1, we referred to the instructional cycle, which includes planning the lesson, presenting the lesson with guided practice and feedback, providing for independent practice, and evaluating the effectiveness of the lesson. In this chapter, we examine some of the decisions teachers must make in the daily teaching process combined with designing lessons that are created using a Universal Design format to ensure the success of all learners. In the daily planning phase, teachers make decisions about instructional time, motivation, and academic content. In presenting the lesson, they make decisions about strategies for presenting new subject content, activities for practice, positive and corrective feedback, and summarization of the content. With questioning and feedback, they evaluate how the lesson is proceeding and the necessity of making changes. During independent practice activities, teachers decide on activities that reinforce the content presented and ways to generalize the information. After the lesson, they make evaluative decisions concerning student performances and the necessity of reteaching the content. They also reflect and self-evaluate. The teacher effectiveness research supports this instructional cycle (Rosenshine, 1995).

We feel this instructional cycle provides a useful framework whether a teacher follows the reductionist or constructivist paradigm. For example, during the lesson presentation, a teacher may present the subject matter (reductionist paradigm) or encourage a classroom dialogue (constructivist paradigm). In a review of validated practices for teaching mathematics to students with learning disabilities, Miller, Butler, and Lee (1998) reported that no matter the intervention—whether direct instruction, strategy instruction, self-regulation, etc.—instructional procedures followed a modeling, guided practice, feedback, independent practice, and evaluation cycle.

A critical part of the planning process is ensuring that lessons are created to maximize the success of all students. This process is referred to most often as Universal Design for Learning. The Center for Applied Special Technology (CAST) defines Universal Design for Learning (UDL) on their website as:

Multiple means of representation, to give learners various ways of acquiring information and knowledge,

Multiple means of expression, to provide learners alternatives for demonstrating what they know, and

Multiple means of engagement, to tap into learners' interests, offer appropriate challenges and increase motivation.

With curriculum design that focuses on the needs of all, Scott, McGuire, and Shaw (2001) expanded upon the principles of UDL to create Universal Design for Instruction (UDI).

Teacher effectiveness research supports the use of the instructional cycle (Rosenshine, 1995) while CAST supports a planning process that considers the range of learners at the conceptualization of lesson content. Throughout this chapter we focus on the planning process embedded within the principles of UDI, which allows students in each phase of the instructional process guaranteed access to learning, instruction, and assessment that will effectively meet their needs.

The instructional cycle also includes independent practice. Teachers would provide universally designed independent practice activities that reinforce the content and ways to generalize the information. In collaboration with the special educator you would first make evaluative decisions concerning student performance and the necessity for teaching the content. Then you would modify future lessons from assessment data on learning outcomes for the lesson presented. Finally, you would reflect on how to improve the overall student learning outcomes in your classroom. We feel the instructional cycle in combination with the principles of Universal Design empowers teachers working across content areas and grade levels to ensure student success.

UNIVERSAL DESIGN FOR LEARNING

The concept of creating lessons that are accessible to all students reflects the passage of the Americans with Disabilities Act (ADA). After the passage of ADA, all buildings were required to be accessible for people with physical disabilities (e.g., ramps instead of stairs). So, if a new building was built or an existing building renovated, the requirements for accessibility outlined in ADA had to be met. Although in theory this was a great way to renovate currently existing buildings, what society quickly learned is that creating buildings that were accessible in the first place was more economical than taking the time and expense to retrofit a building. This cost-saving measure of designing accessible buildings from the beginning is the same concept being applied to lesson preparation. Instead of trying to retrofit instruction (which can be more time-consuming and costly), teachers should create lessons from the start that embrace the needs of all learners. The purpose behind creating instruction that is universally designed parallels the movement of our field to universal access provided with the passage of ADA allowing all populations the ability to navigate the architectural structures of our country. If we create curriculum and instruction in this same manner, then we should be able to meet the needs of all students. Table 5.1 provides an overview of the nine principles related to creating Universally Designed Instruction. As you read in the chapter opener, Mrs. Chen and Mr. Roland plan to use Universal Design to enhance instructional planning for students with diverse needs and all students to ensure that optimal student learning occurs.

According to the Center for Applied Special Technology, Universal Design for Learning is grounded in the philosophy that instruction and teaching must be designed from the outset to meet the needs of the widest plurality of learners. Universal Design for Instruction takes into account the natural diversity present in every classroom and seeks to present content within the following three-tiered framework: multiple means of representation, multiple means of expression, and multiple means of engagement. More specifically, teachers provide learners with myriad opportunities to acquire content, express that acquisition, and explore areas of interest directly connected to life experiences. Hitchcock and Stahl (2003) further explain that a universally designed curriculum creates an exciting variety of opportunities for multiple learners and learning styles.

Table 5.1 Nine Principles of Universally Designed Instruction

The Nine Principles of Universal Design for Instruction©

Principle	Definition
Principle 1: Equitable use	Instruction is designed to be useful to and accessible by people with diverse abilities. Provide the same means of use for all students; identical whenever possible, equivalent when not.
Principle 2: Flexibility in use	Instruction is designed to accommodate a wide range of individual abilities. Provide choice in methods of use.
Principle 3: Simple and intuitive	Instruction is designed in a straightforward and predictable manner, regardless of the student's experience, knowledge, language skills, or current concentration level. Eliminate necessary complexity.
Principle 4: Perceptible	Instruction is designed so that necessary information is communicated effectively to the students, regardless of ambient conditions or the student's sensory ability.
Principle 5: Tolerance for error	Instruction anticipates variation in individual student learning pace and prerequisite skills.
Principle 6: Low physical effort	Instruction is designed to minimize nonessential physical effort in order to allow maximum learning. Note: This principle does not apply when physical effort is integral to essential requirements of a course.
Principle 7: Size and space for approach and use	Instruction is designed with consideration for appropriate size and space for approach, reach, manipulations, and use regardless of a student's body size, posture, mobility, and communication needs.
Principle 8: A community of learners	The instructional environment promotes interaction and communication among students and between students and faculty.
Principle 9: Instructional climate	Instruction is designed to be welcoming and inclusive. High expectations are espoused for all students.

Taken from the article written by McGuire, J, Scott, S., & Shaw, S. (2003). Universal Design for Instruction: The paradigm, its principles, and products for enhancing instructional access. *Journal of Postsecondary Education and Disability, 17*(1), 11–21.

Activity 5.1

Assume you are going to teach a lesson to students on line segments. How would you introduce this lesson for a student who cannot process language, a student who has difficulty sitting in his or her seat, a student who has difficulty with the writing process, or a student for whom English is not the primary language?

(Answers for this and other activities are found in the Instructor's Manual)

PLANNING

When you plan instruction that is universally designed, your first step in introducing the lesson is to catch the students' attention. You might start by asking students to draw a line on their desks using a dry erase marker or throwing a ball to students and asking the person who catches it to name something that is a line segment in the classroom. To engage students of all ages, you need to provide something novel, unexpected, or active, which can often be a great hook. Vacca and Vacca (2006) recommend using real-life motivators (e.g., you just found a billfold with $100) or creating hooks connected to student's lives (e.g., asking students how the price of gas relates to the Great Depression). Sometimes, teachers are in such a hurry to teach a concept that they forget that Jose' isn't going to learn the concept if he is asleep or is talking to Gwenetta or is just not interested in the topic as presented. First, ensure students are engaged and interested in the topic, then begin to teach the concept.

INSTRUCTIONAL TIME

Never in the history of education have stakes been higher, content more compacted, and the value of instructional time at a greater premium. For students with disabilities who are expected to pass high-stakes assessment, the pressure on teachers to maximize student learning is at the center of discussion in every school and classroom (Thurlow, 2002; Thurlow & Johnson, 2000).

Academic Learning Time

Academic learning time (ALT) is the amount of time that students spend engaged in successful completion of relevant learning activities (Wilson, 1987). Cates and Lee (2005) found that academic learning time also relates to behavioral outcomes for students with behavioral issues. In this time of high-stakes testing, effective teachers ensure that they maximize every minute of their ALT.

Time on Task

With more and more students with disabilities being expected to master state standards and being included in the general education setting, time on task is at a premium. Time on task varies, depending on the special education setting and the instructional techniques utilized. The importance of time on task for all students is critical and research indicates that students can only stay on task about 8–10 minutes (Jensen, 1998) without some type of break or summary activity. These short breaks can be connected to the content and still focus on academic learning time, and often it is a good idea to include a physical break. Some ideas for breaks might include having students stand up and talk to a neighbor for 60 seconds about the topic being discussed, or to draw a 2-minute visual image of the content to this point. These breaks reinforce concepts and allow the mind to encode the learning while giving the learner a chance to move within the confines of the lesson.

Activity 5.2

With a peer come up with three or four more examples of breaks you could use during a lesson on the continents. Can you think of at least one activity that promotes physical movement within the lesson?

Figure 5.1 DIMENSIONS OF LEARNING

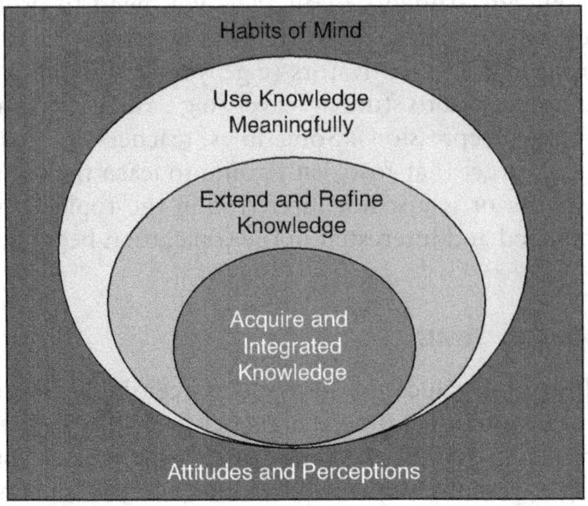

Remember if you have students who make comments off task during a movement break or even during a lecture, redirect them by asking them to talk about the topic later. Then of course remember to talk with these students about the topic they have presented at the time indicated.

MOTIVATION

As a teacher, you will be faced with the challenge of motivating your students, and Marzano, Pickering, and McTighe (1993) offer a diagram related to learning (see Figure 5.1). One component of their diagram related to learning is creating a positive climate, which they state closely relates to motivation.

Positive Learning Environment

Marzano et al. (1993) discuss the importance of the development of a positive learning climate. Even if students can master the learning theory, the importance of students having "positive attitudes and perceptions" about the learning environment is critical. Marzano et al. present aspects of teaching that impact students' "positive attitude and perception" about learning. These aspects focus on creating a positive climate. Climate involves more than just a place for learning and focuses on students being accepted by both their teachers and their peers as well as there being "comfort and order" in the learning environment. Too many times teachers create lessons without considering how to develop a climate of acceptance and support for students to learn.

Task Completion

The second aspect that Marzano et al. describe for students entering the lesson with a "positive attitude and perception" reflects the classroom tasks students are being asked to complete. Marzano et al. (1993) state that if students do not value the task, are not clear about what they are supposed to accomplish, or do not believe they have the ability to complete the task, learning will be greatly compromised. Therefore, keeping these critical foundations in mind as lessons are developed will ensure a more motivated learner who is engaged in instruction. Once students are positive about the task created, then the task must be completed with a high level of accuracy to encode and retain the concepts presented. When answering questions or participating in practice connected with presentation of new material, students should achieve an accuracy level of approximately 80% or greater (Christenson, Thurlow, & Ysseldyke, 1987; Wilson, 1987).

> **Activity 5.3**
> Meet with your peers and develop three ideas for creating a positive learning environment for students at the secondary level and three ideas for the elementary level.

During independent practice you may want to schedule a variety of activities so that students can choose the task they will complete (see Figure 5.2). You may also offer a variety of ways for students to demonstrate their knowledge. One of the most common responses in education is a paper-and-pencil response, which requires students to answer questions on worksheets, workbook pages, or at the end of a chapter (Rieth, Polsgrove, Okolo, Bahr, & Eckert, 1987). The use of exhibitions provided in Chapter 4 as an informal assessment tool breaks away from this more traditional approach. Exhibition assessments provide students with a way to present their knowledge in nontraditional formats. This model allows students to demonstrate their knowledge through their learning style and also allows students to bring their own cultural and background knowledge into the work and complete the activity using their learning preferences.

Figure 5.2 SAMPLE CHOICE SHEET FOR SECONDARY STUDENTS

Name ______________________________

Date ______________________________

I will do ________ of these to show I understand the material found in Chapter

______________________ of ______________________.

________ 1. Take a test.

________ 2. Design a technology presentation of the major points.

________ 3. Write a summary and answer the questions at the end of the chapter.

________ 4. Tape a summary and the answers to the questions at the end of the chapter.

________ 5. Complete ______________ worksheets.

________ 6. Discuss the major points with two peers over a tape recorder.

________ 7. Complete a notebook of major facts.

________ 8. Your option as approved by the teacher ______________________.

(The following numbers are required by all ______________________.)

Personal Relevance

Motivation is enhanced when learning is personally relevant (Good & Brophy, 1984; Ladson-Billings, 2002; Marzano et al., 1993). Teachers who truly understand motivation embrace the richness that children from all cultures and backgrounds bring, rather than emphasizing their deficits (Ladson-Billings, 2004; Rethinking schools online, 2004). The consideration of students' personal interests in the selection of materials motivates students (Zigmond, Sansone, Miller, Donahoe, & Kohnke, 1986). Making a commitment to learning and setting goals give students a sense of participation in the learning process. One of the techniques used in the Strategic Instruction Model from the University of Kansas Center for Research on Learning is to ask adolescents to make a commitment to learning a new strategy before you introduce it. The self-advocacy strategy of the learning strategies curriculum increased adolescents' participation in setting their own goals during IEP conferences (VanReusen & Bos, 1994). In Figure 5.3, we present a sample contract for a secondary student. The student typed his responses using a word-processing program.

In a discussion of the literature concerning motivation for adolescent low achievers, Mercer and Mercer (2001) note the benefit of student involvement. While teaching a secondary basic science class, Ms. Williams motivated students by allowing them to select roles in a cooperative learning strategy called literature circles (Daniels, 2002). She then provided students with several types of books on the assigned topics and let the students select for their literature circles the book they wanted to read as well as their roles in their groups. The teacher in this lesson became a facilitator of learning, while the students were actively engaged in mastering the goal of the lesson throughout the various reading materials. This type of activity allowed students to have their own roles while at the same time allowing students to read an array of materials that they were motivated to read on the topic assigned.

ACADEMIC CONTENT

With the recent changes in legislation in both general and special education, the academic content for students with disabilities is clearly the general education curriculum. All states now have aligned curricular standards in all subject areas, which must be

Figure 5.3 ACADEMIC CONTRACT

Math Contract

Objective I Will Be Working On:

I will learn to add, subtract, multiply, and divide like fractions and reduce the answers to the lowest terms.

Materials and Techniques:

Participation in teacher-directed lessons during the weeks of November 1-29. Completion of all worksheets and assigned activities.

Goal:

90% on at least 1/2 of the worksheets and activities.

80%-90% on the unit exam.

I have selected the goal and feel it is one I can achieve.

Signed Juan H.
(Student)

IMPORTANT POINTS

1. Lessons should be created based on the instructional cycle using universally designed principles to meet the needs of all students.
2. Academic learning time is the amount of time students spend engaged in successful completion of relevant learning activities.
3. Time on task is influenced by setting, instructional strategies, and student motivation during engagement.
4. Teachers should create a positive learning climate, encourage positive student attitudes and value for a task, offer students a variety of task choices and ways to respond, make learning personally relevant, ask students to make commitments and set goals, and actively involve students to achieve academically and to display appropriate behaviors.

considered when selecting appropriate content material. For example, a benchmark for students in PreK–2 to meet the reading standard of "the student uses reading processes effectively" is "students are expected to predict what the content of the text will be from its title or illustrations" (Florida Department of Education, 2006). The benchmark for students in grades 6–8 to meet the same reading standard is "students are expected to predict the content, purpose, and organization of the text based on their background knowledge and their knowledge of text structure" (Florida Department of Education, 2006). Many states link the passage of tests based on standards to promotion, retention, or remediation. Thus, these academic content standards must serve as guidelines for lesson preparation and for creating universally designed instruction, so be certain to check your state standards.

Task Analysis

Many times the tasks students are asked to complete in academic content areas, especially in the higher grade levels, can be overwhelming or too complex for students to succeed. The job of a special educator is to complete a task analysis of the steps in the process. Task analysis involves breaking down a task or objective being taught into simpler components.

To perform a task analysis, you must identify the terminal behavior (the behavior you expect the students to accomplish) and list the necessary prerequisite skills and component skills in sequence (Alberto & Troutman, 2006). Prerequisite skills are skills that students must master *before* they can be taught a terminal behavior. For example, in math, if students are unsuccessful at mastering division problems (the terminal behavior) because they could not subtract or multiply accurately (prerequisite skills), then these skills must be listed and either taught or compensated for to master the next skill. Students may also be unsuccessful with mastering division because you have not identified the component skills that must be mastered *on the way* to reaching the terminal behavior. The component skills may be either parallel or sequential (Desberg & Taylor, 1986). Parallel component skills have no sequential order; it does not matter which component skill you teach first. For example, you may introduce adverbs or adjectives in no particular order. Skills are sequential when each step of the skill must be mastered before the next step can be taught.

Table 5.2 Task Analysis for Reading a Map

Given a map of the local community, can the student:

- Locate their current location
- Locate the compass rose
- Find a location north
- Find a location south
- Find a location east
- Use coordinates to find a location

After completing this simple task analysis, use those skills not mastered to target each student's individual instruction. Then once skills are taught, reassess using the task analysis.

Thus, when completing a task analysis of a skill to master, you must consider prerequisite and component skills. Table 5.2 shows an example of how you might task analyze a skill a student needs to master. In this example, Ms. Martinez decided that she had better emphasize the procedures a student needs to know to understand how to read a map.

Activity 5.4

Using task analysis, identify how you might assess students' skills in these two areas.

1. Preparing for class after going to the locker in middle school.
2. Adding 1 digit numbers up to 10.

Types of Academic Content

The academic content found in today's classrooms is clearly outlined by each state department of education. All academic content found in the state standards represents the following areas: basic concepts, rules, laws, law-like principles, value judgments, and self-help content. Basic concepts are skills that students must master to be successful. Rules are often found in reading, spelling, grammar, and mathematics content; laws in the natural sciences; and law-like principles in social studies. Value judgments are often found in social skills and elective courses. See Table 5.3 for specific guidelines concerning academic content types.

Complexity of Academic Content

Instruction must be developed to meet the wide range of learners in the classroom and reflect the principles of Universal Design for Learning. Within Universally Designed Instruction the difficulty of tasks is controlled as an effective strategy for teaching reading and writing to students with learning disabilities (Vaughn, Gersten, & Chard, 2000). A way to control task difficulty is to present concepts in small steps. For example, after performing a task analysis on counting coins, Ms. Johnson taught the students (1) to count pennies and had them practice that step, (2) to count nickels and had them practice that step, and (3) to count pennies and nickels and had them practice that step. She

Table 5.3 Types of Subject Matter

WHAT CONTENT TO INCLUDE WHEN YOU ARE TEACHING
Basic Concepts or Skills—Simple facts, verbal chains, or verbal associations
The color red (simple fact)
Examples—*red apple, red block, red truck*
Nonexamples—*blue truck, blue block, green square*
Or
The days of the week (verbal chains)
Examples—*Sunday, Monday, Tuesday, Wednesday, Thursday, Friday, & Saturday*
Nonexamples—January, February, March
Or
States and capitals (verbal associations)
Examples—Sacramento, California; Denver, Colorado
Nonexamples—Sacramento, New Mexico; Denver, Rhode Island
Concepts—Abstract or generic idea
Verb (example)
Definition—*A verb is a word that indicates action or state of being*
Examples—*run, jump, is,* and *are*
Nonexamples—*girl, man,* and *to*
Attributes—*Verbs often follow subjects*
Comparisons—*A verb doesn't name a person, place, or thing like a noun does.*
Identify new examples—*Over—no*
Smile—yes
Rule—A prescribed guide for action
A capitalization rule (example)
Rule identification—*Begin a sentence with a capital letter.*
Application items—*The boy is my friend and off the chair.*
Justification of the rule—*Tell why the rule was or was not used.*
Laws or Principles—Explanation of physical behavior
Movement of electricity (example)
Law identification—*Electricity can pass through a closed circuit only.*
Cause and effect—*If the circuit is closed, then electricity can pass through.*
Application items—*Experiment with wires and a battery cell to turn on a light bulb.*
Lawlike Principles—Explanation of human or animal behaviors
Camouflage (example)
Principle identification—*Animals use camouflage to hide from their enemies.*
Cause and effect—*If a chameleon thinks an enemy is near, it will turn the color of its surroundings.*
Application items—*Discover other animals and ways they camouflage themselves.*
Value judgment—Evaluation of the value of things
Pam's behavior was appropriate (example)
Development of criteria—*Calm voice, polite*
Identification of facts—*Pam asked, "May I please borrow a pencil?"*
Comparison—*Calm voice—yes*
Polite—yes

proceeded in small steps until the students were able to count coins from pennies to quarters.

Proponents of the constructivist model feel that teachers should refrain from breaking down complex tasks into small steps, because it results in a lack of meaning (Poplin, 1988; Heshusius, 1989), yet some structure may need to be added for students with cognitive delays to be successful in a constructivist model (Scruggs & Mastropieri, 2003).

Instead, constructivists recommend that teachers use scaffolding strategies to decrease the complexity and preserve the meaning of the academic content. With scaffolding, a teacher supports and guides the learner in taking risks to achieve a task just beyond the learner's capabilities. The teacher provides supports until the student can achieve the task independently. For example, to decrease the complexity involved in counting coins, Ms. Wolfe did not break the content into small steps as Ms. James did. Instead, she decided to present all the coins at once and to provide students with a cue card, which reminded them of the value of each coin, and to sort and count coins in order from largest to smallest.

Count

Quarter—25 cents

Dime—10 cents

Nickel—5 cents

Penny—1 cent

Activity 5.5

Use scaffolding to decrease the complexity for students of learning how to add 1 digit numbers up to 10. Think about how you might use peer support as part of your scaffolding.

Instructional Alignment

Instructional alignment is the amount of congruence among the objectives, instructional procedures, and evaluation procedures of a lesson (Cohen, 1987). The close alignment of daily instruction and instructional materials with local and state assessments are the challenges many teachers face with the emphasis placed on state and local

BOX 5.1

Reflections on Practice

National standards are available in most academic content areas. These standards provide the backbone for state and local standards. The national organizations for academic content areas and special education that are most often consulted for standard development are listed below.

Council for Exceptional Children

National Council of Teachers of Mathematics

National Council of Teachers of English

National Science Teachers Association

National Council for the Social Studies

National Association for Sport and Physical Education

National Music Council

National Art Education Association

accountability from the passage of NCLB and the level of accountability for students with disabilities. What you intend to teach must match what you teach and what you assess (West, Idol, & Cannon, 1989). An example of nonalignment is found in the following lesson. The teacher, Ms. Harper, planned to teach students to identify adjectives. During the lesson, she asked students to circle the adjectives in each sentence, and then during evaluation, she required them to write sentences with adjectives. Ms. Harper has matched the objective to the instructional procedures, but not to the evaluation procedures. Requiring students to write a sentence with *beautiful* in it (the evaluation task) is more difficult than her objective of requiring students to circle the adjective in a sentence, as in, "The beautiful girl is crying." To correct this nonalignment, Ms. Harper should require students to identify adjectives in sentences during evaluation.

IMPORTANT POINTS

1. No Child Left Behind and the Individuals with Disabilities in Education Act Reauthorized 2004 states that students with disabilities should learn the same academic content as their general education peers.
2. Each state has developed clearly articulated standards for each academic content area that provide guidance for the daily planning process.
3. Task analysis requires the identification of prerequisite skills, component skills, and terminal behaviors or objectives.
4. When students are first learning a new skill, effective teachers decrease the complexity of materials by presenting a number of small, sequenced steps or by using scaffolding procedures.

PRESENTATION

Daily instruction that is universally designed and aligned with standards is the next step to ensure student learning. As you think about how you will present your instruction, keep these facts in mind.

Many of your students will come from diverse cultural and linguistic backgrounds (Lue, 2001; Obiakor, 2007). Because of this diversity, cultural discourse between teacher and students may occur. Many of these learners may exhibit a wide range of language, learning, and behavioral characteristics that may present challenges to educators (Heward, 2003). An effective teacher uses the diversity of the learners to create a climate in which students can learn from each other. For example, in a class that contained more than 50% of the students from a different culture, Ms. Grant started a lesson on the Great Depression by asking students about a time when they felt sad, poor, or hungry. She then presented five key points to students about the Great Depression. She asked the students to compare those key points to aspects of their own lives through pictures, words, or drama. Students then shared their life comparisons. This type of presentation took an issue that was key in American history but allowed it to be personalized in the lives of each child from various cultures in the classroom.

The students learned about the Great Depression and at the same time Ms. Grant learned a great deal about the students' lives and cultures.

When presenting the lesson, Archer and Isaacson (1990) recommend dividing lessons into three parts: opening, body, and closing. To these areas, we add guided practice and feedback. Of course, feedback is given throughout the lesson presentation, but is presented as a separate topic to assist in your understanding of the concept.

OPENING

Ms. Grant's lesson demonstrates that in order to teach students, you must *gain their attention*, and for many of our students we must continue to use motivating ideas to keep their attention throughout the lesson. Sometimes the opening can be made exciting for young children by verbally cueing the students with "Look at me" or bringing in an item connected to the story in a paper bag. For older students we know the part of the adolescent brain that grows the most at this age is the area related to risk-taking, aggression, and pleasure (Sousa, 2001). With this knowledge you might consider talking about a movie they liked or something that they enjoy such as "Describe the last time you felt happy" or "Name your favorite _____" related to the topic you are about to discuss. Sometimes nonverbal cues, such as silently waiting or flicking the light switch, are used for younger children, while more dramatic ideas such as putting in a 2-minute movie clip or telling a joke can be used with older students. Hunter (1981) describes an anticipatory set as a statement or an activity that introduces the content, motivates students to learn, and is connected as much as possible to the students' lives. For example, ask students to write down a problem they recently had and how that problem may relate to the problem presented in the first paragraph of the story, or ask students to talk about how they think the topic you are introducing tastes, smells, feels, and looks.

Overview of Instructional Content

Once you have everyone's attention, Rosenshine and Stevens (1986), in their summary of the teacher effectiveness research, suggest beginning a lesson with a *short review of prerequisite skills. Relating the current lesson to previous lessons* is also recommended when introducing a new skill to students with special needs (Cohen, 1986). An introduction that is especially effective for students with problem behaviors is *sharing behavioral expectations* at the beginning of the lesson (Falk, Lane, Strong, & Wehby, 2004; Rosenberg, 1986). One idea to consider is using a T-chart where you draw on the board a T and on one side at the top you draw an eye and on the other side you draw an ear. Then ask students to share instructional expectations for what you as a teacher should see and hear while completing the activity in today's lesson. Sharing behavioral expectations is particularly important at the beginning of the year and when new students enter a program. Many schools use Positive Behavioral Instructional Supports (PBIS) to create a climate of consistency of rules and consequences across the school (see Chapters 2 and 9). Because students come to school with prior information, *activating background knowledge* is an effective way to open a lesson (Palincsar & Brown, 1989). For students who may not have the necessary prior knowledge to understand text information, Hasselbring (1998) recommends the use of *anchoring activities* to help build backgrounds. Anchoring is using real-world situations to develop meaningful knowledge (Bransford, Sherwood, Hasselbring, Kinzer, & Williams, 1990).

Activity 5.6

Part 1: For a group of elementary students with special needs in a cotaught setting, decide how you would open a lesson with the following objective: When presented with two-digit numbers and asked to round them off to the nearest 10, students will round off the numbers at a rate of at least 20 digits correct and no more than 2 digits incorrect per minute for three sessions.

Part 2: For a group of secondary students with special needs in a social studies class, decide how you would open a lesson with the following objective: When presented with a paragraph from a history text, students will paraphrase the content with 100% accuracy.

BODY

In the body of the lesson several types of activities can occur including modeling, teacher–student dialoguing, scaffolding instruction, lecturing, questioning, and guided practice when new information is presented (Christenson, Ysseldyke, & Thurlow, 1989; Larkin, 2001). Peer-mediated instruction may also occur in the body and during guided practice. See Chapter 9 for a detailed discussion of various peer-mediated instructional strategies.

Modeling

In the process of modeling for students, Katims and Harmon (2000) included "think-aloud" and task performance as key variables. In modeling, students are to observe the teacher thinking through the task and problem solving, both verbally and visually. With modeling, visual aids such as cue cards and graphic organizers are provided to enhance comprehension (Bakkan & Wheldon, 2002). Modeling also can be combined with class discussion, the end result being, students learn the skill to a level of automaticity, which means they know the answer instantly (Katims & Harmon, 2000).

Once automaticity is reached, the teacher transfers the responsibility for modeling to the students. Students independently practice the use of the strategy while they review the material. In addition to independent practice, students participate in small- and whole-group practice. Students perform the assigned tasks in small groups, work cooperatively, compare work, and participate in discussions, to name just a few practices that can occur at this stage. Bakkan and Wheldon (2002) point out the importance of providing opportunities for students to have ample practice in a new skill they are trying to master. Teacher modeling is recommended when students are just acquiring a skill (the acquisition stage). Modeling is effective for all levels and ethnic groups of students with special needs (Rivera & Smith, 1988).

Duffy, Roehler, and Rackliff (1986) described a think-aloud for low-achieving readers. In this think-aloud, teachers talk about their thought processes and the steps to the strategy. We have modeled the following think-aloud after theirs.

> Mr. Rodriquez begins: Today, I'd like to share with you a strategy I use when I come to a word that I don't know when I'm reading. I'll think out loud so you can hear my thoughts.
>
> **First,** I read the unknown word in the sentence. The weather forecaster said there will be snow flurries. I know I've heard the word *flurries* before, but I don't know what it means.

My **second** step is to see if there are any other words in that sentence that can help me figure out the word. The word before *flurries* is *snow*, so it has something to do with snow. Hm. It may mean it's going to snow a lot or it may mean it isn't going to snow much.

The **third** step is to read more of the sentences. OK, I'll read on. The next sentence says, "When the little boy heard the weather report, he became angry, because he wanted to build a snowman."

The **fourth** step is to use any background information. I think that sentence can help me figure the word out, because I know that you have to have a lot of snow to build a snowman. My brother and I used to make snowmen all the time.

The **fifth** step is to guess at the meaning. Now I bet I know what *flurries* means. I think it means light snow.

The **last** step is to substitute the meaning and reread the sentences. Let me go back and check. "The weather forecaster said there will be snow flurries or light snow. When the little boy heard the weather report, he became angry, because he wanted to build a snowman." Yep, I'm right.

Teacher–Student Dialoguing

In reciprocal teaching, Palincsar and Brown (1984) teach students to generate their own questions and to ask questions of others as they compose a dialogue to learn new information (see Chapter 7). After writing the following two-syllable words (*chimney, open, coaster, intend*, and *today*) on the overhead, Mr. Leonard asks the students if they think these words are alike in any way. No student replies, so Mr. Leonard continues with, "Any idea of how we might go about figuring it out?" One of the student replies, "Maybe, we should look at individual letters." Another student says, "Maybe, we should try to say the words and that would help." The teacher asks, "Any other ideas?" "Which one do you think we should try?" The class decides, as a group, to pronounce the words and see if that will help. The teacher asks if anyone would like to read the first word. The dialogue continues in the same manner until the class concludes that the commonality is that the words contain two parts and that the parts are called syllables.

Scaffolding Instruction

Previously in the chapter, we discussed how scaffolding can decrease the complexity of subject matter. In this section, we describe some scaffolding procedures that can be used in the body of the lesson. Remember, in scaffolding, teachers assist and support students until students can complete the task independently. Hogan and Pressley (1997) suggest that teachers assist students through prompting, questioning, modeling, telling, and discussing. Rosenshine (1990) recommends the use of procedural facilitators and anticipation of students' errors as specific scaffolding strategies.

Procedural facilitators may include hints or prompts, cue cards, and half-done examples. Listing the steps of rounding hundreds, beginning with the first step of "Look at the number in the tens position" provides hints to students. Montague and Leavell (1994) used grammar cue cards to improve the quality and length of stories by junior high students with learning disabilities. The cue cards contained key words such as *where, when, characters, problem and plan*, and *story ending*. These key words reminded students to include this information in their stories. Half-done examples provide questions or statement starters, such as "That doesn't sound right because *cold* means _____," for students to complete.

In anticipating student errors, effective teachers point out the material that is easily misunderstood. For example, Mr. Anderson, in discussing the spelling of *all right*, mentioned that most students forget that it is two words and spell it as *alright*. It may be difficult to anticipate mistakes at first, but with experience you will begin to recognize content that may prove particularly troublesome for students.

Foorman and Torgesen (2001) describe a scaffolding procedure that directly shows children who are at risk for reading difficulties the thinking or process necessary to complete a reading task successfully. First, the student is presented with a reading task (read the word *emergency*). When the student makes an error or doesn't know how to proceed (reads the word *emergency* as *emercy*), the teacher asks a question that "focuses the child's attention on a first step in the solution process, or that draws attention to the required piece of information" (p. 209). For example, "You are correct on the first part of the word *emer*; let's look at this part, *gency*. Any ideas?" The child responds again. The questioning and prompting continue until the student discovers the information without being told directly.

Lecturing

Often, at the secondary level, especially in an inclusive classroom, you may collaborate with a teacher who presents information through the lecturing technique. During lecturing teachers should limit the time they spend talking, because research shows that active student involvement is essential during lesson presentation (Christenson, Ysseldyke, & Thurlow, 1989).

Some effective adaptations to ensure that students with disabilities are engaged during a lecture is to use the instructional-pause procedure, think-pair-share routine, Numbered Heads Together (NHT; Kagan, 1992), guided note taking, and visual aids (Stringfellow & Miller, 2005).

Instructional-Pause Procedure In the instructional-pause procedure, the teacher lectures and then allows time for student discussion. During the brief discussion, the students may identify the main idea and important points and predict the next section of the lecture, or they may share notes and review information. In a secondary social studies class, the following coteaching instructional-pause procedure was established. The general educator, Mr. Green, lectured for 10 minutes, then had the students repeat the important points in small peer groups for about 3 minutes while he and the special education teacher monitored the comments of the various groups. Both teachers then listed the major points on an overhead projector, asked questions of the groups to summarize the relevant features of the lecture, and clarified any misunderstandings that they heard while monitoring the group discussions.

Think-Pair-Share Routine In the think-pair-share routine, the teacher asks students in pairs to think about the topic for a minute, discuss it, and then share their ideas with the rest of the group. Mr. Green and his coteacher could just as easily incorporate this routine during the social studies class.

Numbered Heads Together To use NHT, teachers divide students into heterogeneous learning teams and have students number themselves 1 to 5. The teacher continues to lecture and ask questions. After asking a question, instead of calling on one student, the teacher directs the students to put their heads together to arrive at the best answer and to make certain that everyone in their group knows and understands the answer. The teacher then randomly calls on different students to respond (all 3s tell the answer). Other class members then argue or expand on the answer. When NHT was used in a third-grade social studies class and a sixth-grade science class, students with and without disabilities performed better on exams and had higher on-task rates than those in whole-group instruction (Maheady, Harper, & Malette, 2001).

Guided Note Taking With guided note taking, students are actively involved during a lecture as they complete a teacher-prepared handout to assist them in taking notes from the lecture. The guided note handout consists of cues and spaces for students to write key facts, concepts, and important relationships while the teacher is lecturing. For example, guided notes concerning the taxes levied by the British on the colonists may include a statement that says:

1. To increase revenue, the British decided to levy _____ on the colonists. Some of the products taxed were
   a. _____
   b. _____
   c. _____

Guided notes resulted in the taking of more accurate notes and in improved quiz scores for middle and secondary students with disabilities (Heward, 1994). Guided notes should include the use of consistent cues (lines, bullets, etc.), more than a simple fill-in-the-blank format, daily quizzes as a follow-up activity, and minimal student writing, along with the inclusion of all facts, concepts, and relationships that students must learn (Boyle & Weishaar, 2001; Hamilton, Seibert, Gardner, & Talbert-Johnson, 2000; Heward, 1994). In Chapter 10, we discuss guided notes in detail with more examples.

Visual Aids With PowerPoint, movie-editing software, and other publishing technology, teachers can easily prepare visual aids and short movies listing the important points of a lecture. The students may either copy notes from the prepared materials or receive copies of the prepared materials (CD of movie or handouts of PowerPoint slides), transparencies. For example, Ms. Montgomery prepared a PowerPoint presentation to correlate with her lecture on the effects of global warming. She also provided students with copies of the handouts in a student packet that contained three slides per page (for handouts choose the 3 slides per page option of the print command of the PowerPoint program). Then, students added any extra points that came up during the discussions.

Questioning

Teachers use questioning during lesson presentation to elicit student involvement (Engelmann & Carnine, 1982), to foster cognitive learning (Florida Performance Measurement System, 1984), to reinforce concepts, and to monitor and adjust instruction (Puntambekar & Kolodner, 2005). Teachers may also teach students to generate their own questions. One teacher uses Solo plastic plates and dry-erase markers daily in her class to allow all students a chance to compose and participate in question development and responses in her classroom. Students are provided an old sock to clean their plate and they are each set to provide answers to all questions posted. In summarizing the critical findings in a synthesis of research conducted with students with learning disabilities, Vaughn, Gersten, and Chard (2000) report that directed response questioning or teaching students to generate their own questions while reading, solving math problems, or composing an essay produced a strong impact on student learning. Teaching students to self-question is discussed extensively in Chapter 7 under metacognition and other cognitive strategies.

Involving Students Questioning students is a way to increase their academic responding time. Academic responding time is the time that students spend making active, overt responses. It is positively related to achievement (Greenwood, Delquadri, & Hall, 1984). Even though teacher questioning can effectively involve all students, low-achieving students are not given as many opportunities to respond in

BOX 5.2

Reflections on Practice

Bloom's Taxonomy of cognitive development was first published in 1956 and in the years hence it has been used extensively as a framework for educational objectives. In 2001 the original Taxonomy was revised to more accurately reflect the continuum of how students progress through stages when learning new concepts (Anderson & Krathwohl, 2001). The revised Taxonomy (as it is referred to) is now a two-dimensional concept, rather than the one-dimensional list it evolved from.

In the original Taxonomy, *knowledge* was the first of six categories. The revised Taxonomy views *knowledge* as one of the two dimensions of learning and breaks it down into four separate categories: *factual knowledge, conceptual knowledge, procedural knowledge,* and *metacognitive knowledge.* The metacognitive category is new to the Taxonomy and reflects what we now know to be an important aspect of learning (Krathwohl, 2002).

The second dimension to the revised Taxonomy is the six categories of *the cognitive process.* These resemble the original six categories, but some have been renamed to better reflect terminology that teachers use, some have been placed in different order, and we now are asked to view the categories as sometimes overlapping rather than discrete stages of learning. The new categories, in order of concrete to abstract, are: *remember, understand, apply, analyze, evaluate,* and *create.* As Table 5.4 illustrates, now that these category names are all verbs, they translate easily into stems for effective questioning before, during, and after instruction.

class as other students (Reid, 1986). Teachers advance the following reasons for not calling on low achievers: to protect the student from embarrassment, to prevent a slowdown of the lesson, and to ensure that everyone will hear a good answer (Christenson, Thurlow, & Ysseldyke, 1987). To ensure that every student is given an opportunity to respond to questions, you may call on students in a fixed order or put each student's name on a Popsicle stick and put them in a cup, then call on the name you pull from the cup. Another strategy to involve all students is to call on students with disabilities first whenever you ask a question with many parts. For example, a question such as "What were the three causes of the uprising?" is easier for a student to answer when first asked than after other students have responded with two causes. You also might provide the student with a disability with a cue (e.g., when I stand near your desk) as to when they might be called upon (LaVoie, 1989). Sousa (2001) reports that anxiety greatly reduces the ability to recall information. See Table 5.4 for sample question stems.

Wait Time Two types of wait time are connected with questioning. One involves the amount of time a teacher waits for a student's response after asking a question. The other concerns the amount of time a teacher waits to ask another question after a student's response. Tobin (1987) in analysis of wait-time research found that, when 3 seconds or more of wait time was used, student learning increased. When teachers increased the amount of wait time, students responded with longer answers, volunteered answers more frequently, and even initiated more questions.

In a review of wait-time research, Tobin (1987) stated that a 3- to 5-second wait time enhanced achievement in all content areas with all levels of students, kindergarten through 12th grade. Wait time is also important for bilingual students who have language-processing difficulties (Watson, Northcutt, & Rydele, 1989).

Table 5.4 Sample Question Stems Based on Bloom's Revised Taxonomy

1. Remember
   Who, what, when, and where
2. Understand
   What is the main idea . . . ? What is meant by . . . ?
3. Apply
   How would you . . . ? What would happen if . . . ?
4. Analyze
   Why? What was the author's purpose in . . . ?
5. Evaluate
   Which is better . . . ? What do you think . . . ? Would you tend to agree that . . . ?
6. Create
   Do you suppose that . . . ? What if . . . ?

Activity 5.7

Ask your peer a lower level question about Bloom's Taxonomy and count the amount of wait time needed for a response.

Now ask a question about Bloom's Taxonomy from the highest level and record the amount of wait time required for a response.

How did this time differ and what implications does this have for you as a teacher?

IMPORTANT POINTS

1. When opening a lesson, gain student attention through an area of interest and connect to the students' lives.
2. Modeling may involve a think-aloud, where teachers or students share their thought processes.
3. Questioning is used to elicit active student involvement, to foster cognitive learning, reinforce concepts, monitor, and adjust instruction.
4. In scaffolding, teachers provide just the right level of support to ensure students' progress towards mastery of a skill.
5. Effective teachers use a wait time of 3–5 seconds.

GUIDED PRACTICE

Guided practice is active participation directed by the teacher. After presenting subject matter, the teacher leads the students in practice of the information. Often, guided practice is alternated with teacher modeling and demonstration, so that presentation and practice appear as one (Rosenshine & Stevens, 1986). A common practice routine in general education classrooms is to call on one student to demonstrate the answer to a problem on the board while other students watch. To increase the active participation of and extra practice for all students, simply have the other students complete the problem at their desks. One of our interns supplied her students with small individual chalkboards while another used small dry-erase boards.

Guided practice activities must align with the objective of the lesson and actively involve the students. Guided practice is used to ensure errorless learning for students with disabilities. Also be certain to provide students with any adaptations that they will be allowed to use on state or local assessments. Students being allowed to use supports such as calculators need to know how to use these accommodations as they are mastering the task in guided practice. For example, if the objective of the lesson is to write a descriptive sentence, then guided practice activities should involve students writing descriptive sentences, not identifying which of two sentences is a descriptive one. If, for this activity, a student will be allowed either a scribe or some type of word-processing tool, then these accommodations should be used during guided practice. Also during guided practice, effective teachers provide prompts, check for understanding, repeat-and-rephrase lesson content, provide examples and nonexamples, and give feedback (Rosenshine & Stevens, 1986). Often, a teacher continues with guided practice until students reach a mastery level, usually 80% (Brophy, 1980).

Active Responding

Students need to be actively involved in responding to questions to allow the teacher to assess students' mastery of content. If wait time and a cue word are not used, the fastest and brightest students often blurt out the answers. Interspersing choral responses or response cards with individual responses tends to keep students actively involved.

Choral Responding Choral responding is an effective strategy for providing practice for students with disabilities (Stringfellow & Miller, 2005). Choral responding was found to be more effective than turn taking in teaching sight words to elementary students with learning disabilities or mild mental disabilities (Sindelar, Bursuck, & Halle, 1986). The normal choral-responding routine is to ask a question or model a response, pause, cue students to respond together, and give feedback (see "Reading Mastery" in Chapter 7). For example, after telling students that an adjective tells which, what kind of, or how many, the teacher signals, pauses, and asks, "On the count of 3 please everyone respond, what does an adjective tell?" Then all the students respond and the teacher acknowledges with feedback, "Absolutely correct, a perfect answer." Notice in the preceding example that a cue word, *everyone*, was used to elicit the group response but wait time was incorporated to allow all students a chance to process the question. Heward, Courson, and Narayan (1989) recommend the use of choral responding when a short and specific answer is required and when presenting information at a fast pace.

Response Cards Response cards may be used instead of oral choral responding. Studies show that elementary and middle school students with or without disabilities participated more, scored higher on quizzes, and preferred response cards as compared to hand raising and one-student-at-a-time recitation in answering teachers' questions during math, social studies, and science classes (Narayan, Heward, Gardner, Courson, & Omness, 1990). Skinner, Pappas, and Davis (2005) talk about how the use of various response techniques including response cards allows students to choose to participate, reducing behavior issues and increasing achievement. Ms. Otto used 3-by-5-inch cards in a nonverbal guided practice activity involving adjectives and adverbs for middle school students. She passed out two cards to each student and had them write ***adjective*** on one card and ***adverb*** on the other. She also made two cards for herself. She read a sentence written on the transparency (e.g., "The dilapidated window shutter was flapping wildly in the breeze."), asked a question (e.g., "What part of speech is ***dilapidated***?"), followed by a pause, then cued the students to respond in unison (e.g., "Now"). Upon hearing the cue word, the students held up one of the cards. At the same time, she held up her adjective card so students could compare their answers with hers.

Other ways to get students to respond include a tool called gel boards that are similar to inexpensive Etch-a-sketches that can fit into students' 3-ring binders. These boards allow all students to respond. Other inexpensive ways to create response boards are to buy either chalkboard contact paper or chalkboard spray paint. Put the material on a sturdy box like a refrigerator box. Provide students with a piece of chalk and an old sock and they are set to respond individually to all questions posed. You may also wish to preprint some general cards for some students such as Yes/No or True/False that students can use for any curriculum. Whatever type of response cards you may choose to use, model several question-and-answer trials first, elicit many responses during a short time period of about 5 or 10 minutes, provide cue words such as *everyone*, give specific feedback based on the majority response, repeat items missed, and allow students to look at their peers' response cards (Heward, Gardner, Cavanaugh, Courson, Grossi, & Barbetta, 1996).

Activity 5.8

How would you correct the following lesson?

The teacher asked students a question and then answered her own question immediately. Next she asked the class a question and after 1 second allowed the first student who raised her hand to answer.

CLOSING

Frequently, the lesson ends with (a) a review of the information presented (Archer & Isaacson, 1990; Schumaker, 1989), (b) a preview of the future use for the information (Archer & Isaacson, 1990; Schumaker, 1989), (c) a statement of expectations (Archer & Isaacson, 1990; Schumaker, 1989), (d) a cue to chart progress or self-evaluate (Palincsar, 1986; Schumaker, 1989), and (e) an introduction of the independent work (Archer & Isaacson, 1990) plus a generalization activity. We like to call this closure with generalization. In this phase of the lesson students are given a task in closing the lesson that will generalize to their home setting or can be used to loop back into class the next day. Following is an example of each feature of closure.

Review

Students or teachers may review the major points of lessons with summaries or by asking questions, for example, "Today we discussed the three types of sentences. What was the first type of sentence, Shari?" or "Shari, please summarize what you learned today." The generalization feature would be to say to all students, "When you go home tonight, try to find one of each of the three types of sentences in the newspaper and share them with a family member." Another review strategy (used by one of our interns) is called "Whip or Pass." The students are all asked to summarize the chapter with two words. This review is conducted at a rapid pace, like a whip, but if students do not know a word, they simply say pass. This strategy allows everyone to participate in a review, but allows students to either repeat an answer they already heard or pass if they cannot think of a two-word summary. To close the review, the teacher instructs the class, "Please remember at least two of the words you heard as your password to come into class tomorrow."

Preview

Teachers frequently use previews to tie together information. One teacher created a visual timeline of each chapter in the science book. The students then previewed past visual images on the timeline and then talked about what they expected to learn next.

Expectations

You may either summarize how students met your behavior expectations or what they may expect as a result of their new knowledge. For example, one of our student teachers, in commenting on behavior expectations of the tenth graders, noted: "You all worked hard today and completed your charts on plant growth. I especially like that you remembered to write down key components about your plants and you listened to others without interruptions as they commented on their plants' changes. Thank you."

Self-Evaluation

You may have students monitor their own progress using any of the procedures discussed in Chapter 4. In the self-advocacy strategy, VanReusen, Bos, Schumaker, and Deshler (1994) have students keep track of their mastery of the strategy using goal dates and completion dates.

FEEDBACK

Feedback often proceeds in the following cycle: Teacher asks a question or elicits a response, students respond, teacher evaluates answer and gives feedback (Pressley, Hogan, Wharton-McDonald, Mistretta, & Ettenberger, 1996). Teachers give feedback by acknowledging, amplifying, rephrasing, and correcting (Anderson, Evertson, & Brophy, 1979; Florida Performance Measurement System, 1984).

Acknowledgment

Acknowledgment involves telling a student that an answer is correct or wrong, such as "Yes, that is correct" or "No, that is not correct." Acknowledgment also involves the use of specific praise. Specific praise requires specification of the appropriate behavior. It is not merely "Terrific," but "Good reading" or "Good remembering." Stating a specific behavior (reading, remembering) helps students recognize why they are receiving positive statements from you. They know the exact behavior that earned the positive statement. In response to a general statement like "Good job," a student may think, "Oh, yes, I read well," or "Oh, the teacher must be in a good mood today." Many students with special needs, especially emotional disturbances, have problems connecting a behavior with the praise when the behavior is not specified. Soldier (1989) recommends praising a student's efforts rather than the product. Positive comments also are extremely important for students who are at risk (Lago-Delello, 1998).

Positive comments may also be made in the feedback of written products. Marking the correct items in color or writing positive comments on the paper ("Excellent printing," "Great idea") take a little more time, but they help students view school more positively.

Amplification and Rephrasing

Amplification is expansion of a student's response by either the teacher or another student, such as "Yes, Jim, you are correct. We do multiply to solve that problem and the reason we do that is . . ." or "Yes, Sue, that is a good start. Now, Pat, would you explain it further?" Amplification is used during the teaching of learning strategies to help students discriminate between good and poor student modeling of the teacher's think-aloud (Schumaker, 1989). Rephrasing is often used to emphasize the steps or methods used to arrive at a correct answer (e.g., "Yes, Jimmy, you first divide and then you multiply.") or to repeat the relevant points of a lesson (e.g., "Yes, that's correct, the rule is *i* before *e* except after *c*.") (Anderson, Evertson, & Brophy, 1979).

Correction

Correcting a wrong response usually follows a supply or scaffolding format, or adaptations of them. A teacher who employs the supply format simply supplies or has another student supply the correct answer. For example, after a student's incorrect response, you or another student model the correct one ("No, the word is *heat*." or "Susie, please read the word."), lead the student ("Let's say it together."), and test the student ("Now, you read the word."). Alternatively, you may just model and test, as in "No, the word is *heat*. What word?" (Engelmann & Carnine, 1982; Meyer, 1986).

With the scaffolding format, the teacher follows up the question with more questions, prompts, and hints "to probe students' understandings and as a guide for individualized instruction, rather than for evaluation only" (Pressley et al., 1996, p. 142). For example, now you may suggest a strategy ("Is this a word that can be sounded out?") or provide information that the student can use to deduce the correct answer ("Try using the silent 'e' rule to sound out the word."). With either format, the process should end with the student responding with the correct answer (Collins, Carnine, & Gersten, 1987).

Activity 5.9

Student Teacher 1 asked a first-grade student to use the word *we* in a sentence. The student said, "We goed to the store." Provide a correction using the supply format; using a scaffolding format.

Student Teacher 2 responded, "That's correct," when a student answered the question about why the moon changes phases while at the same time the student shouted out the answer without raising his hand. How could this teacher use more specific praise?

INDEPENDENT PRACTICE

The final part of lesson instruction should involve students practicing on their own. At this stage, if independence has not occurred then more guided practice is needed.

Introducing the Independent Practice Activity

You should discuss the directions of the activity and then check for student comprehension of the directions. Remember, "Do you understand?" is not an effective question. Remember to complete at least a sample problem in class or provide an example for all students. Many of our students may go home to one of two scenarios. Either they are home alone to complete their homework or many of our curricular standards have increased so greatly that parents may not be able to support students without a model. Don't forget to also build in generalization activities that include the use of the information in the natural setting. For example, in a lesson on nutrition, have students keep track of what they eat for breakfast for a week and then have them sort the foods into groups such as dairy, protein, etc.

When students are making few errors during guided practice, they should move to independent practice activities (Rosenshine & Stevens, 1986). Independent practice activities are completed by students with minimal teacher assistance. Independent practice should result in fluency, maintenance, and generalization of skills. Teachers must design generalization activities, as students with disabilities often have a difficult time relating content they are learning to other settings and situations. For example, if you are teaching the job-related social skill of giving compliments appropriately, you may assign an activity that requires students to record each time they give compliments at home for one week.

Independent practice is not to be confused with a student's interacting with a worksheet. Ineffective teachers often expect students to learn too much from worksheets (Rieth, et al., 1987; Rosenshine & Stevens, 1986). It is appropriate to use worksheets during independent practice, but only to reinforce a concept that has already been taught. Remember, independent practice should relate to objectives and guided practice activities, even though new examples are provided. For example, if the objective of the lesson is to identify possessive nouns, then students should practice the identification of possessive nouns during both guided and independent practice activities. Also remember to consider limiting the amount of independent practice for students who take a great deal of time to complete homework. One teacher and parent had an agreement that the child would do no more than 60 minutes of homework each night. If after working on an assignment for 60 minutes, the student had not completed the task but was giving his maximum effort, then the parent was empowered to sign the remaining work and the student would not be penalized for partial completion of the work. Although homework is important, students with disabilities also need to have a life beyond school, so close communication with parents regarding independent practice is critical.

A success rate of 90% to 100% is suggested for independent practice of basic skills for effective learning (Christenson, Thurlow, & Ysseldyke, 1987). To ensure a 90% success rate, give instructions telling what you expect during the independent activity and, if necessary, adapt the activities. Paik (2003) lists principles that improve learning and focus specifically on the need for direct instruction and independent practice with over a 90% success rate. These strategies include (a) parental involvment and partnerships, (b) homework and feedback, (c) goal setting and time on task, (d) direct teaching, (e) advance organizers, (f) teaching and learning strategies, (g) peer tutoring, (h) cooperative learning, and (i) adaptive education.

Some teachers choose to have students develop creative exhibition types of tasks for homework such as: write a song, create a 3-minute play, draw a CD cover with 10 song titles, all of which can be adapted for any learner. Refer to Chapter 6 for other ways to develop and adapt materials and assignments.

MONITORING STUDENT PRACTICE

Instead of sitting at their desks, effective teachers circulate and give extra help and individual feedback during independent practice (Brophy & Evertson, 1977). However, if you need to spend more than a few minutes explaining a problem to a student, you should probably reteach that lesson. Beginning teachers often run into management problems during independent practice because they spend too much time with one student or they position themselves with their backs to the other students, making it impossible to monitor behaviors. Try playing some classical music during independent practice if you want students to work quietly. Students want to fill silence, so some soft music allows for noise but nothing distracting. Carlson, Gray, Hoffman, and Thompson (2004) found that playing classical music at about 60 beats per minute impacts students' reading gains.

EVALUATION

The last step in the instructional cycle is to evaluate whether students have learned the skills, strategies, and content of the lesson. Chapter 3 provides numerous ideas and techniques for ongoing informal evaluation. The evaluation process is critical to identify mastery as well as gaps in learning, as students and teachers are being held more and more accountable for a level of state and national proficiency on numerous assessments. Evaluation procedures should be aligned with the lesson objectives, guided practice, and independent practice and be ongoing and formative and summative. For example, if the objective of the lesson is to teach students to write descriptive sentences, then students should practice writing descriptive sentences during guided and independent practice activities and be evaluated on how well they write descriptive sentences (formative), but the complexity of sentences, number of paragraphs, and pages of text (depending on the age) students produce over time should also be evaluated (summative). Summative evaluations are at the core of ensuring that students are reaching the benchmarks that will be evaluated on state and local assessments.

In Chapter 4, we discussed different ways to monitor student progress. The procedures of precision teaching, curriculum-based measurements, and numerous alternative assessments are effective methods to evaluate individual lessons. For example, Mr. LaRue has students chart the number of words they read correctly during the reading of a story. Ms. Smythe observes the strategies students use in solving math problems as she moves from one student to another during independent practice. Ms. Gonzalez uses oral questions to check comprehension. Some general evaluation guidelines are to specify the criteria, vary evaluation methods, and teach students to self-evaluate and reflect on the teaching episode.

SPECIFY THE CRITERIA

Students need to know how you plan to evaluate them, especially if the student is being assessed in an alternative format. Too many times we see students receive adapted assessments, tools, or grading criteria but often the students are not informed of this alternative outcome they are expected to meet. One way to share evaluation expectations is to use expert products (Rosenshine, 1990). With expert products, you present the students with a project that you feel demonstrates the quality of work you expect.

Another way to specify criteria is to prepare a holistic or analytic scoring rubric (see Chapter 4). Rubrics are used in most states for assessing proficiency in written language. For example, the organization standard of the essay accounts for 30% of the total score, the sentence structure standard for 25%, usage accounts for 20%, mechanics for 20%, and format for 5%. Now, students know that a high-level score of 5 on the sentence structure standard not only meets the indicator of "sentences are complete and varied in length and structure" but also is worth 25% of the final essay grade. Check the World Wide Web for already developed rubrics and tools to assist you in creating your own rubrics.

One of our student teachers presented students with an evaluation sheet as they began an assignment. Before he divided students into cooperative groups to write a report about Ohio, he presented them with a checklist of items such as (a) Did you describe three of the major occupations of the state? (12 points) and (b) Did you write complete sentences in the two-page report? (10 points). Thus, he shared with his students the information he expected to see on the report and the importance of including it. He also listed the point value for each question on an exam or quiz and taught students to spend more time answering the questions worth more points. Then two students received a modified rubric that said they only had to list two items about Ohio and provide a 3-minute oral report. All of the students were focused on the same goal but the way they demonstrated knowledge of the goal varied.

VARY WAYS TO EVALUATE

Teachers frequently use worksheets or pencil-and-paper tests to evaluate performance. Many other ways exist for students to show what they have learned. You may allow students to give an oral report, complete a homework project, choose from a list of 10 ways to exhibit their knowledge, or prepare a portfolio. In the section on motivation, we presented a sample choice sheet for secondary students to select ways to demonstrate their knowledge. When you give students choices at any level, you are providing for the different learning preferences of students, which makes the experience more meaningful. Evaluation should be linked to meaningful and relevant tasks that allow students to compensate for their disabilities and to show they have achieved the lesson outcomes.

TEACH STUDENTS TO SELF-EVALUATE AND SELF-ADVOCATE

In Chapter 4, we discussed strategies to teach students to self-evaluate as they monitor their progress in the general education classroom setting and as they complete their portfolios. Self-evaluation is an important aspect of authentic evaluation, as evidenced in its use in portfolio assessment, learning logs, and journals. One of our interns required her secondary students to complete a brief daily journal entry. During the last 15 minutes of class, the students independently or in a small group answered the questions: (a) What did you learn today? and (b) Do you have any concerns? She then responded to the entries and used their concerns to reteach any confusing information during the next day's lesson.

Another intern and her primary students listed items for students to evaluate before turning in written assignments. The students answered yes or no to these items on a separate sheet of paper and then attached the paper to their required assignments: (1) Did I use my best handwriting?, (2) Did I remember to write my name and date on the paper?, and (3) Does my paper look neat?

A middle school teacher asked her students to keep ongoing data of their progress and then they prepared a PowerPoint presentation for their IEP meeting to share their strengths, concerns, and vision for their future. Overall the students took great pride and ownership in their presentations and in their education.

BOX 5.3

Reflections on Practice

On the first day of school ask students to fill out an interest inventory, which typically consists of open-ended questions. Include specific questions about their preferences as a learner. For example, you may ask, "How do you like to share what you have learned: (a) write a paper, (b) draw a picture, (c) complete a group project, or (d) other." Also ask the student's parent(s) to write a letter that includes the student's strengths, areas of focus, and any other information they might like to share to help you meet the needs of their child.

In a local high school students were provided with a self-advocacy program in which they were asked to create portfolios and to write a statement for the teachers about their disabilities. Then students made appointments with their general education teachers to advocate for their own needs. This type of self-advocacy program prepares students for accessing services on their own, in the work place, or in college.

COMPLETE A SELF-EVALUATION

Effective teachers frequently reflect on the teaching episode (Costa & Garmston, 1994). The use of videotapes, cognitive coaching, student evaluations, and self-questioning are multiple ways of gathering data for reflection. Schon (1983), in his work on reflection, shares that two types of reflection happen in our field—reflection on action and reflection in action. Some questions you may wish to ask for as part of a reflection are: (a) What did I want to have happen? (b) Is what happened different? (c) What strategy was particularly effective today? (d) What strategy didn't work as well as I thought? (e) How should I change what happened? and (f) What did I learn that I may use in the future?

As discussed previously, teachers constantly monitor the effectiveness of their teaching strategies as the lesson is progressing. However, no matter how carefully a teacher has planned, there are some days that lessons do not go as expected. Some things that can be done when this happens are:

1. Change the grouping structure, directing students to work with partners in completing the task or worksheets, pairing students who understand with those who do not.
2. Stop the lesson and review what was discussed the day before or move on to a different subject area or activity.
3. Before assigning independent work, give a couple of problems for students to complete. Assign independent work to those students who completed the problems correctly on their own, but continue instruction with those students who did not complete the problems correctly.
4. Tell the students that the lesson doesn't seem to be going well and ask if they have any suggestions.
5. Stop the lesson and use an activity to review previously taught skills.

IMPORTANT POINTS

1. Guided practice is teacher-led practice that must be aligned with the objective and independent practice. Examples of guided practice activities are repeated reading, repetitive routines, and choral responding.
2. Frequently, lessons close with a review of the information presented or a preview of the future use for the information.
3. Independent practice activities should relate to objectives; and guided practice activities reinforce previously taught information, even though new examples are provided.
4. Evaluation procedures must be aligned with the lesson objectives, guided practice, and independent practice.
5. General guidelines to follow in evaluation are to specify the criteria, vary evaluation methods, teach students to self-evaluate, and reflect on the teaching episode.

LESSON PLAN

As a way of summarizing the parts of the instructional cycle, Figure 5.4 contains a sample lesson plan. Notice that a short explanation is given in parentheses after each section of the plan.

Figure 5.4 SAMPLE LESSON PLAN

Objective: When presented with an independent practice sheet of 10 fractions, students will write equivalent fractions with 90% accuracy. (Fractions were identified on each of the students' IEPs.)

Subject Matter Content:
For presentation: Concept
Definition—Equivalent fractions are fractions that name the same number (from text, *Applying Mathematics,* 1986, Laidlaw Brothers, p. 538.)
Attribute—Equivalent fractions are equal.
Examples—$1/2 = 2/4 = 4/8 = 8/16$, $1/4 = 2/8 = 4/16$, $1/8 = 2/16$, $2/4 = 4/8 = 8/16$, etc.
Nonexamples—$1/2 = 3/4$, $1/4 = 3/8$, $1/8 = 4/16$, $2/4 = 7/8$, etc.

For review: Basic concept/skill—write fractions from pictures. Examples—see Transparency A.
Basic concept/skill—identification of fraction kits

Curriculum standard: Students in grades 3–5 are expected to recognize and generate equivalent forms of commonly used fractions, decimals, and percents in the understanding numbers standard.

(Since this is a concept, a definition, examples, nonexamples, and attributes were identified. Teacher reviewed prerequisite basic concepts/skills. See Step 4 of the plan and Transparency A. The curriculum standard was adapted from the National Council for Teachers of Mathematics Standards, 2001.)

Questions:
How many eighths are in one-half? How many fourths are in one-sixteenth?
Why aren't $3/4$ and $7/8$ equivalent fractions?
What does *equivalent* mean?
Are $1/2$ and $2/4$ equivalent fractions?
Why are these fractions equal?
How can you prove that the fractions are equal?

(Notice, the teacher identified both low- and high-level questions.)

Feedback:
Correct—You certainly know how to find equivalent fractions, well done, (name). You are absolutely correct, $1/2$ does equal $2/4$.
Incorrect—What was the first step? What fraction pieces do you think you need?

(Notice, the teacher plans to use specific praise and amplification for correct answers and a scaffolding strategy for incorrect.)

Ideas If Plan Is Not Working:
Do more Think-Alouds and modeling with the students drawing more examples on a blank transparency similar to those found on Transparency A, assign two students to work together on the independent practice sheet, or complete the independent practice sheet as a class.

Materials:
Math Journal
Teacher Fraction Kit (same as students' kits, but made from transparencies, produced by a graphics software program and color printer)
Students' Fraction Kits made from construction paper:
One sheet of yellow construction paper represents 1 whole.
One sheet of green construction paper cut into 2 equal pieces represents halves.
One sheet of blue construction paper cut into 4 equal pieces represents fourths.
One sheet of orange construction paper cut into 8 equal pieces represents eighths.
One sheet of purple construction paper cut into 16 equal pieces represents sixteenths.

(continued)

Figure 5.4 SAMPLE LESSON PLAN (*continued*)

Transparency A with pictures for review (Students must write the fraction from the picture.)

Transparency A

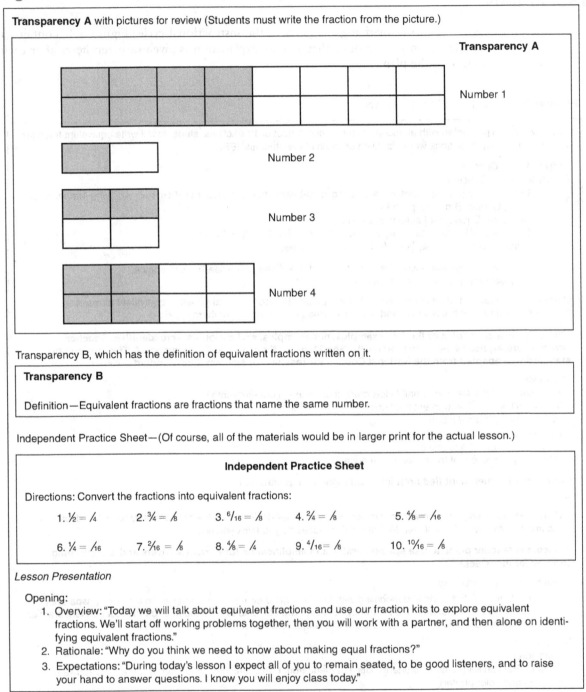

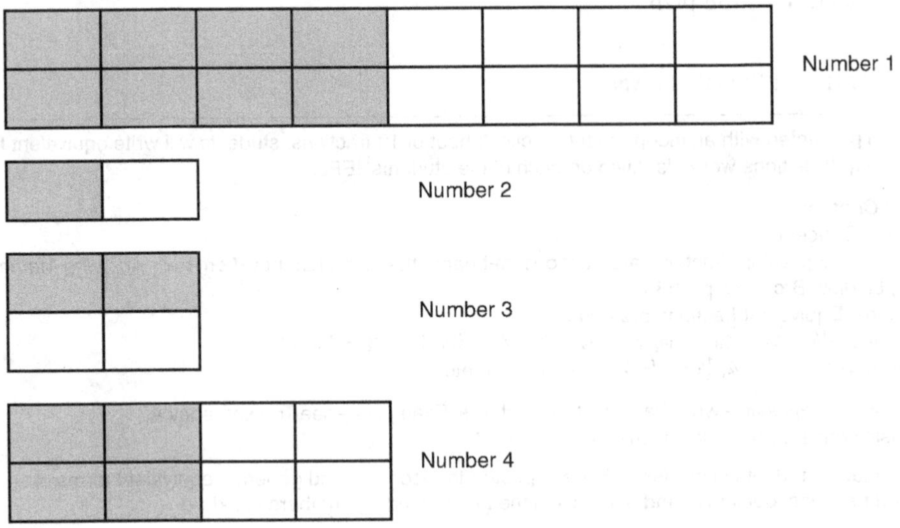

Transparency B, which has the definition of equivalent fractions written on it.

Transparency B

Definition—Equivalent fractions are fractions that name the same number.

Independent Practice Sheet—(Of course, all of the materials would be in larger print for the actual lesson.)

Independent Practice Sheet

Directions: Convert the fractions into equivalent fractions:

1. $\frac{1}{2} = \frac{}{4}$	2. $\frac{3}{4} = \frac{}{8}$	3. $\frac{6}{16} = \frac{}{8}$	4. $\frac{2}{4} = \frac{}{8}$	5. $\frac{4}{8} = \frac{}{16}$
6. $\frac{1}{4} = \frac{}{16}$	7. $\frac{2}{16} = \frac{}{8}$	8. $\frac{4}{8} = \frac{}{4}$	9. $\frac{4}{16} = \frac{}{8}$	10. $\frac{10}{16} = \frac{}{8}$

Lesson Presentation

Opening:

1. Overview: "Today we will talk about equivalent fractions and use our fraction kits to explore equivalent fractions. We'll start off working problems together, then you will work with a partner, and then alone on identifying equivalent fractions."
2. Rationale: "Why do you think we need to know about making equal fractions?"
3. Expectations: "During today's lesson I expect all of you to remain seated, to be good listeners, and to raise your hand to answer questions. I know you will enjoy class today."

Figure 5.4 SAMPLE LESSON PLAN (*continued*)

4. Review: "But, first, let's quickly review writing fractions and our fraction kit values."
   a. Show Transparency A and have students write down fractions on a sheet of paper. Then check with unison response, "Everyone, what is this fraction?" Give feedback.
   b. Hold up yellow construction paper and ask, "What do we call the yellow pieces of our fraction kit, everyone? Blue? Purple? Orange? Green?"

(Notice, the teacher selected overview, rationale, expectations, and review as components to use to introduce this lesson. She cued with "Everyone" in eliciting a student response and then gave feedback.)

Body:

5. After review, state and show the definition of equivalent fraction (Transparency B). Ask students questions about the definition. (Emphasize that they are equal parts of the whole.) Have students copy the definition into their math journals.
6. Model doing an equivalent fraction using Transparency A, Example 2, and fraction kit. "Let's see, I've identified that fraction as $\frac{1}{2}$ so I need to find all the fractions equivalent to $\frac{1}{2}$. Let me start by pulling out my green $\frac{1}{2}$ pieces from my fraction kit. Now, I'll pull out my fourth pieces, the blue ones from the kit. How many fourth pieces do I think equal the $\frac{1}{2}$ piece? Hm, let's try 3. Nope. That doesn't work. They do not fit on top of each other. So $\frac{1}{2}$ doesn't equal 3 pieces of the fourths or $\frac{3}{4}$. Let's try 2 pieces. They fit fine. So $\frac{1}{2}$ equals $\frac{2}{4}$. So $\frac{1}{2}$ and $\frac{2}{4}$ are equivalent fractions; they cover an equal portion of the whole. They are equal." (Write $\frac{1}{2} = \frac{2}{4}$ on the board.).
7. Do another example (Write $\frac{1}{2} = \frac{}{8}$ on the board.), asking students questions as they watch you, beginning with, "Now, I wonder if I can find an equal number of eighths to equal $\frac{1}{2}$. What should I do first, Jack?"

   (The teacher employed a think aloud type of modeling and then involved students in the modeling process.)

Guided Practice:

8. Have students take out their fraction kits. "Let's see if you can find an equal number of sixteenths. (Write $\frac{1}{2} = \frac{}{16}$ on the board.) What should you do first? Yes, start with your green or half sheet."
9. Do two more examples ($\frac{8}{16} = \frac{}{2}$, and $\frac{3}{4} = \frac{}{8}$), asking the students questions.
10. Divide the students into pairs, having one student show one fraction with the kit and another student the equivalent fraction. Model with two students first, "Jim and Jason are partners. They are working the problem of $\frac{6}{16} = \frac{}{8}$. Jason, show us $\frac{6}{16}$ with your fraction kit. Now, Jim, take out your eighths. What do you do now?" (Remember, to have students write both fractions.)
11. Circulate while students are working five more examples (taken from the examples listed in subject matter).
12. Call on each group to write one of the problems, explaining and showing how they got their answers. Then have all students copy the five examples into their Math Journal underneath the definition.

    (The teacher used peer tutoring, discussion, and teacher monitoring.)

Closing:

13. "Let's do a quick review. What is the definition of an equivalent fraction? How do you use your fraction kit to find an equivalent fraction?"
14. Share with students how they met expectations set at the beginning of the lesson.
15. Have students write what they learned from today's Math Lesson in their Math Journal.

    (The teacher asked questions and had students reflect on the lesson.)

Independent Practice:

16. Have the student helper pass out the worksheets. Go over the directions and do the first problem with the students. Remind the students that they may use their fraction kits. (See Independent Practice sheet in Materials section of plant.)
17. Have students interview parents to see how they use equivalent fractions. Write up the results for the 5 points extra credit.

    (The teacher made sure students understood the task using comprehansion checks and completing the first problem. Additionally, the teacher attempted to connect the lesson to real life experiences.)

Evaluation:

18. Circulate as the students are completing the worksheets. Plan to reteach the lesson to any student who scores less than 90%.

PUTTING IT ALL TOGETHER

In this chapter we have discussed the basic components of planning for instruction with critical reflections on the importance of motivation, high-stakes assessments, and the importance of instructional alignment with local and state evaluation procedures. Planning effective instruction aligned with standards is at the core of every school and classroom in our nation. Daily lessons must focus on high levels of questioning and ensure evaluations that monitor student progress toward the goal of proficiency in all content areas. The stakes are high for teachers as well as students in today's schools, and the only way to meet these high-stakes demands is through careful daily planning that maximizes student engagement in a positive learning environment—the art of effective teaching.

DISCUSSION QUESTIONS

1. Discuss how you plan to actively involve **all** your students during lesson presentation.
2. Research shows that motivation is further enhanced when (a) learning is personally relevant for students, (b) the classroom is comfortable and orderly, (c) students are accepted by peers and teachers, (d) the task is something the student values, (e) the students believe they can accomplish the task, and (f) the students are clear about what they are being asked to do. Describe how you plan to address these issues in your classroom.
3. Describe why guided practice is important for all students but especially important for students with special needs.

Websites: Useful websites related to chapter content can be found in Appendix A.

PART

2

Instructional Techniques

CHAPTER

6

Instructional Materials

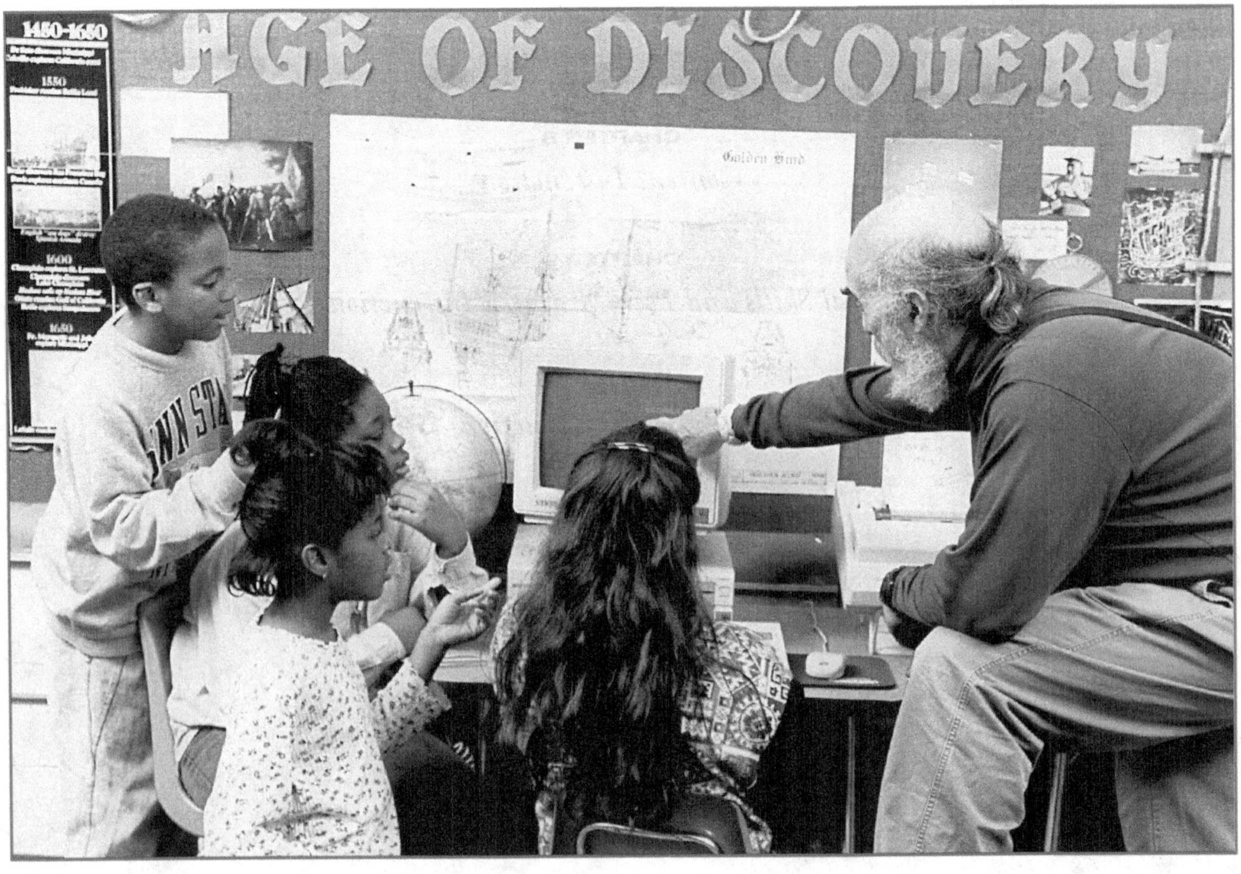

KEY TOPICS

Emily and her third grade-classmates were excitedly leafing through the pages of their new science textbooks on the first day of school. Their teacher, Mr. Alvarez, was pointing out the many beautiful photographs and the "fun facts" that appeared at the beginning of each chapter. After Mr. Alvarez thought that enough time had passed to explore the new textbook, he directed everyone to turn to the first lesson and begin reading Section One silently to themselves. Emily found the correct page and nervously began reading.

Last year Emily experienced many difficulties with reading. It just wasn't as easy for her as it seemed to be for everyone else. By the end of the school year she was diagnosed as having a learning disability, so it was decided that this year she would receive extra help from another teacher, Ms. Jacobs, who would come into Emily's third-grade classroom every day.

Emily tried to read Section One, but it was so hard to keep her eyes on the words with the amazing close-up photograph of the frog in the middle of the page. Actually, she wasn't quite sure which words she should be reading because there was a column of words down the side of the page, more words at the bottom of the page, and the heading for Section One was right over the frog. Emily raised her hand to ask Mr. Alvarez where she should begin just as he announced that it was time to stop reading and talk about what they had read. When Ms. Jacobs arrived, Mr. Alvarez immediately pulled her aside to let her know that Emily had not completed the assigned science reading. Ms. Jacobs could tell that Mr. Alvarez was quite frustrated, not only with Emily, but also with his own ability to keep his class focused on their new textbook. Ms. Jacobs took one look at the new book and smiled. It was easy to see why Mr. Alvarez was having such a hard time.

What do you think Ms. Jacobs noticed right away? If you were in her place, what would you recommend to Mr. Alvarez and, more importantly, what would you do for Emily to help her hold onto her initial enthusiasm for her new book?

Responses to these questions are found in the Instructor's Manual.

INTRODUCTION

The instructional materials you use are the nuts and bolts of your instructional program, the vehicles through which instruction is delivered. If your students are to achieve success in the classroom, the materials they use should produce appropriate learning outcomes, motivate them, and hold their interest. They must also be accessible to a wide range of students (Sperling, 2006).

The increased diversity among students in today's classrooms necessitates the use of adaptations to increase the likelihood that they will experience success in school (Miller, 2002) (see chapter opening scenario about Emily). In school districts where state-adopted textbooks and materials are used, teachers should be adept at modifying and adapting materials. Udvari-Solner (1997) recommends that general and special education teachers collaborate to design adaptations and accommodations as part of the curriculum. In districts where they are given choices in the selection process, teachers should be skilled in making sound choices based on students' needs. In this chapter, we present ways to select, analyze, adapt, and develop instructional materials along with strategies to modify/adapt tests. As you read this chapter, look for ideas that you might use with a student like Emily.

SELECTING INSTRUCTIONAL MATERIALS

The selection of appropriate instructional materials and activities is part of the process of individualizing and planning instruction for students. Many commercially produced instructional materials are available for use with students who have special needs. The suggestions in this section and throughout the chapter are appropriate for teachers to use with students with special needs who are receiving instruction in general education inclusive classrooms as well as in pull-out programs.

FACTORS INFLUENCING THE SELECTION OF INSTRUCTIONAL MATERIALS

Remember to exercise care in your selection of instructional materials. Attention to individual learner needs, interest and motivation levels of materials, opportunities for social interaction, and diversity increases the probability of success with commercially produced instructional materials.

Individual Learner Needs

In choosing materials, you should consider the fact that you will work with students who have a wide variety of needs, abilities, and individual differences and you will be addressing these needs, abilities, and differences in both general and special education settings. Instructional materials should be compatible with diverse learning and presentation styles; adaptable to a variety of disabilities; include supplementary items such as software, manipulatives, and games; allow for monitoring of student progress; and be developmentally, culturally, linguistically, age, gender, and interest appropriate for students.

Interest and Motivation Levels

Materials that are age appropriate, interesting, motivating, appealing, and related to real life are likely to be used by your students, particularly when you have given consideration to cultural backgrounds, gender, and interests. For example, some students benefit from using high-interest, low-vocabulary materials that are age and interest appropriate. Secondary students are often motivated by materials that relate to real life.

Jobe and Dayton-Sakari (2002) have provided a wonderful resource in their book, *Info-Kids: How to Use Nonfiction to Turn Reluctant Readers into Enthusiastic Learners.* This book recommends the use of nonfiction with students who are not interested in reading, but fascinated by facts and information, by giving them materials they will want to read. Examples include *This Book Really Sucks!* (the science behind tornadoes, black holes, vacuum cleaners, and other things that suck) by Jess Brallier; *Factastic Book of Comparisons* by R. Ash; *The Really Wicked Droning Wasp and Other Things that Bite and Sting* by Teresa Greenaway; *The Book of Slime* by Ellen Jackson; and *Animals Eat the Weirdest Things* by Diane Swanson. Be sure to check out their recommended websites. Jobe and Dayton-Sakari (2002) include lists of books in areas such as basketball, baseball, soccer, hockey, science, creatures, biographies, diaries, and much more. Connecting students to motivating reading materials like these gives the students the opportunity to be "the expert" with the facts, a role they may not often play in or out of school or relate to reading.

Many elementary students enjoy reading by themselves or listening to others read commercial materials called predictable books. According to Rhodes and Dudley-Marling (1996), "books are predictable when they enable students to quickly and easily predict what the author's going to say and how the author's going to say it based upon their knowledge of the world" (p. 108). "Predictable text structures, achieved through the use of rhyme, repetition, cumulative patterns, and familiar story lines" (Rhodes & Dudley-Marling, 1996) make predictable books relatively accessible to less skilled readers while still encouraging these students to use a range of textual and phonetic cues (Dudley-Marling & Paugh, 2004, p. 14). Rhodes (1981) identified the characteristics that make books predictable: (a) a match between the content and the reader's experiences; (b) rhythmical, repetitive patterns; and (c) familiar, well-known stories. Examples of books with repetitive patterns (i.e., predictable or pattern books) are *Inside a Zoo in the City* (Capucilli, 2000) and *The Animal Boogie* (Harter, 2005). See Table 6.1 for more examples.

Opportunities for Social Interaction

It is important to emphasize social skills with students in order to help them develop their interpersonal relationships and communication skills (Cohen & Spenciner, 2005). Teachers may use fiction, nonfiction, and high-interest reading materials to facilitate social interactions through peer tutoring, learning center activities, role-playing, group projects, and cooperative learning activities. A technique that is particularly effective in getting middle and high school students involved with young adult literature and engaged in social interactions is the practice of book talks (Ousley, 2006). Book talks should be brief (three to four minutes), and involve props and character interviews to generate student interest. During a book talk, a teacher or student gives the title, author, publisher, length of the book, and recommended audience (e.g., middle school) followed by a brief description and questions to ponder (e.g., Will Marvin and his family be able to battle the flood waters? What will the family do for food and water? Should they stay and wait to be rescued or try to get to higher ground?). Book talks invite social interaction.

Diversity

Instructional materials may be used to help students recognize and celebrate the diversity and variety that exists among individuals and to share information about people from different cultural backgrounds. "Students' contextual, linguistic, and gender characteristics influence how they learn, and the teaching styles that work with one segment

Table 6.1 Predictable Books

Aardema, V. (1981). *Bringing the rain to Kapiti Plain.* New York: Dial.
Barrett, J. (1980). *Animals should definitely not act like people.* New York: Atheneum.
Brett, J. (1999). *Gingerbread baby.* New York: Putnam.
Brown, K. (2001). *What's the time Grandma Wolf?* Atlanta: Peachtree.
Capucilli, A. S. (2000). *Inside a zoo in the city.* New York: Scholastic.
Day, N. R. (2000). *A kitten's year.* New York: HarperCollins.
de Paola, T. (1981). *Now one foot, now the other.* New York: Putnam's Sons.
Fox, M. (1986). *Hattie and the fox.* New York: Simon & Schuster
Harley, B. (1996). Sitting down to eat. Little Rock, AR: August House LittleFolk.
Harter, D. (2005). *The animal boogie.* New York: Barefoot Books.
Kimmel, E. (1988). *Anansi and the moss covered rock.* New York: Holiday House.
Kirk, D. (1994). *Miss Spider's tea party.* New York: Callaway Editions, Scholastic Books.
Leslie, A. (2001). *Who's that scratching at my door?* Brooklyn, NY: Handprint Books.
Lewis, K. (2001). *The lot at the end of my block.* New York: Hyperion Books for Children.
Lobel, A. (1984). *The rose in my garden.* New York: Greenwillow.
Martin, B. (1989). *Chicka chicka boom boom.* New York: Simon & Schuster.
Numeroff, L. (1985). *If you give a mouse a cookie.* New York: Harper & Row.
Plume, I. (1980). *The Bremen-town musicians.* Garden City, NY: Doubleday.
Rosen, M. (1989). *We're going on a bear hunt.* New York: Margaret K. McElderry Books.
Shaw, N. (1991). *Sheep in a shop.* Boston: Houghton Mifflin.
Viorst, J. (1972). *Alexander and the terrible, horrible, no good, very bad day.* New York: Atheneum.

of the population may not work with another" (Winzer & Mazurek, p. 250). As you select materials, make sure that all groups are represented. Under-representation in instructional materials appears to occur most often for minority groups, women, people with disabilities, and older individuals (Gollnick & Chinn, 2002). Make sure to use culturally responsive instructional strategies and materials to meet the needs of students from diverse racial, ethnic, cultural, and linguistic groups (Banks, et al., 2001).

In Mr. Balado's class, students read and discuss books that incorporate different age groups, both males and females, a variety of cultural groups, and people with disabilities. For example, the class examined the problems of the elderly in *Butterfly Boy* (Kroll, 2002), a story about a Hispanic boy and his aging grandfather who can no longer understand what his grandson, Emilio, is saying. The story highlights the special friendship between the grandfather and grandson who may not be able to communicate with words, but who communicate in other ways as they find they still share a passion for the same things. A particular favorite of the class was *Joey Pigza Loses Control* (Gantos, 2000). This Newberry Honor Book is a story about a boy with attention deficit hyperactivity disorder (ADHD).

White Tiger, Blue Serpent (Tseng, 1999) is a beautifully illustrated folktale from China about a boy, Kai, and his mother. Kai's hard work pays off when he overcomes the wrath of a greedy goddess who has stolen a magnificent silk brocade created by Kai's mother (the work of a thousand days and nights) and successfully returns it to her. *The Black Snowman* (Mendez, 1989) describes a young African American boy who discovers the beauty of his heritage and self-worth. *Shabanu, Daughter of the Wind* (Staples, 1989) is the story of a Muslim family preparing for the marriage of its oldest daughter told by the younger sister. For a list of books about a variety of cultural groups, see Table 6.2.

MATERIALS SELECTION AND THE STAGES OF LEARNING

You may use a variety of instructional materials to meet the needs of your students at each of the stages of learning. At the *acquisition* level, materials should provide opportunities for extensive teacher participation. For example, to teach writing skills to your

Table 6.2 Multicultural Literature

AFRICAN AMERICANS

Bial, R. (1995). *The underground railroad.* New York: Houghton Mifflin.
Bridges, R. & Lundell, M. (1999). *Through my eyes: Articles and interviews.* New York: Schoastic.
Chocolate, D. M. (2000). *The piano man.* New York: Walker.
Cole, K. (2001). *No bad news.* Morton Grove, IL: A. Whitman.
Curtis, C. (1999). *Bud, not Buddy.* New York: Delacorte.
Grimes, N. (1998). *Jazmin's notebook.* New York: Penguin Books.
Igus, T. (1998). *I see rhythm.* Connecticut: Children's Press.
Martin, A. M. (2001). *Belle teal.* New York: Scholastic Press.
Morrison, T. (2004). *Remember: The journey to school integration.* New York: Houghton Mifflin.
Pinkney, S. (2000). *Shades of black: A celebration of our children.* New York: Scholastic.
Porter, A. P. (1992). Jump *at de sun: The story of Zora Neale Hurston.* Minneapolis: Carolrhoda Books.
Rinaldi, A. (1996). *Hang a thousand trees with ribbons: The story of Phillis Wheatley.* San Diego, CA: Harcourt Brace & Co.
Ryan, P. M. (2002). *When Marian sang: The true recital of Marian Anderson.* New York: Scholastic Press.
Taylor, M. D. (1997). *Roll of thunder, hear my cry.* New York: Puffin Books.

ASIAN AMERICANS

Coatsworth, E. J. (1990). *The cat who went to heaven.* New York: Aladdin Paperbacks.
Demi. (1998). *The empty pot.* New York: Henry Holt & Company.
Ho, M. (1996). *Maples in the mist: Poems for children from the Tang Dynasty.* New York: Lothrup, Lee & Shepard Books.
Kessler, L. (1994). *Stubborn twig: Three generations in the life of a Japanese American family.* New York: Dutton.
Kimmel, E. A. (1998). *Ten suns: A Chinese legend.* New York: Holiday.
Namioka, L. (1994). *Yang the youngest and his terrible ear.* New York: Bantam Doubleday Dell Books for Young Readers.
Pittman, H. C. (1986). *A grain of rice.* New York: Bantam.
Tseng, G. (1999). *White tiger, blue serpent.* New York: Lee & Shepard.
Vuyon, L. D. (1982). *The brocaded slipper and other Vietnamese tales.* Reading, MA: Addison-Wesley.
Wells, R. (2001). *Yoko's paper cranes.* New York: Hyperion Books for Children.
Yep, L. (1995). *Thief of hearts.* New York: Harper Collins.

HISPANICS

Aardema, V. (1979). *The riddle of the drum: A tale from Tizapan, Mexico.* New York: Four Winds.
Ada, A. F. (1995). *My name is Maria Isabel.* New York: Aladdin Paperbacks.
Bethancourt, T. E. (1987). *The me inside of me.* Neward, DE: Lerner.
Griego y Maetras, J., & Anaya, R. A. (1980). *Cuentos: Tales from the the Hispanic Southwest.* Santa Fe, NM: Museum of New Mexico.
Kroll, V. (1997). *Butterfly boy.* Pennsylvania: Boyd Mills.
Lattimore, D. (1987). *The flame of peace: A tale of the Aztecs.* New York: Harper & Row.
Martinez, V. (1996). *Parrot in the oven: Mi Vida.* New York: Harper Collins.
Ryan, P. (2000). *Esperanza rising.* New York: Scholastic.
Steptoe, J. (1997). *Creativity.* New York: Clarion Books.

NATIVE AMERICANS

Carter, F. (1990). *The education of Little Tree.* Albuquerque, NM: University of New Mexico Press.
Edrich, L. (1999). *The birchback house.* New York: Hyperion.
Freedman, R. (1988). *Buffalo hunt.* New York: Holiday.
George, J. (1987). *Water sky.* New York: Harper & Row.
Highwater, J. (1998). *I wear the morning star.* New York: Harper & Row.
Hortze, S. (1990). *A circle unbroken.* New York: Clarion.
Hudson, J. (1989). *Sweetgrass.* New York: Philomel.
Hudson, J. (1992). *Dawn rider.* New York: Philomel.
Paulsen, G. (1992). *Canyons.* New York: Delacorte.

students, use materials that explain how to write a variety of sentence types and then model for students what to do when writing sentences.

After your students have acquired skills, they need to practice them to gain *fluency*. Students should practice first in a controlled or guided situation under close supervision, then in independent situations. Therefore, you should select and develop a wide variety of materials and provide opportunities for extensive student involvement. Practice materials should foster participation on the part of students. Use workbooks, magazines, practice exercises, software programs, and games to develop fluency in writing. In addition, you may use charts and graphs to monitor each student's progress.

After students have demonstrated fluency, you should provide instructional materials that allow them to maintain their skills. At this stage, provide materials that will encourage frequent use of the skills. Students with special needs can practice writing a variety of things to maintain their skills (such as a letter to the editor). In addition, *maintenance* is frequently enhanced by learning centers or a computer, where students work independently on such skills as writing different sentence types, stories, and reports.

The final stage of learning involves the *generalization* of skills across situations and settings. For example, you should help students identify the opportunities for using writing in real-life materials. Thus, select materials that require students to apply their writing skills to the types of writing they do in content area classes (e.g., English), on the job (e.g., taking orders), and personally (e.g., writing letters).

Activity 6.1

1. Look back at the chapter opening scenario about Emily. Locate a textbook in science, social studies, math, reading, or English at the elementary level and one at middle or high school level.
   a. Describe in what ways the two textbooks would be appropriate or inappropriate for a student like Emily.
   b. What activities (if any) are provided that would interest and motivate students?
   c. What (if any) opportunities are provided for social interaction?
2. Think of a popular teen magazine. What activities (if any) are provided that would interest and motivate students? What opportunities (if any) are provided for social interaction?

(Answers for this and other activities are found in the Instructor's Manual.)

ANALYZING INSTRUCTIONAL MATERIALS

It is important to analyze instructional materials for their appropriateness for students before incorporating them into the instructional program. Many commercial products are not appropriate because they possess characteristics that make their use extremely difficult for students with special needs. Commercial materials, curricula, programs, and textbooks may be ineffective for many reasons:

1. ***The readability of text may be too difficult.*** Many materials are written on a reading level that may be challenging for students with special needs. Sentences may be too long and complex, and vocabulary may be unnecessarily difficult, as in "The man,

addressing the audience before him, told them that he had repented for all of his past offenses" instead of "The man told the people he was sorry for what he did."

2. ***The vocabulary is often highly sophisticated.*** Complex words may be used when easier synonyms would be just as effective (see preceding example). Unfortunately, when technical terms are introduced in some content materials, definitions are omitted or not clearly stated. Wiig and Semel (1984) suggest the use of only five unfamiliar words per lesson for students who have language or learning disabilities.

3. ***Too many concepts may be presented at one time.*** Students with special needs benefit when concepts are introduced one at a time. Unfortunately, math materials sometimes present more than one type of problem on a page. For example, in one text we examined, the division problems (24/8 = _____; 38/5 = _____; and 215/3 = _____) required three different skills and levels of competence but were presented on the same page. Notice that the first problem can be divided evenly, the second has a remainder, and the third involves a two-digit quotient with a remainder. Each type should be mastered before the next is introduced.

4. ***The sequencing of skills may be inappropriate.*** Students with special needs may experience problems when skills are taught out of sequence. For instance, students should be taught initial consonant sounds before they are introduced to the concept of consonant blends (Spache, 1982).

5. ***Directions are not always clear.*** Some materials use different words for the same directions, as in the case of "Circle the best answer" and "Put a line around the best answer." It is less confusing for students if directions are worded consistently on assignments and tests.

6. ***There are insufficient opportunities for practice and review.*** Many workbooks, textbooks, and other printed products move too quickly, failing to provide sufficient practice. For example, students should spend sufficient time learning how to subtract two-digit numbers *without* regrouping before attempting similar problems *with* regrouping. Many commercial materials do not incorporate a review of previously learned skills in practical, relevant situations. For example, once students in an employability skills class have learned the steps for job interviewing, they need to apply those skills through role-playing scenarios and videotaping.

7. ***Key points and terms may not be given adequate emphasis.*** Printed products do not always highlight, print in bold type, print in italics, or define the most important terms and ideas. This may cause difficulty for students who do not easily identify key points and terms.

8. ***Organization, format, and layout are sometimes confusing.*** Printed materials do not always begin with an advance organizer or introduction of what is to come (e.g., list of objectives, key vocabulary list, outline), nor do they conclude with a post-organizer (e.g., summary, list of important points, questions). In addition, when tables, graphs, and illustrations are placed far away from the text that describes them, they may confuse students or be ignored, as the students do not see the connection between the text and the graphic aid. Imagine trying to follow an explanation of how to record checks in a check register, when the instructions are on one page and a diagram of the check register is on another. In addition, pages may be cluttered with too much information. Remember how Emily in our opening chapter scenario struggled with her new science textbook? Crowded formats may confuse students and discourage or prevent them from even beginning a task. Students may be unable to pinpoint relevant

information and screen out nonessential information when a page is overcrowded. Pages with ample white space are more student friendly.

9. ***Materials may be unmotivating and uninteresting.*** Some commercially produced materials simply are not appealing or interesting because of format, level of difficulty, lack of color and illustrations, subject matter, age level targeted, typeface, or lack of relevance and functionality. Thus, they may not hold the learner's attention.

10. ***Materials and text are sometimes too abstract.*** Some written materials contain long passages of text with no clues to the definitions of abstract vocabulary and concepts. For example, a social studies chapter on justice, democracy, and freedom may not make these concepts concrete. Another example is math material that contains the term *congruent* with no examples, definitions, or illustrations of the term.

11. ***Students may be limited in their response modes.*** Unfortunately, some materials require only one type of response from students. For example, a science text that provides only end-of-chapter questions limits response. In contrast, a science text that provides suggestions for experiments, topics for discussion, suggestions for group activities, ideas for field trips, and chapter questions provides a variety of ways for students to respond.

12. ***A variety of ethnic, cultural, and gender groups may not be represented or they may be inaccurately represented.*** Some instructional materials do not include exposure to a variety of ethnic and cultural groups and genders, thereby limiting their appeal. This omission may communicate to students that some ethnic and cultural groups are less important than others (Gollnick & Chinn, 2002). Some materials include descriptions of people and activities that stereotype individuals in terms of culture, ethnic group, religion, gender, age, and vocational or career choice. Biases may occur within both the printed and graphic sections of materials (Baca & Cervantes, 2004). There still exists the lack of Spanish, Polish, African, and other non-Anglo names in materials, as well as feminine pronouns (Gollnick & Chinn, 2002), and Asian Americans, Latinos, Native Americans, and women are underrepresented in instructional materials (Hernandez, 2001).

TEXTBOOK ANALYSIS

Analyzing a textbook as part of your selection process helps you determine the amount of repetition, review, and material that is included. You should be sure that your students can handle the concept load and that the text provides ample opportunities for your students to check their understanding. Supplementary materials may include study aids, activity sheets, and overviews. You should also make sure that the format (layout, print, graphics) is compatible with the needs of your students. By analyzing elementary and secondary textbooks for content, organization, supplementary materials, and format, you can identify elements that cause problems for students and then adapt the textbooks accordingly.

You may also want to check the readability level of your textbooks and other reading materials. Typically, readability formulas are used to evaluate the complexity of the sentences in a passage (e.g., sentence length) and the level of difficulty of the vocabulary (word length or frequency). Figure 6.1 contains the Fry Graph for Estimating Readability. You can use these steps to obtain a general idea of the difficulty level of a passage. Although readability formulas are typically used to determine readability level, they should be used with caution and as only one means of evaluating the appropriateness of a text or reading passage. Standal (1978) recommends using a readability formula as a "general indicator of a possible range of materials" (p. 646) and a good starting point for estimating the readability of a passage.

Figure 6.1 FRY READABILITY FORMULA

GRAPH FOR ESTIMATING READABILITY—EXTENDED

by Edward Fry, Rutgers University Reading Center, New Brunswick, NJ 08904

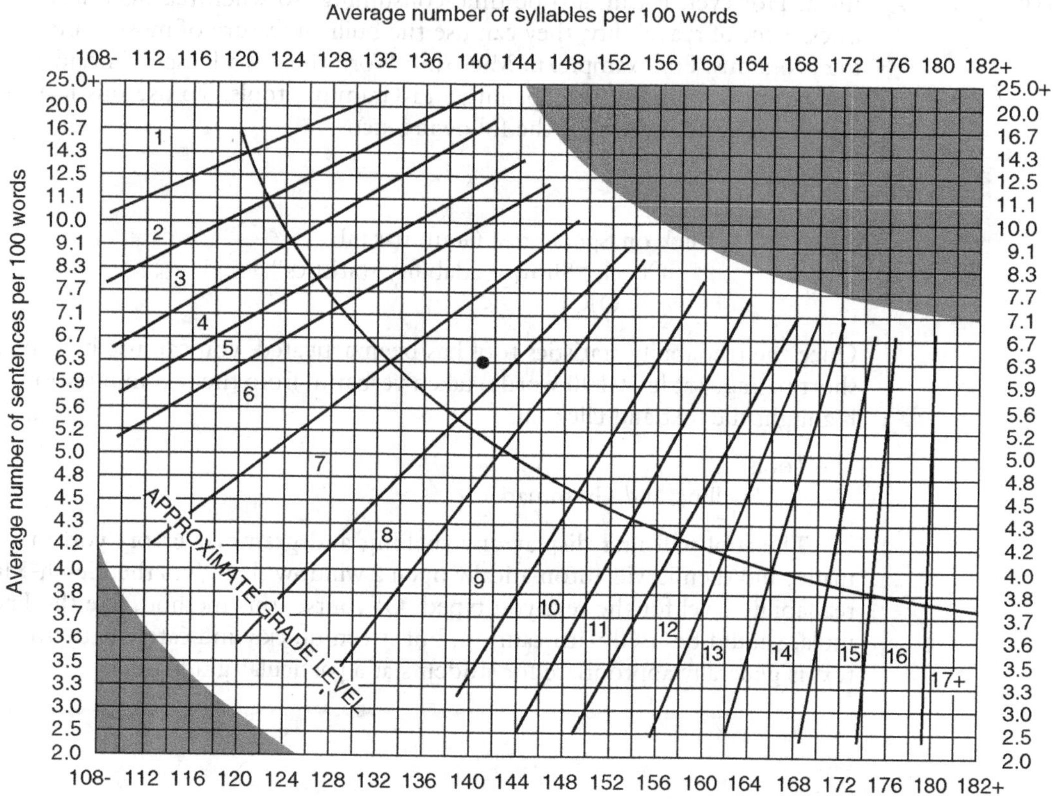

Expanded Directions for Working Readability Graph

1. Randomly select three (3) sample passages and count out exactly 100 words each, beginning with the beginning of a sentence. Do count proper nouns, initializations, and numerals.
2. Count the number of sentences in the hundred words, estimating length of the fraction of the last sentence to the nearest one-tenth.
3. Count the total number of syllables in the 100-word passage. If you don't have a hand counter available, an easy way is to simply put a mark above every syllable over one in each word, then when you get to the end of the passage, count the number of marks and add 100. Small calculators can also be used as counters by pushing numeral 1, then push the + sign for each word or syllable when counting.
4. Enter graph with *average* sentence length and *average* number of syllables; plot dot where the two lines intersect. Area where dot is plotted will give you the approximate grade level.
5. If a great deal of variability is found in syllable count or sentence count, putting more samples into the average is desirable.
6. A word is defined as a group of symbols with a space on either side; thus, *Joe, IRA, 1945,* and *&* are each one word.
7. A syllable is defined as a phonetic syllable. Generally, there are as many syllables as vowel sounds. For example, *stopped* is one syllable and *wanted* is two syllables. When counting syllables for numerals and initializations, count one syllable for each symbol. For example, *1945* is four syllables, *IRA* is three syllables, and *&* is one syllable.

BOX 6.1

Reflections on Practice

Windows Readability Procedure

It is important for teachers to know the steps involved in using a readability formula. However, it can also be time-consuming, so when teachers need a quick assessment of readability, they can use the built-in feature of most word-processing programs. For example, in Microsoft Word there is a Flesch-Kincaid readability feature included in the Spelling and Grammar tools. To use this feature you need to activate it through the following steps:

Tools
  Options
    Click on Spelling & Grammar tab
      Check "Show readability statistics"
        OK

Once the readability statistics tool has been activated, you can use it by typing a short passage (at least 100 words) taken verbatim from the text in question. Then highlight the text and click on:

Tools
  Spelling and Grammar

The tool will first display any spelling and grammar errors you may have made, and then it will automatically open a window that gives the Flesch-Kincaid readability level for the text you typed. Of course, this method, like the Fry formula, should be used with caution, but it can quickly indicate whether or not a text is generally appropriate for students at a particular grade level.

Most readability formulas are based on sentence complexity and vocabulary and do not take into consideration other aspects of a textbook, such as the way it is organized and formatted (headings, graphic aids, important points, definitions in margins, etc.). Bailin and Grafstein (2001) refer to multiple readabilities, varying with the topic, the nature of the text, and the nature of the audience. Beals (1989) suggests that teachers should also evaluate vocabulary load, syntax, and style and recommends the following steps:

1. Determine the reading level of the student who will be using the text/material.
2. Select an easy-to-use readability formula, such as the Fry Readability Formula (Fry, 1968, 2002), to get a general estimate of readability (see Figure 6.1).
3. Examine the passages that you used to determine readability, and mark any words that the student might not understand (those that require direct instruction or use of context).
4. Analyze the syntax in the passage by identifying the basic sentence types.
5. Compare the sentence types typically used by the student (e.g., simple, compound, complex) with those found in the passage.
6. Analyze the style of the writing by looking for anything that might cause problems for the student.

By analyzing material using a readability formula to obtain a general indication of a range of materials (Standal, 1978) and assessing vocabulary load, syntax, and style

(Beals, 1989), you should be able to judge the suitability of reading materials for your students. Remember also to take into consideration the characteristics of the reader as you make your selection of materials that are reader friendly.

Numerous forms and checklists are available, both commercial or teacher-made (such as the one following), for teachers to use when analyzing instructional materials for students. You should use some type of evaluation procedure to help you decide whether to use a given material as it is, use it with modifications, or not use it at all. In addition to evaluating materials themselves, some teachers borrow or obtain sample sets of commercial materials from publishers and ask their students to try them out and provide feedback about them.

Complete the following:

Title: __________

Author: __________

Publisher: __________

Copyright: __________

Cost: __________

Purpose: __________

Rate the following:

	Acceptable	Unacceptable
Directions	____	____
Readability	____	____
Sequencing	____	____
Interest level	____	____
Pace	____	____
Examples	____	____
Opportunities for practice	____	____
Opportunities for self-monitoring	____	____
Use of visual images	____	____
Multicultural emphasis	____	____

Respond to the following:

1. How would you use this material (e.g., supplementary, required, to help with generalization)? __________
2. In what type(s) of instructional arrangement(s) would you use this material (e.g., individual, group)? __________
3. What population of students would be most excited by this material?
4. Are links to appropriate websites provided?
5. Give your overall impression of the material.

Activity 6.2
Find textbooks at the elementary, middle, and high school levels. Use the Fry Readability Formula and the Windows Readability Procedure to determine the readability of the textbooks. Discuss the results and the implications of your findings.

IMPORTANT POINTS

1. When selecting instructional materials, teachers should be aware of individual learner needs, interest and motivation levels of materials, opportunities that materials provide for social interaction, and the level of attention to diversity within the materials.
2. Materials should be developmentally, culturally, linguistically, age, and interest appropriate for students.
3. Instructional materials may be used to address the needs of students at each of the stages of learning (acquisition, fluency, maintenance, and generalization).
4. Readability formulas are used to evaluate the complexity of the sentences in a passage and the level of difficulty of the vocabulary.

ADAPTING MATERIALS

Once you have analyzed materials and identified any shortcomings, you may need to adapt the materials for use with students who have special needs. Materials should be usable under different instructional conditions with students who have varying abilities. If students experience difficulty with assignments or activities, teachers may make changes to help meet their needs. The number of students with disabilities being educated in general education classrooms is continuing to grow (U.S. Department of Education, 2005). Almost half of all students with disabilities were spending 80% or more of the day in general education classrooms during the 2003–04 school year (U.S. Department of Education, 2005). This percentage confirms the need for general education teachers to be knowledgeable about adapting materials and instruction. Unfortunately, observational studies of actual instruction provided by general education teachers to students who are in inclusive classrooms show that few, if any, adaptations in instruction are being made and that general education teachers vary significantly in their ability or willingness to make adaptations (Rotter, 2004). Therefore, one of the most important roles of the special education teacher is to assist general education teachers in the adaptation of materials and instruction to ensure the successful participation of students with special needs in the general classroom community.

Instructional materials include textbooks, workbooks, worksheets, transparencies, kits with cards or written information, and software programs. Following are areas to modify and techniques that you may use to modify materials for students with special needs.

Readability To modify the readability level:

1. Decrease the use of complex language and provide examples that explain statements (Salend, 2005).
2. Provide outlines or study guides to accompany the text.

Figure 6.2 MARGINAL GLOSS TECHNIQUE

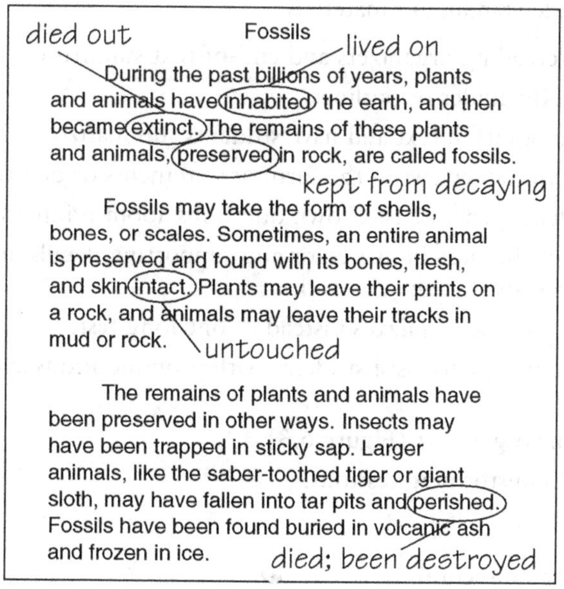
Fossils

During the past billions of years, plants and animals have inhabited the earth, and then became extinct. The remains of these plants and animals, preserved in rock, are called fossils.

Fossils may take the form of shells, bones, or scales. Sometimes, an entire animal is preserved and found with its bones, flesh, and skin intact. Plants may leave their prints on a rock, and animals may leave their tracks in mud or rock.

The remains of plants and animals have been preserved in other ways. Insects may have been trapped in sticky sap. Larger animals, like the saber-toothed tiger or giant sloth, may have fallen into tar pits and perished. Fossils have been found buried in volcanic ash and frozen in ice.

3. Highlight essential information.
4. Limit the amount of information on a page.
5. Have a volunteer write one-sentence summaries on Post-it notes.
6. Make the topic sentence of a paragraph the initial sentence (Wood, 2006).

Vocabulary To modify vocabulary:

1. Use the marginal gloss technique. Write terms and their definitions in the margins of a textbook page (Figure 6.2).
2. Underline or highlight key terms and use erasable highlighters.
3. Locate all boldface, italicized, or new concept words from the text and list them with the corresponding page number (Wood, 2006).
4. Record essential words, definitions, and sentences on language master cards or on audiotapes.
5. Provide vocabulary lists or glossaries with simplified definitions and use the words in sentences.

Presentation of Concepts

To modify the presentation of concepts:

1. Present concepts one at a time.
2. Provide visual supplements, such as transparencies, illustrations, and diagrams.
3. Use modeling and demonstration to clarify concepts.
4. Use games, manipulatives, and hands-on activities to reinforce concepts.
5. Draw upon the different cultural backgrounds and experiences of your students to make concepts meaningful.

General Comprehension
To increase understanding of materials:

1. Include prereading organizers and end-of-text summaries.
2. Provide study guides or outlines.
3. Insert stop points in text and have students summarize what they have read.
4. Include periodic reviews in the form of statements or questions.
5. Have students generate their own questions about printed materials.
6. Highlight main ideas in one color and supporting details in another. Post a key to the coding system in the classroom.
7. Give short, frequent quizzes instead of one long test.
8. Use books on tape to assist students with pronunciations and the understanding of dialects.
9. Use graphic organizers (Figure 6.3).
10. Conduct brainstorming sessions.

Directions
To clarify written directions:

1. Simplify the directions.
2. Shorten the directions.
3. Use concise, boldface directions.
4. Put the words typically used in directions on language master cards or use text to speech software.
5. Highlight the key words in a set of directions (e.g., "**Write** a *t* in the blank if the answer is **true** and an *f* if the answer is **false**.").

Figure 6.3 GRAPHIC ORGANIZER

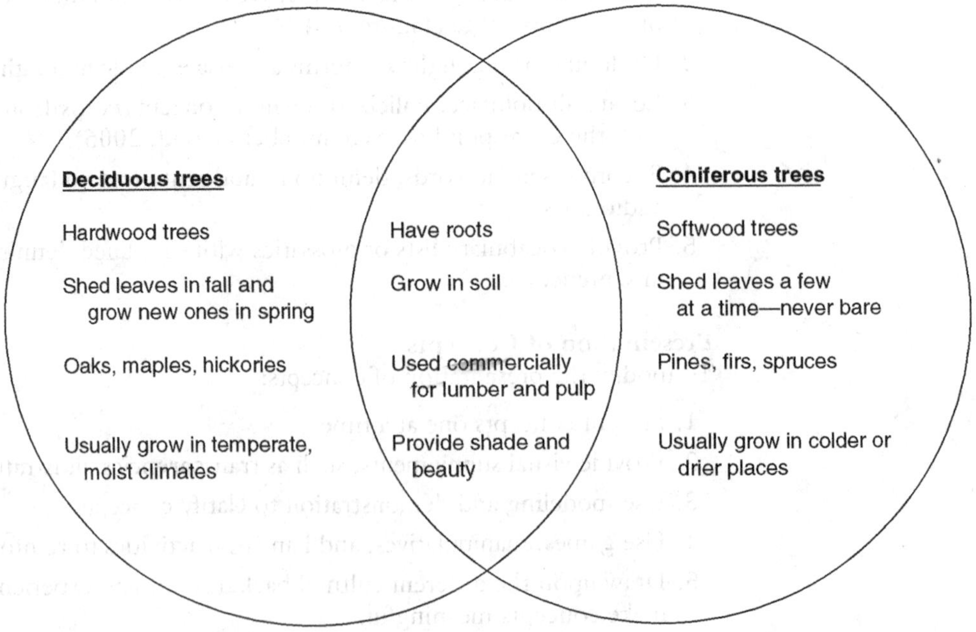

6. Have the students underline what they are supposed to do (e.g., "Write your answer in the blank provided for you.").
7. In a set of multiple directions, use colored dots or numbers to differentiate the separate directions (Lambie, 1980; Salend, 2005).

Practice

To provide sufficient practice:

1. Have students move laterally before they move vertically to a new skill (e.g., have students practice multiplying one-digit numbers by one-digit numbers to mastery level before you teach them to multiply one-digit numbers by two-digit numbers).
2. Supplement practice in printed products with games, audiotapes, and manipulatives.
3. Provide repetition, review, and application of skills.
4. Provide opportunities to practice previously taught skills within learning centers.

Manageability of Assignments

To increase the manageability of assignments:

1. Clip a piece of paper to a page so that it covers half of the page, and have the student complete the other half.
2. Draw a box around the questions that the student should answer (Figure 6.4).
3. Use bookmarks to help students locate words and keep their place.
4. Underline or highlight specific information that is being introduced or emphasized.
5. Mask out certain areas of print material to emphasize specific concepts, eliminate unnecessary visual stimuli, and encourage task performance.
6. Color-code newly introduced material, major concepts, or material to be memorized.
7. During PowerPoint presentations, indicate the important points with one symbol (e.g., highlighting or printing in boldface type) and the details with another (e.g., underlining or italicizing).
8. Give students a list saying what they need to accomplish first, second, third.

Figure 6.4 SHORTENING AN ASSIGNMENT

Name ______________________ Date ______________

Directions: Write your answers to the subtraction problems in the space provided.

Do the problems that are inside the box.

1. $5.10 −2.51	2. $6.28 −2.99	3. $4.43 −1.76	4. $8.11 −5.86
5. $7.56 −6.78	6. $4.41 −3.85	7. $9.05 −2.79	8. $6.43 −4.78
9. $3.10 −2.98	10. $8.83 −5.99	11. $6.76 −3.97	12. $5.20 −4.91
13. $5.84 −1.96	14. $4.12 −3.87	15. $8.03 −5.75	16. $7.07 −2.49

9. Allow students to begin homework in class and provide feedback to ensure that they will complete the assignment correctly when they work on it at home.

Note that some of these recommendations such as items 4–7 can be used with print materials and on the computer.

Organization

To organize print materials in a clear, consistent manner:

1. Use advance and post organizers for each activity (e.g., give students an outline or a set of questions at the beginning of a lesson and print a summary or list important points on a transparency to use for review at the end of a lesson).
2. Reorganize poorly designed worksheets to create simple, easy-to-follow layouts and formats (Figures 6.5 and 6.6).
3. Provide graphics that are clear and understandable. Be sure graphics clarify and support the printed text (e.g., give students a photocopy of a check that has been filled out so that, as they read the text, they can see where the date, amount, signature, etc., belong).

Figure 6.5 EXAMPLE OF A POORLY DESIGNED WORKSHEET

Name ______________________________ Date______________

Read Chapter 5 about the rainforest and answer the following questions.

A. TRUE/FALSE

1. Rainforests are characterized by vast, dry, sunny regions.
2. Destruction of the world's rainforests may affect plants, animals, and climate.
3. It is humid and rains almost every day in a rainforest.
4. Rainforests are dense forests that are found in tropical regions around the equator.
5. Rainforests are very heavily populated areas with many people.
6. The trees of a rainforest grow so close together that sunlight rarely reaches the forest floor.

B. Look up the following words in the Glossary of your social studies book.

1. uninhabited
2. vegetation
3. tropical
4. frontier
5. agriculture
6. lumbering
7. ecologists
8. economy
9. climate
10. temperature
11. Amazon
12. equator
13. continents
14. minerals
15. extinction
16. humidity
17. minerals
18. petroleum
19. resources
20. carbon dioxide

C. Read another story or article about rainforests.Compare the information in Chapter 5 with your new article, or write a story about a rainforest including how it would look,sound,smell,and feel.

Figure 6.6 EXAMPLE OF AN ADAPTED WORKSHEET

Name ______________________ Date __________

The Rainforest

Directions: Read pages 43–52 in Chapter 5 of your social studies book. Then complete Parts I, II, and III about the rainforest.

Part I—True/False

Directions: Read each of the following statements. Write "True" in the box if the statement is true, and "False" if it is false.

☐ 1. Rainforests are characterized by vast, dry, sunny regions.
☐ 2. Destruction of the world's rainforests may affect plants, animals, and climate.
☐ 3. It is humid and rains almost every day in a rainforest.
☐ 4. Rainforests are dense forests that are found in tropical regions around the equator.
☐ 5. Rainforests are very heavily populated areas with many people.
☐ 6. The trees of a rainforest grow so close together that sunlight rarely reaches the forest floor.

Part II—Vocabulary

Directions: Look up the following words in the Glossary in the back of your social studies book. Write the word and its definition in your notebook.

List 1	List 2
1. uninhabited	1. lumbering
2. vegetation	2. ecologists
3. tropical	3. climate
4. agriculture	4. temperature
5. frontier	5. economy

List 3	List 4
1. carbon dioxide	1. extinction
2. Amazon	2. humidity
3. equator	3. petroleum
4. populated	4. resources
5. continents	5. minerals

Part III—Take Your Choice

Directions: Complete *either* Choice #1 or Choice #2.

Choice #1

1st — Read another story or article about rainforests.
2nd — Write two things that are the same as the information in Chapter 5 of your book.
3rd — Write two new things that you learned.

Choice #2

Write a story about a rainforest including how it would look, sound, smell, and feel.

Response Modes

To increase the options for student responses:

1. Allow students to tape their responses on audiocassette.
2. Provide opportunities for students to work in groups with games, flash cards, and hands-on activities in response to printed assignments.
3. Let students dictate stories, themes, and book reports.

4. Allow students to use the computer instead of writing spelling words, themes, and reports.
5. Provide role-play and discussions.
6. Make materials self-correcting.

Motivation

To increase motivation and interest in print materials:

1. Use concrete examples and demonstrations to supplement print materials.
2. Draw upon prior knowledge to make material more interesting to students.
3. Supplement text materials with nontraditional print materials, such as newspapers, magazines, and comic books (e.g., use stories dictated by students about popular athletes and other celebrities to develop reading lessons for students).
4. Allow students to use self-correcting materials and manipulatives.
5. Use materials that interest students while simplifying vocabulary.
6. Use DVDs and computer software to increase interest in print materials.
7. Use think/pair/share—after asking a question, ask students to find a partner, share their response to the question, remember their partner's response, and share with the class.
8. Incorporate multicultural materials into your classroom.
9. Encourage students to select materials for projects.

Abstract Concepts and Materials

To make materials more concrete:

1. Provide demonstrations.
2. Present abstract concepts in the form of concept maps, graphic organizers, or webs.
3. Use role-play.
4. Associate concepts with music or art.
5. Relate materials to students' cultural backgrounds and experiences.

TEST ADAPTATIONS

The increase in the percentage of students with disabilities receiving instruction in general education classrooms for 80% of the day or more has implications for general education teachers (U.S. Department of Education, 2005). Students with disabilities are spending more time with the general education curriculum, including tests. A nationwide survey of general education teachers was conducted regarding their views related to test adaptations for students with disabilities (Jayanthi, Epstein, Polloway, & Bursuck, 1996). The adaptations that were rated by the teachers as being the most helpful for students were assisting students with directions during tests, reading test questions to students, and simplifying the wording of questions. The adaptations rated as the easiest to make included providing extra space for answers, giving open-note and open-book tests, giving practice questions as a study guide, and helping with directions during testing.

In another study, middle school students, including those with high incidence disabilities, were asked to rate each of 23 testing adaptations (Nelson, Jayanthi, Epstein, & Bursuck, 2000). Students indicated a preference for open-note and open-book tests, practice questions, and multiple-choice over short-answer or essay questions, as well as a preference for using a dictionary or calculator, a copy of the test for studying, and extra space for answers. As you might predict, students with disabilities and students with low achievement did show a significantly higher preference for test adaptations than did students with average or above-average achievement. It is also important to know what students do not like or find helpful. "Overwhelmingly, students most frequently chose teacher reading of test questions to students as the least-liked adaptation. Students most often explained their reasons for this choice in terms of the adaptation interfering with their own ways of test taking, particularly pacing, or with their ability to concentrate."

BOX 6.2

Reflections on Practice

After reading the Nelson, et al. (2000) article referred to in this section of the textbook, Beth Christner, a fifth-grade teacher, told us that one of the most frequently used adaptations on the statewide assessment test she administers to her students is *reading the test questions to students*. However, she had always thought that it might be making her students uncomfortable. The article by Nelson and colleagues prompted her to make a change. During her most recent proctoring of the test, she spaced her students' desks far apart and let them work at their own pace, reading the questions to students individually only if they requested it. She felt that because of these adjustments, her students were much more relaxed. (Note: Be sure to check your students' IEPs in case they specify that questions must be read.)

TEACHER-MADE TESTS

In addition to using adaptations, such as providing practice questions and giving open-note and open-book tests, we recommend that you examine your own teacher-made tests and adapt them, if needed, using these suggestions:

1. Type your tests. Tests are more legible when they are typed, not hand-written, and on an easy-to-see background.
2. Use a combination of uppercase and lowercase letters because the combination is easier to read than all capital letters (Salend, 2005).
3. Allow students to write on the test instead of using a separate answer sheet (Salend, 2005). Leave ample extra space for answers.
4. Provide extra paper for students to work out problems, jot down an outline, or make lists of words for later reference.
5. Use separate sheets of paper (not front/back) for each page of the test to make the test easier to follow and to ensure that students do not forget to respond to every page and every question.
6. Vary the response modes by allowing students to spell words aloud to a paraeducator or teacher instead of writing them; dictate written responses into a tape recorder; or use a computer instead of writing an essay by hand.
7. Use cues such as color coding, underlining, or highlighting key words in a test to alert students to specifics about the items, and arrows and stop signs at the bottom of test pages (Salend, 2005).
8. Modify the end-of-chapter questions.
   - Read questions as a class.
   - Ask fewer questions.
   - Reword the questions in simpler terms.
   - Increase response time.

Figure 6.7 CHAPTER QUESTIONS

Directions: Read each question carefully. Next to each question is the page on which the answer may be found.
Find the page in the chapter and look for the answer.
Write your answers at the bottom of this paper.

1. What are bacteria? (Page 16)
2. What shape are bacteria? (Page 16)
3. Where do bacteria live? (Page 17)
4. How are bacteria harmful to us? (Page 19)
5. How are bacteria helpful to us? (Page 21)

- Allow students to work on some of the questions together (e.g., odd-numbered questions) and then complete the remaining questions independently.
- Write the number of the page on which the response can be found next to each question at the end of the chapter (see Figure 6.7). Or next to the response in the chapter, write the number of the question, then highlight the response (Wood & Wooley, 1986). Students may actually spend more time reading the material as they look for the answer to a particular question than they might if you just asked them to read the material.

9. Teachers should consider the readability of test items when they construct tests (Goh, 2004; Salend, 2005). Modify the readability level of a test by rewording the

Table 6.3 Test Questions With Lowered Readability

These are examples of how you can rewrite test questions to lower the readability level. Notice that the original intent of each question is maintained.

Original	Earthquakes are produced by what force within the earth?
Revised	What causes earthquakes?
Original	Compare and contrast the personal attributes and characteristics of Ulysses S. Grant and Robert E. Lee.
Revised	How were Ulysses S. Grant and Robert E. Lee alike? How were they different?
Original	What is the sensation of seeing two objects when only one is viewed?
Revised	What is double vision?
Original	Discuss the rationale of the secessionists in regard to their threat to secede from the Union in 1860.
Revised	Why did the Southern states decide to leave the Union in 1860?
Original	According to the Gadsden Purchase, the United States procured thousands of square miles of unsettled land located in New Mexico and Arizona along the southern borders of both states. Provide a description of how and why this occurred.
Revised	The Gadsden Purchase gave the United States unsettled land along the southern border of New Mexico and Arizona. Tell how and why this happened.
Original	List the four primary taste sensations that are each sensitive to a particular kind of chemical stimulus.
Revised	List the four primary taste sensations.
Original	Describe the three environmental conditions required for the prolific growth of mold and mildew.
Revised	List three things mold and mildew need in order to grow.
Original	Crystal Thompson needs insurance for her personal belongings, but not for her residence, since she lives in an apartment. If her annual insurance premium is $63.00, what amount will she have paid in three years?
Revised	Crystal Thompson lives in an apartment and needs to insure her belongings. The insurance premium costs $63.00 a year (annually). How much will she pay in three years?

Table 6.4 Adapted Essay Question

Key word list
Funnel-shaped, cloud particles, updraft, debris, destruction, kilometers, Doppler radar, meteorologists
Essay question
Gigantic cumulonimbus clouds have been building overhead. The sky is dark with a strange tint of gray and green. The air has become very still and the sound of a siren can be heard. Name and describe the type of severe storm that is about to occur.
Subquestions
In writing your answer, discuss the following:
1. How is this type of storm formed?
2. How can this type of storm be predicted?
3. What are the possible effects of such a storm?
4. What safety measures should you take in this type of storm?

content, shortening sentences, and simplifying vocabulary or asking students to write questions in their own words. Adapted from Murphy, Meyers, Olesen, McKean, and Custer (1995), Table 6.3 provides an example of how to reword test items while maintaining the original intent of the questions.

Many authors have offered guidelines to use in writing or adapting test items such as multiple choice, matching, fill in the blanks, and essay. For example, for multiple-choice questions, you should present the choices vertically; avoid using words such as always, all, never; and make sure the choices are of similar length (Salend, 2005). In constructing matching items, you should list both columns on the same page. For fill-in-the-blank items, you should make the size of the blanks the same. Essay questions are frequently challenging for students because they involve reading, critical thinking, and written expression. There are some things you can do to assist students to respond to an essay item on a test that may result in a more complete and better organized response. After you write the essay question, provide subquestions and a list of key words that the student can include in the response (Salend, 2005) (see Table 6.4). Notice how by structuring the student's response with subquestions and including a key word list, you can assist the student to better analyze the question and organize a well-thought-out written response.

ADDRESSING CULTURAL AND LINGUISTIC DIVERSITY

Because the assessment of students from diverse racial and ethnic groups is influenced by cultural and language differences as well as by varied learning styles, Banks and colleagues (2001) recommend that teachers use multiple, culturally sensitive assessment techniques. They suggest that teachers use formative and summative strategies that include observations, oral tests, and teacher-made and standardized assessments because students acquire and demonstrate competencies in different ways.

In addition to using multiple and appropriate assessment techniques with students from culturally and linguistically diverse groups, teachers must also use meaningful and appropriate instructional materials. In some states, textbooks and other materials are adopted by the state or district, whereas in other states the teacher may have the opportunity to recommend textbooks, supplementary materials, and other printed products. Because many teachers depend on the textbook in determining the curriculum, the way in which textbooks and other printed materials are selected is vitally important in providing multicultural education (Gollnick & Chinn, 2002). Some groups such as women, minority groups, individuals with disabilities, and older persons are underrepresented in materials (Gollnick & Chinn, 2002). Teachers who are sensitive to these omissions will develop strategies for including them as part of instruction. They will use supplementary materials and discussions to overcome biases that are inherent in some instructional materials and ensure that their students are exposed to the multicultural nature of society. For example, in her history class, Ms. Andreas adapts and supplements the history textbook significantly to include the perspective of Native Americans in the study of Western expansion. Gollnick and Chinn (2002) state that textbooks typically present only one perspective and suggest that students should be given the opportunity to read more than one perspective. If the textbook presents only the U.S. government's perspective of treaties and protection, the teacher should also present the Native American perspective, which might examine the topics of broken treaties and the appropriation of lands (Gollnick & Chinn, 2002). To further illustrate this point, a text that is limited to the contributions of the European settlers in the United States does not present a balanced perspective (Gollnick & Chinn, 2002). Many students would fail to learn about the contributions of their own cultural groups in the development of their country. Such a text would have to be significantly modified or supplemented.

Therefore, "just as we adapt the pace and complexity of the instructional format for students with disabilities, so we further adapt to accommodate cultural and linguistic differences" (Winzer & Mazurek, 2000, p. 253). It is recommended that you include the following types of materials in your classroom (Winzer & Mazurek, 1998):

1. Books that are fiction, nonfiction, dual-language texts, poetry, magazines, and newspapers.
2. Books that have predictable features, invite conversation, have meaningful illustrations, support the curriculum, and are linked to the student's culture.
3. Materials that are culturally relevant, meaningful, accurate, and in the student's language.
4. Supplemental materials that include manipulatives, technology, and bulletin boards.

Few curricular materials exist for students with disabilities who are also linguistically diverse (Baca & Cervantes, 2004). Special education teachers, in collaboration with other personnel, may find it helpful to try out different materials, and adapt or supplement until they achieve an appropriate education plan for English language learners (Baca & Cervantes, 2004). This process may begin as part of the IEP development and later continued in the student's various classrooms by teachers and other personnel.

Artiles and Ortiz (2002) recommend that teachers consider certain factors when adapting materials for English language learners:

- Analyze vocabulary and syntax for verbal load and regional forms and rewrite the text if necessary;
- Use textbooks with pictures, media, and action to make the content understandable;
- Provide vocabulary guides, concept maps, semantic webs, and advance organizers to assist students with comprehension of academic content; and
- Use structured study guides, chapter outlines, and summaries.

BOX 6.3

Reflections on Practice

With the cultural and linguistic diversity of our classrooms increasing, it is important for teachers to be aware of and utilize resources that will result in a culturally and linguistically responsive curriculum. We recommend that you follow the suggestions already presented in this chapter and also enhance your curriculum by consulting websites such as the following for the most up-to-date multicultural resources available.

The Multicultural Literacy page at the University of Connecticut website www.literacy.uconn.edu/multilit.htm offers links to multicultural instructional resources, additional background information, and multicultural booklists.

The Teacher's Corner www.theteacherscorner.net/ is a general-purpose teaching site that provides an excellent starting point for lesson plans and additional resources.

Education World www.education-world.com/ is a site designed for all educators to access a wealth of information on many topics, including multicultural issues.

Student magazine subscriptions such as *Time For Kids* and *Scholastic Magazine* offer a multicultural perspective on current events at appropriate readability levels.

For example, Mr. Bonavidez uses DVDs and CD-ROM technology to supplement his discussion of famous inventors. His students are able to see different parts of the United States and the world as each DVD and CD-ROM traces the origin and background of one inventor. In addition, Mr. Bonavidez provides glossaries that contain terms, definitions, and pictures to help students who are not proficient in English.

Activity 6.3

Find an instructional material at the level (elementary, middle, or high school) and subject (reading, biology, algebra) of your choice. Complete an analysis of the material using the materials analysis techniques we have presented in this chapter. If you identify areas for improvement, apply some of the techniques presented in this chapter to make the instructional material more appropriate for students with special needs.

IMPORTANT POINTS

1. Techniques for adapting print products include highlighting, color coding, and simplifying, among others.
2. Test adaptations include typing clear, easy-to-read tests, providing study questions, modifying the readability level, and using visual cues on the test to guide students.
3. Teachers should use multiple, culturally sensitive assessment techniques that include observations, oral tests, and teacher-made and standardized assessments (Banks, et al., 2001).
4. To facilitate the effective and appropriate use of instructional materials with students who are culturally and linguistically diverse, strategies include modification of vocabulary; use of media, pictures, and glossaries; presentation of multiple perspectives; attention to gender, age, individuals with special needs, and inclusion of materials that emphasize different languages and cultures.

DEVELOPING MATERIALS

Some instructional materials cannot be adapted or modified to a level that is acceptable for use with students who have special needs. For example, we have worked with some math and spelling materials that required an almost complete reconstruction because of inappropriate sequencing of skills, problems with format, and print quality. Other materials have been inappropriate because of cultural or gender bias. Still other materials have introduced too much new vocabulary.

Because of these and other problems, you may choose to develop your own materials. When developing instructional materials, avoid the problems that are characteristic of ineffective commercial products. For example, design materials that provide sufficient practice, repetition, and review and consider factors that will affect the performance of your students. Consider how the learner is going to interact with the material. The input may be auditory, with directions given on an audiotape, and the output may be written, with the student required to write something. Vary the input (auditory, visual) and output (written, verbal), depending on the activity and the characteristics of your students. Parallel the types of activities required for students on local and state assessments.

You should also attend to the complexity of the material and match it to the level of your students. Some teachers develop manipulative materials to help their students better grasp abstract concepts. The complexity of the material can also be related to the stages of learning. For example, when Ms. Roberts teaches place value to her students, she gives them popsicle sticks to help them understand the concept (acquisition stage).

As you develop materials, consider how your students will receive feedback. Some of your materials should be self-correcting, so your students can monitor their own performance. In addition, computers can provide automatic feedback.

In materials development, you should give careful consideration to the concept load of the material. This includes the number of new concepts you present at one time, the amount of practice you provide, and the rate of presentation. For example, Mr. Saunders spends a class period with his high school students going over a diagram that he developed after examining several textbooks. He consolidated into one diagram nearly everything he could find on the topic of prejudice. Concentrating on the one concept, the class defines prejudice, identifies characteristics, and gives examples.

In materials development, you should also consider your level of involvement with the materials and whether it is extensive (teacher-directed) or minimal (student-directed, individual, or group). Rewriting materials and then presenting them to your students (teacher-directed) will require quite an investment of your time. Giving the students self-correcting materials requires less teacher interaction and time. Finally, you should consider the affective aspects of materials, such as cultural emphasis, age bias, and gender bias.

TYPES OF TEACHER-MADE MATERIALS

Teacher-made materials may include worksheets, folder activities, educational games, and self-correcting materials. These materials may increase the effectiveness of the overall instructional program because they ensure individualization and because they are designed to reinforce, motivate, and enhance pupil participation. For example, Biamca, a third grader, had trouble learning vocabulary in its written form in her reading workbook. Ms. Melendez made her a word bank that contained the reading vocabulary on language master cards. Biamca practiced her words on the language master, which presented the words to her both visually and aurally. Biamca said each word aloud as she practiced and again, later, as Ms. Melendez checked her. Ms. Melendez noted Biamca's progress on a chart that she created on the computer. Biamca learned the words quickly because she received positive and corrective feedback and found the material interesting and motivating.

Latasha, a seventh-grade student, had just been taught a technique to improve her comprehension of reading material. Because she works successfully in groups and learns well from others, her teacher, Mr. Thurman, grouped her with two other students to practice, repeat, and review the steps of the comprehension monitoring technique. Mr. Thurman developed assignments for the students to use for written practice, let them verbally rehearse the steps with one another, and then, using a teacher-made checklist, evaluated each student for mastery of the steps. Use of the teacher-made materials and attention to affective concerns, in combination with learner interactions with the materials and feedback and evaluation, increased Latasha's opportunities for success.

Worksheets

Because many schools use worksheets, you should know how to recognize and develop effective worksheets. In developing worksheets for students, you should make directions clear and concise and be careful not to overload the page with items. Worksheets should focus on one concept at a time and provide adequate practice. Worksheets should be manageable in appearance, not overwhelming, with a clear, easy-to-follow, inviting format. In addition to developing your own worksheets, you may also need to adapt or rewrite worksheets.

Figure 6.5 contains a sample of a poorly designed worksheet. Figure 6.6 shows how that worksheet has been adapted. Notice how the poorly designed worksheet is crowded and lacks clear, specific directions. For example, there are no directions for Part A (the true/false items), there are incomplete directions for Part B (the vocabulary section), and the directions lack specificity in Part C (the written response section). The list of 20 words looks overwhelming, and the worksheet looks crowded. The adapted worksheet is easier on the eye because of the way it is organized (e.g., boxes around sections and better spacing). Introductory directions are provided and directions for Parts I, II, and III are clear and specific. Part I contains boxes in which students may write their responses, and the directions specify that students are to write *true or false*. The directions for Part II state where to write the words and definitions. The long list of 20 words has been divided into four smaller, more manageable lists. The directions for Part III clearly state that students have a choice of *two* activities for the written response question.

You can make worksheets self-correcting by printing the answers on the back, on the bottom (upside down), or along the right margin (which can be folded over to conceal them). A word of caution: If you plan to use worksheets, be sure they serve a valid purpose and are not used merely to fill time, and make sure you provide feedback to students.

Folder Activities

File folders meet the needs of students by providing opportunities for practice and reinforcement of a wide range of skills. File folders are convenient to use and store, and teachers who float from classroom to classroom can easily transport them. Because folder activities are usually student directed, they should contain clear, concise directions. Many folder activities include some means of self-monitoring, such as access to an answer key.

Folders may be constructed to include activities that are multilevel. For example, in her preparation of a math unit, Mrs. Barkwell set up folder activities that used a restaurant menu. In one folder activity, students were asked to locate the cost of various items, such as hamburgers, soft drinks, french fries, and milkshakes. In another folder activity, students were required to order several items and compute the total cost. In still another activity, students had to figure the total cost plus tax. In a more advanced folder activity, students determined the total cost and tax, then figured out how much change they would receive from \$10 and from \$20. Notice how the difficulty level of the activities varied, making them appropriate for students functioning at several different levels. The activities were set up to be self-correcting, with the answers written on the reverse side (e.g., a card with a picture of a hamburger on one side and the price on the back).

Educational Games

Educational games do not take the place of instruction, but they do provide motivating ways to help reinforce skills (Kellough & Kellough, 2003; Rotter, 2004; Salend, 2005). By creating games, you help students attain skills and solve problems that are important to their success both in and out of school. A teacher-made game must provide (a) a clearly stated purpose or rationale, and outcome; (b) complete yet uncomplicated directions and rules; (c) reinforcement and practice of skills already acquired; and (d) a method of monitoring and evaluating progress.

You may construct your own board game or use a commercial board. Some publishers produce wipe-off game boards, cards, spinners, and game pieces available for purchase. You can use this generic equipment to create your own instructional games to support the sequential development of the academic skills your students need. The game boards can be adapted to any academic skill and content that you want to reinforce, including simplifying fractions, reviewing science vocabulary, and practicing long vowel sounds. You may also construct a spinner for a game by attaching a paper fastener to the center of a transparency. By drawing a circle on the transparency, dividing it into eighths, and writing numbers 1 through 8 in consecutive sections, you can make a generic spinner that is appropriate for use with any game and is usable with the entire class or a small group.

Self-Correcting Materials

Many teachers include a self-correcting component in the materials they develop because of the importance of immediate feedback to learning. Mercer and Mercer (2005) point out some advantages of self-correcting materials:

- Students avoid practicing mistakes.
- Students learn better with immediate rather than delayed feedback.
- Students can function independently.
- Students tend to remain on task with self-correcting materials.

You can develop self-correcting materials in a variety of formats (e.g., answer on the back, audiocassette, matching, etc.). The following ideas are based on suggestions by Mercer, Mercer, and Bott (1984).

Answer on the Back You can write a problem on one side of a card and put the answer on the back. You may use such cards for math facts and their answers or for vocabulary terms and their definitions. Alternatively, you can write terms or math facts and their answers on the same side of the card. Then cut each card in half in a different zigzag pattern, so the question is on one half of the card and the answer is on the other half. That way, the two parts fit together each time your students respond correctly. You may also use this technique for the states and their capitals.

Audiocassette You can use an audiocassette to record a problem, question, or direction, then pause before dictating the answer. This self-correcting technique is also effective with spelling words, science vocabulary, and word problems.

Matching For practicing a word and its abbreviation, a math problem and its answer, or a date in history and the event that took place on that date, prepare sets of cards with a problem or question on one card and the answer on another card. Be sure the back of each pair of cards contains some type of picture completion. After students respond to the problems, they should turn the cards over. If the answer is correct, the pictures should either match or fit together to complete an object or design.

A teacher who has taught in both general and special education settings developed a way to practice vocabulary. She calls it PowerPoint practice. For practicing vocabulary in the content areas, students can create short PowerPoint displays by typing the word on the first slide using WordArt, to look up a visual representation of the word to go on the second slide, and connecting to an online dictionary to look up the definition and type it on the third slide. These PowerPoint shows can then be used over and over to help master difficult vocabualry.

Activity 6.4

Work in a group to develop an educational game for students at the elementary level. Remember, a teacher-made game must provide a clearly stated purpose, uncomplicated directions and rules, reinforcement and practice of acquired skills, and a monitoring method. After you have developed your game, ask another group to try it. Based upon their feedback, what changes (if any) will you make?

IMPORTANT POINTS

1. In developing instructional materials, it is important to provide sufficient practice, repetition, and review.
2. Key variables during materials development include the learner's interactions with the materials, the concept load, the extent of teacher involvement, and affective aspects of materials.
3. Teacher-made materials include worksheets, folder activities, educational games, and self-correcting materials.

PUTTING IT ALL TOGETHER

In this chapter, we have presented a variety of ways to select, analyze, adapt, and develop instructional materials, along with strategies to modify tests. We have also emphasized the importance of having general and special education teachers collaborate in this process. Since instructional materials are the tools that teachers use to implement their instructional programs, the materials must be developmentally, culturally, linguistically, age, gender and interest appropriate for students; based upon need; and incorporated into the IEP process. If instructional materials are not appropriate, it is up to the teacher to modify, adapt, and develop materials so that elementary and secondary students with special needs achieve success within the curriculum.

DISCUSSION QUESTIONS

1. Provide examples to support the statement, "One of the most important roles of the special education teacher is to assist general education teachers in the adaptation of materials and instruction." Once again, think back to the chapter opener about Emily. Respond to this question in the context of Emily's situation with her general and special education teachers. Now think of an example at the secondary level.
2. Discuss how you are going to provide materials in your classroom that are appropriate for culturally and linguistically diverse groups of students.
3. How do you build a classroom community and at the same time provide test adaptations for students with special needs?.

Websites: Useful websites related to chapter content can be found in Appendix A.

CHAPTER

7

Strategy Instruction

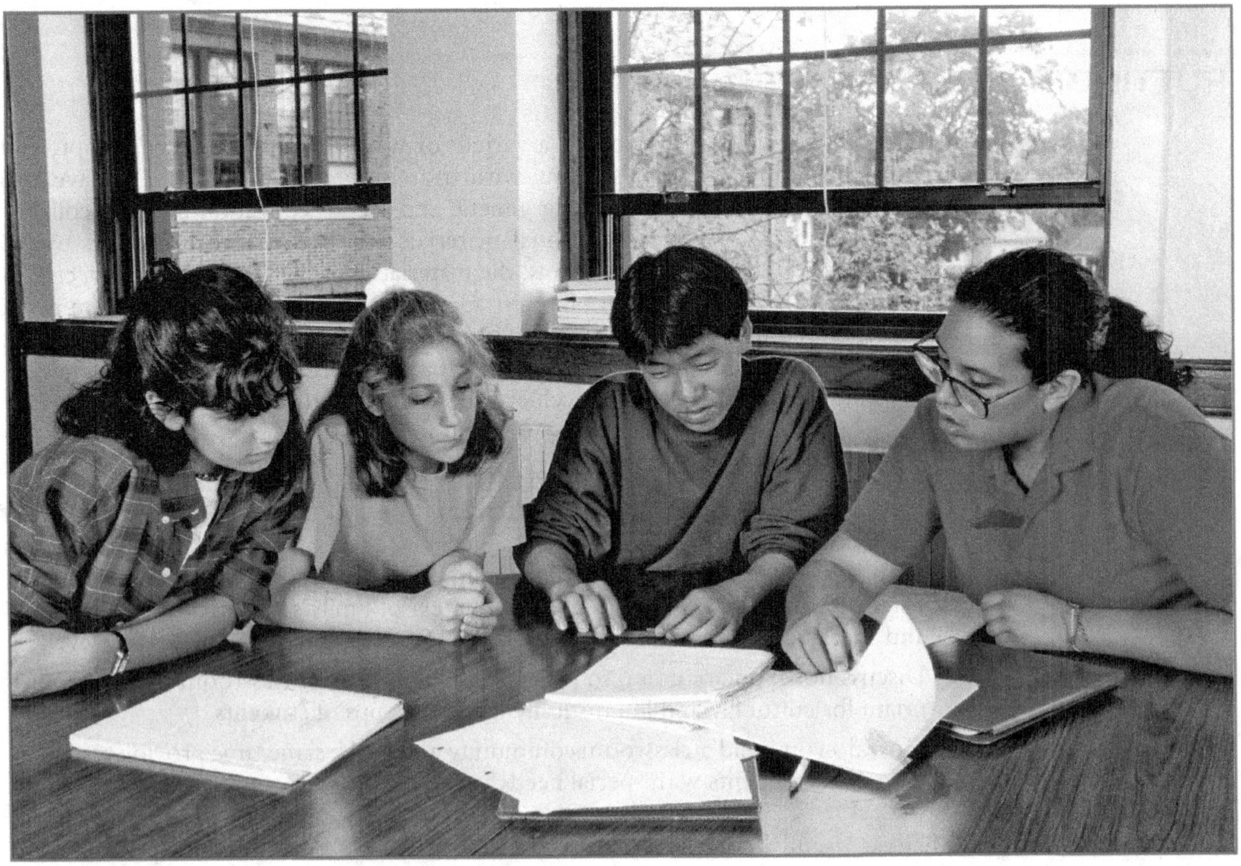

KEY TOPICS

Miguel did not notice the noisy crowd of students around him as he worked his way down the hall to Ms. Crisafi's room at the end of the school day. He had just received his first quarter grade report and a D in Physical Science was the only thing he could see. His first thought when he opened the envelope and scanned down the list of C's to the horrible D was, "My mom is going to kill me!" Miguel had not been diagnosed with a learning disability until the end of fourth grade. By then he had fallen behind the others in his class and each year he struggled to catch up. He was so tired of getting bad grades and by this point in eighth grade, he figured he would never catch up.

Miguel slid into a chair in Ms. Crisafi's classroom and slumped over in a state of defeat. "I have been working so hard, studying every night, turning in most of my homework and this is all I get for it!" he told Ms. Crisafi, his reading intervention teacher. "It's all because that book is too hard to read and my science teacher makes me read it every night. I read a page and when I get to the bottom, I don't remember anything I've read. My mom even paid extra for me to get a tutor and the tutor helps me with the words, but when she leaves, I don't remember them. Then when we have a test, I can't answer the questions. How am I ever going to bring this grade up and keep up with the rest of the class?"

Ms. Crisafi felt as if she too had failed despite working very hard. It was only her second year of teaching and her assignment to teach inclusively in Miguel's science class was her only chance to work with her eighth-grade students within a general education classroom rather than here in her classroom. When she sat down with the science teacher last week to prepare the grade reports, it was easy to see that her students with learning disabilities were really struggling to keep up with their peers. Her coteacher, Mrs. Henry, was also feeling dismayed and the two of them agreed to strategize about how to better meet the needs of their students with disabilities, particularly Miguel.

"Miguel, I want you to know that Mrs. Henry and your mom and I know how hard you have been working" she said. "I know that right now you are feeling very discouraged, but please don't give up. Tomorrow Mrs. Henry and I are going to come up with a plan for you that will help you to be successful for the rest of the school year."

If you were Ms. Crisafi, what would you discuss with Mrs. Henry to improve the chances for Miguel and other students to be successful in class? Hint: The content in this chapter will help you identify strategies for students who are struggling with acquiring, retaining, and expressing information. Think about how you would assist Miguel in both Mrs. Henry's and Ms. Crisafi's class and how you would involve Miguel's mother in the plans for her son.

Responses to these questions are found in the Instructor's Manual.

INTRODUCTION

The adage, "Give me a fish and I eat for a day. Teach me to fish and I eat for a lifetime," exemplifies the need to teach students *how to learn*. If you teach students how to learn, then you will not have to help them prepare for every test, assist them with each report, or help them answer the questions at the end of every chapter they are assigned. In other words, you provide them with the strategies that will empower them to act independently and master skills across a variety of situations and settings. These skills may include paraphrasing a textbook passage, accessing and remembering information, or writing an essay.

In this chapter, we discuss the use of cognitive strategies to teach students with special needs to become strategic information processors and problem solvers. First, we provide a discussion of cognitive strategies in general. Then we describe how cognitive strategies are taught through the use of metacognition, cognitive behavior modification (CBM), reciprocal teaching (RT), the Strategic Instruction Model (SIM), and the Self-Regulated Strategy Development (SRSD) model, all of which include aspects of both the reductionist (scientific) and constructivist (holistic) paradigms described in Chapter 1. These approaches rely on direct instruction, modeling, feedback, and active student involvement—characteristics of the reductionist paradigm. They also place an emphasis on how students think, embed instruction in meaningful contexts, and provide opportunities for students to assume responsibility and advocate for their own learning by setting their own objectives and learning from one another—characteristics of the constructivist paradigm. Metacognition, cognitive behavior modification, reciprocal teaching, the Strategic Instruction Model, and the Self-Regulated Strategy Development model begin with the teacher assuming the major responsibility for teaching, then gradually shifting the responsibility to the students.

COGNITIVE STRATEGIES

Cognitive strategies relate to how we process information (Lenz, Ellis, & Scanlon, 1996). They are the cognitive processes that learners use to influence learning (Mayer, 2001). For example, Joshua may use the cognitive strategy of writing a long-distance phone number five times to help him memorize it, whereas B. J. may use the cognitive strategy of clustering, so the phone number is processed as 702 452 38 10. Cognitive strategy instruction combines the elements of explicit teaching with scaffolding procedures (Ciardello, 1998), and empowers students by giving them access to techniques or methods for acquiring, remembering, and demonstrating information in order to solve problems.

RATIONALE

Some students lack certain strategies, choose inappropriate strategies, or fail to use strategies altogether to tackle a task or help themselves learn on their own (Berry, Hall, & Gildroy, 2004). These same students do not appear to take an active role in their own learning. Others may actually use strategies but may not choose them wisely (as in repeating a long list of words over and over in order to memorize it instead of using mnemonics or visual imagery). Jones, Palincsar, Ogle, and Carr (1987) indicate that if students do not already possess a strategy for completing certain tasks, then teaching an appropriate strategy is likely to improve achievement, especially for less proficient students. Because low-achieving students are not likely to develop cognitive strategies spontaneously, it is important to provide specific strategy instruction (Jones, et al., 1987) by teaching them how to use effective and efficient strategies to enhance their independence (Berry, et al., 2004). Research has shown that students with learning disabilities benefit from cognitive strategy instruction (Montague, 1997), including the use of self-instruction (Van Luit & Naglieri, 1999). Cognitive strategies provide students with a set of self-instructional steps that assist them in addressing a specific need (e.g., writing an essay) and in learning, organizing, retaining, and expressing information. Cognitive strategies offer promise for students with mild disabilities to set goals, devise strategies, and monitor their own progress (Meese, 1994).

In addition to knowing how to use a cognitive strategy, it is important for students to know why the strategy is useful or how to evaluate its effectiveness (Billingsley & Wildman, 1990). Students need to know what the strategy is for; how, when, and where to use the strategy; why the strategy is important and useful; and how to evaluate its effectiveness (Winograd & Hare, 1988). This knowledge is critical to generalization efforts. Studies have shown that cognitive strategy training has a significant impact on academic performance when generalization of the training to natural environments occurs (Lenz, Deshler, & Kissam, 2004). In other words, "the strategy must be generalizable across a variety of settings, situations, and contexts" (Lenz, et al., 1996, p. 16).

STRATEGIC TEACHING AND LEARNING

In classroom settings where strategic teaching and learning are taking place, teachers and students think and make decisions about strategy selection, application, and evaluation. If you walked into a classroom where the teacher was using cognitive strategy instruction, you would notice the **teacher**:

- Tailoring instruction to meet students' needs and difficulties;
- Modeling the use of strategies by "thinking aloud";
- Making sure that students understand the task and the significance of the strategy to the task;
- Actively involving students;
- Helping students create their own strategies;
- Assisting students to personalize the strategies they use;
- Providing feedback regarding students' use of strategies; and
- Gradually transferring the responsibility for teaching and learning to the students.

In that same classroom, you would see **students**:

- Applying strategies to various academic content;
- Actively participating;

- Monitoring their own progress;
- Interacting with teachers and with each other, and
- Taking responsibility for their own learning through self-instruction, self-evaluation, and self-regulation.

In describing strategic teaching and learning, we borrow from the ideas of Jones and associates (1987), along with the principles of effective teaching (Englert, Tarrant, & Mariage, 1992). Strategic teachers:

- Spend time thinking/reflecting about instructional planning and teaching
- Focus on students' prior learning experiences
- Possess a wide variety of strategies and explain to students the purpose and significance of each strategy
- Are rich in content knowledge
- Know how to achieve a balance between strategies and content
- Understand characteristics of learners
- Are knowledgeable about the organization of instructional materials and curriculum
- Actively collaborate with their students in selecting, applying, and monitoring the use of strategies to meet specific goals.

As you read the next sections on metacognition, cognitive behavior modification, reciprocal teaching, the Strategic Instruction Model, and the Self-Regulated Strategy Development model, notice that the strategic teaching and learning behaviors previously described are included in each of them. Both special and general education teachers should be strategic teachers and take an active role in helping students with special needs and others develop good metacognitive skills; utilize the components of cognitive behavior modification to manage their academic and social behaviors; engage in reciprocal teaching activities with students; use strategies that help students learn how to learn; and help students assume more control over their own writing. The special education teacher can focus on these areas of instruction in both pull-out and inclusion settings and the general education teacher can reinforce that instruction in the general education setting and/or initiate it. Thus, the key is to integrate strategy instruction with content instruction and ensure that special and general education teachers have the expertise and opportunity to accomplish this integration.

Metacognition is the knowledge (awareness) and control (monitoring) that individuals have over their learning. Cognitive behavior modification (CBM) teaches self-regulation and problem solving. Reciprocal teaching (RT) involves gaining meaning from text through the use of teacher–student dialogues. Both Strategic Instruction Model (SIM) and Self-Regulated Strategy Development (SRSD) model include how to plan and complete a task, monitor progress, and make adjustments and modifications. Although there are some differences among these five approaches, the many similarities place each of them in the category of cognitive strategies. Each approach (1) has a set of steps or procedures, (2) uses cognitive modeling, (3) involves explicit instruction, (4) includes practice and feedback, (5) incorporates a gradual transfer of responsibility and ownership from teacher to students, and (6) promotes generalization. Table 7.1 provides a comparison of metacognition, CBM, RT, SIM, and the SRSD model in terms of definition, components, instructional procedures, instructional approach, and content taught.

Figure 7.1 illustrates an example of a cognitive/metacognitive strategy for mathematical problem solving (Montague, 1997).

Table 7.1 Comparison of Cognitive Approaches

	Metacognition	Cognitive Behavior Modification	Reciprocal Teaching	Strategic Instruction Model	Self-Regulated Strategy Development Model
Definition	The knowledge (awareness) and control (monitoring) that individuals have over their own thinking and learning	A technique in which the teacher models his or her thinking processes while performing a task; then the student practices overtly and covertly by him or herself	An interactive teaching strategy that takes the form of a dialogue between teachers and students to construct the meaning of text jointly	Learning *how* to learn and perform Focus on tasks and curriculum demands	An integrated approach that assists students in developing composition skills and self-regulation strategies
Components	Active involvement of students Systematic steps or procedures Cognitive modeling Self-awareness Self-monitoring Gradual transfer of ownership and regulation Generalization	Active involvement of students Systematic steps or procedures Cognitive modeling Guided practice Verbalizations Overt and covert processing Gradual transfer of ownership and regulation Generalization	Active involvement of students Systematic steps or procedures Instruction in useful strategies Guided interactive instruction Well-informed learners Readable, meaningful practice materials Scaffolding Cognitive modeling Gradual transfer of ownership and regulation Generalization	Active involvement of students Systematic steps or procedures Cognitive modeling Overt and covert processing Guided and independent practice Gradual transfer of ownership and regulation Generalization	Active involvement of students Systematic steps or procedures Cognitive modeling Overt and covert processing strategies Gradual transfer of ownership and regulation Individualization of instruction Criterion-based instruction Generalization

(*continued*)

Table 7.1 (continued)

	Metacognition	Cognitive Behavior Modification	Reciprocal Teaching	Strategic Instruction Model	Self-Regulated Strategy Development Model
Instructional procedures	Identify task Determine student's performance Select a strategy Teach the strategy Provide practice Provide feedback Teach generalization	Explain strategy Share rationale Perform task while thinking aloud Have student perform task overtly and covertly Provide feedback	Teach summarizing, question generating, clarifying, and predicting Read title, ask for predictions Read a segment of text Ask a question about content Summarize/ask for elaborations Discuss clarifications Discuss predictions regarding next segment Provide feedback	Pretest Describe/obtain commitment Model Verbal practice Controlled practice and feedback Advanced practice and feedback Confirm acquisition and obtain generalization commitment Generalization	Develop background knowledge Discuss it Model it Memorize it Support it Independent performance
Instructional approach	Integration of reductionist and constructivism	Integration of reductionist and constructivism	Integration of reductionist and constructivism	Integration of reductionist and constructivism	Integration of reductionist and constructivism
Content	Academic subjects Social behaviors	Academic subjects Social behaviors	Academic subjects	Academic subjects Social behaviors	Academic subjects Social behaviors

Source: Adapted from Platt, J., & Olson, J., *Teaching Adolescents With Mild Disabilities* 1997. Brooks/Cole Publishing Company, Pacific Grove, CA. Reprinted by permission.

Figure 7.1 A COGNITIVE/METACOGNITIVE STRATEGY FOR MATHEMATICAL PROBLEM SOLVING

Read (for understanding)

Say:	Read the problem. If I don't understand, read it again.
Ask:	Have I read and understood the problem?
Check:	For understanding as I solve the problem.

Paraphrase (your own words)

Say:	Underline the important information. Put the problem in my own words.
Ask:	Have I underlined the important information? What is the question? What am I looking for?
Check:	That the information goes with the question.

Visualize (a picture of a diagram)

Say:	Make a drawing or a diagram.
Ask:	Does the picture fit the problem?
Check:	The picture against the problem information.

Hypothesize (a plan to solve the problem)

Say:	Decide how many steps and operations are needed. Write the operation symbols ($+ - \times \div$).
Ask:	If I do—, what will I get? If I do—, then what do I need to do next? How many steps are needed?
Check:	That the plan makes sense.

Estimate (predict the answer)

Say:	Round the numbers, do the problem in my head, and write the estimate.
Ask:	Did I round up and down? Did I write the estimate?
Check:	That I used the important information.

Compute (do the arithmetic)

Say:	Do the operations in the right order.
Ask:	How does my answer compare with my estimate? Does my answer make sense? Are the decimals or money signs in the right places?
Check:	That all the operations were done in the right order.

Check (make sure everything is right)

Say:	Check the computation.
Ask:	Have I checked every step? Have I checked the computation? Is my answer right?
Check:	That everything is right. If not, go back. Then ask for help if I need it.

Source: From "Cognitive Strategy Instruction in Mathematics for Students with Learning Disabilities" by M. Montague, 1997. *Journal of Learning Disabilities, 30*(2), p. 171. Copyright (1997) by PRO-ED, Inc. Reprinted by permission.

METACOGNITION

The general knowledge (awareness) and control (monitoring) that an individual has over his or her thinking and learning is known as metacognition (Paris, Lipson, Jacobs, Oka, Debritto, & Cross, 1982). Metacognitive strategies relate to how an individual selects, monitors, and uses these strategies (Lenz, et al., 1996). Awareness, the first component of metacognition, involves a person's knowledge about his or her cognitive resources and the relationship between those capabilities and the demands of the task. For example, if you notice that you can study better with the radio off, you are demonstrating an understanding of how you function best in a specific situation or with a certain task. If you are aware of what you need to do to perform effectively, you may be able to regulate and control activities to solve a problem or complete a task. For example, when Rebekah observes that she is more successful in afternoon classes than in morning classes because she performs better in the afternoon, she is demonstrating metacognitive awareness.

The second component of metacognition involves self-regulatory mechanisms that enable a person to monitor, adjust, correct, and control his or her cognitive activities and task performance. For example, when you estimate the length of time it will take to complete an activity and adjust your pace to allow yourself sufficient time to finish, you are exercising control and regulating your actions. You are actively participating in the learning situation and assuming control over it. For example, Rashard has learned self-regulation by adjusting his rate when he reads different materials. He reads *The Sporting News* magazine and the daily comics quickly, but spends more time methodically reading his science textbook, looking back frequently to check his comprehension. Notice how he first demonstrates an awareness of the need to read materials at different rates (metacognitive awareness) and then exercises control over the situation by actually adjusting his reading rate with different materials (metacognitive monitoring). Awareness of one's thinking is necessary in order to monitor one's comprehension (Pressley, Wharton-McDonald, Raphael, Bogner, & Roehrig, 2002).

RATIONALE

The reason we teach metacognitive strategies to students is to influence how students interact with a learning task (Palincsar, 1986a). Metacognitive instruction is designed to empower students to assume control over their own learning and problem solving. It allows students to be more independent, to understand the purpose behind their academic assignments, and to realize the results of their actions. Metacognitive instruction is

Activity 7.1

Part 1: Complete a metacognitive awareness activity by selecting a textbook passage of your own choosing. As you read it, try to observe what you do by asking yourself these questions, which are based on H. A. Robinson's (1975) work:

1. Do I look back at the words I have just read?
2. Do I look at each word?
3. Do I think of other things when I read?
4. Do I read and think about the meaning of every word, or do I put words together into groups?
5. Do I really know what I am reading?

When you finish reading, write down all the things you did while you were reading.

Part 2: Now that you have completed a metacognitive awareness activity, try a metacognitive monitoring activity. If you were to read this passage again, what would you do to improve your reading of it? Jot down any strategies you would use or adjustments you would make. For example, would you slow down? Would you pause during reading to make sure you understood what you just read?

(Answers for this and other activities are found in the Instructor's Manual.)

designed to promote generalization and transfer of skills across content areas and settings and is effective in teaching higher level skills such as summarizing, paragraph writing, and self-questioning. Wong (1986) found that students who believe they are in control of their environment appear to be the most successful learners, and therefore remedial programs for students with learning disabilities should include a metacognitive component to help them become independent learners.

DESCRIPTION

Cognitive psychology is an important source of information for teachers working with students who have special needs. Using the contributions of cognitive psychology, special educators can design interventions that emphasize the maintenance and generalization of metacognitive skills and strategies (Wong, 1986). For example, a self-questioning procedure taught to students with learning disabilities resulted in systematic self-monitoring and enhanced reading comprehension (Wong & Jones, 1982). Other investigations have studied the effects of metacognitive instruction on the memory (Paris, Newman, & McVey, 1982) and written expression skills (Harris & Graham, 1994) of students with academic problems. Researchers in cognitive developmental psychology and instructional psychology have developed systematic procedures for teaching metacognitive strategies (Cooney & Swanson, 1990). Teachers may use these procedures with students who have special needs.

A variety of metacognitive strategies are available for you to use as you work with students with special needs. We can compare a student having a variety of metacognitive strategies to a music group with a repertoire of hits to perform at a concert. Students with special needs require a number of strategies at their disposal to respond to the academic demands of the classroom. Besides knowing a variety of strategies, students need to know which strategies to use and when to use them. The members of the group will consider their audience and the acoustics of the facility in which they are playing (setting demands); the lighting, equipment, their voices, instruments (strengths and weaknesses); and what they are trying to accomplish at each concert they hold, such as fund-raising or plugging a new release (personal goal or objective). Students need to consider the demands and problems they encounter in the classroom, what strengths they bring to a learning activity, what typically gives them problems, and what they are trying to do, such as understand a reading passage, remember a list of words, or write a theme. Successful musicians monitor throughout the concert how they are received by the crowd. They may decide to rearrange the sequence of hits they are performing based on the reaction of the audience, or they may resurrect some of their old classics if they get lots of requests for them or if the new ones are not getting a good reaction. You may have been to a concert that started out in a sequenced and organized manner and then noticed signals being passed among the group members to change the original plan and try something else.

Just as the group members monitored and made adjustments in their performance at the concert, students who are metacognitively aware and know how to regulate their learning make adjustments as they proceed through a task. Karim could not remember what he had read when he got to the bottom of the page in his history book (awareness), so he reread the page, this time pausing after each paragraph to paraphrase what he had just read (monitoring). Mayra was having difficulty studying for tests at the end of a unit because she could not understand her own notes or remember what the teacher had said (awareness). She began to rewrite her notes after each class, thereby engaging in a cumulative review (monitoring). These two students were using metacognitive skills. When students possess good metacognitive skills, they are able to interact effectively with learning situations and perform independently.

IMPLEMENTATION

Teachers initially assume the responsibility for helping students identify tasks for which they need metacognitive instruction. They begin metacognitive instruction by modeling self-regulation activities. Then, gradually, through scaffolding, they shift the responsibility to the students, who participate in applying metacognitive skills. Metacognitive strategies become student-directed when students show independent application of them, or generalization.

A review of the literature in metacognition suggests the existence of specific elements to include in metacognitive instruction. We present the following critical steps adapted from the work of Palincsar and Brown (1987) and Pressley, Borkowski, and O'Sullivan (1984), in combination with our own thoughts.

1. Identify the task.

   Example: Students will remember what was read.
2. Choose a strategy to facilitate completion of the task.

   Example: Insert stop points in a text and then tell students to paraphrase what was read.
3. Explicitly teach the strategy.

   Example: Model for students what they should do when they come to a stop point.
4. Explain the benefits to be expected.

   Example: Describe that grades will improve, frustration will decrease, and reading will be easier and more fun.
5. Provide guided practice.

   Example: Work through an activity with students; have them apply the strategy.
6. Provide feedback.

   Example: Give positive and corrective comments, oral and/or written, regarding consistent and appropriate use of the strategy.
7. Teach students how to generalize the use of the strategy.

   Example: Show students how to use this technique with reading materials in school (content-area subjects) and out of school (magazines, email, written directions).

Let's take a look at a metacognitive intervention for increasing class participation. Ellis's (1989) class participation intervention (CPI) for students with special needs addresses metacognitive awareness ("Am I prepared for class?") and monitoring ("What do I already know? Can I tell three things about the topic?"). CPI consists of four parts (PREP, SLANT, RELATE, and WISE) that teach students to think ahead, think during class discussions, and think after class discussions. PREP (prepare materials, review what you know, establish a positive mindset, and pinpoint goals) activates students to prepare themselves for class discussions. During actual class discussions, SLANT (sit up, lean forward, act like you're interested, nod, and track the teacher) cues students to demonstrate appropriate nonverbal behaviors. RELATE (reveal reasons, echo examples, lasso comparisons, ask questions, tell the main idea, and examine importance) directs students to the verbal behaviors essential for class participation. WISE (were goals met, itemize important information, see how information can be remembered, and explain what was learned) requires students to think back and evaluate their participation after class is over. Figure 7.2 shows the WISE strategy for thinking after a lesson, and Figure 7.3 shows the PREP/WISE score sheet.

Figure 7.2 THE METACOGNITIVE STRATEGY FOR THINKING AFTER A LESSON

Think Back with WISE

Were goals met?

- Did you learn what you wanted to learn?
- Did you meet your participation goals?

Itemize important information

- Review study guide, notes, or textbook
- Mark key information

See how information can be remembered

- Draw graphic displays
- Create mnemonic devices
- Create study cards

Explain what was learned to somebody

- Use your notes to teach somebody about the topic

Source: From "A Metacognitive Intervention for Increasing Participation" by E. S. Ellis, 1989, *Learning Disabilities Focus, 5*(1), p. 37. Reprinted by permission.

Figure 7.3 PREP/WISE EVALUATION SHEET

PREP/WISE score sheet

Student name: ____________________

PREP/WISE Process Score

\# of "yes" boxes / # categories evaluated = ______ Process Score

PREP

Prepare materials for class

yes no N/A

☐ ☐ ☐ Textbook

☐ ☐ ☐ Notebook

☐ ☐ ☐ Pen/pencil

☐ ☐ ☐ Homework

☐ ☐ ☐ Study guide

☐ ☐ ☐ Other ____________

yes no N/A

☐ ☐ ☐ Difficult areas marked on notes/book

Review what you know

(at least 3 items known about topic listed)

yes no N/A

☐ ☐ ☐

What I already know:

1. ____________________
2. ____________________
3. ____________________

Establish positive mindset

yes no

☐ ☐

Positive statement about myself: ____________

Pinpoint goals

Question about the topic has been noted

yes no N/A

☐ ☐ ☐

I want to find out ____________________

____

I found out ☐ I still don't know ☐

yes no N/A

☐ ☐ ☐

Participation goals noted

My participation goal is to ____________________

____

I met my goal ☐ I didn't meet my goal ☐

WISE

Were goals met?

yes no N/A

☐ ☐ ☐ Noted whether topic question had been answered during the lesson/what answer was

Itemize important information

yes no N/A

☐ ☐ ☐ Marked on notes/book perceptions of most important information from lesson

See how information can be remembered

yes no N/A

☐ ☐ ☐ Remembering devices created

Explain what was learned to somebody

yes no N/A

☐ ☐ ☐ Explained what was learned to someone else

Source: From "A Metacognitive Intervention for Increasing Participation" by E. S. Ellis, 1989, *Learning Disabilities Focus, 5*(1), p. 39. Reprinted by permission.

BOX 7.1

Reflections on Practice

The purpose of the Reading First initiative of the No Child Left Behind (NCLB) Act is to ensure the use of scientifically based practices for the instruction of reading. In the state of Florida, the challenge of how to help teachers use best practices when teaching reading led to the creation of the Just Read, Florida! Program. This program maintains a website called "Just Read Now!" which provides:

- Metacognitive reading strategies
- Sample lesson plans implementing reading strategies
- Video demonstrations of teachers modeling strategies
- Tools for integrating reading strategies
- Content area suggestions
- Online professional development courses

You may find the Just Read Now! website to be a valuable resource for the topics discussed in this chapter. Additional websites that reinforce strategy instruction are listed at the end of the chapter.

Ellis recommends teaching PREP and WISE together and, after they are mastered, he recommends teaching SLANT and RELATE together. Ellis specifies that the CPI strategies should be taught by motivating students to learn them; describing and modeling the strategies; requiring verbal elaboration and then rote memorization of the strategies; providing group and individual practice; and periodically checking for maintenance of the strategies. He reports that students who master the CPI strategies come to class better prepared and increase academic responding during class.

IMPORTANT POINTS

1. Cognitive strategies relate to how we process information.
2. Metacognition is the general knowledge (awareness) and control (monitoring) that an individual has over his or her thinking and learning.
3. Metacognitive awareness involves a person's knowledge about his or her own cognitive resources and the relationship between those capabilities and the demands of the task.
4. Metacognitive monitoring involves self-regulatory mechanisms that enable a person to monitor, adjust, correct, and control his or her cognitive activities.
5. Metacognitive teaching procedures include the following steps: (a) identify the task, (b) choose a strategy, (c) teach the strategy, (d) explain the benefits, (e) provide guided practice, (f) provide feedback, and (g) teach generalization.

COGNITIVE BEHAVIOR MODIFICATION (CBM)

Cognitive behavior modification (CBM) involves "specific techniques that teach self-control through increased awareness of cognitive processes and knowledge of how behavior affects academic outcomes" (Swaggert, 1998, p. 235). The teacher models his or her thinking processes in performance of a task and then the student practices the teacher model, overtly with assistance, and then covertly alone. It requires the teacher to analyze the task and the thinking processes involved in performing the task. In turn, the students are active participants as they attempt to change their cognitive behaviors. Students are taught to continuously monitor their progress toward preset goals (Swaggert, 1998). Thus, students are able to regulate their own actions (Fraser, Belzner, & Conte, 1992).

Cognitive behavior modification training was first introduced by Meichenbaum and Goodman (1971) to improve the self-control of children with hyperactivity. Since then, various components of CBM have been found to be effective in developing cognitive, behavior, and academic skills in students with learning and behavior problems (Ager & Cole, 1991).

RATIONALE

One of the premises of CBM is that language is thought to affect the socialization and learning processes (Vygotsky, 1962). According to Vygotsky, children first use language to mediate their actions overtly (e.g., "If I touch the stove, I will get burned."). These overt processes (thinking aloud) eventually change to covert processes (thinking to yourself), and the child no longer uses external language mediation to avoid the hot stove. Overt behavior can be changed by modifying a person's pattern of thoughts; that is, changing the way a person thinks about a task can change how he or she approaches it. As a teacher, you can share your thought processes with students as you attempt to solve problems and complete tasks, providing a model for students to imitate. For example, Mercer and Mercer (2001) suggest that teachers model appropriate actions and language for responding to frustrating situations and dealing with failure.

The procedures used in CBM training can be adapted to fit a variety of tasks (Meese, 1994), situations, and settings. Cognitive behavior modification (CBM) is effective in assisting students to remember the steps needed to solve an academic or a social problem, such as computing a long division problem or responding to peer pressure (Swaggart, 1998). It is also a way for students to improve their self-control (Fraser, et al., 1992).

DESCRIPTION

Cognitive behavior modification (CBM) is an approach that teaches students self-regulation and problem solving. Its essential components are cognitive modeling, guided practice, and verbal mediation.

Cognitive Modeling

Cognitive modeling is used as the primary means of instruction (Bos & Vaughn, 2006). In cognitive modeling, you model your thoughts by thinking aloud for students as you attempt to solve an academic or a social problem. As a first step, Albion (1980) suggests that you identify the specific steps if the task deals with a skill such as dividing numbers or the generic steps if the task deals with such behaviors as being prepared for class. Once the steps are identified, you should reconceptualize them into the conversational styles of the students. For example, Ms. Ruiz used think-aloud procedures as she completed long division problems ("I know I can solve this problem. Let's see . . . first I divide. Yes, that's right. Now, what do I do next? I remember . . . I multiply. Let's see, did I multiply correctly? Yes. Next, I need to subtract. Okay . . . that looks good. Now, the last thing I do is bring down the next number. This looks right . . . I knew I could do it!").

Guided Practice

An adaptation of a training sequence developed by Meichenbaum and Goodman (1971) is usually used to teach students to imitate the teacher's verbalizations (Alberto & Troutman, 2006). The sequence proceeds from overt verbalization (in which students perform out loud the same task that was modeled by the teacher) to covert verbalization (in which students perform the task via private speech). It also moves from external guidance provided by the teacher as he or she assists the students in performing the task to internal guidance in which the students complete the steps alone.

Verbal Mediation

Self-instruction, self-reinforcement, self-regulation, and self-evaluation are generally included individually or in combination as part of the verbal mediation procedure. Self-instruction is the use of language to mediate the completion of a task. Self-reinforcement includes selecting and administering a reinforcer, contingent on meeting some performance standard (Alberto & Troutman, 2006). Self-evaluation refers to monitoring the quality or acceptability of the behavior, whereas self-regulation refers to monitoring whether the strategies are working and changing them if they are not (Paris & Oka, 1986). Examples of these various components follow in our description of a verbal mediation procedure recommended by Meichenbaum and Goodman (1971). Adaptations of the verbal mediation procedure are frequently found in studies that measure the effectiveness of cognitive behavior modification (Alberto & Troutman, 2006). The verbal mediation procedure includes the following steps:

1. ***Problem definition:*** "What is it I have to do?"
2. ***Focusing attention and response guidance:*** "Oh, proofread the paragraph I've just written."
3. ***Self-reinforcement:*** "Good, I'm remembering to check to see if I've capitalized everything I'm supposed to."
4. ***Self-evaluative coping skills and error-correction options:*** "That's okay; even if I make an error, I can go slowly." (p. 23)

You may have noticed that the last step also includes self-regulation, as students are taught how to monitor their errors and how to decrease them (in this case, "go slowly").

IMPLEMENTATION

Like most cognitive strategies, this one should be introduced with an explanation, purpose, and rationale to implement cognitive behavior modification. Then model your strategy and elicit student participation to model the strategy overtly and then covertly. The steps, adapted from Meichenbaum and Goodman (1971), usually proceed in the following manner:

1. ***Explain the technique:*** "You seem to be having a problem with talk-outs, Lupa. I have a strategy I use whenever I am having a problem. Let me show it to you."

2. ***Share the purpose:*** "The strategy should help you stop your talk-outs."
3. ***State its value:*** "Last year it helped one of my students make new friends because she listened to them when they spoke. It should also help you get your work done because you won't talk out as much."
4. ***Select a verbal mediation procedure:*** The teacher selects the steps: 1. Define problem 2. Study problem and its consequences 3. Examine possible solutions 4. Decide 5. Implement.
5. ***Model your thoughts out loud, using appropriate vocabulary:*** "Let's see . . . my first step is to define my problem. Uh, I seem to have difficulty talking out in class." (The teacher continues modeling each of the steps of the problem-solving procedure).
6. ***Prompt and guide the student in imitating your model:*** "What do you plan to do first? What are your options?"
7. ***Have the student practice overtly without guidance, but with feedback:*** "Lupa, you try it alone." "Well done, Lupa, you remembered each of the steps." Or, "Not quite, Lupa, you forgot to look at all the solutions."
8. ***Fade overt practice:*** "Now whisper the problem-solving steps, Lupa."
9. ***Have the student practice the model silently:*** "Practice the problem-solving steps just by thinking about them now, Lupa."

Anita Gearhart, a teacher of middle school students with behavior problems, adapted the technique into a Think Sheet (see Figure 7.4). She has the student identify the problem (My behavior), study the problem (Reasons), and suggest alternative ways to behave (Acceptable alternatives). We added the requirement of selecting a strategy to try the next time a similar incident occurs (Next time, I will try). She has the student take the Think Sheet home for parent signatures.

IMPORTANT POINTS

1. Cognitive behavior modification is a technique in which the teacher models his or her thinking processes in the performance of a task. The student practices overtly with assistance and eventually covertly (internalizing the procedure).
2. Cognitive behavior modification includes the components of cognitive modeling, guided practice, and verbal mediation.
3. Cognitive behavior modification may be implemented by completing the following steps: (a) explain the technique, (b) share its purpose, (c) state its value, (d) select a verbal mediation procedure, (e) model your thoughts using appropriate vocabulary, (f) prompt and guide the student in imitating your model, (g) have the students practice overtly without guidance but with feedback, (h) fade overt practice, and (i) have the student practice the model silently.

Activity 7.2

Work with a partner for this activity and take turns being the teacher and student. Choose an academic or social skill that you want to teach to a fourth-grade student. Teach the skill using the components of cognitive modeling, guided practice, and verbal mediation. Be sure to look back at the Important Points to review the steps used in cognitive behavior modification.

Figure 7.4 THINK SHEET

My behavior: ____

____

____

Rule: I will be held responsible for my own behavior (copy).

____

____

____

Reasons for my behavior: ____

____

____

Acceptable alternatives (acceptable behavior I could have decided on):

____

____

____

____

Next time, I will try (which of the above): ____

____

☐ I am ready to return to task.

Student ______________________

Teacher ______________________

Parent (s) ______________________

RECIPROCAL TEACHING (RT)

Reciprocal teaching (RT) is a research-based instructional procedure designed to encourage students' active participation in lessons (Speece, MacDonald, Kilsheimer, & Krist, 1997). Like the other approaches in this chapter, reciprocal teaching (RT) concentrates on teaching students how to gain meaning from reading text. Essentially, "reciprocal teaching is a dialogue between teachers and students for the purpose of jointly constructing the meaning of the text" (Palincsar, 1986a, p. 119). This approach helps students understand how to study and learn from a text and promotes metacognitive monitoring of comprehension (Palincsar & Brown, 1986, 1987). The instruction is teacher-directed at first, but then a student assumes the teacher's role as other students comment on the student's questions, elaborate on the student's summary, and assist in constructing meaning and predicting new information. Students take turns assuming the role of the teacher as they lead discussions using the four reading strategies of summarizing, questioning, clarifying, and predicting text information (Bos & Anders, 1990). The context in which these four strategies are learned is social, interactive, and holistic in nature (Englert & Palincsar, 1991). To move from teacher-directed to student-directed instruction, the teacher uses a scaffolding procedure, decreasing the intensity and frequency of the prompts and supports (Palincsar & Brown, 1984).

The technique is usually taught to students individually or in groups of four to seven, and the lessons last approximately 30 minutes for 20 days (Palincsar & Brown, 1986, 1988). Many of the techniques identified in the teacher-effectiveness literature (see Chapter 5) are the same as those used in reciprocal teaching, and we point out the similarities in our discussion.

The value of reciprocal teaching (RT) for students with poor comprehension has been documented in the literature (Brown & Palincsar, 1989; Rosenshine & Meister, 1994). In fact, much of the research on the effectiveness of reciprocal teaching (RT) was conducted by the creators of the model with junior high students in remedial reading classes as the subjects, and expository or informational text as the reading material. The students were identified as "adequate decoders but poor comprehenders" (Palincsar & Brown, 1986, p. 775). In the studies (Palincsar & Brown, 1984), students improved in comprehension, measured by daily curriculum-based tests of 450-word passages and 10 comprehension questions. They also improved in comprehension of material presented in their general education classes, demonstrating that reciprocal teaching produced generalization.

Additionally, Palincsar and Brown (1989) found that reciprocal teaching (RT) was effective with first and second graders judged to be at risk for academic failure. In these studies, the teachers, instead of the students, read the text. It was found that 75% of the first-grade children achieved criterion performance on comprehension. In addition, the first-grade children attempted to apply the procedure to spontaneous discussions and were able to maintain the procedures in a follow-up study conducted when the students entered second grade.

RATIONALE

The idea behind reciprocal teaching (RT) is that the teacher is teaching the students strategies that will enable them to learn how to gain information from the printed page. Once the students learn the strategies, they can apply them to different situations without the presence of the teacher. The strategies improve self-concept, because students learn to attribute their success to their ability to use the strategies and not to luck (Palincsar, 1986a). The emphasis on ensuring that the students are well informed about the procedures, purposes, and applications finds its basis in metacognition and in the premise that students with learning problems acquire information more readily when they are well informed (Duffy, Roehler, Meloth, Putnam, & Wesselman, 1986). The interactive nature of the approach, which requires a joint construction of meaning, is based on the belief that students can learn from each other (Palincsar & Brown, 1988).

DESCRIPTION

The essential components of reciprocal teaching (RT) are strategies that teach students how to gain information from text, guide interactive instruction, and inform learners. The teacher instructs the students in the strategies of summarizing, questioning, clarifying, and predicting. In guided interactive instruction, control of the lesson moves from the teacher to the students. Students are informed about the procedures, purposes, and applications.

Strategies
The teacher teaches the four strategies: summarizing, questioning, clarifying, and predicting. For the first 4 days of the procedures, the teacher teaches the students the strategies. On the fifth day, the teacher begins modeling the strategies in constructing a dialogue. For example, Palincsar and Brown (1986) suggest that you teach students to generate information—seeking questions by first asking them to generate questions concerning everyday events, such as, "If you are interested in knowing what time the afternoon movie begins, you call the theater and ask" (p. 773). The teacher spends only about a day introducing each strategy, because the emphasis is on teaching the strategies through the interaction between teacher and students in a dialogue (Palincsar & Brown, 1986).

Summarizing Summarizing involves identifying and paraphrasing the main ideas. Students are taught first to summarize the content in a paragraph or section and then to integrate the content across paragraphs.

Questioning Questioning requires students to question themselves about the content. Students become more involved when they must generate questions than when they merely respond to teacher questions (Palincsar & Brown, 1986). At the beginning, students often generate questions that cannot be answered using the information presented in the text, which is a clue that they are not focusing on the text information (Palincsar & Brown, 1988).

Clarifying Clarifying is discerning when there is a breakdown in comprehension and identifying appropriate strategies to restore meaning. To do this, students must know that they are not comprehending the information (metacognitive awareness). Readers who have comprehension problems often cannot discriminate when they do not understand materials, as they are more interested in decoding words than in making sense of the words (Palincsar & Brown, 1986). At first, students attribute lack of vocabulary knowledge as the cause for not understanding the meaning of a passage, so they focus on the unknown words in a selection for clarification. Eventually, however, they realize that unfamiliar ideas or difficult content may block understanding of the text, so they attempt to clarify these concepts (Palincsar & Brown, 1988).

Predicting Predicting is hypothesizing the next event in the text. Students often use pictures and text structures, such as headings and italicized words, to aid them in making predictions. Predicting requires students to activate background information concerning the passage and to link that information to the author's intent. However, students from different cultural backgrounds often find that their background information does not relate to the classroom materials that they are using, and they have difficulty comprehending the author's message (Ruiz, 1989). For example, if you are reading a selection about plants of the desert, you probably will predict that sometime in the text the author will mention cactus. Think of the advantage for the student who has read about or visited a desert compared with one who has never encountered the desert environment.

Predictions can also let teachers and students know when there is a breakdown in comprehension and a student's background knowledge is incorrect. Palincsar and Brown (1988) relate the example of students not using the facts of a selection to check an incorrect prediction. In reading the title and looking at the picture in the selection "Ships of the Desert," some students predicted that the author would talk about camels storing water in their humps. When asked to summarize, these same students said the author told how camels stored water in their humps, when in fact the author had stated that camels store fat in their humps. The students did not correct their prediction and, thus, didn't glean the correct meaning from the selection. They failed to use metacognitive monitoring to check their incorrect prediction.

Guided Interactive Instruction

During guided interactive instruction, you model the use of the four preceding strategies. Remember, you have already spent 4 days teaching the strategies. During the initial modeling, you attempt to involve the students by having them answer questions, elaborate on your summary, and add predictions and clarifications (Herrmann, 1988). You gradually transfer responsibility for these activities to the students until, eventually, you just provide feedback and coach the students through the dialogue as they interact with each other. For example, if the student discussion leader cannot generate a question, you may prompt by suggesting that the student begin the question with when. If that doesn't work, then you may modify the task by asking the student to identify a fact instead of a question. If that doesn't work, you may model the task: "I might ask the question . . ." You may also give corrective feedback using the prompt format (e.g., "I think you forgot an important point in your summary. Remember . . .") and praise for correct answers (e.g., "Good summary, Monika").

Students who are at risk frequently have difficulty constructing summarizing statements and generating appropriate questions, so during the beginning stages, you should construct paraphrases and questions for the students to mimic (Brown & Palincsar, 1982). Eventually, however, students who are at risk are able to use strategies on their own. In a comparison between student performance on the beginning dialogue sessions (when the teacher assumed most of the responsibility) and the end sessions (when the students assumed most of the responsibility), Brown and Palincsar (1982) report that nonquestions were reduced from 19% to 0%, and student responses needing clarification were reduced from 36% to 4%. Only 11% of the students' summary statements described main ideas in the beginning sessions, whereas 60% of their statements did at the end of the study.

Informed Learners

At the beginning of every RT session, inform learners about the strategies they will be using, the importance of using the strategies, and ways to generalize them. In addition, inform learners of the consequences of learning the strategies. Specifying what happens when a strategy is employed leads to a better understanding of the relationship between the strategic learning and successful performance (Paris & Oka, 1986). Students must feel that the effort of learning the strategies produces success with a task (Paris & Oka, 1986). Direct and frequent measurements are suggested as a means to convince students of the worth of reciprocal teaching (RT) (Palincsar, 1986b). Frequent graphing of the results of comprehension testing, and taping of the reciprocal sessions help prove to students that the use of reciprocal teaching (RT) leads to positive consequences (Palincsar & Brown, 1984).

IMPLEMENTATION

Implementation of reciprocal teaching (RT) requires careful planning and incorporation of the activities of summarizing, questioning, clarifying, and predicting into the lesson presentation. The steps for planning and presentation are adapted from the work of Palincsar and Brown (1986, 1988, 1989) and Herrmann (1988).

Planning

To prepare for an RT session, first select text segments. Criteria for text selection are that the students can decode the material with at least 80 words-per-minute (wpm) accuracy with no more than 2 errors and that the text is representative of the materials that students read and study in the general education class (Palincsar, 1986b). Remember, most RT research has been completed with expository or informational materials. Other planning activities include (a) generating possible predictions, (b) identifying questions, (c) summarizing each section, (d) circling difficult vocabulary or concepts, and (e) identifying supports that students will need to help them learn the information (Hermann, 1988). We present each of these activities with an example in Table 7.2.

Presentation

We suggest the following steps for presentation in an RT lesson during the initial stages of teacher modeling and after the students have been taught the four strategy skills. We follow each step with an example of its implementation in teaching a group of middle school students with special needs. Because this is an initial lesson, the teacher is still facilitating, and the students are participating mostly by answering questions generated

Table 7.2 Planning Steps with Examples for Reciprocal Teaching

1. *Select the text segment for the first modeling.*

   Langston Hughes: He Believed Humor Would Help Defeat Bigotry and Fear by L. Morgan (Ed.). (Seattle, Washington: Turman Publishing Company, 1988)

   > "I've known rivers," wrote Langston Hughes in *The Negro Speaks of Rivers*, one of his best-known poems. "I've known rivers ancient as the world and older than the flow of human blood in human veins. My soul has grown deep like the rivers."
   >
   > Langston, one of America's greatest writers, was a powerful artist. He was able to capture in his writing both the humor and sadness of life.
   >
   > Langston had a very difficult childhood. Not long after he was born in Missouri on February 1, 1901, Langston's father James left home. James had studied law for years and learned he could not become a lawyer because he was black. Angry and bitter, James moved to Mexico to become a lawyer there. (p. 9)

2. *Generate possible predictions.*

   He was an author.

3. *Identify questions.*
   - How do you think Langston's father's leaving affected his writing?
   - Why did Langston's father leave home?
   - Why did his father have to leave for Mexico?
   - Did Langston think life was only funny?
   - What did he compare his soul to?
   - Who is Langston Hughes?

4. *Summarize each section.*

   Include who he was and why he had a difficult childhood.

5. *Circle difficult vocabulary or concepts.*

   Bigotry. "My soul has grown deep like the rivers." Effect that a difficult childhood may have on writing.

6. *Identify supports.*
   - Kendra will need help on questions.
   - All will need a prompt for prediction.

7. *Generate possible predictions for the next section.*

   It will tell more about Langston's childhood.

by the teacher, elaborating on the summary, and adding predictions and clarifications. The teacher explains, instructs, models, guides the students, and praises (Palincsar & Brown, 1986). We use the plan in Table 7.2 to assist in generating the dialogue.

1. Begin with a review of the four strategies, their importance, and the context in which the strategies are useful.
2. Read the title and ask the students to predict what they will learn. For example:

   TEACHER: The title of the passage is *Langston Hughes: He Believed Humor Would Help Defeat Bigotry and Fear.* In your own words, by looking at the pictures, what do you think this story will be about?

   STUDENT 1: A man.

   TEACHER: Correct. Any other predictions?

   STUDENT 2: A black man.

   STUDENT 3: He thinks humor is powerful and can beat fear.

   STUDENT 4: I bet he's a comedian.

   STUDENT 5: No, look at the picture. He's signing autographs. I bet he's a writer.

   TEACHER: Those are excellent predictions. Let's begin.
3. Read a small portion of the text orally or have the students read it silently, depending on the group.
4. Ask a question about the content. In the beginning ask students to answer your question. Then ask if students have any additional questions of their own to ask about the text material. For example:

   TEACHER: After reading the first three paragraphs my question is, Why did Langston's father leave home?

   STUDENT 1: To go to Mexico.

   TEACHER: To do what?

   STUDENT 1: To become a lawyer.

   TEACHER: Why did he go to Mexico?

   STUDENT 1: Because he was black.

   TEACHER: And . . .

   STUDENT 1: Oh, yeah, he couldn't practice law in this country.

   TEACHER: That's correct. Does anyone else have a question to ask?
5. Summarize the section and invite elaboration from the group members. Herrmann (1988) recommends that you also explain how you arrived at the summary. For example:

   TEACHER: My summary begins with the statement that Langston Hughes was a famous black writer who wrote about the humor and sadness in life. He had a difficult childhood. His father left to become a lawyer in Mexico, because he wasn't allowed to practice law in this country. This is a summary because I have included only information that we have already read.
6. Discuss any clarification that needs to be made concerning ideas or words.

   TEACHER: Let me ask you something. Do you know what bigotry in the title means?

STUDENT 1: No.

TEACHER: Let's see if we can find the meaning somewhere in the text. I see an example in the story. Langston's father had to move to Mexico to practice law because he was black. This is an example of bigotry. Does anyone know what it means now?

STUDENT 4: Oh, it's when people do not like you because your skin is black.

TEACHER: Any other ideas?

STUDENT 2: Yes, bigotry means having bad feelings about someone.

TEACHER: I guess you could say that it is having bad feelings without a good reason.

7. Predict the next section of the text.

TEACHER: I think the next part of the story may be about some more unhappy childhood experiences. Anyone have another prediction?

Activity 7.3

Prepare an RT lesson identifying possible predictions, questions, a summary, and difficult words or concepts from the following selection from *Langston Hughes.* Check the plans in Table 7.2.

> Carrie Hughes, Langston's mother, moved to Topeka, Kansas. She worked in a law office. Carrie wanted Langston to go to a public school that did not allow black children. She went to the school board and won her fight to place Langston in the school. Even though his mother won that fight, Langston had to struggle every day to fit in at the school. Many of the children, and one teacher especially, were mean to Langston and made fun of him. Langston later wrote about his school years in *The Big Sea,* a book about his life. (Morgan, 1988, p. 9)

IMPORTANT POINTS

1. The essential components of the RT model are strategies to teach students how to gain information from text, guided interactive instruction, and informed learners.
2. The comprehension and monitoring strategies of summarizing, questioning, clarifying, and predicting are taught to structure the dialogue of reciprocal teaching.
3. Teachers employ a scaffolding procedure, decreasing and adjusting support as they model the techniques, assist the students in the transfer of the technique, and move into a coaching and feedback role.
4. Careful planning includes identification of the text segment, possible predictions, questions, a summary, difficult words or concepts, and supports that students may need.
5. Presentation includes (a) sharing a brief review of the strategies, (b) reading the title for student predictions, (c) reading a small portion of the text, (d) asking questions, (e) summarizing, encouraging the students to elaborate on the summary, and (f) adding clarifications.

STRATEGIC INSTRUCTION MODEL (SIM)

The Strategic Instruction Model (SIM), developed by researchers Donald Deshler, Jean Schumaker, and their colleagues, represents a combination of reductionist and constructivist principles (Deshler, Ellis, & Lenz, 1996). The teaching approach used in the Strategic Instruction Model has changed over the years from one of direct teaching to a combination of direct teaching and a significant amount of student involvement, participation, and commitment in the instructional process (Lenz, et al., 1996). This incorporation of the direct (i.e., the teacher teaches the strategy) and indirect approaches (i.e., the teacher leads the students toward understanding and use of the strategy) has been the result of formal and informal research with students who are at risk for school failure, including those with learning disabilities (Lenz, et al., 1996). The purpose of the Strategic Instruction Model is to teach students how to learn and perform academic, social, and job-related tasks so that they can cope with immediate setting demands and generalize these skills across situations and settings throughout their lives (Deshler & Schumaker, 2006).

RATIONALE

As students with learning disabilities progress through the grades, the gap widens between what they can do (their levels of functioning) and what they are expected to do (curriculum demands), particularly in the later grades (Deshler, Schumaker, Alley, Warner, & Clark, 1982). Research conducted at the University of Kansas Center for Research on Learning demonstrates that students with learning disabilities who are entering ninth grade appear to read at about a fourth grade level (Deshler et al., 2001) and on average are functioning at the fourth-grade level in writing and fifth-grade level in math (Warner, Schumaker, Alley, & Deshler, 1980). It seems appropriate to change the curricular approach to one that teaches students how to learn, solve problems, monitor performance, and take control of their cognitive processing.

Research conducted at the University of Kansas Center for Research on Learning indicates that low-achieving students do not use effective or efficient study techniques, have difficulty completing assignments, do not organize information well, and have problems distinguishing important information from unimportant information (Deshler, Ellis & Lenz, 1996; Lenz, et al., 1996). These problems can be addressed by assisting students to select appropriate strategies, monitor their own execution of the strategies, and generalize the strategies across situations (content) and settings (school, home, work, and community).

Often, students with special needs are not actively involved in, or do not assume responsibility for, learning and applying specific strategies to help themselves acquire the skills needed to meet the demands of the curriculum (Graham, Harris, & Troia, 2000). Research has shown that students with learning disabilities do not typically apply techniques to facilitate their comprehension of reading materials (Wong & Jones, 1982). However, students have shown significant improvement in performance when taught appropriate strategies (Graham, et al., 2000). Through strategic instruction, a teacher actively involves students in learning and gives them opportunities to set their own goals. Many students who are low achieving fail to generalize the skills they have learned to new situations and settings (Lenz, et al., 1996). The Strategic Instruction Model emphasizes mastery and includes specific procedures to promote generalization.

BOX 7.2

Reflections on Practice

As you may recall in our chapter opener, Miguel was an eighth-grade student with learning disabilities who was struggling to understand and remember content in his general education science class. His teachers realized that they would need to use direct instruction of learning strategies in order for Miguel and his peers to be successful. But how realistic is this expectation of success? Can adolescents with learning disabilities succeed across multiple content areas and achieve the goal of a standard diploma?

Deshler (2005) published an article entitled Adolescents with learning disabilities: Unique challenges and reasons for hope. In this article he encouraged practitioners to forge ahead in their efforts to promote strategy instruction for students with learning disabilities at the secondary level. Deshler provided evidence of success, but he also identified several challenges that educators will face as they attempt to sustain this success. One of those challenges is the importance of maintaining the integrity of teacher roles in the future. According to Deshler, the primary role of the special education teacher should be to teach specific skills and strategies that will enable students to be effective learners in their general education classrooms. It is then up to content teachers to use their expertise in their subject matter to convey the most essential information to their students, while prompting the students to make use of the strategy instruction they received. Deshler believes that maintaining these well-defined roles is crucial to the success of the student. He cautions against using the valuable time of the support teacher for tutoring rather than teaching strategies that can help students become independent learners. Obviously for this concept to work well in practice, communication between teachers is a fundamental component of the instructional design.

To access this article in its entirety, consult Deshler, D. (2005). *Learning Disability Quarterly, 28*(2), 122–124.

DESCRIPTION

The Strategic Instruction Model stresses collaboration among support agents: general education teachers, special education teachers, students, parents, and administrators. Ongoing, systematic, collaborative efforts among support agents will assist in ensuring generalization. Special education teachers may be responsible for teaching strategies or coteaching them with general education teachers in inclusive classrooms. General education teachers and parents may be responsible for cueing strategy use and reinforcing students when they apply strategies at school and home. Administrators may promote and reinforce the use of strategies on a schoolwide basis.

The Strategic Instruction Model consists of three components: strategic curriculum (what strategies are taught), strategic instruction (how strategies are taught), and strategic environment (how the environment is arranged to promote and enhance learning) (see Table 7.3).

Strategic Curriculum

The strategic curriculum component consists of four types of strategies: (1) learning strategies (memorizing information, paraphrasing, test taking), (2) social skill strategies

Table 7.3 Components of the Strategic Instruction Model

Strategic Curriculum Component

The Strategic Curriculum Component of the Strategic Instruction Model specifies *what* will be taught to low-achieving or at-risk students. This component consists of four types of strategies.

Learning Strategies: Designed to teach students how to cope with the academic demands encountered across a variety of school, home, community, and employment settings. These learning strategies teach students how to respond to critical reading, writing, listening, remembering, and test-taking demands.

Social Skill Strategies: Designed to teach the student how to interact appropriately across a variety of situations and settings. Strategies such as resisting peer pressure, accepting criticism, negotiating, following directions, and asking for help are included.

Motivation Strategies: Consists of strategies that enable students to become active in planning the direction of their lives. Strategies that teach students how to set, monitor, and attain goals related to important areas of their lives and then communicate these goals to others are included.

Executive Strategies: Designed to teach students how to solve problems independently and generalize learning. These strategies are taught to students after instruction in three to five learning strategies.

Strategic Instruction Component

The Strategic Instruction Component includes procedures for *how* strategies should be taught to students. In addition, it includes procedures for the effective delivery of content to low-achieving and at-risk students.

Acquisition Procedures: Provides teachers with a sequenced set of steps for teaching the strategies to mastery.

Generalization Procedures: Provides teachers with a sequenced set of steps for teaching and ensuring generalization and maintenance of newly acquired strategies to other settings and situations.

Strategic Teaching Behaviors: Provides teachers with the critical teaching behaviors that should be infused throughout all steps and phases of strategy and content instruction to promote maximum learning by low-achieving and at-risk students.

Content Enhancement Procedures: Provides teachers with routines and devices for delivering subject-matter information in a manner that can be understood and remembered by students.

Strategic Environment Component

The Strategic Environment Component deals with how to manage and organize educational settings and programs to promote and prompt strategic learning and performance.

Teaming Techniques: Consists of methods related to teaching teachers, students, parents, and other professionals how to work as a team to bring about maximum student learning.

Management Techniques: Consists of methods related to how to manage materials, time, instructional arrangements, and student behavior to promote student independence and success.

Evaluation Techniques: Consists of systems related to evaluating student performance, program performance, and teacher performance and providing feedback to those involved in a manner that will promote student learning and success.

Development Techniques: Consists of methods related to systematically implementing program components and developing strategies responsive to student needs.

Source: From *Students With Learning Disabilities*, 6th ed. (p. 174), by C. D. Mercer & P. C. Pullen, 2005, Upper Saddle River, NJ: Pearson Education, Inc. Copyright 2005 Pearson Education, Inc. Reprinted by permission.

(getting along, conversational skills, problem solving), (3) motivation strategies (goal setting), and (4) executive strategies (selecting and designing appropriate strategies). Learning strategies are critical for understanding, retaining, and expressing content. Social skill strategies are needed for students to be successful in school, at home, and on the job. Motivation strategies assist students in problem solving and decision making. Executive strategies enable students to create their own strategies, monitor their effectiveness, and make the adaptations necessary to improve the strategy's effectiveness. All four types of strategies are essential for success.

In this section, we focus on strategies that deal specifically with academic content. The learning strategies curriculum is divided into three strands: (1) the acquisition strand helps students acquire information from printed materials, (2) the storage strand helps students store important information, and (3) the expression and demonstration of competence strand helps students with writing, proofreading, and organization (see Table 7.4). The learning strategies curriculum is organized in the form of a series of instructor's manuals with accompanying student activities, detailed lesson plans for teachers, and teaching materials.

Strategic Instruction

The strategic instruction component consists of four stages that are critical to the success of the model: (1) stages of acquisition, (2) stages of generalization, (3) strategic teaching behaviors, and (4) content enhancement procedures. Table 7.5 provides a description of the stages of acquisition (Stages 1–6) and generalization (Stages 7–8) that are used to teach strategies and content to students. It is important to adhere to these stages during instruction if maximum results are to be achieved.

The strategic teaching behaviors are the critical teaching procedures that must be used throughout strategy and content instruction in order to meet the needs of students who are low achieving (Kea, 1987, 1995). Strategy instruction is more effective when teachers actively involve their students and make instruction motivating and interesting. The strategic teaching behaviors include:

- Using advance and post organizers
- Communicating rationales
- Communicating expectations
- Reviewing and checking for understanding
- Facilitating independence
- Ensuring intensity of instruction
- Providing instructional monitoring
- Providing feedback
- Requiring mastery of learning.

Content enhancement procedures are used to help make decisions about what content to teach and how to present it in a meaningful way. Content enhancement procedures provide teachers with planning and teaching routines and devices for presenting content in a way that can be organized, comprehended, and remembered by students. The use of content enhancement planning and teaching routines is based on the premise that students learn more effectively when they are actively involved, abstract concepts are presented in concrete forms, information is organized for them, relationships among pieces of information are made explicit, and important information is distinguished from unimportant information.

- Relationships among pieces of information are made explicit, and
- Important information is distinguished from unimportant information.

Table 7.4 Learning Strategies Curriculum

Acquisition Strand

Word Identification Strategy: Teaches students a problem-solving procedure for quickly attacking and decoding unknown words in reading materials, allowing them to move on quickly for the purpose of comprehending the passage.

Paraphrasing Strategy: Directs students to read a limited section of material, ask themselves the main idea and the details of the section, and put that information in their own words. This strategy is designed to improve comprehension by focusing attention on the important information of a passage and by stimulating active involvement with the passage.

Self-Questioning Strategy: Aids reading comprehension by having students actively ask questions about key pieces of information in a passage and then read to find the answers for these questions.

Visual Imagery Strategy: Designed to improve students' acquisition, storage, and recall of prose material. Students improve reading comprehension by reading short passages and visualizing the scene that is described, incorporating actors, action, and details.

Multipass Strategy: Involves making three passes through a passage for the purpose of focusing attention on key details and main ideas. Students survey a chapter or passage to get an overview, size up sections of the chapter by systematically scanning to locate relevant information that they note, and sort out important information in the chapter by locating answers to specific questions.

Storage Strand

First-Letter Mnemonic Strategy: Designed to aid students in memorizing lists of information by teaching them to design mnemonics or memorization aids, and in finding and making lists of crucial information.

Paired Associates Strategy: Designed to aid students in memorizing parts or small groups of information by using visual imagery, matching pertinent information with familiar objects, coding important dates, and a first-syllable technique.

Vocabulary Learning Strategy: Designed to teach students to learn the meaning of new vocabulary words.

Expression and Demonstration of Competence Strand

Sentence Writing Strategy: Designed to teach students how to recognize and generate four types of sentences: simple, compound, complex, and compound-complex.

Paragraph Writing Strategy: Designed to teach students how to write well-organized, complete paragraphs by outlining ideas, selecting a point of view and tense for the paragraph, sequencing ideas, and checking their work.

Error Monitoring Strategy: Designed to teach students a process for detecting and correcting errors in their writing and for producing a neater written product. Students are taught to locate errors in paragraph organization, sentence structure, capitalization, overall editing and appearance, punctuation, and spelling by asking themselves a series of questions. Students correct their errors and rewrite the passage before submitting it to their teacher. The added component of the INSPECT Strategy helps students detect spelling errors through the use of a spellchecker.

Theme Writing Strategy: Teaches students to write a five-paragraph theme. They learn how to generate ideas for themes and how to organize these ideas into a logical sequence. Then the students learn how to write the paragraphs, monitor errors, and rewrite the theme.

Assignment Completion Strategy: Teaches students to monitor their assignments from the time an assignment is given until it is completed and submitted to the teacher. Students write down assignments; analyze the assignments; schedule various subtasks; complete the subtasks and, ultimately, the entire task; and submit the completed assignment.

Test-Taking Strategy: Designed to be used by the student during a test. The student is taught to allocate time and read instructions and questions carefully. A question is either answered or abandoned for later consideration. The obviously wrong answers are eliminated from the abandoned questions and a reasonable guess is made. The last step is to survey the entire test for unanswered questions.

Source: From the University of Kansas Center for Research on Learning. Reprinted by permission.

Table 7.5 The Stages of Strategy Acquisition and Generalization Developed by the University of Kansas Center for Research on Learning

Stage 1: Pretest and Make Commitments

Purpose: To motivate students to learn a new strategy and establish a baseline for instruction

Phase 1: Orientation and pretest
- Give rationales and overview
- Administer pretest
- Determine whether strategy is appropriate

Phase 2: Awareness and commitment
- Describe:
  - The alternative strategy
  - Results others have achieved
- Ask for a commitment to learn the new strategy

Stage 2: Describe the Strategy

Purpose: To present a clear picture of the overt and covert processes and steps of the new strategy

Phase 1: Orientation and overview
- Give rationales for the strategy
- Describe situations where the strategy can be used

Phase 2: Present the strategy and the remembering system
- Describe the overall strategic processes
- Explain the remembering system and its relationship to self-instruction
- Set goals for learning the strategy

Stage 3: Model the Strategy

Purpose: To demonstrate the cognitive behaviors and physical actions involved in using the strategy

Phase 1: Orientation
- Review previous learning
- State expectations

Phase 2: Presentation
- Think aloud
- Self-monitor
- Perform task

Phase 3: Student enlistment
- Prompt involvement
- Check understanding

Stage 4: Conduct Verbal Elaboration and Rehearsal

Purpose: To ensure comprehension of the strategy and facilitate student mediation

Phase 1: Verbal elaboration
- Have students describe the intent of the strategy and the process involved
- Have students describe what each step is designed to do

Phase 2: Verbal rehearsal
- Require students to name each of the steps at an automatic level

Table 7.5 (continued)

Stage 5: Provide Controlled Practice and Feedback
Purpose: To provide practice in controlled materials, build confidence and fluency, and gradually shift the responsibility for strategy use to students
Phase 1: Orientation and overview
Review the strategy steps
Prompt reports of strategy use and errors
Phase 2: Guided practice
Prompt student completion of activities as teacher models
Prompt increasing student responsibility
Give clear instructions for peer-mediated practice
Stage 6: Provide Advanced Practice and Feedback
Purpose: To provide practice in advanced materials (e.g., regular class, work related) and situations and gradually shift the responsibility for strategy use and feedback to students
The instructional sequence for Advanced Practice and Feedback is the same as the instructional sequence used for Controlled Practice. However, this level of practice should:
Use grade-appropriate or situation-appropriate materials
Fade prompts and cues for use and evaluation
Stage 7: Posttest and Elicit Commitments to Generalize
Purpose: To document mastery and to build a rationale for self-regulated generalization
Phase 1: Confirm and celebrate
Congratulate student on meeting mastery
Discuss achievement and attribution for success
Phase 2: Forecast and commit to generalization
Explain goals of generalization
Explain the phases of generalization
Prompt commitment to generalize
Stage 8: Promote Generalization
Purpose: To ensure the use of the strategy in other settings
Phase 1: Orientation
Prompt students to:
Discuss rationales for strategy use
Identify settings in which the strategy may be used
Discuss how to remember to use the strategy
Evaluate appropriateness of the strategy in various settings and materials
Phase 2: Activation
Prompt and monitor student application across settings
Enlist assistance of other teachers
Prompt students to:
Apply the strategy in a variety of settings, situations, materials, and assignments
Set goals for the use of the strategy

(continued)

Table 7.5 (continued)

Prompt general classroom teachers to:
Understand the strategy
Cue use of strategy
Provide feedback on strategy use
Phase 3: Adaptation
Prompt students to:
Identify where these processes and strategies are required across settings
Identify how the strategy can be modified
Repeat application with the modified strategy
Phase 4: Maintenance
Prompt students to:
Discuss rationales related to long-term use of the strategy
Set goals related to monitoring long-term use
Identify self-reinforcers and self-rewards

Source: From *Students With Learning Disabilities*, 6th ed. (pp. 185–186), by C. D. Mercer & P. C. Pullen, 2005, Upper Saddle River, NJ: Pearson Education, Inc. Copyright 2005 by Pearson Education, Inc. Reprinted by permission.

Strategic Environment

The Strategic Instruction Model consists of four types of techniques designed to promote a learning environment that is strategic: (1) teaming techniques, (2) management techniques, (3) evaluation techniques, and (4) development techniques. Teaming techniques relate to preparing the members of the educational community (teachers, parents, students, psychologists, vocational rehabilitation counselors, and others) to work together cooperatively. Management techniques are related to managing time, materials, and the expertise and contributions of professionals in order to facilitate student learning and performance. Evaluation techniques emphasize the provision of feedback to teachers, students, and families. Finally, development techniques refer to the systematic and continued design and development of strategies and other program components to meet student needs.

IMPLEMENTATION

In teaching learning strategies, follow the stages of strategy acquisition and generalization. You begin by pretesting students and gaining their commitment to learn the strategy. You then describe and model the strategy, conduct verbal elaboration and rehearsal, provide controlled and advanced practice and feedback, administer a posttest, gain student commitment to generalize the strategy, and ensure the use of the strategy in other settings. If you follow these stages, you can teach students such strategies as error monitoring, paraphrasing, sentence writing, and word identification. The following systematic application of these stages is vital to the success of the model (see Table 7.5).

Pretest and Make Commitments (Stage 1)

Establish the student's current level of performance and secure his or her agreement to learn a strategy. For example, after Lashon takes his pretest, he and his teacher, Ms. Johnson, review the results. Perhaps Lashon notices that his written work is messy and contains quite a few capitalization and punctuation errors, or Lashon and Ms. Johnson discover this together. Ms. Johnson makes a commitment to help him improve and motivates Lashon to make a commitment to proofread his work by learning and applying the error monitoring strategy developed by Schumaker, Nolan, and Deshler (1985).

Describe the Strategy (Stage 2)
Discuss or elicit the rationales and benefits for learning the strategy, then carefully describe the steps of the strategy. This step was also included in reciprocal teaching and metacognitive instruction. Ms. Johnson asks and then shows Lashon how the error monitoring strategy will help him improve his grades in school, his chances for employment, and his ability to write error-free emails to his girlfriend. Then she describes and gives examples of each step of the error monitoring strategy.

Model the Strategy (Stage 3)
The modeling stage is based on the premise that students learn a skill better if they see it performed, rather than just hear it described. Therefore, Ms. Johnson models the steps of the strategy by thinking aloud and using self-instruction, self-regulation, and self-monitoring. For example, she says, "Let's see. I will look at this sentence to see if there are any capitalization errors. Hmm, I have capitalized all of the proper nouns. Oh, I forgot to capitalize the first word in the sentence. Good, now I don't have any capitalization errors." After Ms. Johnson models the cognitive processes by thinking aloud as she examines a written passage for errors, she enlists Lashon's participation in finding errors in the passage.

Conduct Verbal Elaboration and Rehearsal (Stage 4)
The next stage consists of two parts—verbal elaboration and rehearsal. With verbal elaboration, you ask questions about the strategy and lead the student to discover how the strategy could be helpful. Ms. Johnson asks, "Why do you think it is important to prepare papers that are error-free and neat in appearance?" "What do you think are the most common mistakes students make in their written work?" "In which of your classes do your teachers penalize you for spelling, punctuation, and grammatical errors?" With verbal rehearsal, you review the steps of the strategy until the student knows them on an automatic level. For example, Lashon and Ms. Johnson practice the steps to error monitoring until he has committed them to memory.

Provide Controlled Practice and Feedback (Stage 5)
Provide ample guided practice in easy materials (controlled) until mastery is reached. Give individual feedback to reinforce efforts and avoid practice of incorrect responses. For example, Ms. Johnson gives Lashon practice exercises and then provides verbal and written feedback regarding his performance of detecting and correcting errors in passages. This type of practice usually begins by having the teacher and students work together, and then with partners or in groups.

Provide Advanced Practice and Feedback (Stage 6)
Provide advanced practice in grade-level materials found in general education classrooms while providing positive and corrective feedback. For example, Ms. Johnson checks some of Lashon's work from selected general education classes and gives him feedback regarding his ability to detect and correct errors in these more difficult materials.

Posttest and Elicit Commitments to Generalize (Stage 7)
Give a posttest to determine progress and to provide feedback. Ask students to agree to generalize use of the strategy to other settings.

Promote Generalization (Stage 8)

After ensuring that students have acquired a strategy, teachers should focus on the stages of generalization. Although teachers should be promoting generalization throughout the teaching of a strategy, they should focus on a systematic set of generalization procedures after they have completed the stages of acquisition. For strategy instruction to be effective, students must generalize the use of strategies. The following stages of generalization provide students with the steps necessary to ensure successful transfer of skills across situations and settings.

Orientation: Make the student aware of the need to apply the strategy. For example, Ms. Johnson and Lashon discuss where Lashon could use the error monitoring strategy, how he will remember to use it, and why it is important to use it in a variety of classes.

Activation: Prompt the student to use the strategy and monitor use of it. For example, Ms. Johnson checks with general education teachers to see if Lashon is using the error monitoring strategy and helps Lashon set goals.

Adaptation: Prompt the student to examine the strategy for the cognitive behaviors he or she is using (e.g., self-questioning) and to modify the strategy to the demands of new situations. For example, Lashon and Ms. Johnson work together to figure out how Lashon can use the error monitoring strategy as he takes tests.

Maintenance: Promote long-term use of the strategy across situations and settings. For example, Ms. Johnson conducts periodic checks to see that Lashon is still using the error monitoring strategy effectively in a variety of situations (home, school, and on the job).

Activity 7.4

Part 1: You are a special education teacher talking to a general education colleague. In this age of high-stakes testing with the focus on the mastery of content, justify to your colleague why he or she should include learning strategy instruction in an already overcrowded academic curriculum in the general education setting.

Part 2: How could you use coteaching to incorporate learning strategies instruction into a social studies classroom?

SELF-REGULATED STRATEGY DEVELOPMENT (SRSD) MODEL

The Self-Regulated Strategy Development (SRSD) model was developed for students with academic learning difficulties and has been used to teach writing strategies and self-regulation procedures to students with and without disabilities (Graham, et al., 2000). Through an integrated approach, students are taught task-specific strategies for planning or revising expository or narrative text (Graham, et al., 2000) and the self-regulation procedures of goal setting, self-monitoring, self-instruction, and self-reinforcement (Harris & Graham, 1996). SRSD provides a way to help students successfully complete an academic task and become more strategic and self-regulatory in their performance of the task (Graham, Harris, & Mason, 2005).

RATIONALE

Many students, particularly those who exhibit significant difficulties with writing, lack self-regulation and composition strategies and skills (De La Paz, 1999; Graham, et al., 2000; Graham & Harris, 2000; Harris, Schmidt, & Graham, 1997). Their compositions do not typically show evidence of planning, effort, and monitoring (Graham & Harris, 1993). Students with problems in reading and writing need structured and explicit instruction in strategies crucial to literacy (Graham & Harris, 1994). Self-regulated strategy training focuses on strategies for planning, writing, editing, and managing the writing process (Harris, Schmidt, & Graham, 1997) as well as on self-regulation strategies such as self-instruction, self-assessment, self-monitoring, and self-reinforcement. The use of Self-Regulated Strategy Development has resulted in improved writing skills of both normally achieving students and students with learning disabilities (De La Paz, 1999; Graham, Harris, MacArthur, & Schwartz, 1991). SRSD has had a significant impact on students' goal setting (Graham, MacArthur, & Schwartz, 1995), self-monitoring (Harris, Graham, Reid, McElroy, & Hamby, 1994), organization of writing content (Sawyer, Graham, & Harris, 1992), and revising of written products (Graham, et al., 1995), among others.

DESCRIPTION

Self-Regulated Strategy Development (SRSD) is an instructional approach that directly addresses students' affective, behavioral, and cognitive characteristics, needs, and strengths (Harris & Graham, 1996). SRSD complements existing effective practices in writing; involves teachers as collaborators in the learning process through dialogues, sharing, and scaffolding; and actively engages students in writing instruction, development of their own strategies, and transfer and generalization of strategies. It is important to note that SRSD is only as explicit and supportive as is required by individual students, due to the fact that students vary in their needs for writing and self-regulation strategies. Harris, Schmidt, and Graham (1997) have worked with students in elementary, middle, and high school as well as with younger children in primary grades including students in urban schools (Graham, et al., 2005).

Characteristics of Self-Regulated Strategy Development

Graham, Harris, and Troia (2000) indicate that five characteristics are essential for the effective implementation of SRSD. We list them here with our own descriptions and support from other researchers:

1. ***Strategies and self-regulation procedures are explicitly taught.*** Students with learning difficulties generally require direct, explicit instruction to acquire and master certain skills. Therefore, strategies are explicitly taught. Later, when students become more skilled, the level of explicitness may be adjusted so that students can be guided to discover a strategy or even create one on their own (Graham, et al., 2000). Schloss, Smith, and Schloss (2001) cite the importance of making instruction explicit so that

students learn efficiently with few errors, but they quote a statement from Harris and Graham (1994): "Explicitness and structure need not equate with decontextualized learning of meaningless skills, passive learning, or the teaching of . . . basic skills as a pre-requisite to higher-order thinking and skills" (p. 238).

2. ***Interactive learning is emphasized.*** As with other types of cognitive strategy instruction discussed in this chapter, the teacher takes the initial responsibility for teaching and learning and then gradually shifts the responsibility to the students. For example, students are seen as active participants who work with each other and the teacher in goal setting, monitoring, executing, and modifying writing strategies.

3. ***Instruction is individualized.*** Instructional decisions are based on the needs of students. For example, students will vary in terms of goals, strategies, pace of instruction, amount of repetition and practice, ability to select and modify strategies, as well as many other considerations.

4. ***Instruction is criterion-based.*** Students progress through the stages at their own pace and focus on their own individual goals. As previously stated, not all students will need to work at each stage.

5. ***The SRSD model represents an ongoing process.*** New strategies are introduced and formerly taught strategies are upgraded (Graham, et al., 2000). For example, a strategy that was previously taught may have been introduced in its simplest form. Now that students have mastered it, additional steps or more complex applications are presented. Each student's developmental level as a writer and as a strategic learner must be considered. As mentioned earlier in this chapter, it is important to help students understand the meaning and significance of strategy use and assist them in making decisions about how and when to apply strategies. Teachers must be knowledgeable about each student's stage of development and how strategies can best assist them at that stage.

IMPLEMENTATION

In teaching SRSD, you generally follow six stages of instruction and choose from a variety of strategies. These strategies may be presented by the teacher or may be developed and/or modified by the students.

Stages of Instruction

Although six stages are provided for the implementation of SRSD, these stages serve only as a general guideline. In other words, some stages will not be needed by some students. Stages may be combined, modified, reordered, or revisited. For example, some students may be able to skip Stage 1, if they already possess sufficient background knowledge. Others may need to revisit Stage 3 for additional instruction or Stage 5 for additional support. The model is flexible and focuses on addressing individual needs of students. Note, for example, in Table 7.6 that some students who are learning an essay writing strategy may need to revisit Stage 5 for additional support. Perhaps, they need more help writing supporting reasons for their premise, or maybe they need additional assistance with self-regulation procedures (e.g., "Slow down and take my time. Then my work will be better."). Students set their own goals and work at their own pace. As with the Strategic Instruction Model, procedures for maintenance and generalization are integrated throughout the six stages of the SRSD model (see Table 7.6).

Table 7.6 Self-Regulated Strategy Development Instructional Stages: Using the TREE Strategy to Teach Essay Writing

Stage 1—Develop Background Knowledge

Find out what students already know about essays and build on it.

Look at samples of well-written essays.

Identify the effective features of these well-written essays.

Look for these features in essays they are reading in class and in essays of classmates.

Using a variety of topics, brainstorm ideas for essay parts.

Stage 2—Discuss It

Have an individual conference with each student to discuss their essays and identify any strategies or self-statements currently being used.

Introduce the idea of a strategy for writing essays along with the self-monitoring components of self-assessment and self-recording.

Discuss the benefits of using the strategy.

Determine each student's current performance.

Set goals.

Describe the TREE strategy (note **T**opic sentence, note **R**easons, **E**xamine reasons, note **E**nding) in an interactive session with students.

Provide strategy charts and lists of self-statements.

Stage 3—Model It

Model the TREE strategy while thinking out loud.

Elicit student help during modeling.

Use self-statements throughout the modeling (e.g., "What do I need to do next?" "Yes, that is a good reason. I'll write that.").

Stage 4—Memorize It

Have students memorize the strategy and practice using self-statements.

Stage 5—Support It

Collaborate with the students in supporting their use of the strategy and the self-regulation procedures.

Revisit the rationale for using the strategy and the self-statements, as needed.

Model the correction of errors in the use of the strategy and include a self-statement (e.g., "I'm going to change this supporting reason. I need to remember to follow all of the steps of the strategy so that I will write a good essay.").

Adjust the level of support as students become more proficient, gradually fading prompts or reminders.

Use goal setting and self-assessment (e.g., Have students assess their work to see if they have met their goals. Have them provide feedback to one another.).

Stage 6—Independent Performance

Have students plan and write essays independently.

Provide positive and constructive feedback.

Encourage students to work without their strategy charts and self-statement lists.

Promote generalization of the strategy and self-regulatory procedures.

Source: Information taken from *Every Child Can Write: Strategies for Composition and Self-Regulation in the Writing Process* by K. Harris, T. Schmidt, & S. Graham (1997). In *Teaching Every Child Every Day: Learning in Diverse Schools and Classrooms* by S. Graham & K. Harris (Eds.). Cambridge, MA: Brookline Books. Reprinted by permission.

BOX 7.3

Reflections on Practice

Students with learning disabilities appear to have difficulty maintaining and generalizing the strategies we teach them (Deshler & Schumaker, 2006). Generalization is often examined by researchers when studying the effectiveness of a particular strategy. Graham, Harris, and Mason (2005) conducted a study of struggling third-grade minority students in an urban setting in order to examine the effectiveness of the Self-Regulated Strategy Development (SRSD) model. The researchers conducted writing lessons using the SRSD stages we have discussed here in Chapter 7, and they tested the additional component of peer support. In this additional component, pairs of students met throughout a writing project to discuss their use of SRSD as they progressed through a particular piece of writing. The student partners used metacognitive techniques including thinking aloud about the planning and execution of the strategies they had been taught. Students were also asked to report back afterwards on how and when they were able to help each other use the strategies.

The conclusion of this study was that students who used the SRSD model, regardless of whether or not it included the component of peer support, significantly outperformed students who used an alternative model of writing instruction. Additionally, those students who were included in the group that used peer support better demonstrated the ability to generalize the strategies they learned to other areas, and they spent more time on their writing than the students who used SRSD but did not have peer support. This finding is also bolstered by the fact that the students reported liking it better when their writing time included the support of fellow students.

To access the 2005 article, Improving the writing performance, knowledge, and self-efficacy of struggling young writers: The effects of self-regulated strategy development, in its entirety, consult *Contemporary Educational Psychology, 30*, 207–241.

Strategies

Harris and Graham (1996) have developed writing strategies in a variety of areas that include but are not limited to planning, brainstorming, story writing, essay writing, and report writing. We provide examples of some of their strategies for assisting students with planning and writing. When teaching these strategies, remember to use the instructional stages noted in Table 7.6.

Three-Step Planning Strategy for Story Writing The teacher introduces a planning and writing strategy to students by explaining that these three steps will help them write better stories and essays. Students are asked to think about who will read the story or essay and why they are writing it. Then the students are instructed to use the SPACE mnemonic, which will help them plan what to say in their story or essay. As they write, they may think of more things to say and should be encouraged to do so.

1. Think.

   Who will read this? Why am I writing this?

2. Plan what to say.

   Use SPACE (Setting, Purpose, Action, Conclusion, Emotions)

3. Write and say more.

Three-Step Writing Strategy This strategy is similar to the planning strategy for story writing. However, this time the mnemonic, TREE, is used to help students make note of their **T**opic sentence (e.g., "My topic sentence is that it is better to be the oldest child in the family instead of the youngest."); note **R**easons (e.g., "One of my reasons is that you get privileges that your younger brothers and sisters do not get. Now, I need to think of others."); **E**xamine reasons (e.g., "Hm, I think I'll cross out the one about getting to boss the others around—that's a little weak."); and note **E**nding (e.g., "Now I need to write a good ending.").

1. Think.

   Who will read this? and Why am I writing it?

2. Plan what to say.

   Use TREE (note Topic sentence, note Reasons, Examine reasons, note Ending).

3. Write and say more.

W-W-W or Story Grammar Strategy This strategy teaches students how to write stories by focusing on seven questions that prompt the story parts. Significant improvements were noted in the quality and length of students' stories after they learned and practiced this strategy.

1. Think of a story you would like to share.
2. Let your mind be free.
3. Write down the story part reminder (W-W-W).

   Who is the main character?

   When does the story take place?

   Where does the story take place?

   What = 2

   What does the main character do or want to do, and what do the other characters do?

   What happens when the main character does or tries to do it, and what happens with other characters?

   How = 2

   How does the story end?

   How does the main character feel, and how do other characters feel?

4. Make notes of your ideas for each part.
5. Write your story—use good parts, add, elaborate, revise as you write or afterwards, and make sense.

STOP and LIST Writing Strategy The strategy of STOP (Stop Think of Purpose) and LIST (List Ideas and Sequence Them) assists students to set goals, brainstorm, and sequence when writing or performing other tasks. It can be used for completing writing assignments, planning a report, or preparing for other activities.

Evaluation Procedures

Harris, Schmidt, and Graham (1997) suggest several basic principles for assessing SRSD methods and procedures:

- Involve students as co-evaluators. Co-evaluation increases the sense of ownership and enriches the evaluation process. Students may use self-assessment, peer evaluation, and other reflective techniques.
- Consider the level of evaluation needed. Harris, Schmidt, and Graham (1997) recommend that teachers find out if students are using the strategy, whether it is having a positive effect on performance, and if students think the strategy is valuable and manageable.
- Assess changes in performance, attitudes, and cognition. It is important to determine changes in the quality and quantity of students' writing and any changes in attitude (e.g., enthusiasm for writing, confidence in writing abilities) and cognitive processes (e.g., spontaneous statements about writing).
- Assess how students actually use the strategy. It is helpful to observe students directly as they write and also to look for evidence of strategy use by examining students' written work.
- Assess students' use of the strategy over time and in new situations. To be sure that students are continuing to use a strategy and use it appropriately, find out how students are using and/or modifying strategies. In other words, conduct spot checks by asking students to share information about using the strategy, asking general education teachers if students are using the strategy in their class, or looking at samples of students' written work.
- Collaborate with colleagues during the evaluation process. It is important to collaborate with other teachers in promoting generalization and in monitoring strategy use in other classroom settings. This teamwork should result in more effective use of strategies by students and more consistent application and generalization of strategies.
- Use portfolio assessment procedures. As it relates to SRSD, portfolio assessment is an excellent way to encourage students to engage in reflection and self-assessment of their writing and self-regulation strategies and to ensure that they are taking more responsibility for their own learning.

Activity 7.5

Your elementary school is having a Young Author's Conference and everyone in the school is expected to write a story. You and your general education coteacher are working with a fifth grade class. Some of the students are having difficulty thinking of a topic for the story, while others are struggling with developing the parts of a story. What elements of Self-Regulated Strategy Development could you use to assist them?

PUTTING IT ALL TOGETHER

In this chapter, we have focused on the use of cognitive strategies to teach students with special needs to become strategic learners and problem solvers. We have recommended that you accomplish this through the use of metacognition, cognitive behavior modification (CBM), reciprocal teaching (RT), the Strategic Instruction Model (SIM), and the Self-Regulated Strategy Development (SRSD) model. As you work with your students, **you** will initially assume the major responsibility for teaching, then gradually shift the responsibility to **your students**. We acknowledge that this takes your time and commitment, but it will reap benefits for your students as they become more independent learners. We feel that strategic teaching and learning can occur in both special and general education settings as well as across content areas and grade levels. By being a strategic teacher (e.g., one who actively collaborates with students, focuses on their prior learning, and possesses a variety of strategies), you will empower your students by giving them access to techniques for acquiring, remembering, and demonstrating information in order to solve problems independently.

IMPORTANT POINTS

1. The Strategic Instruction Model (SIM) includes a strategic curriculum component (what to teach), a strategic instruction component (how to teach), and a strategic environment component (how the environment is arranged to enhance student performance).
2. The teaching approach used in the SIM includes direct teaching of strategies; significant amount of student involvement, participation, and commitment in the instructional process; application of strategies by students to classroom materials; and generalization of strategies across content areas, new situations, and various settings.
3. The Self-Regulated Strategy Development (SRSD) model is an integrated, instructional approach that assists students in developing composition skills and using self-regulation procedures (e.g., goal setting, self-instruction, self-monitoring, self-assessment, and self-reinforcement).
4. The SRSD model directly addresses students' affective, behavioral, and cognitive characteristics, needs, and strengths.
5. The characteristics of SRSD emphasize explicit teaching, interactive learning, individualization, criterion-based instruction, and an ongoing process of learning new strategies and adding to or upgrading previously learned strategies.

DISCUSSION QUESTIONS

1. Differentiate between the reductionist and constructivist elements of cognitive strategy instruction. Be sure to use examples from metacognition, cognitive behavior modification, reciprocal teaching, the SIM, and the SRSD model.
2. Explain the benefits for students when the teacher thinks aloud during instruction. Give three examples of using think-alouds in the general education classroom.
3. Work with a partner to respond to this question. You are a special education teacher and you are explaining to a general education teacher the importance of having students use self-regulation procedures such as self-instruction, self-monitoring, self-assessment, and self-reinforcement. What will you say? Now reverse roles and have your partner convince you of the importance of self-regulation, particularly for students with special needs.

Websites: Useful websites related to chapter content can be found in Appendix A.

CHAPTER

8

Content Instruction

KEY TOPICS

Mr. Gibson has been teaching students who need special education services for nineteen years at Great Valley Middle School. Several years ago he became interested in using Strategy Instruction methods to facilitate his teaching across content areas. He developed a coteaching model that was very effective in meeting his students' needs within their math, language arts, science, and social studies classes. Mr. Gibson, his coteachers, and their students all derived a great deal of satisfaction from this teaching model and, as an added bonus, when the final Part B regulations to implement IDEA 2004 were released, Mr. Gibson found that he already was teaching within the definition of a "highly qualified" special educator.

This year Mr. Gibson will be teaching with the seventh-grade team of teachers for the first time. With two weeks to go before the start of a new school year, the seventh-grade team has assembled to plan for instruction. Mr. Gibson has always believed that the kind of instruction that works for students with special needs is also good for all students. With this philosophy in mind, he is explaining his coteaching methods to his new team.

"I've prepared this schedule for all of you" he says while passing out copies. "Let me know if you see any problems. I used a plan very similar to this one last year with the sixth-grade team."

"But Mr. Gibson," began Mrs. Daviano, the math teacher, "how can you possibly learn all there is to know about teaching seventh-grade mathematics, science, language arts, and social studies?"

"Good question, Mrs. Daviano. I want you all to know that my role as a coteacher is to supplement your content area with skills and strategies to help all our students be more successful. I won't pretend to be an expert in all content areas, but I do know what it takes to help struggling students be successful, across subject areas."

"So what you are telling us is that you will take class time to teach these strategies to all our students, even if they are not on an IEP?" asked Mr. Juarez, the social studies teacher.

"Precisely," replied Mr.Gibson. "Then I will use the independent practice portion of the class period to work with the students who are on IEPs or any student who is struggling. We will practice applying the strategies to the concepts they are trying to master. Some students with IEPs may need more practice than others, so those students will spend an additional period with me in my pull-out setting. The fact that I am in their classroom when they are learning the social studies lesson makes my teaching so much more effective toward supporting their learning."

"Maybe this would be easier for us to understand if you would give us an example Mr.Gibson," said Ms. Simms, the science teacher. "Let's say I have a student on an IEP who has a learning disability and is having a difficult time learning the science vocabulary that is required for a unit test. What exactly would you do?"

Place yourself in the role of Mr. Gibson. How would you answer the question posed by Ms. Simms? Based on what you have read in previous chapters, what strategies would be most effective toward helping the student Ms. Simms describes?

For possible answers to the questions posed by the above scenario, please refer to the Instructor's Manual.

INTRODUCTION

With the emergence of more learning standards and higher-stakes testing across all content areas, teachers who work across or within specific content areas face new challenges. The combination of increased testing, the necessity for students with disabilities to meet state standards, and the requirements of NCLB that special educators be highly qualified in content areas has caused an increase in collaboration across general and special education. These combined challenges have created new issues in all instructional areas and especially in literacy, mathematics, science, and social studies where students throughout the United States are expected to take and pass content-area assessments.

We begin this chapter with an in-depth discussion focused on both Direct Instruction and BALANCED Literacy instruction emphasizing how these techniques relate to high-stakes testing and how they can be used in more inclusive settings. We follow this discussion by taking a general look at approaches related to the numerous content areas and provide research-based practices related to teaching across content areas. Frequently, content area instruction is based on the use of textbooks (Cobb-Morocco, 2001). Therefore, we examine the issues presented in textbooks combined with basic information about key components in each of the content areas.

DIRECT INSTRUCTION

Prior to the passage of NCLB and IDEA, a Direct Instruction model was often used to teach academic content. This model is the basis for various popular commercial reading, mathematics, and spelling curriculum programs such as *Distar Arithmetic, Corrective Spelling Through Morphographs, Reading Mastery,* and *The Corrective Reading Program,* all created by Engelmann, Meyer, Johnson, and Carnine (1988) and *Direct Instruction Reading* by Carnine, Silbert, and Kame'enui (1997), also examples of the Direct Instruction model. These models continue to be considered effective as they are supported as a strong tool for comprehensive school reform by the NorthWest Regional Educational Center (2005) and in numerous studies related to student achievement gains (Carlson & Francis, 2002; MacIver & Kemper, 2002). Another national trend in early literacy instruction is the use of the Dynamic Indicators of Basic Early Literacy Skills (DIBELS) and the Comprehensive Test of Phonological Processing (Hintze, Ryan, & Stoner, 2003), which is strongly supported as an evidence-based practice for early literacy development. The Dynamic Indicators of Basic Early Literacy Skills (DIBELS) are designed to be short measures used to assist teachers in assessing prereading and early reading skills. These assessments were derived from recommendations of the National Reading Panel (2000) and National Research Council (1998).

Direct Instruction and DIBELS can be used to teach and assess students' literacy skills in more self-contained settings or as tools in the general education setting.

Figure 8.1 SAMPLE DI FORMAT FOR TEACHING SOUNDS

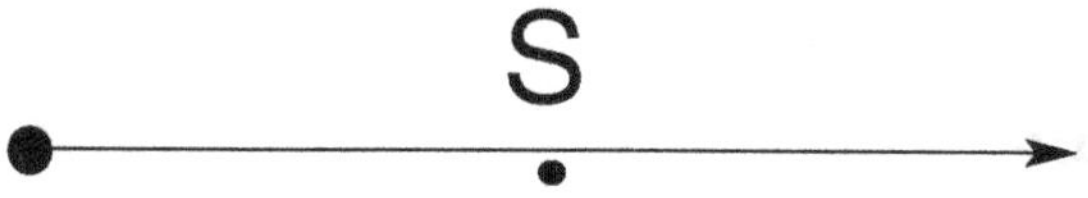

**The teacher models the sound and repeats twice.*

1. Touch the first ball of the arrow. **Here's a new sound. My turn to say it. Get ready.** Move quickly to the second ball. Hold. **sss.**
2. Touch the first ball of the arrow. **My turn again. Get ready.** Move quickly to the second ball. Hold. **sss.**
3. Touch the first ball of the arrow. **My turn again. Get ready**. Move quickly to the second ball. Hold. **sss.**
   **The teacher prompts the students to practice the sounds in unison.*
4. Touch the first ball of the arrow. **Your turn. Get ready.** Move quickly to the second ball. Hold. sss. **Yes, sss.**
5. Touch the first ball of the arrow. **Again. Get ready.** Move quickly to the second ball. Hold. sss. **Yes, sss.**
   **The teacher directs students to repeat sound until firm.*
6. Repeat **5** until firm.
   **The teacher tests individuals.*
7. Call on different children to do **4.**
   **The teacher gives feedback.*
8. **Good saying sss.**

Source: From *Reading Mastery: Distar Reading I* (p. 102) by S. Englemann and E. C. Bruner, 1988. Chicago: Science Research Associates. Copyright 1988 by McGraw-Hill, Inc. Reprinted by permission.

However, with more students being included in the general education setting, Direct Instruction can be more of a challenge to incorporate unless such techniques are being used classroom-wide for all students, which is a phenomenon we see occurring in many states. Direct Instruction (DI) is being used in numerous grade levels to support students in learning all content areas. A wealth of empirical evidence supports the use of the Direct Instruction model with children with disabilities.

The Direct Instruction model began to be used with students in special education elementary classes in the late 1960s to teach basic skills (Gersten, Woodward, & Darch, 1986; Lloyd, Cullinan, Heins, & Epstein, 1980), and continues to be suggested as an evidence-based technique to increase the academic performance of students with mild disabilities (Hudson, Lane, & Pullen, 2005).

A distinct advantage of the DI model is that the scripted lessons allow adults other than teachers to use the program successfully. Combined with peer tutoring, practice activities, and repeated readings, students were found in one research study to improve their reading scores from a pretest score of 2.4 grade level to a posttest score of 3.5 (Gardner, et al., 2001). See Figure 8.1 for an example of a Direct Instruction format for teaching sounds.

RATIONALE

The Direct Instruction model is based on behavioral principles with the fundamental premise that students must master basic academic skills before they can master higher-level cognitive skills. Direct Instruction is considered one of the most effective methods to teach both basic and higher-level skills. Students being supported by DI are carefully presented a sequence of content using task analysis and mastery learning principles.

DESCRIPTION

The Direct Instruction model features a well-designed curriculum and detailed instructional procedures. The curriculum features include sequential order, positive and negative examples, well-constructed formats, prompts, independent practice activities, and mastery learning. All skills are taught directly, with minimal reliance on incidental learning. Each lesson includes teacher-scripted presentations with fast-paced, repetitive formats; individual tests; and independent practice activities. Mastery tests are interspersed throughout the curriculum. The use of scripts permits teachers to focus on monitoring student performance, instead of concentrating on the use of clear instructional language and appropriate examples (Stein, Carnine, & Dixon, 1998).

Effective instructional procedures include cueing attention, modeling, eliciting overt student responding, providing immediate feedback, testing individual children, and teaching to mastery. The teacher usually presents the lesson to small groups of children, which can occur within the general education setting using techniques such as coteaching, or a form of coteaching called alternative teaching (Friend & Cook, 2003).

USE

Many school districts have adopted the previously discussed commercial programs for Direct Instruction in reading, spelling, math, and language. Thus, you may find a kit with a teacher's manual, student workbooks, and other materials in the classroom. Overall though in comparing the outcome for students with learning disabilities across 25 studies, Lloyd (2005) found that Direct Instruction is extremely effective for students with disabilities.

Even if Direct Instruction commercial programs are not available, it is possible to incorporate the curriculum design features and instructional procedures into a lesson. For example, Darch and Gersten (1986) incorporated Direct Instruction procedures as they used an advance organizer with high school students with learning disabilities. They used a well-constructed format, carefully worded definitions, and carefully selected examples to open the science lesson. The format consisted of (a) the teacher reading the item, (b) the teacher cueing responses, (c) the students reading the item in unison, and (d) the teacher asking fast-paced questions of the students after several items were read to check comprehension. The scripted lesson began:

Information about Ocean Currents

I. A current moves like a river.
   A. Water moves in parts of the ocean. These are called ocean currents.
   B. These currents can be very wide—sometimes as wide as 100 miles.

TEACHER: Today we are going to learn about ocean currents and how these currents can affect the weather on land. Everybody look at I. A current moves like a river. Say that.

STUDENTS: A current moves like a river.

TEACHER: Everybody look at IA. Water moves in parts of the ocean. These are called currents. Say that.

STUDENTS: Water moves in parts of the ocean. These are called currents.

TEACHER: Touch IB. These currents can be very wide—sometimes as wide as 100 miles. Say that. . . . Let's review what we have covered so far. Everybody, can an ocean have currents?

STUDENTS: Yes.

TEACHER: Do these currents move?

STUDENTS: Yes.

TEACHER: Everybody, how wide can these currents be?

(Darch & Gersten, 1986, p. 238)

Activity 8.1

Find an example of a Direct Instruction book in your curriculum library related to a topic you are interested in teaching or use the example given above. Participate in a peer talk about how you would use this material in both a pull-out as well as in the general education setting. If you have trouble thinking about a topic, you might consider starting with the topic of teaching students about how the moon changes phases. Be certain to include feedback comments, unison or choral responding, visual prompts, individual tests, mastery learning, and a repetitive format.

Use this example of "Ocean Currents and How Weather on Land Is Affected" to assist you in thinking about how you would use Direct Instruction to teach the phases of the moon.

II. Ocean currents that start in the tropical temperature zone are warm.

A. The Gulf Stream is an example.

B. The current starts in a tropical temperature zone.

C. The Gulf Stream is a warm current.

D. It makes land warmer. (Darch & Gersten, 1986, p. 238)

(Answers for this and other activities are found in the Instructor's Manual.)

BALANCED INSTRUCTION

Balanced Instruction emerged from years of debate over the way students should be taught literacy skills. From an examination of numerous studies dealing with literacy instruction, Pressley (2005) recommends a balanced approach. The balanced approach includes open-ended tasks and self-selection (more aligned with the constructivist paradigm), plus teacher-directed explicit phonics and comprehension instruction (more aligned with the reductionist paradigm). A combination approach for the instruction of bilingual students with disabilities is also recommended from research (Slavin & Cheung, 2004).

In general education, many teachers are finding success with a Balanced Instruction approach that combines literature-based and basal reading programs (Foorman & Torgesen, 2001). Balanced Instruction integrates Direct Instruction commercial reading programs with the whole language or literature-based model (Pressley, 2005). Called BALANCE (*B*lending *A*ll *L*earning *A*ctivities *N*urtures

Classroom Excellence), the program promotes the use of Direct Instruction, precision teaching, quality literature, the writing process, and integrated subjects to enhance the teaching of skills. A sample BALANCE lesson on the unit theme "Accepting Myself and Others" proceeds in the following manner:

Day 1, 50-minute period

10 minutes:	Read *Leo the Late Bloomer* (a trade book)—use Preview and Predict.
5 minutes:	Do character chart of Leo.
20 minutes:	Teach Reading Mastery Lesson 11—use Preview and Predict, model reading, and modify questions from teacher's guide.
5 minutes:	Do character chart of Arf.
5 minutes:	Do precision teaching timing with partners.
5 minutes:	Introduce writing assignment, which students complete on their own. Draw a picture of yourself in a place where you like to spend time.

Homework: Reading Mastery Lesson 11 Take-Home (Hefferan & O'Rear, 1991, p. 1).

Science Research Associates/McGraw-Hill, the publisher of many Direct Instruction commercial materials, also publishes a series of Direct Instruction resource guides that correlate literature to Reading Mastery Plus. The supplemental product, *Language Through Literature* (SRA/McGraw-Hill, 2002) helps children make the connection between basic skills and literature.

Writing activities are also easy to correlate to the Direct Instruction curriculum. Experience stories may be completed after each class period. For example, Ms. Phillips has her students retell the story they read each day. As they are retelling it, she transcribes the story on chart paper. The children then read the story and several are selected to draw a picture to go with the story. The next day, Ms. Phillips begins class by having the students read their own story as a review before reading the new part of the story. Depending on the students, you may want them to write their own story or even think of their own endings.

Ms. Anderson had her children create big books from literature selections that were correlated to a particular theme from the Reading Mastery curriculum. A Big Book is usually made after children are quite familiar with a story. The children retell the story, and the general and special education teachers work together to print one or two sentences at the top of each 12-by-18-inch piece of light cardboard until the children's version of the story is complete. Then the children, either individually or in small groups, draw illustrations that correspond to the text on each page. A cover page with the title and author and a preface page that explains why the children selected the story to retell are also included (Herald-Taylor, 1987). The pages are sequenced by the children and then bound with a heavy-duty stapler or bookbinding tape. A great tool to use for the covers is wallpaper samples.

Activity 8.2

Take the concepts of a BALANCED approach to instruction and create a lesson about the habitats of animals for students at the elementary, middle or high school level.

IMPORTANT POINTS

1. Direct Instruction is a tool that can be used to support students who are struggling in the general or special education setting.
2. The curriculum features of DI include sequential order, positive and negative examples, well-constructed formats, prompts, independent practice activities, and mastery learning.
3. The effective instructional procedures of Direction Instruction include cueing attention, modeling, eliciting overt student responding, providing immediate feedback, testing individual children, and teaching to mastery.
4. Balanced Instruction combines literature-based and basal reading programs. As used in special education, Balanced Instruction integrates Direct Instruction and literature-based materials.

UNIVERSAL DESIGN FOR LEARNING UNITS

The principles of Universal Design for Learning directly relate to the development of a unit and how that structure can support learning outcomes for students with disabilities (Friend & Pope, 2005). In the typical unit or theme approach, students participate in various activities and are exposed to a variety of instructional techniques and arrangements. Depending on the structure of the unit, the unit approach may fall under either the reductionist or constructivist paradigm. Generally, the unit approach promotes meaningful contexts and establishes classroom communities. The teacher's role may vary from the direct purveyor of knowledge to that of a facilitator as students assume responsibility for their own learning. In more inclusive environments the general and special education teacher may develop the unit as a team.

Universal Design principles introduced in Chapter 4 provide a structure to ensure instruction in the unit occurs through multiple means of representation, expression, and engagement (Rose & Meyer, 2000). A sample of a Universally Designed lesson is provided in Table 8.1. This lesson has built-in accommodations for students with academic and behavioral needs as well as providing instruction in science.

The unit approach integrates academic content with a topic, theme, or interest area and is a method typically used in elementary classrooms and middle school teams is emerging at the high school level. With the unit approach, teachers can emphasize higher-order thinking skills linked to standards-based reforms. These higher-order thinking skills may include authentic problem solving, project-based learning, experimentation, prediction, evaluation, and application. For example, instead of teaching students about electricity by having them read page by page in the science text, you may promote higher-order thinking by having students complete a unit on electricity. Students may calculate the average cost of the school's electric bill for the past 6 months and problem solve how to reduce the cost, set up an experiment demonstrating the idea of a circuit, or predict the different types of power that may replace electricity in the future.

Table 8.1 Universally Designed Lesson: Stringing Along—a simulation of adaptations in organisms

Big Idea: Students will simulate different organisms living in the same ecosystem. They will learn the significance of adaptations to a specie's survival. This activity will also illustrate how diversity affects the population of an ecosystem.

What are adaptations? Adaptations are changes made to the environment, curriculum, instruction, and/or assessment practices in order for students to be successful learners. Adaptations are based on students' strengths and needs.

Materials Needed: 100 pieces of yarn or beans (spray painted) in different colors (some colors should blend in with the color of the floor), colored pencils, graph paper, small bags-one per student to gather string or beans, larger bags to hold enough yarn or beans for a small group of students to work together, and rulers.

Procedures *(please indicate amount of time in bold for each procedure)*	**Academic Adaptation**	**Behavioral or Social Adaptation**	**Assistive Technology**
1. Day 1—Tell students that today they will play the role of an animal searching for food. They will be working in groups to complete the activity. They will have roles in the group in order to complete the task efficiently. Assign group members the following roles; task master-this is the person at the table responsible for making sure the group is completing all parts of the activity, clock watcher-will be responsible for keeping track of time, materials handler-will be responsible for gathering and returning materials, and spokesperson-will be responsible for communicating to all other members of the class what the group concluded. **5 minutes**	Explain the roles and review the group roles. Provide written directions.	1. It is important that you have class rules and expectations posted in the class so students know what is expected. Having rules posted can establish boundaries and stop potential problems in the future. 2. When grouping students you may want to think of the following: a. What are the exceptional needs or accommodations stated in the IEP. b. Can you pair higher level students with a student who has an exceptional need? c. Is it better for a student to work alone at this point or for this lab?, d. Can the special education teacher be of assistance?, e. Do you feel the student can make a good choice if he/she is allowed to select a group?	
2. Tell students where their designated "habitat" is. You may choose to have all the tables pushed back and have all students "feed" from the floor in the center of the room OR you may choose to cover their lab tables with a certain color paper or fabric and have that be the "habitat" for the group. **5 minutes**	Try to keep the direct connection between real life and academic studies.		Have students who might struggle with writing record their hypothesis on a tape recorder, or use graph paper and/or spread sheet program to illustrate their hypothesis. (i.e.—Microsoft Excel)
3. Tell students they will have 10 seconds to gather as much "food" as possible. They will then need to record the quantity and color of each piece of food collected in the group. Students will repeat this process of gathering food at least three more times, each time gathering and recording data and observations.		3. When assigning group roles such as the timer, watcher, material person, taskmaster it may be helpful to practice these before doing a lab. Expecting students to simply follow these roles and understand how a group works takes time, practice and patience. Once you feel that the students can do cooperative groups, some roles are better for students with exceptional needs. Being clock watcher may help the student who has trouble with	Have student use a timer to keep time.
4. Have students formulate and record a hypothesis. You may choose to have students construct their data table prior to the beginning of the activity. **10 minutes**			
5. When the class is ready to begin the activity, have the materials handler dump out the bag of string or beans onto the designated "habitat" for feeding. The clock-watcher can tell the students at his/her table when to begin and end	Provide a template for students to record their responses		Have students use a word processing program or portable word processor to write up their reports

Procedures *(please indicate amount of time in bold for each procedure)*	**Academic Adaptation**	**Behavioral or Social Adaptation**	**Assistive Technology**
feedings. You may want to turn off the lights for the feedings depending on the background color you choose. **5–10 minutes**		attention problems, or a student with high levels of energy may work well as a material getter.	(i.e.—Alphasmart, Quick Pad)
6. After each group has recorded at least three rounds of feedings, have the students begin to analyze their data and write their conclusions. Ask, "What kind of graph would be appropriate for this type of data?" (A bar graph is most appropriate due to the comparison of different colored "foods"). **10–15 minutes**		4. When doing steps 2 and 3 there could be potential problems. During these steps it is easy for the students to become very excited. Therefore, it is important for the teacher to monitor the behaviors and interactions through proximity control. This monitoring means you are making observations of the students and re-directing any inappropriate behaviors that may occur. Also it is a time to compliment appropriate behaviors that the students are displaying. When the students record their data, this is a good time to re-group the class and monitor their mood. If the class seems overly excited asking some focused questions will calm them down so they can gain the most from this lesson. Some students may need extended time to complete their assignments. It is best to check with the special education teacher if you are not sure which students need extended time.	
7. Ask the students to complete their lab reports for the next day. Their reports should include the title of the activity, their initial prediction/hypothesis, data and observations, a graph of their data, and a detailed conclusion. **5 minutes**	Provide a scribe to write responses		
1. *Day 2*—Have students share their lab reports with their groups and ask them to come up with a group conclusion to present to the class (the spokesperson). You may want to have students write up their conclusion and draw a graph on an overhead to present to the class. **10–15 minutes**	Provide students with potential language issues talking points		
2. As groups come up to share their findings, make a data chart for the entire class's data. Have a student construct a graph to hang that shows the entire class's data. **15 minutes**			
3. Discuss the similarities and differences between groups after the students have presented their findings. Ask them to use their graphs to answer the following questions; • Which color was gathered the most? • Which color was gathered the least? • Why? • What are some of the possible errors in the simulation? • What were the variables that should have remained constant while doing the simulation? (lights on or off, start with the same amount of "food" each time, etc.) **10–15 minutes**	Provide questions and potentially multiple choice responses to questions as needed	5. When making the class chart on the overhead, use an overhead vs. a blackboard to write notes and monitor the class. There is less chance for the students to act out when using the overhead projector. Finally the key questions related to the chart can be handed out as a worksheet so that the students can focus on their answers rather than copying down the questions and answering the questions. You may need to reduce the number of questions that some students are required to answer such as answer any 3 or specifically assign the ones you feel must be answered. Also, stress that their answers should be complete sentences.	
4. Discuss the significance of the lesson and how it deals with an organism's ability to survive. Discuss how the strings or beans that were not gathered easily will live to survive and reproduce more than the strings or beans that were gathered. Also, bring up "real life" examples of how adaptations aid in an organisms survival such as an owl's ability to hunt small rodents at night due to their eyesight. **10–20 minutes**			

(*continued*)

Table 8.1 (continued)

Components Embedded in the Lesson Procedure

Opening/Stimulus: Take a pair of cheap knit gloves and glue spoons to the ends of the fingers. Have two students come up to the front of the room and ask them both to pick up a pen. Ask the class why it is easier for the student without the "fork hands" to pick up the pen. This will lead to a discussion of what an adaptation is and how an adaptation such as fingers and thumbs allow us and other organisms to survive and reproduce.

Students' Misconceptions: Students may equate the term *adaptation* to *acclimation*. Often students have the misconception that when an organism has an "adaptation" that allows it to survive and reproduce, the organism has the power to decide that it will have that adaptation. For example, students think that when it gets cold outside, we *adapt* during the winter months by putting on coats and scarves. They may also think that giraffes decided to grow long necks so they could reach tall trees for food.

Questions to ask:

- How did color make a difference in the survival of the "food"? (Colors easily seen were eaten first.)
- What if all of the "foods" had an easy-to-see color? (They would all be eaten, which may lead to population problems over time.)
- How would their survival change if they were in a different setting or different background color?
- Can you think of an environment where the piece we collected most would be camouflaged?
- Different animals have different vision; how might that play a role in the prey's survival?
- Why is variation important?

Background Knowledge: As quoted from the *National Science Education Standards*, pp. 157–158.

- *Millions of species of animals, plants, and microorganisms are alive today. Although different species might look dissimilar, the unity among organisms becomes apparent from an analysis of internal structures, the similarity of their chemical processes, and the evidence of common ancestry.*
- *Biological evolution accounts for the diversity of species developed through gradual processes over many generations. Species acquire many of their unique characteristics through biological adaptation, which involves the selection of naturally occurring variations in populations. Biological adaptations include changes in structures, behaviors, or physiology that enhance survival and reproductive success in a particular environment.*
- *All organisms must be able to obtain and use resources, grow, reproduce, and maintain stable internal conditions while living in a constantly changing external environment.*

Staging/Tips/Tricks/Safety: You may want to try this outside using beans spray-painted different colors and have the gathering area set up in the lawn.

Worksheets: none

Other:

Website:

AlphaSmart
http://www.alphasmart.com
Quick Pad
http://h45.com

BOX 8.1

Reflections on Practice

Many science teachers use the stages of the 5E Learning Cycle for a constructivist model to help students discover a concept they plan to present. Here are the stages of the 5E Learning Cycle (Bybee, 1997).

Engage—The teacher tries to capture the students' attention, stimulate their thinking, and help them access prior knowledge related to the topic.

Explore—The teacher gives students time to think, plan, investigate, and organize collected information about the topic.

Explain—Students are involved in an analysis of their exploration. Their understanding is clarified and modified because of reflective activities.

Extend—Students expand and solidify their understanding of the concept and/or apply it to a real-world situation.

Evaluate—Students demonstrate their knowledge and teachers evaluate, typically using some type of rubric.

Mastropieri and Scruggs (1994) posit that students with disabilities are less likely to encounter difficulties with language and literacy demands with a hands-on science approach that includes manipulative activities and thematic units instead of a text-oriented one. Thematic units were part of a school-based literacy learning project that improved the reading and writing performance of students with mild disabilities over that of a control group (Englert, Raphael, & Mariage, 1994). Literature units have been found to contribute to improved assessment results for students from diverse backgrounds (Saunders, 1999).

RATIONALE

Using a unit approach allows students to learn content across disciplines and to assimilate information by actively participating in a variety of activities. If units are created that reflect the principles of Universal Design for Learning then, as mentioned in Chapter 4, these lessons should meet the needs of a range of learners with varying abilities. Integrating content and ensuring access for all learners reflects current brain research that shows the brain does not process information in a step-by-step, one-item-at-a-time process, but by continuously multiprocessing information and emotions through all of our senses at the same time (Jensen, 1998; Sousa, 2001). Furthermore, units are motivational because they can take advantage of a student's special interests, natural curiosity, experiences, and cultural background. Effective units incorporate student choice and have been found to impact the learning of students with disabilities (Gardner, Wissick, Schweder, & Smith-Canter, 2003).

DESCRIPTION

As units are created, they can be either teacher-prepared, teacher-student prepared, or student-prepared. In a teacher-prepared unit, the teacher decides the topics and information to be presented. In a teacher-student-prepared unit, the teacher generally selects the topic but guides the students in their selection of the content and ways to learn the information. In a student-prepared unit, the students decide the topic, ways to learn the information, and how much time to spend on a topic. Units may contain activities centered around different themes, content areas, learning styles, or multiple intelligences, but also are based on state standards.

Units Related to Themes and Content

Thematic units are organized around themes, which provide a point of view or perspective, not topics (Shanahan, Robinson, & Schneider, 1995). Canter, Gardner, Schweder, and Wissick (2003) found that the use of a unit enhanced interdisciplinary instruction in inclusive settings especially when technology was a part of instruction.

Created at the University of Kansas Center for Research on Learning, "The Unit Organizer Routine is a teaching method used to introduce a unit of content to a diverse group of students" (Lenz, Bulgren, Schumaker, Deshler, & Boudah, 1994, p. 5). In *The Unit Organizer Routine*, the teacher and students create a graphic worksheet to identify the important content and relationships of a unit. For example, the Unit Organizer contains (a) key words to identify the theme; (b) lines and labels to help students see connections; (c) schedules of assignments, topics, tasks, and activities; and (d) a list of questions (see Figure 8.2).

Three different teaching routines accompany the visuals: one for introducing the unit (**Cue**), one for daily instruction (**Do**), and one for follow-up (**Review**) (Lenz, et al., 1994). In the **Cue** routine, the teacher explains the purpose of the Unit Organizer and how it will assist the students in learning the information. Then, the teacher distributes copies of the Unit Organizer with the Current Unit and Unit Schedule completed [see (1) and (2) in Figure 8.2]. In the **Do** step, the teacher (a) leads the students to link the Current Unit with the previous and the future units by eliciting summarization and prediction and how all units are related [see (3), (4), and (5)]; (b) leads students in recognizing the major areas, the connecting words, and a summary of unit content [see (6)]; (c) has students identify the relationships to assist in understanding the unit and identifying the information they will need for passing an exam [see (7)]; (d) helps students construct good self-test questions based on the relationships [see (8)]; and (e) relates the content to the assignments and activities listed in the Unit Schedule. In the **Review** step, the teacher reiterates the purpose and how to use the Unit Organizer as a review for the exam, as a basis for expanded maps, and as a reminder of the organization and relationships of the unit content.

When the Unit Organizer Routine was used in secondary science and social studies general education classes, both students with and without learning disabilities increased their scores on unit tests 10 percentage points over baseline (Deshler, Schumaker, Lenz, Bulgren, Hock, Knight, & Ehren, 2001).

Units Related to Learning Styles and Multiple Intelligences

Even though research concerning learning styles and brain hemisphere preferences is controversial (Jensen, 1998; Sousa, 2001), this approach provides teachers with a model for individualizing instruction and honoring diversity. Thinking about learning styles and multiple intelligences reminds us to present information in a variety of ways and to provide students with choices of ways to demonstrate their knowledge.

Multiple Intelligences. Gardner (2006) posits the existence of multiple intelligences that enable people to solve problems. These intelligences are verbal/linguistic, logical/mathematical, visual/spatial, musical/rhythmic, body/kinesthetic, interpersonal, and intrapersonal. Verbal/linguistic is related to words and language; logical/mathematical is related to numbers and the recognition of abstract patterns; visual/spatial includes the ability to create mental images; musical/rhythmic is related to recognition and sensitivity to rhythms and beats; body/kinesthetic includes physical movement and body

Figure 8.2 UNIT ORGANIZER

NAME _____
DATE _____

(3) LAST UNIT/Experience Grasslands		**(1) CURRENT UNIT** Deserts

(5) BIGGER PICTURE
Regions of the World

(4) NEXT UNIT/Experience
Forests

UNIT MAP

is about...

(6)

A dry, barren region where plants, animals, and people find that water is scarce.

Chapter 10

(6) inhabited by

Desert Animals (6)

Mammals (6) Reptiles (6) Insects

(6) covered with

Vegetation (6)

Creosote Bush Mesquite (6) Cactus

(6) divided into

Certain types of deserts (6)

Tropical Temperate (6) Cold (6) Semi-Arid

(7) UNIT RELATIONSHIPS

compare/contrast

cause/effect

descriptive

(2) 4/17	Introduce unit schedule	✓
4/18	Describe types of deserts	✓
4/19	Read pp. 1–6 in Chapter 10	✓
4/20	Make desert collages	
4/21	Show video on desert vegetation	
4/24	Discuss pp. 7–12	
4/25	Complete a cloze activity on desert vegetation	
4/26	Read pp. 12–18	
4/27	Discuss desert animals	
4/28	Construct a bulletin board of desert animals	
5/1	Write a journal entry called: "One Day in the Desert"	
5/2	Review	
5/3	Test	

UNIT SELF-TEST QUESTIONS

(8)

1. In what ways do tropical, temperate, cold, and semi-arid deserts differ?
2. How do desert plants get water?
3. How do desert animals withstand the extreme heat of the desert?
4. What are three examples of desert vegetation?

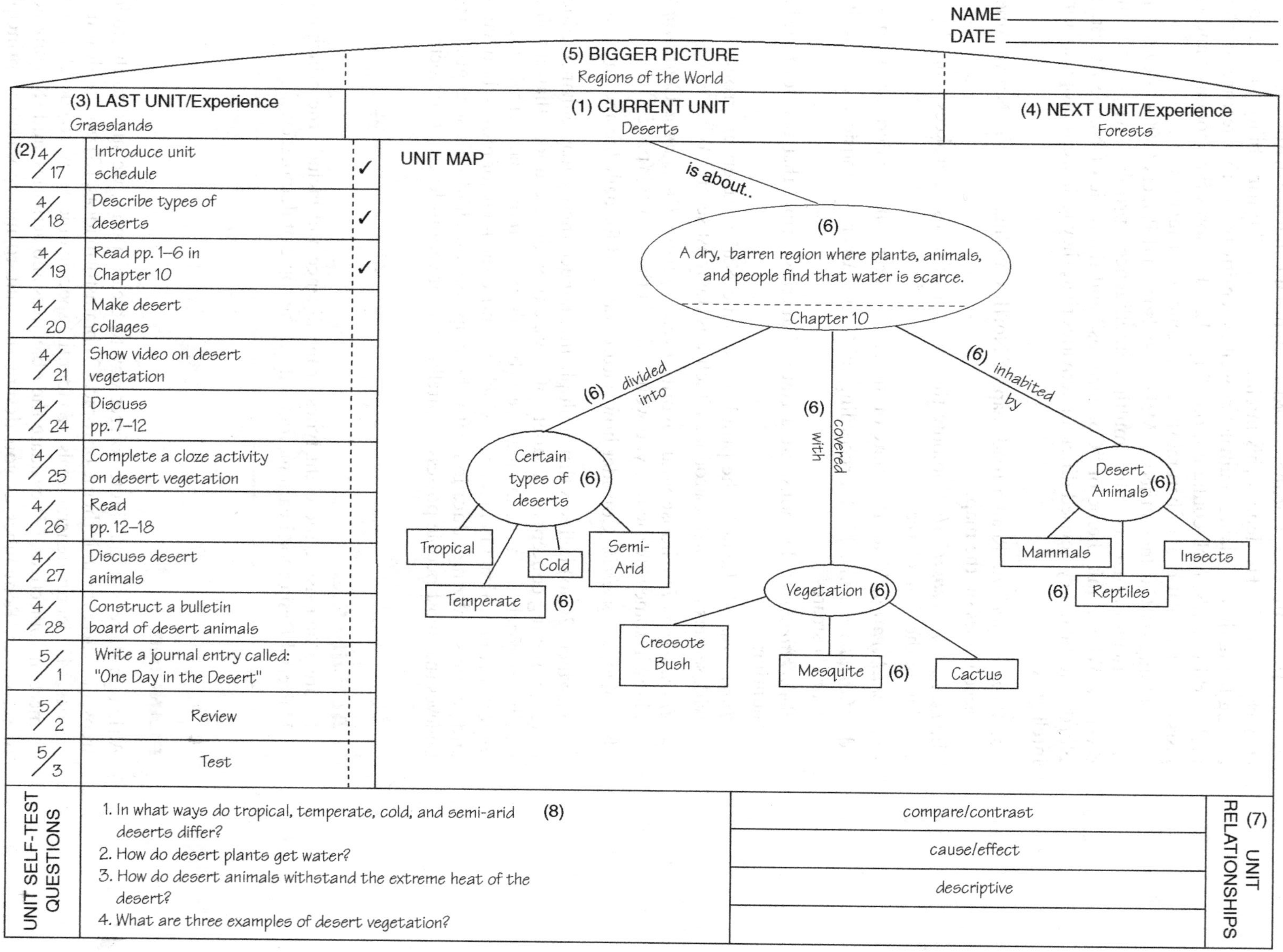

awareness; interpersonal relies on relationships and communications; and intrapersonal centers on metacognition and inner awareness.

In a 1997 interview, Gardner added an eighth intelligence, naturalistic intelligence (Checkley, 1997). He defines this intelligence as "the human ability to discriminate among living things (plants, animals) as well as sensitivity to other features of the natural world (clouds, rock configurations)" (p. 12). He notes that botanists and biologists exhibit a great deal of naturalistic intelligence (Gardner, 2006).

Building on Gardner's theory, Maker, Nielson, and Rogers (1994) devised a thematic curriculum that considers multiple intelligences, problem types, and cultural diversity. With a unit theme of "Connections" and the topic of Native Americans in North Carolina, they devised different activities that, they feel, are appropriate for each intelligence:

a. *Verbal/linguistic:* Read a road map of North Carolina. List the Native American place names on the map.
b. *Logical/mathematical:* Compute the number of miles Cherokees walked per day during the Trail of Tears.
c. *Visual/spatial:* Trace the route of the Trail of Tears on a modern-day map.
d. *Musical/rhythmic:* Find a recording of Native American music and share it with your classmates.
e. *Body/kinesthetic:* Demonstrate a Native American game that teaches the skills of hunting.
f. *Interpersonal:* Identify the problems specific Native American groups have had with settlers in North Carolina. Which was the most severe? Why?
g. *Intrapersonal:* Choose your favorite event(s) from *Knots on a Counting Rope.* Show in some way the role you would play in the event(s) (p. 15).
h. *Natural linguistic:* Consider how nature was used for daily life and survival.

Gardner (2006) believes that multiple intelligence theory may enhance education by (a) presenting concepts in a variety of ways, although he cautions that not all topics may be approached via the intelligences; (b) cultivating more than verbal/linguistic or logical/mathematical intelligences, which comprise the focus of most school curricula; and (c) personalizing education with the emphasis on children's strengths. He also believes that most people possess all intelligences at various levels of competence.

Activity 8.3
Create a unit using the eight types of intelligence and include the principles of Universal Design for Learning focused on the topic of democracy.

PLANNING

Although there is not a single correct way to create a unit, we suggest the following steps: (1) select the unit theme or topic, (2) brainstorm ideas, (3) group ideas into categories, (4) identify general goals, (5) identify specific objectives, (6) develop activities to meet the objectives, (7) evaluate the objectives and activities, and (8) compile a list of resources. Remember as you design the unit to incorporate the principles of

Universal Design for Learning to ensure multiple means of representation, expression, and engagement (Rose & Meyer, 2000). The steps are not always sequential, as sometimes it is easier to identify the activities before the objectives. If the unit is created using Universal Design for Learning principles, then it should not have to be retrofitted when a new student arrives, but should be ready to support all students in the class. We suggest that as you plan lessons to think about creating lessons for students who may come into your classroom with any of these five characteristics:

1. A student who cannot hear
2. A student who cannot physically navigate the environment
3. A student who cannot see
4. A student who does not speak
5. A student who is not behaving

Even though it would be extremely rare to have five students with these characteristics, every student with a disability who enters the classroom will have aspects of the five students mentioned above. For example, a student with autism may be able to speak but may choose to not verbally interact in a lesson. A student who has a learning disability in reading comprehension may not be able to read the text much like a student with a visual impairment. Using these five students as a framework for creating units will ensure that your lessons are accessible to the majority of students who enter the general education setting and save valuable time in that your unit will not need to be redesigned each time as it is prepared for all students from the beginning.

Select the Unit Theme or Topic

The selection of the unit theme or topic is often dictated by local, state, and district standards. Although creativity is a strength, as a new teacher it is critical that lessons be based on these standards as to what students will be expected to know as they progress through the grade levels. If you are coteaching, your unit should be planned in collaboration with the general education teacher. Most content-area textbooks will provide you with units or themes but the challenge as a special educator is that many of these units do not provide adaptations or modifications to the lessons for students' academic or behavioral needs. Therefore, your job as a special education teacher will be to add aspects of Direct Instruction (e.g., incorporating the DIBELS into the unit or aspects of multiple intelligence) to ensure that students with disabilities can be successful in meeting state standards through modalities and styles in which they are comfortable.

Brainstorm Ideas and Group into Categories

After selection of the general theme or topic, the students and teachers list everything that comes to mind. This brainstorming can be created using an effective prereading or writing strategy called semantic maps. Several electronic tools are available to assist in making outlines or semantic maps and one that is most commonly used is a program called *Inspiration*. With young children, you may wish to show pictures or a book to elicit brainstorming due to limited background knowledge.

During this process, you may want to think of your students' IEP objectives, current resources, interests, and literature books, including both fiction or nonfiction titles (Jobe & Dayton-Sakari, 2002). For example, the topic of money or finance may elicit a simple discussion of how money is made or go through a complicated discussion on budgeting for students to be prepared to live on their own. This discussion on budgeting will meet the requirements of the general education curricular standards and at the same time address social and living skills of students with disabilities with a range of needs.

Figure 8.3 SAMPLE SEMANTIC MAP

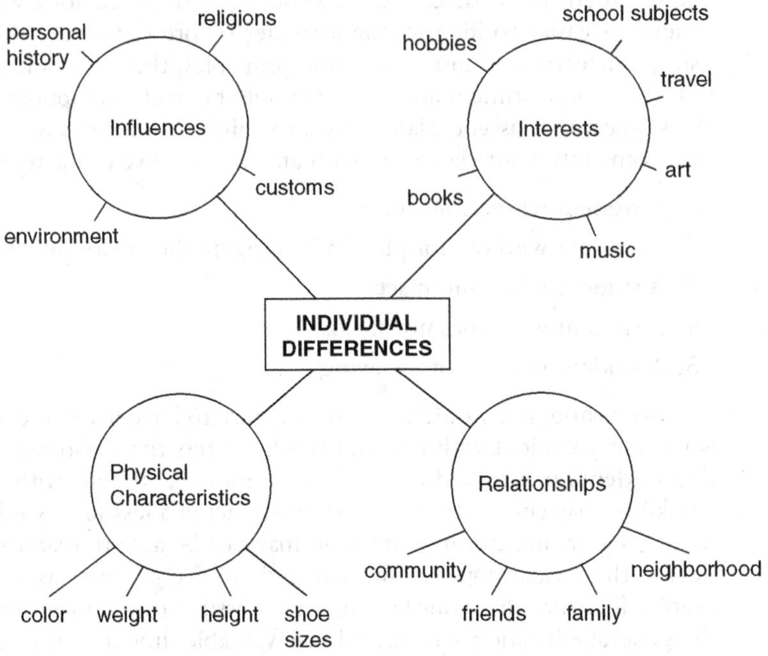

Next, take these ideas and develop them into semantic maps or webs with categories that show relationships (see Figure 8.3 for an example of a semantic map). *Kidspiration* or *Inspiration* both allow the creation of semantic maps electronically and then allow the user to turn the map into an outline format to use for writing stories if needed.

> **Activity 8.4**
> Create two semantic maps—one of words and the other of pictures—to represent how you might start a lesson on the topic of the water cycle.

Identify General Goals

General goals present an overall picture of what you wish the students to accomplish and learn. A general goal for a unit on time may be "to help students understand the role of time in history."

Identify Objectives

Behavioral objectives specify the learner, condition, criterion, and target behavior. They describe outcomes that can be measured and correlated with the categories and the major goals of the unit. For example, an objective for the general goal just discussed may be, "Following an experiment with the water cycle, students will identify the states of water with 100 % accuracy." Students may wish to develop their own objectives based on the questions they would like answered.

Develop Activities and Learning Experiences

Ideas for activities may come from suggested experiments and enrichment activities found in teachers' manuals, your own creativity and experiences, or again, from student interests. Activities should be tied to subject areas, literacy stages, themes, learning styles, and multiple intelligences.

An example of this type of activity that embraces a wide range of learners came from one of our interns. He used this procedure in a cotaught health class on substance abuse. After weeks of researching information, one group wrote a play about the dangers of smoking. Another group presented posters dealing with statistics on teenage substance abuse and a comparison with their own school from interviews and surveys that they had conducted. A third group videotaped a day in the life of a teenage substance abuser, as role-played by a member of the group, emphasizing the effects on work, school, and relationships. After researching the causes of substance abuse, a fourth group wrote ten 2-minute infomercials dealing with handling peer pressure and how to help a friend who may be having difficulties.

Many times, teachers plan a culminating activity to tie together the information and understandings the students have developed in a unit. For example, after studying about Mexico, students in a cotaught class invited parents and members from other classes to visit the various booths designed by each cooperative group. Visitors sampled foods in the food booth, viewed dramatizations in the arts booth, heard oral reports in the government booth, and saw visual displays in the lifestyles booth. The culminating activity was so motivating to one student who was essentially a nonreader that he volunteered to read one of the group-prepared reports. He had memorized the report, but pretended to read from the typed project.

Evaluate Objectives and Activities

Authentic evaluation is recommended as a way to evaluate the learning outcome of students involved with a unit. Students should be allowed to have multiple ways to express what they have learned, a principle of Universal Design for Learning. These evaluation tools could be based upon a rubric where students might be encouraged to create a play, write a story, draw a picture, conduct an interview, or act on numerous formats that celebrate the differences that students bring to the classroom. For example, in a cotaught science lesson, the students and teachers created a rubric to evaluate a student's public speaking as each presented (see Table 8.2). The teacher then brought in two projects from the previous year and students evaluated the projects with the rubric, which helped them understand the general education teacher's expectations and provided a guideline for the special educator who was new to coteaching. The teacher then used the same rubric to evaluate the students' projects.

Compile a List of Resources

Since a single text is typically not used in the unit approach, you need to include many activities and compile a list of resources related to the unit topic. Many of these resources can come from the general education textbooks but also look to outside agencies and community-based businesses to help provide materials for many of the units you develop.

Sometimes, students may secure supplemental materials. One teacher, who organized the social studies curriculum into units with various countries as topics, had the students write to the embassies located in Washington, DC, for information about each country. Frequently, embassies send addresses of other places to write to for free materials as well as free pamphlets about their countries. At the beginning of the school year, this same teacher had parents identify any special skills or topics they or their friends might share from a list of planned unit topics for the coming school year. (See Figure 8.2 for an example of a unit.)

Table 8.2 Science Project Rubric

Student Name____________________ Topic____________________

Focus Area	1	2	3	4	Score
Grammar and Spelling	Very frequent grammar and/or spelling errors.	More than two errors.	Only one or two errors.	All grammar and spelling are correct.	
Research	Does not pose any research question.	Provides a vague research question.	Provides a research question but not clearly defined or connected to the topic.	Provides two or more questions that are logically connected to the topic	
Procedure	Not sequential, most steps are missing or are confusing.	Some of the steps are understandable; most are confusing and lack detail.	Most of the steps are understandable; some lack detail or are confusing.	Presents easy-to-follow steps that are logical and adequately detailed.	
Data Analysis	Data table and/or graph missing information and are inaccurate.	Both complete, minor inaccuracies, and/or illegible characters.	Both accurate, some ill-formed characters.	Data table and graph neatly completed and totally accurate.	
Conclusion	Presents an illogical explanation for findings and does not address questions.	Presents an illogical explanation for findings and addresses few questions.	Presents a logical explanation for findings and addresses some of the questions.	Presents a logical explanation for findings and addresses most of the questions.	

USE OF TEXTBOOKS

In some inclusive settings, teachers rely on the textbook for instructing students. Frequently, the instruction proceeds with students taking turns reading paragraphs orally or reading the text silently and answering questions. For some students with disabilities

BOX 8.2

Reflections on Practice

An ancient tool for having students use the skills of reading, writing, speaking, and art can be found in a practice called Kamishibai. This Japanese tradition came from storytellers who visited villages to sell their candy and share stories. The storyteller would ride a bicycle that had a small stage on the back. Then, after selling candy, he would tell a very engaging story with two or three Kamishibai episodes. He would never tell the whole story so the children would anxiously await his next visit. In this same format Kamishibai can be used with cooperative groups, as part of a unit, or to explore culture while developing skills in storytelling, writing scripts, and creating visual images. Kamishibai can be used for one concept in your curriculum or unit or can be an ongoing set of episodes that students create throughout the year.

who have reading, organization, memory, and attention problems, these instructional strategies are ineffective. Adaptations should be made before, during, and after lesson presentation especially when the general education teacher focuses on more of a textbook-driven type of instruction (see Chapter 6).

BEFORE INSTRUCTION

Some electronic material can be utilized to assist students before instruction. IDEA 2004 requires that all publishers produce textbooks in a standardized electronic file format known as the National Instructional Materials Accessibility Standard (NIMAS) that can be converted into accessible formats such as braille, large print, or electronic text. Each state is required to have a plan to provide textbooks in alternative formats for students who are blind or who have other print-related disabilities. An important point for you to understand as a special education teacher is the loophole that exists in the copyright law. This loophole allows material that is copyrighted to be scanned into a computer or accessed from a nonprofit site called Book Share (http://www.bookshare.org). This website provides books that are in a format called .txt that basically means these files can be opened in most computers and are provided for a nominal fee to allow students with disabilities ways to manipulate text. Text then can be summarized using a feature in Word called "Autosummarize," enlarged, or put into programs such as Write Outloud to allow students with disabilities other venues for accessing content knowledge in textbooks if they have reading difficulties.

If you perceive that students cannot read the content-area text, make sure to check the reading level of the text before the semester begins. Often texts that are supposed to be at a specific grade level are much more difficult than the listed grade level (see Chapter 6). Also examine the practice items and ask yourself the following questions: (a) How are the items presented? (b) Are there enough items? (c) Are the independent practice items aligned with the objectives and content of the lesson and with students' needs and objectives? (d) What do I need to emphasize in the lesson so that my students will successfully complete the items? (e) Does the student text cover the information that my students need to complete the independent practice items successfully?

EXAMPLE:

After rereading the chapter, the special education teacher decided to increase the **vocabulary** items to 10 on the independent practice sheet. To emphasize the problems and care of the skin, hair, and nails, she replaced the comprehension activity with 10 **comprehension** questions, such as, "Why shouldn't you squeeze a pimple or blackhead?" that the students had to answer. She eliminated the **analogies**, as she felt they were not important to her objectives and were not aligned with the information found in the text.

DURING INSTRUCTION

To introduce the lesson, you may wish to ask students questions to bring in their background information, to list important key points or vocabulary, to complete a **K** (Know) -**W** (Want to Learn) -**L** (Learned) (Ogle, 1986) activity, to bring in concrete objects, to act out simulations, or to preview the lesson by attending to the pictures or vocabulary. For example, one of our student teachers brought in Native American artifacts to introduce a chapter on the Plains Indians. Another student teacher had all the students measure their resting heart rate, run in place for 2 minutes, and then measure their heart rate again to introduce a chapter on physical fitness.

Frequent adaptations in the body of the lesson include the use of guided notes, instructional pausing, vocabulary simplification, concrete objects, paraphrasing, questioning, and graphic organizers. Paraphrasing and questioning involve turn-reading, but stopping after a few paragraphs are read and then either the teacher or student paraphrases what was read (paraphrasing) or asks questions after the previously read material (questioning). Some examples of graphic organizers are presented in Figure 8.3 on page 250.

EXAMPLE:

To open the lesson, Ms. Robinson used the **K** column of the **K-W-L** procedure and asked students what they knew about skin, hair, and nail problems and cures. Students looked at the pictures and titles in the text to add ideas. She then directed student attention to the words that they needed to know for successful completion of the independent practice items.

Ms. Robinson next used the instructional pause procedure: One student read two paragraphs and then the students in groups of three discussed the main idea and two details. One of the groups then shared their ideas with the class. Ms. Robinson wrote the main idea on a transparency and students wrote it in their health journal. In her discussion of the details, she referred to the word on the board and listed a short definition or a key word (e.g., bacteria—tiny living things that can lead to sickness; glands—oil and sweat). She also decided to use a graphic organizer for each of the topics, for example:

Hair	
Problems	**Solutions**

To close the lesson, she used the **L** column of the **K-W-L** procedures and had students tell what they had learned about hair, skin, and nail problems and solutions as she wrote the information on an overhead. She then asked them to compare this information to what they listed in the **K** column at the beginning of the lesson. The students then completed the adapted worksheet of 10 vocabulary items and 10 comprehension questions.

Activity 8.5

Find a text at any grade level. Look over the text with a peer and discuss the strengths and weaknesses of the text for students with disabilities. Come up with at least three ways you might support students with disabilities in mastering the content provided in the text by modifying the text or the activities (Hint: Look back at Chapter 6).

AFTER INSTRUCTION

Teachers select activities that reinforce, enrich, generalize, or apply the information. We like to emphasize generalization activities at this time, because generalization of new information or skills is a problem for many students with disabilities.

EXAMPLE:

Ms. Robinson gives a homework assignment that requires students to interview peers or parents to see how they care for certain skin, hair, and nail problems. Each group writes a list of five questions and then presents the list to the entire class. Students may select any five questions for their interviews.

WORKING ACROSS CONTENT AREAS

The changing role of special educators in relation to their role in working with content teachers has made a dramatic shift in the last few years. At the same time many of the practices in various content areas have shifted due to a focus on evidence-based practices and high-stakes testing in all subject areas. This chapter began with a strong focus on literacy instruction; this section provides a summary of the current practices in the content areas of mathematics, science, and social studies, along with a table of practices in each of the respective disciplines. The items in each table are concepts that are critical for special education teachers to understand as they work collaboratively with general education teachers across the content areas.

MATHEMATICS

The field of mathematics has dramatically changed over the past 10 years. In the past completing a problem correctly was considered the most important task to accomplish. Today textbooks place an equal focus on process and product and students are being asked to verbally and in writing tell why the addition of two numbers resulted in a particular sum. Students at all levels are being asked to talk about, read about, and write about mathematical processes. This more verbal approach to mathematics has created problems for students with disabilities who have language-based issues. Yet in contrast, the emphasis in the field of mathematics for more manipulative-based learning has been very beneficial to many students who are more tactile and kinesthetic learners. Table 8.3 provides some of the themes that special education teachers should be aware of in mathematics as well as a few comments related to each point presented.

SCIENCE

The days of reading a science book, answering a few questions at the end of the chapter, and occasionally doing a lab are passé skills in highly effective science lessons. Today state-of-the-art lessons focus on students working in groups, using inquiry-based learning approaches, and constructing their own knowledge about numerous scientific concepts. Table 8.4 provides an overview of current practices in science education that special educators should be ready to support and understand in inclusive settings.

SOCIAL STUDIES

With state assessment in social studies either already in place or becoming a fact for schools in the next few years, this area is regaining emphasis in our nation's classrooms. A strong civic-minded focus is found in many of today's social studies classrooms with

Table 8.3 Mathematics and Special Education

PROBLEM-BASED LEARNING

- Once viewed as a product activity, mathematics today focuses more on how problems are solved not just the final solution to the problem.
- Be prepared to assist students with the higher-level processing that is needed today in mathematics as well as providing support for the complex vocabulary and the need for concrete representations when possible in teaching mathematics.

MANIPULATIVES

- Manipulatives in the past were limited to elementary mathematics, but today these tools are available across grade levels.
- Remember that when manipulatives are being used, plan for any behavioral challenges that might emerge.

ASSESSMENT

- Just completing 20 problems is not enough. Today's mathematics assessments provide as many challenges with language as with numbers. Students with language issues will need support in mathematics just as they do in reading.
- Consider how students with writing or language issues can be supported so they can show how they arrived at their answers on mathematics assessments.

TECHNOLOGY

- Many websites are helpful for the drill-and-practice portion of mathematics. Calculators and other tools such as algebra calculators (many are free on the Web) support students so they can see the steps of the mathematical process.
- Workshops on mathematics and technology and Web searches are helpful in identifying tools that exist to support students.

DISPOSITION

- Mathematics much like science now focuses on students' fears and dispositions about their ability to do mathematics. Gender and culture can be barriers to students believing they can be successful in mathematics.
- Know that many students with disabilities may have negative or erroneous dispositions in mathematics, so focus on ways to make students feel successful.

MENTAL MATH

- Although many teachers grew up using paper and pencil, a strong concept in mathematics is the use of mental math. The logic for the use of mental math is to ensure that students can identify when their answers are not logical. For example, if a student adds 80 + 20 and arrives at 1000, then using mental math the teacher might ask the student to calculate if the answer should be more or less than 100.
- Remember, for many students higher level or mental activities can be difficult. Consider using manipulatives with students who need more concrete examples.

ERROR ANALYSIS

- A common phenomenon for students when they make an error in a mathematical calculation is to ask them to recalculate their answers. This strategy helps students see the error in their thinking patterns.
- A better idea for many students with disabilities is to work with them and analyze the errors in their logic related to the mathematical process. Many times errors in logic are difficult for the student to clarify without direct support from teachers.

Table 8.4 Science and Special Education

- **Constructivist or Inquiry Approach to Teaching**
  - Science has moved to more of a constructivist or inquiry model that may be more difficult for some students with disabilities.
  - With this type of approach, introduce students to the stages of inquiry using a model such as the 5E Learning Cycle as outlined in Reflections on Practice Box 8.1.
- **Cooperative Learning**
  - Many classrooms embrace a more student-friendly inquiry process, which often involves cooperative groups.
  - If cooperative learning is utilized, ensure that students have adequate peer and teacher support.
- **Discussion**
  - Deductive reasoning and cognitive discourse are a part of the inquiry process. Assume that numerous questions and student-focused discussions will occur in a more progressive science classroom.
  - Consider how you might provide some guided discussion questions for students who may have difficulty with open-ended discussions. For example, practice the responses to some questions in an alternative setting or provide students with additional information (e.g., movie) to help them acquire the same knowledge that others might gain from a general discussion.
- **Demonstration**
  - Demonstrations can be teacher directed or student-driven. Teachers may demonstrate an aspect of a scientific process and ask students to talk about what they observed. Students also may be asked to show their logic through demonstrations during labs.
  - Consider having a checklist for students to follow each step of the demonstration and perhaps guided questions or visual supports to help the student understand each step of the demonstration.
- **Laboratory and Safety Issues**
  - With a more hands-on approach and an inquiry-based process, more time is spent on students working in labs. Students with disabilities may need to have lab steps broken down for them or even presented one step at a time for success.
  - As a special educator, be ready to deal with any issues that might arise related to safety and access.
  - Know that students not being able to follow some basic safety procedures may lead to their being denied access to general education content classrooms (e.g., not being able to put on safety goggles).
- **Disposition**
  - Just as background knowledge is important, so is a student's disposition related to science. For example, be aware that females may see themselves as limited in this area and some students with disabilities may have been pulled for resource support during science.
  - Take a measure of how students feel about their skills in science before you start to teach.
- **Technology**
  - Numerous tools exist to help students with sensory or safety issues in science. For example, sites offer activities such as frog dissections online.
  - Investigate sites to help with giving students richer experiences in science.
- **Alternative Assessment**
  - More students are being included in science classrooms because of the constructivist nature and the ability to show multiple means of expression.
  - As a special educator, be ready to provide alternative assessment ideas for a teacher who uses a more traditional approach such as a paper-and-pencil test.

many secondary schools even incorporating service-learning components into their curriculum to raise the civic and cultural awareness of students about life within and around their community. Table 8.5 provides information related to aspects of this content to be aware of in general education classrooms.

Table 8.5 Social Studies and Special Education

Cooperative Learning

- Working on the social structure of groups and cultures is at the core of social studies instruction. Therefore, expect students to do some projects in groups.
- Provide behavioral and academic supports as well as strategically assign students to groups and roles for success.

Experiential Learning—Civic Responsibility

- At the upper grade levels service learning activities may be attached to social studies goals, whereas at the elementary level field trips and community-based activities may be related to social studies.
- As a special educator, you will need to consider any issues that might need to be addressed for students in these activities (e.g., wheelchair access, ability to transition to outside environments, or any communication issues that might arise).

Virtual Field Trips

- Web-based and game-based software programs are being developed that allow students to have virtual experiences related to social studies content.
- Experiences provided by the Harriet Tubman website or other virtual experiences can be used by students to learn about past culture and history.

Geographical Orientation

- With such advanced travel options the world is getting smaller and many teachers have had numerous experiences in travel. Often class discussions are rich in information about various locations that many students have had the chance to visit.
- If students with disabilities have had limited exposure to other states, regions, or countries, be certain to provide concrete supports and tools such as videos, brochures, and rich discussions to assist students in understanding geographical locations as well as cultural differences.

Current Events

- More and more of the discussion focuses on the world around students. Cable in the classroom provides both current and past events that can be incorporated into learning.
- As the special educator, be certain to preview shows, if possible, and determine the supports students might need to learn current events.

PUTTING IT ALL TOGETHER

The role of the special educator in content areas has changed since the passage of No Child Left Behind. The stakes are higher for students with disabilities, but the stakes also are higher for special educators who need to be well versed across content areas to support students with disabilities. The strong emphasis on literacy for all students provides support for using many effective practices adopted in our field for many years, including Direct Instruction, BALANCE Literacy, and DIBELS for early reading intervention. We recommend that teachers think about all content areas in a unit format that is developed to provide access to a range of learning and behavioral needs. We conclude this chapter by providing you with information across content areas emphasizing the importance of the special educator being an equal team member in content-area instruction by understanding emerging and promising practices.

IMPORTANT POINTS

1. The unit approach integrates subject matter with a topic, a theme, or interest areas and may correspond to various subject areas, themes, learning styles, or multiple intelligences.
2. In planning a unit, select the unit theme or topic, brainstorm ideas, group ideas into categories, identify general goals, identify specific objectives, develop activities to meet the objectives, evaluate the objectives, and compile a list of resources.
3. Unit topics may be selected from curriculum guides, classroom texts, children's literature, and students' interests.
4. Teaching content with a single text may require various adaptations, such as using technology to provide alternative ways to learn the content to changing or adding more practice items, or using graphic organizers.
5. As a special educator, you need to be aware of current practices in the content areas and be ready to support general education teachers in inclusive settings.

DISCUSSION QUESTIONS

1. Opponents of the Direct Instruction model frequently assert that the lessons are boring and not motivating to the students due to the constant repetition and controlled vocabulary. How might you respond to such criticism?
2. Discuss how unit planning can be tied to state standards in various content areas.
3. What are some effective methods you might use if you are supporting a coteacher in math, science, or social studies?.

Websites: Useful websites related to chapter content can be found in Appendix A.

CHAPTER

9

Social Skills and Peer-Mediated Instruction

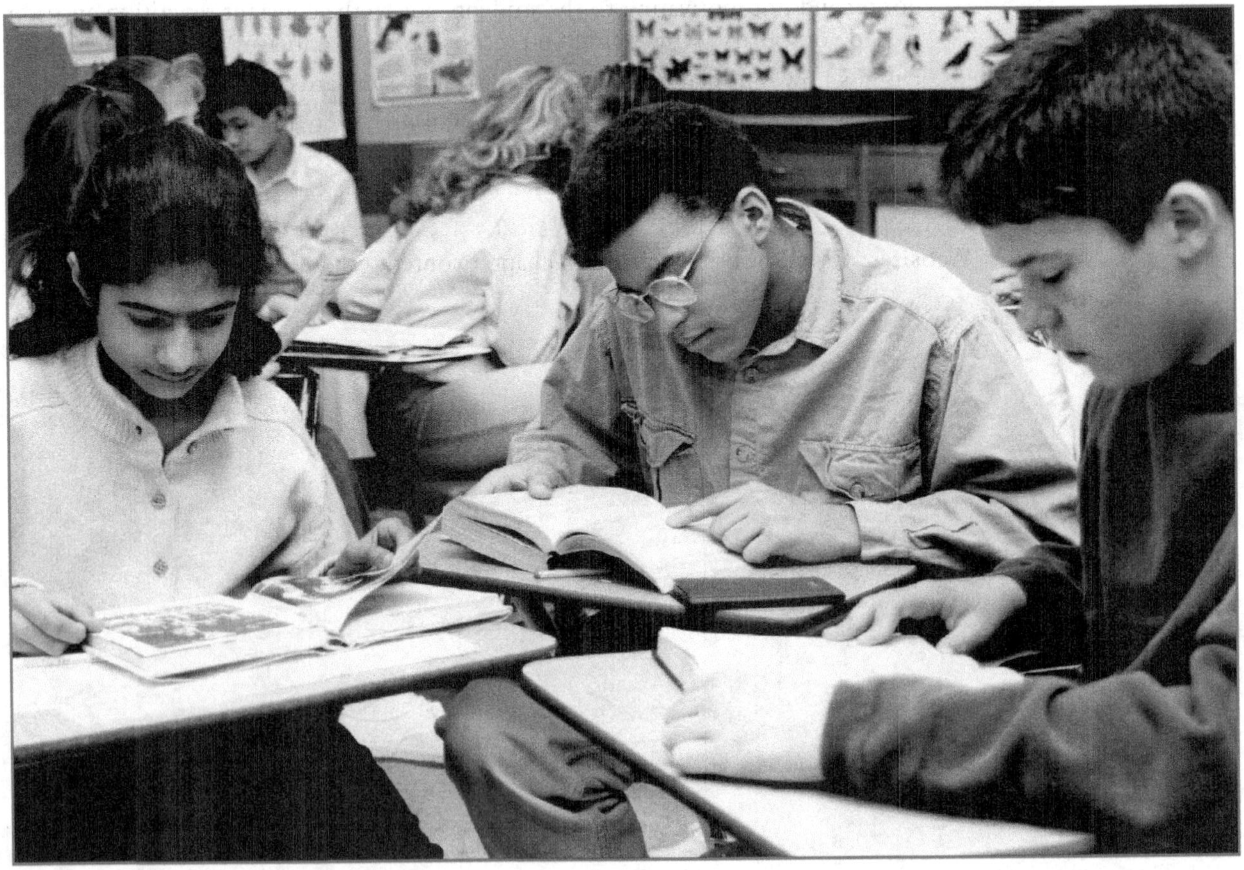

KEY TOPICS

"Mr. Washington, can I have my desk moved?" asked Juanita. "That new kid Andrew keeps getting in my face every time he has a question and I can't get my work done."

"Have you tried asking him to back off a little Juanita?"

"Yes, but he just laughs and then does the same thing to Ashley. He is driving our whole group crazy."

Mr. Washington sighed and looked across the room at his coteacher, Mrs. Shoemaker, a special education teacher. The two of them had been using this model of coteaching fifth grade for the past four years. Andrew was placed in their class because he had been diagnosed in second grade with both ADHD and learning disabilities. Both teachers believed strongly in the power of peers working cooperatively to enhance the social skills of students with mild disabilities. In fact, they had already begun weaving social skills instruction into their first week's lesson plans. However, this wasn't the first complaint they had received about Andrew.

"I'll talk to him about it, but I'm not moving any desks just yet. It is only the first week of school and you have to all learn to get along. Remember that talk we had on the first day about creating a classroom community by cooperating and working as a team?"

"Yes Mr. Washington. I remember. I just wish that being a 'community' wasn't so hard."

If you were Mr. Washington, would you have handled this situation any differently? What do you think he means by "social skills instruction"?

Responses to these questions are found in the Instructor's Manual

INTRODUCTION

The need for all students to learn social skills is critical and peer-mediated strategies that focus on students helping others can make a positive impact on learning outcomes. Both peer tutoring and cooperative learning are strongly supported as evidence-based strategies for inclusive settings (Vaughn, Klinger, & Bryant, 2001). These peer-mediated strategies can accommodate a wide range of cultural, linguistic, and academic diversity found in the current inclusive classroom and provide a great structure to teach many skills needed for success in life.

The power of any type of cooperative structure is that it allows students to work together to accomplish goals and to create collaborative learning communities. Today, as the world of work has changed and with a flurry of research in collaborative structures, there is clear evidence that peer-support structures can impact both student achievement and social interactions in the general education setting. Dieker and Murawski (2003) found that both peer tutoring and cooperative learning are a critical part of any successful secondary school inclusion program.

Students working together reflects the workplaces most students will be expected to survive in once they leave school. Social interactions can be taught and practiced through direct instruction of skills or through the use of peer tutoring, cooperative learning, and direct instruction. Peer tutoring involves students working together, whereas cooperative learning usually occurs in groups of three or more. Peer tutoring and cooperative learning provide tools to address both the high-stakes standards of our curriculum today as well as the social goals often written into a student's IEP. Both tools start with direct instruction of teaching students their role in the process and yet focus on the ultimate goal of increasing students' learning of concepts presented in the classroom. So, before we describe these peer-mediated strategies in-depth, we spend time discussing the importance of teaching social skills in general. Remember, asking students to work together without ensuring social goals and skills are in place could jeopardize both peer relationships as well as student learning. Teachers must teach social skills before and during peer-mediated instruction for effective learning to occur (Allsopp, 1997).

SOCIAL SKILLS

Not always, but many times, students with special needs may display inappropriate social skills. The lack of social skills tends to isolate these students from their peers, prevent positive interactions with teachers, and limit successful transitions to the world of work. Meta-analysis of social skills training finds only a modest effect for both students with learning disabilities and students with emotional disabilities (Kavale, Mathur, Forness, Rutherford, & Quinn, 1997), which may be the result of this training happening in more isolated settings. Factors may include the lack of intensive training as most of the studies in the meta-analysis report an average time of 30 hours in social skills training and the lack of matching interventions to social skills deficits (Gresham, Sugai, & Horner, 2001). As with all intervention strategies, the individual teacher should rely on data collection procedures to monitor the effectiveness of social skills training, as one cannot argue with the necessity of teaching social skills to students with special needs. Yet if we review the state standards for various grade levels and especially at the secondary content levels, minimal to no mention of social skills standards are provided. With the push for high-stakes testing, teachers are very focused on the academic standards provided. Our focus here is to remind you that equal emphasis has to be on the social aspects of learning.

IDENTIFICATION OF SOCIAL SKILLS

An examination of the literature finds varied definitions of social skills. McFall (1982) conceptualized a two-tiered model of social competence and social skills. According to his model, social competence involves the overall effectiveness of social behavior. A person who is socially competent perceives and interprets social situations and knows how to modify behavior when the situation changes (Chadsey-Rusch, 1986). Social skills are the specific strategies (accepting criticism, initiating conversation) and tactics that students must use to negotiate daily social tasks.

BOX 9.1

Reflections on Practice

Review your state standards at any grade level. Think about how these standards relate to the social needs of students. What social skills will students need to master these standards? Consider visiting a general education classroom to observe or interview a general education teacher about the social skills students need to be successful. Great teachers understand that students must be taught these social or sometimes called "soft" skills as much as they need to be taught the general education curriculum.

Remember that in today's world many of our students are learning about social skills via technology. For younger students there are sites such as Webkins www.webkins.com or Club Penguin (www.clubpenguin.com) which are controlled sites that allow students to learn to talk with (limited prompts for discussion) or to care for a pet. For older students there is of course text messaging, online chats, blogs and even the controversial myspace (www.myspace.com). Remember as part of your social skills instruction to include exploring these types of options to talk about social skills, but always be certain to teach Internet safety.

Gresham, Sugai, and Horner (2001) identify three social skills deficits: social skill acquisition deficits, performance deficits, and fluency deficits. Additionally, they recommend the selection of various interventions and settings based on the identification of the deficit (see Table 9.1).

How does a teacher decide which social skills will promote the behaviors necessary for effective peer tutoring and cooperative learning practices? You may want to start by looking at samples of rubrics created by teachers at various grade levels on the Web at sites such as rubric star. These rubrics indicate many of the social skills teachers deem important in their classroom.

A review of the literature reveals that offering encouragement and assistance, accepting compliments and criticism, taking turns, listening to what others are saying,

Table 9.1 Matching of Interventions to Social Skills Deficits

Social Skills Deficit	Definition	Intervention	Setting
Acquisition	Absence of knowledge to execute skill or failure to discriminate which behaviors are appropriate for different situations	Modeling, coaching, behavioral rehearsal, feedback on performance	Small group
Performance	Skill is present but students fail to execute it	Manipulation of antecedents such as teaching strategies (e.g., peer tutoring) or consequences (e.g., contingency contracting)	Naturalistic (e.g., classrooms, playgrounds)
Fluency	Skill is present and student wants to perform, but executes an awkward performance	Behavioral rehearsal and feedback for performance	Small group or natural settings

avoiding sarcasm and criticism, and presenting a positive and friendly manner are frequently mentioned as skills that promote the behaviors necessary for effective peer tutoring and cooperative learning (Mathes, Fuchs, Fuchs, Henley, & Sanders, 1994). To these skills, Wolford, Heward, and Alber (2001) add recruiting positive attention and instructional feedback from peers for students with learning disabilities to have success in peer tutoring and cooperative learning situations. Another activity to consider comes from a study on students with disabilities as they were about to be included in the general education setting (Monda-Amaya, Dieker, & Reed, 1998). The researchers attempted to determine what skills were needed for students to be successfully included in a general education setting. These skills were observed by watching successful students in the classroom and then taught to students with disabilities who were to be included. The social skills observed were turned into student goals that they self-monitored in the general education setting. Most direct social skills training involves four phases: (1) modeling the behavior necessary for success, (2) shaping that behavior for students to demonstrate it in multiple settings, (3) coaching the students as they attempt the new behavior, and (4) generalizing or reinforcing the behavior (Mastroprieri & Scruggs, 2007).

Leffert, Siperstein, and Millikan (2000) emphasize that teachers need to teach students with mental retardation not only discrete observable social behaviors, but also underlying social-cognitive skills, as these students frequently have difficulty participating in cooperative groups (Pomplun, 1997). Students with mental retardation often have difficulty interpreting cues regarding intentions of others and selecting effective social strategies (Leffert, et al., 2000). Wagner (2002) points out that students with autism often have difficulty (1) understanding nonverbal cues, (2) responding to eye contact and facial interactions, (3) showing interest in and/or sharing with others, (4) seeking comfort when hurt and/or comforting others, (5) interacting with others and making friends, and (6) using appropriate social responses. These categories, although originally proposed for students with autism, are also areas of need for many students with a range of disabilities. Students who display socially-valued behaviors are more likely to be accepted by peers. Walker, Schwarz, Nippold, Iroin, Noell (1994) identify compromising, assisting, cooperating, and contributing to achievement of a valued outcome as behaviors that are highly preferred by peers and lead to peer acceptance and popularity. Thus, you may wish to interview your students to identify the social skills they feel are necessary for peer tutoring or cooperative learning to work.

Leffert and Siperstein (2003) recommend the use of packaged social skills curricula with caution for students with learning disabilities. They emphasize that the programs that focus on social skills vary as does the content and method of instruction. Although they recognize the need for students to learn social skills, teachers should be mindful of the skills they teach and gather data on the positive outcomes or lack of growth that occurs using tools like those mentioned in chapter 4.

A way to teach social skills is through peer structures. These structures can be used as a tool to build social and academic skills in inclusive classrooms. Kauffman, Landrum, Mock, Sayeski, and Sayeski (2005) argue that with support and structures like peer tutoring and cooperative learning a broader student population can be served in the general education setting. For example, McMaster, Fuchs, Fuchs, and Compton (2005) found a significant impact on what they refer to as nonresponders (students in the lowest 10% in the area of reading) using peer-support structures. In addition, Ryan, Reid, and Esptein (2004) suggest peer structures such as peer tutoring and cooperative learning as effective practices for students with emotional/behavioral disorders across grade levels.

SOCIAL SKILLS INTERVENTIONS

Social skills interventions generally fall into two areas or combinations of the two areas of skill-based approaches and problem-solving approaches (Walker, et al., 1994). Smith (1995) recommends a skill-based approach for students who demonstrate skill deficits and a problem-solving approach for students who demonstrate performance deficits or self-control deficits. The skill-based approach adheres to the effective teaching strategies mentioned in Chapter 5: (a) teaching definition, steps, and rationale; (b)modeling; (c) presenting examples and nonexamples; (d) scheduling opportunities for students to practice the skill; (e) prompting; (f) giving feedback; (g) providing contingent reinforcement; and (h) teaching generalization of the skill. The problem-solving approach frequently teaches students to identify their feelings, tell what is happening, decide on a goal, identify alternative responses, envision possible outcomes for each response, select the best solution, decide on one solution, emit the behavior, and self-evaluate for future problem solving (Elias & Tobias, 1996). Another practical idea used by a teacher is to have students create social stories. Students write these stories about how they can deal with social issues. For example, "When I forget my homework" might be the title of the story. The story is written about all of the options and the consequences of each of the options the student can pursue. Then when the student forgets his homework, he can read his social story to decide what actions he should take. Other topics that can be covered in a book include getting angry, using negative language with others, arguing with my peers, wasting instructional time, or working in a group. Whether using social stories, the skill-based approach, or the problem-solving approach or elements of all three, teachers should directly teach social skills, provide practice opportunities, integrate social skills with other curriculum, emphasize generalization of the skills to other settings, or just teach the skills in inclusive settings.

Activity 9.1

Select a social skill and design a social story related to students at a grade level of your choice to use with the skill you selected.

(Answers for this and other activities are found in the Instructor's Manual.)

Directly Teach Social Skills

As with academic skills, students with disabilities have difficulty learning social skills incidentally. Teachers should directly teach the skills and then use scaffolding (prompting) to facilitate social skills performance. Adolescents with learning disabilities were successfully trained to directly teach social skills to their peers with learning disabilities (Prater, Serna, & Nakamura, 1999).

Elias and Tobias (1996) recommend teaching students problem-solving strategies by using questioning techniques. They suggest that open-ended questions, such as "What happened? What were you trying to do? How are you feeling? What was the other person doing? What happened before this?" (p. 24) assist students to become competent and independent thinkers. For the resistant or younger child, they suggest teaching students to make choices, such as, "Were you trying to keep the toy for yourself?" or "Did you just want to play with it a little longer?" A two-question rule is used to encourage children to think. For example, before putting children into cooperative groups, you may ask them to think about these questions: "How do you plan to show that you do not agree with your partner's idea? What are some words you could start with?" The idea is to lead students to reflect on their own behaviors.

Goldstein, McGinnis, Sprafklin, Gershaw, and Klein (2002) provide two additional tools that teachers can use to teach social skills one at the elementary level, *Skillstreaming the Elementary Student*, and another at the secondary level, *Skillstreaming the Adolescent*. These books identify at different age levels critical social skills students must master. Two other ideas that can be used classroom-wide to help focus on problem solving are called a problem box and pass the problem. Teachers use the problem box for anyone (including the teacher) who wants to put problems into the box so they can be read to the class. You may finish this activity with a short discussion about the problem as well as suggestions about how to effectively solve the problem. Often one of the issues for students with disabilities is that they often either believe they are the only students who have problems or do not know how others solve problems. One thing a teacher can stress is that everyone has problems but the core of being a capable person is learning to solve problems in effective ways. The same concept can be addressed using pass the problem. In this strategy students write a detailed description of their problem (this strategy is typically used more at the secondary level) and then every student writes a solution to this problem, showing that there are multiple solutions to all problems. These strategies also allow teachers to use problems in relation to the subject they are teaching (e.g., tying a student problem with dating to the novel being read in literature class).

Rosenthal-Malek (1997) used six 10-minute daily instruction periods to teach her preschool children self-interrogation questions, such as "What will happen if _____?" to develop social skills. She asked each child to repeat the questions, she then wrote the questions on the board, and she developed games for application of the questions.

Modeling social skills by both teachers and peers is an effective way to teach these skills directly. Teachers or students may model skills in an appropriate manner and then in an inappropriate manner, and students must discriminate between them. For example, Ms. Trailer modeled the appropriate way to disagree with a peer and then the inappropriate way. The children designed their own evaluation to help discriminate the appropriate example from the inappropriate.

New technological developments also are providing new avenues for teaching social skills. For example, Robins and Dautenhahn (2004) have created a robot to assist students in learning social skills. Rizzo, Schultheis, Kerns, and Mateer (2004) have begun to experiment with the use of virtual environments to impact student learning and social interaction. Elias and Taylor (1995) suggest a tool as simple as the use of videos to teach social skills. They first show a segment of a television program or a movie. Then they ask students to discuss the main characters, the problems they have, their expressed feelings, the character's goals, their solutions, the roadblocks, the plan, and evaluation of the plan. Instead of using a movie, Ms. Fearis videotaped each cooperative group for 5 minutes and then presented the tape to the students and asked them to pinpoint any problems they saw that the group was having, brainstorm some solutions, vote on one solution, and agree to try the solution the next time the group met.

Directly teaching social skills using literature is another effective strategy (Cartledge & Kiarie, 2001; Morris, 2002). Select books that include examples of the social skill you are planning to teach, are not dominated by violence, include brief stories, are culturally diverse, present males and females in nonstereotypical ways, and have minimal text with repetitive refrains for young children or students who are not skilled readers (Cartledge & Kiarie, 2001). Two sources to check for literary materials are Carolhurst Publishing and a book *Cultural Diversity and Social Skills Instruction: Understanding Ethnic and Gender Differences* by Cartledge and Milburn (1996). Carolhurst provides a website with award-winning books correlated to social skills such as how to handle bullies. Each chapter in the Cartledge and Milburn book identifies sample books for various social skills.

Provide Practice Opportunities

Practice for social skills frequently occurs during role-playing. Role-playing allows students to identify and learn skills and to solve problems in a group context with impersonal materials. During role-playing, an effective teacher provides prompts and feedback. Many commercial social skills curriculum kits provide role-playing suggestions. However, you or your students may generate the role-playing situations or observe these actual skills in the general education setting. At the end of one of the peer-tutoring sessions, Ms. Bright had students role-play how to give corrective feedback, as she noticed many tutors were having problems correcting their peers in an effective manner.

Another effective strategy is to provide students with mnemonics to cue students to remember and practice a skill. The SLAM (McIntosh, Vaughn, & Bennerson, 1995) strategy does just that. After skills instruction, teachers may use SLAM to remind students how to handle negative feedback: "**S**top whatever you're doing. **L**ook the person in the eye. **A**sk the person a question to clarify what he or she means. **M**ake an appropriate response to the person."

The importance of direct instruction in the area of social skills is critical for students with disabilities especially as they are included more and more into general education settings. However, these skills cannot be taught in isolation of the standards required of general education teachers as there is already not enough time for teachers to provide the level of direct instruction needed. Therefore, we recommend you consider the following tips related to social skills integration.

- Review students' IEPs and make a list of social skill goals that are listed on the IEPs.
- Take this list of goals and plan for these skills in the same way you would plan for teaching academic skills.
- In the general education setting, think about ways to teach the social skill goal needed by the student with a disability to all class members.
- Use simple techniques like writing a social skill goal daily on the board so everyone in the class is working to accomplish it, or assign as homework a goal for students to use at home. Parents would appreciate it if you assigned as homework the students saying something nice to their sibling(s) or using please and thank you.

Integrate Social Skills With Other Curriculum

If you use peer tutoring and cooperative learning groups frequently in your class, it is easy to integrate social skills, because both arrangements incorporate academic and social skills. The writing process also promotes the use of social skills, especially if you have students evaluate each other's work. During student feedback and evaluation of other students' writings, Zaragoza (1987) teaches her students to react positively to each other's work through the simple steps of TAG: "(a) **T**ell what you like, (b) **A**sk questions, and (c) **G**ive ideas" (p. 293).

Elias and Tobias (1996) suggest that social problem-solving frameworks may be applied to language arts, social studies, and health. For example, a "Book Talk" format brings problem-solving ideas into language arts for young readers:

> My character's problem is . . .
>
> How did your character get into this problem . . .?
>
> How does the character feel?
>
> What does the character want to happen?
>
> What questions would you like to be able to ask the character you picked, one of the other characters, or the author? (p. 109)

Generalize Social Skills

Some students with disabilities have great difficulty in generalizing new information to other situations and settings (Rivera & Smith, 1997). Therefore, you must incorporate generalization strategies into your teaching of social skills or better yet teach the skill to the student in the inclusion class. We assume students are included to the maximum extent appropriate, therefore generalization to this setting is not needed. However, students might need to use the new skills in the cafeteria, in electives, and across numerous teachers. Teaching social skills in isolation of peers and natural settings is not as effective.

Salend, Jantzen, and Giek (1992) found that a peer confrontation system was effective in modifying inappropriate verbalizations and low levels of on-task behavior for students with mild disabilities. Whenever a student displayed either behavior during the language arts classes, the teacher initiated the procedure by asking the group to respond to these questions: "_____ seems to be having a problem. Who can tell _____ what the problem is? Can you tell _____ why that is a problem? Who can tell _____ what he/she needs to do to solve the problem?" (p. 214). The teacher verbally praised appropriate responses to the questions and verbally praised the student who had been confronted for accepting and displaying the alternative suggested by the group. Twelve of the 13 students reported that they felt the teacher should continue the intervention, even though some felt it was embarrassing to be singled out. An adaptation is to direct the confrontation to the group and not a single subject; for example, "Our group seems to be having a problem . . . ."

Another technique is for teachers to give homework assignments for students to generalize social skills in addition to academic skills. Ms. Holt noticed that students were not demonstrating encouraging behavior to each other during group work. Using peer confrontation procedures, the group defined the problem and discussed how to show more encouragement to others. Ms. Holt then gave the students a homework assignment to complete for their social skills journals (see Figure 9.1). Chances are with the peer-mediated strategies of peer tutoring and cooperative learning, social skills instruction will become an integral part of your curriculum.

Activity 9.2

Think of a social behavior that was difficult for you when you were in school. How might you provide students with training in this social skill within your reading or mathematics lesson?

Figure 9.1 SAMPLE SOCIAL SKILLS POSTER FOR PEER-MEDIATED STRATEGIES

ENCOURAGING OTHERS
Sounds Like
Let's try again.
I think we're close to solving it.
We can do this.
Well done! Perfect!
Looks Like
Pat on the back.
Smile.
A-okay sign.
Handshake.

Source: Adapted from Marge Christensen (1992). *Motivational English for At-Risk Students: A Language Arts Course That Works,* Copyright 1992 by the National Education Service, 1252 Loesch Road, Bloomington, IN 47404, Telephone: 800-733-6786. Reprinted by permission.

IMPORTANT POINTS

1. Looking for appropriate peer role models as well as using students' everyday problems can provide a forum for teaching social skills.
2. Peer tutoring and cooperative learning allow for social skills instruction by: (a) recruiting positive attention and instructional feedback from peers for students with learning disabilities (Wolford, et al., 2001), and (b) interpreting cues regarding intentions of others and selecting effective social strategies for students with mental retardation (Leffert, et al., 2000).
3. Teachers must directly teach social skills, provide practice opportunities, integrate social skills with other curriculum, and emphasize generalization of the social skills to other settings.

PEER TUTORING

Peer tutoring consists of one student acting as a tutor, or the person who transmits the information, and one student acting as the tutee, or the person who receives the information. A tutor may be the same age as the tutee (same-age tutoring) or a different age (cross-age tutoring). Students may also assume reciprocal roles: sometimes as a tutor and sometimes as a tutee.

Peer tutoring enjoys much empirical support in the field of special education for students with mild disabilities in both elementary and secondary grades in all subject areas (Maheady, Harper, & Mallette, 2001). Students taught by teacher-directed instruction followed by peer tutoring yielded better mean gain scores in comprehension of material than their counterparts taught by traditional instruction. Peer tutoring was identified as one of the promising interventions from a meta-analysis of special education research (Forness, Kavale, Blum, & Lloyd, 1997) and has received endorsement from the Council for Exceptional Children Division of Learning Disabilities and the Division of Research (Maheady, et al., 2001). In summarizing the research on peer tutoring, Kalkowski (2001) reports its effectiveness in impacting academic and affective areas at all age/grade levels for students with learning disabilities and behavioral disorders as well as other at-risk populations including English language learners. Mastropieri, Scruggs, and Graetz (2005) conducted research on 39 high school students with and without disabilities who participated in a peer-tutoring program. Ten of the students enrolled in the inclusive classes met federal and state criteria for learning disability classification. Their investigation confirmed the effectiveness of peer tutoring in chemistry conducted within a secondary inclusive class. Table 9.2 outlines steps to take to ensure a quality peer-tutoring program is developed.

Not only is peer tutoring effective for students, but both teachers and students appear to like peer tutoring (Mastropieri, et al., 2001). Students prefer it over teacher-led and student-regulated activities (Maheady, et al., 2001). Danville High School in Kentucky has offered an elective course in peer tutoring for 11th and 12th graders to tutor students with moderate and severe disabilities since 1983 (Longwill & Kleinert, 1998). Another school offers this model but students with disabilities can serve as tutors to other students. The criteria to serve as a tutor in this school is that you can only tutor in a class that you have received a B+ or better. In this school several students tutor during first period and then are served by a tutor in second period. This reciprocal tutoring allows students to tutor in an area of strength making tutoring more accepted school-wide while simultaneously boosting the self-esteem of some students with disabilities.

Table 9.2 Guidelines for Using Peer Tutoring

Have each member of the pair share the roles of tutor and tutee, and train them by modeling appropriate behaviors for each. Train each pair in giving feedback and in error correction procedures. Have pairs practice each role, with monitoring by the teacher. Begin tutoring with less complex drill and practice or vocabulary words, then transition to more challenging content when students are proficient at tutoring procedures. Choose materials with the appropriate difficulty level carefully, noting the skills of the tutoring pair.

1. Explain the purpose and rationale for the technique. Stress the idea of increased opportunities for practice and "on-task" behavior.
2. Stress collaboration and cooperation rather than competition.
3. Select the content and instructional materials for tutoring sessions.
4. Train students in the roles of tutor and tutee. Include specific procedures for (a) feedback for correct responses, (b) error correction procedures, and (c) score-keeping.
5. Model appropriate behaviors for tutor and tutee. Demonstrate acceptable ways to give and accept corrective feedback.
6. Provide sample scripts for student practice of roles. Divide the class into practice pairs and teams.
7. Let pairs practice roles of tutor as teacher circulates, provides feedback, and reinforcement.
8. Conduct further discussion regarding constructive and nonconstructive pair behavior. Answer questions and problem-solve as needed.
9. Let pairs switch roles and practice new roles as teacher circulates and provides feedback, and reinforcement. Repeat Step 8.

Source: Fulk, B. M., & King, K. (2001). ClassWide Peer Tutoring at work. *Teaching Exceptional Children, 34* (2), 49–53. Table 4: Guidelines for Using ClassWide Peer Tutoring.

RATIONALE

The rationale behind the use of peer tutoring is that the procedures promote more active student responding, a direct link to higher achievement. Students have more opportunities to correct errors, are given immediate feedback, and are exposed to more social and academic support than in teacher-mediated instruction (King-Sears & Bradley, 1995; Utley, Mortsweet, & Greenwood, 1997). Furthermore, peer tutoring is another way to accomplish individualized instruction, because instructional material may be matched to the learner's interest and ability. Peer tutoring is also an effective way to reinforce concepts previously taught by the teacher. A peer who has similar experiences and is closer to the developmental age of the tutee can often interpret the teacher's ideas or content in that student's language. Peer tutoring is also an economical and teacher-friendly way to accommodate the wide range of cultural, linguistic, and academic diversity found in current inclusive classrooms.

DESCRIPTION

Within peer tutoring, we highlight instructional procedures that involve two peers working together, such as Reciprocal Peer Tutoring (Fantuzzo, King, & Heller, 1992) and the Reciprocal Peer Revision Strategy (MacArthur, Schwartz, & Graham, 1991). Additionally, we present models that involve peers working together as part of a team, such as ClassWide Peer Tutoring (CWPT; Delquadri, Greenwood, Stretton, & Hall, 1983), and Peabody Peer-Assisted Learning Strategies (PALS; Mathes, et al., 1994). We select these particular models to describe, as they are supported in the literature for their effectiveness for students with mild disabilities and students at risk (Utley, et al., 1997).

Reciprocal Peer Tutoring

The routine for Reciprocal Peer Tutoring (RPT) includes 20 minutes of peer tutoring, followed by 7 minutes of testing to teach mathematics and spelling skills. Teachers use modeling and instructional prompts to teach students to follow specific techniques for acting as partners and for managing their own group reward contingencies (Heller & Fantuzzo, 1993). In mathematics tutoring procedures (Dufrene, Duhon, Gilbertson, & Noell, 2005), students are paired randomly in same-age dyads and work with flash cards selected for them individually, based on their scores on a pretest. They also select their rewards and performance goals from teacher-prepared options. Sometimes students begin the procedures by completing a 5-minute multiplication drill, while other times they begin by reminding themselves of their individual and group goals. The tutoring format proceeds in the following manner:

a. Peer teacher presents flash card with answer and strategy on back to student.

b. Student completes problem on a worksheet that is divided into sections (Try 1, Try 2, Help, and Try 3).

c. If student is correct, peer teacher praises and presents next problem.

d. If student is wrong, peer teacher provides structured help (strategy on back of card) and personal suggestions.

e. Student attempts problem again in Try 2 section.

f. If still incorrect, the peer teacher completes the problem, explaining the procedures in the Help section on the worksheet.

g. Student attempts to solve problem again in Try 3 section.

h. At the end of 10 minutes, students change roles.

i. Both students take a 16-problem quiz.
j. Students grade each other's quizzes using an answer sheet.
k. Students compare their team score with the team goal.
l. If the score exceeds the team goal, the students score a "win."
m. After a certain set of "wins," the team earns the predetermined reward.

Dufrene, Duhon, Gilbertson, and Noell (2005) suggest that if students are not progressing using RPT then provide detailed performance feedback to the RPT partners. With all cooperative strategies, setting up the strategy as well as providing ongoing monitoring and feedback is critical and a strong component of all research that has found these structures to make a positive impact on student learning.

Reciprocal Peer Revision Strategy

The Reciprocal Peer Revision Strategy combines strategy instruction and peer interaction. MacArthur, Schwartz, and Graham (1991) designed this highly structured approach to teaching revision skills, which are usually taught more informally in the process approach to writing instruction.

In this strategy the teacher introduces the peer editing strategy, shares its importance, teaches the steps and rationale for each step, models the steps, and provides practice opportunities. At the conclusion of the teacher's instruction, pairs of students work together in a structured routine to improve composition writing.

The routine requires the peer editor to (a) listen and read along as the peer author reads; (b) tell the peer author the main idea of the paper and the part liked best; (c) reread the paper, take notes, and address whether the material is clear and is written with enough details; and (d) discuss suggestions with the peer author. Both students complete Steps (a) and (b) as a peer editor and as a peer author. At Step (c), each student works independently on each other's composition. Students ask two questions during this step: "(1) Is there anything that is not CLEAR? and (2) Where could more DETAILS and information be added?" (MacArthur, et al., 1991, p. 203). They then discuss the suggestions (Step d), and each student revises his/her composition. At the second meeting, they discuss revisions that they made and complete a checklist that concentrates on four types of errors: complete sentences, capitalization (beginning of sentences), punctuation (end-mark), and spelling. The students with learning disabilities in the Reciprocal Peer Revision strategy group made more revisions and produced papers of higher quality with peer support than those who did not participate in the Reciprocal Peer Revision Strategy.

ClassWide Peer Tutoring

Initially developed by researchers to work with children from low socioeconomic and culturally diverse backgrounds, the second phase of the Juniper Garden Children's Project extended the program to special education settings (Greenwood & Delquadri, 1995). Since then, these procedures have demonstrated effective results in both pull-out and inclusive classrooms for students with and without disabilities (Greenwood, 1999). Although many different versions of ClassWide Peer Tutoring (CWPT) are evident in the literature, certain core components are usually incorporated into the various adaptations. These core components include direct teacher presentation of new material to be learned, teacher monitoring of the tutoring process, whole-class instructional activity, explicit presentation formats for peers to follow, active student responding, reciprocal roles in each session, teams competing for the highest team point total, contingent point earning, systematic error correction strategies, public posting of student performance, and social awards for the winning team (Greenwood & Delquadri, 1995). Teachers explain the tutoring methods, model the procedures, have students role-play the procedures, and then give students feedback regarding their performance. When CWPT procedures were instituted in a health education class, the entire class was trained for 15 minutes a day for three consecutive days using role-playing and feedback (Utley, Reddy, Delquadri, Greenwood, Mortsweet, & Bowman, 2001).

We describe the use of CWPT in a secondary social studies inclusive classroom (Maheady, Sacca, & Harper, 1988). However, CWPT has been just as successful with elementary-age students and in mathematics, reading, and spelling.

Maheady, Sacca, and Harper (1988) instituted the following CWPT approach in an inclusive secondary social studies class using study guides developed by the general and special education teachers. On Monday and Tuesday, the general education teacher presented the material; on Wednesday and Thursday, the peer tutoring occurred; on Friday, the students took a quiz during class time. Students with disabilities were paired with general education students. The pair was assigned to one of two teams by randomly drawing colored squares. The students then contributed points to each team as the teams competed with each other. The team membership stayed the same for 2 weeks.

During the 30-minute peer tutoring sessions, the tutor dictated the study guide questions to the tutee, who wrote and said the correct answer. The tutors gave feedback: either "that's right" or "wrong" and the correct answer. Tutees earned three points for each correct answer. When tutees gave an incorrect answer, the tutors instructed them to write the correct answer three times and awarded two points instead of three. After 15 minutes elapsed, the students reversed roles and continued with the same procedures.

The teachers' roles also were structured. Each teacher moved around the classroom and awarded up to 10 bonus points to tutors for following the presentation format. The individual scores of tutor and tutee were totaled for the daily team scores and posted on a chart in front of the class. On Friday, an individual quiz was given, and each student earned five team points for each correct answer. The winning team was announced following the weekly quiz.

A common complaint of teachers in using CWPT is the amount of time that it takes for the score-reporting process and the planning. A computerized system is available that provides support to teachers in both these processes (Greenwood, et al., 1993). The computerized system was used successfully with English language learners in five first- through fifth-grade classrooms to increase sight vocabulary and spelling words (Greenwood, Arreaga-Mayer, Utley, Gavin, & Terry, 2001).

Peabody Peer-Assisted Learning Strategies

In Peabody Peer-Assisted Learning Strategies (PALS), also referred to as the Peabody ClassWide Peer Tutoring procedure, the reading strategies of summarization, main idea identification, and prediction are combined with peer interactions (Mathes et al., 1994). Saenz, Fuchs, and Fuchs (2005) report positive outcomes for using PALS with students who not only have disabilities but also for English language learners. When using PALS, teachers directly instruct the students in the key procedures of the tutoring process and in the strategies.

Once the students are trained in the strategies and the tutoring procedures, PALS typically occurs for three 35-minute periods each week for 15 weeks (Fuchs, Fuchs, Mathes, & Simmons, 1996; Mathes et al., 1994; Saenz, et al., 2005). Each strategy takes about 10 minutes. Readers of various levels work together and assume reciprocal roles. Teachers rank order their students and then split the class into high and low performers. The top-ranked student in the high-performing group is then matched to the top-ranked student in the low-performing group until all students from each group are paired (Mathes, et al., 1994). Pairs may read from different texts.

Each pair is then assigned to one of two teams. Individuals earn points for their teams and then at the end of the week, the teacher's and each student's points are totaled, and the winning team is announced. Teachers may give points to students for following the procedures correctly and for exhibiting cooperative behaviors. The winning team receives applause from the other team. After 4 weeks, new peers and teams are assigned. In Table 9.3, we outline the specific format for peer teaching of the reading strategies.

Table 9.3 Peer Teaching of Reading Strategies

PARTNER READING (MATHES, ET AL., 1994)

The instructional format for partner reading is:

- 5 minutes—Best reader reads orally while worse reader tutors.
- 5 minutes—Worse reader reads the same passage.
- 1 or 2 minutes—Worse reader retells in sequence what is read.
- After the retell sequence, partners reward themselves 10 points if they feel they have worked hard and tried their best.

The routine for correction of word recognition errors for each student is:

- Peer teacher says, "You missed this word. Can you figure it out?" Pauses 4 seconds (p. 45)
- If correct, student rereads sentence.
- If incorrect, peer teacher says, "That word is ____." (p. 46).
- Student rereads the word and then the sentence.
- Peer teacher rewards a point for each sentence read correctly, no matter the trials.

The routine for the retell sequence is:

- Peer teacher says, "What did you learn first?" "What did you learn next?" (p. 46)

If incorrect or the student can't remember, the peer teacher provides the information.

PARAGRAPH SHRINKING (FUCHS, ET AL., 1996)

The instructional format for paragraph shrinking is:

- 5 minutes—Best reader orally reads one paragraph.
- Worse reader prompts tutee to recall main idea by reading cue cards:
  - "Who or what was the paragraph mainly about? Tell the most important thing learned in the paragraph" (p.10).
- Best reader identifies main idea with not more than 10 words.
- Worse reader awards 1 point for correct who or what, 1 point for main idea, and 1 point for shrinking the statement to 10 words.
- 5 minutes—Worse reader reads next paragraph.
- Best reader prompts worse to recall main idea with the same questions.
- Best reader assigns points.

The routine for correction for each student is:

- Incorrect answer, peer teacher says, "Try again."
- Still incorrect answer, peer teacher says, "Read the paragraph silently and try again."
- Still incorrect answer, peer teacher provides the answer.

PREDICTION RELAY (MATHES, ET AL., 1994)

Prediction Relay is introduced after the students become better at summarizing and identifying the main idea.

The instructional format for prediction relay is:

- 5 minutes—Best reader makes a prediction about content, reads half page, confirms or disconfirms prediction, summarizes content in 10 words or less, makes a new prediction about next half page, and continues with routine until 5 minutes are up.
- Worse reader decides if answers are correct and assigns 1 point for each step, totaling 4 points.
- 5 minutes—Roles reverse and same procedures are followed.

There are also PALS procedures for math and group story mapping and writing. PALS is a strategy that researchers have found can be used across grade levels, age levels, and varying types of diversity in the classroom.

Activity 9.3

Look at Table 9.3 that compares each of the types of peer tutoring and explain to a peer how each type differs. Share specific content areas or lessons for which each type would be best.

IMPLEMENTATION

Teachers must carefully plan peer-tutoring activities. Decisions must be made about selecting objectives, selecting and matching students, preparing materials, determining schedules and selecting sites, planning the presentation format, training tutors, monitoring progress, evaluating the tutoring session, and informing significant others. Many of these decisions will be made for you if you select any of the models we have just described. See Table 9.4 for a description of how each model addresses some of these decisions.

Selecting Objectives

Your first step in deciding to institute peer tutoring is to formulate the objectives of the peer-tutoring program. Usually, basic academic skills are taught directly, and positive social interaction is achieved indirectly. IEPs are a good source of objectives for peer tutoring.

Delquadri, Greenwood, Whorton, Carta, and Hall (1986) designated the following target behaviors as appropriate for peer-tutoring selection: "answering comprehension questions; practicing in reading workbooks; practicing spelling word lists; practicing math facts; and practicing words, their meanings, and definitions" (p. 536). Objectives may also include the teaching of strategies such as revision, paragraph shrinking, and others.

Selecting and Matching Students

In a meta-analytic review of grouping practices and reading outcomes for students with learning disabilities and behavior disorders, Elbaum, Vaughn, Hughes, and Moody (1999) report that peer tutoring was an effective grouping whether students with mild disabilities acted in a reciprocal role (both tutor and tutee) or in a tutee role; however, with cross-age tutoring, students with disabilities perform better when they are the tutors. Furthermore, they report that students with disabilities benefit from tutoring younger students at least a grade level below them. You may wish to change your pairing every 3 to 4 weeks and more frequently if you are working with high school students to counteract absences.

Preparing Materials

Either the student or you may prepare the materials depending on the objective. If you target spelling words as the objective for peer tutoring, the tutor may just use the class text. If you select memorizing math facts, the tutor may write each fact on a 3-by-5-inch card. If the objective is studying for a test, you should prepare a study guide. For a shared reading objective, you may guide tutors in selecting a book for the session. Administration of a pretest and the selection of 10 missed items comprised the content for math-tutoring sessions designed by Miller, Barbetta, and Heron (1994). Monitoring sheets may also be prepared by the tutors or by you. This step requires substantial time initially, but materials may be reused. Additionally, written copies of the correction procedures or cue cards for strategies may assist students in remembering the tutoring procedures.

Table 9.4 Comparison of Peer-Tutoring Models to Assist in Teacher Decision Making

Models	Selecting Content as Pertains to Our Descriptions (Objectives)	Matching Students	Preparing Materials	Determining Schedules & Sites	Planning Presentation Format	Training Tutors	Evaluating Sessions
Reciprocal Peer Tutoring	Math facts	Paired randomly; Same age; Reciprocal roles	Flash cards with answer and strategy to solve problem on back of cards; Worksheet divided into Try 1, Try 2, & Try 3	20 minutes for tutoring; 7 minutes for test	Tutee gets three tries to answer problem, gets feedback from tutor for each try following specific procedures; Change role at end of 10 minutes; Both take exam; Earn points for team and then earn reward	Teachers train students to act as partners and to manage their own group reward contingencies through modeling and instructional prompts	Quizzes; Team scores; Goals
Reciprocal Peer Revision Strategy	Written expression	SLD students with non SLD; Reciprocal roles	Individual written assignments; Checklist of four types of errors	None specified	Assumed roles of peer editor and peer author; Both listen to each composition, tell main idea, and what like; Use questions such as "Is there anything that is not CLEAR?" and "Where could more DETAILS and information be added?" to assist in revision	Teachers teach strategies through rationale, modeling, practice, and comparison to students' previous work; Students view and discuss a videotape of two students following the presentation format	Amount of revisions and quality of papers
ClassWide Peer Tutoring	Social studies	Students with disabilities to students without disabilities; Same age; Reciprocal roles	Study guide questions. Cue cards for prompting of procedures	Teacher-directed instruction for two days, peer tutoring (30 minutes) of practice activity for two days, quiz on fifth day	Tutor read study guide question while tutee wrote answer; Tutor awarded points for each correct answer; Tutors gave feedback as either, "That's right" or "That's wrong"; Change role at end of 15 minutes; Individual points totaled	Teachers explain, model, role-play tutoring procedures, and give students feedback on their performances in the role-playing episodes	Bonus points for following presentation format; Individual scores; Team scores

(*continued*)

Table 9.4 (continued)

Models	Selecting Content as Pertains to Our Descriptions (Objectives)	Matching Students	Preparing Materials	Determining Schedules & Sites	Planning Presentation Format	Training Tutors	Evaluating Sessions
					for team; Team scores posted		
Peabody Peer-Assisted Learning Strategies	Reading	Heterogeneous matching by ability highs to lows; Reciprocal roles; Changed after four weeks	Reading texts	Three 35-minute periods each week for 15 weeks	For reading, 10 minutes is spent in teaching each strategy; Best reader reads first or employs the strategy first for 5 minutes, then roles are reversed; Tutor asks specific questions for each strategy; Correction procedures are specified for each strategy; Individual points totaled for team; Team scores posted	Teachers teach students key procedures of the tutoring process and the strategies; Each strategy is taught separately through modeling and practice	Bonus points for following procedures correctly and for exhibiting cooperative behaviors; Individual scores; Team scores

BOX 9.2

Reflections on Practice

Consider making permanent cards (laminated) that you can use for peer-supported strategies such as peer tutoring or cooperative learning. For example, laminate cards for the peer tutor or with the roles for cooperative groups. You could also laminate various checklists such as one for preparing materials for your tutee to allow these cards to be used over and over again. For some students it is helpful to add clip art or photos to show the emotional aspects of how they should look in various roles or during various steps. For example, to illustrate "remember to smile" put a picture of a person with a smile next to the phrase.

Checklists are also effective reminders of essential behaviors. Ms. James prepared the following list for her students: (a) I have all the materials, (b) I have examined the materials, (c) I plan to _____ when my student says something wrong, (d) I know when to say, "Good answer," and other positive things, (e) I will remember to smile, and (f) I will count to five to give my tutee a chance to answer after I ask a question.

Determining Schedules and Selecting Sites

The popular length of a tutoring session is 30 minutes two or three times a week for 5 to 7 weeks, with about 15 to 20 minutes for the actual student contact time (the rest of the time is spent organizing materials). The site should be a place where the tutors and tutees can work together undisturbed. If you use any of the reciprocal peer procedures, tutoring is scheduled as part of the class routine, so there is no problem with site selection; students may just be instructed to move their desks together. Two unsatisfactory areas for peer tutoring are outside the school building and in the hallways, where distractions tend to be excessive.

Planning the Presentation Format

You may decide on the presentation format or you may ask for student input. You may wish to select or adapt any of the well-researched models that we discussed previously (e.g., PALS), where students assume reciprocal roles, or you may adapt those models with only one student acting as the tutor. Remember, you should identify how the tutor retrieves and returns materials, presents the information, gives feedback, and monitors the progress of the tutee. You may even wish to script the procedures. In a case study of a student with behavior disorders, Fulk and King (2001) scripted the correction procedure for the tutor to help the child with behavior disorders accept correction without argument.

Training Tutors

Once you have decided on the presentation format, you must train your tutors to follow the format and to display appropriate teaching behaviors. These behaviors include waiting for the response instead of immediately telling the answer, avoiding sarcasm and criticism, and proceeding in a positive, friendly manner.

You should plan an orientation session in which you share the purpose, responsibilities, general guidelines, and expected outcomes of the tutoring session (Copeland, et al., 2004). This is also a good time to teach the tutors how to set up and put away the tutoring materials.

Following the orientation session, you should model the presentation format including correction procedures, guide the students in their imitation of the model, and point out the important behaviors. In a coteaching situation, modeling is frequently presented with one teacher acting as the tutor and the other as the tutee.

Role-playing positive interactions and negative interactions and having students discriminate between the two are essential.

Monitoring Progress

You should collect academic and social data to document the progress of both tutors and tutees. These data may be particularly helpful to answer any parent concerns about the tutoring process (Durrer & McLaughlin, 1995). It is helpful to have the tutors chart the progress of the tutee. For example, the tutor may count and chart the number of words the student reads correctly each day or the number of addition facts the tutee answers correctly. Be sure to monitor and praise tutors for following the procedures.

Evaluating the Tutoring Session

Both tutors and tutees should evaluate the tutoring session. After each session, you should give tutees forms to mark whether they learned anything and how the session went. See Figure 9.2 for a sample secondary evaluation form.

Informing Significant Others

You should be certain to notify parents of peer-tutoring programs. Parents need to understand when their children come home and talk about working with other students. Tell them why, when, and how tutoring will be used. It is important to indicate that you are still responsible for teaching the children and to document that their children are continuing to learn. You also might involve the parents in a cross-age peer-tutoring program in which students with disabilities are going to work with younger students. Ask parents to practice reading material or design projects for their child to help with tutoring the younger student they are assigned. Here are some tasks parents could help with in a cross-age tutoring program:

> **Activity 9.4**
>
> With a partner, pick either a content-area book or a library book at either the elementary, middle, or secondary level. Using the material selected, refer to Table 9.2 and discuss how you would use these guidelines to help prepare and implement a peer-tutoring program. Remember to think through how you will identify the objective and plan the presentation format for the tutor. Also remember to consider how you will inform and involve parents as part of the process.

Figure 9.2 HOMEWORK ENTRY SOCIAL SKILLS JOURNAL

Date: January 1. 2003 Name: Jason C.

Practice Skill: Encouragement

Where I did it: At home

What I did: I told my brother that he really was a good drawer and I knew he'd draw a good map.

How I felt: Good. Happy.

How it worked: Good. He smiled at me. And Mom told me that I was being thoughtful.

- Providing incentives for the younger student
- Providing materials (e.g., books that are too easy for their child to read could be used in the tutoring program)
- Providing reinforcement of skills that both the tutor and tutee (e.g., social skills and reinforcing academics) are working on in this relationship
- Assisting the tutor in making exciting materials to be used in tutoring pairs (e.g., games or other fun activities).

IMPORTANT POINTS

1. Peer tutoring may consist of one student acting as a tutor, or the person who transmits the information, and one student acting as the tutee, or the person who receives the information, or students may assume reciprocal roles.
2. Reciprocal Peer Tutoring involves students paired randomly in same-age dyads and self-selection of rewards and performance goals.
3. In the Reciprocal Peer Revision Strategy, strategy instruction and peer interaction are combined to teach written revision skills.
4. The Peabody Peer-Assisted Learning Strategies involve/the teaching of both academic skills and strategies in reading, mathematics, story mapping, and writing.
5. The steps for implementing peer-tutoring procedures consist of (a) selecting objectives, (b) selecting and matching students, (c) preparing materials, (d) determining schedules and selecting sites, (e) planning the presentation format, (f) training tutors, (g) monitoring progress, (h) evaluating the tutoring session, and (i) informing significant others.

COOPERATIVE LEARNING

Like peer tutoring, cooperative learning relies on peers working together to solve problems or share information. Cooperative learning groups consist of teams of three or four students working together to master academic tasks or content to meet individual and group goals, rather than just two students as in peer tutoring. The students are usually of varying ability levels, races, and ethnic groups. Slavin, Stevens, and Madden (1988) and Johnson and Johnson (1994) have studied cooperative learning extensively. Cooperative learning has been identified as an evidence-based practice directly impacting the achievement of students with disabilities if a teacher utilizes all of the required components of *true* cooperative learning (McMaster & Fuchs, 2002).

Many classrooms or.schools that we have observed place students in groups but often do not ensure students use the core principles of cooperative learning. According to Johnson and Johnson (1994), there are five basic elements of cooperative learning: positive interdependence, face-to-face interaction, individual accountability, group behaviors, and group processing. Positive interdependence means that students see the importance of working as a team and realize that they are responsible for contributing to the group's effort. Face-to-face interaction means students work in situations that promote eye contact and social exchanges to allow maximum engagement in discussions. Individual accountability suggests that each person is responsible to the group and must be a contributing member. Group behaviors refer to those interpersonal, social, collaborative skills needed to work with others successfully. Finally, group processing is a time after the cooperative learning task is finished when team members reflect on their personal and their group's behavior during the process.

Students are encouraged to work in groups and to actively engage in discussions (similar to the typical workplace) to determine how they might better solve problems presented to them or to learn from each other's perspectives. The natural peer-support structures built into a class using cooperative learning provides a strategy to address a wide range of learners and learning needs (Pisha & Coyne, 2001).

The instructional processes of individual accountability and group rewards are required for positive effects (Stevens & Slavin, 1991). Teacher behaviors that promote effective cooperative learning procedures include (Johnson & Johnson, 1996):

1. Public identification of students who demonstrate cooperative behaviors
2. Validation of low-status students' contributions to the group process
3. Insistence that all students participate
4. Direct instruction of cooperative behaviors and strategies
5. Repeated review and reinforcement of group cooperation
6. Monitoring of cooperative behaviors
7. Explicit explanation of expectations for group process and individual products.

Two common special education practices that seem to defeat the effectiveness of cooperative learning are differential assignments and teacher assistance. O'Connor and Jenkins (1996) found that students with disabilities participated more in cooperative learning groups when their assignments matched those of their peers and that teachers who provided more assistance to students with disabilities or joined the cooperative learning group interfered with peers working together.

RATIONALE

Cooperative learning is proposed as a way to ensure successful inclusion of students with special needs (Johnson & Johnson, 1996; Slavin, 1988a) based on the premise that students who work together tend to come to like each other (Johnson & Johnson, 1980). Cooperative learning also relies on peer pressure, a powerful reinforcer for adolescents in particular (Alberto & Troutman, 1999). Urging other students to complete a task for the good of the group frequently motivates reluctant adolescents. Similar to peer tutoring, cooperative learning, when effective, is an economical and teacher-friendly way to accommodate the wide range of cultural, linguistic, and academic diversity found in the current inclusive classroom.

DESCRIPTION

Our discussion centers around models of cooperative learning that have been shown to be effective with students with mild disabilities and appear in the special education literature or are emerging in general education or more inclusive settings. They were selected because they have been used or we feel could easily be implemented in inclusive classrooms and are detailed enough that they may be implemented. They include ClassWide Student Tutoring Teams (Harper, Mallette, Maheady, & Brennan, 1993), Cooperative Homework Teams (O'Melia and Rosenberg, 1994), and Collaborative Strategic Reading (Klinger & Vaughn, 1996). We also include the Jigsaw Approach (Aronson, 1978), Learning Together (Johnson & Johnson, 1991), and Literature Circles (Daniels, 2002) because we have used these strategies in our own classrooms and have observed their effectiveness. Many of these models are based on the work of Slavin and Johnson and Johnson. The discussion of cooperative learning models is not meant to be exhaustive but to provide practical guidelines for use in your classroom.

ClassWide Student Tutoring Teams

A combination of Slavin's competitive teams programs and the CWPT model, the ClassWide Student Tutoring Teams (CSTT) requires team members to play a game (Maheady, et al., 2001). For example, in a mathematics class, the teacher assigns one student with high ability, one student with low ability, and two students with average ability to each table. At each table is a folder with the task (e.g., study guide, math problems, etc.), answer sheet, paper and pencils, and a deck of cards. The cards contain numbers on them that correspond to the items. Students take turns at being the teacher. The first peer teacher draws a card and reads the corresponding question from the study guide. Each student then writes an answer. The peer teacher checks each answer against the answer sheet and awards five points. If an answer is not correct, the peer teacher gives the correct answer, shares strategies, and awards two points to the students after they successfully write the answer two times. The teaching responsibility is then moved to the next student and the procedures are repeated. The classroom teacher gives bonus points to teams who follow the steps and who demonstrate appropriate interactions. After 20 or 30 minutes, the teacher tallies individual points and converts them into team points, which are displayed on laminated scoreboards within the classroom. The most improved team is recognized, the teams that reached the preset criterion are recognized, and the most outstanding team members are recognized (Utley, et al., 1997). The three- to four-member team composition is usually changed every 4 to 6 weeks.

Cooperative Homework Teams

Based on the guidelines of Slavin's Team-Accelerated Instruction, O'Melia and Rosenberg (1994) designed a Cooperative Homework Teams (CHT) model for secondary students with learning disabilities. The model uses peer teams to grade and make corrections on individual homework assignments. At the end of each mathematics period, the teacher assigns the students eight computation and two story problems. The next day, after opening activities, the CHT groups meet for 10 minutes. Each day, a different student assumes the role of the checker. The checker in each group checks the other students' homework assignments using teacher-made answer sheets, then reports the grades to the teacher and returns the papers to the team members for review and corrections. Students help each other correct the errors before they return the papers to the teacher.

The teacher awards daily points based on the completion of the assignment and the percentage of correct answers. The teacher then converts the mean individual scores to mean team scores and presents certificates to those teams who exceed a certain criterion set by the teacher. With CHT in effect, seventh- and eighth-grade students with mild disabilities completed more homework assignments and increased their accuracy scores (O'Melia & Rosenberg, 1994).

Collaborative Strategic Reading

Collaborative Strategic Reading (CSR) combines components of reciprocal teaching (see Chapter 7) and cooperative learning structures. CSR can be used effectively with different reading programs (literature-based, basal, and balanced), different texts (expository and narrative), and various student populations (students with learning disabilities, students without disabilities, bilingual students, and students at risk for reading difficulties) in inclusive settings (Vaughn, Klinger, & Bryant, 2001).

Using think-alouds, teacher and student modeling, practice, and feedback, teachers directly teach students the four strategies of preview, click and clunk, get the gist, and wrap-up in a whole-class setting before students are assigned to groups. In the preview strategy, students examine headings, bold words, pictures, and so on to make predictions before reading and to activate a "group" background knowledge. If background knowledge concerning a particular topic is limited, Vaughn, Klinger, and Bryant (2001) suggest that the teacher continue to employ the preview strategy with the class as a whole, instead of assigning students to small groups. Click and clunk involve a self-monitoring strategy that students employ as they are reading. The reader "clicks" along with no difficulty in understanding the content and vocabulary, but "clunks" when comprehension breaks down. Students in the group employ fix-up strategies when clunking occurs. Cue cards are given to the students to help them remember some fix-up strategies. Some groups may need teacher assistance at this point. The strategy of get the gist requires students to rephrase the main idea in 10 or fewer words after every two paragraphs. At the end of the selection, the students ask and answer questions to summarize the most significant ideas about the entire passage using the wrap-up strategy. See Figure 9.3 for a more detailed discussion of these strategies.

Once students are taught these strategies and the cooperative procedure, four or five students are randomly assigned to heterogeneous groups. To ensure the participation of all students, the specific roles of leader, clunk expert, announcer, encourager, reporter, and time keeper are assigned (Klinger & Vaughn, 1998). The leader tells the group what to read next and what strategy to apply. The leader asks the teacher for assistance if needed. The clunk expert uses the cue cards to remind students of the fix-up strategy when a word or concept is not understood. The announcer makes certain all students participate and listen to each other. She or he calls on different students to read or share ideas. The encourager gives feedback, praises behavior, encourages students to help each other, evaluates how well the group cooperated, and gives suggestions for improved cooperation. The reporter shares the main ideas of the group to the rest of the class and shares a question the group has generated. The time keeper sets the timer for each portion of CSR and makes certain the group moves on to the next activity. Teachers may take over the role of the leader and time keeper to speed up the procedures (Klinger & Vaughn, 1998; Vaughn, Klinger, & Bryant, 2001).

Roles are assigned for a day or longer and cue sheets are provided to prompt students to remember their responsibilities. For example, the cue sheet reminds the encourager to tell two things that went well with the group and then asks, "Is there anything that would help us do even better next time?" (Klinger & Vaughn, 1998, p. 36). Teachers monitor the group interactions and provide assistance when needed.

Learning logs monitor student progress and suggest follow-up activities. Students are directed to write down the most important ideas that they learned from the day's reading assignment. They then take turns sharing their entries with the rest of the class. Materials that have one main idea in a paragraph, provide cues for prediction, and help students connect information are conducive to strategy application. Klinger and

Figure 9.3 THE FOUR STRATEGIES OF CSR

Before Reading
Examine headings, bold words, pictures, and so on

1. Preview (2–3 minutes)
   a. Brainstorm: What do we already know about the topic?
   b. Predict: What do we expect to learn?

During Reading
Self-monitor understanding after two paragraphs and then at the end

2. Click and Clunk
   a. Keep reading if we understand the content (click).
   b. Were there any words or concepts that were hard to understand (clunks)?
   c. Use fix-up strategies to fix the clunks:
      (1) Reread the sentence and look for key ideas to help you understand the word.
      (2) Reread the sentence with the clunk and the sentences before or after the clunk looking for cues.
      (3) Look for a prefix or suffix in the word.
      (4) Break the word apart and look for smaller words.
3. Get the Gist (answer in 10 words or less)
   a. What is the most important person, place or thing?
   b. What is the most important idea about the person, place, or thing?

After Reading

4. Wrap-Up
   a. Ask questions and answer them;
      Why do you think that?
      How were _____ and _____ the same? How were they different?
      What do you think would happen if _____?
      What do you think caused _____ to happen?
      What might have prevented the problem of _____ from happening?
      What are the strengths and weaknesses of_____?
      What are some other solutions for the problem of _____ ?
   b. b. Review
      Write answer to question, What did we learn in Learning Log, and share entry with class.
   c. Ask questions that begin with what, when, where, why, and how.

Source: Adapted from Figure 1 by Klinger, J. K., & Vaughn, S. (1998). Using collaborative strategic reading. *TEACHING Exceptional Children, 30*(6), 32–37. Reprinted by permission.

Vaughn (1998) recommend that teachers select brief, nonfiction articles such as those found in *Scholastic Reader* when first instituting CSR procedures.

Activity 9.5
Considering the grade level you are most interested in teaching, discuss with a peer which of these types of structures you anticipate trying first in your own classroom and why.
(a) ClassWide Student Tutoring Teams, (b) Cooperative Homework Teams, or (c) Collaborative Strategic Reading

The Jigsaw Approach

In the Jigsaw Approach (Aronson, 1978), each member of the jigsaw group becomes an expert in some aspect of the task or material and teaches the others what he or she knows (Topping, 2005). For example, in preparing a report or answering a worksheet about the life of Martin Luther King, Jr., each student in the group may select to study one aspect of Reverend King's life. Once each student has mastered the specific content, he or she shares the information with the rest of the group. Then the group as a whole combines the individual information for the final project, whether it is a report or a worksheet about King's life.

The idiom of jigsaw is appropriate for this technique, for each student has a puzzle piece (e.g., Hector has information concerning Reverend King's childhood and Lashonda has information concerning King's educational background) that must be joined together with the puzzle pieces of the other students before it is possible to complete the entire puzzle (a report on the life of Martin Luther King, Jr.). But student absenteeism can be a problem in the Jigsaw Approach. If Hector is absent, he cannot contribute the information concerning Reverend King's childhood. Slavin (1988b) suggests assigning two students from each group to the same subtopic (Hector and Kendra would both be assigned to gather information concerning Reverend King's childhood) or selecting an activity that may be completed during one class period if absenteeism is a problem.

A variation of the Jigsaw Approach is a "counterpart" group (Aronson, 1978). In this adaptation, all students working on a particular subtopic meet together. After sharing information on this subtopic, they rejoin their original group members and complete the report.

Learning Together

In Learning Together (Johnson & Johnson, 1991), students pool their knowledge and skills to create a project or complete an assignment often in the areas of social studies and science. These groups are informally structured and usually are organized for a specific task. Noddings (1989) recommends complex tasks such as projects and experiments to increase student participation. For example, Pomplun (1997) describes one such project where fifth-grade students with and without disabilities participated in the Kansas Science Assessment and were assigned a collaborative activity of completing a study. Groups of three, four, or five students were required to develop a hypothesis, study their hypothesis, and reach a conclusion concerning results. For example, with the topic of water waste, each group had to develop a hypothesis about one cause of water waste, study the cause, and develop one solution.

Literature Circles

A general education cooperative learning strategy that is used extensively in the general education setting is called Literature Circles (Daniels, 2002). We introduce this final ClassWide Peer Tutoring strategy as one that is gaining momentum in today's classrooms. Resources for the use of Literature Circles can be found from a web search. The steps to a Literature Circle as introduced by Daniels can be found in Table 9.5

Although this strategy is an excellent tool to use in a reading classroom, the pure components of the strategy are very constructivist in nature, so use caution if students have severe reading or writing disabilities. Dieker and Ousley (2006) suggest a modification of this structure that combines the components of Literature Circles and cooperative learning in a more inclusive setting. In this modified version students can still select the text they would like to read, but instead are assigned specific segments of the text to read, and once they complete the reading of the assigned segment, then they

Table 9.5 Steps for Literature Circles

DEFINING LITERATURE CIRCLES
1. Students **choose** their own reading materials.
2. **Small temporary groups** are formed, based upon book choice.
3. Different groups read **different books.**
4. Groups meet on a **regular, predictable schedule** to discuss their reading.
5. Kids use written or drawn notes to guide both their reading and discussion.
6. Discussion **topics come from the students.**
7. Group meetings aim to be **open, natural conversations about books** so personal connections, digressions, and open-ended questions are welcome.
8. In newly forming groups, students may play a rotating assortment of task **roles.**
9. The teacher serves as a **facilitator**, not a group member or instructor.
10. Evaluation is by **teacher observation and student self-evaluation**.
11. A spirit of **playfulness and fun** pervades the room.
12. When books are finished, **readers share with classmates**, and then **new groups form** around new reading choices.

Retrieved from www.literaturecircles.com in August 2006.

are asked to complete their circle. In the circle students are assigned different roles to assume while reading the text. The various roles are defined differently throughout the literature but these are the roles that we find work well for an inclusive classroom.

1. *Questioner*—This person is to ask the group a question related to the text. The questioner may need further structure and be told to ask a question that is either a "who, what, when, where, or how" type of a question.
2. *Clarifier*—This role is typically assigned to one of the highest readers in an inclusive setting. This student is to clarify any word someone has difficulty pronouncing or to explain any concepts students have difficulty understanding.
3. *Summarizer*—This student's role is to provide a verbal summary of the story. We like to use the strategy provided earlier in "Predictions" of having the student share a summary in 10 words or less.
4. *Predictor*—This student's role is to predict what they think will happen next in the story. This role can be assigned to a lower functioning student because it allows the student to always be successful since a prediction is a student's best guess.
5. *Artist*—This student can be doodling while the reader is reading the story. This role is great for a student who has difficulty attending. We also suggest using a low-odor dry-erase marker and a "Solo" plastic plate for the artist to represent the story.

No matter what type of collaborative structure used, providing students roles for communication, engagement, and positive learning in the area of reading is essential to academic and social learning at all levels.

IMPLEMENTATION

You should follow certain steps when implementing cooperative learning procedures, especially if you are planning to use the less-specific procedures of Jigsaw and Learning Together. Planning is essential for cooperative groups to succeed.

Specifying Objectives
Specify both academic and collaborative objectives. You may emphasize collaborative objectives (such as all students need to know how to do the work and students need to help each other learn). Slavin (1988a) insists that the group objective must be important to the group members and suggests that awarding certificates, free time, or bonus points for appropriate group participation may motivate each group member to cooperate.

Assigning Students to Groups
It is recommended that you assign students of various ethnic backgrounds and ability levels to each group (Johnson & Johnson, 1986; Slavin, 1988a). In an inclusive class, make certain that students with special needs are evenly distributed among the different groups. O'Connor and Jenkins (1996) emphasize that this step is extremely important, as students with disabilities need peers who are both willing and compassionate. Much of the research that shows positive effects for students with special needs has combined two students who are performing the skill or task at a low level and two students who are performing the skill at a higher level in each group (Slavin, 1984; Slavin, Stevens, & Madden, 1988). The recommended size of a group is three to five members (Johnson & Johnson, 1986). To ensure the cohesiveness of the team, Slavin (1988b) stresses that you should make clear to the students that "putdowns, making fun of teammates, or refusing to help them are ineffective ways for teams to be successful and not acceptable kinds of behavior" (p. 52).

Deciding Team Schedules
As with any new technique, you should first try the cooperative learning approach with one class or in one area. Students may stay on one team from 4 to 10 weeks. However, if teams do not work out, reassign the students after 3 or 4 weeks (Slavin, 1988b). The idea is to give every student an opportunity to work with all students in the classroom.

Arranging the Room and Materials
Group members should be close together and groups should be far apart (Schniedewind & Salend, 1987). Johnson and Johnson (1986) recommend a circle arrangement to accommodate student communication. Such an arrangement allows students to share and discuss materials and to maintain eye contact. The physical arrangement also must allow clear access for the teacher. Each group needs an area to store materials or the group project. One teacher bought square laundry baskets that each group decorated and used for the storage of their materials. The decorations were removable to accommodate the frequent changes in group membership.

Guaranteeing Individual Accountability and Participation
Teachers must make certain that each member is participating in the group and that only one or two students are not completing the project or activity. Individual point assignments in CSTT, specific role assignments in CSR, and individual grades and homework assignments in CHT ensure individual accountability and participation.

Johnson and Johnson (1986) recommend assigning the roles of checker, accuracy coach, summarizer, elaboration seeker, and reporter, so that each group member has a specific responsibility. The checker makes certain that all students can understand the information. The accuracy coach corrects any mistakes in another member's explanation or summary. The summarizer restates major conclusions or answers of the group. The elaboration seeker asks members to relate material they previously learned. The reporter writes down the information or completes the worksheet. Assigning a specific role to students is particularly important for cooperative learning activities in an inclusive setting as, often, students with disabilities are left out if no particular role is assigned to them.

Another way to ensure individual accountability and participation is to select only one student's product to represent the group effort (Johnson & Johnson, 1986). Of course, this selection is kept secret until the end of the project. Salend and Allen (1985) ensure participation of all students by limiting the number of times each student may talk. Before the group activity, each member is given a certain number of tokens. Each time a student addresses the group, he or she must surrender a token. Once all of the tokens are used, the student may no longer address the group. A final technique for ensuring group participation is to limit the amount of material given to the group (Slavin, 1988a). If only one worksheet is given to the group, then four members cannot complete the worksheet individually.

Teaching and Role-Playing Cooperative Behaviors

Just placing students with disabilities in cooperative groups is not effective unless they are directly taught the strategies and cooperative skills. In the CSR model, Vaughn, Hughes, and Moody (2001) note that much explicit teaching with modeling and practice is needed before students are assigned to groups. As discussed at the beginning of the chapter, many students with disabilities must also be taught social skills before they can effectively participate in cooperative groups.

For students with mild disabilities, role-playing such cooperative behaviors as "use a quiet voice," "stay with your group," and "say one nice thing to everyone in your group" (Putnam, Rynders, Johnson, & Johnson, 1989) is necessary, because many of these students have an inability to relate to others in socially appropriate ways. Research shows that students with disabilities can be taught the social skills for successful group participation (Prater, et al., 1999; Wolford, et al., 2001). You should model cooperative behavior first. Then have students role-play appropriate and inappropriate ways to show cooperation and evaluate whether the demonstrated behavior is an example of cooperative or uncooperative behavior. Continue to review appropriate cooperative behaviors whenever you plan to form cooperative groups.

You may also use games to teach cooperative behaviors. Cooperative games require players to cooperate in order to overcome some obstacle. For example, Cartledge and Cochran (1993) created a circular game board with the goal that everyone must complete the entire circle before time ran out. Thus, students helped each other complete the game as they raced against time. Students were reinforced for their cooperative interactions instead of win-lose behaviors. Sapon-Shevin (1986) described a nonelimination musical chairs game. The object was to keep everyone in the game as the chairs were eliminated. The children had to find ways to make room for more and more children. The verbal behavior during the game was of a cooperative nature: "Come sit with me," or "Make room for Quentin" (p. 284).

For older students, a checklist of cooperative behaviors for students to self-monitor is often useful. Examples may include (a) I listened to others' opinions, (b) I complimented a person's idea in the group, (c) I spoke in a pleasant voice, (d) I didn't get angry if my ideas weren't used, and (e) I made constructive comments when I thought another student's idea was outrageous or not appropriate.

Monitoring Cooperative Behaviors

Once you have taught the concept or given directions for the required activity or project and modeled cooperative behavior, your role becomes that of a monitor. You monitor each member's cooperative behavior, keep the group on task, and intervene when necessary to provide task assistance. For young students, praise the sharing or helping behaviors publicly (Putnam, et al., 1989) with such comments as "Sunny shared her article with Juan. She was being very cooperative." Your comments should also include validation statements, such as "Matt has the correct idea. He is on target," directed to students with disabilities who are often perceived as incompetent by peers.

One teacher instituted a system for students to self-monitor everyone's participation in the cooperative learning group. On a grid of names of team members and question numbers, one student placed a yellow Post-it note next to a student's name when he or she participated. Strategy cards with a list of questions can remind students to monitor participation and understanding: Am I listening to group members? Do I understand the directions and goal? If not, ask others in the group; if not, ask the teacher? Am I helping group members? (Goor, Schwenn, Elridge, Mallein, & Stauffer, 1996). Students using the cards made more on-task comments and were better able to explain the main idea of the group discussion.

Evaluating Both the Product and the Process

You should evaluate both the product and the process of the group. In the jigsaw or group project approaches, you may elect to grade the group project or the individual student's project selected to represent the group work. Some teachers, when they know what individual members have contributed, grade the students' individual contributions in addition to assigning a group grade. Another strategy is to average the group grade with the individual student's grade. For example, if Joe scored 10 points on his individual project and his group scored 20 points, his final score would be 15.

According to Slavin (1988a), the group grade should be based on an average of the performances of all of the students. Johnson and Johnson (1986) suggest using different criteria to evaluate the project of a student with special needs, giving bonus points to the groups that have members with special needs. Some teachers also give grades for the group process. Remember, Slavin (1988b) recommends giving points to the students for appropriate participation. Even if you don't grade the process, you and the students should evaluate how the group functioned. See Table 9.6 for a sample evaluation form. In fact, you may want to have students role-play problem areas and possible solutions for evaluation of the process.

Table 9.6 Student Evaluation of Cooperative Session

What was learned in the group today?____________________

____

Describe an example of cooperative behavior (a helpful action).

- You did ______________________________

____

- Others did ______________________________

____

Describe an example of uncooperative behavior (not a helpful action).

- You did ______________________________

____

- Others did ______________________________

____

Change the uncooperative behaviors to cooperative ones.

____

____

The completion of this sheet is worth 10 points toward your grade.

Recognizing the Group Effort

Certificates and scoreboards are used to recognize group effort in CHT and CSTT, respectively. In Table 9.7, we present a checklist of decisions you need to make before you use cooperative learning techniques. Remember, teachers make instructional decisions and monitor their effectiveness.

Activity 9.6

In a cooperative group of four using the Jigsaw Approach, select one of the following roles:

1. Review the textbook and come up with five positive aspects of social skills instruction.
2. Make a list of five problems that could arise and potential solutions for using peer-support groups.
3. Clearly describe at least two types of cooperative learning presented in this chapter.
4. Clearly describe at least two types of peer tutoring presented in this chapter.

Once roles are assigned, then use the Jigsaw approach to gather all of the number 1's, 2's, 3's, and 4's in the class to become experts on the topic assigned (approximately 15 minutes).

Once everyone in your number group is an expert on their assigned topic, then return to your original group and share your knowledge related to your assigned role.

Table 9.7 Teacher Checklist

1. Specify group objective.
   Academic:
   ____
   Motivated to attain by:
   _____a. Points
   _____b. Certificates
   _____c. Free time
   _____d. Praise
   _____e. Homework pass
   _____f. Other
2. Specify other group objective.
   Collaborative:
   ____
   Motivated to attain by:
   _____a. Points
   _____b. Certificates
   _____c. Free time
   _____d. Praise
   _____e. Homework pass
   _____f. Other
3. Select model
   _____a. CSTT
   _____b. CHT
   _____c. CSR
   _____d. Jigsaw
   _____e. Learning Together
   _____f. Own Creation
4. Assign students.
   _____a. Even number of girls/boys
   _____b. Two high-level/two low-level
   _____c. Students of various cultures/interests divided
   _____d. Random
5. Decide team schedule.
   Time Frame:
   _____a. No. of weeks
   _____b. No. of days
6. Arrange room materials.
   _____a. Clear access for teacher
   _____b. Storage for materials
7. Guarantee individual accountability.
   _____a. Grade individual quizzes or projects
   _____b. Assign roles
   _____c. Select one student's project
   _____d. Tokens
   _____e. Other

Table 9.7 Teacher Checklist (continued)

8. Have students evaluate their own cooperative behaviors.
   _____a. Complete student evaluation form
   _____b. Answer questions
9. Evaluate the students' work.

The product:	The process:
_____a. Points	_____a. Points
_____b. Grades	_____b. Grades
_____c. Other	_____c. Other

10. Recognize the group effort.
    _____a. Bulletin board
    _____b. Newsletter
    _____c. Other

IMPORTANT POINTS

1. Cooperative learning groups consist of teams of three or four students who work together to master academic tasks or content.
2. Try to use a variety of cooperative learning structures in your classroom: ClassWide Student Tutoring Teams (CSTT), Cooperative Homework Team (CHT), Cooperative Strategic Reading (CSR), the Jigsaw Approach, the Learning Together format, and Literature Circles.
3. To implement cooperative learning, the following steps are recommended: (a) specify objectives, (b) select the model, (c) assign students to groups, (d) decide team schedules, (e) plan room and material arrangements, (f) guarantee individual accountability and participation, (g) role-play cooperative behaviors, (h) monitor cooperative behaviors, (i) evaluate both the product and the process, and (j) recognize the group effort.

PUTTING IT ALL TOGETHER

Students at all levels need to learn to work together to be effective in all aspects of life. Teachers of students with disabilities must provide direct instruction of social skills and find numerous opportunities for students to have these skills incorporated into the general education setting. Consider teaching social skills to all students and putting in place peer tutoring and/or cooperative learning structures into your classes.

The use of groupings sounds like a logical and simple thing to do in a classroom. We recommend that you start with extensive planning as to not only how you will incorporate these effective structures into your classrooms, but also as to the dynamics of the students who will work in peer tutoring or cooperative learning structures. These types of structures are easiest to implement in heterogeneous inclusive settings, and where coteachers are available, there are two adults to help facilitate, evaluate, and ensure that groups are truly collaborative.

DISCUSSION QUESTIONS

1. How might you suggest that social skills instruction be incorporated into the general education curriculum to meet the needs of students with disabilities in the general education setting?
2. When Lashonda went home and told her mother that she was teaching Susanna how to add during mathematics class, her mother immediately called you to complain. She commented that you are the teacher and her child is not. How would you respond to this criticism of peer tutoring?
3. Describe how you might use cooperative learning or peer tutoring if you were coteaching in a general education setting?

Websites: Useful websites related to chapter content can be found in Appendix A.

CHAPTER

10

Study Skills Instruction

KEY TOPICS

It was Thursday afternoon and Jasmine was rushing to her sixth-grade science class. Her teacher, Mrs. Wilmette, had scheduled a unit test for tomorrow, so Jasmine already knew that class time today would be spent reviewing everything they had learned in the last four weeks. Jasmine has a learning disability, and these kinds of review sessions were always long and tedious for her. As she slid into her desk in the last row, she suddenly realized she didn't even have a pencil.

"Psst! Carmen!" she whispered to the girl next to her as the class quieted down and started listening to the teacher give the directions for the day. "Can I borrow a pencil?"

Carmen dug around in her backpack, pulled out a green pen, and handed it to Jasmine. "Here", she mumbled. Jasmine sensed that Carmen was irritated with always having to help her. "Oh well, she'll get over it", she thought.

Jasmine looked around at what everyone else was doing, adjusted her glasses, and started copying down the lengthy paragraphs Mrs. Wilmette had written on the board. Mrs. Wilmette loved to write multi-color paragraphs that seemed to wrap around the room as they continued from one board to the next. The initial sounds of students grumbling gave way to the scratching of pencils on paper. For the next 50 minutes Jasmine struggled to decipher the cursive writing and not leave out any words. When she finished the first board and looked over at Carmen, she suddenly realized that most of the class had finished copying and moved on to their homework assignment. There were only a few minutes of class time remaining.

Jasmine panicked and thought "What am I going to do?" Just then the bell rang and Mrs. Wilmette announced, "Be sure and study tonight boys and girls."

"Hey Carmen," pleaded Jasmine, "Can I borrow your notes after school? You can come to my house to study and we'll order pizza."

Jasmine obviously needs more help with her study skills than Carmen alone can give her. Pretend that you have been hired as the resource teacher assigned to monitor Jasmine's progress in the general education setting. What recommendations would you make if you had observed the above scenario? Be sure to include suggestions for both the teacher and the student in your response.

Responses to these questions are found in the Instructor's Manual.

INTRODUCTION

School settings present many challenges for students with special needs, particularly in view of the practice of including students with disabilities in general education settings: the expectation that all students must pass standards-based assessment tests (Salend, 2005) and the requirement that students with disabilities successfully access and master the general education curriculum (Deshler & Schumaker, 2006). During a typical school day, students in K–12 settings may be asked to acquire new content; demonstrate understanding and mastery of the content through completion of tests, projects, or other assignments; demonstrate good work habits; and perhaps work with several school professionals who may have different expectations and requirements and whose teaching styles may vary. Students with special needs may have problems meeting these expectations because they lack strategies for organizing and remembering information (Wood, 2006), taking tests (Hoover & Rabideau, 1995) and listening (Hoover, 2005). It has been suggested that integrated study skills programs be provided throughout students' schooling and as lifelong skills (Hoover, 2005) to help students meet these expectations. The purpose of this chapter is to present study skills and strategies that will assist students with special needs to acquire information, organize it, and express it so they will be successful in general education settings and with standards-based assessments.

RATIONALE FOR STUDY SKILLS INSTRUCTION

"Study skills are those competencies associated with acquiring, recording, organizing, synthesizing, remembering, and using information and ideas" (Hoover, 2005, p. 442). They typically include listening, note taking, outlining, textbook usage, test taking, reference skills, and others that are needed for success in academic (e.g., science class) and nonacademic (e.g., the workplace) settings (Platt & Olson, 1997). In other words, study skills assist students to acquire, retain, and express information (Mercer & Mercer, 2005; Polloway, Patton, & Serna, 2005). Utilization of study skills may lead students with special needs to exhibit more active learning styles and to demonstrate proactive approaches to academic tasks. Incorporation of study skills instruction into the curriculum may help students attribute their learning successes to the systematic selection and application of study strategies instead of luck or the assistance of others. Study skills represent the key to independent learning by helping students acquire and use information effectively (Bos & Vaughn, 2006).

Because evidence suggests the need for study skills in elementary and secondary settings for students with special needs (Hoover, 2005), we recommend the introduction of study skills instruction at the elementary level followed by continuous instruction and monitoring throughout middle and high school. Systematic instruction in study skills can show students the relationship between their approach to a learning task and the result of that approach (e.g., using a mnemonic device to memorize a list of words may facilitate memorization of that list better than simply repeating the words in the list). The application of study skills may, therefore, increase the independent functioning of learners.

COMPONENTS OF STUDY SKILLS INSTRUCTION

For study skills instruction to be effective, teachers must be aware of the components that contribute to its success. The following five components derived from Paris (1988) should be included in study skills instruction. These criteria are similar to the critical features of strategy instruction that we presented in Chapter 7. Notice how the teacher's role may incorporate elements of both the reductionist and constructivist paradigms. For example, it is recommended that study skills instruction be direct, informed, and explanatory with the teacher providing instruction in small sequential steps (i.e., reductionist). However, notice also that the teacher may engage students in dialogue following the modeling of various study skills, thus allowing students to draw their own conclusions about the usefulness of study skills (i.e., constructivist). The teacher can also seek elaboration of students' initial responses (Brooks & Brooks, 2001) in regard to what strategies they already employ and what strategies might be helpful for them to try (i.e., constructivist). The five components of inclusion in study skills instruction include:

1. ***Study skills should be functional and meaningful.*** Identify your students' needs and determine the study skills that would be most effective in meeting those needs. For example, if Jesse is required to memorize lists of terms for his fourth-grade health class, you may want to teach him a mnemonic strategy to help him memorize material and prepare for tests. Suppose Jesse has to memorize the parts of the digestive system. He may make a list with all the parts and then look at the first letter of each of the words. Perhaps they spell a word, or maybe he can make a sentence out of them.

2. ***Students should believe that study skills are useful and necessary.*** Your students must be convinced that study skills are important, necessary for success, worth using, and effective in solving problems; therefore, it is helpful to demonstrate to your students that their current methods may not be effective and to explain the rationale for each specific strategy (Alley & Deshler, 1979). For example, Mr. Benevidez asked his students to take notes on one of his math lessons. When he evaluated their notes with them, he pointed out any shortcomings or ineffective practices that he noted. He elicited from the students the rationale for taking effective notes and had them suggest situations in which they might need to use this skill. One student mentioned she could use it in her social studies class, and another said that it would help him as a reporter for the school newspaper. Then Mr. Benevidez presented some effective note-taking techniques to the class. By first demonstrating how note-taking techniques are useful and necessary, he was able to motivate and interest the students in note taking.

3. ***Instruction should be direct, informed, and explanatory.*** According to Rosenshine (1983), instruction should include (a) presenting material in small steps, (b) focusing on one aspect at a time, (c) organizing the material sequentially for mastery, (d) modeling the skill, (e) presenting many examples, (f) providing detailed explanations for difficult points, and (g) monitoring student progress. For example, in their instruction of report writing, Ms. Greene and Ms. Lopez took their cotaught fifth-grade class to the media center and modeled the steps that they wanted the students to follow as they used reference materials. They provided several different topics and modeled the steps sequentially for each one. They spent time teaching the students how to use the automated card catalog or similar computer system before they assigned them topics to look up. Then, as the students worked through the steps they had modeled, the two teachers carefully monitored their progress. Remember to provide opportunities for the practice of study skills and monitor student use of study skills (Hoover, 2005).

4. ***Instruction should demonstrate what study skills can be used, how they can be applied, and when and why they are helpful.*** For example, Mr. Ortiz, working with his high school students on test taking, taught the students study skills to apply when taking tests. Next, he elicited from the students when and why the study skills would be helpful (content classes, job seeking, and taking the driver's test or the test for the

military). Finally, he showed the students how to apply the study skills to each of the situations they had identified.

5. ***Instructional materials must be lucid and enjoyable.*** The materials you use as part of study skills instruction must be motivating, meaningful, relevant, and easy to understand. For example, working with a group of fifth graders in a general education classroom, Ms. Barnhart incorporated information about the students into a lesson that showed them how to use the graphic aids in textbooks. She taught her fifth-grade students to read graphs by graphing several topics of their own choosing—the students' birthdays, their favorite movies and television shows, and their interests and hobbies. These activities were instrumental in holding student interest and attention.

Because we believe the preceding components of effective study skills instruction should be included in the teaching of all of the study skills presented in this chapter, we do not mention them each time a new study skill is introduced. However, we urge you to incorporate them into your instruction. We hope that you will look back frequently at this section of the chapter as you reflect on how you will teach study skills to students.

ACQUISITION OF INFORMATION

Students with special needs often have difficulty with reading, mathematics, oral and written language, attending, and organizing. Therefore, they must be taught techniques to help them acquire the skills and content expected of them. In this section, we present strategies for listening, taking notes, and comprehending.

LISTENING

Students spend approximately two thirds of their time in school in listening-related activities (Gearheart, Weishahn, & Gearheart, 1995). In fact, listening skills are needed to complete most academic tasks or requirements (Hoover, 2005). Students with special needs should be made aware of the fact that listening is more than hearing words, and it may require practice and training (Masters, Mori, & Mori, 1999). Listening can be improved through systematic teaching and practice (Devine, 1987). The following suggestions are provided for students who have difficulty listening effectively, have developed poor listening habits, do not attend to relevant stimuli, or are inattentive.

1. Make sure students are seated where they can listen, attend, and concentrate.

2. Use verbal and nonverbal cues at the beginning of and throughout a lesson to get attention (e.g., standing at the front of class, making eye contact, using a phrase that signals you are ready to begin).

3. Alert your students before they listen to a class presentation that there will be at least one factual error in the presentation. Ask the students to write down the error(s) after the information has been presented (Hammill & Bartel, 2004). For example, during a presentation on the size, population, major cities, and important industries of New Jersey, Mr. Feldman erroneously identified the capital as Newark. We recommend telling the students what the error is if they cannot identify it themselves.

4. Prior to a lecture or presentation, list the five most important points of the talk on the board, PowerPoint, or a handout. Then ask your students to listen for those five

points and arrange them in the correct sequence before the conclusion of the presentation (Devine, 1987).

5. Periodically, stop your presentation and ask students to construct summary statements (e.g., "The subject of a sentence tells whom or what the sentence is about"; "Stacy constantly struggled with her own feelings because she was torn between her Chinese and American cultures").

6. Show a DVD containing subject matter that is interesting and age appropriate. Ask the students to listen for specific information, such as the speaker's intent; definitions of certain words and how context affects them; factual information; the general theme; or the multiple perspectives that were generated by the subject matter. You may stop the DVD at any time to ask questions about the content or ask for predictions of what will happen next. For example, Mr. Johnson showed a series of DVD presentations to his students about the lives of four African Americans who made great contributions to our country: (a) Paul Lawrence Dunbar, (b) Harriet Tubman, (c) Dr. Martin Luther King, Jr., and (d) Dr. George Washington Carver. He periodically stopped the presentation to ask open-ended questions and to give his students a specific fact to listen for.

7. Ask your students to listen to television or radio advertisements and explain how the advertisers are trying to influence listeners to buy their products. For example, some advertisers ask celebrities to advertise and endorse their products, others use catchy tunes, and some tell about the money you will save.

Listening is essential for students both in their schoolwork and in their overall development and transition to independent living (Hammill & Bartel, 2004). Students need to learn how to listen effectively and practice the skill of listening just as they practice other skills.

Activity 10.1

Part 1: Think back to a class you attended recently. Share with another class member the verbal and nonverbal cues the instructor used. Discuss the cues that assisted you to listen effectively.

Part 2: Look back at the chapter opening scenario about Jasmine. What ideas have you read in the section on listening that might assist her?

(Answers for this and other activities are found in the Instructor's Manual.)

NOTE TAKING

The inclusion of students with learning problems in general education classrooms where they must meet the demands of that environment, combined with the fact that college is a viable option for many students with learning disabilities, has increased the need for learning how to take notes during class presentations (Czarnecki, Rosko, & Fine, 1998). In general education settings, high school teachers spend at least half of their class time presenting content through lectures (Putnam, Deshler, & Schumaker, 1993). Although many students without disabilities develop note-taking skills on their own (Beirne-Smith, 1989), many students with learning disabilities may not develop note-taking skills or may have deficient note-taking skills (Suritsky & Hughes, 1996). "Many students in inclusive settings have difficulty taking notes because of their

BOX 10.1

Reflections on Practice

Often when we think of the need for study skills, we tend to think of older students (e.g., middle and high school). However, it is important to begin teaching study skills to students in the elementary grades and it is never too early to teach listening skills. If you are looking for a creative way to help elementary school students practice their listening skills, you could use an audio version of *Peter and the Wolf.* For those of you who may be unfamiliar with this piece, it is a classic children's tale that unfolds through a combination of narration and orchestra music in which each character is represented by a different musical instrument. Students must rely solely on listening skills to comprehend the message of the tale.

Research confirms the positive impact that music has had on students' cognitive development (Sze & Yu, 2004). Utilizing music to practice listening skills, therefore, provides a natural bridge to learning. Prior to listening to the CD, display a prompt such as: "Based on the sound of his instrument, what do you think Peter is feeling in this next section?" This sets a purpose for listening, much in the same way as you would set a purpose for reading to encourage comprehension. You could ask students to create illustrations while they listen, or you could periodically pause the CD and give them time to write down what they think is happening in response to what they have heard.

Students with special needs can be paired with students who have stronger listening skills for the writing portion of the activity to encourage collaboration in crafting responses. Another approach to the lesson would be to assign peer partners a question to respond to at the end of the CD, with each set of partners receiving a different question. In this approach the oral responses to the different questions provide a comprehensive review of the tale.

There are many versions of *Peter and the Wolf* currently on the CD market. To locate one, we recommend visiting the amazon.com website, or the website of your favorite music store, and conduct a title search.

Sze, S., & Yu, S. (2004). *Educational benefits of music in an inclusive classroom.* Retrieved June 19, 2006 from http://search.epnet.com/login.aspx?direct=true&db=eric&an=ED490348

inability to organize ideas or concepts, distinguish main points or ideas, or transfer information from written or oral formats" (Wood, 2006, p. 325). Consequently, many of them do not take notes in class. You may need to convince your students of the importance of taking notes. One effective way is to make them aware of what they currently do during a lecture or after reading a textbook chapter. For example, Ms. Walker presented information on the recycling of products as a way to protect the environment. She asked her students to take notes during her presentation, using the activity as a pretest to show the students that improvement might be needed. After instruction in note-taking techniques, she used the activity as a posttest to show the students their improvement in note taking.

Non-note takers tend to forget 80% of a lecture within two weeks (Pauk, 1989). Pauk and Owens (2005) reported a study in which individuals who read a chapter forgot 46% of the content after 1 day, 79% after 14 days, and 81% after 28 days. The only way to ensure that you do not forget is by taking notes and then going over them (Pauk & Owens, 2005). Therefore, it is important for teachers to teach note taking directly and to reinforce its use. Many strategies are available to improve note taking, although no one approach is considered to be superior (Mercer & Mercer, 2005). You may want to show your students a variety of ways to take notes so that they can find the ways that are most effective for them.

Guided Notes

For students who have difficulty taking notes, it is helpful to begin with guided notes, because students do not have to generate all of the notes themselves. Guided notes are the skeleton outlines that contain the main ideas and related concepts of a lecture or reading passage, including designated spaces for students to complete as the lecture or reading passage progresses (Lazarus, 1991, 1996). These notes are prepared by the teacher to guide students through a lecture, presentation, or reading assignment (Schloss, Smith, & Schloss, 2001). Guided notes assist students who have mild disabilities to participate actively in note taking, follow along with the sequence of the lecture or reading passage, and write useful notes for later review (Lazarus, 1991). First, the teacher provides the students with a structured outline of a class presentation or reading passage (Shields & Heron, 1989). As the information is presented by the teacher or in a textbook, the students follow the outline and fill in missing words, underline key words, and mark the important points. The advantages of guided notes include their applicability across subject areas and settings, their emphasis on the major points of a topic, their assistance with retention of information, and the opportunities for student involvement (Kline, 1986).

Shields and Heron (1989) recommend including three components in a set of guided notes, as illustrated by this example of a presentation on ecosystems:

1. ***Key terms.*** ecology, ecosystem, atmosphere, hydrosphere, geosphere, biosphere, ecosphere, energy, matter, and organisms.
2. ***Two brief paragraphs that provide definitions of the terms and explain the key concepts.*** For example, the goal of *ecology* is to discover how air, water, soil, and organisms work and how they sustain themselves.
3. ***Several questions that the student must answer after reading the notes.*** What is an ecosystem and what are its most important living and nonliving components? What roles do different organisms play in an ecosystem, and how do they interact?

Figure 10.1 contains an example of another approach to using guided notes. This example illustrates what a teacher might give to students at the beginning of a lecture/presentation. Notice that the student's copy of the guided notes contains main ideas and key concepts and follows a specific sequence. It contains a minimal amount of information, giving students maximal opportunities and flexibility to respond (Lazarus, 1996). Note how Lazarus includes cues (e.g., blanks, labels, etc.) along with a review tally so that students can self-record how many times they review their own notes. Figure 10.2 contains an example of the teacher's completed notes on transparencies or PowerPoint, which may be shown to students before the lecture/presentation to introduce and provide an overview of a lesson/unit and communicate the expectation that students will complete their own notes. The completed notes may be shown to students during and after a lecture/presentation so that students can monitor the accuracy of their own work and teachers can provide immediate feedback regarding students' notes. After the lecture or presentation, the completed notes may be used to review the material together as a class or in small groups. Studies have shown that the use of guided notes has resulted in improved academic performance of students with and without disabilities (Lazarus, 1996).

Figure 10.1 STUDENT'S COPY OF GUIDED NOTES WITH CUES AND REVIEW TALLY

Review Tally

Chapter 20

Cell Reproduction

I. All life starts out as a _____ ____.

A. ---------------------

B.

II. ____ ______ are formed by ____ _______.

III. Types of cell division.

A. Mitosis—DEFINITION:

1. Mitosis is used for replacement of:

a.

b.

c.

d.

e.

2.

3.

Source: From "Flexible Skeletons, Guided Notes for Adolescents with Mild Disabilities" by B. D. Lazarus, *Teaching Exceptional Children, 28*(3), 1996, 38. Copyright (1996) by The Council for Children. Reprinted by permission.

The Five-Step Method for Taking Lecture Notes

The five-step method for taking lecture notes (Bragstad & Stumpf, 1987) includes the following:

1. ***Surveying.*** Many teachers give an advance organizer or preview of what they are going to cover. Students can take notes on these points, thereby alerting themselves to what to expect during the lecture.

2. ***Questioning.*** Encourage your students to have a questioning attitude to help them focus on what is happening in the presentation. They may ask themselves, What is the main idea of this presentation? What am I supposed to know when the speaker is finished? What is being said about the topic? Effective ways to teach students to have a questioning attitude during a lecture presentation include (a) modeling question asking for them and (b) setting up role-plays so that they can practice with each other.

3. ***Listening.*** Encourage students to employ listening strategies to help them listen carefully for content, cues, organization, main points, and supporting statements.

4. ***Organizing.*** Have your students determine how you are organizing the information being presented. Perhaps you use the board, PowerPoint, or handouts to organize

Figure 10.2 TEACHER'S TRANSPARENCIES WITH COMPLETED GUIDED NOTES THAT CORRESPOND WITH THE STUDENTS' COPIES

Chapter 20

Cell Reproduction

I. All life starts out as a <u>single</u> <u>cell.</u>

   A. single cells ------------------------- millions of cells

   B. Humans have millions of cells.

II. <u>New</u> <u>cells</u> are formed by <u>cell</u> <u>division.</u>

III. Types of cell division.

   A. Mitosis—DEFINITION: process of cell division in which two cells are formed from one cell.

      1. Mitosis is used for replacement of:

         a. red blood cells

         b. skin cells

         c. muscle cells

         d. root tips

         e. leaf cells

      2. Before cells divide, the cell parts are copied so the result is two identical cells.

      3. Mitosis is a series of steps.

Source: From "Flexible Skeletons, Guided Notes for Adolescents with Mild Disabilities" by B. D. Lazarus, *Teaching Exceptional Children, 28*(3), 1996, 38. Copyright (1996) by The Council for Exceptional Children. Reprinted by permission.

content. If you do not provide these clues, you could ask your students to listen for verbal cues to organization, such as, "The most important point to remember is . . . " or "Note this . . . " You may also repeat important points or say them slowly with emphasis and then a pause.

5. ***Reviewing and revising.*** As soon after the lecture or presentation as possible, your students should review their notes. In this way, they can add, change, or delete material while the information is still fresh in their minds. Encourage your students to conduct frequent cumulative reviews of their notes. By going back over that day's notes along with all previous notes after each class session, your students will be committing the material to memory.

Two- and Three-Column Methods of Note Taking

Two- and three-column methods of note taking provide opportunities for students to interact with content. The two-column method (Bragstad & Stumpf, 1987) may be varied and modified for individual purposes. With this system, students divide their papers into two sections by drawing a line from top to bottom, thus forming two columns. The narrower column is used to record the teacher's ideas as presented in class. The wider column is used after the lecture to write questions or to summarize the major points and ideas. For example, Ms. Tuttle asked one of her students to read

Figure 10.3 TWO-COLUMN METHOD OF NOTE TAKING

Teacher's Comments	Student's Summary Statements and Questions
<u>Bats</u>	
-Mammals	-All of these animals are classified as mammals.
• Bats	
• People	
• Dogs	
• Mice	
-Nurse young	-How are bats like all other mammals?
-Bear living young	
-Have hair on bodies	
-Fly	-How are bats different than other mammals?

the following information about bats while she took notes using the two-column method.

> Today we are going to talk about bats. Bats are classified as mammals—a group of vertebrates that include people, dogs, and mice. Like all mammals, bats nurse their young on milk. Like most mammals, they bear living young and have hair on their bodies. However, in one way, bats are different from all other mammals, because bats can fly! Bats fly through the air with wings. . . .

Ms. Tuttle shared with the class what she wrote in each column. First, she filled out the "Teacher's Comments" column by writing down information from the presentation in the form of key words. Next, she filled out the "Student's Summary Statements and Questions" column with words, phrases, and sentences that clarified what she had written under "Teacher's Comments." It is helpful if teachers give students class time to fill in their summary statements and questions (see Figure 10.3), so that students can remember how the information in the two columns is related. They can also use this time to connect the information in their textbook to the notes in class by jotting down additional material from the text.

Some students prefer to have a third narrow column to define key terms or to paraphrase material from the class presentation. Students in Ms. Tuttle's class preferred a third column to write the definition of terms (e.g., mammals—any of the group of vertebrate animals, including humans, that nourish their young with milk) and to paraphrase information (e.g., Bats are like other mammals except that bats can fly).

Additional Note-Taking Tips

In teaching note taking to students, you should model effective note taking. Bragstad and Stumpf (1987) suggest playing a tape of a lecture and while the class is watching, taking notes on an overhead projector so the students can see what you write. At the conclusion of the demonstration, you and your students can discuss the note-taking techniques that you utilized.

You should provide your students with ample practice in note taking before asking them to take notes in general education classes. Devine (1987) recommends using how-to-do-it presentations, such as how to change a tire, how to look up a word in the dictionary, or how to make a peanut butter sandwich. Have your students take notes as you present one of these topics.

Bragstad and Stumpf (1987) recommend giving students a set of notes that contains errors. Then have the students work in groups to correct the errors and to improve the notes. Remember to provide positive and corrective feedback to students, so they will know what they did well and will be aware of exactly where the errors were. To reinforce the importance of taking notes, Devine (1987) recommends having a note-taking contest in which main ideas and supporting details are each worth a specified number of points. Then have the students calculate the scores of the different sets of notes. You may also specify other aspects to look for in a set of notes, such as underlining of key points or defining of technical vocabulary in the margins, and then ask the students to judge which notes contain all of the important elements.

Czarnecki, Rosko, and Fine (1998) developed two note-taking strategies for middle and high school students with special needs. The first, CALL UP, was designed for students to use while they are taking notes in class. The second, "A" NOTES, was created for students to use when reviewing notes after a lecture/presentation. They developed these strategies so that students with special needs participating in inclusive settings would be able to take notes in their general education classes. After instruction, both teachers and students reported greater competency in taking notes (Czarnecki, et al., 1998).

Call Up

Copy from board or transparency.

Add details.

Listen and write the question.

Listen and write the answer.

Utilize the text.

Put it in your own words.

A Notes

Ask yourself if you have a date and a topic.

Name the main ideas and details.

Observe ideas also in text.

Try margin notes and use SAND strategy.
- **S**tar important ideas.
- **A**rrange arrows to connect ideas.
- **N**umber key points in order.
- **D**evise abbreviations.

Examine for omissions or unclear ideas.

Summarize key points.

In addition to teaching one or more of the previous note-taking strategies, you may wish to share the following general note-taking tips with your students to help them organize, understand, and retain information for later recall (Platt & Olson, 1997).

1. Before going to class, review notes from the previous class, review vocabulary, read assigned pages, and think about the topic that will be covered.
2. Use a looseleaf notebook so that you can keep notes, handouts, and tests in order and together. You can take out materials, add materials, and move them around as needed.
3. Divide your notebook into different sections for each class, or use a different notebook for each class.
4. Bring materials to class each day (pens, pencils, highlighters, calculator, etc.).
5. Sit in front where you can see and hear, away from distractions, and pay close attention.
6. Write the name of your class and the date at the top of the paper and number each page.
7. Write on only one side of the paper.
8. Write quickly but clearly and legibly. Do not write everything the teacher says—just key words and phrases.
9. Write a main idea. Then indent details under the main idea in outline form. Add an example of your own or one of the teacher's. Skip a line or two before moving to another idea.
10. Leave a blank column on your paper to record your own questions and ideas. Take advantage of pauses in the presentation to make your own notes.
11. Put a question mark by items that you do not understand or that you need more information about, and ask the teacher for clarification.
12. Put a blank where you missed a word and check on it later.
13. Use a marking system to distinguish main ideas from details and examples, perhaps by drawing a box around main ideas and underlining, highlighting, or color coding certain items.
14. Use abbreviations:

e.g. = example	p = page	# = number
> = greater than	< = less than	vs = versus

15. Listen and look for verbal and nonverbal cues.
    - Points that are repeated
    - Key points ("The most important point to remember is . . . ")
    - Definitions
    - A change in the speaker's volume, rate, and posture
    - Gestures used to emphasize points
    - Information that is written on the board, overhead, or PowerPoint presentation
    - Use of absolute words (all, always, never, none, best)
    - Words and phrases that signal or alert you to something:

_____ In conclusion	_____ In summary
_____ Finally	_____ For example
_____ The opposite of	_____ Remember

16. After class, fill in any missed information, and ask the teacher to clarify anything you did not understand.
17. Make sure your notes are organized chronologically along with supporting handouts.
18. As soon as possible after class, examine your notes and check to see how they support, supplement, and/or explain the information in your textbook.

19. Review your notes before the next class. Cumulative review assists with understanding, retention, and test preparation.
20. Compare your notes to those of a peer and check for accuracy and consistency, consulting your textbook if necessary.

IMPORTANT POINTS

1. The components of effective study skills instruction include: (a) study skills should be functional and meaningful; (b) students should believe that study skills are useful and necessary; (c) instruction should be direct, informed, and explanatory; (d) instruction should demonstrate what study skills can be used, how they can be applied, and when and why they are helpful; and (e) instructional materials must be lucid and enjoyable.
2. Teachers can help students develop better listening skills by (a) using verbal and nonverbal cues, (b) alerting students to listen for factual errors in a presentation, (c) listing the five most important points of a lesson and directing the students to listen for those points, (d) asking students to listen for certain information as they view a video presentation, (e) having students listen to advertisements to determine how consumers are being influenced to buy products, and (f) using a pause procedure to assist students with recall of information.
3. Guided notes consist of a teacher-prepared, structured, sequenced outline of a class presentation or reading passage. Students follow along, fill in missing words, underline or write key words, and mark important points.
4. A five-step method of taking notes includes (1) surveying, (2) questioning, (3) listening, (4) organizing, and (5) reviewing and revising.
5. General note-taking tips for students include following an outline, using abbreviations, listening and looking for cues, leaving blanks where you missed something, using a marking system to distinguish main ideas from details and examples, and organizing notes chronologically.

Comprehension

To succeed in content classes, students with special needs are expected to acquire information from textbooks and from material presented orally in class discussions, demonstrations, and student presentations (Faber, Morris, & Lieberman, 2000; Mercer & Mercer, 2005). "Many secondary students with disabilities have difficulty in reading from content area textbooks" (Schloss, et al., 2001, p. 266). Because your students may lack a systematic approach to comprehending content material, or have difficulty reading and comprehending text, you must provide specific strategies to help them structure their efforts. In this section we present study skills and strategies that will improve comprehension such as the use of advance organizers, mapping, concept teaching, and textbook usage.

Advance Organizers

An advance organizer is material that is presented "in advance of, and at a higher level of generality, inclusiveness, and abstraction than, the learning task itself" (Ausubel & Robinson, 1969, p. 606). Advance organizers may be verbal or written statements, activities, or illustrations that assist students in identifying and understanding essential information in a learning activity (Munk, Bruckert, Call, Stoehrmann, & Radant, 1998). Used at the beginning of a lesson, advance organizers orient students to the content that will be presented (Salend, 2005), and may include a review of the last lesson, along with the purpose, rationale, and expectations of the current lesson (Swanson & Deshler, 2003).

An advance organizer may also consist of an activity for obtaining student attention, a statement of the lesson objectives, a confirmation of the teacher's expectations, or a presentation of a graphic organizer (Putnam & Wesson, 1990). Mr. Ruiz used a written advance organizer in the form of a handout to introduce a lesson on the parts of a story. The first part of the handout contained the lesson objectives, and the second part listed the parts of a story and then identified them in an actual story. While coteaching with a general education teacher, Mr. Dunn used a verbal and visual advance organizer to introduce a lesson on rocks. He began by showing the students a display of different kinds of rock formations and then said, "Today we are going to learn about the three types of rocks: igneous, sedimentary, and metamorphic. Tell me what you already know about these three types of rocks and make some predictions about them now that you have seen and touched them." In both of these classrooms, the teachers used advance organizers to provide clues to important information that they wanted their students to acquire and to inquire about.

Mapping

Mapping is making a word picture of ideas. It involves structuring information on a topic into categories using a graphic or web (Bulgren & Lenz, 1996). Maps may have boxes, arrows, lines, or other figures; they are visual representations that show relationships among conceptual ideas. Mapping is an excellent method for acquiring information from printed materials. It enhances learning (Lenz, Adams, Bulgren, Poulliot, & Laraux, 2002), allows students to think about the relationships among concepts and ideas, and facilitates the condensing of material to be studied.

A type of mapping technique that promotes comprehension of reading content involves the use of a character web. A character web is a type of map that allows students to study characters, their traits, and examples of those traits. Figure 10.4 contains a character web that the teacher and class co-constructed about Big Anthony, a character in *Strega Nona* by Tomie dePaola. This is a folktale about an elderly woman with special magical powers and the young man who takes care of her and helps her with her house. When Strega Nona leaves him alone with her magic pasta pot, Big Anthony is

Figure 10.4 CHARACTER WEB

CHARACTER	TRAITS	EXAMPLES
Big Anthony	Likeable	He means well and tries hard to do the right thing.
	Lazy	He wanted the magic pasta pot to do his work for him.
	Show-off	He bragged that he could make the magic pasta pot work.
	Poor Listener	He did not listen to Strega Nona about how to make the magic pasta pot work.

determined to show the townspeople how it works. The story goes on to describe what happens when Big Anthony tries to show off for the town instead of listening to Strega Nona. Note how the use of this web with second graders enhances their understanding of the story and opens up opportunities for lessons in character and career education. After initial instruction in how to develop a character web, students can construct them independently, with a peer, or in a cooperative group.

Concept Teaching

Concept teaching possesses many of the same characteristics as mapping. The Concept Mastery Routine, which utilizes Concept Diagrams (Bulgren, Deshler, & Schumaker, 1993), is effective for helping students acquire and organize information. This teaching routine is particularly useful in facilitating the comprehension of content material (e.g., science, social studies). It requires the teacher to select and become familiar with textbook or unit content before initiating instruction with students.

The Concept Mastery Routine, developed at the University of Kansas Center for Research on Learning, consists of (a) a visual device called a Concept Diagram (see Figure 10.5), (b) a set of linking steps used to develop the Concept Diagram (see the seven steps listed below and represented by the acronym CONCEPT), and (c) instructional procedures that help the teacher cue the students to use the Concept Mastery Routine, interact with the students in completing the Concept Diagram, and review understanding of the concept (i.e., Cue-Do-Review). For a detailed description of this teaching routine, please contact the University of Kansas Center for Research on Learning in Lawrence, Kansas. Bulgren, Schumaker, and Deshler (1988) successfully assisted general education teachers in using Concept Diagrams with students with learning disabilities and with other students by using the following procedures (CONCEPT):

1. *Convey the targeted concept.* Name a word or phrase that represents a category or idea. *Example:* cooperation.
2. *Offer the overall concept.* Explain the category into which the targeted concept can be grouped. *Example:* a way to do tasks.
3. *Note key words.* List words or phrases that are related to the concept. *Examples:* sports team, lab partners in science, rewards, two or more people, no competition.
4. *Classify characteristics as always, sometimes, or never present.* For each word or phrase that is classified as a characteristic, decide whether it is always, sometimes, or never present. *Example:* two or more people—always-present characteristic of cooperation; study—sometimes-present characteristic of cooperation; only individual—never-present characteristic of cooperation.
5. *Explore examples and nonexamples.* Decide which words or phrases represent examples or nonexamples. *Examples:* lab partners in a science class—example of cooperation; a person playing golf—nonexample of cooperation.
6. *Practice with a new example.* Generate your own examples and nonexamples of the concept. These are words or phrases that were not on the original key word list. *Example:* construction team—example of cooperation; movie theater audience—nonexample of cooperation.
7. *Tie down a definition.* Use the always-present characteristics and the overall concept to form a definition. *Example:* Cooperation is a way to do tasks that involves two or more people with shared goals, tasks, rewards, and responsibilities.

The preceding information is plotted in Figure 10.5. The sixth step, practice with a new example, gives you and your students the opportunity to generate additional

Figure 10.5 CONCEPT DIAGRAM

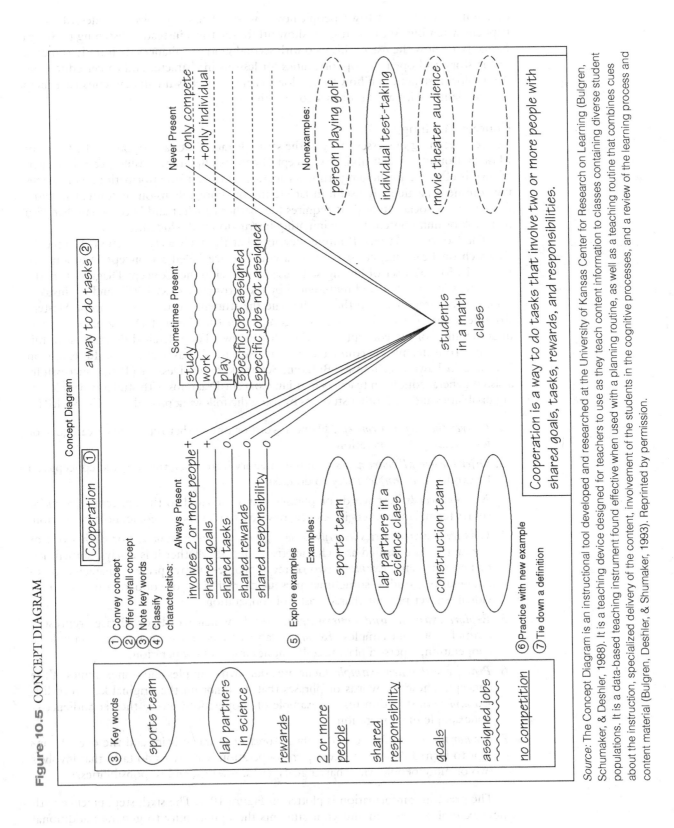

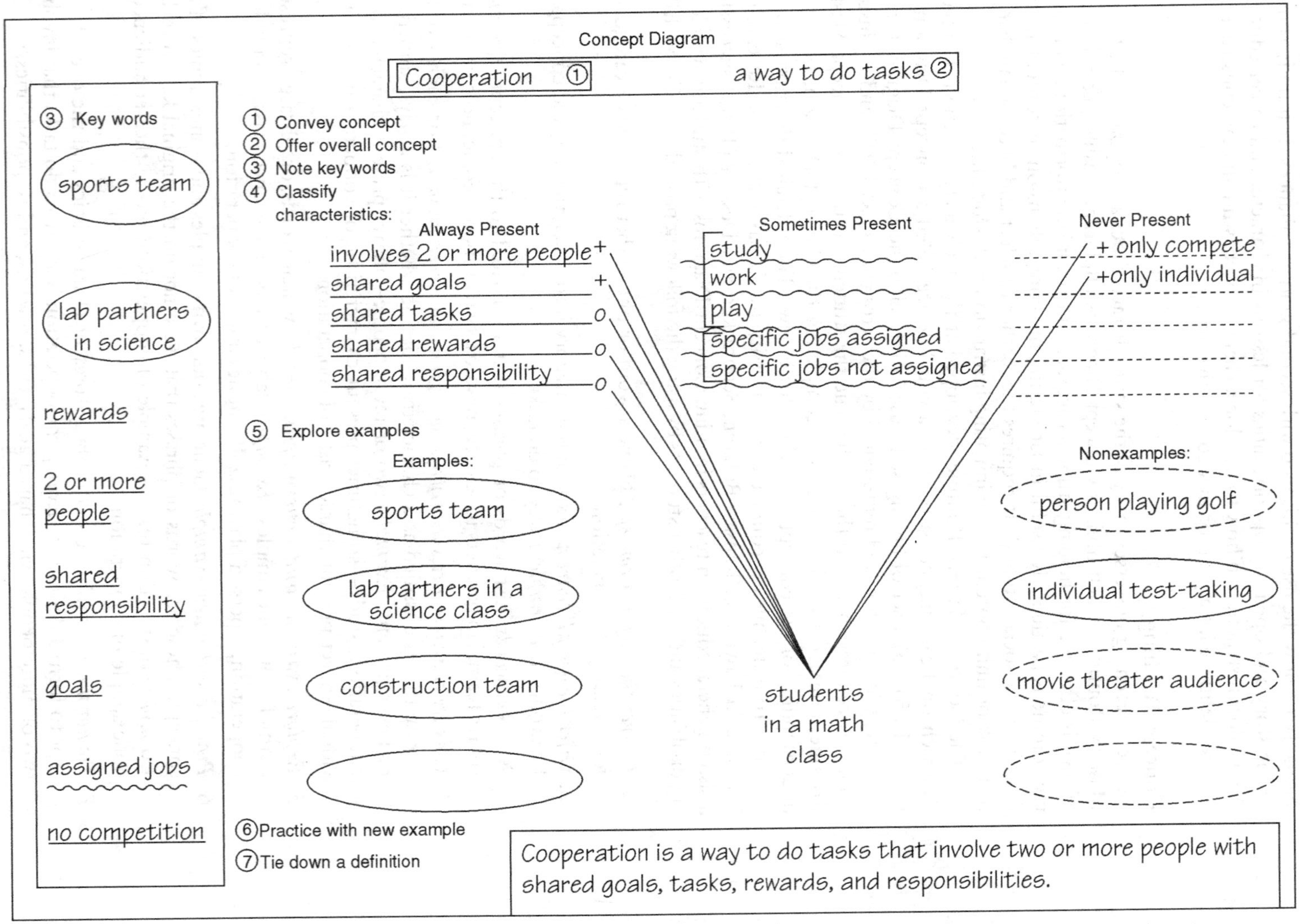

Source: The Concept Diagram is an instructional tool developed and researched at the University of Kansas Center for Research on Learning (Bulgren, Schumaker, & Deshler, 1988). It is a teaching device designed for teachers to use as they teach content information to classes containing diverse student populations. It is a data-based teaching instrument found effective when used with a planning routine, as well as a teaching routine that combines cues about the instruction, specialized delivery of the content, involvement of the students in the cognitive processes, and a review of the learning process and content material (Bulgren, Deshler, & Shumaker, 1993). Reprinted by permission.

examples and nonexamples. For example, in Figure 10.5 you will note that + (yes) or 0 (no) is used to decide whether *students in a math class* is an example or a nonexample of *cooperation.* An example has all the always-present characteristics, none of the never-present characteristics, and possibly some of the sometimes-present characteristics. A nonexample lacks at least one of the always-present characteristics or has at least one of the never-present characteristics. *Students in a math class* is a nonexample, because it meets these criteria. Remember, the Concept Mastery Routine is intended to be dynamic, with a great deal of teacher and student interaction with the concept being studied. The Concept Diagram has not been shown to be an effective tool if it is simply distributed to students. Instead, teachers should follow a Cue-Do-Review sequence as recommended by the authors cueing students to use the Concept Diagram, working with them, and reviewing the steps, what has been learned, and where the information may be applied (King-Sears & Mooney, 2004). Like mapping, concept teaching routines help students comprehend content material. Concept Diagrams condense material into manageable chunks and facilitate the acquisition of information.

Activity 10.2

Work with a group to describe how you would use the concept teaching routine to teach an abstract concept to a high school science class. Choose a concept (e.g., photosynthesis) and complete a concept diagram.

Textbook Usage

Almost 44% of the information students are responsible for learning is contained in textbooks but is not discussed in class (Zigmond, Levin, & Laurie, 1985), and yet, textbooks have been found to be the primary instructional tool that is used (Okolo & Ferretti, 1996). Many secondary students with disabilities experience difficulty reading (Mastropieri, Scruggs, & Graetz, 2003; Schloss, et al., 2001) and comprehending content-area textbooks (Meese, 1994). Strategies in textbook usage can provide valuable assistance, particularly to students who are expected to use textbooks independently in general education classes. We present suggestions for previewing textbooks, surveying textbooks and textbook chapters, and using graphic aids.

Textbook Previewing. Davis and Clark (1981) indicate that by focusing on 10 specific aspects of a textbook, students concentrate on the fewest number of words that contain the greatest amount of information. After previewing these 10 components, your students will know a great deal about the textbook (Davis & Clark, 1981):

1. Title
2. Introduction
3. Summary
4. Pictures and maps
5. Chapter questions
6. Subtopic titles
7. First paragraphs following topics
8. First sentences of paragraphs
9. Special print
10. Bold print

Another way to preview a textbook is to conduct a textbook feature analysis (Burke, 2001). This activity could be completed first by the teacher and then by the students.

Textbook and Chapter Surveying. Prior to using a new textbook, a valuable activity for your students to perform is surveying that textbook. This technique allows the students to become familiar with the parts of a textbook: table of contents, preface, glossary, appendix, bibliography, and index. This activity may be performed in small groups, thus encourging students to ask questions of each other, or individually.

After a textbook is surveyed and students become familiar with its contents, surveying a chapter may be performed. This procedure allows students to predict from the title and their prior knowledge what the chapter is about, turn headings into questions, identify study aids (e.g., bold print, italics, graphs, and charts), and divide the chapter into manageable sections. Class discussions, cooperative learning activities, and class presentations may facilitate sharing information about the chapter before the students read and study it. These discussions and activities allow students to test their initial hypotheses regarding the chapter content. Another way to survey a chapter is to use the chapter survey routine called TRIMS (Schumaker, Deshler, & McKnight, 1989):

Title
Relationship
Introduction
Main parts
Summary

An important part of TRIMS involves identifying the common relationship structures and signal words associated with these relationship structures (Bulgren & Lenz, 1996). These include listing, compare/contrast, cause/effect, and general/specific. These structures are organized on a worksheet that the teacher and students can use to complete a TRIMS of the chapter. For a thorough description of the procedures involved in using TRIMS, consult the work of Lenz, Deshler, and Kissam (2004).

Table 10.1 illustrates textbook and chapter surveying. If students know how to use a textbook and are aware of how to read and study individual chapters, they are more apt to interact with the content presented. This interaction may promote more independent functioning in both pull-out and inclusive settings.

Activity 10.3

Complete a textbook and chapter survey by finding a content-area textbook at the elementary or secondary level. Use the form in Table 10.1 to survey the textbook and one of its chapters.

Graphic Aids. Many students with learning problems do not automatically activate and utilize strategies to help them acquire information from text (Stanovitch, 1986) and therefore, struggle in content classes (DiCecco & Gleason, 2002). This problem is intensified in their content classes because of the prevalence of inconsiderate text (e.g., a text that lacks structure, unity, coherence, and audience appropriateness) (Schloss, et al., 2001). For students to be successful in content classes, teachers must present information in a clear and organized manner (Dye, 2000). The use of graphic aids may alleviate the problems inherent in content-area textbooks, and may assist teachers to organize material for students. Graphic aids may take the form of a table of contents, chapter headings, tables, a glossary, an appendix, a bibliography, or an index, as well as maps, semantic webs, Venn diagrams (see Figure 10.3), graphs, illustrations, or other visual displays. These graphic aids help students gather clues about the content of the text and organize facts so that they are easy to understand.

Table 10.1 Surveying a Textbook and Chapter

Surveying Your Textbook

1. Name of textbook
2. Author(s)
3. List two things you can tell about the book by its title.
4. List three points that the author makes in the introduction.
5. Look at the table of contents. List three things you know about the textbook by reading the chapter titles.
6. Does the textbook contain an index, glossary, and appendix? If so, how will you use each of them?

Surveying a Textbook Chapter

1. Title of chapter
2. List two things that the chapter title suggests.
3. Read the first and last paragraphs and the boldface headings in the chapter. What do you think the author wants you to learn?
4. What graphic aids does the chapter contain?

_____ maps	_____ italics
_____ graphs	_____ questions
_____ charts	_____ definitions
_____ illustrations	_____ bold print
_____ diagrams	_____ other

5. What other clues does the chapter have that might help you understand it?

Traditionally, students with problems in academic areas have demonstrated greater difficulty managing abstract writing concepts that teachers have not explicitly taught to them (Berninger, et al., 1998). We recommend that you specifically teach the use of each graphic aid rather than assume that your students know how and when to use them to acquire information, and include the five components of study skill instruction presented at the beginning of the chapter. For example, Mr. Alonzo taught beginning map skills to his primary students by drawing a map of the neighborhood around the school. He showed the students how to use the compass rose (i.e., the symbol with lines or arrows that point in the four main directions on the map). He gave them many opportunities to practice by asking them questions, such as "If you wanted to walk from East Main Street in front of the school to Spruce Street behind the school, in which direction would you walk?" Next, he showed them how to use the distance scale (1 inch = 3 miles) on the map to determine the distance between streets and between stores. After modeling how to figure distance with the distance scale and a ruler, he asked them questions, such as "If I live on Bellvedere Street and I want to walk to school, how far will I have to walk?"

In large part, gains made by students with special needs have been linked to the use of a specific type of graphic aid, the graphic organizer (Griffin, Malone, & Kame'enui, 1995; Robinson & Keiwra, 1995). In a review of research, Anderson, Yilmaz, and Washburn-Moses (2004) reported that graphic organizers can be used successfully to improve the understanding of concepts by middle and high school students. The graphic organizer is a visual representation that shows relationships, and serves as a means for organizing material to be learned. There are many varieties of graphic organizers and different ways to use them. Alvermann and Phelps (2005) suggest that graphic organizers be prepared in their entirety and presented ahead of time as an introduction to a lesson or unit, or be partially completed by the teacher, and then students can help complete the sections during a discussion with the teacher. In the latter case, the graphic organizer contains empty spaces to represent missing information for

Figure 10.6 TREE DIAGRAM

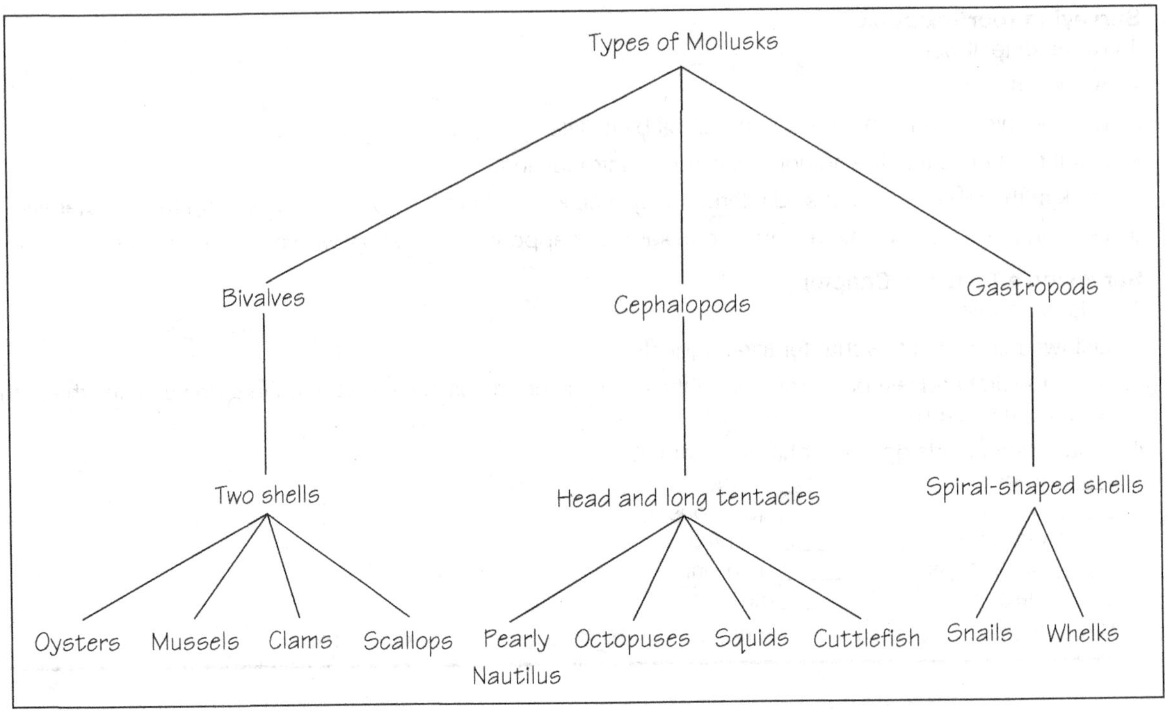

students to fill in while reading their textbooks or interacting with the teacher. This method ensures the students' involvement by requiring them to search for missing information. Imagine if Figure 10.6 on mollusks contained empty spaces. You could engage your students at the beginning of a lesson in predicting what the empty spaces might contain, or ask students what they already know about mollusks and fill in the empty spaces. At the end of the lesson or textbook chapter, the students would be able to see if their predictions were correct.

Merkley and Jefferies (2001) recommend following specific guidelines when using graphic organizers in instruction. We present their instructional guidelines with our own examples from Figure 10.6.

1. ***Verbalize relationships (links) concepts expressed by the visual.*** ("Notice, the graphic organizer describes the different types of mollusks with examples.")
2. ***Provide opportunity for student input.*** ("Should we add any other examples of mollusks?")
3. ***Connect new information to past learning.*** ("How would you compare mollusks to the types of sea life that we studied in the last section?")
4. ***Make reference to the upcoming text.*** ("As you read, look for the three types of mollusks and prepare to tell something about each one.")
5. ***Seize opportunities to reinforce decoding and structural analysis.*** ("Remember that the letters "ph" make the sound that "f" makes. Look at cephalopods. If you have trouble pronouncing a word, try dividing it into syllables.")

Once you have taught the use of graphic aids, be sure to provide opportunities for practice. For example, Dye (2000) constructed an organizer to use for a lesson about flight, which compared the early attempts at flight made by people in the United States with those made by people in Europe. She left some blank spaces on the graphic organizer so that students could add to it as the lesson progressed.

Initially, the teacher may assume responsibility for constructing the graphic organizer in order to assist students with the understanding of concepts, the meaning of vocabulary, the relationship among terms and ideas, and the organization of textbook material. Eventually, students will be able to construct these diagrams in collaboration with the teacher and, finally, on their own. To construct a graphic organizer, you should follow these steps adapted from Alvermann (1983):

1. ***Choose the portion of a textbook chapter* (e.g., a few pages) *that you are ready to teach next.*** Let's continue to use the topic of mollusks, which we introduced with our discussion of graphic organizers (see Figure 10.6).
2. ***Write down the words that represent your topic* (e.g., types of mollusks).**

mantle	clams	cuttlefish
bivalves	scallops	tentacles
oysters	cephalopods	gastropods
pearly nautilus	octopuses	mussels
whelks	snails	squids

3. ***Arrange the words in a diagram to show their relationship to the concept* (e.g., types of mollusks).** You may need to add or delete words to connect terms and ideas and to clarify relationships. We added *two shells* to describe *bivalves, head and long tentacles* to describe *cephalopods*, and *spiral-shaped shells* to describe *gastropods.* We deleted *mantle.*
4. ***Draw your diagram on the board or overhead transparency to discuss with the students.*** We recommend giving each student a copy. If you use a modified graphic organizer (a graphic organizer with some empty spaces), give students a copy so they can supply the missing information.
5. ***Demonstrate for the students how the information on the diagram simplifies, clarifies and relates to the information in the textbook.***

IMPORTANT POINTS

1. An advance organizer is used at the beginning of a lesson, may be verbal or written, and consists of an activity for obtaining student attention; a statement of the lesson objectives; the teacher s expectations; a presentation of a graphic organizer; a review of the last lesson; and/or the purpose and rationale for the current lesson.
2. Maps are visual representations that show relationships among concepts.
3. The Concept Mastery Routine consists of selecting the targeted and overall concept; selecting key words or phrases; identifying characteristics as always, sometimes, or never present; identifying examples, nonexamples, and new examples; defining the concept; and plotting this information on a Concept Diagram.
4. Students may preview a textbook by examining the title, introduction, summary, pictures and maps, chapter questions, subtopic titles, first paragraphs following subtopics, first sentences of paragraphs, italics, and bold print.
5. Surveying a textbook allows students to become familiar with the table of contents, preface, glossary, appendix, bibliography, and index before they begin reading.

ORGANIZATION AND MEMORIZATION OF INFORMATION

In this section, strategies are presented that relate to how students organize and memorize information. We describe mnemonic and general memory strategies, underlining and highlighting, and study guides.

MEMORY/MNEMONICS

Memory plays an important part in the academic success of students. Memory skills affect the organization and storage of information for later retrieval and are among the most commonly reported areas of weakness among students with learning disabilities (Mastropieri & Scruggs, 1998) and students in special education and remedial classes (Scruggs & Mastropieri, 1984). Students with disabilities may have difficulty memorizing information for tests, presentations, and written work (Ashbaker & Swanson, 1996) as well as everyday functional information (McNamara & Wong, 2003). Consequently, it is important to teach specific strategies that will enhance memory skills.

Mnemonics facilitate the organization, storage, and retrieval of information (Masters, Mori, & Mori, 1999). *Mnemonics* comes from a Greek term and refers to the art of improving memory by using formulae or other aids (Bragstad & Stumpf, 1987).

Keyword Method The keyword mnemonic method has been used successfully for learning and recalling information (Mastropieri, Scruggs, & Levin, 1986b); remembering foreign language vocabulary (McLoone, Scruggs, Mastropieri, & Zucker, 1986); and remembering abstract English vocabulary (Mastropieri, Scruggs, & Fulk, 1990; Mastropieri & Scruggs, 2004). Additionally the keyword method has been used in teaching history and science to students with learning disabilities (Veit, Scruggs, & Mastropieri, 1986).

The keyword method is a mnemonic strategy that assists in the retention of facts by using auditory and visual cues as well as visual imagery (Mastropieri, 1988). It employs the steps of recoding, relating, and retrieving. In recoding, an unfamiliar word is associated with a familiar, acoustically similar keyword. The relating element allows the learner to link the keyword to the actual word through a picture or image. Finally, the retrieving component enables the learner to call to mind systematically the original word (Mastropieri, Scruggs, & Levin, 1986a). For example, Mastropieri (1988) suggests that to learn the word *apex*, you recode it to a word that sounds similar, like *ape*. This is a good keyword for students who are familiar with the concept of ape. Next, relate the keyword, *ape*, by creating an image of the keyword and the definition of the word *apex*. Since *apex* means highest point, you would picture an ape at a highest point. A good interactive image may be an ape (possibly King Kong) sitting on the highest point of something, for example, the Empire State Building. To retrieve the word *apex* and its definition, you would tell the student to think of the keyword, think back to the picture, and state the definition. It is important to consider students' experiential and cultural backgrounds when choosing keywords. You want to be sure to include concepts with which they are familiar.

Pegword Method A method for learning and remembering a list of items is the number rhyme, or pegword method. A pegword is a rhyming word for the numbers from 1 to 10:

BOX 10.2

Reflections on Practice

One of the dilemmas facing educational researchers today is how to best inform pre-professionals and practicing educators about research results. You may have already discovered that visiting the websites of organizations such as the Council for Learning Disabilities (CLD) is an excellent way to quickly stay abreast of the latest strategies for effective instruction. Recently the CLD website featured several journal articles in their "Scholarly Initiatives" section. One of those articles is reviewed here as an example of how to connect research to practice.

In *Memory for Everyday Information in Students with Learning Disabilities*, McNamara and Wong (2003) report the results of a study they conducted to examine how students with learning disabilities process everyday information. Their premise was that research had already proven how memory deficits impact students with learning disabilities academically, but do those same deficits affect these students in their everyday working memory? The 60 participants in this study were 20 students identified as having learning disabilities, 20 students who were nondisabled and matched in age to the students with learning disabilities, and 20 students who were nondisabled and matched in reading level to the students with learning disabilities. The everyday information that these students were asked to remember fell into three groups: common objects (a touch-tone telephone), procedures (checking a book out of the library), and episodes (learning a dance).

The results of the study indicated that students with learning disabilities perform even more poorly on everyday information memory processing than they do when asked to recall academic information in a laboratory setting. In addition, a second part of this study attempted to discover whether students with learning disabilities were experiencing memory deficits due to problems with storage of the information or problems with retrieval of the information. The findings indicated that the greater difficulty is with retrieval of the information once it is stored. Proof of this is seen when students with learning disabilities are given cues prior to being asked to recall information and their ability to recall increases. Interestingly enough, when appropriate cues were used, their recall of information matched that of their nondisabled peers.

As a teacher of students with special needs, you can benefit from this important research in many ways. Your awareness of the everyday struggles your students' experience will help you hone your teaching style to better match their needs. The authors state that "it is important to recognize that difficulties associated with learning disabilities may not be limited to reading or math" (p. 405). Consequently, students with learning disabilities may not be exhibiting purposeful behavior when they forget to take home their math book or continually arrive late for science because they can't remember the correct hallway to turn down to get there. If you add the use of verbal cues prior to requesting information recall from your students with learning disabilities, you will be adjusting your teaching style in a manner that will have a direct, positive impact on your students. And if you combine the use of metacognitive strategies with direct instruction in cueing, you may well equip your students with strategies and skills that will benefit them throughout their lives.

To access the article, please see McNamara, J. K., & Wong, B. (2003). Memory for everyday information in students with learning disabilities. *Journal of Learning Disabilities, 36*(5), 394.

1. Bun
2. Shoe
3. Tree
4. Door
5. Hive
6. Sticks
7. Heaven
8. Gate
9. Vine
10. Hen

To learn a list of words, you create an image that associates the number 1, the word *bun*, and the first word on the list of items to be learned. For example, if you wanted to remember the five senses (sight, hearing, smell, taste, and touch), you would picture (1) a large bun wearing glasses, (2) a shoe with big ears, (3) a tree with an oversized nose sniffing its blossoms, (4) a door with an open mouth licking its lips, and (5) a beehive with long arms extending from its sides that were getting stung by bees because they kept touching the hive. This technique utilizes the visualizing and associative potential of the learner to help aid memory.

Other Mnemonic Aids Although mnemonic aids are not to be used as a substitute for studying and understanding, they may provide useful cues for students who are required to memorize lists, items, causes, laws, or equations. Some commonly used mnemonics are suggested:

1. Directions (north, east, south, west)—*Never eat soggy waffles*
2. Parts of the atom (proton, electron, neutron, shell)—*PENS*
3. Colors of the spectrum (red, orange, yellow, green, blue, indigo, violet)—*Roy G. Biv*
4. Time changes—Spring forward, fall back
5. Coordinating conjunctions (for, and, nor, but, or, yet, so)—*fan boys.*

Activity 10.4

Use the information from this chapter to complete the following activity:

1. The endocrine glands assist in coordinating the body's activities and response systems (usual and stressful). Develop a mnemonic strategy to remember the names of the endocrine glands (pituitary gland, thyroid gland, parathyroid glands, adrenal glands, and pancreas).
2. Think back to your study of the colonization of the United States and develop a mnemonic strategy to memorize the thirteen original colonies (Connecticut, Delaware, Georgia, Maryland, Massachusetts, New Hampshire, New Jersey, New York, North Carolina, South Carolina, Pennsylvania, Rhode Island, and Virginia).

UNDERLINING AND HIGHLIGHTING

Some study strategies help students organize information by physically altering the text or material. Underlining is one of the most popular and frequently used study strategies (Anderson & Armbruster, 1984) and is accomplished by drawing a line under the important text. Highlighting is accomplished by going over the text with a transparent marker. Particularly useful with consumable materials, underlining and highlighting may facilitate studying by isolating the information to be recalled (Blanchard, 1985) and may help focus student attention on the most significant information (Sabornie & deBettencourt, 2004). Highlighting is particularly helpful in an inclusive setting for students who have difficulty with vocabulary and for English language learners. You should underline only after you have read the material by going back and picking out a few words (not whole sentences) that summarize the author's main point (Murphy, Meyers, Olesen, McKean, & Custer, 1996). Effective underlining identifies the main ideas and supporting statements in a passage and conveys the same meaning as the entire passage (Raygor, 1970). For example, consider the following passage that Ms. Rodriguez used with her students:

> Every now and then, a moving light may appear in the night sky. That light may be a comet. A comet has a head and a tail. The head of the comet is made up of a large cloud of gases called the coma. The tail actually forms when the cloud of gases is blown back by the wind.

Notice that the same meaning is conveyed when you read the entire passage and when you read only the underlined portions. The results of many of the studies conducted in the area of underlining (Anderson & Armbruster, 1980) suggest that teachers should do the following:

1. Give preunderlined material whenever possible.
2. Provide training in effective underlining.
3. Encourage students to underline important general ideas.
4. Remind students that with underlining, less is more.
5. Encourage students to use the time saved by underlining to study the material.

For example, Ms. Rodriguez frequently gives handouts to her students to accompany their fifth-grade science textbook chapters. Her handouts contain sections that she has underlined prior to assigning the chapter. These handouts help her students focus on important concepts, key terms and their definitions, study questions, and other elements that she wants them to study in preparation for a quiz or test. Sometimes, she passes out handouts that have not been underlined and models for her students what they should underline. She uses cognitive modeling techniques to demonstrate by saying, "I am going to underline moving light and night sky because it is important to know that comets move and that we can see them against the dark sky at night. I will underline comet, head, and tail because I need to remember that a comet has a head and tail. I am going to underline head made up of gases called coma so that I will remember what the head is composed of. That sounds as if it might be a test question."

After modeling for her students, she gives them another handout and asks them to practice underlining the way she has shown them. When Ms. Rodriguez began this procedure, her students tended to underline almost everything on a page, but after repeated practice, the amount of underlining decreased and was limited to the most essential information.

STUDY GUIDES

Study guides help students organize visual (e.g., reading assignment, board work, PowerPoint presentation, laboratory work) and auditory (e.g., lecture and audio recording) information. They help students develop a plan for reviewing and studying information (Wood, 2006). By directing attention to specific points, study guides provide organized ways to view video presentations or listen to audio presentations. They are also valuable to students as a tool for reviewing for tests.

Study guides may be used with elementary and secondary students before, during, and after instruction. A child in the elementary grades may benefit from a guide illustrating the four steps in long division or an outline with the names of the five parts of a friendly letter and an example of each. Mario, a second-grade student, was given a study guide with the five short vowels (*a, e, i, o, u*) on it. Next to each vowel was a picture that represented the sound that the vowel made (apple, elephant, igloo, octopus, umbrella). Bonita, a fifth-grade student, received the following guide prepared by her teacher:

Topic	Writing four types of sentences
Terms	Declarative, interrogative, exclamatory, and imperative
Definitions	Declarative: a sentence that states or declares something. Interrogative: a sentence that asks a question. Exclamatory: a sentence that expresses emotion or surprise. Imperative: a sentence that gives a command or order.
Examples	Don ran all the way home from Bob's house. (declarative) Do you think I could have left my notebook in school? (interrogative) I'll never do that again as long as I live! (exclamatory) Close the door. (imperative)

Riegel, Mayle, and McCarthy-Henkel (1988) recommended different levels of study guides depending on a student's reading level. Table 10.2 illustrates three different types of study guides. The ***independent*** study guide includes critical information and is appropriate for students who have good reading and study skills, know how to use an index, can skim and scan for information, and can make inferences (Riegel et al., 1988). The ***prompted*** study guide includes critical information and prompts (e.g., page numbers) to help students locate the information. The ***directed*** study guide identifies, provides prompts for, and defines critical information.

Students at the secondary level may profit from a listing of (1) title or subject, (2) purpose, (3) key vocabulary and definitions, (4) a brief outline of subject matter, (5) questions, and (6) text references with pages. For example, Leroy needed to prepare for a test on Japan. Utilizing the six elements just listed, his teacher, Ms. Delgado, developed a study guide to help structure his studying and organize the information.

1. ***Title/Subject*** The island of Japan
2. ***Purpose*** To describe the environment of Japan and the way of life of its people
3. ***Key vocabulary and definitions***

bonsai:	potted plants and trees kept small through specific cultivation techniques
monsoon:	a periodic wind that reverses direction seasonally
archipelago:	a body of salt water interspersed with numerous islands
typhoon:	a tropical cyclone that occurs in the western Pacific
tsunami:	a huge wave caused by an underwater disturbance

4. ***A brief outline***

   I. Climate
   II. Population distribution
   III. Landforms
      A. Mountains
      B. Plateaus
      C. Plains
   IV. Natural resources

V. Life in Japan
    A. Urban
    B. Rural

5. ***Questions*** What are the advantages and disadvantages of Japan's location? What are Japan's greatest natural resources? Describe urban and rural life in Japan.
6. ***Text references***

    World Cultures, pages 56–67
    Japan Today, page 34 and pages 117–129

Table 10.2 Independent, Prompted, and Directed Study Guides

Sample Independent Study Guide

Define the following terms:

1. axis
2. blitzkrieg
3. neutral
4. isolation

Answer the following questions:

1. What happened on December 7, 1941?
2. Describe two factors that contributed to war in Europe.

Sample Prompted Study Guide

Define the following terms:

1. axis (page 123)
2. blitzkrieg (page 130)
3. neutral (page 129)
4. isolation (page 125)

Answer the following questions:

1. What happened on December 7, 1941? (page 132)
2. Describe two factors that contributed to war in Europe. (pages 121 & 122)

Sample Directed Study Guide

Define the following terms:

1. axis (page 123)—Germany and its allies
2. blitzkrieg (page 130)—lightning warfare
3. neutral (page 129)—to take no side between nations at war
4. isolation (page 125)—a belief that a nation should not become involved in foreign (other countries') problems

Answer the following questions:

1. What happened on December 7, 1941? (page 132) The Japanese bombed Pearl Harbor, Hawaii.
2. Describe two factors that contributed to war in Europe. (pages 121 & 122) Economic factors and political conditions contributed to war in Europe.

Source: From *Beyond Maladies and Remedies: Suggestions and Guidelines for Adapting Materials for Students With Special Needs in the Regular Class* by R. H. Riegel, J. A. Mayle, & J. McCarthy-Henkel, 1988. Novi, MI: RHR Consultation Services. Reprinted by permission.

Table 10.3 Study Guide to Assist with Reading Assignments

Questions to Guide Your Reading about Wild Plants and Animals

Directions: Read this study guide before you begin reading the material or responding to the questions.

1. The main idea can be found in the first paragraph. Write it in your own words. (p. 68)
2. Read pp. 68–73 and then stop and write in your own words two major points the author is making. Now read pp. 74–79 and do the same.
3. Terms you should know are: (pp. 68–79)

extinct	wildlife management
species	wildlife refuges
depleted	ethics
resources	predator
endangered	poaching
threatened	migration

   Be prepared to use them meaningfully in a class discussion.
4. What wild plants and animals are in danger of becoming extinct? Six are listed on pp. 70–75.
5. The author gives three reasons why we should not let these endangered species die. Write them and give one of your own. (Hint: Think about our speaker from the Audubon Society as well as the debate we had in class.)
6. Make sure you read the captions under the pictures. They give excellent descriptions of the California condor, snow leopard, whooping crane, black-footed ferret, Florida manatee, and black lace cactus.
7. Write down any words that you are unsure of and bring them to class. Remember first to use context clues and the glossary in the back of the book to help figure them out.
8. Think about what you have read and how this material relates to the previous unit on land and water resources. List at least two things in the previous unit that helped you with this unit.

A couple of weeks after Leroy has become used to the format of the study guide, Ms. Delgado will leave some blanks in his study guide and require him to fill in these sections, increasing his involvement with the material. Perhaps he will supply some of the definitions, generate some questions about the topic, or fill in parts of the outline.

Students at both elementary and secondary levels may benefit from study guides to assist them with school or home reading assignments. For example, Ms. Donahue gave her students a reading assignment on wild plants and animals and prepared a study guide to accompany their reading (see Table 10.3). Notice how Ms. Donahue made this reading assignment meaningful by developing a study guide to accompany it.

Study guides may take many different forms, depending on the age of the student, the purpose of the guide, the subject matter, and the needs of the students. They provide an excellent way to facilitate the organization of information for students with special needs and all students in inclusive settings.

Activity 10.5

Choose a content-area textbook at the elementary, middle, or high school level and develop a study guide for one of the chapters. Use the suggestions in this chapter to help you construct your guide. Work with a partner and describe how your study guides will assist a student with special needs in an inclusive classroom.

IMPORTANT POINTS

1. Mnemonics facilitate the organization, storage, and retrieval of information.
2. Underlining and highlighting help students organize information to be studied by physically altering the material.
3. Study guides help students organize information presented visually (in reading assignments, on the board, in a PowerPoint presentation, in laboratory work) and auditorily (through lectures and audio presentations).
4. Independent study guides include critical information and are appropriate for students who have good reading and study skills, know how to use an index, can skim and scan for information, and can make inferences. Prompted study guides include critical information and prompts; directed study guides identify, provide prompts for, and define critical information.

EXPRESSION OF INFORMATION

In this section, we present study skills and strategies that relate to how students express information. Students are expected to possess skills that will enable them to demonstrate their knowledge and mastery of content in school. Therefore, in this section, we provide techniques to improve two skill areas important for success in school and later at work and in life: test preparation and test taking, and report writing and presentation.

TEST PREPARATION AND TEST TAKING

Most students are required to take tests before they enter elementary school, during the elementary and secondary years in school, and before they leave high school. Even though students spend their school years taking quizzes, unit tests, minimum competency tests, and state assessments, they are not necessarily proficient at doing so. Students with special needs encounter problems preparing for and taking tests because of difficulties with organization, comprehension, memory, task completion within time limits, studying, self-confidence, and test-wiseness.

Just as you prepare your students in computation, handwriting, and theme writing, you may also prepare them to take tests. After all, your students are tested in every aspect of the curriculum, from reading to vocational skills. We present several suggestions to help your students improve their skills in test taking. Studying the content, using the study skills previously mentioned in this chapter (e.g., listening, note taking, memory techniques, study guides), and using these test-taking tips should help your students improve their performance on tests. The following suggestions, adapted from the work of Bos and Vaughn (2006), Bragstad and Stumpf (1987), and Mercer and Mercer (2005), may assist your students before they take a test, during the completion of a test, and after a test is returned.

Before the Test

Teach both general and specific strategies to help students prepare for a test.

General Strategies Students typically need to spend a significant amount of time trying to comprehend and retain information in order to take tests (Hughes, 1996). Therefore, it is extremely important for them to have good test preparation skills that they can use across content areas and in a variety of situations and settings. Following are some general procedures you may suggest to your students as they prepare for a test.

1. ***Keep reviewing.*** Students should review after each class, week, or section. A spaced or cumulative review is more effective than a massed review of the information just before a test. You may suggest that your students keep a study log to help keep up with information. The study log may contain things to do, such as review prior work, rewrite notes, or highlight important information.

2. ***Determine the specifics about the test.*** Suggest that your students find out the following from the teacher: date of test, sources to be studied (e.g., text, notes, presentations), and types of questions (e.g., objective, essay), and time allowed.

3. ***Guesstimate about the test.*** Prompt your students to use past tests and quizzes, clues from their teachers, and brainstorming with other students to predict questions on the test.

4. ***Think positive thoughts.*** Encourage your students to tell themselves that they will do well because they have studied the right sources of information, prepared for specific types of questions, and thought about how to allot their time.

Specific Strategies. Specific strategies include **EASY**, **RCRC**, and the use of flash cards.

Easy. Ellis and Lenz (1987) developed a strategy for students to use independently to prepare for tests by organizing and prioritizing information.

E = Elicit "Wh" questions (who, what, when, where, why) to identify important information.

A = Ask yourself which information is the least troublesome.

S = Study the easy parts first and the hardest parts last.

Y = Say **"Yes"** to self-reinforcement (p. 99).

RCRC. Archer and Gleason (1994) developed the **RCRC** strategy that students can use independently to prepare for tests by verbally rehearsing information from class presentations, notes, handouts, and textbooks.

R = Read. Read a section of material from the textbook, notes, or handouts and read it again.

C = Cover. Cover the material so you cannot see it.

R = Recite. Tell yourself what you have read.

C = Check. Uncover the material and check to see if you are right.

Flash Cards. McCarney and Tucci (1991) suggest putting information to be learned for tests on flash cards using a who, what, where, when, how, and why format. The questions are written on one side, with the answers written on the back, and may be prepared by the teacher, a teaching assistant, or the students themselves. Students can study independently or with a partner. This technique can be adapted for younger children by using pictures instead of words. Our example shows a sample of the flash cards a fifth-grade teacher had his students use to study for a test on a unit about heroes and heroines.

Who

Front: Who was Molly Pitcher?

Back: Molly Hays McCauley (called Molly Pitcher) was a heroine of the Revolutionary War.

What

Front: What did she do to help the soldiers during the Revolutionary War?

Back: She cooked for and fed the soldiers and the wounded during the Revolutionary War.

Where

Front: Where was she born?

Back: She was born in New Jersey.

When

Front: When did she live?

Back: She lived from 1754 to 1832.

How

Front: How did she earn her nickname, Molly Pitcher?

Back: She got her nickname by carrying pitchers of water to the wounded during the Battle of Monmouth. They called, "Molly, pitcher!"

Why

Front: Why was she proclaimed a heroine at the Battle of Monmouth?

Back: She fought side by side with the soldiers by loading and firing cannons during the Battle of Monmouth.

During the Test

You may teach some general and specific strategies to assist students during a test. We discuss some general strategies first followed by a discussion of the specific strategy of **SCORER.**

General Strategies Following are techniques your students can use as they take a test:

1. ***Situate yourself where you can concentrate.*** If seats are not assigned, remind the students to choose one that will allow them to concentrate. For some it will be in the back and for others in the front—away from friends, noise, or other distractions.

2. ***Survey the test.*** Suggest that the students take a few deep breaths before starting. They should then put their names on their tests and look over the entire test before beginning. This will help them decide how much time to spend on each section and how the points are allocated. If this is not clear to them, they should ask the teacher.

3. ***Complete the test.*** Alert the students to read the directions carefully and to respond as directed, since failure to do so may result in a loss of points. They should answer the easy questions first (to earn points quickly and gain confidence) and place a mark by each question they are unsure of. Then they can go back later to the questions they left unanswered. Unless there is a penalty for guessing, they should answer all of the questions, even if they must guess.

4. ***Review the test.*** Remind the students that after they have completed the test, they should look it over again. They should have followed the directions, answered all

of the questions, and put their name on the test. They should check to see if their writing is legible and all words are spelled correctly. Caution the students to change an answer only if they are absolutely certain it is incorrect.

SCORER Carman and Adams (1972) designed a technique called **SCORER** for students to use when they take tests. We discuss each step of the SCORER technique in detail to assist students in using the test-taking strategies.

1. **S**chedule time
2. **C**lue words
3. **O**mit difficult questions
4. **R**ead carefully
5. **E**stimate answers
6. **R**eview the work

Schedule Time. Students should begin their test by looking it over and planning how much time they will spend on each section. They can determine this by identifying the items that are easy and difficult for them, the point values of items, and how many items are on the test.

Clue Words. Students should look for clue words in multiple-choice and true-false items. Words like *never*, *none*, *every*, *always*, *all*, and *only* are "100 percent words," which imply that the response is true 100 percent of the time (Pauk & Owens, 2005). In most cases, students should avoid choosing responses that contain these words in multiple-choice items, and should answer *false* to true-false items containing these words.

Omit Difficult Questions. A good rule of thumb in taking tests is to answer the questions you know first and mark the ones you do not know. Come back later to the marked questions. Sometimes a question that a student has already answered on the test contains information that will help with an abandoned item.

Read Carefully. It is important that students read directions and test items carefully so they will not miss points because they did not follow the directions, answer the actual question, or answer all parts of a question.

Estimate Answers. Carman and Adams (1972) suggest that students performing mathematical calculations should estimate the answer before performing the calculation in order to avoid careless errors. Mercer and Mercer (2005) suggest that if guessing is not penalized, students should eliminate obvious choices and make their best guess.

Review the Work. Students should go back over the entire test to make sure they have followed directions accurately, answered all abandoned items, and responded to all questions.

Lee and Alley (1981) found that junior high students with learning disabilities demonstrated significantly improved unit test scores using the SCORER approach. Ritter and Idol-Maestas (1986) used SCORER with high school students with mental disabilities and found the students who received instruction in SCORER performed better than the control group in content tests.

After the Test

Following are some of the suggestions you can give to your students after they turn in their tests. Have the students systematically analyze their test-taking strengths and weaknesses.

Directions: To analyze your test-taking performance, please mark ***Yes*** or ***No*** for each of the following statements.

	Yes	No
1. Studied for test		
2. Put name on paper		
3. Surveyed test		
4. Decided order to do test		
5. Read and followed directions		
6. Answered easy questions first		
7. Marked/left difficult questions		
8. Went back to unanswered questions		
9. Answered all questions		
10. Proofread test		

Managing Instructional Language and Terms

Tests and quizzes are accompanied by directions that contain key words requiring students to respond in a specific way. It is vital for students to have a clear understanding of these words in order to complete short-answer and essay questions accurately. Several authors have identified commonly used terms (Bos & Vaughn, 2006; Pauk & Owens, 2005), many of which we have listed in Table 10.4. To check for understanding of these terms, Bos and Vaughn (2006) recommend asking students to respond to test items that use different instructional language. This technique enables students to see how varying the instructional language varies their responses. Consider the different responses you would get to the following two instructions: *Define* autocratic. *Discuss* autocratic.

Table 10.4 Instructional Language of Tests

Apply	Using examples, explain how an idea or concept would work.
Compare	Show similarities and differences of two or more things.
Contrast	Highlight just the differences of two or more concepts.
Define	Provide a general description of the concept.
Discuss	Provide a more detailed description, including pros and cons.
Evaluate	Discuss the concept, including your opinion and the facts to support the opinion.
Explain	Tell why something occurred.
Illustrate	Use examples, including diagrams and pictures, to explain your idea further.
Justify	Offer reasons and provide facts to support your statements.
Outline	Condense material into major topics with their subpoints underneath.
Relate	Show the connection between several thoughts and ideas.
Solve	Arrive at a desired outcome using facts and knowledge.
State	Offer main point without providing details.
Summarize	Bring knowledge together with emphasis on main points only.

Activity 10.6

Part 1: In this age of high-stakes testing, describe how you would use the test-taking strategies in this chapter to assist students with special needs in general education classrooms.

Part 2: Think back to Jasmine in the chapter opening scenario. What techniques could she use "before a test" in her science class to help her prepare? In what ways could her teacher, Mrs. Wilmette, assist her?

REPORT WRITING AND PRESENTATION

Students are frequently required to express information through the writing and presenting of reports. This expectation begins in elementary school, with children in the primary grades using show-and-tell activities and writing and illustrating simple stories and with students in the intermediate grades creating short stories, book reports, and

BOX 10.3

Reflections on Practice

Now more than ever before, teachers are aware of the importance of working as a team to ensure the success of students. The parents or guardians of your students are a critical part of that team, and you will benefit as a teacher if you communicate with them frequently and recommend resources that are easy for parents to access and use.

One such resource is a website that has been in existence for many years called "LD OnLine." This site is designed to assist parents and teachers of students who have learning disabilities and/or related disabilities. The site is an easy-to-use storehouse of information that has proven to be helpful to thousands of parents of struggling students.

Consider the following scenario: You have just given your fourth weekly vocabulary test and James, who has a learning disability, has earned a D on every one of them. On this particular day, your students have been home for about 30 minutes and you are still at school preparing for the next day's lessons when your phone rings. It is James's mom and, among other things, she wants to know what she can do to help him prepare for the next vocabulary test. You schedule a conference when she can come in with James to review his note-taking and test preparation techniques, but it is two weeks away due to her work schedule.

Rather than leave her feeling helpless for two weeks, you refer her to the LD OnLine website. Once there, she will discover a section entitled "LD in Depth," which has links to pages on "Study Skills" and "Homework Help," both of which would help James's mother to immediately know how to assist him to prepare for his next test. For example, the section on Study Skills contains a link to commonly asked questions and answers about how students with learning disabilities can improve their memory, and there is a list of recommended books and copies of articles that can be directly accessed. For a parent who does not have access to a computer, it would be very easy for you to print out this information to send home. This action by the teacher does not replace the parent-teacher interactions that occur during conferences, but recommending websites and other resources is an effective way to empower parents to help their children when they cannot work directly with the teacher.

themes. Students in middle and high school express themselves in writing (through theme writing, journal writing, and preparation of written reports and research papers requiring extensive use of references) and orally (through the presentation of themes, reports, and research papers).

It is helpful for students to have a time line to follow in the development of a paper or report. Some teachers ask for a topic, outline, and first draft by specific dates. These deadlines may be planned cooperatively with students, thus involving them in setting their own goals. You may want to instruct your students in how to do the following:

1. ***Choose a topic.*** When possible, topic choices should reflect student interests. For example, Mr. Bruno wanted his elementary students to write a report in his science class. He gave his students several choices of topics (e.g., the greenhouse effect, environmental pollution, depletion of resources, waste disposal) to motivate them to do the research and prepare the report. With choices, students had more involvement in the assignment from the start.

2. ***Use reference materials in the media center*** (e.g., Reader's Guide, encyclopedia, fiction and nonfiction, and technology resources—World Wide Web, CD-ROMs, software, etc.). It may be necessary to demonstrate for students how to locate reference materials and use them effectively. Some teachers take their classes to the media center during class time to review how to use the library catalog and conduct a search on the Internet, and to introduce the students to current websites that may be helpful to their research. Ms. Taylor took her 10th-grade students to the media center to give them guided practice in using reference materials and technology resources. She showed them how to make a card or create a file online for each reference they used. This helped them later as they put together their bibliographies.

3. ***Prepare an outline (for organization and prioritization) and submit it for approval.*** Many teachers require their students to submit outlines of their reports prior to the preparation of the actual report. This technique is an excellent way to monitor the progress of your students and to guide them in organizing and expressing themselves. For example, Mr. Tseng helped two of his students sequence the events of the Civil War by changing the order of the items on their outlines.

4. ***Write and submit a thesis statement.*** Your students should begin with a thesis statement and make sure that all of their information contributes to and supports that thesis. Show your students how to write a sample thesis statement such as "Insects have an effect on people and the environment." Then list several facts about insects, and ask your students to decide which statements contribute to the thesis.

- Insects have three body regions: the head, thorax, and abdomen.
- Insects are the largest class of organisms, including three-fourths to five-sixths of all known types of animals.
- Some insects transmit diseases to humans, plants, or animals.
- Some insects feed on crops and stored products.
- The expense in combating insects and the cost in loss or damages is at least $4 billion per year.
- Insects play an important role in soil improvement.

This step helps your students organize their writing so that what they write relates to and supports the thesis statement.

5. ***Prepare a rough draft of the report.*** Many teachers require a rough draft of a report as a monitoring device. They assign points or credit to emphasize its importance in the preparation of a report. Suggestions, adjustments, and corrections can result in an improved final product. For example, out of a possible 300 points, Jeremy received 30 points for his outline, 90 points for his rough draft, 15 points for his bibliography, and 110 points for his final report.

6. ***Prepare a bibliography.*** Your students should include a list of the references and resources they used in completing their reports. This task is made easier when they make a card for each of their references as they find them.

7. ***Develop a final copy of the report.*** By incorporating any changes suggested during the rough draft stage of the report preparation, students have the opportunity to earn the maximum points possible. If students voice reluctance with "doing the report twice," remind them that their work will be more complete and polished and more likely to earn them a better grade when they complete the final copy.

8. ***Proofread all work.*** Some teachers award extra points when students turn in perfect papers because this indicates that they have proofread their work.

9. ***Submit the paper or give the report orally.*** You may require a written paper or an oral report as a final product. Either way, it is helpful for students to follow a well-sequenced, systematic set of procedures. Smith, Boone, and Higgins (1998) suggest that students may want to share their reports with students in other schools, states, or countries by posting it to a school or classroom website. This technique is an excellent way for students to receive feedback about their work from a variety of sources and to disseminate their research and writing to others.

Whether your students are presenting the information orally or in writing, they should follow the preceding steps. You may want to give your students the nine points listed above in the form of a checklist. Let this form serve as a monitoring tool for your students as they complete each stage of the presentation or the report.

Activity 10.7

Practice writing a thesis statement on a topic of your choice. List several facts about the topic including both extraneous and relevant issues. Justify which ones relate to the thesis statement and which ones do not.

PUTTING IT ALL TOGETHER

We have included a wide variety of study skills in this chapter. Now, it is up to you. Schloss, Smith, and Schloss (2001) state that students who have not been taught study skills will not learn them on their own. Therefore, students need to be specifically taught study skills and strategies in listening, note taking, outlining, test taking, report writing, and other areas, so that they can meet the expectations of general education settings (i.e., to acquire, organize, remember, and express information); access and master the general education curriculum; and pass standards-based assessments. We urge you to use the five components of study skills instruction we presented at the beginning of the chapter for every study skill you teach. Remember that study skills should be functional and meaningful; students should believe that study skills are useful and necessary; instruction should be direct, informed, and explanatory; instruction should demonstrate what study skills can be used, how they can be applied, and when and why they are helpful; and instructional materials must be lucid and enjoyable (Paris, 1988). These components represent the keys to the successful implementation of a study skills program, and it is the teacher's role to ensure that they are implemented.

IMPORTANT POINTS

1. Techniques to use before taking a test are to review using a study log, determine specifics about the test, guesstimate about the test, and think positive thoughts.
2. Techniques to use during a test are to sit where it is possible to concentrate, survey the test, complete the test, and review the test.
3. A suggestion to use after taking a test is to analyze test-taking performance, including strengths and weaknesses.
4. The steps for developing an oral or written report are to choose a topic, use reference materials, prepare an outline, write a thesis statement, prepare a rough draft, prepare a bibliography, develop a final copy, proofread all work, and submit or give the report.

DISCUSSION QUESTIONS

1. Justify the inclusion of study skills instruction in an already overcrowded curriculum.
2. Describe what you would include in a study skills program in elementary, middle, and high school. Think back to Jasmine in the chapter opening scenario and consider what you would include for her.
3. Why do you think some students leave high school without a repertoire of study skills to enhance their success in postsecondary education? What can be done about it?

Websites: Useful websites related to chapter content can be found in Appendix A.

PART

3

Factors Affecting Instruction

CHAPTER

11

Technology for Teaching and Learning

Colleen Klein-Ezell
Dan Ezell

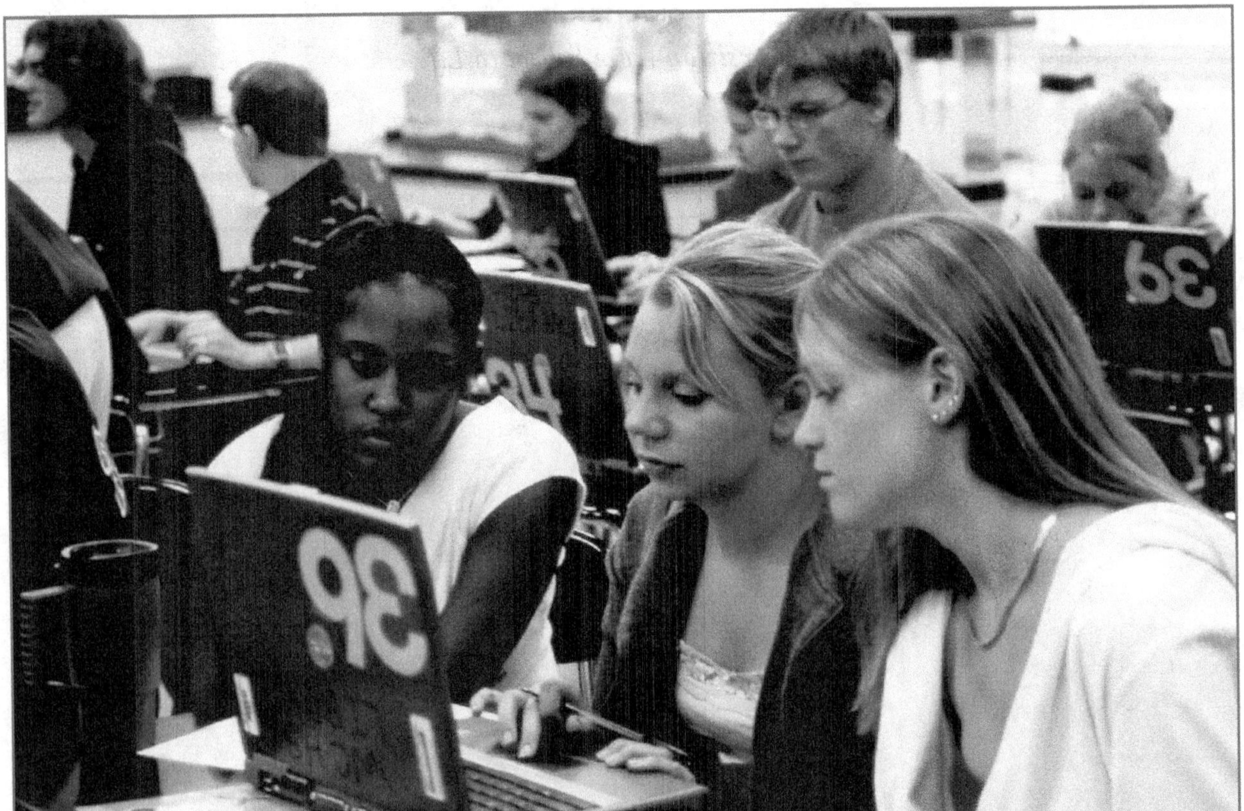

KEY TOPICS

"I have one more question for you Ms. Howard. Like many other schools in this area we only have enough funds for two computers per classroom. If I hire you as our new fourth- and fifth-grade special education teacher, how will you utilize technology in your classroom?"

"Well, first of all, Dr. Wentworth, when I think of using technology in my role as a teacher, I would begin by studying my students' IEPs to see what kinds of accommodations are listed that might require technology to meet goals and objectives. For example, if I have students with an audio-processing disorder, they will need some sort of FM system. I may have other students with extreme handwriting or spelling concerns who would benefit from an AlphaSmart for writing activities, or I could have students who need me to write on a whiteboard rather than a blackboard. I would become aware of these kinds of needs and locate the resources through our county office."

"Of course," Ms. Howard continued, "the two computers you mentioned could be effectively used by one or two students at a time for instructional activities. With their parents' permission, I could have students using the Internet to conduct a webquest, do research for a report they are writing, or download podcasts on topics they want to know more about.

"If the school has a video camera," she continued, "My students could even create their own podcasts. Using that camcorder to pre-record oral book reports and other presentations is a teaching strategy that is very effective in an inclusive classroom. It gives all students a choice of how they will present, and levels the playing field for students with disabilities."

"I don't have much experience with podcasts", replied the principal. "Another principal I know was telling me that she uses them as a sort of video newsletter for the parents at her school."

"That would be easy to do, Dr. Wentworth", said Ms. Howard. "If you hire me, I'll be happy to help you get started with that project."

"Well I guess I do have just one more question for you, Ms. Howard. Can you start next week?"

Ms. Howard had some good ideas about how to use technology to meet the needs of her students. One thing she did not mention though was how she could use technology to make her job easier. Brainstorm several ways to use technology to assist in the administration of your job as a teacher.

INTRODUCTION

The use of technology is widespread in classrooms at all levels—as a tool for teachers to develop, monitor, and provide instruction and as a tool for students to access and engage in learning. Today technologies play a critical role in the education of all students, including students with disabilities. Technology can offer students with disabilities alternative ways to showcase their capabilities and can provide teachers with tools to enhance their instruction and support student learning (Lewis, 2000). Unmotivated students suddenly become interested in the task of writing a friendly letter when given the option of using a word-processing program and adding graphics. Students whose spelling problems interfered with their writing skills are suddenly turning in papers free of spelling errors. New technology guides students through the writing process and assists with choosing words, correcting their spelling and grammar, and even lets them hear what they wrote.

The purpose of this chapter is to focus on technology as a tool for students and teachers. We first examine the legislation that promoted the use of technology. We next discuss technology tools as powerful enablers that help students access curriculum, engage in learning, meet required outcomes, and transition to the workplace. Then, we discuss technology tools as an integral part of the curriculum to support effective instructional interventions. Finally, we describe assistive technology tools that make a positive impact on the lives of children and adolescents.

We include computers, DVDs, and the Internet, plus assistive technology devices in our discussion of technology applications. Technology has tremendous potential for enhancing the capabilities of individuals with disabilities (Zhang, 2000). Technology can be used as a support for completing assignments or learning new information and can be used to help students access the general education curriculum and enjoy full inclusion and benefit from an education (Alper & Raharinirina, 2006).

A caveat in writing any chapter on technology is the impossibility of presenting current information, because technology is always changing. Two months later, that powerful computer is no longer so powerful, as another computer is on the market with more RAM (random access memory) and faster processor speeds (megahertz). The Internet site that last month provided you with valuable lesson plans and information has disappeared. Please remember this caveat as you read this chapter and continue to stay current by reading professional journals, participating in professional organizations, visiting new websites, and taking technology classes.

TECHNOLOGY LEGISLATION

Legislation was instrumental in promoting the use of technology tools for children and adolescents with disabilities. PL 99–457, Part G of the Education for All Handicapped Children Act of 1986, authorized the Technology, Educational Media, and Materials Program for Individuals with Disabilities to research and develop technology tools for students with disabilities (Hauser & Malouf, 1996). PL 100–407, the Technology-Related Assistance for Individuals with Disabilities Act (Tech Act) of 1988, was designed to enhance the availability and quality of assistive technology (AT) devices and services to all individuals and their families throughout the United States (Behrmann, 1995). The Assistive Technology Act of 1998 (AT Act), PL 105–394 (S.2432), replaced the Tech Act and created discretionary activities for states to fund, such as alternative financing systems to increase access to assistive technology. In addition, provisions of the AT Act included promoting public awareness; providing technical assistance, training, and outreach; and promoting interagency collaboration.

The No Child Left Behind Act (2001), which revised the Elementary and Secondary Education Act of 1965, provides incentives to use technology in the education of students and their teachers. The Individuals with Disabilities Education Improvement Act (IDEA, 2004) provides an emphasis on the accessibility of the general education curriculum for students with disabilities and updates the mandates of IDEA 1990 and 1997.

The Technology Education and Copyright Harmonization Act of 2002 (TEACH Act) allows teachers and faculty to use copyrighted materials in the "digital classroom" without prior permission from the copyright holder as long as certain measures are met. Additional information about the inclusions and exclusions of the TEACH Act may be found at http://www.ala.org/washoff/teach.html. See Table 11.1 for a summary of legislation affecting assistive technology.

Table 11.1 Federal Legislation that Applies to Assistive Technology

Legislation	Date	Basic Content Related to Assistive Technology (AT)
Rehabilitation Act 93–112	1973	Reasonable accommodations and LRE mandated in federally funded employment and higher education—AT devices and services required
Vocational Rehabilitation Act, Section 504	1973	AT can be used as an accommodation to allow individuals with disabilities who are not in special education programs to take part in activities
Education for All Handicapped Children Act (EHA) 94–142	1975	Reasonable accommodations and LRE are extended to all school age children, IEP mandated, AT plays a major role in gaining access to educational programs
Preschool and Infant/Toddler Program (amendments to EHA)	1986	Reasonable accommodations and LRE are extended to children ages 3–5, expands emphasis on educationally related assistive technologies
Technology-Related Assistance for Individuals with Disabilities Act (Tech Act) 100–407	1988	First federal legislation directly related to assistive technology, stresses consumer-driven services and systems change, Section 508 extended to all states
Reauthorization of the Rehabilitation Act	1990	Formally adopted the same definitions and terminology as IDEA, also mandated that rehabilitation technology be seen as "a primary benefit" to be included in the IWRP

(*continued*)

Table 11.1 (continued)

Legislation	Date	Basic Content Related to Assistive Technology (AT)
Americans with Disabilities Act (ADA) 101–336	1990	Provisions including assistive technology are recognized in the areas of public accommodations, private employment, transportation, and telecommunications—extends 503, 504, and 508 to all citizens
Individuals with Disabilities Education Act (IDEA) 101–496	1990	Specifically defined assistive technology devices and services as well as carefully delineating how they apply to education
Reauthorization of the Individuals with Disabilities Education Act (IDEA) 105–17	1997	Assistive technology needs must be considered during the discussions involving a student's IEP—an indication during these discussions that AT might be needed leads to an evaluation of needs
Assistive Technology Act of 1998 PL 105–394	1998	Extended funding of the 1988 Tech Act to assist states in enhancing AT awareness, technical assistance, and interagency collaboration
No Child Left Behind Act PL 107–110	2001	Revised the 1965 Elementary and Secondary Education Act (ESEA) providing incentives to use technology in the education of students and their teachers
Individuals with Disabilities Education Improvement Act (IDEIA) PL 108–446	2004	Emphasized the potential of AT to assist students with disabilities in accessing the general education curriculum

Source: Adapted from Judith P. Sweeney (2006) http://www.onionmountaintech.com/files/AT%Laws%20Table%202006.pdf Reprinted by permission.

TECHNOLOGY AS A WAY FOR STUDENTS TO ACCESS THE CURRICULUM

Throughout this textbook, we have discussed how students with disabilities can access the general education curriculum. Technology plays a vital role in assisting students with disabilities to gain access to the general education curriculum. Inclusion is a reality and teachers have more demands placed upon their time and expertise in making the curriculum meaningful and accessible to all students (Harden & Rosenberg, 2001).

The myriad functions and potentials of technology in the realm of student instruction is endless. In an adaptation of Means' (1997) classification scheme for technologies, we suggest the broad categories of traditional, exploratory, tool, and communication applications. Although these categories are not mutually exclusive, they highlight the differences in instructional applications.

TRADITIONAL APPLICATIONS

Tutorial, drill and practice, simulation, and problem solving are examples of traditional applications of software. This use of software represents the traditional view of learning where information is transmitted to the student.

Tutorial Programs

Tutorials are designed to teach new concepts and skills. They may be simple to very complex in design. They may be linear, with all students completing the same program, although the pace may be different for each student. More complex programs may offer multiple branching opportunities, with different responses taking students to different parts of the program for review, remediation, or advanced information. Good interactive tutorials can provide students with disabilities the kind of individual instruction that matches learner needs to a specific concept or skill.

Drill-and-Practice Programs

Drill-and-practice programs give students opportunities to practice skills and concepts. Good drill-and-practice programs offer corrections, hints for improvement, and even simple reteaching. They provide immediate feedback and do not allow students to make the same mistakes over and over again. When well designed and used as an integral part of the curriculum, drill-and-practice programs can help students with disabilities gain fluency in required skills. When poorly designed and used without instructional planning, drill-and-practice programs can be an inappropriate use of a powerful computer and a student's academic time.

Simulation Programs

Simulation programs offer students opportunities to see the consequence of their choices. These programs model reality and allow students to use their skills to make decisions and solve problems in a safe learning environment. Well-designed simulation programs provide some of the authentic experiences students need to succeed outside school (e.g., vocational, educational, and transitional). They may provide opportunities for instruction in settings that may not generally be available in schools.

Problem-Solving Programs

Problem-solving programs generally give students practice in identifying a problem, finding alternative solutions, selecting appropriate strategies, and evaluating results of the decisions made. Students may need to collect information, take notes, discover patterns, make generalizations, chart data, apply strategies, use inductive or deductive reasoning, or create a product. Some of these programs encourage students to work together in pairs or teams. Problem-solving software can offer students with disabilities the opportunity to develop and apply the higher-order thinking skills that are required for success in school and in the world of work. Although it is critical that students have the prerequisite skills for using the program, teachers need to remember that students with disabilities may be capable of solving more complex problems than their mastery of basic skills indicates.

EXPLORATORY APPLICATIONS

Exploratory application software allows the student to navigate through a program and select information for learning. Examples are electronic encyclopedias, atlases, and multimedia databases of animals, plants, people, places, and things. Today, the ability to access and manage information is a required skill for success in school and in the world of work.

TOOL APPLICATIONS

These programs include the familiar applications like the word processor, database, and spreadsheet. Here, the technology facilitates the performance of such tasks as writing, organizing, and presenting information. All students and teachers need tools. Students with disabilities may need special tools or need to use common tools in a special way. Technology tools provide access to the curriculum, offer alternative experiences for learning, allow students to demonstrate performance, and provide alternative options for assessment.

COMMUNICATION APPLICATIONS

These applications allow students to send and receive information from anywhere in the world. They include interactive distance learning, e-mail, and electronic field trips. As wider access to the Internet is available across classrooms and families, students with disabilities are getting the opportunity to participate in the technologies that can minimize differences.

> **Activity 11.1**
> Describe when you might use a more traditional application versus an exploratory application with students. Share your ideas with a partner.
>
> (Answers for this and other activities are found in the Instructor's Manual.)

TECHNOLOGY AS A TOOL FOR STUDENTS

Technology advancements such as the widespread availability of digital materials and rapid computer networks coupled with Universal Design principles are making the general education curriculum more accessible to students with special needs. The Center for Applied Special Technology (CAST) and the National Center to Improve the Tools of Educators (NCITE) at the University of Oregon have pioneered the application of the principle of Universal Design for Learning. The premise of Universal Design for Learning (UDL) is that instructional materials can be designed so that learning goals may be achieved by individuals, no matter their disability, cultural background, or experiential background. CAST indicates that UDL calls for multiple ways learners can acquire information and knowledge, demonstrate what they know, and various means of engaging them in their learning (CAST Inc., 2006). Through the use of technology, these outcomes can be realized.

With technology, accommodations such as reading the text to students, highlighting important words or phrases, controlling the speed of presentation, changing print size, presenting advance and post organizers, and allowing students to record compositions are features that can be built into a text, instead of added as an after-thought. With these accommodations, students with disabilities may interact successfully with the general education curriculum and are no longer stigmatized because they are using different texts or materials than their peers without disabilities.

Two software programs that use the principles of Universal Design are Wiggleworks (Scholastic) and the ULTimate Reader (Universal Learning Technology). With Wiggleworks, an early literacy software program, the text may be enlarged, read aloud, and highlighted, and students may express themselves by typing, drawing, recording, and other ways. With the ULTimate Reader software, any text may be digitized and loaded into the program. Created by CAST, the program provides many accommodations such as adding spoken voice and visual highlights to the electronic text. With the text in digital form, students may accomplish the traditional task of answering questions at the end of the chapter by dragging and dropping whole paragraphs for use in the answer, allowing more time for instruction in higher-order thinking skills. To learn more about UDL, visit the Center for Applied Special Technology (CAST) (http://www.cast.org) or ERIC/OSEP Special Project for the ERIC Clearinghouse on Disabilities and Gifted Education (ERIC EC) for a topical brief on Universal Design principles (http://ericec.org/osep/recon5/rc5cov.html).

Technology may assist students with mild disabilities in organization, note taking, the writing process, productivity, accessibility to reference materials, and cognitive assistance (Lahm & Morrisette, 1994). Each of these areas has a wide range of technology available, from no-tech and low-tech tools to more sophisticated tools that may require the use of a computer.

ORGANIZATION

No-tech (nonelectronic) solutions for improving your students' organizational skills include teaching organizational strategies such as flowcharting, task analysis, webbing, and outlining. These organizational strategies could also entail the use of high-tech items such as specialized graphic, software-based organizers. By using software-based organizers, students may make changes to the generated items more easily with the use of the computer as noted at the end of this section. Your students may also benefit from low-tech electronic organizers that are commonly available in office supply and major discount stores. These small portable planners, referred to as personal digital assistants (PDAs), and the more advanced ones that are referred to as handheld computers can help compensate for poor organizational skills, illegible handwriting, and memory deficits. Students can use a variety of inexpensive PDAs and handheld computers to keep track of homework assignments or due dates for projects, write to-do lists, store short notes or spelling words, consult a calendar, or set an alarm as a cue to perform some task such as stopping to check for understanding. The website http://www.k12handhelds.com/gettingstarted.php#software has a link to click on that lists 101 educational uses for the handheld computer and has case studies of how teachers are using them in the classroom.

Activity 11.2
Go to the website http://www.k12handhelds.com/gettingstarted.php#software and list five education uses for the handheld computer.

High-tech organization tools enable your students to organize and communicate their thoughts with story webs, character charts, tree diagrams, time lines, and other graphic organizers. Two examples of high-tech organization tools are the software programs of Kidspiration (for K–5 students by Inspiration), Inspiration (for 6–12 students by Inspiration), and TimeLiner (for K–12 by Tom Snyder Productions). Kidspiration and Inspiration allow students to create a picture of ideas or concepts in a diagram (see Figure 11.1). Using TimeLiner, students can print out a visual display of critical dates on a time line.

One of our student teachers assigned students to organize their personal histories or life maps using TimeLiner and then to relate their own time lines to events in American history.

NOTE TAKING

Note taking is a skill that is beneficial to all of us to help us remember. Note taking can assist students in understanding lecture information and provide reference material for studying purposes (Boyle, 2001). Taking notes is a way to actively engage students in their learning and enhance their long-term memory. A no-tech approach to note taking for your students is to provide detailed outlines of the instructional materials in which they can add information as needed. Other means of note taking could include such low- and high-tech methods as videotaping class sessions for playback or streaming at a later time, translating print-based notes to voice by using software programs such as ULTimate Reader (Universal Learning Technology), using laptop computers,

Figure 11.1 SAMPLE GRAPHIC ORGANIZERS FROM INSPIRATION SOFTWARE

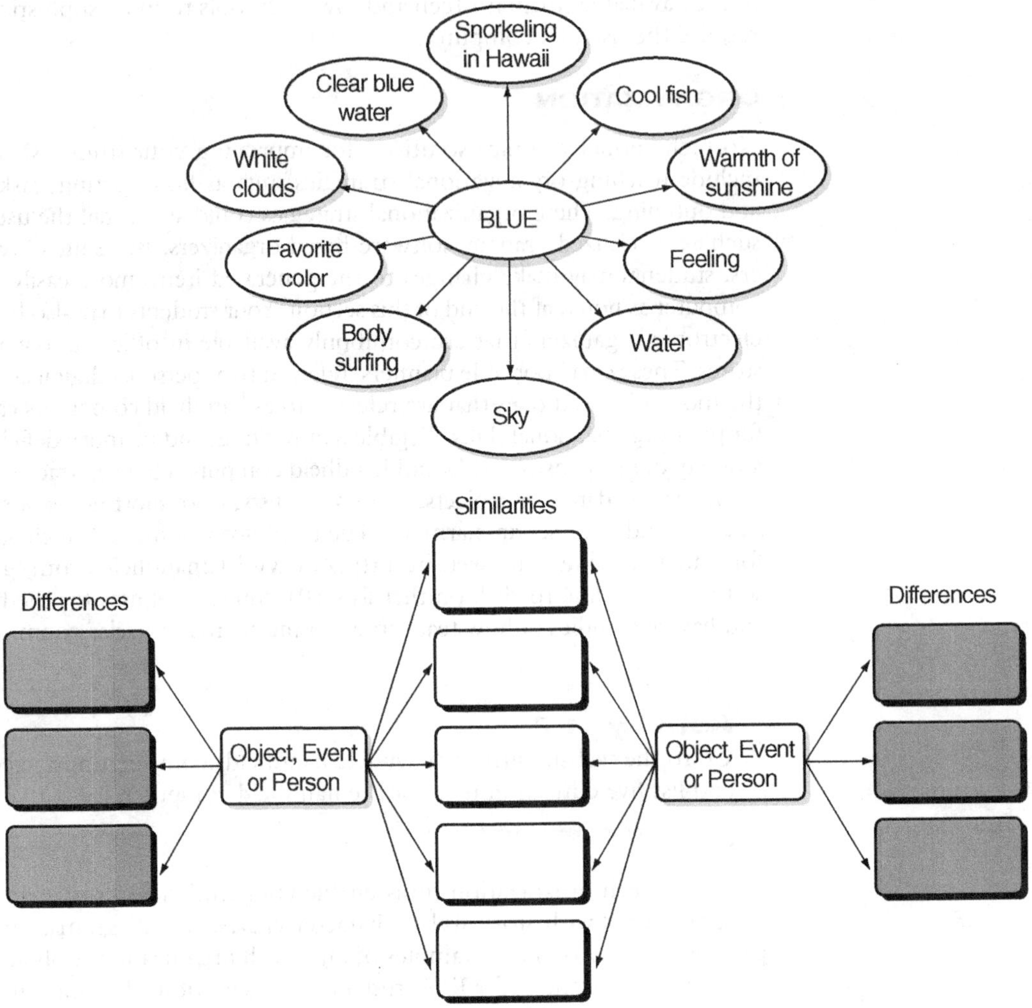

Source: From Inspiration Software, 7412 SW Beaverton, Hillsdale Hwy., Suite 102, Portland, OR 97225. Reprinted by permission.

PDAs, or portable word-processing keyboards to help students with the note-taking process. An additional option would be to use voice recognition software to automatically create notes as the student or teacher talks or lectures.

THE WRITING PROCESS

Word processing may be the most important application of technology for students with disabilities. Students having difficulty in the writing process may encounter barriers including the mechanics of writing (spelling, grammar, and punctuation), the process of writing, and/or motivation. DVDs, computers, digital cameras, and the Internet are invaluable tools to assist students with disabilities in the steps of the writing process: prewriting, writing, editing and revising, and publishing as well as increase their interest or motivation in writing.

In the **prewriting** stage, instead of reading resource books or magazines, students may collect information by clicking on a link to a website, viewing a video, using pictures from digital cameras, or inserting a DVD. For example, in Ms. Zelk's class, students used digital pictures they had taken during a field trip to assist in constructing a story.

In the **writing** stage, instead of paper and pencil, students may use word processing, word predictions, abbreviation expansion programs, or voice recognition software (e.g., Dragon Naturally Speaking). Even young children can begin to use word processors such as ClarisWorks for Kids (Apple Computer, Inc.), Word (Microsoft), and Kid Works 2 (Knowledge Adventure). Using the "Write" command of Wiggleworks software (Scholastic), students may type, record, or place words from a word list into their composition to assist in the writing stage.

Word prediction and abbreviation expansion help students with disabilities compose text and overcome problems with word recall, spelling, and keyboarding. For example, in word prediction, students enter the beginning letters of a desired word. The program produces a list of predicted words that begin with that letter. For example, if the student enters "th," a predicted list might look like:

1. them	4. think
2. then	5. thing
3. their	6. this

When students see or hear the word that they want from the list, they enter the corresponding number, and the word is added to their text. If the word is not on the list, students keep typing the next letter until the word appears.

In programs with abbreviation expansion, a long word or phrase can be coded using a few consonants. When the word or phrase is needed, students type the code, and the full word or phrase is entered into the text. For example, if Jim is writing a story about Tyrannosaurus rex and doesn't want to type out the word each time, he can type in a code such as TYR, and the full name (Tyrannosaurus rex) will appear in the body of the text. Co:Writer (Don Johnston, Inc.), TypeIt4Me by Riccardo Ettore (Shareware), E Z Keys (Words +, Inc.), and Telepathic II (Madenta Communication, Inc.) are word prediction programs that allow for abbreviation expansion and may be used in conjunction with any word processors.

Students who are struggling with reading or writing may use "talking" word processors during the writing stage. Such programs as Write: Out Loud (Don Johnston, Inc.), Intellitalk II (Intelli-Tools), and Kid Works Deluxe (Knowledge Adventure) help students make critical connections among saying, writing, and reading words. Students of all ages can enter their own words into the program, hear the computer say them, and print them out to be read. Free programs such as Readplease.com or the TextEdit on Mac computers can also read text aloud.

A technology solution that may help some students overcome difficulties related to the physical process of writing is the portable keyboard. It is a low-cost and lightweight alternative to a computer. Students may type on the portable keyboard conveniently at their desks without laboriously having to go through the process of physically writing letters and words. Several models are available, including the AlphaSmart, DreamWriter, Laser PC6, the QuickPad, and The Writer. The student turns the keyboard on, does some typing, and turns it off. The system saves several files, which allows for students to share the keyboard. The files will load into any computer word-processing file by attaching a cable from the portable word processor to the computer. The student can then use spell check and other features of the word-processing software. The Writer has a feature to teach keyboarding skills as well as word prediction software. Word prediction software predicts the next potential word and students just pick a number for the word instead of typing an entire word, saving keystrokes and assisting with spelling issues.

AlphaSmart has launched a new affordable laptop alternative called the Dana. The Dana features Palm OS operating system and includes a full-size keyboard and screen. Just like a PDA you can enter data by writing with the Dana stylus directly on the screen, or, like the AlphaSmart, you can use the keyboard. All Palm applications are compatible, and the Dana is expandable to add memory and devices. The Dana can print to your printer and easily synchronizes data with a computer just like a PDA. The writing stylus feature will be most beneficial to students who have difficulty using traditional keyboards. In addition, AlphaSmart produces the Neo, which was especially designed for school use, has a full-sized keyboard and a large LCD screen. The Neo has adaptive key features, flexible keyboard layouts, and larger font sizes.

The orbiTouch Keyless Keyboard (Keybowl, Inc.) allows you to type and use the mouse without having to move your hands off the keyboard. This innovative keyboard eliminates the fine-motor skills required for traditional types of keyboards. The orbiTouch uses two ergonomically sculpted domes for typing and mouse functions, which only require using gentle sliding motions once the hands are placed on the domes.

Once students have entered text they move to the **revision** and **editing** stages. During these stages Smith, Boone, and Higgins (1998) suggest that students paste their word-processed story into a Web publishing program called Home Page (Claris Corporation). Next, they select graphics and create a hypertext link to other websites. They also e-mail their draft to other students or to experts for help in the revision process. Smith and colleagues (1998) relate how Billy, at this stage, selects the word *skull* from his story and links the word to a website that has a picture of a dinosaur's head. When the teacher and his peers read Billy's story, they may click on the underlined word *skull* and see the close-up picture of the head of the dinosaur from another website. Spelling and grammar check programs are also invaluable at this step. The **publishing** stage provides for an exciting use of technology. Smith and colleagues (1998) suggest that students now establish a website address, or URL, and register the story for international access.

A publishing alternative is to use software programs that create a multimedia presentation such as HyperStudio (Knowledge Adventure), PowerPoint (Microsoft), and LinkWay Live! (IBM). Students may use these programs to build interactive presentations that combine text, graphics, sound, animation, and movie clips to present ideas and information. Students create a stack of screens or slides that are interrelated and cross-referenced by hot spots or buttons on each card (Ray & Warden, 1995). Students may easily program buttons to perform functions such as move to another card, play a sound, play a QuickTime movie, play a DVD, start an animation, keep a running test score, or direct an Internet browser to open a specific home page or site on the Internet. For example, Sherry published her story about plant-eating dinosaurs using HyperStudio. On her first card, she located a button on her dinosaur picture. A click on the button took the reader to a QuickTime movie of a dinosaur eating plants.

Many other software programs are available that make the writing process motivational. EasyBook Deluxe (Sunburst) allows students to make double-sided books by writing and illustrating each page. Clicker 5 (Crick Software) can be used from preschool through adulthood for writing, reading, communicating, and making multimedia presentations and is adaptable for use with students who have physical and/or sensory disabilities. Hollywood High (Theatrix) lets adolescent students write a script with 10 characters and 20 places designed to reflect typical high school hangouts, including a mall, the arcade, or the beach.

Customizing features of various multimedia publishing software programs often increase students' motivation to write. Graphic images, video, and audio can provide interest or highlight specific aspects of the students' written work and motivate students to generate new ideas and stories. Due to the versatility of the various software programs, even younger writers can publish by utilizing pictures or symbols as well as text.

> **Activity 11.3**
> Your school just received a substantial technology grant to enhance students' writing performance skills. You have been given the opportunity to order $20,000 worth of technology and software for your classroom of 18 students. Identify what you would purchase and justify how it will be incorporated in your writing instruction. Develop a student writing activity utilizing some of the purchased items.

PRODUCTIVITY TOOLS

Students with disabilities need to use productivity tools to become independent lifelong learners. An ever-increasing number of productivity tools is available to enable your students to work effectively in all subject areas ranging from hardware-based, software-based, or both. They may be handheld devices like the Bookman Speaking Merriam Webster Dictionary and Thesaurus from Franklin Learning. Students type in a word, such as *enuf,* and see the word, *enough,* on the screen and hear the word pronounced. Students can also store the word in a customized list to practice for a spelling test. Optional headphones eliminate classroom noise and provide privacy. Another productivity tool is The Visual Thesaurus software (Thinkmap), which creates an animated display of words and meanings. A free online web dictionary and thesaurus can be found at http://www.voycabulary.com, which can transform words on any web page into links to definitions and word lookups in the *Webster Dictionary.*

Other handheld devices include calculators or spreadsheet programs. Simple calculators perform rote tasks while students use higher-order thinking skills to solve real math problems. Graphing calculators may help students who are visual learners "see" abstract algebraic concepts. Talking calculators may assist students who transpose digits to verify the sequence of their numbers.

For students with special needs, "an electronic spreadsheet helps students organize their math problems and print them out so they can be read. Since computers do most of the calculations, students can only get the correct answer by understanding how to set up the problem, a key thinking and problem-solving skill" (Male, 1988, p. 68). The Cruncher (Davidson & Associates) is a full-featured, easy-to-use spreadsheet for young children through adults. It includes tutorials to introduce students to spreadsheet functions and enables students to add sound effects and animation to their work in addition to reading text and numbers out loud. Students can use mental math to verify that the formulas and spreadsheets are accurate.

There are many opportunities to learn to work with spreadsheets in any classroom. Using a spreadsheet, a student can keep track of expenses for a field trip or project. The student can estimate expenses item by item, calculate the actual total, and compare the differences. A unit on weather yields many statistics that can be stored, sorted, calculated, and analyzed. Hypotheses can be tested. Which month has the hottest average temperature in Arizona? Is it the same month as it is in Alaska? Are warm months windier than cool months?

Many students who have poor math skills have excellent abilities to recall and interpret sports statistics. Spreadsheets may be used to record statistics from the daily paper, make comparisons, and predict outcomes. Who will have the best batting average? Which team had the most touchdowns at the end of the season? Students can also use spreadsheets to manage their allowances and prepare personal budgets or keep statistics during simulations.

REFERENCE MATERIAL TOOLS

Access to the general education curriculum is emphasized by IDEA (2004) and entails not only the ability to obtain materials but to also understand and use them. As we discussed in the prewriting stage of the writing process, technology has given students other ways to gain information in addition to the library book. The explosion of CD-ROM technologies has made electronic access to encyclopedias, atlases, dictionaries, and other reference materials a common occurrence in school media centers and classrooms. Most of the electronic encyclopedias provide basic information on a wide range of topics. They may contain a speech output option where the program will read selected passages to students. Most offer Internet links to websites for additional information.

To select effective reference materials, you should check such features as the reading comprehension level of the material; the ease of searching for information; the ability to cut and paste pictures and text into a word processor; and the use of video, sound, animation, charts, and illustrations to bring content alive. If your students cannot access the reference material because they cannot read the passages (and the program will not read it to them), you can use a tool such as the ULTimate Reader (Universal Learning Technology). Remember, this program allows students to import the text from CD-ROMs or other files and have the text read to them. Other tools such as Write: OutLoud (Don Johnston, Inc.) or readplease.com can also be beneficial.

COGNITIVE ASSISTANCE TOOLS

Many technology tools are available to help students develop and improve cognitive and problem-solving skills. Well-designed, multimedia systems support students in learning both basic and more complex literacy skills. Videotape technology has also been effective in assisting students in the self-monitoring of their behavior (Sturmey, 2003; Wert & Neisworth, 2003).

Through multimedia presentations students see the text and hear it read aloud. Simultaneous presentation of written words and sounds assists students in building decoding skills. An example of this technology is the interactive book. With an interactive book, students can follow the highlighted text as the passage is read. Then they can click on individual words to hear them pronounced. They can also explore the engaging

BOX 11.1

Reflections on Practice

The Peabody Learning Lab, a multimedia software program developed for middle school students from disadvantaged backgrounds who have reading and spelling problems, enlists a virtual peer tutor to take students through a series of skill-development activities in reading, spelling, and writing. First, the students watch a segment of a video, which gives them some background for their upcoming reading. After students view the video, they may either read a related text passage, with the peer tutor helping them with individual words, or they may ask the peer tutor to read the passage slowly (word by word) or fluently (sentence by sentence) to them. The Orange County Literacy Program in Florida used the Peabody Learning Labs for five years with approximately 10,000 students. Since its inception, students' gains averaged 1–2 years growth in their reading grade level each year (Taylor, 2001).

hot spots on each page. For example, in *Just Grandma and Me* by Mercer Mayer (Broderbund), the student can click on the cow to see and hear it moo.

One of the suggestions Sturmey (2003) makes for the use of videotapes with students with a variety of disabilities is to use them as a means to provide positive behavior support and models of appropriate language behavior. Wert and Neisworth (2003) also advocate using video feedback for self-monitoring techniques.

Activity 11.4

Describe how the following technology tools can be used to assist students with disabilities. The first one is completed for you.

1. A word prediction program (This program is used for students with spelling problems because they can enter the beginning letters of the word that they do not know how to spell and then the program will produce a list of possibilities.)
2. Dana
3. A multimedia presentation such as Hyperstudio and EasyBook Deluxe
4. An electronic spreadsheet
5. The ULTimate Reader

IMPORTANT POINTS

1. Legislation such as PL 99–457 and PL 100–407 have been instrumental in promoting the use of technology tools for children and adolescents with disabilities.
2. An adaptation of Means' classification scheme includes the broad categories of traditional, exploratory, tool, and communication technology applications.
3. The premise of Universal Design for Learning (UDL) is that instructional materials can be designed so that learning goals may be achieved by individuals, no matter their disability, cultural background, or experiential background.
4. Authentic uses of technology provide students with experiences that include features such as (a) supporting the use of technology for tasks that are similar to tasks performed by workers in nonschool settings, (b) integrating technology into activities that are a core part of the classroom curriculum, and (c) treating technology as a tool to accomplish a complex task.
5. Videotapes, DVDs, and other multimedia systems support students in learning both basic and more complex literacy skills.

SOFTWARE SELECTION

Selecting software for the instruction of students with disabilities is an important task. Thousands of software programs are available for teachers and students to use. Many schools or districts purchase site licenses for software packages for everyone to use. The daunting task is to match the appropriate software to the curriculum and students' needs. Komoski (1995) recommends seven steps to responsible software selection:

Step 1—Analyze Needs: The major question to ask here is whether the computer is the most appropriate medium to meet the instructional goals and objectives or if other strategies are more efficient.

Step 2—Specify Requirements: Questions here involve analyzing learners' characteristics and needs and matching the software to these characteristics and needs. Komoski (1995) also recommends thinking about compatibility of software to current hardware, user friendliness, and access to technical support. For new multimedia programs in which students are developing their own presentations, questions may include: How easy is the program for students to use? Can students incorporate the elements they need to produce an effective presentation? What is the learning time required? Does the program work consistently well so that the students do not have downtime when the program crashes?

Step 3—Identify Promising Software: Sources such as *Closing the Gap* and *Technology and Learning* frequently provide listings of software appropriate to a particular subject area or unit of instruction. The Technology and Media Division of the Council for Exceptional Children also includes information about computer software in its journal. These sources and others frequently present ideas for integrating computers into the curriculum and for using application programs in the classroom.

Another source for finding software is software advertisements. You should carefully examine the advertising claims about the effectiveness or the content of software, as believing all of the claims may lead to disappointment. Remember, software producers are not likely to identify the poor qualities or limitations of the program in an advertisement.

Step 4—Read Relevant Reviews: Software reviews are reports of evaluations by experts. However, even a piece of software that has received a good review may not be appropriate for a particular situation or student. It is important to consider the needs, strengths, and weaknesses of students as well as the expert's viewpoint of the software.

Step 5—Preview Software: Many companies now let you download a demonstration version of their software from their website that you can preview before you decide to purchase it. The most effective way to preview software is to watch students as they interact with the program.

Step 6—Make Recommendations: At this step, Komoski (1995) suggests teachers complete an evaluation form (see Table 11.2 for a sample one) and also keep a record of the optimal uses for the piece of software.

Step 7—Get Post-Use Feedback: Accountability requires a check that the software program is meeting the instructional goals and objectives identified in Step 1 and the needs of the students.

The following are additional criteria to consider when selecting software for students with special needs (Lewis, 1993):

1. ***Flexibility:*** Can the software be used by many students? Can it be used by a single student many times? Does the software offer a large variety of formats and contexts to facilitate the acquisition of new skills and maintain learner attention?

2. ***Student or teacher control of the presentation of the materials:*** Can students work at their own pace? Is the rate of movement through the program, response controlled rather than time controlled? Can the response time be set at a very slow rate appropriate for the students? Can the rate be increased in small increments?

Table 11.2 Software Evaluation Form

Title ______________________ Date ______________
Publisher ______________________
Address ______________________
Subject Area ____ Grade Level
________ Price ________
Directions: Place a check mark under Y if yes, N if no, or NA if not applicable.

	Y	N	NA
Appropriateness:			
• Age	___	___	___
• Interest	___	___	___
• Level	___	___	___
Hardware Considerations:			
• Compatible with computer	___	___	___
• Sufficient memory	___	___	___
• Peripherals required (printer, mouse, etc.)	___	___	___
Documentation:			
• Manual provided	___	___	___
• Additional materials included (worksheets/websites)	___	___	___
• Adaptations suggested	___	___	___
Program			
• Content interesting	___	___	___
• Content accurate	___	___	___
• Information up to date	___	___	___
• Information Free from stereotypes	___	___	___
• Content well-organized	___	___	___
Interaction			
• Active participation required of learner	___	___	___
• Varying levels of difficulty available	___	___	___
• Learner control of presentation rate	___	___	___
• Learner control of exit function	___	___	___
• Feedback provided	___	___	___
• Concepts and skills reinforced	___	___	___
Technical Considerations:			
• User friendly	___	___	___
• Sound optional	___	___	___
• High-quality graphics	___	___	___
Record Keeping:			
• Reporting of scores option	___	___	___
• Capable of printing out scores	___	___	___
• Parent reports	___	___	___

3. ***Number of problems or length of lesson:*** Can you control the number of problems presented so that students are challenged but attention is maintained? Are students able to stop a program and continue it later from the same point?
4. ***Type of feedback:*** Does feedback include an indication of correct responses, incorrect responses, and reasons why a response is incorrect? Does the feedback compare an incorrect response with the correct response? Is feedback intermittent

and varied? Does the program refrain from negative feedback? Are prompts and hints provided?

5. ***Program content:*** Is the software built on clearly specified learning objectives? Is the reading level of information presented in the program carefully controlled and specified in the program manual? Do supplementary materials that provide extensive and varied practice accompany the software? Do the content and the presentation meet the needs of the students? Do they fit the curriculum?
6. ***Screen design:*** Is the screen display simple and uncluttered? Is color used to add interest, motivation, and complement the content? Are relevant stimuli clearly identified and emphasized through flashing, underlining, color, or contrast? Are graphics utilized to provide realistic and concrete illustrations of abstract concepts?

INTERNET

The Internet is a network of computers throughout the world that are connected to each other to share information. On May 4, 2006, comScore Networks (2006) estimated the number of Internet users worldwide over the age of 15 as 694 million people. In this section, we discuss general information, instructional use, professional development, and safeguards of the Internet.

GENERAL INFORMATION

Most schools have access to the Internet either through local area networks (LANs) or an Internet service provider (ISP). Many school districts have a dedicated computer that has been assigned as a gateway ISP to connect to the Internet for their teachers, staff, and students. It is important to note that even in this day and time of vast technology access, many students are still without computer access in their homes (Alper & Raharinirina, 2006). Information on the Internet is basically organized by a website of individual web pages that pertain to a similar subject. Free browsers (software programs such as Netscape Navigator and Microsoft Internet Explorer, Safari, and Foxfire) allow you to move from page to page and site to site.

On the web page, you may see some text that is highlighted in different colors or highlighted and underlined. By clicking your mouse on this highlighted text, you are automatically connected to different pages or sites. All web pages at a site have addresses or URLs (uniform resource locators). For example, if you wish to go to the Council for Exceptional Children (CEC) website, you would type the URL of http://www.cec.sped.org/ in the location box and find information concerning CEC divisions and other special education information. In Table 11.3, we describe some popular websites.

Let's say that you do not have a specific site in mind, but you want to explore a general topic. You can access directories such as Yahoo or Yahooligans (a directory for children ages 8 to 12) or such search engines as AltaVista, Google, or Ask Jeeves to find sites that contain information concerning your topic.

INSTRUCTIONAL USE

Learning on the Internet is occurring on a daily basis in many classrooms across the nation. As advances are made in technology, the selection of information on the Internet steadily increases. Materials may be downloaded from the Net to enhance

Table 11.3 Sample Internet Sites

Site Name	Internet (URL) Address	Description
The Educator's Reference Desk	http://www.eduref.org	Lesson plans for all levels and content, education information, search engine for educational professional literature
ATEN	http://www.aten.scps.k12.fl.us	Resources and links for assistive technology
BCK2SKOL Lessons	http://www.sc.edu/bck2skol/fall/fall.html	Lessons on using the Web and search engines
Busy Teachers' WebSite K–12	http://www.ceismc.gatech.edu/busyt/	Materials, lesson plans, class activities, interactive Web projects for students
Classroom Connect	http://www.classroom.net/	Site for K–12 educators and students
Education World	http://www.educationworld.com/	Lesson plans, templates, professional information
About Learning (4MAT)	http://www.aboutlearning.com/	Information on teaching/learning, lesson exchange
Internet Island—Miami Science Center	http://www.miamisci.org/ii/	Teaches students to use the Internet via a story
Multicultural Pavilion	http://curry.edschool.virginia.edu/go/multicultural/teachers.html	Links to multicultural sites
The Online Books Page	http://onlinebooks.library.upenn.edu/	Source of online books and out of copyright ones

Note: Site addresses may change without notice. If you are unable to find the site, use Web search engines and search by subject area(s).

lessons. For example, one special education intern in a coteaching setting downloaded the production graph from the M & M Corporation. The students then compared their class graph of the various M & M colors to the company's production graph. Wissick and Gardner (1998) recommend the Internet for designing thematic units. They give an example of how the topic of whales quickly leads to various sites, information, and integrated activities. The Educator's Toolkit (http://www.eagle.ca/~matink/) and Thematic Units (http://www.ed.sc.edu/caw/toolboxtheme.html) are two sites that provide a hotlist of sites grouped thematically (Wissick & Gardner, 1998). WebQuests, virtual tours and field trips, and research projects are other ways to incorporate the Internet into classroom instruction.

Created by Dodge and March in 1995, WebQuests is an inquiry-oriented activity in which most or all of the information used by learners is drawn from the Web. WebQuests is designed to use learners' time well, to focus on using information rather than looking for it, and to support learners' thinking at the levels of analysis, synthesis, and evaluation (Dodge, 1995). A visit to the website at http://webquest.org finds a variety of WebQuests in different grade levels and content areas. For example, a click on the content area of Art and Music for Grades K–2 finds eleven WebQuests. A click on one of the eleven WebQuests, Dino Show, results in twelve links for teachers, a suggested lesson sequence, plus more traditional resources. Using these Internet resources, students create their own "DinoShow" museum attraction. Students do Internet research on one of eight dinosaurs and then use that information to create a diorama, an audio tour, and a brochure. Then, the students open their dinosaur room displays to show other students.

Even though typical WebQuests may be used successfully for all students, some accommodations and modifications may be necessary for students with special needs. Vocabulary may need to be modified by hyperlinking (linking to another resource or document for further information). Difficult vocabulary words in the passage can be hyperlinked to their definitions (Hasselbring & Glaser, 2000). This will give the children an easy and quick way to look up words they do not know. More prompts may also be needed to assist students in completing the projects. Additionally, Hines and Hall (2000) recommend the following accommodations for students with special needs: (a) design simple backgrounds with few distractions, (b) use a consistent page layout, (c) create large buttons for easy navigation, and (d) leave plenty of white space to increase readability. If you plan to design your own WebQuests, the website http://webquest.org/questgarden/author/outlines steps for you to follow.

Virtual tours or field trips allow students to visit places they have never before visited without leaving the classroom. Even though virtual tours and field trips are not the same as actual travel experiences, Roblyer and Edwards (2000) suggest that virtual field trips give students a chance to discover new places worldwide and share their experiences with others. Virtual tours and field trips also give students access to places they otherwise could not go, such as to the sun, to the moon, or to a planet. Virtual tours and field trips involve active learning and encourage student interaction and collaboration. Students can take a tour of the White House (http://www.whitehouse.gov/history/whtour/), the mall of Washington, DC (http://ahp.gatech.edu/dc_map.html), the South Pole (http://astro.uchicago.edu/cara/vtour/pole/), or the nine planets (http://seds.lpl.arizona.edu/billa/tnp/).

Teachers can get ideas for lesson plans on virtual field trips such as a tour of Antarctica (http://www.education-world.com/a lesson/lesson042.shtml), download a virtual permission slip (http://www.field-guides.com/PermissionSlip.pdf), or browse through some examples at http://www.sesd.sk.ca/teacherresource/virtualtour/ virtualtours.htm.

Teachers may also develop their own virtual tours or field trips to match their instructional content. Specific websites can be arranged so students can journey from site to site, adding meaning to teachers' lessons. Students can experience the site through virtual pictures or video. Some software allows the user to manipulate pictures of objects in a museum so that they can look at the object from all angles. Even if the students were to visit a museum, they wouldn't be allowed to pick up or touch a valuable artifact. The other way virtual tours are useful is in performing tasks such as dissecting a virtual frog or other scientific experiments that may be too costly or too dangerous to perform in a classroom setting.

Students can also use the Internet to enhance their research skills. Teachers can guide students to specific Internet sites to locate information on particular research questions. Since many students with disabilities have difficulty with organization, software programs such as Research Assistant for Students and Teachers (Visions Technology in Education) can be a valuable tool to assist students in gathering and organizing information and storing it on the computer. Research Assistant for Students and Teachers references the sources in a bibliographical format after the student plugs in the necessary information.

In searching the Internet for information for research purposes, students need to be aware of specific strategies and tools to locate their own websites for their particular research topic. Students should be taught Boolean terminology, which can enhance their search endeavors. Boolean operators such as *and*, *or*, and *not* between key words will provide the students with more efficient searching power. A good website for assistance in understanding how Boolean terminology enhances research searches is http://library.albany.edu/internet/boolean.html.

Through these Internet connections, students and teachers are able to tap into resources previously unavailable. There are online dictionaries, encyclopedias, databases, picture databases, movie clips, sound clips, and chat rooms with subject area experts.

PROFESSIONAL DEVELOPMENT

The Internet enables educators to access current, up-to-date information from professional organizations; listservs and Usenet Newsgroups may provide support and encouragement to teachers. Professional organizations, such as the Council for Exceptional Children (CEC), maintain websites that house a wealth of information concerning professional development opportunities in exceptional education and information on disabilities.

The Internet offers innovative ways to communicate with persons in various settings and places. E-mail, chat rooms, listservs, Usenet Newsgroups, and videoconferencing are used daily to connect professionals with one another. Jonassen, Howland, Moore, and Marra (2003) suggest that these various forms of communication can be used to form relationships that can potentially provide information, support, and unique perspectives on various topics.

Listservs provide forums for discussing topics with people who have similar interests (Jonassen, et al., 2002). People subscribe to a listserv, read messages, and send messages to the listserv. A valuable website for educational listservs is http://www.greece.k12.ny.us/taylor/suny/listservs.htm. Usenet Newsgroups are an electronic bulletin board system that consists of discussion forums on thousands of topics (Morgan, 1997). Using e-mail or videoconferencing, teachers can interact with other professionals in solving everyday problems.

The Internet may also enhance background information for many special educators who may feel at a disadvantage in subject matter knowledge in a coteaching setting. For example, when Mr. Sams, the special education teacher, was coteaching a unit on the American Revolution with Ms. James, the history teacher, he decided to upgrade his subject knowledge by checking the Internet for information on famous generals of the Revolution. A useful website to check out is http://www.specialconnections.ku.edu, which connects teachers to strategies that help students with special needs be successful across the curriculum.

BOX 11.2

Reflections of Practice

Although many schools have enlisted the aid of software that helps create a safer Internet environment, students can still get to sites that are not appropriate. It is important to teach students "Net safety" in the same manner that they are taught drug safety and stranger safety (Bakken & Aloia, 1998; Goldstein, 1998). Some general precautions to teach students are that they should (a) let teachers know if any e-mail message or website information is inappropriate or makes them feel uncomfortable, (b) not believe everything that is on the Internet, (c) not give out personal information, and (d) not agree to meet anyone face-to-face (Bakken & Aloia, 1998; Goldstein, 1998). We want to reiterate the idea of evaluating carefully what you find on the Internet. Anyone can put information on the Internet without having it checked for accuracy, validity, or appropriateness. The American Library Association (2006) has a website that lists several Internet safety links for young people and their parents.

Activity 11.5

Part 1: Find two Internet sites and tell how you might use the information in your class. Share your site with a peer.

Part 2: Using the Internet, download a demonstration version of a talking word processor such as Write: Out Loud from Don Johnston, Inc. Describe the features of the program and its advantages for students who have reading and writing problems.

Part 3: Using the WebQuests website, http://webquest.org, select one of the WebQuests examples and describe at least three accommodations that can be made for students with disabilities.

IMPORTANT POINTS

1. Komoski (1995) identifies the following steps for analyzing software: (1) analyze needs, (2) specify requirements, (3) identify promising software, (4) read relevant reviews, (5) preview software, (6) make recommendations, and (7) get post-use feedback.
2. Several ways in which the Internet can be used to enhance student instruction include WebQuests, virtual tours and field trips, and research projects.
3. Students should be taught Boolean operators such as *and, or,* and *not* between key words for more efficient searching power.
4. Some general precautions to teach students are to let their teachers know if any e-mail message or website information is inappropriate or makes them feel uncomfortable, and to not believe everything that is on the Internet, give out personal information, and agree to meet anyone face-to-face (Bakken & Aloia, 1998; Goldstein, 1998).

TECHNOLOGY AS A TOOL FOR TEACHERS

Technology has become an ever-present tool for teachers and students (Behrmann & Jerome, 2002). As technology becomes more common in the classroom, teachers are looking beyond school boundaries for new and innovative ways to integrate and infuse that technology into the curriculum (Craig, 1997). As previously discussed, online access to the Internet is helping teachers bring boundless resources to the classroom. Technology applications that can be used as a tool or a communication vehicle (word processing, spreadsheet, drawing program, and network) can support any curriculum and can be fully assimilated into a teacher's ongoing core practice (Means et al, 1993). Using technology to meet educational standards can enhance students' skills and understanding. Since technology can be learner-focused and authentic, and encourages critical thinking, it can make instruction motivating to the learner (Krueger & Sutton, 2001).

When instruction incorporates concept-based, integrated curricula and focuses on relevant issues, problems, and ideas, learning acquires a new depth (Erickson, 1995).

When such instruction is paired with telecommunications and technology, students make the connection between academics and the world outside the classroom. This relevancy has a lasting impact on student learning. Teachers need to utilize available assistive technology to assist in achieving skill maintenance and generalization across the curriculum (Alper, Mull, & Soenksen, 2004).

PLANNING

Good planning is critical to successful instruction. Because any word-processing program allows you to enter, edit, format, print, and save text, you can easily produce lesson plans that are professional-looking, easily revised, and available when you need to retrieve them. By using a template, which is like filling in a blank form, you can develop a format that meets your needs and simplifies entering new lessons. Or you may want to develop a simple database of lesson plans. A database will allow you to categorize your plans according to such areas as content, objectives, developmental level, themes, and instructional strategies. Integrated programs such as AppleWorks (Apple Computer, Inc.), Microsoft Works, and Microsoft Word will allow you to pursue either option.

You may prefer to use a graphic organizer, such as Inspiration (see Figure 11.1), which allows you to map or diagram your lesson plans. This is a powerful tool for planning and developing integrated thematic units.

IEP GENERATION

Special education teachers generally spend over 10% of their time completing paperwork (SPeNSE, 2002; Coleman, 2000). Some of that paperwork involves the development of Individualized Education Programs (IEPs). A popular use of technology in classrooms with students who have special needs is developing and producing IEPs. You can use your own word processor or database to enter, store, retrieve, and modify your required form, or you can use an IEP generation program. However, more and more districts and states are developing their own computerized IEPs or customizing commercial products to meet federal, state, and local requirements. Computerized IEPs offer the ability to enter data and edit without retyping. Larger systems may provide access to databases of annual goals and objectives, resources that have been correlated to local curriculum, and assessment data. They also allow generation of a variety of reports.

Some computerized IEP programs are meeting the challenge of producing IEPs that adhere to IDEA mandates and increase the efficiency of the IEP process. Prior to choosing a computerized IEP program, school districts and teachers need to work together to try out the program, seek input from prospective stakeholder groups, and compare the IEPs produced with other programs (Wilson, Michaels, & Margolis, 2005). According to CEC Today (2003), computerized IEP programs have become popular and many major special education advocacy organizations are advocating for their use. It is important to remember that IEPs should be written by teams of people, and computerization should not reduce the individualization of the process (Wilson, Michaels, & Margolis, 2005).

RECORD KEEPING AND CLASSROOM MANAGEMENT

Technology can help you manage your classroom. You can improve your record keeping by using a simple spreadsheet program or a spreadsheet template that is available with some integrated programs for educators, such as Microsoft Excel, AppleWorks, and Microsoft Works. You may be interested in a comprehensive classroom management program that includes grading, seating charts, and lesson plans, such as Gradebook2 from Excelsior Software. Many school districts have adopted systems to manage grades, attendance, and student performance data.

Programs are also available for sampling language and testing readability. Many schools are using programs like the Accelerated Reader (Advantage) to track the books students are reading and to measure comprehension of the material they read. It is important to examine informal or formal assessment programs for their appropriateness to current curriculum goals and instructional practices.

Because the thinking behind how we deliver and measure learning is changing, digital or electronic portfolios for students are becoming more common as tools for assessment in many schools. Digital portfolios incorporate graphics, video, and audio. While developing their own digital portfolios, students are also learning valuable computer skills (Venn, 2007). The Grady Profile: Portfolio Assessment is one electronic portfolio software program that encourages student reflection and provides student feedback. An example of an entry in an electronic portfolio is found in Figure 11.2. Check the website www.aurbach.com for more information and examples.

The PowerPoint program may also be used to create portfolios. You may easily include the literature-based portfolio components within a PowerPoint presentation. Once completed, you can burn the PowerPoint portfolio collection on a CD. Within the PowerPoint presentation you can go to google images and also include pictures, video clips, voice recording of the child, charts, scanned student work samples, and much more just as you can with commercially made electronic portfolio software. We have found that taking a picture of the students' work samples using a digital camera is easier than using a scanner to scan the work sample. In addition, we have found that the difference in quality between scanning and using the digital camera is minimal.

You can also save your PowerPoint presentation using the Autorun CD Project Creator Pro, which will allow the parent/guardian to view the PowerPoint presentation on any computer without having the PowerPoint software or a presentation reader (see the website, www.soniacoleman.com and click on tutorials for more information). Many parents may have the technology skills to go to the Internet and find a free presentation reader to download, but using the Autorun CD Project Creator Pro will eliminate this step. The parent can simply place the CD in the computer and wait 30 seconds and the child's portfolio collection will appear. You can opt to set the presentation to automatically scroll if you do not want the parent to have to click to go to the next slide. Encourage the parents to go to the local library or other community facilities if they do not have a computer at home. We have found that many parents are excited to view their child's work electronically.

In addition, you may use videotaping in the classroom setting. Videotaping may be used to document academic and behavior growth during the year and assist students in assessing their own behaviors and learning. Videotapes may also be used to inform and involve families in monitoring their child's IEP goals and increase their knowledge of daily activities their child encounters in the classroom (Hundt, 2002).

It is extremely important that teachers obtain written permission from the families of their students prior to using videotaping. We would suggest that you develop your own form in addition to the permission form routinely sent to parents at the beginning of the year that is generally housed in the school office. The form should specifically address the purpose and use of the videotaping to prevent any misunderstandings. Students whose families object to videotaping should be excluded from this process.

Figure 11.2 ELECTRONIC PORTFOLIO ENTRY

Einstein's Academy for the Advancement of Science and Violin Middle School Division

Demo-Student, Ann | **Work Sample—Graphic**

Assignment
The student was asked to explain some math problems. The goal of the exercise was to assess the student's ability to verbalize the operations performed.

Draft
X Final
Typical
Atypical
X Printing
Cursive

Legend
− = performance does not meet expectation
√ = performance meets expectation
\+ = performance exceeds expectation

Title: 3/02/94—math problems
Evaluator: Ms. A. Nelson
Skill-Set: Mathematics
Date: 9/25/98

Student	Parent	Teacher	
+		+	Explanation shows math understanding
+		+	Explanation is accurate
+		+	Explanation is thorough

Ann
2) $(5^3+25)+(50+50)=250$
3) $7\cdot 6^3-(42-36)-150=1{,}356$
4) $9\cdot 3-9\div 3+3=27$
5) $6\cdot 3\div 2+2^2=36$

Reflections
My teacher asked me to give an example of my best math work this quarter and write a complete explanation. I picked these problems because they show that I know how to write long problems. I know that you are supposed to do the work inside the parentheses before you follow the signs outside them. Then you do multiplication first before the adding to get the right answer. I know how to use an integer (that's the little number three up in the air by the 5 in problem #2). That means to multiply that number by itself three times. Another word for that is cubed. If that number is a 2, it's called squared. You do this cubing or squaring first before you multiply. So here's the order you should go in if you get a problem like this. First look at stuff in parentheses and get those answers done. If there's an integer do that the very first. Then follow the math directions outside the parentheses. Do times and dividing first, then add or subtract. You'll get the right answer every time!

Miscellaneous Remarks
This is the first semester report for all students at Einstein. We the faculty hope you like our new output format. It is part of our new student profile system.

Notes
3/6/94 Ann shows understanding of the process of grouping and order of operations. She also understands squaring and cubing. I'd like her to learn to use the word "operation." Alice Nelson.

Source: Grady Profile Portfolio Assessment Software (1998). Aurbach & Associates, Inc.; St. Louis, MO. Reprinted by permission.

PRESENTATION TOOLS

You may use a combination of graphics, text, sound, and video to introduce new topics, deliver necessary information, explain examples, demonstrate problems, and review previously covered material. Your computer presentations can be viewed by individual students or small groups or you can project them for larger groups. Many teachers are exploring ways to use presentation tools in collaborative learning activities in the classroom (Rogers, 2002).

PowerPoint software has been predominately used as a presentation tool. Many teacher presentations include real pictures, sound, and colorful graphics that enhance their presentations. We feel teachers should continue this effective instructional method, but should also explore creating Interactive PowerPoint activities that are student directed and provide student choices.

Interactive PowerPoint presentations, intended for use by an individual student or small group of students, allow students to navigate through the lesson by clicking on various hyperlinks. For example, a vocabulary word within the text may be linked to a definition slide or a picture slide with an explanation of the vocabulary word. Content may be further explained or examples added using hyperlinks. Action Buttons that have the forward arrows or backward arrows help students navigate from slide to slide.

The teacher may easily modify the lesson to include the specific learning needs of the student by allowing students to select hyperlinks. Individual students who know the definition will probably not click on the hyperlink. The more sophisticated you become in creating interactive PowerPoint presentations, the more options you will be able to provide your students. You can create learning tracks that will be tailored to the individual level of your students based on the options selected by the students.

You can develop slides that check for understanding. These slides can ask questions using multiple-choice options. If the child answers the question incorrectly, you should link it to a feedback slide that will then be linked to review slides. If the student answers the question correctly, the slide should be linked to a feedback slide that would then be linked to the rest of the new material to be learned. It is important to have several review slides that emphasize the important points. We also suggest that you end interactive PowerPoint activities with a multiple-choice interactive quiz.

In addition, the use of sound, colorful graphics, and real pictures can enhance the overall lesson. Caution: Because the PowerPoint software is designed to advance to the next slide with the click of the mouse, some students may be tempted to repeatedly click the mouse without using the Interactive Action Buttons. As a precautionary measure, the teacher should create dummy slides that would direct the child to click the Action Button to return to the appropriate slide (e.g., "Johnny, you are on the wrong slide. Do not click the mouse repeatedly. Please return to the lesson by clicking the arrow below."). Some teachers choose to attach an alarm sound to the dummy slides so when the student repeatedly clicks the mouse, the sound alerts the teacher that the student is merely clicking the mouse and advancing out of sequence. When the teacher hears the sound, he/she can quickly go to the computer and get the student back on track.

Creating interactive PowerPoint activities may be accomplished following some simple steps. Different versions of PowerPoint have various menu options, but the following outlines the basic steps that should work for all versions. We recommend that you create and save all of your slides before you attempt to make them interactive.

Steps to create hyperlinked Action Buttons within the PowerPoint are:

Step 1: From the PowerPoint menu, click AutoShapes.

Step 2: From the AutoShapes menu, click the Action Button and then select the appropriate Action Button for your activity (e.g., forward arrow button or backward arrow button).

Step 3: Move the cursor to the PowerPoint slide and then left-click the mouse, hold and then drag the mouse to create the Action Button to the size you desire, and then release the left mouse click. We suggest you use the larger Action Buttons since they will be easier to navigate.

Step 4: After you release the left mouse in Step 3, an Action Settings box will appear. In the Action Setting box locate the "Hyperlink to:" option. This is where you will select the slide that you wish to be linked. You can scroll down the slide options by clicking the arrow that is next to the "Hyperlink to:" option. You can hyperlink to the previous slide, first slide, last slide, or other slides. After you select the slide to be linked, click OK.

Note: If you want to select the slide based on the title of the slide, click on the word *slide* and then the titles will appear. Click on the slide title you want to be linked and then click OK.

Alternative to Steps 3 and 4: After you have clicked on AutoShapes, selected the Action Button and moved your cursor to the slide, you can right-click the mouse, hold, and drag to create the size of the button. Then click the "Hyperlink to:" option, click "Place in this Document" and then select the slide you want to be linked.

Steps to hyperlink a word within the text to a slide within the PowerPoint are:

Step 1: Highlight the word to be linked.

Step 2: Right-click the mouse.

Step 3: Select the hyperlink option.

Step 4: Click Place in this Document.

Step 5: Select the slide for linkage.

Step 6: Click OK.

Note: If Step 2 does not work, try pressing the Control Key and *k* after highlighting the word. Then, at the hyperlink option, fill in the Named Location in File box with the number of the slide for linkage or click on Browse and select the slide title. After you have created all of the interactive links, be sure to run the PowerPoint show and check the accuracy of all the links prior to using with your students.

Technological innovations have advanced with digital projectors being installed in classrooms and CD-ROMs and DVDs accompanying many school texts. Multimedia presentations have an "entertainment" value for students and several studies have indicated that motivation is higher in classes that use multimedia materials (Astleitner & Wiesner, 2004; Yarbrough, 2001). "If done well, multimedia content organized with a slideware tool can generate productive and stimulating presentations that lead to greater retention, application to new situations, and performance on assessments" (Ludwig, Daniel, Froman, & Mathie, 2004, p.6).

Activity 11.6

Create six slides with PowerPoint and insert Action Buttons to hyperlink two of the slides, add sound to two of the slides, and include two graphics.

PREPARATION OF CLASSROOM MATERIALS

Technology can enhance instruction by helping you prepare materials for your classroom environment and curriculum. Technology today allows teacher-made materials such as worksheets, tests, certificates, templates, games, and learning cards to be created with ease and style or downloaded from the Internet already developed.

Computers can help you generate worksheets that match student needs for practice of skills and concepts. Programs such as Worksheet Magic Plus (Gamco) allow you to produce a variety of creative formats, including crossword puzzles, scrambled words, word searches, and secret codes. Math Worksheet Generator (Garner Systems) and Fraction Worksheet Generator (S & S Software) will help you develop pretests, posttests, and practice problems to meet individual student needs. Problems can be printed horizontally or vertically, with or without answers, with the procedure being shown, or with an example problem. A favorite website of teachers is www.ed.sc.edu/caw/toolboxcreateyourown.html where links are found for teachers to create their own quizzes, games, lesson plans, rubrics, and flashcards. Another website, rubistar.4teachers.org features a free tool to create quality rubrics. Many software programs offer interpretation of test results, information management of test results and data, report writing, and generation of goals, objectives, and instructional strategies (Wilson, Michaels, & Margolis, 2005).

You can create certificates, awards, banners, signs, bookmarks, and bulletin board signs to enhance your themes, and instructional activities on such programs as Print Shop Deluxe (Broderbund) and PrintMaster Gold (Mindscape). Colored paper, special certificate paper, or color printers will add to the appearance of your products.

With desktop publishing programs you can add a professional polish to instructional materials and reports. Templates for newsletters in many word-processing programs will allow you to add columns, rules, boxes, and shading to your work. Programs like Publisher (Microsoft) and the more professional PageMaker (Adobe) will offer more publishing options. You can find templates on the Internet for letters, forms, certificates, and seating charts, saving you the time normally spent in developing these items from scratch. A popular website for teacher templates is http://www.educationworld.com.

Interactive file folder games may be created to meet the individual needs of students. Technology is a great resource to help create games. Once you know the content you want to teach, a new game is merely a few clicks of the computer mouse from creation. You may use word-processing software, such as Microsoft Word, to integrate various graphics and clip art. A variety of font colors and sizes enhances the overall appearance of the games, and the AutoShapes options and WordArt options add colorful detail. In addition, software such as Inspiration, KidPix, Kidspiration, and BoardMaker picture symbols may be used in designing games. Teachers may also use the Internet to download clip art items to meet the goal of the game or download actual photographs of items that can be used to help the games provide authentic learning.

In addition to interactive file folder games, teachers may create learning cards, which present information to be learned in a self-correction card format. The content is presented with the answers. Usually learning cards include pictures to enhance the learning process, but they may be used without pictures. Learning card templates may be created using Microsoft Word. Once you have a general format saved, you may easily insert various content into the templates. The content to be learned should guide how you present it on the learning card and can be placed in the format of your preference. To create the template, you will need to become familiar with the Text Box feature on the Microsoft Word software. An example of the learning card format may be found in Figure 11.3.

Follow these simple directions to begin developing your learning card template:

Step 1: From the pull-down menu click on Insert.

Step 2: Scroll down and click on Text Box.

Step 3: Drag the Text Box to the desired place on the page.

Step 4: Right-click on the Text Box and then click on Format Text Box, which will give you many preferences including the thickness and colors of the Text Box lines.

Figure 11.3 LEARNING CARD TEMPLATE

Learning Card

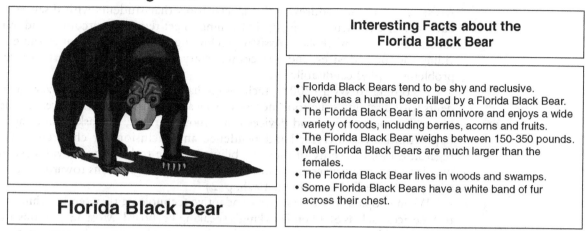

Florida Black Bear

Interesting Facts about the Florida Black Bear

- Florida Black Bears tend to be shy and reclusive.
- Never has a human been killed by a Florida Black Bear.
- The Florida Black Bear is an omnivore and enjoys a wide variety of foods, including berries, acorns and fruits.
- The Florida Black Bear weighs between 150-350 pounds.
- Male Florida Black Bears are much larger than the females.
- The Florida Black Bear lives in woods and swamps.
- Some Florida Black Bears have a white band of fur across their chest.

An important point to remember is that technology should enhance the content, not distract from it. The first step should always be to review the objectives to be taught and then explore one of the technology tools to see whether it can enhance the learning. Never start with a technology tool and then try to find content to fit into the tool. When the latter occurs, there is a high risk of using a wonderful technology tool without a content match. More importantly, there is a higher risk of introducing objectives out of sequence. A teacher may be tempted to select an objective that is out of sequence in order to integrate the new technology in the lesson. It is easy to get sidetracked with the motivational aspect of new technology, but if teachers are enticed by the newest technology tool without first looking at the content, many difficulties may follow and technology may distract instead of enhance the learning process.

IMPORTANT POINTS

1. Technology can assist teachers in planning, IEP generation, record keeping and classroom management, lesson presentation, and material preparation.
2. It is important to remember that IEPs should be written by teams of people, and computerization should not reduce the individualization of the process (Krivacska, 1986; Maddux, 1986).
3. It is extremely important that teachers obtain written permission from the families of their students prior to using videotaping.
4. Interactive PowerPoint activities should be designed so that students can easily navigate through the lesson by clicking on hyperlinks placed throughout the slides, which are linked to slides that further explain or provide additional examples of the content.
5. Software programs are available to assist teachers in preparing individualized worksheets, tests, certificates, templates, games, and learning cards.
6. The first step in using technology should be to review the objective for the lesson and then explore one of the technology tools to see whether it enhances the objective.

ASSISTIVE TECHNOLOGY

Assistive technology addresses the special tools that students with disabilities must have to access curriculum, engage in learning, meet required outcomes, and transition successfully to the workplace. Assistive technology augments student learning by providing the tools, devices, and services necessary for circumventing particular learning problems or physical disabilities.

According to Wyer (2001), technology has become a great equalizer, giving students with disabilities the tools necessary to learn and participate. "Access to the assistive technology services and devices can remove barriers, unmask abilities and create opportunities for increased independence and inclusion for children and adults, regardless of the severity of their disability. Assistive technology provides avenues for people to increase expectations and to stretch their imaginations toward a future filled with possibilities" (Hasselbring, 1998, p. 2).

When people think of assistive or adaptive technology, they tend to think of high-tech devices such as Stephen Hawking's speaking keyboard. Most adaptations are more basic and address issues such as relocating the on/off button of the computer or pressing two keys at once or picking up a disk to slide into the drive. A pencil grip would qualify as assistive technology if it assists a student with writing problems to write better! Assistive technology is technology that allows the student to do something that he/she would not be able to accomplish otherwise.

As discussed previously, legislation promoted the use of assistive technology in the classroom. The definition of assistive technology includes both devices and services.

ASSISTIVE TECHNOLOGY DEVICES

IDEA (2004) defines assistive technology devices as "any item, piece of equipment or product system, whether acquired commercially off the shelf, modified, or customized, that is used to increase, maintain, or improve functional capabilities of a child with a disability" (20 U.S.C. 1400, SECTION § 602(1)). This definition is broad and includes many of the modifications, adaptations, and accommodations made to help a student participate in a Free Appropriate Public Education (FAPE). As discussed previously, the devices may range from no tech or low technology to high technology. With this definition, assistive technology does not have to be electronic or mechanical.

A useful source of information on assistive devices is the ABLEDATA website at http://www.abledata.com. The ABLEDATA site contains detailed descriptions of approximately 32,000 assistive technology products from over 2,000 different manufacturers.

ASSISTIVE TECHNOLOGY SERVICES

IDEA (2004) defines assistive technology service as "any service that directly assists an individual with a disability in the selection, acquisition, or use of an assistive technology device" (20 U.S.C. 1400, SECTION § 602(2). Specifically, this service must include (a) evaluating an individual's assistive technology needs; (b) purchasing, leasing, or providing for acquisition of devices; (c) selecting, designing, adapting, maintaining, repairing, or replacing devices; (d) coordinating therapies, interventions, or services; (e) providing training and technical assistance for the individual and/or family; and (f) providing training and technical assistance for professionals. School districts are responsible for helping individuals with disabilities select and acquire an appropriate assistive technology device and assist in training them to use it.

Students, parents, and professionals together decide on the assistive technology needs of an individual student. Professionals who may be included are the teacher, speech therapist, occupational therapist, physical therapist, paraprofessional, and any other person who works with the student.

MODIFICATIONS

As we discussed previously, assistive technology may also include simple, no-tech or low-tech modifications. Simple modifications are sometimes all that is needed to allow a student to use the computer software program. Some students may benefit from the use of bright stickers to code keys that are frequently used with a program. You may use word-processing or graphics software to produce some special help cards for use at the computer. These cards can list frequently used commands or summarize directions in large, clear print with illustrations. Using screen-capturing features of the computer allows you to print or download the image that appears on the screen. You can use screen-capturing features to produce flash cards, prepare transparencies and task cards for a computer program, display and file exemplary work, and incorporate actual software graphics into student-produced presentations.

When considering the use of assistive technology, teachers should begin with simple, inexpensive no-tech or low-tech options first to prevent wasting extra time and money on high-tech solutions. One option for teachers in trying no-tech or low-tech solutions is the LoTTIE Kits—Low Tech Tools for Inclusive Education (Onion Mountain Technology, Inc.). These kits contain a collection of easy-to-use assistive technology tools. LoTTIE Kits contain tools such as colored filters, pencil grips, handheld devices, raised paper, and rubber letter and number stamps. These tools allow the teacher to conduct informal assessments by trying out simple devices prior to trying more expensive ones. In addition to the tools, the kits also include notebooks detailing the contents along with strategies for using these no-tech and low-tech tools. All of these simple tools are stored in a handy carrying container for ease of use—all at your fingertips at a moment's notice. A variety of LoTTIE Kits are available, including the basic kit as well as one specifically designed for literacy and one specifically designed for math. A total of six LoTTIE kits are available for students ranging from K–12 with a new kit available for young kids that focuses on sensory, language, and motor skills.

The operating systems of computers have accessibility features either built into the system software or available at no cost. These features provide simple modifications that make using the computer more accessible to students. The features were designed primarily for individuals with motion-related disabilities who may have difficulty using the computer keyboard or mouse, for individuals who prefer visual feedback in place of sounds, and for some low-vision students. However, many of these features make the computer more user friendly for other students as well. The terminology for these features may vary from one computer system to another, but the accessibility features are offered in most of the system software. Speech recognition (voice) and language translation is now built into Word 2003.

Both the Mac and Windows operating systems include built-in controls that make standard functions simpler for individuals with special needs. For example, Ms. Perez slows down the speed at which the mouse pointer moves for Kimberly, who has some eye–hand coordination difficulties. More examples of built-in controls appear in Table 11.4.

Many programs give you and your students the option of using various peripheral devices to enhance instruction or provide the student with special access to use the

Table 11.4 Sample Operating Systems Built-In Controls

These built-in controls include:

- The capability of switching from mouse control to keyboard control using the numeric keypad
- Control of the speed at which the mouse pointer moves
- Allowance for control key combinations to be pressed consecutively rather than simultaneously
- Use of the keyboard keys to select menu functions
- Adjustment of icons for size, spacing, and title next
- Change of the background screen color
- Custom features for controlling your mouse, trackball, or operating system
- An audible cue to tell when either the Caps Lock, Num Lock, or Scroll Lock keys have been made active or inactive
- A visual alert for persons with hearing disabilities or for those who are too easily distracted by the alert sounds
- Voice and language translation—now available in Word 2003.

program. Adapted standard computer input devices include different sizes of a mouse or a trackball, and different size or different key layouts of keyboards. Other examples include keyguards, touch-sensitive screens, alternate or adapted keyboards, switches, and voice entry systems.

Students usually respond to instructional software programs by typing on the computer keyboard. **Keyguards** reduce the possibility of hitting the wrong keys as students attempt to enter information. Keyguards fit over the regular computer keyboard and have holes cut out for the individual to access the keys on the keyboard with a finger, stylus, or stick. Keyguards may also have a latching key on certain function keys, such as the shift or control. With **touch-sensitive screens** (e.g., Touch Window, Edmark), students use a finger or stylus for input. To make a selection, the student simply points at the computer screen with a finger or a special pen-like device. This feature often allows students who have fine-motor problems, inaccurate keyboard skills, or problems with spelling to complete programs without frustration.

Alternative or adapted keyboards, such as IntelliKeys (Intellitools) and Discover:Board (Madentec), offer input methods that can be customized to a student's needs. Many of the same features that are system accessibility features are also included in these alternate keyboards. Most of these alternate keyboards have software that allows you to make customized overlays for the keyboards that will correspond to the specific software that the student is using.

The use of on-screen keyboards is an alternative input method that is software and hardware controlled. A graphical representation of the keyboard is displayed on the computer screen to allow individuals who cannot type with a standard keyboard to enter text using a pointing device (e.g., mouse, switch, or trackball).

Software devices such as IntelliSwitch (Madentec) used with Discover Pro 2.0 software allows switch activation and a communication device to act in place of the computer keyboard. With switch activation, the software that comes with the specific device displays the computer keyboard. A switch activation signals the computer to start scanning the on-screen keyboard by row, column, or individual character. The scan can be customized for rate of scanning and activation as well as for different placements of characters on the on-screen keyboard. The simplest communication device activates a switch for selecting an actual object, whereas more advanced devices use intricate symbol codes to produce words on a display or for voice output. IntelliSwitch is compatible with Discover (Matendec) and Intellitools (Intellitools) software, and most self-scanning software.

Voice entry systems allow students to enter information into the computer simply by speaking into a microphone attached to the computer. Voice entry software is available as an alternative input system. Some computer systems have built-in systems providing voice access to the functions of the computer, but do not necessarily allow voice input of data. An individual may give a voice command, such as "Computer, open hard drive," and other commands to control the computer functions. However, the individual cannot tell the computer to enter the data. Instead, specific voice input software, such as Dragon NaturallySpeaking, ViaVoice, or PowerSecretary, can be installed to provide for data input. These programs are fairly sensitive to voice discrepancies of different students. Therefore, they must be programmed to be used by one student at a time and in a fairly quiet environment. For some students with written expression problems, voice input can expedite the entering of text. To be successful, individuals who use voice input must have a fairly high cognitive level as well as extreme patience in working with the software.

For English language learners, it may be necessary to provide tools for translation. Some popular word-processing software programs, such as Word 2003, have built-in features that can convert or translate text in some languages. A popular text translation website is www.babelfish.altavista.com. This website can assist in translating a block of text or an entire web page.

An assistive technology continuum may help you in selecting the type of assistive devices to utilize (see Figure 11.4). To use the continuum, the teacher or IEP team identifies the task (e.g., reading), the needs (e.g., comprehension), and the environment (e.g., classroom). Next, the teacher or IEP team selects the tech tools beginning with low-tech

Activity 11.7

With a colleague, list five modifications that you may make for your students using assistive technology.

IMPORTANT POINTS

1. Assistive technology addresses the special tools that students with disabilities must have to access curriculum, engage in learning, meet required outcomes, and transition successfully to the workplace.
2. Examples of assistive technology range from a high-technology solution such as a speaking keyboard to a low-technology or no-tech solution such as a pencil grip.
3. Teachers should begin with simple, inexpensive low-tech options first to prevent wasting extra time and money on high-tech solutions that may not be necessary.
4. The operating systems of the computers have had accessibility features either built into the system software or are available at no cost that provide simple modifications that make using the computer more accessible to students.

Figure 11.4 THE ASSISTIVE TECHNOLOGY CONTINUUM

The Assistive Technology Continuum

Devices to try if a student has problems with

Tasks	Needs	Environments
reading	faster work	classroom
writing	legible, understandable work	resource/study hall
spelling/grammar	comprehension	therapy
communication	same work as everyone else	home
worksheet completion	modified, shortened, parallel work	community
math	visual/graphic/auditory presentations	
mapping	independent work	
note-taking	fine motor practice	
organization/planning	sharing of knowledge	
learning another language	correct grammar/spelling	

Problems → **Success Independence**

Low Tech Tools	Mid Tech Tools	High Tech Tools
specialized pens/pencils/crayons/markers/grips	tape recorders	alternative keyboard/alternative cursor control
specialized erasers, correction tapes	digital recorders	word processing
raised line paper, grid paper, colored papers	calculators	word prediction
highlighters, highlighter tapes	spell checker, dictionary/thesaurus (talking)	brainstorming, graphic organization
color coding	dedicated word processor	spell checker, grammar checker
Post-It notes, flags, arrows	electronic organizer	word banks (on-screen, overlays)
colored filters, page overlays (clear acetate sheets)	audio books	text readers
NCR paper	music (tapes/CDs)	on-screen math, computer calcuators
reading/writing guides	electronic eraser, stapler	communications devices/software
slanted surfaces, dycem, copy holder	mini-book lights	internet access
white board, markers, crayons	switch operated toys and appliances	CD reference (maps, encyclopedias)
magnetic letters, tactile letters		CAI
magnifiers		environmental control devices
rubber stamps, labels		
specialized measuring and cutting tools		

Source: Judith P. Sweeney (2002). Onion Mountain Technology, Inc. http:www.onionmountaintech.PDFfiles/banner.pdf. Reprinted by permission.

tools (e.g., reading guides) to mid-tech tools (e.g., audio books) to high-tech tools (e.g., text readers) until the student is successful. For further information on a variety of low-tech tools and their implementation, visit http://www.onionmountaintech.com.

PUTTING IT ALL TOGETHER

In this chapter, we have shown how technology can be used by teachers to support the curriculum and assist in planning, managing, and preparing instruction on a daily basis. We have also described how technology can be an effective tool to support and enhance student learning and attainment of instructional goals. Creative ways to enhance instruction using assistive technology as tools to engage learners were also addressed. We believe that technology is a viable tool for providing access to the general education curriculum for students with special needs.

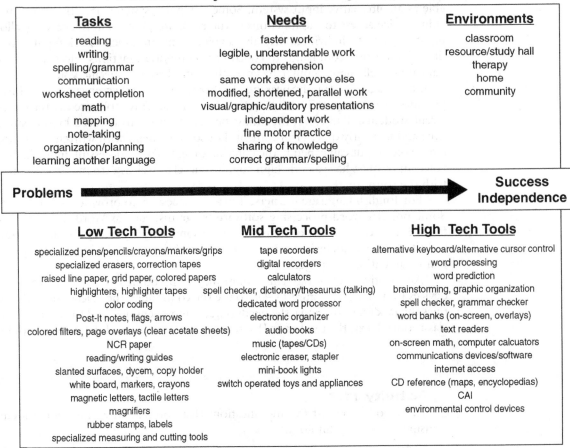

DISCUSSION QUESTIONS

1. Given the budget constraints placed on schools, make a case for expenditures in the area of technology, perhaps at the expense of other types of instructional materials.
2. Predict how students with special needs and their teachers will be using technology 5 years from now.
3. Describe how you will use technology to enhance your roles in teaching and learning.

Websites: Usefule websites related to chapter content can be found in Appendix A.

CHAPTER

12

Transition from School to Life

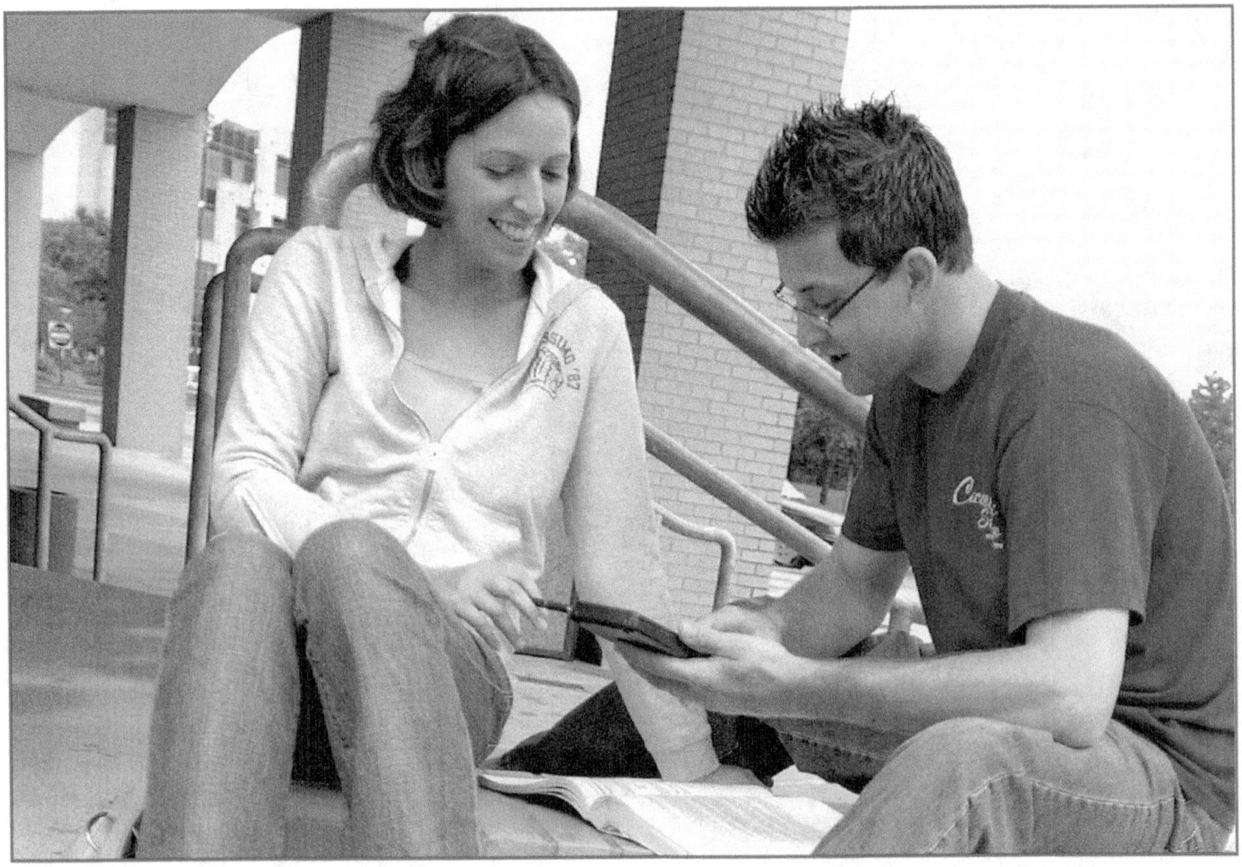

KEY TOPICS

Best Practices in Transition

Preparing for Transition
- Career Education
- High-Stakes Testing

Planning for Transition
- The Individuals with Disabilities Education Act and Transition
- Other Laws Related to Transition

Teaching for Transition
- Instruction
- Related Services
- Community Experiences
- Postschool Adult Living
- Social and Interpersonal Skills
- Employment
- Functional Vocational Assessment
- Daily Living Skills

Linking for Transition
- Family Linkages
- Intraagency Linkages
- General Education Linkages
- Interagency Linkages

Putting It All Together

"Good morning, Mr. and Mrs. Diamante and Josh. As always, it is so nice to see all of you." Mr. Webster, the principal of Orange City High School extended his hand in greeting as all the assembled members of the IEP team found a place to sit and the meeting began. "Josh, why don't we begin with you giving us an update on how your sophomore year is going so far?"

"Everything is great, Mr. Webster. Since we've only been in school for a few weeks, classes aren't too tough yet. Swim team practice is keeping me busy after school, but I haven't missed any homework assignments. Mom helps me stay organized and makes me get started on studying as soon as I get home."

"That's right," said Mrs. Diamante. "As you all know, Josh has been determined since he was a kid to go to college to be a news reporter. His dad and I want to help make that happen, in spite of his learning disabilities. We came in today because we have a lot of questions for all of you about his transition plan and how we should begin to look for the right college for Josh."

"You have already done many things correctly," began the guidance counselor. "You started with a transition plan in middle school that placed Josh on track for a standard diploma. His IEP goals and objectives have reflected this and Josh has worked very hard. This is definitely the ideal time to begin looking for the right college."

"I agree," said the Intensive Reading teacher, Ms. McCool. "Josh has made good use of his time in my class and his good grades in his general education classes reflect how well his accommodations are working for him. I'm sure the before-school tutoring program has helped a lot, and Josh is to be commended for how much effort it takes to get up that early three mornings a week!"

"But we are afraid that after high school his accommodations will no longer be allowed," said Mr. Diamante. "How do we make sure that Josh can still have things like additional time to take tests and guided notes when he is in college? And even though his grades are good, they aren't straight-A's. Will he even be able to get into a college? He thinks he would like to go away to the state university but my wife and

I are thinking he may benefit more from staying at home and attending the community college for his first two years. What do you all think?"

"Most definitely he can get into college," replied the guidance counselor, "and you are wise to consider things like whether or not he is ready to live on his own. Ultimately, you will need to make that decision as a family, but I can offer guidance on which colleges provide the best disability services. Josh, it is important for you to understand that since you won't be on an IEP any longer it will be up to you to contact the office of disability services at each college you consider applying to. They are legally required to assist you, but it is up to you to take the first step and provide them with proof of your disability. Do this right from the start. Don't wait until after you have already received some bad grades to identify your needs, because colleges aren't required to go back and make up for anything that happens before you tell them that you need assistance. Also colleges are allowed to set a minimum GPA that you must stay above in order to stay in school."

"I understand, Mr. Victorino," said Josh. "Ms. McCool has talked to our class about how important it is for students with learning disabilities to understand our strengths and weaknesses. I may be a great swimmer, but I'm not so good at telling people that I need something different, and I know I need to do that if I'm going to make it in college. Right now though, I'm mostly worried about taking the SAT next year."

"If it helps any, *all* the sophomores who sign up worry about taking that test!" said Ms. McCool. "You scored just fine on the practice test we took during tutoring this year and your IEP ensures that when you take the real SAT you will be given the same accommodations you have been allowed to use on other standardized tests, so you will do fine."

"Mr. Diamante, let's go back to your question about Josh's accommodations," said Mr. Victorino. "The law states that every institution must at least have a contact person designated to ensure that individuals with disabilities receive necessary, reasonable accommodations. Some colleges go beyond this minimum requirement and offer additional services to assist students like Josh. A good place to start when you are looking at colleges is to find out exactly what the school has to offer. You may be surprised at how much these programs differ from one school to the next. Any reasonable accommodations should be free for Josh, but you should expect that some services, like the additional tutoring you are used to, may require an additional fee."

"That's good to know," said Josh's dad. "Can Josh expect to get any kind of special consideration when he applies to colleges?"

"Unfortunately not," said Mr. Victorino. "Josh will need to depend on his good grades, SAT scores, and a resumé of activities just like any other student." Turning to Josh he continued, "A good idea, Josh, would be for you to mention your disability in the personal statement that you write for your applications because some schools may be impressed when they see all that you have accomplished even though you have a learning disability. But I need to stress that it is entirely up to you to decide if you want to disclose your disability or not. You don't have to. One other thing that might really help is that I believe several people in this room would be willing to write glowing letters of recommendation for you."

The above scenario reflects a rather ideal situation that we educators would like to envision for all our students with disabilities. Josh has obviously had a great deal of support and encouragement over the years from his parents, teachers, coaches, and administrators, and his potential for future success appears to be quite good. Unfortunately, the data on high school graduation rates for students with disabilities suggests that scenarios like Josh's are not the norm. Why do you think that is the case? Consider the grade level(s) that you are interested in teaching and think about what you as an educator can do to positively impact transition services for your students.

INTRODUCTION

Children with disabilities grow up. They grow up to become adolescents and adults with disabilities. One of the critical turning points in the lives of young people is the transition from secondary school to life as an adult. Knowing yourself well enough to develop independence, determine how to best use one's talents and interests, and decide a career path is a daunting task for all students but especially challenging for many students with disabilities. Many students with any type of disability are unemployed or underemployed at a rate higher than their nondisabled peers. Many students tend to drop out of school before graduation, or are involved with the criminal justice system to a higher degree. Even if students do graduate, they tend to be dependent upon their parents longer than their nondisabled peers (Wagner & Blackorby, 1996). With the greater demands of high-stakes testing brought about by No Child Left Behind, student success in the general education curriculum is at the forefront for any teacher working with students with disabilities. Ensuring that students finish high school is a critical part of the transition process. Although most teachers see transition as a skill taught in the secondary classroom, the building of self-esteem and creating students who believe they can go to college and be successful despite their disabilities must start from birth and be nurtured by classroom teachers and family members throughout the child's life.

Therefore, the purpose of this chapter is to provide teachers with information and strategies to prepare students with special needs to make a successful transition from school to life. We begin this chapter with a summary of best practices in transition found in the literature. Then we suggest activities for students during early school years to prepare them for the more intense transition programming during the late middle and high school years. Next, we suggest practical approaches to assist students with special needs to complete high school, become employable, and emerge as independent and productive members of society. In the last section of the chapter, we provide guidance in developing and maintaining linkages with families and with other people and agencies within the school, and in the larger community. Two values underlie the content of this chapter. One is that students and their families must be at the center of planning for success to occur. Second, preparing students for transition is a life-long process and is the responsibility of elementary, middle, and secondary teachers to ensure that students leave school with the self-determination and self-esteem needed for success in life.

BEST PRACTICES IN TRANSITION

The transition literature suggests many "best practices" in the area of transition from school to community living. Unfortunately, many of these best practices have not been substantiated by empirical, student outcomes research (Sorrells, Reith, & Sindelar, 2004). A meta-analysis of various studies (Kohler, 1993) found that of the many practices thought to be critical, only four had been substantiated through data-driven studies of student outcomes. These four are vocational training, parent involvement, paid work, and social skills training. However, several additional practices were strongly implied to be critical. These were interagency collaboration, individualized plans/planning, community-based instruction, community-referenced curriculum, follow-up employment services, integration, and vocational assessment. Although many students with learning disabilities are encouraged to pursue vocational education rather than to attend 4-year colleges (Janiga & Costenbader, 2002), areas that are important to teach to students who plan to continue their education at colleges, universities, or vocational-technical schools include self-awareness and advocacy (Blalock & Patton, 1996), social-interpersonal (Aune, 1991), independent living (Brinkerhoff, Shaw, & McGuire, 1992), and academic skills.

PREPARING FOR TRANSITION

Preparing for life after school really starts the day a child is born. For a child who is born with any type of disability or challenge, the need to ensure that essential academic, social, and life skills are taught is at the core of the Individualized Education Program. A desirable long-term goal for all individuals is that they will become productive members of society. Because children and adolescents with special needs may require a longer time to attain this goal, there are activities parents and teachers may do at school and at home to set the stage for the more direct and intense transition experience that will occur later in high school. We suggest that teachers consider the following activities for prekindergarten, elementary, and middle school. These are the types of activities that were used by Josh's teachers and parents over the years to help prepare him for his future career as a news reporter (see the chapter opening scenario).

Prekindergarten

1. Design activities that encourage children to become more independent.
2. Involve children in activities that build self-esteem and self-direction.
3. Take young children into the community so they may see and learn about many possible careers and lifestyles.
4. Share at a child's level their strengths and a beginning understanding of any challenges that might exist (e.g., "Honey, you have to wear glasses to help you learn to read.")
5. Spend time talking to children about what they might like to do when they grow older.
6. Model a good work ethic and a joy of productive engagement.

Elementary Years

1. Assign jobs to students within the classroom (or at home). Encourage completion of work in a timely and accurate manner.
2. Notice and praise good grooming and hygiene.
3. Work closely with parents to ensure that your teaching is helping students feel successful in life.
4. Show DVDs, bring in guest speakers, or visit different work sites where people with and without disabilities from different career fields are employed.
5. Encourage students to talk about what jobs they might like and, as appropriate, their abilities and concerns.

Middle School

1. Complete vocational aptitude and interest inventories for each student.
2. Address transition service needs on the IEP.
3. Encourage students to attend their IEP meetings and even consider having them open the meeting with PowerPoint slides sharing their strengths and areas of concern.
4. Identify adult agencies from whom students may need assistance in the future.
5. Engage students in career exploration activities. Become familiar with high school exit options (from employment to various college programs) and the advantages and disadvantages of each.

CAREER EDUCATION

A great way to ensure you are focusing on transition skills across the age span and curriculum is through career education. This term was introduced into American education in 1971 (Brolin, 1995) and has been defined in several ways, but the basic concepts remain the same: Career education is an *ongoing* process that *infuses* an emphasis on careers in *all subjects, K–12.* Career education includes employment and job-specific training as well as training in areas that prepare the student for many adult roles. Career education develops within stages:

Grades K–5: Self and Career Awareness

Self, career, and technology awareness activities are infused into the curriculum.

Grade 6: Personal Assessment and Technology Literacy

At this age, most students continue the process of assessing their academic, physical, and social/emotional strengths and weaknesses. They should have intense technological literacy instruction.

Grades 7 and 8: Career Orientation and Exploration

During this period, students identify broad goals to work toward. Four-year plans for grades 9–12 are developed with input from the students, families, and school personnel.

Grades 9–12: Academic and Specialized Skills Development

During high school, students attain the competencies necessary to go on for further education, training, and employment. This is done through academic programs and vocational programs and through applied learning in the community.

Postsecondary: Skills Development and Career Advancement

Career education is not a process that ends with high school. Many students choose to go on for further education or training either immediately after high school or at some point as adults.

Many elements of career education are found in functional curriculum, supported employment, and other transition-related programs. One of the best-known and most widely used curricula for career education is the Life Centered Career Education (LCCE) Curriculum (Brolin, 1993). LCCE is a K–12 curriculum model that focuses on what an individual needs to know to function in society. It incorporates the basic tenets of the career education concept and provides teachers with a scope and sequence around which to teach children and young adults of all ages. A useful addition to the original LCCE, which targets students with mild disabilities, has been an edition of the LCCE for students with moderate disabilities.

Activity 12.1

As you return from work or class today, make a list of all of the skills you needed during the day. Then turn the various skills you used that day into a lesson plan to support students at either the first or sixth grade to assist them with the transition from school to life.

(Answers for this and other activities are found in the Instructor's Manual.)

HIGH-STAKES TESTING

Current school reform efforts, including stricter high school graduation requirements, are having a powerful impact on the paths students take to attain a high school diploma. High-stakes requirements are of particular concern for students with disabilities (Johnson, Stodden, Emanuel, Luecking, & Mack, 2002).

The National Longitudinal Study II being conducted by the United States Department of Education focuses on gathering transition data from a sample of students who are 13 to 16 years of age as they move from secondary school into adult roles. From this research the field has found an increase over time in the percentage of youth with disabilities who complete high school with the range being as high as 95% for students with visual impairments to as low as 56% for students with emotional disabilities. Overall, the graduation rate of students with disabilities has increased but students with sensory or orthopedic impairments graduate at a much higher rate than students with multiple disabilities or emotional disturbances.

BOX 12.1

Reflections on Practice

Visit the National Longitudinal Study II reports by doing a search on the Web. Numerous documents are being created daily from this project supported by the United States Department of Education Institute of Education Sciences. Take some time to explore their reports and databases to look for potential trends in areas you are interested in teaching. Also notice the strong family component that is embraced in this research. Always remember as an educator that the student and their family will be a unit of support long after you leave their life as a teacher. Consider how you will make families and students the center of the transition process.

Knowing the trends in the field of special education is very important as our field changes and aligns more and more with the general education curriculum. A major concern in the field of special education is the impact of new regulations brought forward in No Child Left Behind related to students with disabilities receiving diplomas and meeting competencies for graduation often tied to passing high-stakes tests. Today, more than ever, great caution must be used in assigning students to a self-contained classroom or a modified curriculum because their chances of mastering the competencies associated with a standard diploma are limited. If a diploma with an academic emphasis is not possible, then students should seek a graduation option that includes increased opportunities for meaningful employment training and experiences (Thurlow & Johnson, 2000).

PLANNING FOR TRANSITION

The planning for the transition process for students with disabilities must start from day one when they are identified with a disability and must be at the forefront of every academic and social decision made throughout the child's school life. The evolving importance of transition planning is evident when looking at the initial passage of the Education for All Handicapped Children's Act, PL 94-142, and the current reauthorization of IDEA 2004. In the initial law was a focus to increase students' independence and productivity to the current reauthorization mandating a "coordinating set of activities," which must be in place "beginning not later than the first IEP to be in effect when the child is 16" (Section 614, VII). This set of coordinated services and plan in place are critical since studies continue to show some improvement in the employment percentages for students with disabilities after they had been out of school 3 to 5 years; however, they still lag substantially behind their peers without disabilities in all areas.

THE INDIVIDUALS WITH DISABILITIES EDUCATION ACT AND TRANSITION

In 1990, PL 94-142 was amended and became the Individuals with Disabilities Education Act or IDEA (PL 101-476). IDEA required schools to address the transition needs of students in the Individualized Education Program (IEP) to help them plan for life after high school. The law contained a specific definition of transition services and mandated that all IEPs address needed transition services no later than age 16 and annually thereafter. IDEA defined transition services as follows:

> Transition services are a *coordinated set of activities* for a student, designed within an *outcome-oriented process,* which promote movement from *school to postschool* activities, including post-secondary education, vocational training, integrated employment (including supported employment), continuing and adult education, adult services, independent living, or community participation. The coordinated set of activities shall be *based upon the individual student's needs, taking into account the student's preferences and interests,* and shall include *instruction, community experiences,* the development of *employment* and other *post-school adult living* objectives, and, when appropriate, acquisition of *daily living skills* and *functional vocational evaluation.* (IDEA, PL 101-476) (italics added for emphasis by the authors).

The 1997 amendments to IDEA (PL 105-17) made small but important changes to the part of the law addressing transition from school to community living. The new amendments added language requiring that "beginning at age 14 and updated annually, each student's IEP must include a statement of the transition service needs under applicable components of the child's IEP that focuses on the child's courses of study" [Sec. 300.347 (b) (i)]. Then in 2004 this language was amended to mandate a plan for coordinated services by no later than age 16. This coordinated service plan could and should include both in-school supports as well as outside activities as deemed appropriate by the Individualized Education Program. For example, a student who is interested in a career in technology may have a statement connected to technology course work, and be aligned to take a community college course in his or her senior year.

Activity 12.2

Think of an in-school and out-of-school activity you might list on a student's transition plan if they had the following dreams or goals.

To be a math teacher

To be an engineer

To be an athlete

To be a zookeeper

To run a business

OTHER LAWS RELATED TO TRANSITION

IDEA mandates the provision of supports and services for eligible students with disabilities pre-K through 12th grade. Once a young adult graduates, permanently drops out, or "ages out," that student is no longer eligible under IDEA. The student may, however, come under the auspices of other related laws that support persons with disabilities. Some of these laws provide legal protection through the transition process for students while they are enrolled in school and other laws provide legal protection for the individual's lifetime. Table 12.1 describes some of the major laws related to transition.

Two of these laws, the Rehabilitation Act of 1973 and the Carl D. Perkins Vocational Education Act of 1984, were passed several years ago but were amended in the 1990s. Table 12.1 reflects just the amendments of these older laws. Section 504 of the Rehabilitation Act of 1973 is not listed because its substance is covered under the Americans with Disabilities Act (ADA).

Table 12.1 Legislation Since 1990 Affecting Transition for Students with Special Needs

Name	Year	Major Purpose (relating to transition)
Americans With Disabilities Act (ADA), PL 101-336	1990	ADA protects people with disabilities from discrimination in employment, public accommodations (including schools), state and local government services (including transportation), and telecommunications relay services. It also requires employers to make "reasonable accommodations" for employees with a disability.
Rehabilitation Act Amendments, PL 102-69	1992	New language in the Rehabilitation Act emphasizes that a person with a disability, regardless of the severity of that disability, can attain employment and other life goals if appropriate supports and services are made available.
Carl D. Perkins Vocational Education and Applied Technology Education Amendments, PL 101-392	1990	The new amendments replace set-asides mandated by the previous legislation with strong assurances and guarantees for equal access to services and support supplementary services for "special populations" (including students with disabilities). Controversy exists about the elimination of the set-asides for special populations.
School-to-Work Opportunities Act (STW), PL 103-239	1994	The purpose of STW is to establish a national framework to expand educational and career opportunities for all youth (including young people with special needs). States may be funded to plan and develop a system that helps ensure a seamless transition from secondary education to meaningful, high-quality employment and continuing education.
Title I of the No Child Left Behind Act	2001	This act increased students with disabilities access to more rigorous academic curriculum and highly qualified teachers. It also increased the accountability of schools in educating students with disabilities. At the same time many states increased their graduation requirements and assessment outcomes for students to obtain a regular diploma.
Individuals with Disabilities Act 2004, PL 101-476	2004	Changed language related to services "beginning no later than the first IEP to be in effect when the child is 16" and added language on role of these students, and coordinated activities and results-oriented process.

The Transition Individualized Education Program (TIEP)

There are many similarities and a few important differences between Transition IEPs and the IEPs completed for students before they need transition services. Table 12.2 summarizes the components of the IEP process that are different for students in need of transition services under IDEA. The components that are required for all IEPs before transition planning remain in effect.

The TIEP is different from a student's previous IEP in that participants now include the student and agency representatives, as appropriate, and the content must address postschool desires and needs. Many local school districts develop Individualized Transition Programs (ITPs) separate from the IEPs. Some choose to incorporate transition planning into the student's IEP, but with more emphasis on preparing students to attain their desired postschool outcomes. Regardless of the way your school district elects to accomplish transition planning, you will be responsible for writing goals that address the postschool needs of your students. Depending on the individual student, these objectives may include skills to prepare them for postsecondary education, competitive employment, and/or community participation.

We encourage you to contact your local school district for copies of local transition guidelines and secondary IEP/Transition Planning formats. Examples of selected sections

Table 12.2 Transition-Related Elements of the IEP Process

CONTENT OF *IEP*

- A statement of transition services needs that focus on the student's existing program or courses (beginning no later than the first IEP to be in effect when the child is 16).
- A statement of needed transition services.
- A statement of each agency's responsibilities and/or linkages.
- Goals and objectives addressing instruction, related services, community experiences, employment, postschool adult living (and, if appropriate, daily living skills and functional vocational evaluation).
- A statement of the students' desired postschool outcome.

Participants of IEP Meeting

- The students must be invited.
- Representatives from agencies responsible for providing or paying for transition services.

Notice of Meetings

- An indication that a purpose of the meeting is to consider transition services for the student.
- Beginning at least 1 year before the student reaches the age of majority, the student is informed of his or her rights as an adult (including signing the IEP).

of TIEPs for two students appear in Figure 12.1. In our two examples, Latasha G. is in 11th grade and working toward an alternate diploma. Her exceptionality is mild cognitive delay. George B. is in 10th grade and working toward a standard diploma. His exceptionality is behavior disorder.

As a teacher of adolescents with special needs, you will be involved in helping your students and their parents make informed choices as they plan for transition. Part of your role involves helping students understand the different diploma options available to them, which vary state by state, and the consequences of leaving school with a document other than a standard diploma. For example, without a standard high school diploma, it is more difficult to access many postsecondary education options such as a community college or university. The armed services usually will not accept anything except a standard diploma (or its equivalent), and some employers are reluctant to hire people who do not have one. Although you may not be responsible for the entire transition planning process, you will be a key player. So your knowing, understanding, and advocating for the transition services available for the students you serve as a special education teacher is critical to their future success beyond school into life.

IMPORTANT POINTS

1. The transition process and ongoing planning should start as soon as a student is diagnosed with a disability and be ongoing throughout the student's life.
2. Career education is based on the infusion of critical skills for living and working throughout the school day from the earliest years and throughout a student's school life.
3. The Transition IEP is different from a student's previous IEP in that participants now include the student and agency representatives, as appropriate, and the content must address postschool desires and needs.

Figure 12.1 SAMPLE TRANSITION IEP FOR TWO STUDENTS

Desired Postschool Outcome is an expression of the student's dreams/visions 1 to 3 years after high school in the areas of employment, postsecondary education, community participation, residential preferences, etc. (i.e., life, work, and play).

Latasha desires to enroll in a postsecondary program to be a child-care worker, continue to live at home, learn to drive a car, and participate in her church choir.

George wants to live at home while he attends community college, continue his involvement with an online gaming group, and get a job at a local electronics superstore.

The *Present Level of Performance* describes how the student is currently functioning. It should be stated so that the relationship between the student's current level of functioning and future level of functioning required to achieve the desired postschool outcome is apparent. It should include what the student *can do* and what the student *needs.* Test scores are acceptable if they are accompanied by an explanation of why they are important.

Based on student and parent interviews, past IEP summaries, other school records, and observation, **Latasha** is on track to meet the requirements for an alternate diploma. She has mastered the performance objectives in the areas of functional academics at the independent level. Latasha has volunteered at the on-campus day-care center and is near successful completion of the special needs vocational program in this area. She needs to investigate postschool training options available to her and have some paid work experiences. Latasha is independent in all daily living and most postschool adult living skills, but still has problems with budgeting money. She has taken Driver's Education, but has not applied for her restricted license. Latasha goes to church with her siblings but has not started to sing in her church choir. Her **priority transition needs are to (1) participate in a work experience program (preferably one that is paid), (2) apply for her restricted driver's license, (3) learn money management skills, and (4) sign up for her church choir.**

Based on prior IEPs and school records, George is somewhat successful with his academic work, but continues to display inappropriate behaviors throughout the day. George has difficulty with student-teacher interactions despite being popular and well liked by his peers. George has difficulty with time management. He had investigated some of the community colleges in the area, but has not selected his career. George is involved with an online gaming group and enjoys daily interactions with the online community. His parents report that he does not complete his chores at home. Vocational evaluations indicate that George has strengths in the areas of creativity and design/drawing. He has good personal hygiene but does not follow through on assigned tasks without repeated prompts. George works well alone and is still working on his ability to control his temper in the classroom setting when he deals with adults. According to his counselor, George can state the appropriate social skills for group participation in all settings. Although he has some informal job experience, usually working for relatives, he has not had any formal employment experience. George needs to **improve his social skills when dealing with adults, time management skills, and select a career.**

Annual Goals address discrepancies between the desired postschool outcomes and the present level of performance. All activity areas must be addressed either as a goal or statement of why the IEP team feels a goal is not needed.

We present **Sample annual goals** for each student.

Latasha will find paid work experience.

George will demonstrate appropriate social skills when interacting with adults in a variety of settings.

Short-Term objectives must relate directly to the annual goal and must be measurable. We also include the criteria, schedule, and responsible person or persons.

(*continued*)

Figure 12.1 SAMPLE TRANSITION IEP FOR TWO STUDENTS (continued)

To achieve the goal of paid work experience:

Objective 1: Using classified ads, **Latasha** will find five employment opportunities by November 15. The OT instructor will assist Latasha.

Objective 2: Given five possible employment opportunities, Latasha will fill out and submit five applications without spelling and grammar errors by December 2. The OT instructor will assist Latasha.

Objective 3: When invited to interview, Latasha will meet with the interviewers and secure a position by January 15. The OT will assist Latasha.

Objective 4: When requested, Latasha will provide evidence of her ongoing employment on a monthly basis from February through May. The OT will assist Latasha.

To achieve the goal of displaying appropriate social skills in various settings:

Objective 1: In a pull-out group setting supervised by the school counselor, **George** will successfully role-play appropriate social skills 90% of the time by September 2.

Objective 2: In all inclusive class settings supervised by the special educational teacher, George will demonstrate appropriate social skills 90% of the time by February 2.

Objective 3: In all inclusive and pull-out class settings, George will demonstrate appropriate social skills 90% of the time as monitored by the special education teacher by April 2.

TEACHING FOR TRANSITION

At the core of teaching for transition is for the teacher to understand the meaning of an important and current term in our field called self-determination. Basically self-determination means teaching individuals the skills needed to take control over one's own decision-making and essential life skills. In the literature self-determination is defined as the "skills, knowledge and beliefs that enable a person to engage in goal-directed, self-regulated, autonomous behavior . . . " (Field, Martin, Miller, Ward, & Whemeyer, 1998). The specific skills needed by a student with special needs to prepare for life after school depends on the desired postschool outcomes of that individual. Remember, as the teacher you are important to the process, but Trainor (2005) in a research study found that students relied upon themselves and their families more than their teachers in the transition process.

In this section, we address the transition process in the context of the following transition domains of IDEA: Instruction, Related Services, Community Experiences, Postschool Adult Living, Social and Interpersonal Skills, Employment, and as appropriate, Functional Vocational Assessment and Daily Living Skills. We also describe general skill areas for students in transition and list some specific skills for transition to postsecondary educational settings and employment. Additionally, we describe commercially available programs for teaching these and other important life and transition skills.

INSTRUCTION

The importance of having an integrated transition planning process is especially relevant for students who are going on to postsecondary education. In this time of high-stakes testing, many students will be provided instruction in content areas which is critical if students are going to have any chance of receiving a standard diploma. Therefore, these skills are essential to transition into most postsecondary educational settings or to secure higher levels of employment. Since this textbook focuses on students with mild to moderate disabilities, we encourage you to make postsecondary education and higher level employment a consideration for all students. Many students do not access higher education for many reasons, but one reason we have seen as an issue is special education teachers not knowing how to support students to access the general education curriculum and the supports they will need to be successful in college. If the academic component of the TIEP is not developed in the context of the student's desired postschool outcomes, the student may not be adequately prepared for postsecondary education. Although most high school curricula are set up to be "college prep," teachers and parents must make sure not only that students enroll in the appropriate courses, but also that they are provided with supports and services to pass those courses. Necessary accommodations and modifications should be documented on each student's TIEP. This approach helps ensure that the student will have a sufficient grade point average for college admission and be prepared academically for college-level work. Additionally, teachers, parents, and students should make formal preparation to take college entrance exams, including investigating possible testing accommodations that are available to students with documented disabilities (Hicks-Cooley & Kurtz, 1997).

BOX 12.2

Reflections on Practice

Do you know what services are available for students with disabilities on your college campus? Do you know what is needed for students with disabilities to have adaptations on the SAT or ACT tests? Do you know what documentation students with disabilities need to provide for entrance to and access for services at local colleges? Consider taking a field trip to either your accessibility office on your campus or to a nearby campus to learn what is needed for students to go to college. Many times students are admitted to college but do not have appropriate documentation or self-advocacy skills to access and utilize these services. Remember college is a privilege not a right for students with disabilities and so their needs being met at a technical school, college, or university does not fall under the rules of IDEA, but they still cannot be discriminated against in these institutions. Therefore, you need to be educated so you can inform your students and their families about how to access future postsecondary options.

For an overview of the process, see an article published in *Teaching Exceptional Children*, Navigating the College Transition Maze: A Guide for Students With Learning Disabilities by Madaus (2005).

Part of academic preparation for postsecondary education is getting students ready for the increased study and organizational demands. Students need to be taught study and work habits that will allow them to balance the demands of school with the need for some personal freedom and relationship building as a young adult. Students who transition to a postsecondary institution benefit from participating in activities that help them develop skills in academic, career, and personal or social areas (ASCA, 2003).

The pivotal SCANS (Secretary's Commission on Achieving Necessary Skills) Report conducted in 1991 identifies academic skill areas critical to functioning in the world of work. These skills include reading and writing on the job, figuring computations, estimating, making change, and using time wisely. Yet many students with special needs are not being exposed to high enough curricula to allow them access to college or functional enough curricula that prepares them for employment. Students with special needs often have difficulty generalizing traditional academics to the real world of employment and adult living (Taylor & O'Reilly, 2000). Therefore, job-related functional academics such as calculating net and gross pay, having positive interactions with coworkers and being punctual and responsible must be infused into existing courses and practiced in school.

RELATED SERVICES

Equally important to job-related skills is ensuring students have access to related services they might need for success in going to college, living independently, or accessing employment. The term *related services* is defined as "transportation and such developmental, corrective, and other supportive services as are required to assist a child with a disability to benefit from special education . . . " (Sec. 300.22). Related services have been a required part of every student's IEP since the original PL 94-142 legislation. Examples of related services that may be especially important for students in transition include transportation to a community-based instruction site, accommodations to a workplace environment, and parent counseling regarding the impact of a student's job on the income of the family. Related services are usually listed on the IEP separate from goals and objectives. These services, if not listed, may mean that the students have the skills to be employed but not the access.

COMMUNITY EXPERIENCES

Most job-related skills can be taught in school but are even more appropriate to teach in community-related experiences. These experiences could be service-learning projects to actual transition experiences created at the school level. When creating experiences that are community-based instruction (CBI) or community-referenced instruction (CRI), teachers should determine: (a) who should receive the instruction, (b) how much instruction is appropriate, (c) which skills should be taught in the community, and (d) what is the impact from these experiences versus students being in academic content (Rose, Rainforth, & Steere, 2002).

The amount of time spent in CRI should vary inversely with the student's ability to generalize postschool plans. For example, a student who wants to attend college and can generalize school experiences to life should not be pulled from a foreign language class (Madaus, 2005). The more a student generalizes academic and social skills from school to nonschool settings, the less community-referenced instruction is needed. Conversely, the less a student demonstrates skills in real-life application situations, the more the student needs CRI.

Many school systems, community colleges, and colleges are promoting community service for *all* students. Community service projects are a positive step toward giving all students opportunities to feel connected to their communities. For example, in one school the students (all students with and without disabilities) go to a local nursery and grow a garden. They then sell these plants to people in the community, and yet provide additional food to people who are poor or homeless learning about both making a profit and being a good member of society.

POSTSCHOOL ADULT LIVING

Postschool adult living is a broad area that encompasses the skills and knowledge required in the adult world outside of work and school. As adults, we shop for groceries, balance our checkbooks, make dental appointments, vote, and participate in community volunteer activities. We form and maintain relationships with others and make lifestyle decisions that affect our lives for years to come. Some students learn the skills to perform these activities through family modeling or incidental learning without direct instruction. Other students will need guidance and support in applying skills learned in and out of school to their own situations in the community. Finding instructional time to address postschool adult living skills when the emphasis is almost exclusively on rigorous academics and higher graduation requirements may be difficult but can be helpful to all students. In the larger scheme of life, learning these skills may be critical to students' survival after high school (Steere, Rose, & Cacaiuolo, 2007). This section suggests possible ways to teach critical postschool adult living skills. It also addresses self-determination and interpersonal skills, which are critical for successful postschool adult living.

Life Skills

There are two basic ways to approach the teaching of life skills in the school setting. One way is to embed life skills into academic instruction. The other is to embed academics in life skills instruction. The approach you choose depends on several factors. If students who have mild disabilities have opportunities to practice adult living skills at home and in the community, and are in a school setting that stresses academic instruction, then you will probably want to teach academics and application opportunities in simulated or actual community settings. If students are able to give you specific examples of how they might use this knowledge and skills in various settings in the community (use language to mediate the generalization), you can be fairly certain they will most likely use the skills in places outside the classroom.

If, on the other hand, the students are enrolled in a life skills curriculum and have great difficulty applying the skills in real-life settings, then you will probably want to teach life skills explicitly and embed the necessary functional academics into this instruction. Below are examples of these two different approaches.

EXAMPLE 1: Embedding Life Skills Into Academics

Teach a lesson on fractions using direct instruction. As part of connecting the fractions lesson to prior learning, ask students why they think knowing about fractions might be useful in everyday life.

Follow the lesson on fractions with a discussion about how fractions could be used in everyday activities (measurements for cooking, measurements for building, fractions of an hour to calculate pay). Or, give a homework assignment to identify three ways fractions are used in their home.

EXAMPLE 2: Embedding Academics Into Life Skills Lessons

Teach a lesson on physical fitness. Use direct instruction to teach students about taking their pulse rate when exercising. Using a model heart, talk about the chambers of the heart and how blood flows throughout the body. For guided practice, you might ask students to exercise for five minutes and then as a group take their pulse rate. Then ask students to talk about the process of blood flowing through their body related to their beginning and ending pulse rate. For independent practice, assign each student to do a different type of exercise for five minutes at home that night (e.g., one student walk, one do jumping jacks, one clean the house) and then to be prepared to come back tomorrow to compare their pulse rates and how blood flowed through their body and the relation to the chambers of the heart.

Even if students demonstrate mastery of taking a pulse rate, there is no assurance that students, especially students with moderate cognitive disabilities, will apply this concept in science class or the importance of exercising daily without some additional steps, so remember repetition must be built into your lesson planning structure. Also remember that your instruction should always focus on students becoming independent learners in the skills you are teaching for transition. Often as a component of the lesson, you will want to include skills in self-advocacy and self-determination.

Self-Advocacy and Self-Determination

In the past, teachers, agency personnel, and parents completed transition planning without much student input. Yet today many curricula are available that use a variety of approaches to help students develop self-determination skills. Table 12.3 lists and describes several of these curricula. Research indicates a relationship between positive postschool outcomes and self-determination for individuals with mild disabilities is critical to success (Miller, Lombard, & Corbey, 2007).

Students at all ages should be encouraged to participate in the planning for transition. At the elementary level they may share a list of strengths and weaknesses and read over their IEP with their teacher. As students progress in age, they should attend and even lead their IEP meetings to prepare them to be their own advocate in postschool activities. Unfortunately, many students do not see themselves as an integral part of the transition planning process, some professionals do not see students as active participants, and sometimes parents are hesitant to have their child participate. Test, Mason, Huges, Konrad, Neale, and Wood (2004) analyzed 16 studies related to the involvement of students with disabilities in the IEP process. Their analysis indicated that students with a wide range of disabilities can be taught to be active participants in the IEP process. Suggestions for ensuring student involvement in TIEP development include (a) have students write a rough draft of their own TIEP as a written class assignment, (b) encourage students to make a list of their strengths and weaknesses, (c) ask students to prepare a tentative list of their own transition goals to bring to the TIEP meeting, (d) allow students to be the prime decision makers relative to the time and place scheduled for their TIEP meeting, and (e) ensure that no TIEP meeting is held unless the students can be in attendance. See Figure 12.2 for an example of a way of involving students in the TIEP process.

Table 12.3 Sample Self-Determination Curricula

Title/Date	Author	Target Population	Comments
NEXT S.T.E.P.: Student Transition Educational Planning (2000)	Halpren, Herr, Doren, & Wolf	High school students	Has 16 lessons focused on self-evaluation, goal setting, self-determination, and progress monitoring.
Student-Led IEP's: A Guide for Student Involvement (2002)	McGahee, Mason, Wallace, & Jones	All ages	Assists students in being at the center of the IEP process and helping write their IEP goals.
It's My Life (1995)	Curtis	Middle and high school students	Materials are designed to be fun for students (i.e., a card deck)
Whose Future Is It Anyway? (1995)	Wehmeyer	Students with mental disabilities	A student-directed transition planning process that is age and developmentally appropriate
Choicemaker Self-Determination Transition Curriculum (1996)	Martin, Huber, Marshall, Maxson & Jerman	One part targets high school students with disabilities; other parts target all students	Comprehensive (and field tested) includes *Self-directed IEP, Choosing Employment Goals,* and *Take Action*

Figure 12.2 GOALS FOR MY FUTURE

Directions: Read each question and answer it to the best of your ability.

The thing I like most about myself is ______________________________.

My favorite classes in school are ______________________________.

My favorite class is ____________________ because ____________________.

My least favorite class is ____________________ because ____________________.

I get along with teachers who ____________________ because ____________________.

I am better in (math, reading, writing, science).

The most difficult subjects for me are ____________________.

I have these accommodations listed on my IEP ____________________.

I am interested in attending:

____________________Four-year college/university

____________________Two-year community college

____________________Vocational School

____________________Military

____________________Other: ____________________

In order to go to college/vocational school/the military I have to ____________________ by (date) ____________________.

My backup plan is ____________________.

I would like to have ____________________ job because ____________________.

I have worked at ____________________, where part of my responsibilities were ____________________.

If I had to pick six adjectives to describe myself, they would be ____________________.

In one year I see myself doing ____________________, living ____________________, and ____________________.

In three years, I would like to be ____________________.

In five years, I will be ____________________.

Activity 12.3

Interview an elementary and a secondary student about their disability (with parent permission, of course). After the interview share what you learned with a peer. Discuss if you feel these students are being prepared to advocate for their needs beyond school, and if not, what more you could do as a teacher to help the students. (see Figure 12.2).

Self-Advocacy and Self-Determination in Postsecondary Education. The biggest difference between high school and postsecondary education is that the burden of advocacy shifts away from teachers and parents to the student. Under IDEA, schools and parents form a partnership to provide a free and appropriate education for the student. As discussed previously, students in postsecondary educational institutions have rights under ADA and Section 504, but they must be able to advocate for themselves.

The first step in preparing for postsecondary education for young people with disabilities is to open them up to the possibility and desirability of continuing education.

Going on to college may not seem like a very good idea to high school students who struggle daily with academic work. Teachers and parents can promote continuing education by (a) helping the young person set and work toward goals, (b) pointing out people with similar disabilities who have entered and completed college and done well, and (c) helping the student develop a more positive self-concept. In order for students to be successful in college, they need to know how they learn best and to understand why various strategies are critical for their success as adults. Students must realize that their disabilities will not disappear, but that they will be responsible for managing and choosing tasks and activities that complement their strengths and to access supports in areas of weakness.

Good self-esteem and a realistic self-image are not enough, however. Students must also be effective at advocating for themselves for success in postsecondary education (Dowdy & Evers, 1996). Overall, students need to:

1. Be aware of their strengths, weaknesses, and learning preferences.
2. Understand their legal rights (federal laws and regulations such as ADA and applicable state laws).
3. Understand the circumstances under which they can and should request accommodations.
4. Maintain records that document their disability (e.g., IEP, medical records, descriptions of accommodations provided in high school).
5. Identify the types of supports and services that will help them most in their chosen postsecondary setting (e.g., note takers, readers, transportation, etc.).
6. Identify specific services and resources available in the postsecondary institution they wish to attend.
7. Identify the specific people or offices they should contact before, during, and after admission to their school of choice.

Most colleges and universities, including community colleges and vocational technical schools, have written policies regarding students with disabilities. As part of the transition planning process, teachers and guidance counselors should make students and their parents aware that these policies are usually found in the college catalog and/or on the college website. Examples of typical supports and services for students with documented disabilities include note takers, special testing conditions (e.g., extended time, quiet setting, etc.), sign-language interpreters, and readers.

Self-Advocacy and Self-Determination Skills in Employment. Self-advocacy and self-determination skills are important to the worker with a disability. Some of these skills are more critical during the job-seeking process and others are needed to help workers maintain employment and feel good about their jobs. In a three-year study of three schools that established teams to increase students' levels of self-determination skills, researchers found that with this systematic approach, schoolwide change did occur for students with mild disabilities related to their ability to self-advocate (Lehmann, Bassett, Sands, Spencer, & Gliner, 1999). In addition, Konrad and Tests (2004) found that simply providing instruction to middle school students with disabilities on how to write their IEPs increased student's participation in the process and their self-determination skills. In the area of employment, the following self-advocacy skills are suggested:

1. Listing strengths and accomplishments (e.g., writing a job application or in person during an interview).
2. Discussing the disability and requesting appropriate accommodations.

3. Responding to criticism in an appropriate manner.
4. Self-evaluating performance, monitoring task completion, and providing self-feedback.
5. Goal setting, including developing short- and long-term goals, and monitoring progress.
6. Developing a vocational plan that includes goals for career advancement and job upgrading.
7. Standing up for one's rights on the job (e.g., not being taken advantage of).

SOCIAL AND INTERPERSONAL SKILLS

Interacting with other people is something we do every day in almost every aspect of our lives. Some of us are more socially adept than others. We seldom think of our social skills consciously. Research and anecdotal reports have clearly shown that for many students with disabilities, socialization is not a naturally occurring process (Chandler & Pankaskie, 1997). Lack of appropriate social skills may result in social isolation in the community and, worse, involvement with the criminal justice system. If we do not provide systematic instruction in social skills for students with disabilities, we may be preparing students to fail in school and in the broader world of work and community.

There are many commercially available curricula that address many aspects of social-interpersonal skills. Some of these programs are listed and described in Table 12.4.

Social and Interpersonal Skills for Postsecondary Education

In addition to self-advocacy and academic skills, students in postsecondary educational settings need appropriate interpersonal skills (Field, Sarver, & Shaw, 2003). Social skills essential for postsecondary educational settings may include the ability to (a) use strategies to manage frustration and anger, (b) speak in a way that conveys a positive yet realistic self-image, (c) show awareness and concerns for the feelings of others, and (d) interact positively with college instructors, administrators, staff, and peers.

Table 12.4 Sample Social Skills Curricula for Transition

Title/Author/Date	Description
ASSET Hazel, Schumaker, Sherman, & Sheldon-Widgen (1981)	A social skills program for adolescents age 13–18. It has a leader's guide, group activities, videotapes, and audiotapes.
Social Skills in the School and Community, Sargent (ed.) (1991)	A CEC publication for mainstreamed primary, intermediate, junior, and senior high school levels.
Teaching Social Skills, Rutherford, Chipman, DiGangi, & Anderson (1992)	A CEC publication that teaches socialization instructional approach.
Skillstreaming the Adolescent. A Structural Learning Approach to Teaching Prosocial Skills, Goldstein, Sprafkin, Gershaw, & Klein (2002)	One of the most widely used, this curriculum provides a five-phase sequence to teach students critical social skills: (1) introduce the steps of the skills, (2) teach the steps, (3) demonstrate the skill, (4) have students rehearse and practice the skill, and (5) teach maintenance and generalization of the skill.

Activity 12.4

In a small group identify 10 social skills that you believe are important for success in today's workforce. Then talk about how you would incorporate teaching these skills in a secondary English classroom.

Social and Interpersonal Skills for Employment

Lack of social and interpersonal skills is often cited as the primary reason for unemployment and underemployment of individuals with special needs (Sitlington, Clark, & Kolstoe, 2000). The specific skills related to successful employment are (a) independently managing one's activities, (b) meeting minimal cleanliness and dress requirements, (c) getting along with supervisors, (d) getting along with coworkers, (e) following directions, (f) being punctual, (g) managing time effectively and efficiently, (h) keeping an orderly work environment, (i) being friendly on the job, and (j) maintaining a moral work ethic (Archer & Gleason, 1994).

EMPLOYMENT

Knowing how to seek, find, and acquire employment are critical elements in transition programs for high school students with special needs and the ultimate outcome of education at all levels (Steere, Rose, & Cacaiuolo, 2007). Adolescents with disabilities need instruction in all aspects of post-education and work-related skills for success. Some guidelines for infusing these components into the high school curriculum are listed below.

1. Include in your school's curriculum for all students how to search for employment by examining job applications, job announcements, and interviewing employers.
2. Include as part of the curriculum resumé development. Although young people may not have prior work experience, they do have life experiences or service learning and volunteer activities that are transferable to the workplace.
3. Include instruction in filling out job applications neatly, accurately, and completely.
4. Include instruction in how to interview for a job in all content areas. For example, how does an interview for a job in business differ from a job in engineering, teaching, or hospitality management. Provide both instruction and modeling related to the interview process.
5. Include instruction on what essential documents are needed for getting a job. Cover what documents are necessary (e.g., birth certificate, state ID card, work permit, Social Security card), and how to obtain these documents.

If students are not given the skills as to how to access employment, then having the skills to be employed is irrelevant. Therefore, having an equal balance of seeking a job as well as keeping a job should be the focus of employment because job success depends equally on job maintenance skills (such as communication and interpersonal skills and good work habits) and actual job skills (Montague, 1988). Employers consider worker behaviors and attitudes to be important or essential to job performance (Sitlington, Clark, & Kolstoe, 2000). When employers were asked to rank factors judged critical to job success for workers with disabilities, the five highest-ranking factors were (1) getting along well with others, (2) interest in the job, (3) efficiency, (4) dependability, and (5) being able to adapt to new work situations (Chamberlain, 1988).

Activity 12.5

Obtain job applications from three local businesses (try to go to a range of businesses from low level—food preparation to higher level—executive positions). Review these applications and talk with a peer about how students might be destined for certain jobs if some specific job skills are not taught. Also discuss what is needed for students to complete both the application process and possible interview questions that might emerge from each position.

FUNCTIONAL VOCATIONAL ASSESSMENT

Appropriate, functional vocational assessment is required but not defined in IDEA. IDEA requires that the interests and preferences of each student be considered in planning for transition. Vocational aptitude and interest inventories can provide much of this information. In the following sections, we describe curriculum-based vocational assessment and situational assessment, two specific types of vocational assessment that have this orientation. We also discuss portfolio assessment. Any of these assessments meet the original IDEA requirements for a "functional vocational assessment" and provide a way of assessing student progress in ways more useful (functional) than more formal, standardized testing. Note how the results of each type of assessment are incorporated in the present level of performance in the sample Transition IEPs found in Figure 12.1.

Curriculum-Based Vocational Assessment (CBVA)

CBVA is similar to curriculum-based measurement, which we described in Chapter 4, but has some unique characteristics. The main purpose of CBVA is to determine the career development and vocational instruction needs of students based on their ongoing performance within existing course content and curriculum. CBVA provides an alternative to the more traditional vocational assessment process. This type of assessment has been found especially useful with students for whom written and simulated manipulation assessments are not appropriate. Table 12.5 provides a comparison of CBVA and traditional vocational evaluation.

Table 12.5 Comparison of Two Vocational Assessment Approaches

Traditional Vocational Work Evaluation	Curriculum-Based Vocational Assessment
Requires a trained work evaluator experienced with special populations	Uses existing personnel such as vocational and special education teachers
Has high start-up costs and ongoing maintenance expenses	Has minimal start-up and maintenance costs
Includes a "snapshot" of a student's abilities at the time of the evaluation	Includes ongoing assessments from middle school through high school
Tends to result in very technical reports that require interpretation by a work evaluator	Tends to results in reports easily understood by parents and teachers
Has little or no relevance to what goes on in the classroom	Focuses on performance of course objectives and work-related outcomes
Provides information at the time of the work evaluation report	Provides a current base of information useful for transition planning

CBVA includes three general assessment areas: work-related behaviors, generalized skill outcomes, and specific skill outcomes. *Work-related behaviors* are the attitudinal, problem-solving, and interpersonal behaviors that are critical for student success both in classroom and community job settings. *Generalized skill outcomes* are the prerequisite concepts and knowledge necessary for students to perform successfully skills required in many occupational areas. These skills include oral and written communication, math computation, and social-personal and problem solving. *Specific skill outcomes* are those skills needed for a particular occupational area. For example, in the area of technology, students may be observed for mastery of their skills in using all aspects of the Microsoft suite as an entry-level skill base.

The results of CBVA should assist teachers, students, and their families in developing transition statements that create meaningful TIEP goals. Keep in mind the cultural backgrounds of families and be certain to not impose your perspective of success from your culture (Rueda, Monzo, Shapiro, Gomez, & Blacher, 2005). These goals should provide the platform for determining exit competencies for each outcome area.

Situational Assessment

Situational assessment is a system for evaluating work-related behaviors by observing a student in a controlled or somewhat controlled work environment. A situational assessment is different from a CBVA in that the assessed variables may be controlled during the assessment process. Situational assessment may be performed in contrived or simulated settings, such as a mock workstation in a classroom, or in a real work setting. The underlying purposes of situational assessment are to observe and assess the individual in the work situation and provide feedback to the person and other interested parties about demonstrated work-related behaviors. The steps in a strong situational assessment are:

1. Planning (considerations such as a work site that is of interest to the student, appropriate supervision, and a means for gathering information that can be used in vocational planning and feedback)
2. Scheduling (consideration of the dates and times of the observations, number of observations, and total time period of the observation—not longer than one month)
3. Recording (describing behaviors in observable, measurable terms; providing information about the work environment; recording the frequency, rate, or duration of behaviors when they occur)
4. Reporting (summarizing the observations and making recommendations, including job placement, work adjustment training, or another situational assessment in the same or different environment).

The outcome of a situational assessment should be that specific skills targeted for instruction can then be assessed at a later date in that same situation. The use of a pre- and post-assessment technique is typically used in situational assessment to ensure the outcome of instruction does provide a generalization of the targeted skill in the actual work setting.

Portfolio Assessment

Although portfolio assessments have been in the academic setting, this tool can also be used for work, college, and employment-related settings. Students as well as their general and special education classroom teachers may provide samples of work to show both student strengths and examples of successes when appropriate supports are provided. Kortering and Braziel (2000) found that adolescents with learning disabilities often had a misperception about the career options available to them after graduation. For example, in a transition portfolio students might show a handwritten paper and then show the same paper that has been typed and edited by the students demonstrating that they can be successful in the area of writing and spelling with a basic tool such as a computer. The portfolio should be created to demonstrate to employers that the students have the skills and knowledge of how they will support areas of weakness to be successful in college or the workforce. Krebs (2002) agreed that future success is facilitated by the development of self-advocacy skills, and a portfolio is an excellent tool to encourage these areas to develop in students.

BOX 12.3

Reflections on Practice

Reflect on your own areas of strengths and weaknesses. How have you learned to compensate for areas of weakness and how have you either sought employment related to your area of strength or showcased your areas of strength in seeking a job?

Now think about how you might both assess that for students with disabilities in your classroom or how you might provide examples in a portfolio. As you reflect upon these skills, think about where they might be logically taught in the curriculum.

Next, review the state standards in a selected secondary academic area. Consider for a moment how you might teach work-related skills as well as gather documentation or work samples of skills in the standards for a specific academic area.

Remember preparing students for the transition from school to work requires an equal commitment to the process by teachers, students, and their families. As you create your transition and work-related plans, be certain students are at the center of the process.

DAILY LIVING SKILLS

Consider for a moment the number of skills that we learn from the day we are born until we are gainfully employed. Most of the time these skills develop naturally as a member of society. Yet for many students with disabilities, they may need to be taught a range of daily living skills. These skills could include maintaining good health, working with others, and managing resources (money, time, and people). Most students with mild disabilities or emotional needs do not need direct instruction in daily living skills. They learn them, as most children do, through observation and guidance from teachers and family members. However, some students (e.g., students with physical disabilities, severe emotional needs, or with moderate to severe mental disabilities) may need direct instruction in the how, where, and when of daily living skills.

Several curricula offer guidance in teaching daily living skills. One of the most popular is the Life Centered Career Education (LCCE) Curriculum (Brolin & Lloyd, 2004). This curriculum contains 10 questions in each of the 21 competencies found in the mild curriculum area. The Adaptive Living Skills Curriculum (ALSC) (Bruinicks, Moreau, Gilman, & Anderson, 1991) covers personal living skills as well as skills for home living, community living, and employment.

The instruction of daily living skills should not occur in the vacuum of only school. These targeted skills should be shared as goals with students, their families, and employers to ensure that during the high school years these skills are not just learned, but mastered.

IMPORTANT POINTS

1. Transition domains under IDEA include instruction, related services, community experience, postschool adult living, social and interpersonal skills, employment, and as appropriate, functional vocational assessment and daily living skills.
2. Although most high school curricula are set up to be "college prep," teachers and parents must make sure not only that students with disabilities enroll in the appropriate courses, but also that they are provided with supports and services to pass those courses.
3. Self-determination and self-advocacy skills will be needed by all young adults, whether they are going on to postsecondary education or directly into employment. The specific skills, however, may be somewhat different.
4. Lack of adequate social and interpersonal skills is often cited as the primary reason for unemployment and underemployment of individuals with special needs.
5. Alternative functional vocational assessments include curriculum-based vocational assessment, situational assessment, and portfolio assessment.

LINKING FOR TRANSITION

Planning and implementing transition supports and services is not something that can or should be done only by schools and teachers. Schools must join with *families*, *intraagency* personnel (i.e., people inside the school system such as general education teachers and guidance counselors), and *interagency* personnel (i.e., people from the wider community, such as representatives from adult service agencies and employers). In this section, we provide ideas about how to connect or link with these key stakeholders for the success of students with disabilities.

FAMILY LINKAGES

Many families and guardians are very involved with children during the early years, as often, parents of children with disabilities are overly committed to their child's successful beginning in the educational setting. Young children require care and attention, and those with special needs may evoke more nurturing and protective impulses in families than typical children. By the time students reach high school, however, family involvement in the IEP process typically declines (Thorin, Yovanoff, & Irvin, 1996). The 1990 amendments to IDEA attempted to reemphasize the importance of family involvement by including a requirement of special notification to families when the purpose of the IEP meeting was to discuss transition services. Salembier and Furney (1997) list three reasons about the importance of family involvement in the transition planning and implementation process:

1. Families know more about their adolescents' needs, interests, and preferences.
2. The transition process prepares family members to think about the new roles and responsibilities they will have when their adolescent leaves the protective atmosphere of high school and the entitlement of IDEA.
3. If done correctly, involvement can empower the family to advocate for the adolescent during and after high school.

Families can be involved in many ways during transition. They may be involved in creating a vision, in the transition planning process, and in facilitating self-determination (Morningstar, Turnbull, & Turnbull, 1996). Many students with disabilities need their parents to become active partners in the transition from school to life and for some students throughout their lives. Family members need to be provided information on the process to access services specific to their adolescent's transition needs.

INTRAAGENCY LINKAGES

You as the teacher as well as students with disabilities and their families need to develop linkages with people inside the school environment, which typically means general education teachers, school psychologists, and guidance counselors. Remember, successful transition takes a team approach and cannot start with just postschool experiences if students are to be successful. Individuals within the school environment are the ones who can help students acquire the knowledge and skills that will allow them access to successful postschool experiences.

General Education Linkages

In this time of high-stakes testing and alternative diploma options, special education teachers must understand and articulate to general education teachers the importance of access and mastery of the general education curriculum. Students who wish to pursue postsecondary education must first obtain a standard high school diploma or its equivalent. Making linkages with general education teachers therefore is critical. Although ways to collaborate with general education teachers and to support students academically in inclusive settings are discussed elsewhere in this text, it is important to remember that this collaboration is also part of the transition process.

School-to-Work Programs. One of the most exciting initiatives related to transition is the School-to-Work Opportunities Act. The purpose of the School-to-Work (STW) Opportunities Act is to establish a national framework to broaden educational, career, and economic opportunities for all youth through partnerships among business, schools, community-based organizations, and state and local governments. "All youth" includes young people with special needs (e.g., students with disabilities, disadvantaged youth, and youth with limited English proficiency). STW was designed to help states develop an integrated system that would provide students with a seamless transition from secondary education to meaningful, high-quality employment and continuing education. Successful school-to-work programs have three core components:

1. School-based learning (e.g., programs in which students learn math, science, language arts, technology, and other skills and standards in the context of the work world)
2. Work-based learning (e.g., programs in which students gain practical experience and training)
3. Connecting activities (e.g., links between employers, schools, teachers, students, and others).

These three components should be incorporated in kindergarten through postsecondary educational programs and should be based upon students' interests and future desires.

Work Experiences. Despite the common perception that work experience is effective in promoting future employment success, the National Longitudinal Transition Study (Wagner & Blackorby, 1996) found only a slight difference in the percentage of students (10.4%) competitively employed after high school between students with mild disabilities who did and did not have work experience. However, paid work experiences while in high school do make a difference in postschool outcomes (Rabren, Dunn, & Chambers, 2002). Students with disabilities who engage in paid employment before high school completion are more likely to stay in school, remain employed after school completion, seek postsecondary education opportunities, and become self-supporting adults (Edgar, 1987).

Guidance and Counseling

School counselors often take an active role in career planning for students with disabilities and initiate early career planning with parents and students. Students need to become aware of the many programs that can help them beyond high school, including community college programs, counseling and testing, student disability services, occupational preparation programs, vocational training programs, and adult agency services.

School counselors should become an integral part of the transition team so they are informed and knowledgeable about the multitude of postschool program options for this group of students. High school special education teachers, job coaches, and other special education support personnel can play a vital role in collaborating with school counselors and soliciting their support on behalf of students with special needs in their quest for successful employment and adult living.

Activity 12.6

Talk to guidance counselors about their role in the transition process. Ask how they collaborate with special education teachers and students with disabilities. If their collaboration is limited, ask why they think it is and how collaboration could be improved.

INTERAGENCY LINKAGES

Under IDEA, schools must provide a description of "interagency responsibilities and/or linkages" needed before a student leaves school. This aspect of the law implies that schools need to have a working knowledge of and relationship with the public or private agencies that might provide or pay for services needed during transition. Unfortunately, students with disabilities often have little contact with representatives from postsecondary education, social, or rehabilitation agencies during their high school years (Roessler, Brolin, & Johnson, 1990).

The referral process to adult agencies must begin early so school personnel can assist with the application process and ensure active service status with the appropriate adult agency before graduation. Once a student with special needs graduates, there are a multitude of adult agencies to access. However, most of the agencies are burdened with high caseloads, bureaucratic complexities, discrepant eligibility criteria, and voluminous paperwork. Most adult agencies (such as state vocational rehabilitation agencies) require a formal application, medical exam, psychological exam, permission to access existing assessment information, interviews with the agency representative, eligibility determination, vocational evaluation, and/or extended vocational evaluation. This process can take anywhere from 12 to 24 months. A planned and systematic process of adult agency referral should be included in the student's TIEP during the tenth grade. The ultimate goal must be active client status with the adult agency, including postsecondary institutions, before the student's graduation date.

Once students with disabilities have completed the period of eligibility under IDEA (usually through age 21 or high school graduation, whichever comes first), they are no longer guaranteed services. The young adult will have to undergo the eligibility determination process for whatever adult services are desired. If determined eligible, the person may receive services from that agency as long as adequate state or federal funding is available or until the eligibility is reversed. There are many challenges in finding and getting the services necessary for young adults to make a successful transition. IDEA makes it clear that meeting these challenges is the shared responsibility of schools, parents, students, and agency personnel.

The most often accessed adult service agencies are listed and described in Table 12.6. This list is not intended to be exhaustive but instead a beginning place for teachers, transition specialists, parents, and students.

Welfare reform is rapidly changing the types of programs available to people with limited means, including those with disabilities. As the federal government gives more and more discretion to state and local governments, fewer and fewer general statements can be made about national programs. You will need to become familiar with state requirements, especially for the programs described in Table 12.6. Because regulations

Table 12.6 Adult Agencies That Serve Students With Disabilities in Transition

Agency	Description
Vocational Rehabilitation (VR)	VR's primary purpose is to assist eligible recipients to attain vocational goals and thereby become more economically self-sufficient. To be eligible for VR, a person must (1) have a physical and/or mental impairment that constitutes a substantial impediment to employment, and (2) be able to benefit from employment outcomes. VR is a federally funded program (80%) with state match.
Job/Employment Services Job Training Partnership Act (JTPA)	Job or Employment Services are often administered by the same state agency that administers VR. The Job Training Partnership Act (JTPA) may also be in this agency (JTPA may be referred to by different names in different localities). This act provides job training services for economically disadvantage adults and others who face significant employment barriers.
Developmental Disabilities (DD) Services	Developmental disabilities services may include services in the areas of employment, residential, advocacy, and day activity programs. The most common developmental disabilities are mental retardation, autism, cerebral palsy, and epilepsy.
Community Colleges and Vocational Technical Schools	Community colleges and vocational technical schools typically have open enrollment and serve high school graduates from a certain area. They can provide information about financial aid, academic counseling and guidance, special supports for students with disabilities, and, of course, an array of programs that usually include both terminal degrees with certifications or two-year programs that will allow students to go on to upper-division colleges and universities.
Social Security Administration (SSA)	The SSA is responsible for administering many federal and state funds for eligible elderly persons and persons with disabilities. The ones that may affect students in transition are: Income Programs [e.g., Supplemental Security Income Benefits (SSI)], Medical Programs [e.g., Medicare and Medicaid], Work Incentive Programs [e.g., Plans for Achieving Self-Support (PASS), Impairment-Related Work Expenses (IRWE), Student Earned Income Exclusion, etc.].
Accessibility Office	If a student plans to attend college, make an appointment in their sophomore year to talk with the student accessibility office. Help the student learn about the supports they can use to be successful in college and areas of independence they still need to gain as they prepare to graduate from high school.

change, including eligibility requirements, you should stay in close contact with local representatives of these agencies. For the most current and detailed information related to Social Security programs, contact your local Social Security Administration (SSA) office. You may locate the SSA office closest to you by calling 1-800-772-1213.

IMPORTANT POINTS

1. For effective transition to occur, families, intraagency personnel such as people inside the school system, and interagency personnel such as representatives from adult service agencies must work together.
2. Family members need to be taught the process of adult agency referral, the mechanics of developing a TIEP, effective strategies for supporting the efforts of a working student, strategies for accessing adult community services, and other information specific to their adolescent's transition from school to the adult community.
3. Under IDEA, schools must provide a description of "interagency responsibilities and/or linkages" needed before a student leaves school.
4. Once students with disabilities complete the period of eligibility under IDEA (usually through age 21 or high school graduation, whichever comes first), they are no longer guaranteed services.

PUTTING IT ALL TOGETHER

When parents learn their child has a disability, they often begin to worry about how they and the school will meet their child's unique learning or behavioral needs. The role of the special educator is to help parents, family members, and the student to achieve success in the school setting.

Yet special education teachers must also focus on results beyond the school setting. From data related to postschool outcomes for students with disabilities we know that just focusing on school is not enough. As a special educator at any grade level, you will need to also help students and their families see into the future related to success in life beyond school. Remember, as the special education teacher, there are numerous supports available at the community college and university levels, in the community and within the school to assist with the transition process and to ensure successful outcomes for students with disabilities. The most important steps to take as a teacher are to learn about and connect students and their families to those resources, include within your instruction, both the academic and social skills students will need to be successful in school and life, teach students to self-advocate for their own needs and keep students at the center of planning for transitions at all levels. If students with disabilities are armed with the skills they need for success in life, then that is the real measure of success of public education.

DISCUSSION QUESTIONS

1. Why do you think students with disabilities do not access college at the same level as their nondisabled peers? Why do you think many students with disabilities are underemployed or unemployed and who is responsible to help close this gap?
2. Do a Google search and look at the data gathered from the National Longitudinal Transition Study II. Which population of students needs the most support from

this study related to transition, and why do you think this population continues to be at risk?

3. You are asked to help write standards for your state in middle school math. How would you include work-related skills in your discussion about state standards?

Websites: Usefule websites related to chapter content can be found in Appendix A.

APPENDIX A: WEBSITES

CHAPTER 1

Center on Instruction–Devoted to disseminating research-based best practices, including a section on Special Education.

http://www.centeroninstruction.org/index.cfm

Circle of Inclusion–This web site offers demonstrations of and information about the effective practices of inclusive educational programs for children from birth through age eight.

http://circleofinclusion.org/

Concept to Classroom: A Series of Workshops–Free professional development self-paced modules on a variety of hot topics in education.

http://www.thirteen.org/edonline/concept2class/index.html

IDEA Partnership–A collaboration of organizations dedicated to providing information and resources relevant to IDEA and NCLB.

http://www.ideapartnership.org/

Inclusion–A wealth of information about planning for inclusive education.

http://www.uni.edu/coe/inclusion/

Inclusion.com–Offers links to resources on inclusion.

http://www.inclusion.com/

Learning Disabilities Online–Offers resources for teachers and families of students with learning disabilities, learning disorders, and learning differences.

http://www.ldonline.org

Wikipedia–A free on-line encyclopedia that has an excellent entry on the use of constructivist teaching.

http://en.wikipedia.org/wiki/Constructivist_teaching_methods

CHAPTER 2

Florida Center for Reading Research–Established at Florida State University as a means of conducting research on reading and making it accessible it to the public.

http://www.fcrr.org/index.htm

Guide to the Individualized Education Program–The U.S. Department of Education link.

http://www.ed.gov/parents/needs/speced/iepguide/index.html

Special Connections–A source of research-based strategies in special education. Organized into four categories; Instruction, Collaboration, Assessment, and Behavior.

http://www.specialconnections.ku.edu/cgi-bin/cgiwrap/specconn/index.php

Special Education Resources on the Internet–A multi-purpose site that would be good for special educators to refer to their general educator colleagues.

http://seriweb.com/

Teachers.net–Contains many teacher resources including free lesson plans

http://www.teachers.net/

CHAPTER 3

Council for Exceptional Education–Sign up for their "Smart Briefs" updates to be delivered to your inbox. The briefs will keep you up-to-date on the latest news in the world of exceptional education.

http://www.cec.sped.org

Education World–A multi-purpose website for teachers. Great for lesson planning and professional development.

http://www.education-world.com/

ESchool News Online–this site provides the latest news and information about the use of technology in schools. Links are provided to available grants and professional development.

http://www.eschoolnews.com/

MarcoPolo–Provides information on how to access quality internet content and professional development.

http://www.marcopolo-education.org/home.aspx

National Education Association–Has a section devoted to paraprofessionals.

http://www.nea.org/index.html

Power of 2–Resources and information on effective inclusion and the collaborative model.

http://www.powerof2.org

CHAPTER 4

4Teachers–A multi-purpose site that assists teachers in the use of technology in their classrooms. Offers free online tools and resources, including printable checklists.

http://4teachers.org/

Easy Test Maker–Allows teachers to make test in varying formats at no cost.

http://www.easytestmaker.com

Fun Brain–Lots of fun assessment types of games and tools.

http://www.funbrain.com

Quia–Assists in making and redesigning quizzes

http://www.quia.com

Quiz Center–Allows you to administer and grade quizzes online.

http://school.discovery.com/quizcenter/quizcenter.html

QuizStar–A free service that allows teachers to give online quizzes.

http://quizstar.4teachers.org

Sheppard Software–A site dedicated to making learning fun. Offers free online games, quizzes, and software.

http://www.sheppardsoftware.com/

CHAPTER 5

Audible.com–A source for downloading audible books, which are a good example of establishing Universal Design for Learning

http://www.audible.com

Cliffsnotes–This site provides short summaries of stories that are excellent for students with disabilities to read instead of entire novels.

http://www.cliffsnotes.com

Free Book Notes–A guide to free book notes, free book summaries, literature notes, and study guides for over 1600 books, plays, and poems.

http://www.freebooknotes.com

Library of Congress–This site houses thousands of pictures and artifacts that can be used to enrich social studies lessons or provide daily writing prompts.

http://www.loc.gov

Spark Notes–This site provides study guides related to classic novels and other areas often covered at the secondary level.

http://www.sparknotes.com

Teachers Helping Teachers–Includes a section on Special Education that has many tips from practicing professionals

http://www.pacificnet.net/~mandel/

Windows of Universe–A user-friendly learning system covering the Earth and Space sciences.

http://www.windows.ucar.edu

CHAPTER 6

iDictate–For a small fee students who need a scribe for their writing can dictate any document using a telephone, fax machine, or dictation device, and then receive the completed job back for editing via e-mail.

http://www.idictate.com

Novel Guide–This site is a free source for literary analysis on the web to assist students in better understand both classic and contemporary text.

http://www.novelguide.com

Paragraph Writing–This web site takes users through the actual steps of writing a basic paragraph.

http://www.paragraphpunch.com

The Teacher's Corner–A multi-purpose site with links to a variety of resources.

http://www.theteacherscorner.net/

VoyCabulary–Makes the words on any webpage into links so you can look them up in a dictionary or other word-reference-site of your choice, by simply clicking on the words.

http://www.voycabulary.com/

What Works Clearinghouse–Established by the U.S. Department of Education's Institute of Education Sciences (IES) to provide scientific evidence of what works in education.

http://www.w-w-c.org/

CHAPTER 7

Center on Accelerating Student Learning (CASL)–Defines the purpose and goals of CASL with links to lesson plans.

http://kc.vanderbilt.edu/casl/index.html

Dr. Mel Levine's site for Understanding Differences in Learning–Includes articles, video clips, a parent toolkit, etc.

http://www.allkindsofminds.org/

Maryland Literacy Research Center at the University of Maryland–Additional information on SRSD and CASL.

http://www.education.umd.edu/literacy/srsd/srsd.htm

ReadWriteThink–The International Reading Association (IRA), and the National Council of Teachers of English (NCTE) partnered to offer this site dedicated to improving reading and language arts instruction.

http://readwritethink.org/

University of Kansas Center for Research on Learning–Information on SIM.

http://www.ku-crl.org/

CHAPTER 8

About Learning–Offers information and resources about different learning styles.

http://www.aboutlearning.com/

BrainPOP–An educational program, providing content spanning 6 main subjects including: Science, Math, English, Social Studies, Health and Technology. May be used at school or at home.

http://www.brainpop.com

Discovery.com–Website for the popular television channel. Links to educational resources, many of which are science related. Excellent video downloads available.

http://www.discovery.com/

National Council for the Social Studies

http://www.socialstudies.org

National Geographic–the popular magazine website offers a wealth of social studies and science resources that can be used in the classroom. Amazing photography and video available for free downloads.

http://www.nationalgeographic.com/index.html

National Science Teachers Association

http://nsta.org

Newseum–An interactive museum of the news.

http://www.newseum.org/

Newsmap–A different approach to presenting the headlines of the day.

http://www.marumushi.com/apps/newsmap/newsmap.cfm

CHAPTER 9

Center for Evidence-Based Practice: Young Children with Challenging Behavior–This site is funded by the U.S. Department of Education's Office of Special Education Programs (OSEP).

http://challengingbehavior.fmhi.usf.edu/resources.html

Dr. Mac's Amazing Behavior Management Advice Site–A very user-friendly site that offers tips on classroom management of challenging behaviors.

http://www.behavioradvisor.com/

Office of Special Education Programs (OSEP) Technical Assistance Center on Positive Behavioral Interventions and Support–Offers effective school-wide interventions backed by scientific research.

http://www.pbis.org/main.htm

Text aloud–Lists books that lend themselves to being read aloud and directly links to the purchase site. A great source to share with students and families and good to use for cross-age peer tutoring.

http://www.readaloud.com

CHAPTER 10

Education World–A helpful site for teachers and parents that has a section on special education resources.

http://www.education-world.com/special_ed/mild/learning.shtml

Graphic Organizers–Free downloads of graphic organizers.

http://www.graphicorganizers.com

Homework Help–Offers unlimited, free, self-paced modules to assist with a variety of subjects. There is a charge if you would prefer live on-line tutoring.

www.homeworkhelp.com

Kidspiration/Inspiration–A great tool to use to help students organize notes for any class or to use as a prewriting strategy. This tool basically creates semantic maps.

http://www.inspiration.com

Teacher Vision–Multi-purpose website for teachers and parents that includes free downloads of graphic organizers. Great for new teachers.

http://teachervision.com/

CHAPTER 11

Assistive Technology Training Online Project–Provides information on AT applications that help students with disabilities learn in elementary classrooms.

www.atto.buffalo.edu/

The connSENSE Bulletin–Assistive technology project provides training, tutorials, and information.

www.connsensebulletin.com/gap2005.html

Education 4 Kids–Drill games related to math, language, social studies, and science.

http://www.edu4kids.com/

Georgia Project for Assistive Technology–Provides information on support strategies and assistive technology solutions.

http://www.gpat.org

Internet Resource for Special Children–A variety of resources for those who work with children with special needs.

http://www.irsc.org

LD Resources–Resources and articles about learning disabilities including hints related to technology.

http://www.ldresources.com

Text-to-speech web browsers–These sites all provide tools to assist students in having text read to them.

- **CAST eReader**–http://www.cast.org
- **IBM's Home Page Reader**–http://www-3.ib.com/able/
- **PwWebSpeak**–http://www.soundlinks.com/pwgen.htm
- **Babel Fish**–http://bablfish.altavista.com–Assists with translation of materials when English is not primary language
- **NextUp**–http://nextup.com/

CHAPTER 12

Abledata- Database of currently available Assistive Technology (AT) devices, and useful information about AT.

http://www.abledata.com

Academy of Achievement–Inspirational site that encourages students to strive to do their best. Students can search for achievers who faced struggles similar to their own.

http://www.achievement.org/autodoc/pagegen/index.html

Council for Exceptional Children–A valuable resource for teachers, students, and their families.

http://www.cec.sped.org/

National Center for Learning Disabilities–Has a section on High School and Adulthood with information on available scholarships and awards.

http://www.ncld.org

National Dissemination Center for Children with Disabilities (NICHCY)–Provides links to assist students and their families.

http://www.nichcy.org/

REFERENCES

CHAPTER 1

Allen, J., & Hermann-Wilmarth, J. (2004). Cultural construction zones. *Journal of Teacher Education, 55* (3), 214–226.

Baca, L. M., & Cervantes, H. (1998). *The bilingual special education interface* (3rd ed.). Upper Saddle River, NJ: Prentice Hall.

Bloomfield, D. C., & Cooper, B. S. (2003). Making sense of NCLB. *T.H.E. Journal, 30*(10), 6–32.

Council for Exceptional Children. (1995). *Mission statement.* Retrieved November 1, 2006, from www.cec.sped.org

Council For Exceptional Children. (2003). *What every special educator must know: The international standards for the preparation and certification of special education teachers* (5th ed.). Arlington, VA: Author.

Darling-Hammond, L., Chung, R., & Frelow, F. (2002). Variation in teacher preparation how well do different pathways prepare teachers to teach? *Journal of Teacher Education, 53,* 286–302.

Delpit, L. D. (2002). *The skin that we speak: Thoughts on language and culture in the classroom.* New York: New Press.

Dieker, L. A. (2007). *Demystifying secondary inclusion: Powerful school-wide and classroom strategies.* Port Chester, NY: NPR, 3399Inc.

Ehren, B. J., Lenz, B. K., & Deshler, D. (2005). The content literacy continuum: A school reform framework for improving adolescent literacy for all students. *TEACHING Exceptional Children, 37*(6), 60–63.

Englert, C. S., Tarrant, K. L., & Mariage, T. V. (1992). Defining and redefining instructional practice in special education: Perspectives on good teaching. *Teacher Education and Special Education, 15*(2), 62–87.

Fact Sheet: No Child Left Behind (2002). Retrieved November 1, 2006, from http://www.whitehouse.gov/news/releases/2002/01/20020108.html

Forness, S. R., Kavale, K. A., Blum, I. M., & Lloyd, J. W. (1997). Mega-analysis of meta-analyses: What works in special education and related services. *TEACHING Exceptional Children, 29*(6), 4–9.

Friedman, T. L. (2005). The world is flat: A brief history of the twenty-first century. New York: Farrar, Straus & Giroux.

Fuchs, L. S., & Fuchs, D. (2001). Helping teachers formulate sound test accommodation decisions for students with learning disabilities. *Learning Disabilities Research and Practice, 16*(4), 174–181.

Gersten, R., & Baker, S. (2000). What we know about effective instructional practices for English-language learners. *Exceptional Children, 66*(4), 454–470.

Gollnick, D. M., & Chinn, P. C. (2002). *Multicultural education in a pluralistic society* (6th ed.). Upper Saddle River, NJ: Merrill/Prentice Hall.

Harris, K. R., & Graham, S. (1994). Constructivism: Principles, paradigms, and integration. *The Journal of Special Education, 28*(3), 233–247.

Hitchcock, C., Meyer, A., Rose, D., & Jackson, R. (2002). *Technical brief: Access, participation, and progress in the general curriculum.* Peabody, MA: National Center on Accessing the General Curriculum. Retrieved October 25, 2006, from http://www.cast.org/ncac/index.cfm?i=2830

Hodgkinson, H. (2002). Demographics and teacher education. *Journal of Teacher Education, 53*(2), 102–105.

Howell, K. W., Fox, S. L., & Morehead, M. K. (1993). *Curriculum-based evaluation: Teaching decision making* (2nd ed.). Pacific Grove, CA: Brooks/Cole.

Individuals with Disabilities Education Improvement Act of 2004. Public Law 108–446. (2005) Washington, D.C.: U.S. Government Printing Office.

Individuals with Disabilities Education Act of 1997, 20 U.S.C. (Section) 1401–1485.

Irmsher, K. (1996). Inclusive education in practice. In Educational Resources Information Center, U.S. Department of Education (Ed.), *Inclusion, 4*(3), 18–19.

Johnson, M. J. (2004). Constructivist remediation: Correction in context. *International Journal of Special Education, 19*(1), 72–88.

Kavale, K. A., & Forness, S. R. (2000). History, rhetoric, and reality: Analysis of the inclusion debate. *Remedial and Special Education, 21*(5), 279–296.

King-Sears, M. E. (1997). Best academic practices for inclusive classrooms. *Focus on Exceptional Children, 29*(7), 1–22.

Lenz, B. K., Deshler, D. & Kissam, B. R. (2005). *Teaching content to all: Evidence-based practices in middle and secondary schools.* Boston: Pearson.

National Clearinghouse for English Language Acquisition. *Glossary of terms.* Retrieved October 17, 2002, from the World Wide Web: http://www.ncela.gwu.edu/askncela/glossary.htm

Nieto, S. (2000). *Affirming diversity: The sociopolitical context of multicultural education* (3rd ed.). White Plains, NY: Longman.

Nieto, S. (2004). *Affirming diversity: The sociopolitical context of multicultural education* (4th ed.). Boston: Pearson.

No Child Left Behind Act of 2001, Pub. L. No. 107–110. [On-line] Available: http://thomas.loc.gov/

Platt, J. M., & Olson, J. (1997). *Teaching adolescents with mild disabilities.* Pacific Grove, CA: Brooks/Cole.

Rodriguez, D., Parmar, R. S., & Signer, B. R. (2001). Fourth-grade culturally and linguistically diverse exceptional students' concepts of number lines. *Exceptional Children, 67,* 199–210.

Salend, S. J. (2005). *Creating inclusive classrooms: Effective and reflective practices for all students* (5th ed.). Columbus, OH: Merrill/Prentice Hall.

Schug, M., Tarver, S., & Western, R. (2001). Direct instruction and the teaching of early reading. *Wisconsin Policy Research Institute Report, 14*(2). Thiensville, WI: Wisconsin Policy Research Institute.

Stanovich, K. (1994). Constructivism in reading education. *The Journal of Special Education, 28*(3), 259–274.

U.S. Department of Education. (2000). To assure the free appropriate public education of all children with disabilities. *Twenty-second Annual Report to Congress on the Individuals with Disabilities Education Act.* Washington, DC: U.S. Government Printing Office.

U.S. Department of Education. (2002). *Twenty-fourth annual report to congress on implementation of the Individuals with Disabilities Education Act.* Washington, DC: Author.

U.S. Department of Education (2005). *Individuals with Disabilities Education Improvement Act of 2004.* Washington, DC: Authors.

Vaughn, S., & Schumm, J. S. (1995). Responsible inclusion for students with learning disabilities. *Journal of Learning Disabilities, 28*(5), 264–270, 290.

Weiner, H. M. (2003). Effective inclusion: Professional development in the context of the classroom. *Teaching Exceptional Children, 35*(6), 12–18.

Working Forum on Inclusive Schools. (1994). *Creating schools for all our students: What 12 schools have to say.* Reston, VA: Council for Exceptional Children. (ERIC Document Reproduction Service No. ED377633).

Zigmond, N., & Magiera, K. (2001). *A focus on co-teaching: Use caution.* (No. 6): Division of Learning Disabilities and Division of Research of the Council of Exceptional Children.

CHAPTER 2

Alberto, P. A., & Troutman, A. C. (2006). *Applied behavior analysis for teachers* (7th ed.). Upper Saddle River, NJ: Pearson Education, Inc.

Ammer, J. J., Platt, J. C., & Cornett, J. W. (2004). Course planning: Knowing yourself and your students to guide learning. In B. K. Lenz, D. D. Deshler, & B. R. Kissam (Eds.), *Teaching content to all: Evidence-based inclusive practices in middle and secondary schools* (pp. 138–161). Boston: Pearson Education, Inc.

Burns, E. (2006). *IEP-2005: Writing and implementing individualized education programs (IEPs).* Springfield, IL: Charles C. Thomas, Publisher, Ltd.

Bursuck, W. D. & Munk, D. D. (1997). Can grades be helpful and fair? Educational Leadership, 55(4), 44–47.

Bursuck, W., Polloway, E. A., Plante, L., Epstein, M. H., Jayanthi, M., & McConeghy, J. (1996). Report card grading and adaptations: A national survey of classroom practices. *Exceptional Children, 62*(4), 301–318.

Callahan, J. F., Clark, L. H., & Kellough, R. D. (1998). *Teaching in the middle and secondary schools* (6th ed.). Upper Saddle River, NJ: Merrill/Prentice Hall.

Carnine, D., Silbert, J., & Kame'enui, E. J. (1997). *Direct instruction reading* (3rd ed.). Upper Saddle River, NJ: Merrill/Prentice Hall.

Carnine, D. W., Silbert, J., Kame'enui, E. J., & Tarver, S. G. (2004). *Direct instruction reading* (4th ed.). Upper Saddle River, NJ: Pearson Education, Inc.

Cegelka, P. T. (1995). Structuring the classroom for effective instruction. In P. T. Cegelka & W. H. Berdine (Eds.), *Effective instruction for students with learning difficulties* (pp. 135–159). Needham Heights, MA: Allyn & Bacon.

Christenson, S. L., Thurlow, M. L., & Ysseldyke, J. E. (1987). *Instructional effectiveness: Implications for effective instruction of handicapped students* (Monograph No. 4). Minneapolis, MN: University of Minnesota, Instructional Alternatives Project.

Cohen, L., & Spenciner, L. J. (2005). *Teaching students with mild and moderate disabilities: Research-based practices.* Upper Saddle River, NJ: Pearson.

Council for Exceptional Children. (2003). *What every special educator must know: Ethics, standards, and guidelines for special educators* (5th ed.). Arlington, VA: Author.

Deshler, D. D., & Schumaker, J. B. (2006). *Teaching adolescents with disabilities: Accessing the general education curriculum.* Thousand Oaks, CA: Corwin Press.

Dettmer, P., Thurston, L. P., & Dyck, N. (2005). *Consultation, collaboration, and teamwork for students with special needs* (5th ed.). Boston: Pearson Publishing, Inc.

Dyck, N., Sundbye, N., & Pemberton, J. (1997). A recipe for efficient co-teaching. *TEACHING Exceptional Children, 30*(2), 42–45.

Eisenman, L., Chamberlin, M., & McGahee-Kovac, M. (2005). A teacher inquiry group on student-led IEPs: Starting small to make a difference. *Teacher Education and Special Education, 28*(3–4), 195.

Emmer, E. T., Evertson, C. M., & Worsham, M. E. (2006). *Classroom management for middle and high school teachers* (7th ed.). Boston: Pearson Education, Inc.

Engelmann, S., & Carnine, D. (1991). *Theory of instruction: Principles and applications* (Rev. ed.). Eugene, OR: ADI Press.

Englert, C. S., & Thomas, C. C. (1982). Management of task involvement in special education classrooms:

Implications for teacher preparation. *Teacher Education and Special Education, 5*(1), 3–10.

Etscheidt, S. K., & Bartlett, L. (1999). The IDEA amendments: A four step approach for determining supplementary aids and services. *Exceptional Children, 65*, 163–174.

Fister, S. L., & Kemp, K. A. (1995). *TGIF: But what will I do on Monday?* Longmont, CO: Sopris West.

Friend, M., & Bursuck, W. D. (2006). *Including students with special needs: A practical guide for classroom teachers* (4th ed.). Boston: Pearson Education, Inc.

Good, T. L., & Brophy, J. E. (2003). *Looking in classrooms* (9th ed.). Boston: Pearson Publishing, Inc.

Graves, D. K., & Bradley, D. F. (1997). Establishing the classroom as a community. In D. F. Bradley, M. K. King-Sears, & D. M. Tessier-Switlick (Eds.), *Teaching students in inclusive settings: From theory to practice* (pp. 365–383). Needham Heights, MA: Allyn & Bacon.

Guskey, T. R., & Bailey, J. M. (2001). *Developing grading and reporting systems for student learning. Experts in assessment.* Thousand Oaks, CA: Corwin Press, Inc.

Heron, T. E., & Harris, K. C. (1987). *The educational consultant* (2nd ed.). Austin, TX: PRO-ED.

Katsiyannis, A., Ellenburg, J. S., & Acton, O. M. (2000). Address individual needs, the role of general educators. *Intervention in School and Clinic, 36*(2), 116–121.

Kellough, R. D., & Carjuzaa, J. (2006). *Teaching in the middle and secondary schools* (8th ed.). Upper Saddle River, NJ: Pearson Education, Inc.

Kupper, L., & McGahee-Kovac, M. (2002). *Helping students develop their IEPs. Technical assistance guide* (2nd ed.) [and] *A student's guide to the IEP* (2nd ed.). Washington, DC: NICHCY.

Lewis, R. B., & Doorlag, D. H. (2006). *Teaching special students in general education classrooms* (7th ed.). Upper Saddle River, NJ: Pearson Education, Inc.

Mason, C. Y., McGahee-Kovac, M., & Johnson, L. (2004). How to help students lead their IEP meetings. *TEACHING Exceptional Children, 36*(3), 18.

Mason, C. Y., McGahee-Kovac, M., Johnson, L., & Stillerman, S. (2002). Implementing student-led IEPs: Student participation and student and teacher reactions. *Career Development for Exceptional Individuals, 25*(2), 171.

Mercer, C. D., & Mercer, A. R. (2005). *Teaching students with learning problems* (7th ed.). Upper Saddle River, N.J: Merrill/Prentice Hall.

Miller, S. P. (2002). *Validated practices for teaching students with diverse needs and abilities.* Boston, MA: Allyn & Bacon.

Morgan, D. P., & Jenson, W. R. (1988). *Teaching behaviorally disordered students: Preferred practices.* Upper Saddle River, NJ: Merrill/Prentice Hall.

Munk, D. D. (2003). *Solving the grading puzzle for students with disabilities.* Whitefish Bay, WI: Knowledge by Design, Inc.

Munk, D. D., & Bursuck, W. D. (1997). Can grades be helpful and fair? *Educational Leadership, 55*(4), 44–47.

Munk, D. D., & Bursuck, W. D. (2004). Personalized grading plans: A systematic approach to making the grades of included students more accurate and meaningful. *Focus on Exceptional Children, 36*(9), 1.

Nougaret, A. A., Scruggs, T. E., & Mastropieri, M. A. (2005). Does teacher education produce better special education teachers? *Exceptional Children, 71*(3), 217.

Polloway, E. A., Epstein, M. H., Bursuck, W. D., Roderique, T. W., McConeghy, J., & Jayanthi, M. (1994). Classroom grading: A national survey of policies. *Remedial and Special Education, 15*, 162–170.

Polloway, E. A., Patton, J. R., & Serna, L. (2005). *Strategies for teaching learners with special needs* (8th ed.). Upper Saddle River, NJ: Pearson Education, Inc.

Pugach, M. C., & Warger, C. L. (2001). Curriculum matters. *Remedial and Special Education, 22*(4), 194–196.

Rich, H. L., & Ross, S. M. (1989). Student's time on learning tasks in special education. *Exceptional Child, 55*(6), 508–515.

Rieth, H. J., Polsgrove, L., Okolo, C., Bahr, C., & Eckert, R. (1987). An analysis of the secondary special education classroom ecology with implications for teacher training. *Teacher Education and Special Education, 10*(3), 113–119.

Rosenshine, B. (1990). How time is spent in elementary classrooms. In C. Denharm & A. Lieberman (Eds.), *Time to learn.* Washington, DC: National Institute of Education.

Salend, S., & Duhaney, L. (2002). Grading students in inclusive settings. *TEACHING Exceptional Children, 34*(8), 8–15.

Smith, T. E. C. (2005). IDEA 2004: Another round in the reauthorization process. *Remedial & Special Education, 26*(6), 314.

Sprick, R. S. (1981). *The solution book: A guide to classroom discipline.* Chicago: Science Research Associates.

Sprick, R. S. (1985). *Discipline in the secondary classroom: A problem-by-problem survival guide.* West Nyack, NY: Center for Applied Research in Education.

Sprick, R. S. (2006). *Discipline in the secondary classroom: A positive approach to behavior management* (2nd ed.). San Francisco, CA: Jossey-Bass.

Vaughn, S., Hughes, M. T., & Moody, S. W. (2001). Instructional grouping for students with LD: Implications for practice. *Intervention in School and Clinic, 36*(3), 131–137.

Vaughn, S., Schumm, J. S., Klingner, J., & Saumell, L. (1995). Students' views of instructional practices: Implications for inclusion. *Learning Disability Quarterly, 18*(3), 236–248.

CHAPTER 3

Ascher, C. (1987). *Trends and issues in urban and minority education.* New York: ERIC Clearinghouse on Urban Education.

Baca, L., & Almanza, E. (1991). Language minority students with disabilities. *Council for Exceptional Children.* Reston, VA.

Bauwens, J., Hourcade, J. J., & Friend, M. (1989). Cooperative teaching: A model for general and special education integration. *Remedial and Special Education, 10*(2), 17–22.

Beale, E. W. (2001). Analysis of state standards for paraprofessionals. *Journal of Instructional Psychology, 28*(4), 244–248.

Berdine, W. H., & Cegelka, P. T. (1995). Collaborative consultation: A key to effective educational delivery. In P. T. Cegelka & W. H. Berdine (Eds.), *Effective instruction for students with learning difficulties* (pp. 19–43). Needham Heights, MA: Allyn & Bacon.

Blackhurst, A. E., & Berdine, W. H. (1993). *An introduction to special education* (3rd ed.). New York: HarperCollins.

Blalock, G. (1991). Paraprofessionals: Critical team members in our special education programs. *Intervention in School and Clinic, 26*(4), 200–214.

Blalock, G. (1993). Strategies for school collaboration. In E. S. Polloway & J. R. Patton (Eds.), *Strategies for teaching learners with special needs* (5th ed., pp. 123–143). New York: Merrill.

Blalock, G. (1997). Strategies for school consultation and collaboration. In E. A. Polloway & J. R. Patton (Eds.), *Strategies for teaching learners with special needs* (pp. 520–550). Upper Saddle River, NJ: Merrill/Prentice Hall.

Blalock, G. (2001). Strategies for collaboration. In E. A. Polloway & J. R. Patton (Eds.), *Strategies for teaching learners with special needs* (pp. 125–160). Upper Saddle River, NJ: Merrill/Prentice Hall.

Bondy, E., & Brownell, M. T. (1997). Overcoming barriers to collaboration. *Intervention in School and Clinic, 33*(2), 112–115.

Bondy, E., Ross, D. D., Sindelar, P. T., & Griffin, C. (1995). Elementary and special educators learning to work together: Team building processes. *Teacher Education and Special Education, 18*(2), 91–102.

Bos, C. S., & Vaughn, S. (2002). *Strategies for teaching students with learning and behavior problems* (5th ed.). Needham Heights, MA: Allyn & Bacon.

Bos, C. S., & Vaughn, S. (2006). *Strategies for teaching students with learning and behavior problems* (6th ed.). Boston: Pearson Education, Inc.

Briganti, M. (1989). *An ESE teacher's guide for working with the limited English proficient student.* Orlando, FL: Orange County Public Schools.

Brown-Chidsey, R. & Steege, M. W. (2005) Response to intervention: Principles and strategies for effective practice. New York: Guilford Press.

Bulusu, A. S. (1998). Barriers of proxemics and kinesics faced by management with an applicant from a different culture during a selection interview. *Annual Meeting of the Southern States Communication Association.* San Antonio, TX.

Chalfant, J. C., & Pysh, M. V. (1981, November). Teacher assistance teams: A model for within-building problem solving. *Counterpoint*, pp. 1–4.

Chalfant, J. C., & Pysh, M. V. (1989). Teacher assistance teams: Five descriptive studies on 96 teams. *Remedial and Special Education, 10*(6), 49–58.

Chesebro, J. L., & McCroskey, J. C. (Eds.). (2002). *Communication for teachers.* Boston: Allyn and Bacon.

Chinn, P. C., & Plata, M. (1987). Perspectives and educational implications of southeast Asian students. In M. K. Kitano & P. C. Chinn (Eds.), *Exceptional Asian children and youth* (pp. 12–28). Reston, VA: The Council for Exceptional Children.

Cohen, L., & Spenciner, L. J. (2005). *Teaching students with mild and moderate disabilities: Research-based practices.* Upper Saddle River, NJ: Pearson.

Costa, A. L., & Garmston, R. J. (1994). *Cognitive coaching: A foundation for renaissance schools.* Norwood, MA: Christopher-Gordon Publishers.

Craig, S., Hull, K., Haggart, A. G., & Perez-Selles, M. (2000). Promoting cultural competence through teacher assistance teams. *TEACHING Exceptional Children, 32*(3), 6–12.

Demchak, M., & Morgan, C. R. (1998). Effective collaboration between professionals and paraprofessionals. *Rural Special Education Quarterly, 17*(2), 10–15.

Deshler, D. D., & Schumaker, J. B. (2006). *Teaching adolescents with disabilities: Accessing the general education curriculum.* Thousand Oaks, CA: Corwin Press.

Dettmer, P., Thurston, L. P., & Dyck, N. (2002). *Consultation, collaboration, and teamwork for students with special needs* (4th ed.). Boston, MA: Allyn & Bacon.

Dettmer, P., Thurston, L. P., & Dyck, N. (2005). *Consultation, collaboration, and teamwork for students with special needs* (5th ed.). Boston: Pearson Publishing, Inc.

Drecktrah, M. E. (2000). Preservice teachers' preparation to work with paraeducators. *Teacher Education and Special Education, 23*(2), 157–164.

Dyck, N., Sundbye, N., & Pemberton, J. (1997). A recipe for efficient co-teaching. *TEACHING Exceptional Children, 30*(2), 42–45.

Dynak, J., Whitten, E., & Dynak, D. (1997). Refining the general education student teaching experience through the use of special education collaborative teaching models. *Action in Teacher Education, 19*(1), 64–74.

Elliott, S. N., & Sheridan, S. M. (1992). Consultation and teaming: Problem solving among educators, parents, and support personnel. *The Elementary School Journal, 92*(3), 315–338.

French, N. K. (2001). Supervising paraprofessionals: A survey of teacher practices. *Journal of Special Education, 30*(1), 41–53.

French, N. K. (2002). 20 ways to maximize paraprofessional services for students with learning disabilities. *Intervention in School and Clinic, 38*(1), 50–55.

Friend, M., & Bursuck, W. (2006). *Including students with special needs: A practical guide for classroom teachers* (4th ed.). Boston: Allyn & Bacon.

Friend, M., & Cook, L. (1992). *Interactions: Collaboration skills for professionals.* New York: Longman.

Friend, M., & Cook, L. (2003). *Interactions: Collaboration skills for school professionals* (4th ed.). Boston: Pearson Education, Inc.

Friend, M., & Cook, L. (2006). *Interactions: Collaboration skills for school professionals* (5th ed.). Boston: Pearson Education, Inc.

Frith, G. H., & Mims, A. (1985). Burnout among special education paraprofessionals. *TEACHING Exceptional Children, 17*(3), 225–227.

Fuchs, D., Mock, D., Morgan, P.L., & Young, C.L. (2003) Responsiveness-to-intervention: Definitions, evidence, and implications for the learning disabilities construct. Learning Disabilities Research & Practice (Blackwell Publishing Limited), 18(3), 157–171.

Glatthorn, A. A. (1990). Cooperative professional development: Facilitating the growth of the special education teacher and the classroom teacher. *Remedial and Special Education, 11*(3), 29–50.

Graden, J. L. (1989). Redefining "prereferral" intervention as instructional assistance: Collaboration between general and special education. *Exceptional Children, 56*(3), 227–231.

Harry, B. (1992). *Cultural diversity, families, and the special education system: Communication and empowerment.* New York: Teachers College Press.

Harry, B., Allen, N., & McLaughlin, M. (1995). Communication versus compliance: African American parents' involvement in special education. *Exceptional Children, 61*(4), 364–377.

Hayek, R. A. (1987). The teacher assistance team: A prereferral support system. *Focus on Exceptional Children, 20*(1), 1–7.

Hepworth, D. H., Rooney, R. H., & Larsen, J. (2002). *Direct social work practice: Theory and skills* (6th ed.). Pacific Grove, CA: Brooks/Cole-Thomson Learning.

Hernandez, H. (2001). *Multicultural education: A teacher's guide to linking context, process, and content* (2nd ed.). Upper Saddle River, NJ: Prentice Hall.

Hilton, A., & Gerlach, K. (1997). Employment, preparation and management of paraeducators: Challenges to appropriate service for students with developmental disabilities. *Education and Training in Mental Retardation and Developmental Disabilities, 32*(6), 71–76.

Hoover-Dempsey, K. V., Walker, J. M. T., Sandler, H. M., Whetsel, D., Green, C. L., Wilkins, A. S., et al. (2005). Why do parents become involved? Research findings and implications. *Elementary School Journal, 106*(2), 105–130.

Hourcade, J. J., & Bauwens, J. (2001). Cooperative teaching: The renewal of teachers [electronic version]. *Clearing House, 74*(5), 242–247.

Hunt, P. (1995). *Collaboration: What does it take? What's working: Transition in Minnesota*, p. 1. Minneapolis: University of Minnesota Institute on Community Integration.

Idol, L. (1986). *Collaborative school consultation* (Report of the National Task Force on School Consultation). Reston, VA: Teacher Education Division, The Council for Exceptional Children.

Idol, L. (1988). A rationale and guidelines for establishing a special education consultation program. *Remedial and Special Education Program, 9*(6), 48–62.

Idol, L., Nevin, A., & Paolucci-Whitcomb, P. (2000). *Collaborative consultation* (3rd ed.). Austin, TX: PRO-ED.

Idol, L., Paolucci-Whitcomb, P., & Nevin, A. (1994). *Collaboration consultation* (2nd ed.). Austin, TX: PRO-ED.

Individuals with Disabilities Education Act of 1997, 20 U.S.C. (Section) 1401–1485.

Johnson, L. J., Pugach, M. C., & Hawkins, A. (2004). School-family collaboration: A partnership. *Focus on Exceptional Children, 36*(5), 1–12.

Kamens, M. W. (1997). A model for introducing student teachers to collaboration. *The Teacher Educator, 33*(2), 90–102.

Killoran, J., Templeman, T. P., Peters, J., & Udell, T. (2001). Identifying paraprofessional competencies for early intervention and early childhood special education. *TEACHING Exceptional Children, 34*(1), 68–73.

Knackendoffel, E. A. (1996). Collaborative teaming in the secondary school. In D. D. Deshler, E. S. Ellis, & B. K. Lenz (Eds.), *Adolescents with learning disabilities* (2nd ed., pp. 579–616). Denver, CO: Love.

Kroth, R. L., & Edge, D. (1997). *Strategies for communicating with parents and families of exceptional children* (3rd ed.). Denver, CO: Love.

Kuykendall, C. (1992). *From rage to hope: Strategies for reclaiming Black & Hispanic students.* Bloomington, IN: National Educational Service.

Lieberman, A. (1995). Practices that support teacher development: Transforming conceptions of professional learning. *Phi Delta Kappan, 76*(8), 591–596.

Lincoln, M. (2002). *Conflict resolution communication: Patterns promoting peaceful schools.* Lanham, MD: Scarecrow Press, Inc.

Lindsey, J. D. (1983). Paraprofessionals in learning disabilities. *Journal of Learning Disabilities, 16*, 467–472.

Marchant, G. J. (2002). Professional development schools and indicators of student achievement. *Teacher Educator, 38*(2), 112–125.

Melamed, J. C., & Reiman, J. W. (2000). Collaboration and conflict resolution in education. *High School Magazine, 7*(7), 16–20.

Miramontes, O. B. (1990). Organizing for effective paraprofessional services in special education: A multilingual multiethnic instructional service team model. *Remedial and Special Education, 12*(1), 29–36.

Mitchell, A. (1997). Teacher identity: A key to increased collaboration. *Action in Teacher Education, 19*(3), 1–14.

Morgan, D. P., & Jensen, W. R. (1988). *Teaching behaviorally disordered students: Preferred practices.* Upper Saddle River, NJ: Merrill/Prentice Hall.

Myles, B. S., & Kasselman, C. J. (1990). *Collaborative consultation: The regular educator's view.* Manuscript submitted for publication.

National Joint Committee on Learning Disabilities (NJCLD). (1999). Learning disabilities: Use of paraprofessionals. *Learning Disability Quarterly, 22*, 23–30.

National Joint Committee on Learning Disabilities (NJCLD). (2005) Responsiveness to intervention and learning disabilities. Learning Disability Quarterly, 28, 249–260.

New report discusses response to intervention. (August/September 2005). Reading Today, 23(1), 3.

Nowacek, J. E. (1992). Professional talk about teaching together: Interviews with five collaborating teachers. *Intervention in School & Clinic, 27*, 262–276.

Ohtake, Y., Fowler, S. A., & Santos, R. M. (2001). *Working with interpreters to plan early childhood services with limited-English-proficient families.* Champaign, IL: Illinois Univ., Early Childhood Research Inst. on Culturally and Linguistically Appropriate Services.

Olion, L. (1989). Enhancing the involvement of Black parents of adolescents with handicaps. In A. A. Ortiz & B. A. Ramirez (Eds.), *Schools and the culturally diverse exceptional students: Promising practices and future directions* (pp. 96–103). Reston, VA: Council for Exceptional Children.

Olson, J., & Platt, J. (2004). *Teaching children and adolescents with special needs* (4th ed.). Upper Saddle River, NJ: Merrill/Prentice Hall.

Ortiz, A. A., & Garcia, S. B. (1989). A preferral process for preventing inappropriate referrals of Hispanic students to special education. In A. A. Ortiz & B. A. Ramirez (Eds.), *Schools and the culturally diverse exceptional student: Promising practices and future directions* (pp. 6–18). Reston, VA: Council for Exceptional Children.

Phillips, V., & McCullough, L. (1990). Consultation-based programming: Instituting the collaborative ethic in schools. *Exceptional Children, 56*(4), 291–304.

Pickett, A. L. (1996). *A state of the art report on paraeducators in education and related services.* New York: National Resource Center for Paraprofessionals, Center for Advanced Study in Education, City University of New York.

Platt, J. M., & Olson, J. (1997). *Teaching adolescents with mild disabilities.* Pacific Grove, CA: Brooks/Cole.

Pugach, M. C., & Johnson, L. J. (1995). *Collaborative practitioners, collaborative schools.* Denver, CO: Love.

Pugach, M.C., & Johnson, L.J. (2002). Collaborative practitioners, collaborative schools. (2nd ed.). Denver, Co: Love.

Pysh, M.V.D. & Chalfant, J.C. (1997). Teacher assistance teams: A system for supporting classroom teacher's in China or The United States. Beijing: China-U.S. Conference on Education.

Riggs, C. G. (2001). Ask the paraprofessionals: What are your training needs? *TEACHING Exceptional Children, 33*(3), 78–83.

Roache, M., Shore, J., Gouleta, E., & Butkevich, E. D. O. (2003). An investigation of collaboration among school professionals in serving culturally and linguistically diverse students with exceptionalities. *Bilingual Research Journal, 27*(1), 117–136.

Rounds, K. A., Weil, M., & Bishop, K. K. (1994), Practice with culturally diverse families of young children with disabilities. *Families and Society: The Journal of Contemporary Human Services, 75*(1), 3–14.

Safran, S. P., & Safran, J. S. (1996). Intervention assistance programs and prereferral teams: Directions for the twenty-first century. *Remedial and Special Education, 17*, 363–369.

Salend, S. J. (2001). *Creating inclusive classrooms: Effective and reflective practices* (4th ed.). Upper Saddle River, NJ: Prentice Hall.

Salend, S. J. (2005). *Creating inclusive classrooms: Effective and reflective practices for all students* (5th ed.). Upper Saddle River, NJ: Prentice Hall.

Saver, K., & Downes, B. (1991). PIT crew: A model for teacher collaboration in an elementary school. *Intervention in School and Clinic, 27*(2), 116–120.

Scott, G. G. (1990). *Resolving conflict with others and within yourself.* Oakland, CA: New Harbinger Publications, Inc.

Showers, B. (1985). Teachers coaching teachers. *Educational Leadership, 42*(7), 43–48.

Showers, B. (1990). Aiming for superior classroom instruction for all children: A comprehensive staff development model. *Remedial and Special Education, 11*(3), 50–53

Sindelar, P. T., Griffin, C. C., Smith, S. W., & Watanabe, A. K. (1992). Prereferral intervention: Encouraging notes on preliminary findings. *The Elementary School Journal, 92*(3), 245–259.

Skelton, K. J. (1997). *Paraprofessionals in education.* Delmar Publishers.

Snell, M. E. & Janney, R. (2000). *Collaborative teaming,* Baltimore, MD: Paul H. Brooks Publishing Co.

Stanovich, P. J. (1996). Collaboration—The key to successful instruction in today's inclusive schools. *Intervention in School and Clinic, 32*(1), 39–42.

Tillery, C. Y., Werts, M. G., Roark, R., & Harris, S. (2003). Perceptions of paraeducators on job retention. *Teacher Education and Special Education, 26* (2), 118–127.

Turnbull, A., & Turnbull, H. R. (2005). *Families, professionals and exceptionality: Positive outcomes through partnership and trust* (5th ed.). Boston: Pearson Education, Inc.

United States Office of Special Education Programs. (2001, December). *SPeNSE fact sheet: The role of paraprofessionals in special education.* Retrieved August 1, 2006, from Study of Personnel Needs in Special Education website at http://www.spense.org

Vaughn, S., & Fuchs, L. S. (2003). Redefining learning disabilities as inadequate responses to instruction: The promise and Potential Problems *Learning Disabilities Research and Practice, 18,* 137–146.

Villa, R. A., Thousand, J. S., & Nevin, A. (2004). *A guide to co-teaching: Practical tips for facilitating student learning.* Thousand Oaks, CA: Corwin Press.

Voltz, D. L. (2003). Collaborative infusion: An emerging approach to teacher preparation for inclusive education. *Action in Teacher Education, 25*(1), 5–13.

Voltz, D. L., Brazil, N., & Ford, A. (2001). What matters most in inclusive education: A practical guide for moving forward. *Intervention in School and Clinic, 37*(1), 23–30.

Wadsworth, D. E., & Knight, D. (1996). Paraprofessionals: The bridge to successful full inclusion. *Intervention in School and Clinic, 30*(3), 166–171.

Wallace, T., Shin, J., Bartholomay, T., & Stahl, B. (2001). Knowledge and skills for teachers supervising the work of paraprofessionals. *Exceptional Children, 67(4),* 520–533.

Walker, J. L. (1988). Young American Indian children. *TEACHING Exceptional Children, 20*(4), 50–51.

Wehmeyer, M. L., Morningstar, M., & Husted, D. (1999). *Family involvement in transition planning and implementation.* Austin, TX: PRO-ED.

Weiss, M. P., & Lloyd, J. W. (2002). Congruence between roles and actions of secondary special educators in co-taught and special education settings. *Journal of Special Education, 36*(2), 58–68.

Welch, M., Judge, T., Anderson, J., Bray, J., Child, B., & Franke, L. (1990). COOP: A tool for implementing prereferral consultation. *Teaching Exceptional Children, 22*(2), 30–31.

Werts, M. G., Harris, S., Tillery, C. Y., & Roark, R. (2004). What parents tell us about paraeducators. *Remedial and Special Education, 25*(4), 232–239.

West, J. F. & Idol, L. (1990). Collaborative consultation in the education of mildly handicapped and at-risk students. *Remedial & Special Education, 11,* 22–31.

Westling, D. L., Herzog, M. J., Cooper-Duffy, K., Prohn, K., & Ray, M. (2006). The teacher support program: A proposed resource for the special education profession and an initial validation. *Remedial and Special Education, 27*(3), 136–147.

White, A. E., & White, L. L. (1992). A collaborative model for students with mild disabilities in middle schools. *Focus on Exceptional Children, 24*(9), 1–10.

Winzer, M. A., & Mazurek, K. (1998). *Special education in multicultural contexts.* Upper Saddle River, NJ: Merrill/Prentice Hall.

Wood, J. W. (2006). *Teaching students in inclusive settings: Adapting and accommodating instruction* (5th ed.). Upper Saddle River, NJ: Merrill/Prentice Hall.

CHAPTER 4

Allinder, R. M. (1996). When some is not better than none: Effects of differential implementation of curriculum-based measurement. *Exceptional Children, 62*(6), 525–536.

Anderson-Inman, L. (1986). Bridging the gap: Student-centered strategies for promoting the transfer of learning. *Exceptional Children, 52*(6), 562–572.

Baskwill, J., & Whitman, P. (1988). *New direction-evaluation: Whole language, whole child.* New York: Scholastic.

Binder, C., Haughton, E., & Eyk, D. V. (1990). Increasing endurance by building fluency: Precision teaching attention span. *TEACHING Exceptional Children, 22*(3), 24–27.

Bott, D. A. (1990). Managing CBA in the classroom. In J. Salvia & C. Hughes (Eds.), *Curriculum-based assessment: Testing what is taught* (pp. 270–294). New York: Macmillan.

Brigance, A. (1999). *BRIGANCE Diagnostic Comprehensive Inventory of Basic Skills (CIBS)—Revised.* North Billerica, MA: Curriculum Associates.

Calkins, L. M. (1986). *The art of teaching writing.* Portsmouth, NH: Heinemann.

Chan, S. (1987). Parents of exceptional Asian children. In M. K. Kitano & P. C. Chinn (Eds.), *Exceptional Asian children and youth* (pp. 36–53). Reston, VA: Council for Exceptional Children.

Christenson, S. L., Thurlow, M. L., & Ysseldyke, J. E. (1987). *Instructional effectiveness: Implications for effective instruction of handicapped students* (Monograph No. 4). Minneapolis, MN: University of Minnesota, Instructional Alternatives Project.

Coalition for Essential Schools. Retrieved October 8, 2006 from www.essentialschools.org.

Cohen, E. G. (1994). Restructuring the classroom: Conditions for productive small groups. *Review of Educational Research, 64,* 1–35.

Cohen, L. G., & Spencimer, L. J. (1998). *Assessment of children and youth.* New York: Longman.

Deno, S. L. (1985). Curriculum-based measurement: The emerging alternative. Exceptional Children, 52(3), 219–232.

Deno, S. L., & Fuchs, L. S. (1987). Developing curriculum-based measurement systems for data-based special education problem solving. *Focus on Exceptional Children, 19*(8), 1–16.

Deno, S. L., Marston, D., & Mirkin, P. (1982). Valid measurement procedures for continuous evaluation of written expression. *Exceptional Children, 48,* 368–371.

Deno, S. L., Mirkin, P., & Wesson, C. (1984). How to write effective data based IEPs. *TEACHING Exceptional Children, 16*(2), 99–104.

Deno, S., Fuchs, L., & Marston, D. (2001). Using curriculum-based measurement to establish growth standards for students with learning disabilities. *The School Psychology Review, 30*(4), 507–524.

Drasgow, E., & Yell, M. (2001). Functional behavior assessments: Legal requirements and challenges. *The School Psychology Review, 30*(2), 239–251.

Eaton, M. D. (1978). Data decisions and evaluation. In N. G. Haring, T. C. Lovitt, M. D. Eaton, & C. L. Hansen

(Eds.), *The fourth R: Research in the classroom* (pp. 167–190). Upper Saddle River, NJ: Merrill/Prentice Hall.

Elliott, S. (1998). Performance assessment of students' achievement: Research and practice. *Learning Disabilities Research & Practice, 13*(4), 233–241.

Evans, S. S., Evans, W. H., & Mercer, C. E. (1986). *Assessment for instruction.* Needham Heights, MA: Allyn & Bacon.

Farr, R. F. (1989). A response from Robert Farr. In K. S. Jongsma (Ed.), Questions & answers: Portfolio assessment. *The Reading Teacher, 43*(3), 264–265.

Fewster, S., & MacMillan, P. (2002). School-based evidence for the validity of curriculum-based measurement of reading and writing. *Remedial and Special Education, 23*(3), 149–156.

Flood, J., & Lapp, D. (1989). Reporting reading progress: A comparison portfolio for parents. *The Reading Teacher, 42*(7), 508–514.

Frisby, C. (1987). Alternative assessment committee report: Curriculum-based assessment. *CASP Today, 36,* 15–26.

Fuchs, L. S., & Deno, S. L. (1991). Paradigmatic distinctions between instructionally relevant measurement models. *Exceptional Children, 57*(6), 488–500.

Fuchs, L. S., Fuchs, D., & Hamlett, C. L. (1989). Effects of alternative goal structures within curriculum-based measurement. *Exceptional Children, 55*(5), 429–438.

Fuchs, L. S., Fuchs, D., Hamlett, C. L., & Stecker, P. M. (1991). Effects of curriculum-based measurement and consultation on teacher planning and student achievement in mathematics operations. *American Educational Research Journal, 28*(3), 617–641.

Fuchs, L. S., Fuchs, D., Hamlett, C. L., & Whinnery, K. (1991). Effects of goal line feedback on level, slope, and stability of performance within curriculum-based measurement. *Learning Disabilities Research & Practice, 6*(2), 66–74.

Fuchs, L. S., Hamlett, C. L., & Fuchs, D. (1990). *Monitoring basic skills growth.* Austin, TX: PRO-ED.

Fuchs, L. S., & Shinn, M. R. (1989). Writing CBM IEP objectives. In M. R. Shinn (Ed.), *Curriculum-based measurement: Assessing special children* (pp. 130–152). New York: The Guilford Press.

Gartin, B., & Murdick, N. (2001). A new IDEA mandate: The use of functional assessment of behavior and positive behavior supports. *Remedial and Special Education, 22*(6), 344–349.

Goldberg, M. (2005). Test mess 2: Are we doing better a year later? *Phi Delta Kappan, 86*(5), 389.

Gollnick, D.M., & Chinn, P.C. (2002). *Multicultural education in a pluralistic society* (6th ed.). Upper Saddle River, NJ: Merrill/Prentice Hall.

Goodrich, H. (December 1996–January 1997). Understanding rubrics. *Educational Leadership, 54*(4), 14–17.

Grossman, H. (1994). *Special education in a diverse society.* Needham Heights, MA: Allyn & Bacon.

Haring, N. G., & Eaton, M. (1978). Systematic instructional procedures: An instructional hierarchy. In N. Haring, T. Lovitt, M. Eaton, & C. Hansen (Eds.), *The fourth R: Research in the classroom* (pp. 23–40). Upper Saddle River, NJ: Merrill/Prentice Hall.

Haring, N. G., & Gentry, N. D. (1976). Direct and individualized instructional procedures. In N. G. Haring & R. L. Schiefelbusch (Eds.), *TEACHING special children* (pp. 77–111). New York: McGraw-Hill.

Hasbrouck, J. E., & Tindal, G. (1992). Curriculum-based oral reading fluency norms for students in grades 2 through 5. *TEACHING Exceptional Children, 24*(3), 41–44.

Hefferan, M., & Diviaio, L. (1989). *A resource manual for the development and evaluation of special programs for exceptional students, Volume V-D: Techniques of precision teaching, Part 1: Training manual.* Tallahassee, FL: Bureau of Education for Exceptional Students.

Heshusius, L. (1989). The Newtonian mechanistic paradigm, special education and contours of alternatives: An Overview. *Journal of Learning Disabilities, 22*(7), 403–415.

Hughes, C. A., Ruhl, K. L., & Peterson, S. K. (1988). Promising practices: Teaching self-management skills. *TEACHING Exceptional Children, 20*(2), 70–72.

Individuals with Disabilities Education Act of 1997, 20 U.S.C. (Section) 1401–1485.

Johnson, E. & Arnold, N. (2004). Validating on alternate assessment. Remedial and Special Education, 25(5), 266–275.

Jones, C. J. (2001(a)). CBAs that work: Assessing student's math content-reading levels. *Teaching Exceptional Children,* 34(1), 24–28.

Jones, C. J. (2001(b)). Teacher-friendly curriculum-based assessment in spelling. *Teaching Exceptional Children,* 34(2), 32–38.

Keel, M., Dangel, H., & Owens, S. (1999). Selecting instructional interventions for students with mild disabilities in inclusive classrooms. *Focus on Exceptional Children, 31*(8), 1–16.

Keeley, P., Eberlee, F., & Farrin, L. (2005). *Uncovering students' ideas in science.* Washington, DC: National Science Teachers Association.

Kleinert, H., Haig, J., Kerns, J., & Kennedy, S. (2000). Alternate assessments: Lessons learned and roads to be taken. *Exceptional Children, 7*(1), 51–66.

Koorland, M. A., Keel, M. C., & Ueberhorst, P. (1990). Setting aims for precision learning. *Teaching Exceptional Children, 22*(3), 64–68.

Leslie, L., & Caldwell, J. (2006). *Qualitative reading inventory* (4th ed.). Reading, WA: Pearson Publishing Inc.

Lindsley, O. R. (1990). Precision teaching: By teachers for children. *TEACHING Exceptional Children, 22*(3), 10–15.

Marston, D., Dement, K., Allen, D., & Allen, L. (1992). Monitoring pupil progress in reading. *Preventing School Failure, 36*(2), 21–25.

Marston, D., & Magnusson, D. (1985). Implementing curriculum-based measurement in special and regular education settings. *Exceptional Children, 52*(3), 266–276.

Marzano, R., Pickering, D., & McTighe, J. (1993). *Assessing outcomes: Performance assessment using dimensions of learning model.* Alexandria, VA: Association for Supervision and Curriculum Development.

McDougal, D., & Brady, M. P. (1998). Initiating and fading self-management interventions to increase math fluency in general education classes. *Exceptional Children, 64*(2), 151–166.

McRobbie, J. (1992). *Using portfolios to assess student performance, knowledge brief, #9.* San Francisco, CA: Far West Laboratory for Educational Research and Development.

Mercer, C. D. (1992). *Students with learning disabilities* (4th ed.). Upper Saddle River, NJ: Merrill/Prentice Hall.

Mercer, C. D., & Mercer, A. R. (2001). *Teaching students with learning problems* (6th ed.). Upper Saddle River, NJ: Prentice Hall.

Ortiz, A. A., & Polyzoi, E. (1989). Language assessment of Hispanic learning disabled and speech and language handicapped students: Research in progress. In A. A. Ortiz & B. A. Ramirez (Eds.), *Schools and the culturally diverse exceptional student: Promising practices and future directions* (pp. 32–44). Reston, VA: Council for Exceptional Children.

OSEP Doc: IDEA '97 Final Regulations Major Issues. Retrieved September 18, 2002, from the World WideWeb: http://www.ideapractices.org/law/addl_material/major issues.php

Pearlman, B. (2002). Designing, and making the new American high school. *Technos, 11(1)*, 14–19.

Pearson, P. D., & Johnson, D. (1978). *Teaching reading comprehension.* New York: Holt, Rinehart, & Winston.

Reid, R., & Nelson, J. (2002). The utility, acceptability, and practicality of functional behavior assessment for students with high-incidence problem behaviors. *Remedial and Special Education, 23*(1), 15–23.

Roberts, G. H. (1968). The failure strategies of third grade arithmetic pupils. *The Arithmetic Teacher, 15,* 442–446.

Salend, S. (2000). Strategies and resources to evaluate the impact of inclusion programs on students. *Intervention in School and Clinic, 35*(5), 264–270.

Salvia, J., & Hughes, C. (1990). *Curriculum-based assessment: Testing what is taught.* New York: Macmillan.

Shin, J., Deno, S., & Espin, C. (2000). Technical adequacy of the maze task for curriculum-based measurement of reading growth. *The Journal of Special Education, 34*(3), 164–172.

Shinn, M. (Ed.). (1989). *Curriculum-based measurement: Assessing special children.* New York: The Guilford Press.

Stump, C., Lovitt, T., Fister, S., Kemp, K., Moore, R., & Schroeder, B. (1992). Vocabulary intervention for secondary-level youth. *Learning Disability Quarterly, 15,* 207–222.

Sugai, G., Maheady, L., & Skouge, J. (1989). Best assessment practices for students with behavioral disorders: Accommodation to cultural diversity and individual differences. *Behavioral Disorders, 14*(4), 263–278.

Thurlow, M. L., Lazarus, S. S., & Thompson, S. J. (2005). State policies on assessment participation and accommodations for students with disabilities. *The Journal of Special Education, 38,* 232–240.

Tindal, G. A., & Marston, D. B. (1990). *Classroom-based assessment: Evaluating instructional outcomes.* Upper Saddle River, NJ: Merrill/Prentice Hall.

Trammel, D. L., Schloss, P. T., & Alper, S. (1994). Using self-recording, evaluation, and graphing to increase completion of homework assignments. *Journal of Learning Disabilities, 27*(2), 75–81.

U.S. Department of Education (2005). *Individuals with Disabilities Education Improvement Act 2004.* Washington, DC: Authors.

Valencia, S. (1990). A portfolio approach to classroom reading assessment: The whys, whats, and hows. *The Reading Teacher, 43*(4), 338–340.

Van Acker, R. Borenson, L. Gable, R. A. & Potterton T. (2005). Are we on the right course? Lessons learned from current FBA/BIP practices in schools. *Journal of Behavioral Education, 14*(1), 1–71.

Wesson, C. L. (1987). Increasing efficiency. *TEACHING Exceptional Children, 20*(1), 46.

Wesson, C. L., & King, R. P. (1996). Portfolio assessment and special education students. *TEACHING Exceptional Children, 28*(2), 44–48.

West, R. P., Young, K. R., & Spooner, F. (1990). Precision teaching: An introduction. *TEACHING Exceptional Children, 22*(3), 4–9.

White, O. R., & Haring, N. G. (1976). *Exceptional teaching.* Upper Saddle River, NJ: Merrill/Prentice Hall.

White, O. R., & Haring, N. G. (1980). *Exceptional teaching* (2nd ed.). Upper Saddle River, NJ: Merrill/Prentice Hall.

Wolf, D. P. (1989). Portfolio assessment: Sampling student work. *Educational Leadership, 46*(7), 35–39.

Wood, J. W. (2006). *Teaching students in inclusive settings: Adapting and accommodating instruction* (5th ed.). Upper Saddle River, N.J: Merrill/Prentice Hall.

Zrebiec Uberti, H., Mastropieri, M. A., & Scruggs, T. E. (2004). Check it off: Individualizing a math algorithm for students with disabilities via self-monitoring checklists. *Intervention in School and Clinic, 39*(5), 269–275.

CHAPTER 5

Alberto, P., & Troutman, A. (2006). *Applied behavior analysis for teachers* (7th ed.). Upper Saddle River, NJ: Prentice-Hall.

Anderson, L., Evertson, C., & Brophy, J. (1979). An experimental study of effective teaching in first grade reading groups. *Elementary School Journal, 79,* 193–223.

Anderson, L., & Krathwohl, D. R. (2001). *A taxonomy for learning, teaching and assessing: A revision of Bloom's taxonomy of educational objectives.* New York: Longman.

Archer, A. L., & Isaacson, S. L. (1990). Teaching others how to teach strategies. *Teacher Education and Special Education, 13*(2), 63–72.

Bakken J. P., & Wheldon, C. K. (2002). Teaching text structure to improve reading comprehension. *Intervention in School and Clinic, 37,* 229–233.

Bloom, B. S. (Ed.), Engelhart, M. D., Furst, E. J., Hill, W. H., & Krathwohl, D. R. (1956). *Taxonomy of educational objectives: The classification of educational goals. Handbook 1: Cognitive domain.* New York: David McKay.

Boyle, J. R. & Weishaar, M. (2001). The effects of strategic notetaking on the recall and comprehension of lecture information for high school students with learning disabilities. *Learning Disabilities Research & Practice, 16,* 133–141.

Bransford, J. D., Sherwood, R. S., Hasselbring, T. S., Kinzer, C. K., & Williams, S. M. (1990). Anchored instruction: Why we need it and how technology can help. In D. Nix & R. Spiro (Eds.), *Cognitive, education, and multimedia exploration in high technology* (pp. 115–142). Hillsdale, NJ: Erlbaum.

Brophy, J. E. (1980). *Recent research on teaching.* East Lansing, MI: Institute for Research on Teaching, Michigan State University.

Brophy, J. E., & Evertson, C. (1977). Teacher behaviors and student learning in second and third grades. In G. D. Borich (Ed.), *The appraisal of teaching: Concepts and process* (pp. 117–139). Reading, MA: Addison-Wesley.

Carlson, J. K., Gray, J., Hoffman D., & Thompson, A. (2004). A musical interlude: Using music and relaxation to improve reading performance. *Intervention in School & Clinic, 39*(4), 246–251.

Cates, G. L., & Lee, D. L. (2005). Increasing learning by getting students to choose to complete more work introduction to a special issue on interspersing procedures, *Journal of Behavioral Education, 14,* 223–225.

Christenson, S. L., Thurlow, M. L., & Ysseldyke, J. E. (1987). *Instructional effectiveness: Implications for effective instruction of handicapped students* (Monograph No. 4). Minneapolis, MN: University of Minnesota, Instructional Alternatives Project.

Christenson, S. L., Ysseldyke, J. E., & Thurlow, M. L. (1989). Critical instructional factors for students with mild handicaps: An integrative review. *Remedial and Special Education, 10*(5), 21–29.

Cohen, S. A. (1987). Instructional alignment: Searching for the magic bullet. *Exceptional Researcher, 16*(8), 16–20.

Cohen, S. B. (1986). Teaching new material. *TEACHING Exceptional Children, 19*(1), 50–51.

Collins, M., Carnine, D., & Gersten, R. (1987). Elaborated corrective feedback and the acquisition of reasoning skills: A study of computer-assisted instruction. *Exceptional Children, 54*(3), 254–262.

Costa, A. L., & Garmston, R. J. (1994). *Cognitive coaching: A foundation for renaissance schools.* Norwood, MA: Christopher-Gordon Publishers.

Daniels, H. (2002). Expository text in lierature circles. *Voices from the Middle,* 9(4). 7–14.

Daniels, V. I., & Vaughn, S. (1999). A tool to encourage "best practice" in full inclusion. *TEACHING Exceptional Children, 31*(5), 48–55.

Darling-Hammond, L. (2002). *Redesigning schools: What matters and what works.* Stanford, CA: School Redesign Network at Stanford University.

Darling-Hammond, L. (2004). Standards, accountability, and school reform. *Teachers College Record, 106*(6), 1047–1085.

Desberg, P., & Taylor, J. H. (1986). *Essentials of task analysis.* Lanham, MD: University Press of America.

Duffy, G., Roehler, L., & Rackliff, G. (1986). How teachers' instructional talk influences students' understanding of lesson content. *Elementary School Journal, 87*(1), 3–16.

Engelmann, S., & Carnine, D. (1982). *Theory of instruction: Principles and applications.* New York: Irvington Publishers.

Falk, K. B., Lane, K. L., Strong, A. C., & Wehby, J. H. (2004). The impact of a structured reading curriculum and repeated reading on the performance of junior high students with emotional and behavioral disorders. *School Psychology Review, 33,* 561–581.

Florida Performance Measurement System (FPMS). (1984). *Domains: Knowledge base of the Florida Performance Measurement System.* Tallahassee, FL: Florida Coalition for the Development of a Performance Measurement System, Office of Teacher Education, Certification and Inservice Staff Development.

Florida Department of Education (2006). *Sunshine State Standards.* Retrieved April 27, 2007 from http://www.firn.edu/doe/curric/prek12/frame2.htm

Foorman, B., & Torgesen, J. (2001). Critical elements of classroom and small-group instruction promote reading success in all children. *Learning Disabilities Research & Practice, 16*(4), 203–212.

Good, T. L., & Brophy, J.E. (1984). *Looking in classrooms* (3rd ed.). New York: Harper & Row.

Greenwood, C. R., Delquadri, J., & Hall, R. V. (1984). Opportunity to respond and student academic performance. In W. L. Heward, T. E. Heron, J. Trap-Porter, & D. S. Hill (Eds.), *Focus on behavior analysis in education* (pp. 58–88). Upper Saddle River, NJ: Merrill/Prentice Hall.

Hamilton, S.L., Seibert, M.A., Gardner, R., III, & Talbert-Johnson, C. (2000). Using guided notes to improve the academic achievement of incarcerated adolescents with learning and behavior problems. *Remedial and Special Education, 21*(3), 133–170.

Hasselbring, T. S. (1998). *The future of special education and the role of technology.* Peabody College of Vanderbilt

University. Retrieved July 15, 1998, from the World Wide Web: http://peabody.vanderbilt.edu/ltc/hasselbringt/futute.html

Herrmann, B. A. (1988). Two approaches for helping poor readers. *Reading Teacher, 42*(1), 25–28.

Heshusias, L. (1989). The Newtonian mechanistic paradigm, special education, and contours of alternatives: An overview. *Journal of Learning Disabilities, 22*(7), 403–415.

Heward, W. L. (1994). Three "low-tech" strategies for increasing the frequency of active student response during group instruction. In R. Gardner III, D. M. Sainato, J. O. Cooper, T. E. Heron, W. L. Heward, J. Eshleman, & T. A. Grossi (Eds.), *Behavior analysis in education: Focus on measurably superior instruction* (pp. 283–320). Monterey, CA: Brooks/Cole.

Heward, W. L. (2000). *Exceptional children: An introduction to special education* (6th ed.). Upper Saddle River, NJ: Prentice Hall.

Heward, W.L. (2003). Ten faulty notions about teaching and learning that hinder the effectiveness of special education. *Journal of Special Education, 36*, 186–205.

Heward, W. L., Courson, F. H., & Narayan, J. S. (1989). Using choral responding to increase active student response during group instruction. *TEACHING Exceptional Children, 21*(3), 72–75.

Heward, W. L., Gardner, R., Cavanaugh, R. A., Courson, F. H., Grossi, T. A., & Barbetta, P. M. (1996). Everyone participates in this class. *TEACHING Exceptional Children, 28*(2), 4–10.

Hitchcock, C., & Stahl, S. (2003). Assistive technology, universal design, Universal Design for Learning: Improved opportunities. *Journal of Special Education Technology, 18*(4), 1–9.

Hogan, K., & Pressley, M. (1997). Scaffolding scientific competencies within classroom communities of inquiry. In K. Hogan & M. Pressley (Eds.), *Scaffolding student learning: Instructional approaches & issues* (pp. 74–107). Cambridge, MA: Brookline Books.

Hunter, M. (1981). *Increasing your teaching effectiveness.* Palo Alto, CA: Learning Institute.

Jensen, E, (1998). *Teaching with the brain and mind.* Alexandria, VA: Association of Supervision and Curriculum Development.

Kagan, S. (1992). *Cooperative learning.* San Juan Capistrano, CA: Kagan Cooperative Learning.

Katims, D. S., & Harmon, J. M. (2000). Strategic instruction in middle school social studies: Enhancing academic and literacy outcomes for at-risk students. *Intervention in School and Clinic, 35*(5), 280–289.

Krathwohl, D. R. (2002). A revision of Bloom's taxonomy: An overview. *Theory into Practice, 41*(4), 212–218.

Ladson-Billings, G. (2001). Crossing over into Canaan. The journey of new teachers in diverse classrooms. San Francisco, CA: Jossey-Bass.

Ladson-Billings, G.J. (2002). I aint writin' nuttin': Permission to fail and demands to succeed in urban classrooms. In L. Delpit & J.K. Dowdy (Eds.), *The skin that we speak* (pp. 109–120). New York, NY: the New Press.

Ladson-Billings, G. (2004). Foreword. In "Is This English?" Race, Language, and Culture in the Classroom, by B. Fecho, xi–xii. New York: Teachers College Press.

Lago-Delello. (1998). Classroom dynamics and the development of serious emotional disturbance. *Exceptional Children, 64*(4), 479–492.

Larkin, M. (2001). Providing support for student independence through scaffolded instruction. *TEACHING Exceptional Children, 34*(1), 30–34.

Lavoie, R. (Writer). (1989). *How difficult can this be: The F.A.T. city workshop* [DVD]. (Available from LD online Store, Po Box 2284, Burlington, VT 05407)

Lue, M. (2001). *A survey of communication disorders for the classroom teacher.* Boston, MA: Allyn & Bacon.

Marzano, R. J., Pickering, D. J., & McTighe, J. (1993). *Assessing students outcomes: Performance assessment using the dimensions of learning model.* Alexandria, VA: Association of Supervision and Curriculum Development.

Mercer, C. D., & Mercer, A. R. (2001). *Teaching students with learning problems* (6th ed.). Upper Saddle River, NJ: Prentice Hall.

Meyer, L. A. (1986). Strategies for correcting students' wrong responses. *Elementary School Journal, 87*(2), 227–241.

Miller, S. P., Butler, F. M., & Lee, K. (1998) Validated practices for teaching mathematics to students with learning disabilities: A review of literature. *Focus on Exceptional Children, 31*(1), 1–24.

Montague, M., & Leavell, A. G. (1994). Improving the narrative writing of students with learning disabilities. *RASE, 15*(1), 21–33.

Narayan, J. S., Heward, W. L., Gardner, R., III, Courson, F. H., & Omness, C. (1990). Using response cards to increase student participation in an elementary classroom. *Journal of Applied Behavior Analysis, 23*, 483–490.

Obiakor, F. E. (2007). *Multicultural special education: Culturally responsive teaching.* Upper Saddle River, NJ: Prentice-Hall.

Paik, S. J. (2003). Ten strategies that improve learning. *Educational Horizons, 81*(2), 83–85.

Palincsar, A. S. (1986). The role of dialogue in scaffolded instruction. *Educational Psychologist, 21*, 73–98.

Palincsar, A. S., & Brown, A. L. (1984). The reciprocal teaching of comprehension fostering and comprehension monitoring activities. *Cognition and Instruction, 1*, 117–175.

Palincsar, A. S., & Brown, A. L. (1989). Instruction for self-regulated reading. In L. B. Resnick & L. E. Klopfer (Eds.), *Toward the thinking curriculum: Current cognitive research: 1989 ASCD yearbook* (pp. 19–39). Alexandria, VA: Association for Supervision and Curriculum Development.

Poplin, M. S. (1988). Holistic/constructivist principles of the teaching/learning process: Implications for the field of learning disabilities. *Journal of Learning Disabilities, 21*(7), 389–400.

Pressley, M., Hogan, K., Wharton-McDonald, R., Mistretta, J., & Ettenberger, S. (1996). The challenges of instructional scaffolding: The challenges of instruction that supports student thinking. *Learning Disabilities Research & Practice, 11*(3), 138–146.

Puntambekar, S., & Kolodner, J. L. (2005). Toward implementing distributed scaffolding: Helping students learn science from design. *Journal of Research in Science Teaching, 42*, 185–217.

Reid, E. (1986). Practicing effective instruction: The exemplary center for reading instruction approach. *Exceptional Children, 52*(6), 510–517.

Rethinking Schools Online (2004). Milwaukee, WI: Author.

Rieth, H. J., Polsgrove, L., Okolo, C., Bahr, C., & Eckert, R. (1987). An analysis of the secondary special education classroom ecology with implications for teacher training. *Teacher Education and Special Education, 10*(3), 113–119.

Rivera, D. P., & Smith, D. D. (1988). Using a demonstration strategy to teach midschool students with learning disabilities how to compute long division. *Journal of Learning Disabilities, 21*(2), 77–81.

Rosenberg, M. S. (1986). Maximizing the effectiveness of structured classroom management programs: Implementing rule-review procedures with disruptive and distractible students. *Behavioral Disorders, 11*(4), 239–248.

Rosenshine, B. (1990). How time is spent in elementary classrooms. In C. Denharm & A. Lieberman (Eds.), *Time to learn*. Washington, DC: National Institute of Education.

Rosenshine, B. (1995). Advances in research on instruction. *Journal of Educational Research, 88*, 262–268.

Rosenshine, B., & Stevens, R. (1986). Teaching functions. In M. Wittrock (Ed.), *Third handbook of research on teaching* (pp. 376–391). New York: Macmillan.

Schon, D. (1983). *The reflective practitioner*. New York: Basic Books, Inc.

Schumaker, J. B. (1989). The heart of strategy instruction. *Strategram: Strategies intervention model, 1*(4). Kansas City, KS: The University of Kansas Institute for Research in Learning Disabilities, pp. 1–5.

Scott, S.S., McGuire, J. M., & Shaw, S. F. (2001) *Principles of Universal Design for Instruction*. Storrs, CT: University of Connecticut, Center on Postsecondary Education and Disability.

Scruggs, T. E., & Mastropieri, M. A. (2003). Recent research applications in secondary content areas for students with learning and behavioral disabilities. In T. E. Scruggs & M. A. Mastropieri (Eds.), *Identification and assessment of learning disorders: Advances in learning and behavioral disabilities* (Vol. 16, pp. 223–230). Oxford, UK: Elsevier Science/JAI Press.

Sindelar, P. T., Bursuck, W. D., & Halle, J. W. (1986). The effects of two variations of teacher questioning on student performance. *Education and Treatment of Children, 9*(1), 56–66.

Skinner, C. H., Pappas, D. N., & Davis, K. A. (2005). Enhancing academic engagement: Providing opportunities for responding and influencing students to choose to respond. *Psychology in the Schools, 42*, 389–403.

Soldier, L. L. (1989). Language learning of Native American students. *Educational Leadership, 46*(5), 74–75.

Sousa, D. A. (2001). *How the special needs brain learns.* Thousand Oaks, CA: Corwin Press, Inc.

Stringfellow, J. L., & Miller, S. P. (2005). Enhancing student performance in secondary classrooms while providing access to the general education curriculum using lecture formats. *TEACHING Exceptional Children Plus, 1*(6), Article 1. Retrieved October 30, 2006 from http://escholarship.bc.edu/education/tecplus/vol1/iss6/1

Thurlow, M. L. (2002). Positive educational results for all students: The promise of standards-based reform. *Remedial and Special Education, 23*(4), 195–202.

Thurlow, M. L., & Johnson, D. R. (2000). High-stakes testing of students with disabilities. *Journal of Teacher Education, 51*(4), 305–314. Minneapolis, MN: University of Minnesota, National Center on Educational Outcomes.

Tobin, K. (1987) The role of wait time in higher cognitive level learning. *Review of Educational Research, 57* (1), 69–95.

Vacca, R., & Vacca, J. (2006). *Content area reading* (7th ed.). New York: Longman. New York.

VanReusen, A. K., & Bos, C. S. (1994). Facilitating student participation in individualized education programs through motivation strategy instruction. *Exceptional Children, 60*(5), 466–475.

VanReusen, A. K., Bos, C. S., Schumaker, J. B., & Deshler, D. D. (1994). *The self-advocacy strategy for education and transition planning.* Lawrence, KS: Edge Enterprises.

Vaughn, S., Gersten, R., & Chard, D. (2000). The underlying message in LD intervention research: Findings from research syntheses. *Exceptional Children, 67*(1), 99–114.

Watson, D. L., Northcutt, L., & Rydele, L. (1989). Teaching bilingual students successfully. *Educational Leadership, 46*(5), 59–61.

West, J. F., Idol, L., & Cannon, G. (1989). *Collaboration in the schools: An inservice and preservice curriculum for teacher, support staff, and administrators.* Austin, TX: PRO-ED.

Wilson, R. (1987). Direct observation of academic learning time. *TEACHING Exceptional Children, 19*(2), 13–17.

Zigmond, N., Sansone, J., Miller, S. E., Donahoe, K. R., & Kohnke, R. (1986). *Teaching learning disabled students at the secondary school level.* Reston, VA: Council for Exceptional Children.

CHAPTER 6

Artiles, A. J., & Ortiz, A. A. (2002). *English language learners with special education needs.* Washington, DC: Center for Applied Linguistics.

Baca, L. M., & Cervantes, H. T. (2004). *The bilingual special education interface* (4 ed.). Upper Saddle River, NJ: Merrill/Prentice Hall.

Bailin, A., & Grafstein, A. (2001). The linguistic assumptions underlying readability formulae: A critique. *Language and Communication, 21*, 285–301.

Baker, J., & Zigmond, N. (1990). Are regular education classes equipped to accommodate students with learning disabilities? *Exceptional Children, 56*(6), 515–526.

Banks, J. A., Cookson, P., Gay, G., Hawley, W. D., Irvine, J. J., Nieto, S., Schofield, J. W., et al. (2001). Diversity within unity: Essential principles for teaching and learning in a multicultural society. *Phi Delta Kappan, 83*(3), 196–203.

Beals, D. E. (1989). A practical guide for estimating readability. *TEACHING Exceptional Children, 21*(3), 24–27.

Birdseye, T. (1990). *A song of stars.* New York: Holiday House.

Burnette, J. (1987). *Adapting instructional materials for mainstreamed students.* Washington, DC: Office of Special Education Programs, United States Department of Education.

Byars, B. (1974). *Summers of swans.* New York: Avon.

Cohen, L., & Spenciner, L. J. (2005). *Teaching students with mild and moderate disabilities.* Upper Saddle River, NJ: Merrill/Prentice Hall.

Demi. (1990). *The empty pot.* New York: Henry Holt.

Dudley-Marling, C., & Paugh, P. C. (2004). *A classroom teacher's guide to stuggling readers* (Vol. 1). Portsmouth: Heinemann.

Ellis, E. S. (1989). A metacognitive intervention for increasing class participation, *Learning Disabilities Focus, 5*(1), 36–46.

Fry, E. (1968). A readability formula that saves time. *Journal of Reading, 11*(7), 513–516, 575–578.

Fry, E. (2002). Readability versus leveling. *Reading Teacher, 56*(3), 286.

Gantos, J. (2000). *Joey Pigza loses control.* New York: Harper Collins Publisher Inc.

George, J. C. (1987). *Water sky.* New York: Harper & Row.

Goh, D. S. (2004). *Assessment accommodations for diverse learners.* Boston, MA: Pearson Education, Inc.

Gollnick, D. M., & Chinn, P. C. (2002). *Multicultural education in a pluralistic society* (6th ed.). Upper Saddle River, NJ: Merrill/Prentice Hall.

Hernandez, H. (2001). *Multicultural education: A teacher's guide to linking context, process, and content* (2nd ed.). Upper Saddle River, NJ: Prentice Hall.

Jayanthi, M., Epstein, M. H., Polloway, E. A., & Bursuck, W. D. (1996). A national survey of general education teachers' perceptions of testing adaptations. *Journal of Special Education, 30*(1), 99–115.

Jobe, R., & Daytona-Sakari, M. (2002). *Info-kids: How to use nonfiction to turn reluctant readers into enthusiastic learners* (1st ed.). Ontario, Canada: Pembroke Publishers.

Kellogg, S. (1984). *Paul Bunyan: A tall tale.* New York: William Morrow.

Kellough, R. D., & Kellough, N. G. (2003) *Secondary school teaching: A guide to methods and resources.* Upper Saddle River, NJ: Merril/Prentice Hall.

Kroll, V. L. (2002). *Butterfly Boy.* Boyds Mills Press: Honesdale, PA.

Lambie, R. A. (1980). A systematic approach for changing materials, instruction, and assignments to meet individual needs. *Focus on Exceptional Children, 12*(1), 1–12.

Martin, B. (1970). *Brown bear, brown bear, what do you see?* New York: Holt, Rinehart, & Winston.

McIntosh, R., Vaughn, S., Schumm, J., Haager, D., & Lee, O. (1993). Observations of students with learning disabilities in general education classrooms. *Exceptional Children, 60*(3), 249–261.

Mendez, P. (1989). *The black snowman.* New York: Scholastic.

Mercer, C. D., & Mercer, A. R. (2005). *Teaching students with learning problems* (7th ed.). Upper Saddle River, NJ: Merrill/ Prentice Hall.

Mercer, C. D., Mercer, A. R., & Bott, D. A. (1984). *Self-correcting learning materials for the classroom.* Columbus, OH: Charles E. Merrill.

Miller, S. P. (2002). *Validated practices for teaching students with diverse needs and abilities.* Boston, MA: Allyn & Bacon.

Murphy, D. A., Meyers, C. C., Olesen, S., McKean, K., & Custer, S. H. (1995). *Exceptions: A handbook of inclusion activities for teachers of students at grades 6–12 with mild disabilities.* Longmont, CO: Sopris Press.

Nelson, J. S., Jayanthi, M., Epstein, M. H., & Bursuck, W. D. (2000). Student preferences for adaptations in classroom testing. *Remedial and Special Education, 21*(1), 41–52.

Ousley, D. (2006). Teachers' Corner: How Young Adult Literature Offers Global Perspectives for Struggling Readers. *Journal of International Special Needs Education, 9*, 53–56.

Rhodes, L. K. (1981). I can read: Predictable books as resources for reading and writing instruction. *The Reading Teacher, 34*(5), 511–518.

Rhodes, L. K., & Dudley-Marling, C. (1996). *Readers and writers make a difference: A holistic approach to teaching learning disabled and remedial students* (2nd ed.). Portsmouth, NH: Heinemann.

Rotter, K. M. (2004). Simple techniques to improve teacher-made instructional material for use by pupils with disabilities. *Preventing School Failure, 48*(2), 38–43.

Salend, S. J. (2005). *Creating inclusive classrooms: Effective and reflective practices for all students* (5th ed.). Upper Saddle River, NJ: Merrill/Prentice Hall.

Schloss, P. J., & Schloss, C. N. (1987). A critical review of social skills research in mental retardation. In R. P. Barrett & J. L. Matson (Eds.), *Advances in developmental disorders* (pp. 107–151). Greenwich, CT: JAI Press.

Spache, E. B. (1982). *Reading activities for child involvement.* Boston, MA: Allyn & Bacon.

Sperling, R. A. (2006). Assessing reading materials for students who are learning disabled. *Intervention in School & Clinic, 41*(3), 138.

Standal, T. (1978). Readability formulas: What's out, what's in? *The Reading Teacher, 21*, 642–646.

Staples, S. F. (1989). Shabanu: Daughter of the wind Laurel Leaf Publishers. Grinnel: IA.

Steptoe, J. (1987). *Mufaro's beautiful daughters.* New York: Lothrop, Lee, & Shepard.

Tolan, S. S. (1978). *Grandpa and me.* New York: Charles Scribner's Sons.

Udvari-Solner, A. (1997). Effective accommodations for students with exceptionalities. *CEC Today, 4*(3), 1, 9–15.

U.S. Department of Education, National Center for Education Statistics. (2005). *The Condition of Education 2005*, NCES 2005–094, Washington, DC: U.S. Government Printing Office.

Viorst, J. (1972). *Alexander and the terrible, horrible, no-good, very bad day.* New York: Atheneum.

Wiig, E., & Semel, E. (1984). *Language assessment and intervention for the learning disabled.* (2nd ed.). Upper Saddle River, NJ: Merrill/Prentice Hall.

Winzer, M. A., & Mazurek, K. (1998). *Special education in multicultural contexts.* Upper Saddle River, NJ: Merrill/Prentice Hall.

Winzer, M. A., & Mazurek, K. (2000). *Special education in the 21st century: Issues of inclusion and reform.* Washington, DC: Gallaudet University Press.

Wood, J. W. (2006). *Teaching students in inclusive settings: Adapting and accommodating instruction* (5th ed.). Upper Saddle River, NJ: Merrill/ Prentice Hall.

Wood, J. W., & Wooley, J. A. (1986). Adapting textbooks. *Clearing House, 59*(7), 332–335.

CHAPTER 7

Ager, C. L., & Cole, C. L. (1991). A review of cognitive-behavioral interventions for children and adolescents with behavioral disorders. *Behavioral Disorders, 16*, 276–287.

Alberto, P. A., & Troutman, A. C. (2006). *Applied behavior analysis for teachers* (7th ed.). Upper Saddle River, NJ: Pearson Education, Inc.

Albion, F. M. (1980, April). *Development and implementation of self-monitoring/self-instruction procedures in the classroom.* Paper presented at CEC's 58th Annual International Convention, Philadelphia, PA.

Baker, L., & Brown, A. L. (1980). *Metacognitive skills and reading* (Technical Report No. 188). Urbana, IL: University of Illinois, Center for the Study of Reading.

Berry, G., Hall, D., & Gildroy, P. G. (2004). Teaching learning strategies. In B. K. Lenz & D. D. Deshler (Eds.) *Teaching content to all: Evidence-based inclusive practices in middle and secondary schools.* Boston, MA: Allyn and Bacon.

Billingsley, B. S., & Wildman, T. W. (1990). Facilitating reading comprehension in learning disabled students: Metacognitive goals and instructional strategies. *Remedial and Special Education, 11*(2), 18–31.

Bos, C. S., & Anders, P. L. (1990). Interactive practices for teaching content and strategic knowledge. In T. E. Scruggs & B. Y. L. Wong (Eds.), *Intervention research in learning disabilities* (pp. 116–185). New York: Springer-Verlag.

Bos, C. S., & Vaughn, S. (2006). *Strategies for teaching students with learning and behavior problems* (6th ed.). Boston: Pearson Education, Inc.

Brown, A. L., & Palincsar, A. S. (1982). Inducing strategic learning from texts by means of informed, self-control training. *Topics in Learning and Learning Disabilities, 2*(1), 1–17.

Brown, A. L., & Palincsar, A. S. (1989). Guided, cooperative learning, and individual knowledge acquisition. In L. B. Resnick (Ed.), *Knowing, learning, and instruction: Essays in honor of Robert Glaser* (pp. 393–451). Mahwah, NJ: Erlbaum.

Ciardello, A. V. (1998). Did you ask a good question today? Alternative cognitive and metacognitive strategies. *Journal of Adolescent & Adult Literacy, 42*, 210–219.

Cooney, J. B., & Swanson, H. L. (1990). Individual differences in memory for mathematical story problems: Memory span and problem perception. *Journal of Educational Psychology, 82*, 570–577.

De La Paz, S. (1999). Self-regulated strategy instruction in regular education settings: Improving outcomes for students with and without learning disabilities. *Learning Disabilities Research and Practice, 14*, 92–106.

Deshler, D. D. (2005). Adolescents with learning disabilities: Unique challenges and reasons for hope. *Learning Disability Quarterly, 28*(2), 122–124.

Deshler, D. D., Ellis, E. S., & Lenz, B. K. (1996). *Teaching adolescents with learning disabilities* (2nd ed.). Denver: Love Publishing.

Deshler, D. D., & Schumaker, J. B. (2006). *Teaching adolescents with disabilities: Accessing the general education curriculum.* Thousand Oaks, CA: Corwin Press.

Deshler, D. D., Schumaker, J. B., Alley, G. R., Warner, M. M., & Clark, F. L. (1982). Learning disabilities in adolescents and young adult populations: Research implications (part I). *Focus on Exceptional Children, 15*(1), 1–12.

Deshler, D. D., Schumaker, J. B., Lenz, B. K., Bulgren, J. A., Hock, M. F., Knight, J., et al. (2001). Ensuring content-area learning by secondary students with learning disabilities. *Learning Disabilities Research & Practice, 16*(2), 96–108.

Duffy, G. G., Roehler, L. R., Meloth, M. S., Putnam, J., & Wesselman, R. (1986). The relationship between explicit verbal explanations during reading-skill instruction and student awareness and achievement: A study of reading teacher effects. *Reading Research Quarterly, 21*(3), 237–252.

Ellis, E. S. (1989). A metacognitive intervention for increasing class participation. *Learning Disabilities Focus, 5*(1), 36–46.

Englert, C. S., & Palincsar, A. S. (1991). Reconsidering instructional research in literacy from a sociocultural perspective. *Learning Disabilities Research and Practice, 6*, 225–229.

Englert, C. S., Tarrant, K. L., & Mariage, T. V. (1992). Defining and redefining instructional practice in special education: Perspectives on good teaching. *Teacher Education and Special Education, 15*(2), 62–87.

Fraser, C., Belzner, R., & Conte, R. (1992). Attention deficit hyperactivity disorder and self-control. *School Psychology International, 13*, 339–345.

Graham, S., & Harris, K. R. (1993). Self-regulated strategy development: Helping students with learning problems develop as writers. *Elementary School Journal, 94*, 169–181.

Graham, S., & Harris, K. R. (1994). The effects of whole language on children's writing: A review of literature. *Educational Psychologist, 29*, 187–192.

Graham, S., & Harris, K. R. (2000). The role of self-regulation and transcription skills in writing and writing development. *Educational Psychologist, 35*(1), 3–12.

Graham, S., Harris, K. R., MacArthur, C., & Schwartz, S. (1991). Writing and writing instruction with students with learning disabilities: A review of a program of research. *Learning Disability Quarterly, 14*, 89–114.

Graham, S., & Harris, K. R., & Mason, L. (2005). Improving the writing performance, knowledge, and self-efficacy of struggling young writers: The effects of self-regulated strategy development. *Contemporary Educational Psychology, 30*, 207–241.

Graham, S., Harris, K. R., & Troia, G. A. (2000). Self-regulated strategy development revisited: Teaching writing strategies to struggling writers. *Topics In Language Disorders, 20*(4), 1–14.

Graham, S., MacArthur, C., & Schwartz, S. (1995). The effects of goal setting and procedural facilitation on the revising behavior and writing performance of students with writing and learning problems. *Journal of Educational Psychology, 87*(2), 230–240.

Harris, K. R., & Graham, S. (1994). Constructivism: Principles, paradigms, and integration. *The Journal of Special Education, 28*(3), 233–247.

Harris, K. R., & Graham, S. (1996). *Making the writing process work: Strategies for composition and self-regulation.* Cambridge, MA: Brookline.

Harris, K. R., Graham, S., Reid, R., McElroy, K., & Hamby, R. (1994). Self-monitoring of attention versus self-monitoring of performance: Replication and cross-task comparison studies. *Learning Disability Quarterly, 17*, 121–139.

Harris, K. R., Schmidt, T., & Graham, S. (1997). *Every child can write: Strategies for composition and self-regulation in the classroom. Every child every day: Learning in diverse schools and classrooms.* Cambridge, MA: Brookline Books.

Herrmann, B. A. (1988). Two approaches for helping poor readers. *Reading Teacher, 42*(1), 25–28.

Jones, B. F., Palincsar, A. S., Ogle, D. S., & Carr, E. G. (1987). *Strategic teaching and learning: Cognitive instruction in the content areas.* Alexandria, VA: Association for Supervision and Curriculum Development.

Kea, C. D. (1987). *An analysis of critical teaching behaviors employed by teachers of students with mild handicaps.* Unpublished doctoral dissertation. The University of Kansas, Lawrence.

Kea, C. D. (1995, July). Critical teaching behaviors. *Strategram, 7*(6), 1–8.

Lenz, B. K., Deshler, D. D., & Kissam, B. R. (2004). *Teaching content to all.* Boston, MA: Pearson Education, Inc.

Lenz, B. K., Ellis, E. S., & Scanlon, D. (1996). *Teaching learning strategies to adolescents and adults with learning disabilities.* Austin, TX: PRO-ED.

Mayer, R. E. (2001). What good is educational psychology? The case of cognition and instruction. *Educational Psychologist, 36*(2), 83–88.

Meese, R. (1994). *Teaching learners with mild disabilities: Integrating research and practice.* Pacific Grove, CA: Brooks/Cole.

Meichenbaum, D., & Goodman, J. (1971). Training impulsive children to talk to themselves: A means of developing self-control. *Journal of Abnormal Psychology, 77*, 115–126.

Mercer, C. D., & Mercer, A. R. (2001). *Teaching students with learning problems* (6th ed.). Upper Saddle River, NJ: Prentice Hall.

Mercer, C. D., & Pullen, P. C. (2005). *Students with learning disabilities* (6th ed.). Upper Saddle River, NJ: Pearson Education, Inc.

Montague, M. (1997). Cognitive strategy instruction in mathematics for students with learning disabilities. *Journal of Learning Disabilities, 30*(2), 164–177.

Morgan, L. (Ed.). (1988). *Langston Hughes: He believed humor would help defeat bigotry and fear.* Seattle: Turman.

Palincsar, A. S. (1986a). Metacognitive strategy instruction. *Exceptional Children, 53*(2), 118–124.

Palincsar, A. S. (1986b). The role of dialogue in scaffolded instruction. *Educational Psychologist, 21*, 73–98.

Palincsar, A. S., & Brown, A. L. (1984). The reciprocal teaching of comprehension fostering and comprehension monitoring activities. *Cognition and Instruction, 1*, 117–175.

Palincsar, A. S., & Brown, A. L. (1986). Interactive teaching to promote independent learning from text. *The Reading Teacher, 39*(8), 771–777.

Palincsar, A. S., & Brown, A. L. (1987). Enhancing instructional time through attention to metacognition. *Journal of Learning Disabilities, 20*(2), 66–75.

Palincsar, A. S., & Brown, A. L. (1988). Teaching and practicing thinking skills to promote comprehension in the context of group problem solving. *Remedial and Special Education, 9*(1), 53–59.

Palincsar, A. S., & Brown, A. L. (1989). Instruction for self-regulated reading. In L. B. Resnick & L. E. Klopfer (Eds.), *Toward the thinking curriculum: Current cognitive research: 1989 ASCD yearbook* (pp. 19–39). Alexandria, VA: Association for Supervision and Curriculum Development.

Paris, S. G., Lipson, M. Y., Jacobs, J., Oka, E., Debritto, A. M., & Cross, D. (1982, April). *Metacognition and reading comprehension.* Symposium conducted at the annual meeting of the International Reading Association, Chicago, IL.

Paris, S. G., Newman, R., & McVey, K. (1982). Learning the functional significance of mnemonic actions: A microgenetic study of strategy acquisition. *Journal of Experimental Child Psychology, 34*, 490–509.

Paris, S. G., & Oka, E. R. (1986). Self-regulated learning among exceptional children. *Exceptional Children, 53*(2), 103–108.

Platt, J. M., & Olson, J. (1997). *Teaching adolescents with mild disabilities.* Pacific Grove, CA: Brooks/Cole.

Pressley, M., Borkowski, J. G., & O'Sullivan, J. T. (1984). Memory strategy instruction is made of this: Metamemory and durable strategy use. *Educational Psychologist, 1*, 94–107.

Pressley, M., Wharton-McDonald, R., Raphael, L. M., Bogner, K., & Roehrig, A. (2002). Exemplary first-grade teaching. In B. M. Taylor & P. D. Pearson (Eds.), *Teaching reading: Effective schools, accomplished teachers* (pp. 73–88). Mahwah, NJ: L. Erlbaum Associates.

Robinson, H. A. (1975). *Teaching reading and study strategies: The content areas.* Needham Heights, MA: Allyn & Bacon.

Rosenshine, B., & Meister, C. (1994). Reciprocal teaching: A review of the research. *Review of Educational Research, 64*, 479–530.

Ruiz, N. T. (1989). An optimal learning environment for Rosemary. *Exceptional Child, 56*(2), 130–144.

Sawyer, R., Graham, S., & Harris, K. R. (1992). Direct teaching, strategy instruction, and strategy instruction with explicit self-regulation: Effects on learning disabled students' compositions and self-efficacy. *Journal of Educational Psychology, 84*, 340–352.

Schloss, P. J., Smith, M. A., & Schloss, C. N. (2001). *Instructional methods for secondary students with learning and behavior problems* (3rd ed.). Needham Heights, MA: Allyn & Bacon.

Schumaker, J. B., Nolan, S. M., & Deshler, D. D. (1985). *The error monitoring strategy.* Lawrence, KA: The University of Kansas.

Speece, D. L., MacDonald, V., Kilsheimer, L., & Krist, J. (1997). Research to practice: Preservice teachers reflect on reciprocal teaching. *Learning Disabilities Practice, 12*(3), 177–187.

Swaggert, B. L. (1998). Implementing a cognitive behavior management program. *Intervention School and Clinic, 33*(4), 235–238.

Van Luit, J. E. H., & Naglieri, J. A. (1999). Effectiveness of the MASTER program for teaching special children multiplication and division. *Journal of Learning Disabilities, 32*(2), 98–107.

Vygotsky, L. S. (1962). *Thought and language.* New York: Wiley.

Warner, M. M., Schumaker, J. B., Alley, G. R., & Deshler, D. D. (1980). Learning disabled adolescents in public schools: Are they different from other low achievers? *Exceptional education Quarterly, 1*(2), 27–35.

Winograd, P., & Hare, V. C. (1988). Direct instruction of reading comprehension strategies: The nature of teacher explanation. In E. T. Goetz, P. Alexander, & C. Weinstein (Eds.), *Learning and study strategies: Assessment, instruction, and evaluation* (pp. 25–56). New York: Academic Press.

Wong, B. Y. L. (1986). Metacognition and special education: A review of a view. *The Journal of Special Education, 20*(1), 9–29.

Wong, B. Y. L., & Jones, W. (1982). Increasing metacomprehension in learning-disabled and normally-achieving students through self-questioning training. *Learning Disability Quarterly, 5*, 228–240.

CHAPTER 8

Bybee, R. W. (1997). *Achieving scientific literacy.* Portsmouth, NH: Heinemann.

Canter, L. S., Gardner, J. E., Schweder, W., & Wissick, C. A. (2003). Enhancing interdisciplinary instruction in general and special education: Thematic units and technology. *Remedial and Special Education, 24*, 161–172.

Carlson, C. D., & Francis, D. J. (2002). Increasing the reading achievement of at-risk children through Direct Instruction: Evaluation of the Rodeo Institute for Teacher Excellence (RITE). *Journal of Education for Students Placed At Risk, 7*(2), 141–166.

Carnine, D., Silbert, J., & Kame'enui, E. J. (1997). *Direct instruction reading* (3rd ed.). Upper Saddle River, NJ: Merrill/Prentice Hall.

Checkley, K. (1997). The first seven. *Educational Leadership, 55*(1), 8–13.

Cobb-Morocco, C. (2001). Teaching for understanding with students with disabilities: New directions for research on access to the general education curriculum. *Learning Disabilities Quarterly, 24*, 5–13.

Darch, C., & Gersten, R. (1986). Direction-setting activities in reading comprehension: A comparison of two approaches. *Learning Disabilities Quarterly, 9*(3), 235–243.

Deshler, D. D., Schumaker, J. B., Lenz, B. K., Bulgren, J. A., Hock, M. F., Knight, J., & Ehren, B. J. (2001). Ensuring content-area learning by secondary students with learning disabilities. *Learning Disabilities Research & Practice, 16*(2), 96–108.

Englemann, et al., 1990

Engelmann, S., Meyer, L., Johnson, G., & Carnine, L. (1988). *Corrective reading: Skills applications, decoding c.* Chicago: Scientific Research Associates.

Englert, C. S., Raphael, T. E., & Mariage, T. V. (1994). Developing a school-based discourse for literacy learning: A principled search for understanding. *Learning Disability Quarterly, 17,* 2–32.

Foorman, B., & Torgesen, J. (2001). Critical elements of classroom and small-group instruction promote reading success in all children. *Learning Disabilities Research & Practice, 16*(4), 203–212.

Friend, M., & Cook, L. (2003). *Interactions: Collaboration skills for school professionals* (4th ed.). Boston: Allyn and Bacon.

Friend, M., & Pope, K. L. (2005). Creating schools in which all students can succeed. *Kappa Delta Pi, 41*(2), 56–61.

Gardner, H. (1983). *Frames of mind: The theory of multiple intelligences.* New York: Basic Books.

Gardner, H. (1995). Reflections on multiple intelligences: Myths and messages. *Phi Delta Kappan, 77*(3), 200–209.

Gardner, H. (2006). *Multiple intelligence.* Jackson, TN: Perseus Books Group.

Gardner, R. III, Cartledge, G., Seidl, B., Woodsey, L., Schley, S., & Utley, C. (2001). Mt. Olivet After-School Program: Peer-mediated intervention for at risk students. *Remedial and Special Education, 22*(1), 34–47.

Gardner, J. E., Wissick, C. A., Schweder, W. G., & Smith-Canter, L. L. (2003). Enhancing interdisciplinary instruction in general and special education. *Remedial and Special Education, 24*(3), 161–172.

Gersten, R., Woodward, J., & Darch, C. (1986). Direct instruction: A research-based approach to curriculum design and teaching. *Exceptional Children, 53*(1), 17–31.

Hefferan, M., & O'Rear, S. (1991). *B.A.L.A.N.C.E. training manual.* Orlando, FL: FDLRS/Action.

Herald-Taylor, G. (1987). How to use predictable books for K–2 language arts instruction. *The Reading Teacher, 40*(7), 656–663.

Hintze, J. M., Ryan, A. L., & Stoner, G. (2003). Concurrent validity and diagnostic accuracy of the *Dynamic Indicators of Basic Early Literacy Skills and the Comprehensive Test of Phonological Processing. School Psychology Review, 32,* 541–556.

Hudson, R. F., Lane, H. B., & Pullen, P. C. (2005). Reading fluency assessment and instruction: What, why, and how? *The Reading Teacher, 58,* 702–714.

Jensen, E. (1998). *Teaching with the brain in mind.* Alexandria, VA: Association for Supervision and Curriculum Development.

Jobe, R. & Dayton-Sakari, M. (2002). *Info-Kids: How to use nonfiction to turn reluctant readers into enthusiastic learners.* Ontario: Pembroke.

Language Through Literature. (2002). Desoto, TX: SRA/McGraw-Hill, Author.

Lenz, B. K., Bulgren, J. A., Schumaker, J. B., Deshler, D. D., & Boudah, D. A. (1994). *The unit organizer routine* (Instructor's Manual). Lawrence, KS: Edge Enterprises.

Lloyd, J. L. (2005). *Characteristics of effective promising and not-so-promising approaches. A summary of the reading programs.* January 25, 2005 Teleconference for the State-to-State Information Sharing Community. Retrieved October 31, 2006, from http://www.behavior-analyst-today.com/JEIBI-VOL-3/JEIBI-3-1.pdf

Lloyd, J., Cullinan, D., Heins, E. D., & Epstein, M. H. (1980). Direct instruction: Effects on oral and written language comprehension. *Learning Disabilities Quarterly, 3*(4), 70–76.

Mac Iver, M. A., & Kemper, E. (2002). The impact of Direct Instruction on elementary students' reading achievement in an urban school district. *Journal of Education for Students Placed At Risk, 7*(2), 197–220.

Maker, C. J., Nielson, A. B., & Rogers, J. A. (1994). Multiple intelligences: Giftedness, diversity, and problem-solving. *TEACHING Exceptional Children, 27*(1), 4–19.

Mastropieri, M. A., & Scruggs, T. E. (1994). Text versus hands-on science curriculum: Implications for students with disabilities. *Remedial and Special Education, 15,* 72–85.

National Reading Panel [cited in text as "Subgroups"]. (2000). *Report of the National Reading Panel: An evidence-based assessment of the scientific research literature on reading and its implications for reading instruction, reports of the subgroups.* Washington, DC: National Institute of Child Health and Human Development. Retrieved October 31, 2006, from http://www.nichd.nih.gov/publications/nrp/report.htm

National Research Council. (1998). *Preventing reading difficulties in young children* (Committee on the Prevention of Reading Difficulties in Young Children; C. E. Snow, M. S. Burns, & P. Griffin, Eds.). Washington, DC: National Academy Press.

Northwest Regional Educational Laboratory. (2005). *Direct Instruction Models (K–8).* Retrieved October 31, 2006, from http://www.nwrel.org/scpd/catalog/ModelDetails.asp?ModelID=13

Ogle, D. M. (1986). K-W-L: A teaching model that develops active reading of expository text. *The Reading Teacher, 39,* 564–570.

Pressley, M. (2005). *Reading instruction that works: The case for balanced teaching.* New York: Guilford Publications.

Rose, D. H., & Meyer, A. (2000). Universal Design for Learning. *Journal of Special Education Technology, 15*(1): 67–70.

Saunders, S. (1999). *Look and learn!: Using picture books in grades five through eight.* Portsmouth, NH: Heinemann.

Shanahan, T., Robinson, B., & Schneider, M. (1995). Integrating curriculum: Avoiding some of the pitfalls of thematic units. *The Reading Teacher, 48*(8), 718–719.

Slavin, R. & Cheung, A. (2004). How do English language learners learn to read? *Educational Leadership, 61*(6), 52–57.

Sousa, D. A. (2001). *How the special needs brain learns.* Thousand Oaks, CA: Corwin Press, Inc.

Stein, M., Carnine, D., & Dixon, R. (1998). Direct instruction: Integrating curriculum design and effective teaching practice. *Intervention in School and Clinic, 33*(4), 227–234.

CHAPTER 9

Alberto, P. A., & Troutman, A. C. (1999). *Applied behavior analysis for teachers* (5th ed.). Upper Saddle River, NJ: Merrill/Prentice Hall.

Allsopp, D. H. (1997). Using classwide peer tutoring to teach beginning algebra problem-solving skills in heterogeneous classrooms. *Remedial and Special Education, 18*(6), 367–379.

Aronson, E. (1978). *The jigsaw classroom.* Beverly Hills, CA: Sage.

Cartledge, G., & Cochran, L. L. (1993). Developing cooperative learning behaviors in students with behavior disorders. *Preventing School Failure, 37,* 5–10.

Cartledge, G., & Kiarie, M. W. (2001). Learning social skills through literature for children and adolescents. *TEACHING Exceptional Children, 34*(2), 40–47.

Cartledge, G., & Milburn, J. F. (1996). Cultural diversity and social skills instruction: Understanding ethnic and gender differences.

Chadsey-Rusch, J. (1986). Identifying and teaching valued social behaviors. In F. R. Rusch (Ed.), *Competitive employment issues and strategies* (pp. 273–287). Baltimore: Paul H. Brookes.

Christensen, M. (1992). *Motivational English for at-risk students.* Bloomington, IA: National Educational Service.

Copeland, S. R., Hughes, C., Carter, E. W., Guth, C., Presley, J. A., Williams, C. R., & Fowler, S. E. (2004). Increasing access to general education: Perspectives of participants in a high school peer support program. *Remedial and Special Education, 25* (6), 342–352.

Daniels, H. (2002). *Literature circles: Voice and choice in book clubs and reading groups* (3rd ed.). Portland, ME: Stenhouse.

Delquadri, J., Greenwood, C. R., Whorton, D., Carta, J. J., & Hall, R. V. (1986). Classwide peer tutoring. *Exceptional Children, 52*(6), 535–542.

Dieker, L., & Ousley, D. (2006). Speaking the same language: Bringing together highly-qualified secondary English and special education teachers. *Teaching Exceptional Children Plus,* http://escholarship.bc.edu/education/tecplus/vol2/iss4/art3

Dufrene, B. A., Duhon, G. J., Gilbertson, D. N., & Noell, G. H. (2005). Monitoring implementation of reciprocal peer tutoring: Identifying and intervening with students who do not maintain accurate implementation. *School Psychology Review, 34,* 74–86.

Durrer, B., & McLaughlin, T. F. (1995). The use of peer tutoring interventions involving students with behaviour disorders. *B. C. Journal of Special Education, 19*(1), 20–27.

Elbaum, B., Vaughn, S., Hughes, M., & Moody, S. W. (1999). Grouping practices and reading outcomes for students with disabilities. *Exceptional Children, 25*(3), 399–415.

Elias, M. J., & Taylor, M. E. (1995). Building social and academic skills via problem solving videos. *TEACHING Exceptional Children, 27*(3), 14–17.

Elias, M. J., & Tobias, S. E. (1996). *Social problem Solving: Interventions in the Schools.* New York: The Guilford Press.

Fantuzzo, J. W., King, J. A., & Heller, L. R. (1992). Effects of reciprocal peer tutoring on mathematics and school adjustment: A component analysis. *Journal of Educational Psychology, 84*(3), 331–339.

Forness, S. R., Kavale, K. A., Blum, I. M., & Lloyd, J. W. (1997). Mega-analysis of meta-analyses: What works in special education and related services. *TEACHING Exceptional Children, 29*(6), 4–9.

Fuchs, D., Fuchs, L. S., Mathes, P. G., & Simmons, D. C. (1996). *Peer-assisted learning strategies: Making classrooms more responsive to diversity.* (Report No. NCRTL-EC-304-716). East Lansing, MI: National Center for Research on Teacher Learning. (ERIC Document Reproduction Service No. ED393269).

Fulk, B. M., & King, K. (2001). Classwide peer tutoring at work. *TEACHING Exceptional Children, 34*(2), 49–53.

Goldstein, A. P., McGinnis, E., Sprafklin, R. P., Gershaw, N. J., & Klein, P. (2002). *Skillstreaming the adolescent: A structured learning approach to teaching prosocial skills.* Chicago, IL: Research Park. www.skillstreaming.com

Goor, M., Schwenn, J., Elridge, A., Mallein, D., & Stauffer, J. (1996). Using strategy cards to enhance cooperative learning for students with disabilities. *TEACHING Exceptional Children, 29*(1), 66–70.

Greenwood, C. R. (1999). Reflections on a research career: Perspective on 35 years of research at the Juniper Gardens Children's Project. *Exceptional Children, 66*(1), 7–21.

Greenwood, C. R., Arreaga-Mayer, C., Utley, C. A., Gavin, K. M., & Terry, B. J. (2001). Classwide peer-tutoring learning management system: Applications with elementary-level English language learners. *Remedial & Special Education, 22*(1), 34–47.

Greenwood, C. R., & Delquadri, J. (1995). ClassWide peer tutoring and the prevention of school failure. *Preventing School Failure, 39*(4), 21–25.

Gresham, F. M., Sugai, G. H., & Horner, R. H. (2001). Interpreting outcomes of social skills training for students with high-incidence disabilities. *Exceptional Children, 67*(3), 331–344. Guilford Press.

Harper, G. F., Mallette, B., Maheady, L., & Brennan, G. (1993). Classwide student tutoring teams and direct instruction as a combined instructional program to teach generalizable strategies for mathematics word problems. *Education & Treatment of Children, 16,* 115–134.

Heller, L., & Fantuzzo, J. (1993). Reciprocal peer tutoring and parent partnerships: Does parent involvement make a difference? *School Psychology Review, 22*(3), 517–535.

Johnson, D. W., & Johnson, R. T. (1980). Integrating handicapped children into the mainstream. *Exceptional Children, 47,* 90–98.

Johnson, D. W., & Johnson, R. T. (1986). Mainstreaming and cooperative learning strategies. *Exceptional Children, 52*(6), 553–561.

Johnson, D. W., & Johnson, R. T. (1991). *Learning together and alone: Cooperative, competitive, and individualistic learning* (3rd ed.). Englewood Cliffs, NJ: Prentice Hall.

Johnson, D. W., & Johnson, R. T. (1996). The role of cooperative learning in assessing and communicating student learning. In T. R. Guskey (Ed.), *ASCD Yearbook 1996* (pp. 25–46). Alexandria, VA: ASCD.

Johnson, R. T., & Johnson, D. W. (1994). An overview of cooperative learning. In J. Thousand, A. Villa, & A. Nevin (Eds.), *Creativity and collaborative learning.* Baltimore: Brookes Press.

Kauffman, J., Landrum, T., Mock, D., Sayeski, B., & Sayeski, K. (2005). Diverse knowledge and skills require a diversity of instruction groups: A position statement. *Remedial and Special Education, 26,* 2–6.

Kavale, K. A., Mathur, S. R., Forness, S. R., Rutherford, R. B., & Quinn, M. M. (1997). Effectiveness of social skills training for students with behavior disorders: A meta-analysis. In T. Scruggs & M. Mastropieri (Eds.), *Advances in learning and behavioral disabilities* (Vol. 11, pp. 293–312). Greenwich, CT: JAI Press.

King-Sears, M. E., & Bradley, D. F. (1995). ClassWide peer tutoring: Heterogeneous instruction in general education classrooms. *Preventing School Failure, 40*(1), 29–35.

Klinger, J. K., & Vaughn, S. (1996). Reciprocal teaching of reading comprehension strategies for students with learning disabilities who use English as a second language. *Elementary School Journal, 96,* 275–293.

Klinger, J. K., & Vaughn, S. (1998). Using collaborative strategic reading. *TEACHING Exceptional Children, 30*(6), 32–37.

Leffert, J. S., Siperstein, G. N., & Millikan, E. (2000). Understanding social adaptation in children with mental retardation: A social-cognitive perspective. *Exceptional Children, 66*(4), 530–545.

Leffert, J. S., & Siperstein, G. N. (2003). *Social skills instruction for students with learning disabilities. Current Practice Alert Series.* Reston, VA: Council for Exceptional Children.

Longwill, A., & Kleinert, H. (1998). The unexpected benefits of high school peer tutoring. *TEACHING Exceptional Children, 30*(4), 60–65.

MacArthur, C. A., Schwartz, S. S., & Graham, S. (1991). Effects of a reciprocal peer revision strategy in special education classrooms. *Learning Disabilities Research & Practice, 6*(4), 201–218.

Maheady, L., Harper, G. F., & Mallette, B. (2001). Peer-mediated instruction and interventions and students with mild disabilities. *Remedial and Special Education, 22*(1), 4–14.

Maheady, L., Sacca, M. K., & Harper, G. F. (1988). Classwide peer tutoring with mildly handicapped high school students. *Exceptional Children, 55*(1), 52–59.

Mastropieri, M., & Scruggs, T. E. (2005). Feasibility and consequences of response to intervention: Examination of the issues and scientific evidence as a model for the identification of individuals with learning disabilities. *Journal of Learning Disabilities,* 38(6), 525–531.

Mastropieri, M. A., & Scruggs, T. E. (2007). *The inclusive classroom: Strategies for effective instruction* (3rd ed.). Upper Saddle River, NJ: Pearson Education, Inc.)

Mathes, P. G., Fuchs, D., Fuchs, L. S., Henley, A. M., & Sanders, A. (1994). Increasing strategic reading practice with Peabody ClassWide Peer Tutoring. *Learning Disabilities Research and Practice, 9*(1), 44–48.

McFall, R. M. (1982). A review and reformulation of the concept of social skills. *Behavioral Assessment, 4,* 1–33.

McIntosh, R., Vaughn, S., & Bennerson, D. (1995). FAST social skills with a SLAM and a RAP. *TEACHING Exceptional Children, 28*(1), 37–41.

McMaster, K. N., & Fuchs, D. (2002). Effects of cooperative learning on the academic achievement of students with learning disabilities: An update of Tateyama-Sniezek's review. *Learning Disabilities Research and Practice, 17*(2), 107–117.

McMaster, K. N., Fuchs, D., Fuchs, L. S., & Compton, D. L. (2005). Responding to nonresponders: An experimental field trial of identification and intervention methods. *Exceptional Children, 71,* 445–463.

Miller, A. D., Barbetta, P. M., & Heron, T. E. (1994). START tutoring: Designing, training, implementing, adapting, and evaluating tutoring programs for school and home settings. In D. M. Gardner, III, J. O. Sainato, T. E. Cooper, W. L. Heron, J. W. Heward, & T. A. Eshelman (Eds.), *Behavior analysis in education: Focus on measurably superior instruction* (pp. 265–282). Pacific Grove, CA: Brooks/Cole.

Monda-Amaya, L., Dieker, L., & Reed, F. (1998). Preparing students with learning disabilities to participate in inclusive classrooms. *Learning Disabilities Research and Practice, 13,* 169–182.

Morris, S. (2002). Promoting social skills among students with nonverbal learning disabilities. *TEACHING Exceptional Children, 34*(3), 66–70.

Murawski, W. W., & Dieker, L. A. (2004). Co-teaching at the secondary level: Unique issues, current trends, and suggestions for success. *Teaching Exceptional Children, 36(5),* 52–58.

Noddings, N. (1989). Theoretical and practical concerns about small groups in mathematics. *The Elementary School Journal, 89,* 607–623.

O'Connor, R. E., & Jenkins, J. R. (1996). Cooperative learning as an inclusion strategy: A closer look. *Exceptionality, 6*(1), 29–51.

O'Melia, M. C., & Rosenberg, M. S. (1994). Effects of Cooperative Homework Teams on the acquisition of mathematics skills by secondary students with mild disabilities. *Exceptional Children, 60*(6), 538–548.

Pomplun, M. (1997). When students with disabilities participate in cooperative groups. *Exceptional Children, 64*(10), 49–58.

Prater, M. A., Serna, L., & Nakamura, K. K. (1999). Impact of peer teaching on the acquisition of social skills by adolescents with learning disabilities. *Education & Treatment of Children, 22*(1), 19–35.

Putnam, J. W., Rynders, J. E., Johnson, R. T., & Johnson, D. W. (1989). Collaborative skill instruction for promoting positive interactions between mentally handicapped and nonhandicapped children. *Exceptional Children, 55*(6), 550–558.

Rivera, D. P., & Smith, D. D. (1997). *Teaching students with learning and behavior problems.* Needham Heights, MA: Allyn & Bacon.

Rizzo, A. A., Schultheis, M. T., Kerns, K., & and Mateer, C. (2004). Analysis of assets for virtual reality applications in neuropsychology. *Neuropsychological Rehabilitation, 14(1)*, 207–239.

Robins, B., Dautenhahn K., Boekhorst, Rt, & Billiard, A. (2004). Effects of repeated exposure to a humanoid robot on children with autism. In S. Keates, J. Clarkson, P. Langdon & P. Robinson (Eds.), London: Springer Verlag. *Designing a More Inclusive World.*

Rosenthal-Malek, A. L. (1997). STOP and THINK: Using metacognitive strategies to teach students social skills. *TEACHING Exceptional Children, 29*(3), 29–31.

Ryan, J. P., Reid, R., & Epstein, M. H. (2004). Peer-mediated intervention studies on academic achievement for students with EBD: A review. *Remedial and Special Education, 25* (6), 330–341(12)

Saenz, L. M., Fuchs, L. S., & Fuchs, D. (2005). Peer-assisted learning strategies for English language learners with learning disabilities. *Exceptional Children, 71*, 231–247.

Salend, S. J., & Allen, E. M. (1985). A comparison of self-managed and externally managed response cost systems on learning disabled children. *Journal of School Psychology, 23*, 59–67.

Salend, S. J., Jantzen, N. R., & Giek, K. (1992). Using a peer confrontation system in a group setting. *Behavioral Disorders, 17*(3), 211–218.

Sapon-Shevin, M. (1986). Teaching cooperation. In G. Cartledge & J. F. Milburn (Eds.), *Teaching social skills to children: Innovative approaches* (3rd ed.). Elmsford, NY: Pergamon.

Schniedewind, N., & Salend, S. J. (1987). Cooperative learning works. *TEACHING Exceptional Children, 19*(2), 22–25.

Slavin, R. E. (1984). Team-assisted individualization: Cooperative learning and individualized instruction in the mainstreamed classroom. *Remedial and Special Education, 5*(6), 33–42.

Slavin, R. E. (1988a). Cooperative learning and student achievement. *Educational Leadership, 46*(2), 31–33.

Slavin, R. E. (1988b). *Student team learning: An overview and practical guide* (2nd ed.). Washington, DC: National Education Association.

Slavin, R. E., Stevens, R. J., & Madden, N. A. (1988). Accommodating student diversity in reading and writing instruction: A cooperative learning approach. *Remedial and Special Education, 9*(1), 60–66.

Smith, J. O. (1995). Getting to the bottom of social skills deficits. *LD Forum, 21*(1), 23–26.

Stevens, R. J., & Slavin, R. E. (1991). When cooperative learning improves the achievement of students with mild disabilities: A response to Tateyama-Sniezek. *Exceptional Children, 57*(3), 276–280.

Topping, K. J. (2005). Trends in peer learning. *Educational Psychology, 25*(6), 631–645.

Utley, C. A., Mortsweet, S. L., & Greenwood, C. R. (1997). Peer-mediated instruction and interventions. *Focus on Exceptional Children, 29*(5), 1–23.

Utley, C., Reddy, S., Delquadri, J., Greenwood, C., Mortsweet, S., & Bowman, V. (2001). ClassWide peer tutoring: An effective teaching procedure for facilitating the acquisition of health education and safety facts with students with developmental disabilities. *Education & Treatment of Children, 24*(1), 1–28.

Vaughn, S., Hughes, M. T., & Moody, S. W. (2001). Instructional grouping for students with LD: Implications for practice. *Intervention in School and Clinic, 36*(3), 131–137.

Vaughn, S., Klinger, J., & Bryant, D. (2001). Collaborative strategic reading as a means to enhance peer-mediated instruction for reading comprehension and content-area learning. *Remedial and Special Education, 22*(2), 66–74.

Wagner, S. (2002). *Inclusive programming for middle school students with autism/Asperger's syndrome.* Arlington, TX: Future Horizons.

Walker, D. M., Schwarz, I. E., Nippold, M. S., Irvin, L. K., & Noell, J. W. (1994). Social skills in school-age children and youth: Issues and best practices in assessment and intervention. *Topics in Language Disorders, 14*(3), 70–82.

Wolford, P. L., Heward, W. L., & Alber, S. R. (2001a). Teaching middle school students with learning disabilities to recruit peer assistance during cooperative learning group activities. *Learning Disabilities Research & Practice, 16*(3), 161–173.

Zaragoza, N. (1987). Process writing for high-risk and learning-disabled students. *Reading Research and Instruction, 26*(4), 290–301.

CHAPTER 10

Alley, G. R., & Deshler, D. D. (1979). *Teaching students with learning problems* (3rd ed.). New York: Merrill/Macmillan.

Alvermann, D. E., & Phelps, S. F. (2005). *Content reading and literacy: Succeeding in today's diverse classrooms* (4th ed.). Boston: Pearson Education, Inc.

Anderson, T. H., & Armbruster, B. B. (1980). *Studying* (Report No. CS 005-205). Arlington, VA. (ERIC Document Reproduction Service No. ED181427)

Anderson, T. H., & Armbruster, B. B. (1984). Studying. In P. D. Pearson (Ed.), *Handbook of reading research* (pp. 657–679). New York: Longman.

Anderson, S., Yilmaz, O., & Washburn-Moses, L. (2004). Middle and high school students with learning disabilities: Practical academic interventions for general education teachers—A review of the literature. *American Secondary Education, 32*(2), 19–38.

Archer, A. L., & Gleason, M. M. (1994). *Skills for school success* (2nd ed.). North Billerica, MA: Curriculum Associates.

Ashbaker, M. H., & Swanson, H. L. (1996). Short term memory operations and their contribution to reading in adolescents with and without learning disabilities. *Learning Disabilities Research and Practice, 11,* 206–213.

Ausubel, D. P., & Robinson, F. G. (1969). *School learning: An introduction to educational psychology.* New York: Holt, Rinehart, & Winston.

Beirne-Smith, M. (1989). A systematic approach for teaching notetaking skills to students with mild handicaps. *Academic Therapy, 24,* 425–437.

Berninger, V., Abbott, R., Rogan, L., Reed, E., Abbott, S., Brooks, A., et al. (1998). Teaching spelling to children with specific learning disabilities: The mind's ear and eye beat the computer or pencil. *Learning Disability Quarterly, 21,* 106–122.

Blanchard, J. S. (1985). What to tell students about underlining . . . and why. *Journal of Reading,* 199–203.

Bos, C. S., & Vaughn, S. (2006). *Strategies for teaching students with learning and behavior problems* (6th ed.). Boston: Pearson Education, Inc.

Bos, C. S., & Vaughn, S. (2002). *Strategies for teaching students with learning and behavior problems* (5th ed.). Needham Heights, MA: Allyn & Bacon.

Bragstad, B. J., & Stumpf, S. M. (1987). *A guidebook for teaching study skills and motivation.* Needham Heights, MA: Allyn & Bacon.

Brooks, J. G., & Brooks, M. G. (2001). *In search of understanding: The case for constructivist classrooms.* Upper Saddle River, NJ: Prentice Hall.

Bulgren, J., Deshler, D. D., & Schumaker, J. B. (1993). *The content enhancement series: The concept mastery routine.* Lawrence, KS: Edge Enterprises.

Bulgren, J., & Lenz, B. K. (1996). Strategic instruction in the content areas. In D. D. Deshler, E. S. Ellis, & B. K. Lenz (Eds.), *Adolescents with learning disabilities: Strategies and methods* (2nd ed.). Denver: Love.

Bulgren, J., Schumaker, J. B., & Deshler, D. D. (1988). Effectiveness of a concept teaching routine in enhancing the performance of LD students in secondary-level mainstream classes. *Learning Disability Quarterly, 11,* 3–17.

Burke, J. (2001). *ACCESS: Textbook feature analysis.* Retrieved July 24, 2006, from http://www.englishcompanion.com/pdfDocs/textbookanalysis.pdf

Carman, R. A., & Adams, W. R. (1972). *Study skills: A student's guide for survival.* New York: Wiley.

Czarnecki, E., Rosko, D., & Fine, E. (1998). How to call up notetaking skills. *Teaching Exceptional Children, 30*(6), 14–19.

Davis, A., & Clark, E. (1981, October). *High-yield study skills instruction.* (Report No. CS 006-323). Paper presented at the annual meeting of the Plains Regional Conference of the International Reading Association, Des Moines. (ERIC Document Reproduction Service No. ED208372)

Deshler, D. D., & Schumaker, J. B. (2006). *Teaching adolescents with disabilities: Accessing the general education curriculum.* Thousand Oaks, CA: Corwin Press.

Devine, T. G. (1987). *Teaching study skills: A guide for teachers* (2nd ed.). Boston: Allyn & Bacon.

DiCecco, V. M., & Gleason, M. M. (2002). Using graphic organizers to attain relational knowledge from expository text. *Journal of Learning Disabilities, 35*(4), 306–320.

Dye, G. A. (2000). Graphic organizers to the rescue: Helping students link and remember information. *TEACHING Exceptional Children, 32*(3), 72–76.

Ellis, E. S., & Lenz, B. K. (1987). A component analysis of effective learning strategies for LD students. *Learning Disabilities Focus, 2,* 94–107.

Faber, J. E., Morris, J. D., & Lieberman, M. G. (2000). The effect of note taking on ninth grade students' comprehension. *Reading Psychology, 21*(3), 257–270.

Gearheart, B. R., Weishahn, M. W., & Gearheart, D. (1995). *The exceptional student in the regular classroom* (4th ed.). Upper Saddle River, NJ: Merrill/Prentice Hall.

Griffin, C. C., Malone, L. D., Kame'enui, E. J. (1995). Effects of graphic organizer instruction on fifth-grade students. *Journal of Educational Research, 89*(2), 98–107.

Hammill, D. D., & Bartel, N. R. (2004). *Teaching students with learning and behavior problems* (7th ed.). Austin, TX: PRO-ED.

Hoover, J. J. (2005). Study skills. In E. A. Polloway, J. R. Patton & L. Serna (Eds.), *Strategies for teaching learners with special needs* (8th ed.). Upper Saddle River, NJ: Pearson Education, Inc.

Hoover, J. J., & Rabideau, D. K. (1995). Semantic webs and study skills. *Intervention in School and Clinic, 30*(5), 292–296.

Hughes, C. A. (1996). Memory and test-taking strategies. In D. D. Deshler, E. S. Ellis, & B. K. Lenz (Eds.), *Adolescents with learning disabilities: Strategies and methods* (2nd ed., pp. 209–266). Denver: Love.

King-Sears, M. E. & Mooney, J. F. (2004). Teaching content in an academically diverse class. In B. K. Lenz, D. D. Deshler, & B. R. Kissam (Eds.), *Teaching content to all: Evidence-based inclusive practices in middle and secondary schools.* Boston: Pearson Education, Inc.

Kline, C. S. (1986). *Effects of guided notes on academic achievement of learning disabled high school students.* Unpublished master's thesis: The Ohio State University, Columbus.

Lazarus, B. D. (1991). Guided notes, review, and achievement of learning disabled adolescents in secondary mainstream settings. *Education and Treatment of Children, 14,* 112–127.

Lazarus, B. D. (1996). Flexible skeletons: Guided notes for adolescents with mild disabilities. *TEACHING Exceptional Children, 28*(3), 36–40.

Lee, P., & Alley, G. R. (1981). *Training junior high LD students to use a test-taking strategy* (Research Report No. 38). Lawrence, KS: University of Kansas, Institute for Research in Learning Disabilities.

Lenz, B. K., Adams, G., Bulgren, J. A., Poulliot, N., & Laraux, M. (2002). *The effects of curriculum maps and guiding questions on the test performance of adolescents with learning disabilities* (Research Report No. BBB-37242). Lawrence: Kansas University, Institute for Academic Access. (ERIC Document Reproduction Service No. ED469292)

Lenz, B. K., Deshler, D. D., & Kissam, B. R. (2004). *Teaching content to all: Evidence-based inclusive practices in middle and secondary schools.* Boston: Pearson/Allyn and Bacon.

Masters, L. F., Mori, B. A., & Mori, A. A. (1999). *Teaching secondary students with mild learning and behavior problems: Methods, materials, strategies* (3rd ed.). Austin, TX: PRO-ED.

Mastropieri, M. A. (1988). Using the keyword method. *TEACHING Exceptional Children, 20*(2), 4–8.

Mastropieri, M. A., & Scruggs, T. E. (1998). Constructing more meaningful relationships in the classroom: Mnemonic research into practice. *Learning Disabilities Research and Practice, 13,* 138–145.

Mastropieri, M. A., & Scruggs, T. E. (2004). *The inclusive classroom: Strategies for effective instruction* (2nd ed.). Upper Saddle River, NJ: Pearson Education, Inc.

Mastropieri, M. A., Scruggs, T. E., & Fulk, B. J. (1990). Teaching abstract vocabulary with the keyword method: Effects on recall and comprehension. *Journal of Learning Disabilities, 23*(2), 92–96.

Mastropieri, M. A., Scruggs, T. E., & Graetz, J. E. (2003). Reading comprehension instruction for secondary students: Challenges for struggling students and teachers. *Learning Disability Quarterly, 26*(2), 103–116.

Mastropieri, M. A., Scruggs, T. E., & Levin, J. R. (1986a). Direct vs. mnemonic instruction: Relative benefits for exceptional learners. *Journal of Special Education, 20*(3), 299–308.

Mastropieri, M. A., Scruggs, T. E., & Levin, J. R. (1986b). Maximizing what exceptional students can learn: A review of keyword and other mnemonic strategy research. *Remedial and Special Education, 6*(2), 39–45.

McCarney, S. B., & Tucci, J. K. (1991). *Study skills for students in our schools: Study, skills and intervention strategies for elementary and secondary students.* Columbia, MO: Hawthorne.

McLoone, B. B., Scruggs, T. E., Mastropieri, M. A., & Zucker, S. F. (1986). Memory strategy instruction and training with LD adolescents. *Learning Disabilities Research, 2,* 45–63.

McNamara, J. K., & Wong, B. (2003). Memory for everyday information in students with learning disabilities. *Journal of Learning Disabilities, 36*(5), 394–406.

Meese, R. (1994). *Teaching learners with mild disabilities: Integrating research and practice.* Pacific Grove, CA: Brooks/Cole.

Mercer, C. D., & Mercer, A. R. (2005). *Teaching students with learning problems* (7th ed.). Upper Saddle River, NJ: Merrill/Prentice Hall.

Merkley, D. M., & Jefferies, D. (2001). Guidelines for implementing a graphic organizer. *The Reading Teacher, 54*(4), 350–357.

Munk, D. D., Bruckert, J., Call, D. T., Stoehrmann, T., & Randandt, E. (1998). Strategies for enhancing the performance of students with LD in inclusive science classes. *Intervention in School and Clinic, 34*(2), 73–78.

Murphy, D. A., Meyers, C. C., Olesen, S., McKean, K., & Custer, S. H. (1996). *Exceptions: A handbook of inclusion activities for teachers of students at grades 6–12 with mild disabilities.* Longmont, CO: Sopris Press.

Okolo, C. M., & Ferretti, R. P. (1996). Knowledge acquisition and technology-supported projects in the social studies for students with learning disabilities. *Journal of Special Education Technology, 13*(2), 91–103.

Paris, S. G. (1988). Models and metaphors of learning strategies. In C. E. Weinstein, E. T. Goetz, & P. A. Alexander (Eds.), *Learning and study strategies: Issues in assessment, instruction, and evaluation* (pp. 299–321). San Diego: Academic Press.

Pauk, W. (1989). *How to study in college* (4th ed.). Boston: Houghton Mifflin.

Pauk, W., & Owens, R. J. Q. (2005). *How to study in college* (8th ed.). Boston: Houghton Mifflin.

Platt, J. M., & Olson, J. (1997). *Teaching adolescents with mild disabilities.* Pacific Grove, CA: Brooks/Cole.

Polloway, E. A., Patton, J. R., & Serna, L. (2005). *Strategies for teaching learners with special needs* (8th ed.). Upper Saddle River, NJ: Pearson Education, Inc.

Putnam, M. L., Deshler, D. D., & Schumaker, J. B. (1993). The investigation of setting demands: A missing link in learning strategy instruction. In L. S. Meltzer (Ed.), *Strategy assessment and instruction for students with learning disabilities* (pp. 325–354). Austin, TX: PRO-ED.

Putnam, M. L., & Wesson, C. L. (1990). The teacher's role in teaching content-area information. *LD Forum, 16*(1), 55–60.

Raygor, A. L. (1970). *Study skills test: Form A*. New York: McGraw-Hill.

Riegel, R. H., Mayle, J. A., & McCarthy-Henkel, J. (1988). *Beyond maladies and remedies*. Novi, MI: RHR Consultation Services.

Ritter, S., & Idol-Maestas, L. (1986). Teaching middle school students to use a test-taking strategy. *Journal of Educational Research, 79*(6), 350–357.

Robinson, D. H., & Keiwra, K. A. (1995). Visual argument: Graphic organizers are superior outlines in improving learning from text. *Journal of Educational Psychology, 78*(3), 455–467.

Rosenshine, B. (1983). Teaching functions in instructional programs. *Elementary School Journal, 83*, 335–351.

Sabornie, E. J., & deBettencourt, L. U. (2004). *Teaching students with mild and high-incidence disabilities at the secondary level* (2nd ed.). Upper Saddle River, NJ: Merrill/Prentice Hall.

Salend, S. J. (2005). *Creating inclusive classrooms: Effective and reflective practices for all students* (5th ed.). Upper Saddle River, NJ: Pearson/Merrill/Prentice Hall.

Schloss, P. J., Smith, M. A., & Schloss, C. N. (2001). *Instructional methods for secondary students with learning and behavior problems* (3rd ed.). Needham Heights, MA: Allyn & Bacon.

Schumaker, J. B., Deshler, D. D., & McKnight, P. (1989). *Teaching routines to enhance the mainstream performance of adolescents with learning disabilities*. Final report submitted to U.S. Department of Education, Special Education Services.

Scruggs, T. E., & Mastropieri, M. A. (1984). Improving memory for facts: The "keyword" method. *Academic Therapy, 20*(2), 159–166.

Shields, J. M., & Heron, T. E. (1989). Teaching organizational skills to students with learning disabilities. *TEACHING Exceptional Children, 21*(2), 8–13.

Smith, S., Boone, R., & Higgins, K. (1998). Expanding the writing process to the web. *TEACHING Exceptional Children, 30*(5), 22–26.

Stanovich, K. (1986). Cognitive processes and the reading problems of learning disabled children: Evaluating the assumptions of specificity. In J. K. Torgesen & B. Y. L. Wong (Eds.), *Psychological and educational perspectives on learning disabilities* (pp. 85–131). Orlando, FL: Academic Press.

Suritsky, S. K., & Hughes, C. A. (1996). Notetaking strategy instruction. In D. D. Deshler, E. S. Ellis, & B. K. Lenz (Eds.), *Adolescents with learning disabilities: Strategies and methods* (2nd ed.) Denver, CO: Love.

Swanson, H. L., & Deshler, D. (2003). Instructing adolescents with learning disabilities: Converting a meta-analysis to practice. *Journal of Learning Disabilities, 36*(2), 124–135.

Sze, S., & Yu, S. (2004). *Educational benefits of music in an inclusive classroom*. Retrieved June 19, 2006, from http://search.epnet.com/login.aspx?direct=true&db=eric&an=ED490348

Veit, D. T., Scruggs, T. E., & Mastropieri, M. A. (1986). Extended mnemonic instruction with learning disabled students. *Journal of Educational Psychology, 78*, 300–308.

Wood, J. W. (2006). *Teaching students in inclusive settings: Adapting and accommodating instruction* (5th ed.). Upper Saddle River, N.J: Merrill/Prentice Hall.

Zigmond, N., Levin, E., & Laurie, T. (1985). Managing the mainstream: An analysis of teacher attitudes and student performance in mainstream high school programs. *Journal of Learning Disabilities, 18*, 535–541.

CHAPTER 11

Alper, S., Mull, C., & Soenksen, D. (2004). *Enhancing inclusion and access through assistive technology*. Unpublished manuscript, University of Northern Iowa, Cedar Falls, IA.

Alper, S., & Raharinirina, S. (2006). Assistive technology for individuals with disabilities: A review and synthesis of the literature. *Journal of Special Education Technology, 21*(2), 47–64.

American Library Association. (2006). *Especially for young people and their parents*. Retrieved October 18, 2006, from www.ala.org/foryoungpeople/youngpeopleparents/especiallyyoungpeople.htm

Astleitner, H., & Wiesner, C. (2004). An integrated model of multimedia learning and motivation. *Journal of Educational Multimedia and Hypermedia, 13*, 3–21.

Bakken, J. P., & Aloia, G. F. (1998). Evaluating the world wide web. *Teaching Exceptional Children, 30*(5), 48–53.

Behrmann, M. M. (1995). *Assistive technology for students with mild disabilities* (ERIC Digest No. E529). Syracuse, NY: ERIC Clearinghouse on Information and Technology.

Behrmann, M., & Jerone, M. K. (2002). *Assistive technology for students with mild disabilities: Update 2002*. (ERIC EC Digest No. E529)

Boyle, J. R. (2001). Enhancing the note-taking skills of students with mild disabilities. *Intervention in School and Clinic, 36*, 221–224.

Coleman, M. R. (2000). *Conditions for special education teaching: Council for Exceptional Children Commission technical report.* Special Education Teaching Conditions Initiative.

Craig, D. V. (1997). Telecurricular teaching and learning: The impact of World Wide Web access on the instructional process. *Telecommunications in Education News, 8*(3), 1.

Erikson, H. L. (1995). *Stirring the head, heart, and soul.* Thousand Oaks, CA: Corwin Press.

Goldstein, C. (1998). Learning at CyberCamp. *TEACHING Exceptional Children, 30*(5), 16–21.

Harden, B., & Rosenberg, G. (2001). Bringing technology to the classroom. *ASHA Leader, 6*(14), 5–6.

Hasselbring, T. S. (1998). *The future of special education and the role of technology.* Peabody College of Vanderbilt University. Retrieved July 15, 1998, from the World Wide Web: http://peabody.vanderbilt.edu/ltc/hasselbringt/future.html

Hasselbring, T. D., & Glaser, C. H. W. (2000, Autumn–Winter). Use of computer technology to help students with special needs. *The Future of Children, 20*(2), 102–122.

Hauser, J., & Malouf, D. B. (1996). A federal perspective on special education technology. *Journal of Learning Disabilities, 29*(5), 504–511.

Hines, R. A., & Hall, K. S. (2000). Assistive technology. *Journal of Special Education Technology, 15*(4), 37–39.

Hundt, T. A. (2002). Videotaping young children in the classroom: Parents as partners. *TEACHING Exceptional Children, 34*(3), 38–43.

Jonassen, D., Howland, J., Moore, J., & Marra, R. (2003). *Learning to solve problems with technology: A constructivist perspective.* Upper Saddle River, NJ: Merrill Prentice Hall.

Komoski, K. (1995). *Seven steps to responsible software selection.* Syracuse, NY: ERIC Clearinghouse on Information and Technology. (ERIC Digest No. EDOIR956)

Krivacska, J. J. (1986). Selection of the IEP management systems. *Computers in the Schools, 3*(3), 91–95.

Krueger, A., & Sutton, J. (Eds.). (2001). *EDThoughts: What we know about science teaching and learning.* Aurora, CO: Mid-Continent Research for Education and Learning.

Lewis, M. B. (1993). *Thematic methods and strategies in learning disabilities: Textbook for practitioners.* San Diego, CA: Singular Publishing Group.

Lewis, R. (2000). Musings on technology and learning disabilities on the occasion of the new millennium. *Journal of Special Education Technology, 15*(2), 5–12.

Ludwig, T. E., Daniel, D. B., Froman, R., & Mathie, V. A. (2004). *Using multimedia in classroom presentation: Best principles.* Report prepared for the Society for the Teaching of Psychology: Pedagogical Innovations Task Force.

Maddux, C. D. (1986). Issues and concerns in special education microcomputing. *Computers in the Schools, 3*(3), 1–19.

Male, M. (1988). *Special magic: Computers, classroom strategies, and exceptional students.* Mountain View, CA: Mayfield.

Means, B., Blando, J., Olson, K., Middleton, T., Moroacco, C., Remz, A. R., & Zorfass, J. (1993). *Using technology to support education reform.* Washington, DC: U.S. Government Printing Office, 1993.

Morgan, N. A. (1997). *An introduction to Internet resources for K12 educators: Part II: Question answering, listservs, discussion groups, update 1997.* Syracuse, NY: ERIC Clearing house on Information and Technology. (ERIC Digest No. EDOIR9704)

Ray, J., & Warden, M. K. (1995). *Technology, computers, and the special needs learner.* Albany, NY: Delmar.

Roblyer, M., & Edwards, J. (2000). *Integrating educational technology into teaching.* Upper Saddle River, NJ: Prentice-Hall.

Rogers, P. L. (Ed.). (2002). *Designing instruction for technology-enhanced learning.* Hershey, PA: Idea Group Publishing.

Smith, S., Boone, R., & Higgins, K. (1998). Expanding the writing process to the web. *TEACHING Exceptional Children, 30*(5), 22–26.

SPeNSE. (2002). *Paperwork in special education.* Retrieved September 3, 2006, from www.spense.org

Sturmey, P. (2003). Video technology and persons with autism and other developmental disabilities: An emerging technology of positive behavioral support. *Journal of Positive Behavior Interventions,* (5), 5–10.

Sweeney, J. (2006). *U.S. federal legislation and policy which applies to assistive technology.* Retrieved September 3, 2006, from http://www.onionmountaintech.com/files/AT%20Laws%20Table%202006.pdf

Technology—the great equalizer. (2003, November-December). *CEC Today.*

Venn, J. J. (2007). *Assessing students with special needs* (4th Ed.). Upper Saddle River, NJ: Pearson.

Wilson, G. L., Michaels, C. A., & Margolis, H. (2005). Form versus function: Using technology to develop Individualized Education Programs for students with disabilities. *Journal of Special Education Technology, 20*(2), 37–46.

Wissick, C. A., & Gardner, J. E. (1998). A learner's permit to the World Wide Web. *TEACHING Exceptional Children, 30*(5), 8–15.

Wyer, K. (2001). The great equalizer. *Teaching Tolerance, 19,* 1–5.

Zhang, Y. (2000). Technology and the writing skills of students with learning disabilities. *Journal of Research on Computing in Education, 32*(4), 467–479.

CHAPTER 12

American School Counselor Association. (2003). *The ASCA national model: A framework for school counseling programs.* Alexandria, VA: Author.

Archer, A. L., & Gleason, M. M. (1994). *Skills for school success* (2nd ed.). North Billerica, MA: Curriculum Associates.

Aune, E. (1991). A transitional model for postsecondary-bound students with learning disabilities. *Learning Disabilities Research and Practice, 6,* 177–187.

Blalock, G., & Patton, J. R. (1996). Transition and students with learning disabilities: Creating sound futures. *Journal of Learning Disabilities, 29,* 7–16.

Brinkerhoff, L. C., Shaw, S. F., & McGuire, J. M. (1992). Promoting access, accommodations and independence for college students with learning disabilities. *Journal of Learning Disabilities, 25*(7), 417–429.

Brolin, D. E. (1993). *Life centered career education: A competency-based approach* (4th ed.). Reston, VA: Council for Exceptional Children.

Brolin, D. E. (1995). *Career education.* Upper Saddle River, NJ: Prentice Hall.

Bruinicks, R. H., Moreau, L., Gilman, C. J., & Anderson, J. L. (1991). *Adaptive living skills curriculum.* Itasca, IL: Riverside Publications.

Brolin, D. E., & Lloyd, R. J. (2004). *Career development and transition services: A functional life skills approach* (4th ed.). Upper Saddle River, NJ: Pearson, Merrill and Prentice Hall.

Chamberlain, M. (1988). Employers' rankings of factors judged to be critical to job success for individuals with severe disabilities. *Career Development for Exceptional Individuals, 11*(3), 141–147.

Chandler, S. K., & Pankaskie, S. C. (1997). Socialization, peer relationships, and self-esteem. In P. Wehman & J. Kregel (Eds.), *Functional curriculum for elementary, middle, and secondary age students with special needs* (pp. 123–153). Austin: PRO-ED.

Dowdy, C. A., & Evers, R. B. (1996). Preparing students for transitions: A teacher primer on vocational education and rehabilitation. *Intervention in School and Clinic, 31,* 197–208.

Durodoye, B., Combes, B., & Bryant, R. (2004). Counselor intervention in the post-secondary planning of African American students with learning disabilities. *Professional School Counseling, 7*(3), 133–140.

Edgar, E. (1987). Secondary programs in special education: Are many of them justifiable? *Exceptional Children, 53*(5), 555–561.

Field, M. D., Sarver, S. F., & Shaw, S. F., (2003). Self-determination: A key to success in postsecondary education for students with learning disabilities. *Remedial and Special Education, 24,* 339–349.

Gerber, P., Price, L., Mulligan, R., & Shessel, I. (2004). Beyond transition: A comparison of the employment experiences of American and Canadian adults with LD. *Journal of Learning Disabilities, 37*(4), 283–291.

Hicks-Cooley, A., & Kurtz, P. D. (1997). Preparing students with learning disabilities for success in postsecondary education: Needs and services. *Social Work in Education, 19*(1), 13–45.

Janiga, S. J., & Costenbader, V. (2002). The transition from high school to postsecondary education for students with learning disabilities: A survey of college service coordinators. *Journal of Learning Disabilities, 35,* 462–468.

Johnson, D. R., Stodden, R. A., Emanual, E. J., Luecking, R., & Mack, M. (2002). Current challenges facing secondary education and transition services: What research tells us. *Exceptional Children, 68*(4), 519–531.

Kohler, P. (1993). Best practices in transition: Substantiated or implied? *Career Development for Exceptional Individuals, 16,* 107–121.

Konrad, M., & Tests, D. (2004). Teaching middle school students with disabilities to use an IEP template. *Career Development of Exceptional Individuals, 27,* 101–104.

Kortering, L., & Braziel, P. (2000). A look at the expressed career ambitions of youth with disabilities. *Journal of Vocational Special Needs Education, 23* (1), 24–33.

Krebs, C. S. (2002). Self-advocacy skills: A portfolio approach. *RE: view, 33,* 160–163.

Madaus, J. R. (2005). Navigating the college transition maze: A guide for students with learning disabilities. *Exceptional Children, 37*(3), 32–37.

Miller, R. J., Lombard, R. C., & Corbey, S. A. (2007). *Transition assessment: Planning transition and IEP development for you with mild to moderate disabilities.* Boston: Pearson, Allyn & Bacon.

Montague, M. (1988). Job-related social skills training for adolescents with handicaps. *Career Development for Exceptional Individuals, 11*(1), 26–41.

Morningstar, M. E., Turnbull, A. P., & Turnbull, N. R., III. (1996). What do students with disabilities tell us about the importance of family involvement in the transition from school to adult life? *Exceptional Children, 62*(3), 249–260.

Rabren, K., Dunn, C., & Chambers, D. (2002). Predictors of post-high school employment among young adults with disabilities. *Career Development for Exceptional Individuals, 25*(1), 25–40.

Roessler, R. R., Brolin, D. E., & Johnson, J. M. (1990). Factors affecting employment success and quality of life: A one year follow-up of students in special education. *Career Development for Exceptional Individuals, 13*(2), 95–107.

Rose, E., Rainforth, B., & Steere, D. (2002). Guiding principles for the education of children and youth with severe and multiple disabilities. In F. Obiakor, C. Utley, & A. Rotatori (Eds.), *Advances in special education: Psychology of effective education for learners with exceptionalities.* Stanford, CT: JAI Press, Inc.

Rueda, R., Monzo, L., Shapiro, J., Gomez, J., & Blacher, J. (2005). Cultural models of transition: Latina mothers of young adults with developmental disabilities. *Exceptional Children, 71,* 401–404.

Salembier, G., & Furney, K. S. (1997). Facilitating participation: Parents' perceptions of their involvement in the IEP/transition planning process. *Career Development for Exceptional Individuals, 20,* 29–42.

Secretary's Commission on Achieving Necessary Skills (SCANS). (1991). *What work requires of schools.* Washington, DC: U.S. Department of Labor.

Sorrells, A. M., Reith, H. J., & Sindelar, P. T. (2004). *Critical issues in special education: Access, diversity and accountability.* Boston: Allyn & Bacon.

Steere, D. E., Rose, E., & Cacaiuolo, D. (2007). *Growing up: Transition to adult life for students with disabilities.* Boston: Pearson, Allyn & Bacon.

Taylor, I., & O'Reilly, M. F. (2000). Generalization of supermarket shopping skills for individuals with mild intellectual disabilities using stimulus equivalence training. *The Psychological Record, 50*(1), 49–62.

Test, D., Mason, C., Hughes, C., Konrad, M., Neale, M., & Wood, W. (2004). Student involvement in individualized education program meetings. *Exceptional Children, 70,* 391–412.

Thorin, E., Yovanoff, P., & Irvin, L. (1996). Dilemmas faced by families during their young adults' transitions to adulthood: A brief report. *Mental Retardation, 34*(2), 117–120.

Trainor, A. (2005). Self-determination perceptions and behaviors of diverse students with LD during the transition planning process. *Journal of Learning Disabilities, 38*(3), 233–249.

Wagner, M. M., & Blackorby, J. (1996). Transition from high school to work or college: How special education students fare. *The Future of Children,* 103–120.

NAME INDEX

SUBJECT INDEX